SOCIAL COGNITION AND CLINICAL PSYCHOLOGY

SOCIAL COGNITION AND CLINICAL PSYCHOLOGY
A Synthesis

Edited by
LYN Y. ABRAMSON
University of Wisconsin–Madison

THE GUILFORD PRESS
New York   London

To DOLORES AND LEROY.—*Lyn Y. Abramson*

© 1988 The Guilford Press
A Division of Guilford Publications, Inc.
72 Spring Street, New York, NY 10012

Printed in the United States of America

Last digit is print number: 9 8 7 6 5 4 3 2 1

Library of Congress Cataloging-in-Publication Data
Social cognition and clinical psychology.
   Includes bibliographies and index.
   1. Clinical psychology.   2. Social perception.
3. Attribution (Social psychology)   4. Self.
5. Cognitive therapy.   6. Psychotherapist and patient.
I. Abramson, Lyn. [DNLM: 1. Cognition.   2. Psychology,
Clinical.   3. Psychotherapy.   4. Social Perception.
WM 105 S6777]
RC467.S58   1988   155.9′2   86-18453
ISBN 0-89862-011-2

Contributors

LYN Y. ABRAMSON, PhD, Department of Psychology, University of Wisconsin–Madison, Madison, Wisconsin

LAUREN B. ALLOY, PhD, Department of Psychology, Northwestern University, Evanston, Illinois

JUDY GARBER, PhD, Department of Psychology and Human Development, Vanderbilt University, Nashville, Tennessee

BARBARA H. HANUSA, PhD, School of Public Health, University of Pittsburgh, Pittsburgh, Pennsylvania

STEVEN D. HOLLON, PhD, Department of Psychology, Vanderbilt University, Nashville, Tennessee

WILLIAM ICKES, PhD, Department of Psychology, University of Texas at Arlington, Arlington, Texas

YORAM JAFFE, PhD, Department of Psychology, University of Southern California, Los Angeles, California

RONNIE JANOFF-BULMAN, PhD, Department of Psychology, University of Massachusetts, Amherst, Massachusetts

NAOMI TABACHNIK KAYNE, PhD, Columbus, Ohio

JURGIS KARUZA, JR, PhD, The Western New York Geriatric Education Center, SUNY at Buffalo, and Department of Psychology, State University College at Buffalo, Buffalo, New York

ARIE W. KRUGLANSKI, PhD, Department of Psychology, University of Maryland, College Park, Maryland

LINDA LANG-GUNN, PhD, Belchertown, Massachusetts

ELLEN J. LANGER, PhD, Department of Psychology and Social Relations, Harvard University, Cambridge, Massachusetts

GERALD I. METALSKY, PhD, Department of Psychology, University of Texas at Austin, Austin, Texas

DALE T. MILLER, PhD, Department of Psychology, Princeton University, Princeton, New Jersey

HELEN M. NEWMAN, PhD, Department of Communications, Hunter College, New York, New York

CAROL A. PORTER, PhD, Department of Psychology, Princeton University, Princeton, New Jersey

VITA C. RABINOWITZ, PhD, Department of Psychology, Hunter College, New York, New York

RICHARD SCHULZ, PhD, Departments of Psychiatry and University Center for Social and Urban Research, Pittsburgh, Pennsylvania

MICHAEL A. ZEVON, PhD, Department of Psychology, Roswell Park Memorial Institute, Buffalo, New York

Preface

Over the past 15 years, social and personality psychologists have made major advances in understanding human cognition about the self and other people. During the same time, many experimental psychopathologists and clinical psychologists have emphasized the importance of cognitive processes in the etiology, maintenance, and treatment of a wide variety of psychological problems. The purpose of this book is to synthesize these exciting developments in social, personality, and clinical psychology. This volume's contributors are leading investigators in these areas, whose common goal is to achieve such a synthesis. As their chapters show, such a synthesis not only facilitates application of basic work in psychology to the clinical setting but also allows the study of clinical phenomena to enrich general psychology.

The first chapter, by Miller and Porter, describes errors and biases in the causal attribution process and explores their relevance to a variety of clinical phenomena. Miller and Porter suggest that errors in information-processing contribute to the cause and/or maintenance of many kinds of psychological disorders, including paranoia, anxiety, and depression.

Chapters 2 through 6 examine psychological health and maladjustment from the perspective of work on social cognition. In Chapter 2, Abramson, Metalsky, and Alloy present a restatement and clarification of the hopelessness theory of depression, which relies heavily on basic work in social psychology on the causal attribution process. These authors come to the disturbing conclusion that the research strategies utilized over the past 10 years to test the theory do not test it adequately. In suggesting more appropriate research strategies, the authors propose that a major challenge for future work is to determine whether or not hopelessness depression, a theory-based subtype of depression, exists in nature and conforms to its description in the hopelessness theory.

In Chapter 3, Ickes traces the historical antecedents of the concept of attributional style and relates this concept to self-esteem. Ickes concludes by suggesting that the links between attributional styles and behavior may have implications for a number of clinical phenomena, including depression and learned helplessness, "deviant" personalities, neurotic ego defense, interpersonal conflict, and anxiety.

As Schulz and Hanusa note in Chapter 4, investigators of learned helplessness are placing an increased emphasis on cognitive mediators of uncontrollable events. In this chapter, Schulz and Hanusa present a research study that examines information-seeking strategies used by people exposed to uncontrollable events. In discussing their results, the authors propose the intriguing hypothesis that some of the behaviors that have been identified as "helpless" are not due to expectations of no control but instead may be strategies aimed at maintaining or enhancing self-esteem.

In Chapter 5, Janoff-Bulman and Lang-Gunn raise the paradox that although the popular conception is that self-blame is psychologically damaging, disease and accident victims often obtain psychological benefits from blaming themselves for their misfortune. To resolve this paradox, Janoff-Bulman and Lang-Gunn propose two types of self-blame: characterological versus behavioral self-blame. Whereas characterological self-blame is maladaptive, behavioral self-blame is not.

Newman and Langer present an intriguing analysis of the role of cognitive processes in the development, course, and termination of intimate relationships in Chapter 6. In particular, these authors argue that causal attribution patterns and levels of mindfulness affect the development of dysfunctional patterns of interaction and interpersonal conflict in intimate relationships.

Chapters 7 through 9 examine psychotherapy from a social cognition perspective. In Chapter 7, Rabinowitz, Zevon, and Karuza analyze psychotherapies in terms of four different helping models. In this view, schools of therapy differ in regard to judgments about the client's responsibility for the origin and solution to his or her problem. The authors suggest that the attributional assumptions of different psychotherapies may cause each therapy to be more or less appropriate in treating particular kinds of psychological disorders.

In Chapter 8, Hollon and Garber analyze cognitive therapy from the perspective of recent advances in social cognition. They propose a provocative hypothesis: Cognitive therapy may seek to induce clients to believe what other people believe by virtue of engaging in cognitive processes that few people actually engage in. More generally, Hollon and Garber examine what cognitive changes actually are being produced by cognitive therapy.

In Chapter 9, Kruglanski and Jaffe present the lay epistemic approach developed by Kruglanski and his colleagues to the theory and practice of therapy. The lay epistemic approach is radical in that it challenges several basic assumptions typically made by contemporary cognitive therapists: (1) that veridical or realistic conceptions are functional for people and contribute to their well being; (2) that normals are generally more accurate in their judgments than neurotics; and (3) that veridical judgments are more likely to be made if people utilize scientific methods of inference. According to the lay epistemic approach, the adaptiveness of a belief derives from its content rather than from its truth value.

Finally, in Chapter 10, Kayne and Alloy examine the clinician and patient as aberrant actuaries. These authors speculate on how the cognitive biases of clients might interact with the cognitive biases of therapists.

I would like to thank Kerry Wanek, Judy Markgraf, and Marie Kestol for secretarial assistance. Special thanks go to Seymour Weingarten, Editor-in-Chief of The Guilford Press, for his editorial and intellectual contributions to the book. I also would like to thank the MacArthur Foundation for financial support of my research with Lauren Alloy. Finally, I would like to thank the authors for their thoughtful and thought-provoking contributions. Their work will help in building a much needed bridge between clinical and general psychology.

Contents

I

*Overview of Attributional Biases
and Clinical Psychology*

1

Errors and Biases
in the Attribution Process

DALE T. MILLER
CAROL A. PORTER

When our actions or those of others puzzle us, we seek to explain them. The principles that people follow in seeking answers to their causal questions constitute what has come to be known as "attribution theory" (Harvey & Weary, 1981; Jones *et al.*, 1971; Ross & Fletcher, 1985; Shaver, 1975). The seminal attributional formulations of Heider (1958), Jones and Davis (1965) and Kelley (1967, 1972) all contend that people follow rational, "common-sense" rules of inference in interpreting their world. In fact, Kelley characterizes man's method of causal inference as that of a "naive scientist."

Our primarily rational approach to the causal analyses of events and human behavior generally yields accurate explanations. We sometimes make errors, however. The question of how errors, especially systematic or frequent errors, arise in our causal attributions has sparked much interest among social psychologists. In the present chapter we will describe a number of such errors and biases and explore their relevance to a variety of clinical phenomena.

Although the terms "error" and "bias" generally are used interchangeably by social psychologists, we will distinguish between the two in our discussion. The term "error" will be applied to an attribution or inference that can be demonstrated to deviate from a statistical or "normative" standard (Funder, 1987; Nisbett & Ross, 1980). The term "bias" will be used in instances where an attributional divergence occurs between individuals with different perspectives or outcomes but where no normative standard exists to help assess the relative accuracy of the different attributions.

As our discussion will show, there is considerable controversy over both the prevalence and the origins of attributional errors and biases. For most errors and biases, there are generally two interpretations offered—one "hot" and one "cool" (Nisbett & Ross, 1980). "Hot theories are those positing that errors and biases occur when some need or motive in a person interferes with his or her normal attributional processes. These theories have their roots in the psychodynamic and related traditions that emphasize the prepotency of

3

emotions over intellectual functioning (Dawes, 1976). "Cool" theories, on the other hand, contend that attributional errors and biases stem from limitations inherent in the human cognitive apparatus. These theories are inspired by a model of man emerging from the human judgment literature. According to this model, people are rational, but their rationality is "bounded" (Simon, 1957). The principles and heuristics they use to process and simplify the information confronting them, though generally serving them well, also predispose them to make certain errors (Kahneman, Slovic, & Tversky, 1982; Tversky & Kahneman, 1973). The conviction that errors and biases need not reflect motivationally induced distortion is a distinguishing characteristic of contemporary cognitive social psychology (Fiske & Taylor, 1984; Markus & Zajonc, 1985).

ATTRIBUTIONAL BIASES AND CLINICAL PSYCHOLOGY

As the present volume aims to demonstrate, attribution theory holds considerable relevance for contemporary clinical psychology. That part of attribution theory focusing on attributional errors and biases converges with the concerns of clinical psychology at a number of points. There is, for instance, a growing consensus among clinical psychologists that many forms of psychological dysfunction, such as paranoia, anxiety, stress, and depression are partially caused, or at least sustained, by errors in information-processing (e.g., Beck, 1967, 1976; Ellis & Grieger, 1977; Hollon & Kriss, 1984). Moreover, there are a growing number of therapies that attempt to help clients become more "rational," "logical," or "realistic" in their interpretation of their social world (e.g., Beck, Rush, Shaw, & Emery, 1979; Goldfried & Davison, 1976). Contemporary clinical and social psychology also share increasing comfort with cool as opposed to hot explanations of inferential errors and biases (Alloy, 1988).

In its focus on causal explanations of behavior, attribution theory is also relevant to the fundamental clinical debate over the origins of deviant or psychopathological behavior (Ullman & Krasner, 1969). To ask whether abnormal behavior is due to factors within the person (internal causes) or factors operating in the person's environment (external causes) is, in effect, to ask an *attributional* question. Consequently, it is appropriate to ask about the possible attributional errors or biases that clinical diagnosis and therapy might reflect. Put bluntly, we can ask, "Who is more accurate in making causal attributions for abnormal behavior: the psychoanalysts, who emphasize intrapsychic factors, or the behaviorists, who emphasize environmental contingencies?"

Our plan for the present chapter is, first, to examine the various empirical phenomena that have been labeled attributional errors or biases and to discuss their hot and cool interpretations. Second, we will consider the potential relevance of these errors and biases for an understanding of various clinical phenomena. Finally, we will offer some suggestions for countering these errors and biases. We begin our discussion with the most heavily researched attributional bias.

THE SELF-SERVING ATTRIBUTIONAL BIAS

A great many of the events or outcomes with which a person is associated can be viewed as constituting a success or failure experience, or as having some positive or negative valence. Social psychologists have discovered that people often explain their successes and their failures in different terms. Most commonly, people take personal responsibility for their successes (positive events) but attribute their failures (negative events) to external factors. This tendency to credit ability or effort for success and blame luck or task difficulty for failure is not always encountered, but it is encountered sufficiently often in both laboratory and field conditions to justify its designation as an attributional bias.

Until recently, this bias was generally believed to stem from a psychological need to bolster or protect one's ego or self-esteem (Hastorf, Schneider, & Polefka, 1970). Versions of this hypothesis have been offered by psychologists of diverse theoretical orientation (e.g., Allport, 1937; Heider, 1958; Murphy, 1947). The "self-serving" hypothesis is an intuitively appealing one, and few lay persons would dispute that such a bias exists in most people's, at least most other people's, responses to everyday successes and failures.

Over a decade ago, Miller and Ross (1975) contended that the empirical findings adduced in support of the self-serving hypothesis could actually be explained more parsimoniously by cool information-processing concepts. More specifically, Miller and Ross proposed that three factors operating in isolation or in combination may cause individuals to take more personal responsibility for success than failure. First, individuals are more likely to accept responsibility for expected outcomes than unexpected outcomes and, in general, people expect success rather than failure. Second, individuals discern a closer covariation between behavior and outcomes in the case of increasing success than in the case of constant failure, where changes in behavior are not perceived to be associated with changes in outcomes. Third, individuals tend to hold an erroneous conception of contingency, which leads them to associate control primarily with the occurrence of the desired (successful) outcome.

Since Miller and Ross's review, research and controversy in this area have continued to flourish. A number of studies have sought stronger evidence for the self-serving hypothesis. In a study reported by Miller (1976), reactions to success and failure under two levels of ego involvement were observed. The task was a multiple-choice test of social perceptiveness. Subjects answered questions based on case studies. In order to ensure that the manipulation of involvement did not produce any difference in effort or any other feature of performance, this manipulation did not occur until after the subjects had completed the test. At this point, they were told either that the test was well validated as a measure of "intelligence, personal and marital happiness, and job satisfaction" (high involvement) or that the test was new and its validity "still very much in doubt" (low involvement). Subjects thereafter received false success or failure feedback. The results revealed a general tendency for subjects to take more personal responsibility for success than for failure, but this asymmetry was much greater under the high-involvement condition. Miller interpreted these results as supporting the motivational hypothesis because the condition in which ego involvement was highest also produced the most pronounced success–failure difference. On the basis of this study and others, more recent reviews (e.g., Snyder, Stephan, & Rosenfield, 1978; Zuckerman, 1979) have tended to side with the motivational hypothesis, although the controversy is far from over and may well prove unresolvable (see Tetlock & Levi, 1982).

Aside from the issue of what factors account for the success–failure attributional differences, we can inquire into the consequences of such a bias. Both the affective and behavioral consequences of achievement-oriented attributions have been explored. Evidence provided by Weiner and his colleagues (Russell & McAuley, 1986; Weiner, Russell, & Lerman, 1978, 1979) suggests that people who make external attributions for failure experience more positive moods than individuals making internal attributions. Moreover, successful subjects who make internal attributions experience more positive feelings than successful subjects who make external attributions.

Further evidence on the relationship between attributional biases and affective states comes from laboratory studies that have examined the relationship between depression and causal attributions for task success and failure (Kuiper, 1978; Metalsky, Abramson, Seligman, Semmel, & Peterson, 1982; Rizley, 1978; Seligman, Abramson, Semmel, & von Baeyer, 1979; Sharp & Tennen, 1983; Zemore & Johansen, 1980). In general, these studies show that nondepressives engage in more self-flattering attributions than do depressed individuals (Coyne & Gotlib, 1983; Miller & Moretti, 1988). This pattern has also been observed in explanations for past real-life interpersonal successes and failures. For example, Girodo, Dotzenroth, and Stein (1981) reported that individuals who had low self-esteem and who described themselves as shy tended to attribute their interpersonal failures to internal factors and their successes to external ones, whereas the opposite pattern of attributions was found for individuals with high self-esteem who described themselves as not shy.

Unfortunately, one cannot confidently conclude from these correlational studies that the direction of causality is from causal attributions to affective states (see Brewin, 1985). It may well be that the different affective states predispose people to different causal attributions. More specifically, people may tend to make attributions that are congruent with their affective state

(Clark & Isen, 1982). If a person who succeeds continues to be depressed, for instance, he or she may reasonably infer that this success did not reflect on him or her personally but rather on the fact that he or she was lucky or that it was an easy task (cf. Bem, 1972). It is, of course, also possible that the relationship between affect and attribution is bidirectional, with a certain affective state leading to certain attributions which in turn serve to maintain or intensify the affective state (Miller & Moretti, 1988). A final possibility is that there is no causal relationship between attributions and affective state, and that a third variable accounts for the association.

There are at least two reasons to expect that causal attributions for success and failure will be related to subsequent behavior. First, the explanation of past behavior is related to the prediction of future behavior, and such predictions often become self-fulfilling prophecies (Archibald, 1974). Individuals who attribute success internally and failure externally are probably both more optimistic about future success and more likely to achieve such success than are individuals who attribute success externally and failure internally (Forsterling, 1985; Weiner, 1974). Second, to the extent that causal attributions affect mood, it is reasonable to expect that subsequent behavior, in turn, will be affected.

Implications

On the basis of the foregoing discussion, the self-serving attributional bias would appear to have a number of possible adaptive consequences for individuals. There are clear limitations to the adaptiveness of such a bias, however. If a person is truly responsible for his or her failure and can take steps to avoid further failures, it is likely to be maladaptive for the person to deny causal responsibility. Learning from one's mistakes generally will be more adaptive than denying them. Moreover, some types of internal attributions for failure may be more adaptive than others (Miller & Porter, 1983). Blaming failure on one's ability (a stable, internal, global factor) may be more psychologically damaging than blaming failure on one's effort or preparation (unstable, internal, specific factors) (Abramson, Seligman, & Teasdale, 1978; Janoff-Bulman, 1979; Janoff-Bulman & Lang-Gunn, Chapter 5, this volume; Peterson & Seligman, 1984). And, of course, in some circumstances it will be more adaptive to admit to ability deficiencies than to persist in activities at which one is doomed to fail (Wortman & Brehm, 1975).

A consideration of interpersonal successes and failures introduces some further complexities (see Newman & Langer, Chapter 6, this volume). With interpersonal failures, such as an unsuccessful marriage, two types of external factors can be blamed: personal factors (e.g., spouse) and impersonal factors (circumstances, stage of life, etc.). Attributions to the two types of external factors may have different consequences. In this connection, Newman and

Langer (1981) reported that divorced individuals who blamed their failed marriage on situational factors were happier, more confident, more active, and more optimistic about future relationships than were individuals who blamed either themselves or their ex-spouse.

Another important aspect of self-serving attributions is their susceptibility to change over time. Miller and Porter (1980) have shown that people's causal attributions for events undergo systematic changes with the passage of time. Specifically, people tend to see events as more inevitable and situationally produced as time passes. None of the situations focused on by Miller and Porter involved outcomes of different valences, but it is not unreasonable to expect time-related changes here as well. A study by Miller (1982a) pursued this possibility. Students' attributions for their exam performance were collected both immediately after they received feedback on their performance and 10 days afterward. There was a clear reduction in attributional self-servingness over the 10-day interval. Even more interesting are the findings bearing on the relationship between attributional self-servingness and performance on the next exam. Attributional self-servingness evidenced in the *immediate* condition was not predictive of subsequent performance. However, self-servingness observed after 10 days was significantly negatively correlated with performance on the second test.

The interesting, though clearly speculative, inference to be drawn from these results is that while initial self-serving attributions may be adaptive, persistent attributions of this type actually may be highly maladaptive. When counseling someone, for example a partner in an unsuccessful marriage, it may be of little harm and could be of some benefit to allow him or her to indulge in defensive attributions at the time the marriage breaks up. If the person persists in making defensive attributions, however, and refuses to admit to any responsibility for the failure of the marriage, this may impair his or her ability to both accurately comprehend the marriage and prepare for subsequent relationships.

People's explanations for repeated failures may not show the same temporal pattern as their explanation for a single failure. Thus, while Miller and Porter (1980) reported that individuals' explanations for a single event became more situational with time, Burke and Peplau (1976) found that explanations for loneliness and social isolation became more internal the longer the conditions persisted. It appears that the plausibility of an external explanation for a negative experience diminishes the more often the outcome occurs or the experience is repeated. Ironically, the tendency to externalize responsibility for social or task failure probably increases the likelihood that one will, in fact, fail again.

In summary, the literature on the self-serving attribution bias appears to have a number of implications for clinical psychology. Interesting questions exist concerning the prevalence of this bias in various clinical populations, as well as its affective and behavioral consequences for different groups of individuals. The resolution of the debate over the origin of this bias would be of considerable relevance for clinical psychologists. If the bias proves to be basically cool in nature, this might suggest that individuals who fail to show this bias (e.g., depressives) do so because they do not expect success or, alternatively, because they do not associate control with the occurrence of desired outcomes. On the other hand, if the hot interpretation of the self-serving attribution bias is correct, a very different set of possibilities emerges. From this perspective it might be argued that depressives do not show a self-serving bias because they either do not share the nondepressive's need for high self-esteem or because they have not learned how the attribution process can serve them in this regard (Miller & Moretti, 1988). Such alternative possibilities might also exist for individuals such as paranoids, who show an exaggerated form of the self-serving bias. Social psychological research may be able to offer some insight into the question of whether the paranoid's attributional errors are hot or cool in origin (see Abramson & Alloy, 1981).

THE NEED FOR EFFECTIVE CONTROL

Kelley (1972) has argued that the attribution process not only helps the individual comprehend and understand his or her environment, but also serves to promote a sense of effective control over it. He contends, for instance, that assuming responsibility for success and disclaiming it for failure may serve to strengthen a person's belief in his or her control.

Many other attributional formulations feature the need for personal control as affecting and biasing the attribution process (Wortman, 1976). Lerner's (1970) "belief in a just world hypothesis," for instance, contends that people's attributions of responsibility for the fates of others is often biased by a wish to believe that there is a contingency between a person's actions or character and his or her fate. Confidence in the existence of this contingency is presumed to be essential to the belief that one has control over one's life and that one can effect desired outcomes and avoid undesirable ones.

The best-known finding associated with Lerner's theory is the tendency to derogate innocent victims (see Lerner & Miller, 1978, for a review of this literature). It is Lerner's contention that by finding fault with the actions of victims or by devaluing their character, we protect our belief that the world is a stable and orderly place where we can escape similar fates if we are good and avoid mistakes. Although the phenomenon of victim derogation appears firmly established, the underlying mechanism, as with the success–failure asymmetry, is disputed. Lerner clearly views the process as a hot one, based on the *need* to believe in a just world. Other theorists, however, contend that the tendency to assume a relationship between inputs and fates may reflect a general cognitive disposition to match causes and effects (Brewer, 1977; Kahneman & Miller, 1986) and is in essence a cool phenomenon. Still others have argued that it is quite rational and valid in most instances to blame victims for their fates.

The consequences of the "just world" bias are numerous and often quite devastating. For victims, one consequence is that they often do not get sympathy or aid and may actually be stigmatized and punished further. The history of oppressed minority groups reveals this pattern, as does the experience of many individual victims. Rape victims, for example, are frequently the target of this type of attributional bias, and much of the psychological pain they experience derives from the negative reactions of society as well as of friends and family (Janoff-Bulman, 1979). Once again, the presumed explanation for victim derogation is that the attributors shield themselves from the fact that a similar fate could befall them, as well as from the guilt associated with not helping the victim more (Kalish, 1977). Interestingly, as Wortman and Dunkel-Schetter (1979) report, one of the most insidious aspects of this phenomenon is that the more severe the victim's suffering, the greater is the inclination to derogate and avoid the victim.

A second consequence of unjustifiably blaming others for their fates is that the resultant sense of personal invulnerability may prevent people from taking concrete actions to avoid similar fates. For example, women who believe that rape victims are either women of questionable virtue or women who provoke their assailants, may fail to take the necessary precautions to ensure that they themselves do not become victims. Similarly, the tendency for people to derogate or otherwise blame victims of illnesses such as heart disease or cancer may prevent the individuals from taking actions that would reduce their own chances of suffering a similar fate. That people greatly underestimate the likelihood of contracting and dying from diseases such as cancer is well established (Knopf, 1976; Weinstein, 1984), and workers in the health field are continually frustrated by people's beliefs that they are invulnerable ("It can't happen to me") and that there is a difference between themselves and "victims" (Perloff & Fetzer, 1986). A sense of security and invulnerability may have many adaptive aspects, but if it is maintained through a distortion of reality it may be profoundly maladaptive (Perloff, 1983).

Another distressing aspect of the just world bias is that it appears to lead to self-derogation. There is a large and diverse literature suggesting that people often blame themselves unjustifiably for negative events (see Coates, Wortman, & Abbey, 1979; and Lerner & Miller, 1978, for reviews). Consistent with the phenomenon of other-blame, self-blame can take the form of finding fault with one's behavior or one's character. Self-blame, of course, is one of the most common problems that clinicians confront. People often blame themselves unjustifiably for health problems, interpersonal problems, and career problems, to name a few. One explanation of this phenomenon is that victims come, over time, to internalize the negative views that others have of them (Goffman, 1963; Kleiman, Mantell, & Alexander, 1977). From the perspective of the effective control or just world hypothesis, however, self-blame occurs because it imposes an order or structure on one's fate. The alternative of blaming misfortune on others or fate diminishes the individual's perception of personal control.

The question of adaptiveness as applied to self-blame is a complex one. If such blame is valid and does not involve distortion, it may well prove adaptive if the individual takes steps to avoid similar mistakes in the future. This possibility is obviously more applicable to behavioral than characterological blame (Janoff-Bulman, 1979; Janoff-Bulman & Lang-Gunn, Chapter 5, this volume; Tennen, Affleck, & Gershman, 1986). Even if the self-blame involves distortion, however, there may be instances in which it has adaptive consequences. As Wortman (1976) and Kubler-Ross (1969) have shown, the perception that no one is responsible for a traumatic life event such as terminal illness, is so psychologically disconcerting that victims may gain solace and comfort from blaming themselves. Inappropriate guilt can sometimes be preferable to a sense of randomness or chaos.

Bulman and Wortman's (1977) work with paraplegic accident victims provides empirical evidence that accepting behavioral responsibility for misfortunes is sometimes associated with greater subsequent coping. Here again, if individuals accept that they were responsible for their past (e.g., their accident), then they may also assume that their future fate is in their own hands. Unfortunately, while Bulman and Wortman's findings are most interesting, there is an interpretation problem concerning the issue of attributional accuracy. It is possible that those taking personal responsibility were in fact responsible for their fates and that their attributions do not reflect any bias. It remains to be shown, therefore, that individuals who take more responsibility for their fate than is objectively warranted are subsequently better able to cope.

A Paradox

There is an apparent inconsistency between the self-derogation and success–failure literatures. Specifically, how is it that people are motivated both to accept responsibility for negative outcomes such as illness or injury and to deny responsibility for negative outcomes such as task failure? One possible resolution of this apparent paradox focuses on the nature of the fate to be explained.

The dominant element in the negative affect associated with failure experiences (e.g., failed exams, failed marriages) is the threat to self-esteem. There are obviously other painful consequences to a failed marriage and even to some exam failures (not getting into medical school, for instance), but in most failure contexts, especially those created in the laboratory, it is the threat to self-esteem that is dominant. Externalizing responsibility for failure is presumably effective in forestalling this type of negative affect.

The negative affect associated with being a victim of an accident or illness is quite different from that associated with failure. Self-esteem is generally much less relevant in the case of an accident. To deny responsibility for accidents or illness is not likely to make one feel better. In fact, as noted earlier, such externalization may actually make a person feel worse by rendering his or her fate less explicable and less just. Externalizing blame for an accident, crime, or illness is of only limited explanatory value. It may explain why an event has happened by not why it has happened to you (Janoff-Bulman & Lang-Gunn, Chapter 5, this volume; Miller & Porter, 1983).

In this regard, the case of rape victims is particularly interesting. The experience of rape seems to involve threats both to self-esteem and to a sense of control. The self-concept of the rape victim may well be threatened by the act of rape, but reestablishing her self-esteem after the experience of rape is unlikely to eliminate all or even most of her psychological pain. The haunting question of "Why me?" would still persist, as would the accompanying sense of vulnerability and lack of control. Although it may lower one's self-concept, self-derogation at least helps counter those threats that may ultimately be the ones with which it is most difficult to cope. The conflict between the need for effective control and the need for high self-esteem may also have relevance for an understanding of chronic self-derogators, such as depressives (Beck, 1967). The need for control may be so great in depressive individuals that they are prepared to accept self-blame rather than admit that they are controlled by external influences.

UNDERESTIMATION OF SITUATIONAL INFLUENCE

Gustav Icheiser (1949) was the first to point out that people often underestimate the causal influence that situational factors have on other people's behavior. So pervasive is this error that Ross (1977) has labeled it the "fundamental attribution error." Again and again we overestimate the dispositional basis of a person's behavior and underestimate the causal role of situational factors. A person who behaves aggressively, selfishly, or compliantly is thought to do so because he or she has an aggressive, selfish, or compliant personality, rather than because aspects of the situations provoked this behavior. Another manifestation of this error is the assumption people make about the consistency of another's behavior. Although research indicates that cross-situational consistency coefficients are usually low, suggesting little behavioral consistency, we typically assume that a person's behavior will be consistent. When we see an example of a person's behavior we believe that it is an expression of a stable trait in the person and that similar behavior can be expected in the future. A further feature of this attributional error is that we often underestimate how similar the behavior of others in the same situation would be to that of the person we are observing.

As noted earlier, some authorities, notably behavior therapists and cognitive behavior therapists, have accused traditional psychologists of falling prey to the fundamental attribution error in explaining deviant behavior. Whether this accusation is true or not, it is certainly the case that traditional clinical assessment techniques (e.g., Rorschach, TAT, MMPI) are more appropriate for assessing the person than the situation.

The basis of the fundamental attribution error is not clear and may well be multiply determined. From the motivational perspective, it can be argued that such an error facilitates the perception of stability, predictability, and control over the environment. If we can assume that others possess traits and will behave similarly in the future, it is much easier to know how to respond to them. Support for the motivational hypothesis comes from research showing that people are more likely to infer a dispositional basis from a person's behavior if they are interacting with the person, or if they expect to interact with the person in the future, than if they are simply observing the person interact with another (Miller & Norman, 1975; Miller, Norman, & Wright, 1978). Also, it appears that the tendency to emphasize dispositional causality is greater in those whose need for effective control over their environment is high rather than low (Miller *et al.*, 1978).

There are reasons other than motivational ones for this error, however (Jones, 1979). As observers, we typically focus on the behavior of others, not on situational contingencies. This is especially true if the contingencies are not salient. Sometimes we are not even aware of all the situational influences on a person's behavior. Moreover, one often has no knowledge of the antecedent situational conditions that are responsible for a person's present behavior. In addition to differential knowledge and attention, there is a stronger perceptual link between a person and his or her behavior than between a situation and a person's behavior.

Overestimates of the presence of dispositional influence are particularly likely to occur in three contexts. The first of these contexts concerns role-guided behavior. Much has been written of the influence that roles and role requirements have on people's behavior (e.g., Sarbin & Allen, 1968). A role can be construed as a situational constraint; it normalizes the behavior of the individuals who occupy it, although some roles are certainly less constraining than others (e.g., parent vs. bank teller). Despite the impact of roles, it appears that people often fail to take sufficient account of a person's role when interpreting that person's behavior (Holmes & Miller, 1976). The person in the role is generally aware of its constraints, however, and often points out this fact (e.g., "I'm only doing my job"). Part of the experience of moving from one position in a role relationship (e.g., student, child) to another position in the relationship (e.g., teacher, parent) is the recognition of how much of the behavior we observed others perform in the role is in fact role prescribed.

A second context in which an undue degree of dispositional knowledge is inferred is that situation wherein the situational influence is the observer's own behavior. We often fail to recognize how our behavior influences the behavior of others (Kelley & Stahelski, 1970; Miller & Holmes, 1975; Miller & Turnbull, 1986; Snyder, 1985). There are probably at least two reasons for this error. First, we are not in a very good position to recognize the connections between our own behavior and the behavior of others. We are focused primarily on their behavior. Second, we tend to think that our behavior has only the effects we intend it to have. If we did not intend to influence a person's behavior in a certain way, we find it difficult to believe that we are responsible for such behavior. Ironically, people are generally quick to point out that their own behavior is a reaction to the behavior of others. This tendency to believe that one's own behavior is more influenced than influencing occurs at the inter-group and international levels as well as at the interpersonal level (Jervis, 1976; Tetlock & McGuire, 1986).

A third and related context for situational underestimation occurs with behavior directed toward oneself. People tend to infer more dispositional information from behavior directed toward them than from that same behavior directed toward others (Jones & Davis, 1965). Valins and Nisbett (1971) provide an interesting illustration of this bias. It seems that army psychiatrists in Vietnam observed that men in long-established combat units were in the habit of greeting new arrivals with strong suspicion and hostility. The new men, ignorant of battle and the unwritten rules of this unit, seemed stupid and unsocialized to their seasoned but uncharitable companions. The pattern that the psychiatrists labeled the "f.n.g." (for "f. . . new guy") syndrome, produced a considerable number of psychiatric casualties among the new men. To help them cope with this problem, the psychiatrists began equipping them with the attribution "They hate the f.n.g.," instead of the far more distressing attribution "They hate me." The impact of this shift was dramatic.

There are two important consequences of the fundamental attribution error. First, we may treat others inappropriately, even unjustly, because we fail to recognize the situational determinants of their behavior. Second, we may fail to learn from others what to expect from a situation when we are in it. The behavior of others often tells us much more about what our own behavior in a situation would be like, and much less about the personality characteristics of others, than we think.

A variant of the fundamental attribution error is the tendency to infer more dispositional knowledge from a person's fate than is warranted. A number of psychologists have observed that there is a tendency to blame persons rather than impersonal forces for negative outcomes such as accidents or misfortunes; further, the more negative the outcome, the greater is the tendency to assign responsibility to personal forces (Kelley, 1971; Lerner & Miller, 1978; Shaver, 1985; Walster, 1966). Whether this phenomenon has a hot basis or a cool one is unclear. The hot or motivational explanation is that a sense of personal control is facilitated by holding people responsible for outcomes, especially extreme ones, because people generally can be influenced more than situations can be. Also, one can more satisfactorily direct anger and hostility at people than at circumstances (Miller & Vidmar, 1981; Vidmar & Miller, 1980). The cool interpretation of this phenomenon is that individuals consider people to be more potent causal agents than circumstances because people are invariably seen as more directly linked with an act than are situational forces. The more extreme the outcome, the more compelling it is to assume that a person has been principally responsible.

In conflict situations, this bias has pernicious effects. Because people assume that *someone* must be responsible for the problems they are having, they infer (once they have absolved themselves of responsibility) that the other party "must be" responsible. They often do not even consider that an environmental condition might be responsible. Of course, people are generally also guilty of absolving themselves from responsibility too quickly, either because they are defensive or because they assume that if their motives and intentions are good their behavior cannot be at fault. This last error would seem primarily logical rather than motivational in origin.

SELF–OTHER DIFFERENCES IN CAUSAL ATTRIBUTIONS

Another attributional bias, strongly hinted at in the preceding section, concerns differences in the perceptions of one's own behavior and the behavior of others. In one of the most influential attributional formulations of the 1970s, Jones and Nisbett (1971) proposed that an initiator of an event (an actor) and an observer of that event will have "divergent perceptions" of the causes of that action. Actors will tend to attribute the behavior to the present situational conditions, whereas observers will tend to attribute the same behavior to the enduring dispositions of the actor. A voluminous literature has now been generated, the bulk of which supports the Jones and Nisbett hypothesis (Watson, 1981) and indicates that people are, in effect, S-R theorists when explaining their behavior and trait theorists when explaining the behavior of others.

As with other biases we have discussed, a number of factors probably underlie this one. First, the motivational account suggests that our need for effective control may be best served by seeing the behavior of others as stable and predictable, while seeing our own behavior as flexible and sensitive to situational requirements. But nonmotivational factors are probably even more important in explaining this bias. As Jones and Nisbett (1971) pointed out, the perspectives of the actor and of the observer are quite different. The actor is focused outward, at the situation, while the observer is focused on the actor, unaware of situational factors to which the actor is responding. Strong evidence that this "divergent perspective" contributes to the actor–observer effect comes from a study by Storms (1973), which revealed that when actor and observer were shown each other's perspective through the use of videotape, the biases all but disappeared.

Another important difference between actors and observers, noted by Jones and Nisbett (1971), is that actors have historical knowledge that observers generally do not. Actors may know, for instance, that they do not always act as they are currently acting. Although this last point implies that actors are more accurate interpreters of their own behavior, this is not necessarily the case. We still have much to learn about the relative accuracy of the perceptions of actors and observers (Funder, 1982, 1987; Kahneman & Miller, 1986; Monson & Snyder, 1977).

We have discussed the problems that can arise from seeing another's behavior as dispositionally based. Seeing our own behavior as situationally based, when combined with this other bias, produces considerable potential for interpersonal conflict. Disagreements and conflict will tend to be seen as the fault of the other person and his or her personal characteristics. Our own behavior will not be seen as reflecting our personal characteristics or wishes so much as reasonable responses to aspects of the situation, including the behavior of the other.

Orvis, Kelley, and Butler (1976) conducted a study of young couples and found impressive evidence of this type of attributional bias. Partners tended to explain their own actions in terms of external causes, such as the state of the environment, external objects, or events. In contrast, explanations of the spouse's behavior tended to focus on his or her characteristics. This bias was particularly prevalent for negative behaviors and clearly contributed to much of the conflict that the couples were experiencing. More recent evidence suggests that the tendency to attribute the negative behavior of one's spouse to his or her disposition is especially pronounced in distressed couples (Fincham, Beach, & Baucom, 1987).

One implication of this research for marital therapy is that partners should be made aware of their divergent perceptions, encouraged to talk to each other about them, and helped to see how and why they emerge (Fincham, 1985). Role-taking exercises (Beck *et al.*, 1979) should also help individuals understand and cope with the actor–observer bias.

The actor–observer bias often finds its way into the clinician's office. Progress in therapy may be impeded to the extent that the clinician and the client disagree on the dispositional as opposed to situational basis of the client's behavior. For instance, the clinician may view the client's tendency to explain his or her behavior in situational terms as defensive, while the client may view the clinician's dispositional attributions as unsympathetic.

The tendency of individuals to take more responsibility for joint products than is objectively justified (Ross & Sicoly, 1979) represents another type of self–other bias. Whether asked to account for the individual's own contribution to a seminar discussion, a basketball game, or household chores, Ross and Sicoly found a tendency for people to take more responsibility than they assigned to the other participants. This bias is obviously compatible with the motivational hypothesis that people are egocentric and like to see themselves as causally potent and effective in their environment. Ross and Sicoly (1979) favor another interpretation, however. They argue that the tendency to overestimate our own contributions is actually a cool bias and reflects the fact that it is easier to recall our own actions than the actions of others. The tendency to assume prevalence or causal responsibility by ease of availability in memory was first identified by Tversky and Kahneman (1973) and has been found to account for a variety of judgmental errors and biases (see Fiske & Taylor, 1984; Nisbett & Ross, 1980). The potential of this bias for disagreement, misunderstanding, and conflict is clear.

THE MISPERCEPTION OF SELF–OTHER SIMILARITY

While people appear to interpret the behavior of others differently than they do their own behavior, they also appear to expect that others generally will behave the same way they do. In fact, people generally assume that others are more like them in behavioral predispositions as well as in attitudes and feelings than they in fact are. This bias has been documented by many investigators (e.g., Holmes, 1968; Katz & Allport, 1931) and has been labeled the "false consensus effect" by Ross, Greene, and House (1976).

The interpretation of this phenomenon is subject to considerable controversy. Traditional explanations of it have emphasized motivational processes, such as ego defensiveness or dissonance-reduction (Bramel, 1962; Edlow & Kiesler, 1966). These formulations assume that such "projection," especially in the case of negative characteristics, leaves one feeling better about oneself. Ross *et al.* (1976), in contrast, contend that assumed self–other similarity may be a cool error, due in large part to more frequent exposure to people who are similar rather than dissimilar to ourselves, and also to the greater ease with which we can recall or imagine similar as opposed to dissimilar behavior (see also Sherman, Chassin, Presson, & Agostinelli, 1984). A study by Miller (1982b) shows that the tendency to assume self–other similarity is greater in the case of emotional reactions than of behavioral reactions. This finding probably reflects people's assumption that emotional reactions are more situationally determined than are behavioral reactions.

The consequences of the false consensus effect are numerous. Because people expect "normal" others to behave as they do or would, they may consider dissimilar behavior in another to be especially revealing of *unique* dispositional qualities (Ross *et al.*, 1976). Conflict and embarrassment will also be frequent consequences of the tendency to overestimate self–other similarity. The erroneous assumption that another person shares one's opinions or views can produce conflict in subtle ways, as suggested in a study on couples reported by Harvey, Wells, and Alvarez (1978). The results of this study indicated that members of couples tend to exaggerate the degree of similarity between their own view and their partner's view on various issues. Moreover, Harvey and colleagues offer the interesting suggestion that not knowing there is a divergence of opinion when there is may well lead to more conflict than the divergence itself. Another's hostile or uncooperative behavior is often much more easily explained and handled when self-other differences are recognized than when they are not. In the latter case, a person may be puzzled as to why someone sharing the same values and feelings would do something that he or she would never do.

The tendency to assume that others are similar to oneself is certainly prevalent, but people also often assume that others are more different from themselves than is justified (Campbell, 1986; Valins & Nisbett, 1971). This latter effect, or what we will term the "false uniqueness effect," is particularly likely to find its way into the clinician's office as a source of disturbance. Much therapy and counseling are directed toward helping people see that their reactions or feelings are not only normal but common, and that these emotions do not reflect a unique or even unusual characteristic of theirs. The use of support groups can be very beneficial in this area (Coates & Winston, 1983; Wortman & Dintzer, 1978).

FALSE CONSENSUS AND FALSE UNIQUENESS EFFECTS:
A RECONCILIATION

The existence of both the *false consensus* and *false uniqueness* effects is intriguing, especially because they both have such strong intuitive appeal. A possible reconciliation of the two effects emerges from a closer examination of the situations in which each of them occurs. Our analysis at this point, unfortunately, can only be speculative.

The false consensus effect—assuming greater similarity to others than is justified—is likely the most prevalent of the two errors (Mullen *et al.*, 1985). The false uniqueness effect, however, may actually have more serious consequences. The unjustified perception of uniqueness is particularly likely to occur in two circumstances. In the first of these the individual has little information about the reactions of others and finds himself or herself responding in a way that, while actually similar to others, surprises the individual and does not seem situationally explicable. Without accurate knowledge of how others respond in the situation and without a comprehensible situational explanation, the individual assumes that his or her reactions reflect something dispositional or unique. If this characteristic is perceived to be negative, serious consequences can ensue. The lack of knowledge about the reactions of others and of a compelling situational explanation for one's own reaction are closely related determinants of the false uniqueness effect. It is frequently the knowledge or assumption that others have the same behavioral or emotional reaction to a similar situation that leads people to attribute their reactions to situational causes. If there is a conspiracy of silence by individuals, some people may well conclude incorrectly that their experiences or reactions are unique. Situations that frequently lead to both a reluctance to share experiences and a sense of false uniqueness include socially unacceptable behavior (e.g., incest, wife abuse) and certain major life events (e.g., postpartum or postretirement depression). The mistaken sense that one's behavior or experiences are unique or that one's difficulty in coping is greater than other people's greatly aggravates the distress felt in many situations (Coates & Winston, 1983).

People often err in thinking not only that their behavior is more exceptional than it is but also that the reasons or causes for their behavior are less common than they are. Beckman (1979), for instance, has found that alcoholics tend to believe that their alcoholism is due in greater part to internal factors than is the alcoholism of others. This error may add to the alcoholic's burden by increasing his or her guilt and anxiety.

In attempting to convince people of the ordinariness of their feelings or behaviors, it is particularly important to explain to them why they and others behave or feel the way they do. To tell a new mother that it is common to feel ambivalence toward a child or a recently divorced person that his or her feelings of inadequacy are nothing unusual is likely to have limited effect unless accompanied by an explanation of why this is the case. People believe they are unique in part because they do not understand the psychological forces at play in a situation, and simply telling them that others have the same reactions will not remedy their ignorance of these forces.[1]

A second circumstance that facilitates the illusion of uniqueness is where shyness or fear of embarrassment produce a discrepancy between people's public behavior and their private feelings or perceptions. People recognize the role that shyness and fear of embarrassment play in their own behavior, but not in the behavior of others. It is as though they say to themselves, "I'm indicating that I understand the professor's explanation because I do not want to look stupid, but the others are indicating that they understand it because they really do understand it" or "I'm not trying to find out if that person needs help because I do not want to be seen as an alarmist, but the others aren't approaching because they have decided it isn't an emergency." The tendency to see ourselves as shyer and more fearful of embarrassment than others leads us to view these characteristics as more potent causes of our own behaviors than the behaviors of others (Miller & McFarland, 1987). We assume their behavior must be due to something else.

---

1. Of course, many cases of depression or agitation are not caused or aggravated by a sense of uniqueness, and in these cases it will make little difference if people are told their reaction is shared and predictable. For example, Nisbett, Borgida, Crandall, and Reed (1976) attempted unsuccessfully to alleviate various depressive states, including that of first-year faculty members, by informing the sufferers of the universal nature of these feelings. The probable reason this strategy was *ineffective* is that the individuals already knew that others felt the same way they did or were disturbed by something other than a sense of uniqueness.

This dynamic often can lead to interpersonal conflict. Two people who have had a disagreement, for instance, may both show hesitancy to apologize, yet each may assume that the other's hesitancy reflects a different motivation. They may interpret their own hesitancy as motivated by caution, while interpreting the other's as motivated by continuing hostility.

CONCLUSIONS

In this chapter we have identified a variety of common attributional errors and biases, as follows:

1. the self-serving attributional bias for success and failure
2. the need for effective control and the biasing of attributions
3. underestimation of the causal influence of situations
4. self–other differences in causal attributions
5. the misperception of self–other similarity

We also have speculated about their possible basis and described their various consequences.

TYPES OF ERRORS AND BIASES

The errors and biases we have identified can be described generally as taking one of three different forms, with each one involving a different aspect of the causal sequence (situation/disposition → intention → action → outcome). The first type of bias concerns the inferences about causal antecedents that individuals make on the basis of their knowledge of outcomes. People make very different assumptions about the causal role of dispositions, intentions, and situations depending on whether they succeeded or failed at an activity. It is not easy to tell whether the bias occurs in the explaining of success, failure, or both, but because they are explained differently it is assumed that a bias exists in some form. The tendency to assume a relation between actions or dispositions and "chance" negative outcomes (e.g., victim derogation) is another example of this type of bias, which is particularly strong when the negative outcomes are severe. Thus, this category of bias subsumes the first two items in the list above.

A second type of error concerns the amount of dispositional information one infers from a person's actions. Ross (1977) has contended that the "fundamental attribution error" is the tendency of observers to underestimate the influence of situations on action and overestimate the amount of dispositional information revealed in the actor's behavior (items 3 and 4 in the preceding list). If observers err generally in inferring too much disposition from the actions of actors, actors themselves appear frequently to underestimate the amount of dispositional information revealed in their behavior.

The third type of error involves assumptions about the similarity between one's own actions, dispositions, or intentions and those of others (item 5 in the list). Within this category we described people's tendency, in some circumstances, to overestimate the similarity between their own actions or dispositions and those of others and, in other circumstances, to underestimate the degree of such similarity. Also included in this category is the tendency to exaggerate the role of one's own actions in determining a joint outcome.

ORIGINS OF ERRORS AND BIAS

Different explanations have been proposed for each of the errors and biases we have discussed, but all of them can be subsumed under two generic categories. The first class we have termed the hot or motivational theories because they propose that errors and biases in attribution result from the interference of various psychological needs. These motives, such as the need for high self-esteem and the need for effective control, are believed to subvert the otherwise rational attribution process and yield attributions congruent with themselves. The second class of explanations, the cool or nonmotivational theories, contend that errors and biases arise from the holding of erroneous causal theories, the application of invalid inferential strategies, or the misapplication of valid inferential strategies.

Hot and cool explanations have been provided for each of the errors and biases we have discussed. Clearly, it is exceedingly difficult to determine the relative validity of the two perspectives. Perhaps neither perspective is equally applicable to all types of errors and biases, some classes of errors and biases may be hot and others cool. The debate over the origins of errors will no doubt continue to be vigorous. Resolving it will require each side to be more precise in formulating its position and in specifying what would constitute disconfirming evidence.

The ultimate conclusion may well be that many errors and biases reflect the influence of both hot and cool processes. For example, while our needs or wishes may bias us toward the consideration of certain hypotheses (e.g., the victim was at fault, the task was too hard), it may be the basic features of human information-processing that are responsible for the biased manner in which we select and process the information pertinent to these hypotheses (Kunda, 1987).

CONSEQUENCES OF ATTRIBUTIONAL ERRORS AND BIASES

Attributional errors and biases can have both affective and behavioral consequences. Depending on our attributions, we can feel hopeful, proud, and competent, or pessimistic, ashamed, and helpless. Examples of biases presumed to facilitate positive feelings or prevent negative feelings are those involving the externalizing of responsibility for failure and the derogation of innocent victims. Unfounded feelings of uniqueness and self-blame for misfortunes are examples of errors that yield negative affective states.

The finding that errors and biases have affective consequences would seem to have relevance for the debate concerning their origin. For instance, one might ask whether the fact that people feel better when they make erroneous attributions supports the contention that such errors and biases are motivational in origin. We think not. This result is certainly compatible with the motivational account, but it is *not inconsistent* with nonmotivational explanations. There is no reason why a nonmotivationally produced error or bias cannot have motivational consequences.

It is even possible that hot errors or biases may have weaker affective consequences than cool ones. Findings relevant to this possibility have been reported by Miller (1979). Not even the most ardent proponent of the motivational position would argue that all internal–success and external–failure attributions are motivationally based; therefore, Miller argued that one must be able to distinguish between attributions of this type that are hot and those that are cool in order to perform an adequate test of the motivational hypothesis. He approached this problem by examining the relationship between attribution and mood under two levels of ego involvement. Miller predicted that not only would there be a more pronounced attribution bias in the high- than in the low-involvement condition, as he (Miller, 1976) previously reported, but also that a greater proportion of attributions occurring in the high-involvement condition would be hot. Once again, the assumption is that the greater the ego involvement, the greater the arousal of self-serving tendencies.

Under low-involvement conditions, the pattern of correlations was very similar to that reported by Weiner and his colleagues (Weiner, Russell, & Lerman, 1979), with external–failure and internal–success attributions being associated with the most positive mood ratings. Under high-involvement conditions, however, a very different pattern emerged. Here, the more subjects externalized responsibility for failure, the *lower* their mood ratings. Successful subjects' attributions were not correlated with mood ratings.

How are we to interpret these findings? If it is correct to assume that many more of the attributions offered by subjects in the high-involvement condition are hot cognitions, the results may suggest that such cognitions are not effective in bolstering self-esteem. In other words, hot cognitions may not cool a person off. At the very least, at this point it seems premature to conclude that "defensive" attributions succeed in defending a person.

In many instances, the affective consequences of attributional errors and biases will lead to behavioral consequences. Anger, fear, pride, and shame are all emotional states having behavioral sequelae. Even when there are no obvious affective consequences of attributional errors, behavioral consequences may emerge. A person's erroneous assumption that others will respond to a situation as he or she would may not have strong affective consequences, but it is likely to affect the individual's reaction in that situation. And the tendency to externalize responsiblity for failure experiences is likely to increase the probability that a person will behave in a way that invites similar experiences in the future.

Some errors or biases have more enduring or severe consequences than others. A moderate degree of illusion, if it makes us think well of ourselves, may be adaptive (Taylor & Brown, in press). This speculation is similar to Freud's contention that defense mechanisms can be adaptive if they are used sparingly. We probably survive most errors and biases quite well. Other errors and biases, especially persistently erroneous attributional styles (see Anderson & Arnoult, 1985; Ickes, Chapter 3, this volume; Metalsky & Abramson, 1980) may have profoundly negative consequences.

COUNTERING ERRORS AND BIASES

Because many attributional errors and biases have negative consequences for either the attributor or the target of the attributions, it seems important to consider the means of countering them. The ways one might go about correcting an error or bias depend on both its type and its presumed origins. If the error or bias stems from a person's needs or emotional state, the potential for debiasing would seem low. Unless one could modify the motivational state itself, it seems unlikely that the error or bias could be reduced. Simply enlightening the individual as to the existence and motivational basis of the error is not certain to be productive. Katz and Stotland (1959), for instance, attempted with little success to reduce prejudice in people by explaining the motivational basis of prejudice to them. Some errors and biases may, of course, disappear naturally as the emotional conditions that spawned them dissipate. A person who no longer feels pain over a divorce, for example, may cease to externalize responsibility.

If an error or bias does not have hot origins, the potential for debiasing is perhaps greater, at least in some cases. The tendency to infer more dispositional knowledge from people's behavior than is warranted, for instance, may be modifiable if people are informed about the potency of certain roles or situational pressures. Similarly, actor–observer differences may be narrowed if people are taught to imagine themselves in the role of others. Certain types of erroneous causal inferences, therefore, may be correctable.

Other types are not easily corrected. Misinformation or erroneous theories are more easily modified than are standard inferential strategies. When such strategies or heuristics are responsible for an error, it is exceedingly difficult to modify the error (Kahneman & Tversky, 1979). Let us take as an example the error of assuming more personal responsibility for joint outcomes than is warranted. Recall that the cool explanation for this error is that an individual's own actions or contributions are more "available" from memory than are the actions and contributions of others. How could one modify this error? The basis of the error, the tendency to infer proportion or dominance from availability in memory, is a basic feature of our cognitive functioning and cannot be modified. In fact, we probably would not even want to modify this heuristic because, for the most part, it serves us well and generally leads to correct inferences. The problem is that just as our perceptual system can sometimes lead to perceptual illusions, so our cognitive system can sometimes lead to "cognitive illusions." If a visual illusion is explained to people, they may be able to correct for it, but the "correct" view will still not seem "right" to them. Similarly, once told of the availability heuristic, people may be able to partially adjust for its effects, but this adjustment is unlikely to ever "feel" right." For example, an individual may have great difficulty convincing himself or herself that despite a strong conviction that he or she does 70 percent of the household chores, this percentage is almost certainly inflated because of the availability heuristic.

CLINICAL IMPLICATIONS

Although individuals' causal interpretations of their own behavior and the behavior of others are probably accurate more often than not, the attributional errors and biases that do occur have considerable import for the understanding and treatment of various forms of psychological disturbance. The interface between clinical psychology and attribution theory merits further exploration. Among the most important issues for clinical psychology to consider are the following: (1) Do the information-processing and inferential errors and biases that seem to be key symptoms of psychopathology have hot or cool origins? (2) Are these errors and biases qualitatively different from those that occur in normal individuals or are they simply exaggerated in form? (3) If the latter is the case, when do errors and biases become pathological? Finally, (4) What are the causal relationships between these errors and biases and various forms of psychopathology? Recent research reported in this volume and elsewhere (Alloy, 1988; Coyne & Gotlib, 1983; Peterson & Seligman, 1984) has already begun to shed light on these questions.

ACKNOWLEDGMENTS

Portions of this chapter were written while the first author was a Fellow at the Center for Advanced Study in the Behavioral Sciences. Support was provided by National Science Foundation Grant BNS-76 22943 and SSHRC Grants 410-78-0583 and 410-83-1347. The authors wish to thank Lyn Abramson, Mig Farina, Philip Kendall, and Mark Snyder for their helpful comments on an earlier version of this chapter.

REFERENCES

Abramson, L. Y., & Alloy, L. B. (1981). Depression, nondepression and cognitive illusions: A reply to Schwartz. *Journal of Experimental Psychology: General, 110,* 436–447.

Abramson, L. Y., Seligman, M. E. P., & Teasdale, J. D. (1978). Learned helplessness in humans: Critique and reformulation. *Journal of Abnormal Psychology, 87,* 49–74.

Alloy, L. B. (Ed.). (1988). *Cognitive processes in depression.* New York: Guilford.

Allport, G. W. (1937). *Personality: A psychological interpretation.* New York: Holt.

Anderson, C. A., & Arnoult, L. H. (1985). Attribution style and everyday problems in living: Depression, loneliness and shyness. *Social Cognition, 3,* 16–35.

Archibald, W. P. (1974). Alternative explanations for self-fulfilling prophecy. *Psychological Bulletin, 81,* 74–84.

Beck, A. T. (1967). *Depression: Clinical, experimental, and theoretical aspects.* New York: Harper & Row.

Beck, A. T. (1976). *Cognitive therapy and the emotional disorders.* New York: International Universities Press.

Beck, A. T., Rush, A. J., Shaw, B. F., & Emery, G. (1979). *Cognitive therapy of depression: A treatment manual.* New York: Guilford.

Beckman, L. J. (1979). Beliefs about the causes of alcohol-related problems among alcoholic and nonalcoholic women. *Journal of Clinical Psychology, 35,* 663–670.

Bem, D. J. (1972). Self-perception theory. In L. Berkowitz (Ed.), *Advances in experimental social psychology* (Vol. 6). New York: Academic.

Bramel, D. (1962). A dissonance theory approach to defensive projection. *Journal of Abnormal and Social Psychology, 64,* 121–129.

Brewer, M. B. (1977). An information-processing approach to attribution of responsibility. *Journal of Experimental Social Psychology, 13,* 58–69.

Brewin, C. R. (1985). Depression and causal attributions: What is their relation? *Psychological Bulletin, 98,* 297–309.

Bulman, R. J., & Wortman, C. B. (1977). Attributions of blame and coping in the "real world": Severe accident victims react to their lot. *Journal of Personality and Social Psychology, 35,* 351–363.

Burke, B., & Peplau, L. A. (1976, April). *Loneliness in the university.* Paper presented at the annual meeting of the Western Psychological Association, Los Angeles.

Campbell, J. D. (1986). Similarity and uniqueness: The effects of attribute type, relevance, and individual differences in self-esteem and depression. *Journal of Personality and Social Psychology, 50,* 281–294.

Clark, M., & Isen, A. M. (1982). Toward understanding the relationship between feeling states and social behavior. In A. Hastorf & A. Isen (Eds.), *Cognitive social psychology.* New York: Elsevier.

Coates, D., & Winston, T. (1983). Counteracting the deviance of depression: Peer support groups for victims. *Journal of Social Issues, 39*(2), 169–194.

Coates, D., Wortman, C. B., & Abbey, A. (1979). Reactions to victims. In I. H. Frieze, D. Bartal, & J. S. Carroll (Eds.), *New approaches to social problems.* San Francisco: Jossey-Bass.

Coyne, J. C., & Gotlib, I. H. (1983). The role of cognition in depression: A critical appraisal. *Psychological Bulletin, 94,* 472–505.

Dawes, R. (1976). Shallow psychology. In J. S. Carroll & J. W. Payne (Eds.), *Cognition and social behavior.* Hillsdale, NJ: Erlbaum.

Edlow, D., & Kiesler, C. (1966). Ease of denial and defensive projection. *Journal of Experimental Social Psychology, 2,* 56–69.

Ellis, A., & Grieger, R. (1977). *Handbook of rational-emotive therapy.* New York: Springer.

Fincham, F. D. (1985). Attributions in close relationships. In J. H. Harvey & G. Weary (Eds.), *Attribution: Basic issues and applications.* New York: Academic Press.

Fincham, F. D., Beach, S. R., & Baucom, D. H. (1987). Attribution processes in distressed and nondistressed couples: Self–partner attribution differences. *Journal of Personality and Social Psychology, 52*, 739–748.

Fiske, S., & Taylor, S. E. (1984). *Social cognition.* Reading, MA: Addison-Wesley.

Forsterling, F. (1985). Attributional retraining: A review. *Psychological Bulletin, 98*, 495–512.

Funder, D. C. (1982). On the accuracy of dispositional versus situational attributions. *Social Cognition, 1*, 205–222.

Funder, D. C. (1987). Errors and mistakes: Evaluating the accuracy of social judgment. *Psychological Bulletin, 101*, 75–90.

Girodo, M., Dotzenroth, S., & Stein, D. (1981). Causal attribution bias in shy males: Implications for self-esteem and self-confidence. *Cognitive Therapy and Research, 5*, 325–338.

Goffman, E. (1963). *Stigma: Notes on the management of spoiled identity.* Englewood Cliffs, NJ: Prentice-Hall.

Goldfried, M. R., & Davison, G. C. (1976). *Clinical behavior therapy.* New York: Holt.

Harvey, J. H., & Weary, G. (1981). *Perspectives on attributional processes.* Dubuque, IA: William C. Brown.

Harvey, J. H., Wells, G. L., & Alvarez, M. D. (1978). Attribution in the context of conflict and separation in close relationships. In J. H. Harvey, W. Ickes, & R. F. Kidd (Eds.), *New directions in attribution research* (Vol. 2). Hillsdale, NJ: Erlbaum.

Hastorf, A., Schneider, D., & Polefka, J. (1970). *Person perception.* Reading, MA: Addison-Wesley.

Heider, F. (1958). *The psychology of interpersonal relations.* New York: Wiley.

Hollon, S. D., & Kriss, M. R. (1984). Cognitive factors in clinical research and practice. *Clinical Psychology Review, 4*, 35–76.

Holmes, D. S. (1978). Projection as a defense mechanism. *Psychological Bulletin, 85*, 677–688.

Holmes, J. G., & Miller, D. T. (1976). Interpersonal conflict. In J. W. Thibaut, J. T. Spence, & R. C. Carson (Eds.), *Contemporary topics in social psychology.* Morristown, NJ: General Learning Press.

Icheiser, G. (1949). Misunderstandings in human relations: A study in false social perception. *American Journal of Sociology, 55*(Part 2), 1–70.

Janoff-Bulman, R. (1979). Characterological versus behavioral self-blame: Inquiries into depression and rape. *Journal of Personality and Social Psychology, 37*, 1798–1809.

Jervis, R. (1976). *Perception and misperception in international relations.* Princeton, NJ: Princeton University Press.

Jones, E. E. (1979). The rocky road from acts to dispositions. *American Psychologist, 34*, 107–117.

Jones, E. E., & Davis, K. (1965). From acts to dispositions: The attribution process in person perception. In L. Berkowitz (Ed.), *Advances in experimental social psychology* (Vol. 2). New York: Academic Press.

Jones, E. E., Kanouse, D. E., Kelley, H. H., Nisbett, R. E., Valins, S., & Weiner, B. (Eds.), *Attribution: Perceiving the causes of behavior.* Morristown, NJ: General Learning Press.

Jones, E. E., & Nisbett, R. E. (1971). *The actor and the observer: Divergent perceptions of the causes of behavior.* Morristown, NJ: General Learning Press.

Kahneman, D., & Miller, D. T. (1986). Norm theory: Comparing reality to its alternatives. *Psychological Review, 93*, 136–153.

Kahneman, D., Slovic, P., & Tversky, A. (Eds.). (1982). *Judgment under uncertainty: Heuristics and biases.* Cambridge, MA: Cambridge University Press.

Kahneman, D., & Tversky, A. (1979). Intuitive prediction: Biases and corrective procedures. *Management Science, 12*, 313–327.

Kalish, R. A. (1977). Dying and preparing for death: A view of families. In H. Feifel (Ed.), *New meanings of death.* New York: McGraw-Hill.

Katz, D., & Allport, F. (1931). *Students' attitudes.* Syracuse, NY: Craftsman.

Katz, D., & Stotland, E. (1959). A preliminary statement to a theory of attitude structure and change. In S. Koch (Ed.), *Psychology: A study of a science* (Vol. 3). New York: McGraw-Hill.

Kelley, H. H. (1967). Attribution theory in social psychology. In D. Levine (Ed.), *Nebraska symposium on motivation*. Lincoln, NE: University of Nebraska Press.

Kelley, H. H. (1972). *Attribution in social interaction*. Morristown, NJ: General Learning Press.

Kelley, H. H., & Stahelski, A. (1970). The social interaction basis of cooperators' and competitors' beliefs about others. *Journal of Personality and Social Psychology, 16*, 66–91.

Kleiman, M. A., Mantell, J. E., & Alexander, E. S. (1977). Collaboration and its discontents: The perils of partnership. *Journal of Applied Behavior Science, 13*, 403–410.

Knopf, A. (1976). Changes in women's opinions about cancer. *Social Science and Medicine, 13*, 403–410.

Kubler-Ross, E. (1969). *On death and dying*. New York: Macmillan.

Kuiper, N. A. (1978). Depression and causal attributions for success and failure. *Journal of Personality and Social Psychology, 36*, 236–246.

Kunda, Z. (1987). Motivated inference: Self-serving generation and evaluation of causal theories. *Journal of Personality and Social Psychology, 53*, 636–647.

Lerner, M. J. (1970). The desire for justice and reactions to victims. In J. Macaulay & L. Berkowitz (Eds.), *Altruism and helping behavior*. New York: Academic Press.

Lerner, M. J., & Miller, D. T. (1978). Just world research and the attribution process: Looking back and ahead. *Psychological Bulletin, 85*, 1030–1051.

Markus, H., & Zajonc, R. B. (1985). The cognitive perspective in social psychology. In. G. Lindzey & E. Aronson (Eds.), *Handbook of social psychology* (3rd ed.). New York: Random House.

Metalsky, G. I., & Abramson, L. Y. (1980). Attributional styles: Toward a framework for conceptualization and assessment. In P. C. Kendall & S. D. Hollon (Eds.), *Cognitive-behavioral interventions: Assessment methods*. New York: Academic.

Metalsky, G. I., Abramson, L. Y., Seligman, M. E. P., Semmel, A., & Peterson, C. (1982). Attributional styles and life events in the classroom: Vulnerability and invulnerability to depressive mood reactions. *Journal of Personality and Social Psychology, 43*, 612–617.

Miller, D. T. (1976). Ego involvement and attributions for success and failure. *Journal of Personality and Social Psychology, 34*, 901–906.

Miller, D. T. (1979, June). *The relation between causal attributions and affect: Do hot cognitions cool you off?* Paper presented at the Annual Meeting of the Canadian Psychological Association, Quebec.

Miller, D. T. (1982a). *Effects on performance of self-serving attributions*. Unpublished manuscript, Simon Fraser University, Canada.

Miller, D. T. (1982b). *False consensus effects in behavioral and emotional reactions*. Unpublished manuscript, Simon Fraser University, Canada.

Miller, D. T., & Holmes, J. G. (1975). The role of situational restrictiveness on self-fulfilling prophecies: A theoretical and empirical extension of Kelley and Stahelski's triangle hypothesis. *Journal of Personality and Social Psychology, 31*, 661–673.

Miller, D. T., & McFarland, C. (1987). Pluralistic ignorance: When similarity is interpreted as dissimilarity. *Journal of Personality and Social Psychology, 53*, 298–305.

Miller, D. T., & Moretti, M. M. (1988). The causal attributions of depressives: Self-serving or self-disserving. In L. Alloy (Ed.), *Cognitive processes in depression*. New York: Guilford.

Miller, D. T., & Norman, S. A. (1975). Actor–observer differences in perceptions of effective control. *Journal of Personality and Social Psychology, 31*, 503–515.

Miller, D. T., Norman, S. A., & Wright, F. (1978). Distortion in person perception as a consequence of the need for effective control. *Journal of Personality and Social Psychology, 36*, 598–607.

Miller, D. T., & Porter, C. A. (1980). Effects of temporal perspective on the attribution process. *Journal of Personality and Social Psychology, 39*, 532–541.

Miller, D. T., & Porter, C. A. (1983). Self-blame in victims of violence. *Journal of Social Issues*, *39*(2), 139–152.

Miller, D. T., & Ross, M. (1975). Self-serving biases in the attribution of causality: Fact or fiction? *Psychological Bulletin, 82*, 213–225.

Miller, D. T., & Turnbull, W. (1986). Expectancy effects in interpersonal relations. In M. R. Rozenzweig & L. M. Porter (Eds.), *Annual Review of Psychology* (Vol. 37). Palo Alto, CA: Annual Reviews.

Miller, D. T., & Vidmar, N. (1981). A social psychological analysis of punishment reactions. In M. J. Lerner & S. Lerner (Eds.), *The justice motive in social behavior*. New York: Plenum.

Monson, T. C., & Snyder, M. (1977). Actors, observers, and the attribution process: Toward a reconceptualization. *Journal of Experimental Social Psychology, 13*, 89–111.

Mullen, B., Atkins, J. L., Champion, D. S., Edwards, C., Hardy, D., Story, J. E., & Vanderklok, M. (1985). The false consensus effect: A meta-analysis of 115 hypothesis tests. *Journal of Experimental Social Psychology, 21*, 262–283.

Murphy, G. (1947). *Personality*. New York: Harper & Row.

Newman, H. M., & Langer, E. J. (1981). Post-divorce adaptation and the attribution of responsibility. *Sex Roles: A Journal of Research, 7*, 223–232.

Nisbett, R. E., Borgida, E., Crandall, R., & Reed, H. (1976). Popular induction: Information is not necessarily informative. In J. S. Carroll & W. Payne (Eds.), *Cognition and social behavior*. Hillsdale, NJ: Erlbaum.

Nisbett, R. E., & Ross, L. (1980). *Human inference: Strategies and shortcomings in social judgment*. Englewood Cliffs, NJ: Prentice-Hall.

Orvis, B. R., Kelley, H. H., & Butler, D. (1976). Attributional conflict in young couples. In J. Harvey, W. Ickes, & R. Kidd (Eds.), *New directions in attributional research* (Vol. 1). Hillsdale, NJ: Erlbaum.

Perloff, L. S. (1983). Perceptions of vulnerability to victimization. *Journal of Social Issues, 39*(2), 41–62.

Perloff, L. S., & Fetzer, B. K. (1986). Self–other judgments and perceived vulnerability to victimization. *Journal of Personality and Social Psychology, 50*, 502–510.

Peterson, C., & Seligman, M. E. P. (1984). Causal explanations as risk factors for depression: Theory and evidence. *Psychological Review, 91*, 347–374.

Rizley, R. (1978). Depression and distortion in the attribution of causality. *Journal of Abnormal Psychology, 87*, 32–48.

Ross, L. (1977). The intuitive psychologist and his shortcomings: Distortions in the attribution process. In L. Berkowitz (Ed.), *Advances in experimental social psychology* (Vol. 11). New York: Academic.

Ross, L., Green, D., & House, P. (1977). The "false consensus effect": An egocentric bias in social perception and attribution processes. *Journal of Experimental Social Psychology, 13*, 279–301.

Ross, M., & Fletcher, G. (1985). Social perception. In G. Lindzey & E. Aronson (Eds.), *Handbook of social psychology*. Reading, MA: Addison-Wesley.

Ross, M., & Sicoly, F. (1979). Egocentric biases in availability and attribution. *Journal of Personality and Social Psychology, 37*, 322–336.

Russell, D., & McAuley, E. (1986). Causal attributions, causal dimensions, and affective reactions to success and failure. *Journal of Personality and Social Psychology, 50*, 1174–1185.

Sarbin, T. R., & Allen, V. L. (1968). Role theory. In G. Lindzey & E. Aronson (Eds.), *Handbook of social psychology* (Vol. 1). Reading, MA: Addison-Wesley.

Seligman, M. E. P., Abramson, L. Y., Semmel, A., & Von Baeyer, C. (1979). Depressive attributional style. *Journal of Abnormal Psychology, 88*, 242–247.

Sharp, J., & Tennen, H. (1983). Attributional bias in depression: The role of cue perception. *Cognitive Therapy and Research, 7*, 325–332.

Shaver, K. G. (1975). *An introduction to attribution process*. Cambridge, MA: Winthrop.

Shaver, K. G. (1985). *The attribution of blame: Causality, responsibility and blameworthiness.* New York: Springer-Verlag.

Sherman, S. J., Chassin, L., Presson, C. C., & Agostinelli, G. (1984). The role of evaluation and similarity principles in the false consensus effect. *Journal of Personality and Social Psychology, 47,* 1244–1262.

Simon, H. A. (1957). *Models of man.* New York: Wiley.

Snyder, M. (1985). When belief meets reality. In L. Berkowitz (Ed.), *Advances in experimental social psychology* (Vol. 18). New York: Academic Press.

Snyder, M. L., Stephan, W. G., & Rosenfield, D. (1978). Attributional egotism. In J. Harvey, W. Ickes, & R. Kidd (Eds.), *New directions in attribution research* (Vol. 2). Hillsdale, NJ: Erlbaum.

Storms, M. D. (1973). Videotape and the attribution process: Reversing actors' and observers' points of view. *Journal of Personality and Social Psychology, 27,* 165–175.

Taylor, S. E., & Brown, J. (in press). Illusion and well being: Some social psychological contributions to a theory of mental health. *Psychological Bulletin.*

Tennen, H., Affleck, G., & Gershman, K. (1986). Self-blame among parents of infants with perinatal complications: The role of self-protective motives. *Journal of Personality and Social Psychology, 50,* 690–696.

Tetlock, P. E., & Levi, A. (1982). Attribution bias: On the inconclusiveness of the cognition–motivation debates. *Journal of Experimental Social Psychology, 18,* 68–88.

Tetlock, P. E., & McGuire, C. (1986). Cognitive perspectives on foreign policy. In S. Long (Ed.), *Political behavior annual* (Vol. 1). Boulder, CO: Westview.

Tversky, A., & Kahneman, D. (1973). Availability: A heuristic for judging frequency and probability. *Cognitive Psychology, 5,* 207–232.

Ullman, L. P., & Krasner, L. (1969). *A psychological approach to abnormal behavior.* Englewood Cliffs, NJ: Prentice-Hall.

Valins, S., & Nisbett, R. E. (1971). *Attribution processes in the development and treatment of emotional disorders.* Morristown, NJ: General Learning Press.

Vidmar, N., & Miller, D. T. (1980). Social psychological processes underlying attitudes toward legal punishment. *Law and Society Review, 14*(3), 401–439.

Walster, E. (1966). Assignment of responsibility for an accident. *Journal of Personality and Social Psychology, 3,* 73–79.

Watson, D. (1981). The actor and the observer: How are their perceptions of causality divergent? *Psychological Bulletin, 92,* 682–700.

Weimer, B. (1974). Achievement motivation as conceptualized by an attribution theorist. In B. Weiner (Ed.), *Achievement motivation and attribution theory.* Morristown, NJ: General Learning Press.

Weiner, B., Russell, D., & Lerman, D. (1978). Affective consequences of causal ascriptions. In J. Harvey, W. Ickes, & R. Kidd (Eds.), *New directions in attribution research* (Vol. 2). Hillsdale, NJ: Erlbaum.

Weiner, B., Russell, D., & Lerman, D. (1979). The cognition–emotion process in achievement-related contexts. *Journal of Personality and Social Psychology, 37,* 1211–1220.

Weinstein, N. D. (1984). Why it won't happen to me: Perceptions of risk factors and susceptibility. *Health Psychology, 3,* 431–457.

Wortman, C. B. (1976). Causal attributions and personal control. In J. Harvey, W. Ickes, & R. Kidd (Eds.), *New directions in attribution research* (Vol. 1). Hillsdale, NJ: Erlbaum.

Wortman, C., & Brehm, J. W. (1975). Response to uncontrollable outcomes: An integration of reactance theory and the learned helplessness model. In L. Berkowitz (Ed.), *Advances in experimental social psychology* (Vol. 8). New York: Academic.

Wortman, C. B., & Dintzer, L. (1978). Is an attributional analysis of the learned helplessness phenomenon viable? A critique of the Abramson–Seligman–Teasdale reformulation. *Journal of Abnormal Psychology, 87,* 75–90.

Wortman, C. B., & Dunkel-Schetter, C. (1979). Interpersonal relationships and cancer: A theoretical analysis. *Journal of Social Issues, 35,* 120–155.

Zemore, R., & Johansen, L. Y. (1980). Depression, helplessness and failure attributions. *Canadian Journal of Behavioral Science, 12,* 167–174.

Zuckerman, M. (1979). Attribution and success and failure revisited or: The attributional bias is alive and well in attribution theory. *Journal of Personality, 47,* 245–287.

II

*A Social Cognition Perspective
on Psychological Health
and Maladjustment*

2

The Hopelessness Theory of Depression: Does the Research Test the Theory?

LYN Y. ABRAMSON
GERALD I. METALSKY
LAUREN B. ALLOY

Depression is one of the most common psychological disorders. During any given year, about 15 percent of all adults between 18 and 74 may suffer significant depressive symptoms (Secunda, Katz, & Friedman, 1973). Many people recover from depression, but unlike most other forms of psychopathology, it can be lethal. One out of every 100 people with a depressive disorder dies by suicide (Williams, Friedman, & Secunda, 1970). The economic cost of depression also is great. In the United States alone, the annual financial cost of depression has been estimated to be between 0.3 billion and 0.9 billion dollars (Secunda *et al.*, 1973).

Despite the fact that depression has been recognized as an important form of psychopathology for centuries, researchers are only just beginning to make progress in understanding this disorder. Within experimental psychopathology, it is only in the past 20 years that research on depression has burgeoned. During this time, many investigators have emphasized the importance of cognitive processes in the etiology, maintenance, and treatment of depression (e.g., Abramson & Martin, 1981; Abramson, Seligman, & Teasdale, 1978; Alloy, 1982; Alloy & Abramson, 1979; Beck, 1967, 1976; Beck, Rush, Shaw, & Emery, 1979; Derry & Kuiper, 1981; Kovacs, Rush, Beck, & Hollon, 1981; Krantz & Hammen, 1979; Peterson & Seligman, 1984; Seligman, 1975). The now demonstrated efficacy of cognitive therapy for at least some forms of depression provides clinical support for a cognitive approach to depression (e.g., Beck *et al.*, 1979; Blackburn, Bishop, Glen, Whalley, & Christie, 1981; Kovacs *et al.*, 1981). In this chapter we evaluate the current status of one of the cognitive theories of depression, previously called the reformulated theory of human helplessness and depression (Abramson *et al.*, 1978). For reasons that

33

soon will become clear, we refer to this theory as the hopelessness theory of depression (see also Halberstadt, Mukherji, & Abramson, 1988).

The hopelessness theory of depression was proposed to resolve a number of conceptual and empirical inadequacies associated with the original theory of learned helplessness and depression (Seligman, 1975). The hopelessness theory, which relies heavily on basic work in social psychology on the causal attribution process, captured the attention of many depression researchers and has generated a considerable amount of empirical work. Perhaps because the theory stands at the crossroads of clinical and social psychology, it has been of interest to a diverse group of investigators. In evaluating work on the theory, we have arrived at a very disturbing conclusion: The various research *strategies* utilized over the course of the past 10 years to test the hopelessness theory of depression do not provide an adequate test of its basic postulates. Furthermore, if investigators rely on the robustness and consistency of results obtained with these research strategies as the criterion against which to evaluate the validity of the theory, they may be seriously misled.

In our view, the problems associated with previous studies result, in part, from investigators' failure to appreciate the full methodological implications of the kinds of causal relations specified in the hopelessness theory (e.g., sufficient-but-not-necessary proximal cause, diathesis-stress, and so forth). As a corollary, this limitation also may have contributed to researchers' failure to appreciate the heterogeneity that may exist among the depressive disorders. Consequently, one purpose of this chapter is to restate and clarify the basic postulates of the hopelessness theory and to place it more explicitly in the context of work in descriptive psychiatry about such heterogeneity (see Depue & Monroe, 1978). We suggest that the hopelessness theory hypothesizes the existence of an as yet unidentified subtype of depression—"hopelessness depression," and we elaborate, with respect to hypothesized cause, symptoms, course, variants, therapy, and prevention, the nomological network in which the concept of hopelessness depression is embedded. A second purpose of this chapter is to critique work to test the hopelessness theory conducted to date and to explicate the limitations in the existing research strategies. Third, we suggest more adequate strategies and discuss conceptual issues that will arise in conducting such tests. Finally, we conclude by discussing the general implications of our analysis for research on other theories of depression.

PRELIMINARY CONCEPTS

Before presenting a restatement and clarification of the hopelessness theory of depression, it is useful to distinguish among the concepts of *necessary* cause, *sufficient* cause, and *contributory* cause with regard to the occurrence of symptoms. Although the reader may be familiar with these concepts, it is important to illustrate their defining features because their methodological implications often have not been appreciated fully in hopelessness theory research.

A necessary cause of some set of symptoms is an etiological factor that must be present or have occurred in order for the symptoms to occur. In terms of formal logic, if the presence or occurrence of the etiological facter E is necessary for the occurrence of the set of symptoms S, this means: If S, then E or, mathematically speaking, Probability $(E/S) = 1.00$.[1] An additional feature of such a necessary causal relationship is that the symptoms cannot occur if the etiological factor is absent or has not occurred (i.e., If $\bar{E}$, then $\bar{S}$; Probability $(S/\bar{E}) = 0.00$). It is important to note that such a necessary causal relationship does not require the symptoms always to occur when the etiological factor is present or has occurred.

A sufficient cause of some set of symptoms is an etiological factor whose presence or occurrence guarantees the occurrence of the symptoms. In terms of formal logic, if the presence or occurrence of the etiological factor E is sufficient for the occurrence of the set of symptoms S, this means: If E, then S or, mathematically speaking, Probability $(S/E) = 1.00$. An additional feature of such a sufficient causal relationship is that if the symptoms do not occur, then the etiological factor cannot be present or have occurred (i.e., If $\bar{S}$, then $\bar{E}$; Probability $(E/\bar{S}) = 0.00$). It is important to note that such a sufficient causal relationship does not require the etiological factor always to have occurred or to be present for the symptoms to occur.

A contributory cause of some set of symptoms is an etiological factor that increases the likelihood of the occurrence of the symptoms but is neither necessary nor sufficient for their occurrence. Mathematically speaking, if the presence or occurrence of the etiological facter E contributes to the occurrence of the set of symptoms S, this means: Probability $(S/E) >$ Probability $(S/\bar{E})$, where Probability $(E/S) < 1.00$ (i.e., not necessary) and Probability $(S/E) < 1.00$ (i.e., not sufficient).

It is useful to discuss the possible relationships among the three types of causes described above. Of course, by definition, if a cause is contributory, it cannot be necessary or sufficient. Similarly, if a cause is necessary or sufficient, it cannot be contributory. In contrast, a particular etiological factor E may be necessary and sufficient, necessary but not sufficient, or sufficient but not necessary for the occurrence of the set of symptoms S.

In addition to varying in their formal relationship to the occurrence of symptoms (necessary, sufficient, or contributory), causes also may vary in their sequential relationship to the occurrence of symptoms. If one thinks of an etiological chain or sequence of events culminating in the occurrence of a set of

1. This conditional probability should read, "The probability of the presence (or occurrence) of the etiological factor given the presence (or occurrence) of the set of symptoms is equal to 1.00." Note, in this paper, we denote the *absence* (or lack of occurrence) of the etiological factor and the set of symptoms as $\bar{E}$ and $\bar{S}$, respectively.

symptoms, then some causes may operate toward the end of the chain, proximate to the occurrence of symptoms, whereas other causes may operate toward the beginning of the chain, distant from the occurrence of symptoms. We characterize the former as *proximal* causes and the latter as *distal* causes. It is important to recognize that, strictly speaking, the formal and sequential relationships of causes and symptoms are not orthogonal (i.e., independent) because a cause cannot be both sufficient and distal.[2]

It is useful to classify causes both in terms of their formal and sequential relationship to a set of symptoms. Of course, the concepts of necessary, sufficient, and contributory in conjunction with the concepts of proximal and distal do not exhaust the possible kinds of relationships that may obtain between causes and symptoms. For example, complex causal feedback loops involving threshold effects and so on may be involved in the production of a set of symptoms. However, at minimum, the reader must have mastered the concepts of necessary, sufficient, contributory, proximal, and distal causes in order to understand the postulates of the hopelessness theory of depression and our critique of work conducted to test this theory. If future work using more adequate research strategies (see the section, "A Proposal for a Research Strategy") fails to corroborate the current statement of the hopelessness theory, then further revisions of it, involving more complex (e.g., nonlinear) causal chains may be in order.

STATEMENT AND CLARIFICATION OF THE ETIOLOGICAL POSTULATES OF THE HOPELESSNESS THEORY

In our view, the etiological postulates of the hopelessness theory of depression can be understood best in terms of the concepts discussed in the previous section. Broadly stated, the hopelessness theory specifies a chain of distal and proximal contributory causes hypothesized to culminate in a proximal sufficient cause of depression.

A PROXIMAL SUFFICIENT CAUSE

According to Abramson *et al.* (1978), a proximal sufficient cause of depression is an expectation that highly desired outcomes are unlikely to occur or that

---

2. For simplicity of exposition, we have presented the proximal–distal distinction in terms of a dichotomy: proximal versus distal. Strictly speaking, however, it is more appropriate to think in terms of a proximal–distal continuum.

highly aversive outcomes are likely to occur and that no response in one's repertoire will change their likelihood of occurrence.[3] We view Abramson and colleagues' theory of depression as a *hopelessness* one because the connotations of this term capture the core elements of the proximal sufficient cause featured in the theory. Throughout the remainder of this chapter, we frequently use, for brevity, the phrase "hopelessness" to refer to this proximal sufficient cause.

It is instructive to compare the proximal sufficient cause of depression postulated in the hopelessness theory with the proximal sufficient cause in the original learned helplessness theory of depression (Seligman, 1975). In the latter, a proximal sufficient cause of depression was the expectation that one cannot control outcomes regardless of their hedonic valence or their likelihood of occurrence; hence the characterization of this theory as a helplessness one. In essence, Abramson *et al.* (1978) viewed only a subset of cases of expected lack of control, those involving negative expectations about the occurrence of highly valued or important events, as resulting in depression. In this regard, the hopelessness theory is more similar to other cognitive theories of depression (e.g., Beck, 1967; Brown & Harris, 1978; Melges & Bowlby, 1969) than was the original theory. Indeed, based on their epidemiological studies of the social origins of depression, Brown and Harris (1978) concluded, "It is such *generalization* of hopelessness that we believe forms the central core of a depressive disorder. It is this that sets the rest of the syndrome in train" (p. 235).

It is important to emphasize that Abramson *et al.* (1978) hypothesized that hopelessness is a proximal sufficient, but not a necessary, cause of depression. Explicitly recognizing that depression may be a heterogeneous disorder, they allowed for the possibility that other factors, such as genetic vulnerability, norepinephrine depletion, or loss of interest in reinforcers, also may be sufficient to cause depression (see Alloy, 1982, for a similar analysis of the learned helplessness phenomenon). Thus, Abramson *et al.* presented an etiological account of one hypothesized subtype of depression, defined in part by its

---

3. Abramson *et al.* (1978) cautioned that a basic problem existed in the statement of the proximal sufficient cause of depression featured in their hopelessness theory. They illustrated the problem as follows (Abramson *et al.*, 1978, p. 65): It is a "highly desired" outcome that the editor of this journal give us each 1 million dollars, but we believe this outcome has a very low probability and that there is nothing we can do to increase its probability. Yet we do not become depressed by this realization. In explanation, Abramson *et al.* suggested that some notion such as Klinger's (1975) "current concerns" is needed in the statement of the proximal sufficient cause. We feel depressed about the nonoccurrence of highly desired outcomes that we believe we cannot obtain only when they are "on our mind," "in the realm of possibility," "troubling us now," and so on. Although Abramson and colleagues found Klinger's concept heuristic, they felt it was not sufficiently well defined to be incorporated into the hopelessness theory. The problem of current concerns still remains to be solved.

proximal sufficient cause, which we term "hopelessness depression."[4] In a later section of this chapter ("Hopelessness depression: A Theory-based Subtype of Depression"), we more fully elaborate the concept of hopelessness depression and place it in the context of work in descriptive psychiatry about heterogeneity among the depressive disorders.

One Hypothesized Causal Pathway

An important advantage of the hopelessness theory, compared to the original helplessness theory, is that it not only specifies a proximal sufficient cause of depression but also specifies a sequence of events in a causal chain hypothesized to culminate in this proximal sufficient cause. As can be seen in Figure 2-1, the hypothesized causal chain begins with the occurrence of negative life events (or nonoccurrence of positive life events) and ends with the production of depressive symptoms (specifically, symptoms of hopelessness depression).[5] Each event in the chain leading to the proximal sufficient cause is a contributory cause of depression because it increases the likelihood of, but is neither necessary nor sufficient for, the occurrence of depressive symptoms. In addition, these contributory causes vary in how proximal they are to the occurrence of depressive symptoms.

PROXIMAL CONTRIBUTORY CAUSES

According to Abramson *et al.* (1978), once people perceive that particular negative life events have occurred, the kinds of causal attributions they make for these events and the degree of importance they attach to the events are important factors contributing to whether or not they develop hopelessness and, in turn, depressive symptoms. Although these contributory causes are distal to hopelessness, we refer to them as proximal contributory causes in order to distinguish them from other, more distal contributory causes of depressive symptoms, which are discussed below (e.g., see Depressogenic attributional style in Figure 2-1). These causes have been examined by social

4. Note that Abramson *et al.* (1978) and Seligman (1978) referred to this subtype as "helplessness depression." We prefer the term "hopelessness depression" because it better describes the hypothesized cause of this disorder.

5. For the sake of brevity, throughout the remainder of the chapter, we will use the phrase "negative life events" to refer to both the occurrence of negative life events *and* the nonoccurrence of positive life events. Note that Abramson *et al.* (1978) began the causal chain with the occurrence of uncontrollable events rather than the occurrence of negative life events. However, because the majority of subsequent studies focused on the latter rather than the former, we chose to begin the causal chain with the occurrence of negative life events. Moreover, the logic of the hopelessness theory requires only the occurrence of a negative event, rather than the occurrence of an uncontrollable event, to initiate the series of inferences hypothesized to culminate in hopelessness.

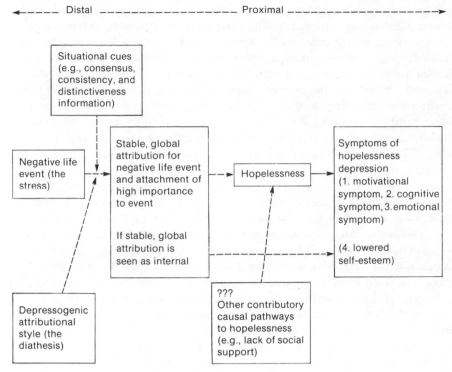

FIGURE 2-1. Causal chain specified in the hopelessness theory of depression. (Arrows with solid lines indicate sufficient causes. Arrows with broken lines indicate contributory causes.)

psychologists, who have begun to specify when people ask "why" questions or make causal attributions for events (e.g., Enzle & Schopflocher, 1978; Pittman & Pittman, 1980; Pyszczynski & Greenberg, 1981; Wong & Weiner, 1981). A major determinant of the onset of spontaneous causal analyses identified in this research is the occurrence of a negative event (Wong & Weiner, 1981), precisely the initiating event in the causal chain postulated by the hopelessness theory.

Abramson *et al.* (1978) postulated that two attributional dimensions are crucial for understanding how negative life events may contribute to the formation of hopelessness: stable–unstable and global–specific. In brief, these investigators suggested that hopelessness and, in turn, depressive symptoms are more likely to occur when negative life events are attributed to stable (i.e., enduring) and global (i.e., likely to affect many outcomes) causes and viewed as important than when they are attributed to unstable, specific causes and viewed as unimportant. Moreover, when negative life events are attributed to internal, stable, global causes, Abramson *et al.* hypothesized that hopelessness will be accompanied by lowered self-esteem. On the other hand, self-esteem should remain intact when negative events are attributed to external causes. For example, an argument with a spouse attributed to a basic flaw in one's character (e.g., I'm unlovable), as opposed to a transient, specific factor about the spouse (e.g., his or her temporary bad mood), should both increase the likelihood of viewing the marriage and perhaps other important close social relationships as being doomed to failure and lower one's self-esteem. It is worth noting that the logic of the hopelessness theory about the link between causal attributions and expectations is very similar to the logic used in Weiner's (1972, 1974) attributional account of achievement motivation. In addition, like many depression researchers in the field of life stress (e.g., Paykel, 1979; Sarason, Johnson, & Siegel, 1978), Abramson *et al.* emphasized people's appraisals of and inferences derived from negative life events, rather than the mere occurrence of such events, as a determinant of depressive reactions.

If causal attributions for negative events do modulate the likelihood of forming hopelessness and developing lowered self-esteem, then it is important to describe the variables that influence the kinds of causal attributions people make in a given situation. A shortcoming in Abramson and colleagues' (1978) statement of the hopelessness theory is that with the exception of their discussion of the relevance of the self–other comparison for making an internal attribution, they failed to specify how situational variables guide the causal attribution process (Alloy & Tabachnik, 1984; Metalsky & Abramson, 1981; Wortman & Dintzer, 1978). Instead, they discussed individual difference variables that may affect the attribution process (e.g., see "Distal Contributory Causes," below).

Fortunately, over the past 20 years social psychologists have conducted studies showing that causal attributions for events are, in part, a function of the situational information people confront (Kelley, 1967; McArthur, 1972). In particular, this line of work suggests that individuals will tend to attribute an event to the factor or factors with which it covaries. In this view, people would be predicted to make internal, stable, and global attributions for an event when they are confronted with situational information suggesting that the event is low in consensus (e.g., failing a math exam while others do well), high in consistency (e.g., typically failing exams in math), and low in distinctiveness (e.g., typically failing exams in other subjects as well as math) (Kelley, 1967; Metalsky & Abramson, 1981). Thus, informational cues present in a particular situation constrain the attribution process by making some causal attributions for particular life events more plausible than others and some not plausible at all (see also Hammen & Mayol, 1982). It should be noted that social psychologists have identified a number of additional factors that may guide the causal attribution process, including the motivation to protect or enhance one's self-esteem, focus of attention, salience of a potential causal factor, and self-presentational concerns, among others (Bradley, 1978; Harvey, Ickes, & Kidd,

1976, 1978, 1981; Harvey & Weary, 1981; Heider, 1958; Miller, 1976; Miller & Ross, 1975; Nisbett & Ross, 1980; Snyder, Stephan, & Rosenfield, 1978; Stevens & Jones, 1976; Weary, 1979; Zuckerman, 1979).

DISTAL CONTRIBUTORY CAUSES

Abramson *et al.* (1978) identified a more distal factor that also may constrain the attribution process and influence the content of causal attributions for a particular event: individual differences in attributional style (see also Ickes & Layden, 1978). Abramson *et al.* speculated that *some* people exhibit a general tendency to attribute negative events to internal, stable, global factors and to view these events as very important. Throughout this chapter we frequently use the phrase "hypothesized depressogenic attributional style" or "attributional diathesis" to refer to this tendency.

According to Abramson *et al.* (1978), individuals who exhibit the hypothesized depressogenic attributional style should be more likely than individuals who do not to attribute any particular negative event they confront to internal, stable, global factors and to view the event as very important, thereby incrementing the likelihood of forming hopelessness and, in turn, depressive symptoms. However, in the presence of positive life events or in the absence of negative life events, people exhibiting the hypothesized depressogenic attributional style should be no more likely to develop hopelessness, and therefore depression, than people not exhibiting this attributional style. According to Metalsky *et al.* (1982), this aspect of the hopelessness theory is conceptualized usefully as a diathesis-stress component. That is, the depressogenic attributional style is a distal contributory cause of depression that operates in the presence, but not in the absence, of negative life events (see also Kayne, Alloy, Romer, & Crocker, 1988; Metalsky, Halberstadt, & Abramson, 1987).

ATTRIBUTIONAL STYLES AND CAUSAL ATTRIBUTIONS

It is important to note that exhibiting the hypothesized depressogenic attributional style is not viewed as a sufficient condition for attributing any particular negative life event to an internal, stable, and global cause (see Figure 2-1). In some situations, environmental cues about the cause of a negative event (e.g., consensus, consistency, and distinctiveness information) (see Kelley, 1967) or other factors may be present and override attributional style as an influence on the content of the particular attribution (Alloy & Tabachnik, 1984; Metalsky & Abramson, 1981). However, on the average, individuals who exhibit the hypothesized depressogenic attributional style should be more likely to make internal, stable, and global causal attributions for negative life events than individuals who do not (cf. Epstein, 1979, 1980).

CAUSAL ATTRIBUTIONS AND HOPELESSNESS

Abramson *et al.* (1978) cautioned that (as Figure 2-1 suggests) negative life events attributed to internal, stable, and global causes and viewed as important increase the probability of, but are not sufficient for, development of hopelessness. Situational information or other factors may intervene between the causal attribution and the expectation (see Alloy, 1982).

THE CONTRIBUTORY CAUSAL PATHWAY AND HOPELESSNESS

We emphasize that the contributory causal pathway featured in the hopelessness theory is not viewed as necessary for formation of hopelessness (see Figure 2-1). Thus, future extensions of the hopelessness theory need to incorporate factors in addition to causal attributions for negative life events that also may modulate the likelihood that a given person will become hopeless (see the section "Hypothesized Cause, Symptoms, Course, and Variants" for some suggestions).

HOPELESSNESS DEPRESSION: A THEORY-BASED SUBTYPE

Over the course of the past 80 years, clinicians have suggested that depression probably is not a single disorder but instead may be a group of disorders that are heterogeneous with respect to symptoms, cause, course, therapy, and prevention (e.g., Beck, 1967; Depue & Monroe, 1978; Gillespie, 1929; Kendell, 1968; Kraepelin, 1913). Consequently, within the clinical tradition, much controversy has centered on the topic of which classification system most meaningfully subdivides the depressive disorders, or best "carves depression at its joints." Historically, a wide variety of nosological distinctions have been proposed to classify the depressive disorders, such as bipolar–unipolar, endogenous–reactive, endogenous–neurotic, psychotic–neurotic, major–minor, and character spectrum–pure dysthymic disorder. In the main, the various classifications proposed to subdivide the depressive disorders have arisen from insights gleaned in clinical practice or from numerical taxonometric procedures such as cluster analysis (Kendell, 1968; Skinner, 1981). We suggest that as a complement to these empirically based approaches to the classification of depression, the hopelessness theory represents a *theory-based* approach to the classification of a subset of the depressive disorders (see also Seligman, 1978). In essence, the hopelessness theory postulates the existence in nature of an as yet unidentified subtype of depression: hopelessness depression.

Consistent with Skinner (1981), we utilize a construct validation approach that emphasizes a continual interplay between theory development and empirical analyses as an organizational framework for elaborating the concept of hopelessness depression. We emphasize that hopelessness depression is an open concept (Cronbach & Meehl, 1955; Hempel, 1952; Meehl, 1972; Pap, 1953) that is defined in terms of the laws or nomological network in which it is embedded. This concept is open rather than closed because we have not defined it exhaustively. Borrowing Cronbach and Meehl's terminology, we will be able to say "what hopelessness depression is" (i.e., define it exhaustively) only when we know all of the laws involving it. Until then, hopelessness depression will remain an open concept.

THE NOMOLOGICAL NETWORK OF HOPELESSNESS DEPRESSION

Hypothesized Cause, Symptoms, Course, and Variants

In contrast to the majority of approaches to the classification of the depressive disorders that are based on differences in symptom clusters among depressed individuals (see Kendell, 1968), *cause* figures prominently in the definition of hopelessness depression. Few clinicians or researchers would disagree that, when possible, classification of psychopathologies by etiology in addition to other factors is more desirable than classification by symptoms alone, insofar as the former generally has more direct implications for cure and prevention than the latter. In this regard, it is of interest that the historical trend in medicine has been from symptom-based classifications of disorders to more etiology-based classifications (Hempel, 1965).

It is important to emphasize that whereas Abramson *et al.* (1978) viewed hopelessness as a proximal sufficient cause of *depression*, we regard this expectation as a proximal sufficient *and* necessary cause of the hypothesized *hopelessness subtype of depression*. An analogy from work on mental retardation helps to illustrate this point. Whereas extreme hypothyroidism is sufficient but not necessary to produce mental retardation, this deficiency is a sufficient *and* necessary cause of cretinism, a relatively well-defined subtype of mental retardation. In general, the history of medicine reveals that whereas the proximal causes of a heterogeneous disorder often are stated in terms of sufficiency but not necessity, the proximal causes of well-defined subtypes of the heterogeneous disorder often are stated in terms of both sufficiency and necessity.

We described relatively more distal contributory causes of hopelessness depression above. Although the hopelessness theory identifies one contributory causal pathway hypothesized to culminate in hopelessness and, in turn, the symptoms of hopelessness depression, this pathway is not viewed as necessary for formation of hopelessness. Therefore, it is important to elaborate further that aspect of the nomological network of the theory involving the contributory causal pathway.

Along these lines, Hammen and her colleagues (e.g., Gong-Guy & Hammen, 1980: Hammen & Cochran, 1981; Hammen & deMayo, 1982) have argued that the *inferred consequences* of negative events, independently of causal attributions for these events, may modulate the likelihood that people will become depressed when confronted with a negative life event. To illustrate the distinction between inferred consequences and causal attributions, it is useful to consider the example, provided by Abramson *et al.* (1978, pp. 57–58), of a student who took the math portion of the Graduate Record Examination (GRE) and believed he did very poorly. He may conclude that he did poorly because everyone's copy of the math GRE was blurred (an external, unstable, specific attribution) but infer that a consequence of his poor performance on the math GRE is that he never will be admitted to a graduate program in mathematics, his preferred career choice. We suggest that inferred consequences moderate the relationship between negative life events and depressive symptoms by affecting the likelihood of formation of hopelessness.

In addition to inferred consequences of negative events, we suggest that the *inferred diagnosticity* of these events also may modulate the likelihood of formation of hopelessness and, in turn, hopelessness depression (see Trope, 1975; Trope & Brickman, 1975). In our usage, the concept of inferred diagnosticity refers to the inferences a person draws about his or her own worth or abilities from the occurrence of a particular negative life event. The concept of inferred diagnosticity of negative events is central to Beck's (1967) description of cognitive processes hypothesized to contribute to the development of depression, and his clinical anecdotes vividly illustrate this concept. For example, Beck (1976, pp. 99–100) reported the case of a depressed suicidal woman who previously had had a breach in her relationship with her lover, Raymond, and therefore concluded, "I am worthless." When the therapist asked the patient why she believed she was worthless, she replied, "If I don't have love, I am worthless," as if it were a universal truth. It is possible that inferred diagnosticity of negative events is not independent of causal attributions for these events, but we believe it is useful to conceptualize and operationalize the former as distinct from the latter. As Abramson *et al.* (1978) hypothesized with respect to causal attributions, individual differences may exist in the general tendency to infer negative consequences and make negative diagnoses about the self given the occurrence of negative life events. We do not know whether or not such cognitive styles are independent of the hypothesized depressogenic attributional style.

In addition to the cognitive factors described above, social (e.g., social support), developmental (e.g., death of mother during the child's early years), and even genetic factors also may modulate the likelihood that a person will become hopeless and, in turn, experience the symptoms of hopelessness depression (see Tiger, 1979, for an intriguing discussion of the possible role of genetic and biological factors in the development of hope and hopelessness). We eagerly await an elaboration of the theoretical statement of the causal pathway to the symptoms of hopelessness depression that includes cognitive, social, and other variables not previously included in our statement of the theory.

The nomological network surrounding the concept of hopelessness depression suggests that this subtype should be characterized by at least three major *symptoms*: (1) retarded initiation of voluntary responses (motivational symptom); (2) difficulty in seeing that one's responses control outcomes related or similar to the outcome about which one feels hopeless (cognitive symptom); and (3) sad affect (emotional symptom). In addition, hopelessness depression will include a fourth symptom, lowered self-esteem, when individuals expect that other people can or could attain the important outcome(s) which they feel hopeless to attain.

In addition to these symptoms of hopelessness depression enumerated in the hopelessness theory, it is possible that this hypothesized subtype of depression is characterized by other symptoms as well. In particular, Beck and others have demonstrated that hopelessness is a key factor in serious suicide attempts and suicidal ideation (Beck, Kovacs, & Weissman, 1975; Kazdin, French, Unis, Esveldt-Dawson, & Sherick, 1983; Minkoff, Bergman, Beck, & Beck, 1973; Petrie & Chamberlain, 1983). Thus, it is possible that serious suicide attempts and suicidal ideation are core symptoms of hopelessness depression.

Insofar as hopelessness is viewed as a proximal sufficient and necessary cause of hopelessness depression, the *course* or duration of an episode of hopelessness depression should be influenced by how long this expectation is present. The longer the time over which an individual exhibits hopelessness, the longer the duration of the episode of hopelessness depression triggered by the expectation. Although not discussed by Abramson *et al.* (1968), the possibility exists that once an individual develops hopelessness, some biological or psychological processes are triggered that need to "run their course" and do not dissipate as quickly as hopelessness.

Inspection of the contributory causal pathway hypothesized to culminate in hopelessness suggests that at least two distinct *variants* of hopelessness depression may exist (see Figure 2-1). We call the first theoretical variant *attributional style–event hopelessness depression*. This variant of hopelessness depression would develop in an individual who exhibits the hypothesized depressogenic attributional style and is confronted with a negative life event which by itself may not be sufficient to trigger hopelessness in most people, but when interpreted or explained by an individual with this attributional style is sufficient to do so. An example is a person who exhibits a style of attributing negative interpersonal events to internal, stable, global factors and viewing these events as very important. The person doesn't have a date on a Friday night, concludes that the cause of being alone on a Friday night is having a flawed personality, and therefore expects never to have a satisfactory close relationship with another individual. The person becomes hopeless and, in turn, depressed. We suggest that when other cognitive styles (e.g., generalized tendency to infer negative consequences from the occurrence of negative events) are incorporated in the hopelessness theory, it may be most appropriate to term this variant *cognitive style–event hopelessness depression.*

A second variant of hopelessness depression suggested by the hopelessness theory is labeled usefully as *event hopelessness depression.* This theoretical variant of hopelessness depression would develop in an individual who does not exhibit the hypothesized depressogenic attributional style or other depressogenic cognitive styles but who is confronted with an event sufficient to engender hopelessness in most people. An extreme example might be an individual who is put in a concentration camp and repeatedly told by the guards that the only way to leave the camp is as a corpse. In the case in which an individual repeatedly is confronted with negative events sufficient to engender hopelessness in most people, we may speak of *recurrent event hopelessness depression.*

Hopelessness Depression and Other Categories of Depression

It is useful to ask which diagnostic categories of unipolar depression, if any, involve different etiological processes, and perhaps symptoms and therapy, than those involved in hopelessness depression. Klein's (1974) concept of endogenomorphic depression may be fundamentally distinct from the concept of hopelessness depression. The hypothesized core process in endogenomorphic depressions is impairment of the capacity to experience pleasure, leading to a profound lack of interest and investment in the environment (e.g., inability to enjoy food or sex). Klein's concept of endogenomorphic depression appears very similar to Costello's (1972) concept of reinforcer ineffectiveness and to the DSM-III category of major depressive episode, with melancholia.

Klein distinguishes endogenomorphic depressions, hypothesized to be responsive to imipramine drug therapy, from the categories of "acute dysphoria" and "chronic overreactive dysphoria" which he believes are fundamentally different depressive disorders. A close reading of Klein's paper suggests that the category of acute dysphoria significantly overlaps with our category of event hopelessness depression, while that of chronic overreactive dysphoria significantly corresponds to cognitive style–event hopelessness depression. Other types of depression, such as character spectrum disorder (e.g., Akiskal, 1983) also may involve different processes than does hopelessness depression. A crucial task for future research is to determine whether or not fundamentally different types of nonbipolar depression actually exist: some characterized by hopelessness, some characterized by a breakdown of the pleasure centers, and still others characterized by additional psychological or biological processes.

Cure and Prevention of Hopelessness Depression

An important function of the hopelessness theory of depression is to serve as an organizing rationale for the derivation of predictions about therapeutic interventions for hopelessness depression (Alloy, Clements, & Kolden, 1985; Beach, Abramson, & Levine, 1981; Halberstadt, Andrews, Metalsky, & Abramson, 1984). Because the theory specifies a chain of events that are hypothesized to contribute to the development of hopelessness and, in turn, the syndrome of hopelessness depression, each link in the chain suggests a point for clinical intervention (Alloy *et al.*, 1985; Beach *et al.*, 1981; Halberstadt *et al.*, 1984). A major advantage of using the proximal–distal continuum to order the events that cause hopelessness depression is that this hypothesized causal pathway not only suggests points of intervention for reversing current episodes of hopelessness depression but also suggests points of intervention for decreasing vulnerability both to depressive episodes and to the development of depression-proneness. We will not present the therapeutic and preventive implications of the hopelessness theory here because we have detailed them elsewhere (cf. Alloy *et al.*, 1985; Beach *et al.*, 1981; Halberstadt *et al.*, 1984). Again, however, bear in mind that hopelessness depression is an open concept and that the part of the nomological network involving its cure and prevention is in need of elaboration. We emphasize that, like the etiological predictions about hopelessness depression, the clinical predictions about this disorder only can be corroborated or discorroborated by empirical test.

CRITIQUE OF RESEARCH STRATEGIES

A useful way to begin our critique is to delineate the defining features of the cross-sectional and prospective research strategies typically used for assessing the validity of the hopelessness theory. In the cross-sectional studies, investigators often have attempted to test the theory by examining the magnitude and consistency across studies of the differences in attributional styles between groups of depressed and nondepressed individuals selected from various populations. For example, a wide variety of investigators have examined attributional styles in depressed versus nondepressed people drawn from college student samples (e.g., Barthé & Hammen, 1981; Blaney, Behar, & Head, 1980; Hammen & Cochran, 1981; Hammen, Krantz, & Cochran, 1981; Harvey, 1981; Peterson, Schwartz, & Seligman, 1981; Seligman, Abramson, Semmel, & von Baeyer, 1979), patient samples (e.g., Gong-Guy & Hammen, 1980; Hamilton & Abramson, 1983; Miller, Klee, & Norman, 1982; Raps, Peterson, Reinhard, Abramson, & Seligman, 1982), and other samples (e.g., Feather & Barber, 1983; Hammen & deMayo, 1982; Seligman *et al.*, 1984).

Investigators using prospective research strategies have attempted to assess the validity of the hopelessness theory by examining the magnitude and consistency across studies of the difference in attributional styles measured at one point in time (Time 1) between two groups of individuals: a group that was not depressed at Time 1 but later became depressed at Time 2 (the future depressed group) and a second group that was not depressed at Time 1 and did not become depressed at Time 2 (the future nondepressed group). A prototypical study of this type was conducted by Lewinsohn, Steinmetz, Larson, and Frankin (1981), who asked whether cognitions known to be correlated with depression (e.g., expectancies of positive and negative outcomes, irrational beliefs, and so forth) precede, accompany, or follow an episode of depression.

A variation on the basic prospective research strategy consists of administering measures of attributional styles and depression at two points in time and using cross-lagged panel correlational analysis to test hypotheses about temporal precedence (e.g., Golin, Sweeney, & Shaeffer, 1981). A second variant of the prospective research strategy consists of examining attributional styles in individuals when they are suffering from a depressive episode as well as when they recover from the depressive episode. (Eaves & Rush, 1984; Hamilton & Abramson, 1983).

As other investigators have argued, prospective research strategies provide an important improvement over cross-sectional ones in that an observed difference in attributional style between future depressives versus future nondepressives at Time 1 or correlation between attributional style at Time 1 and depression at Time 2 cannot be attributed to depressed subjects acquiring the hypothesized depressogenic attributional style as a consequence of being in the depressed state (Golin *et al.*, 1981; Lewinsohn *et al.*, 1981; Seligman *et al.*, 1979). However, we emphasize that with respect to our critique, the cross-sectional and prospective research strategies fundamentally are similar in that they rely on the same criterion for assessing the validity of the hopelessness theory: *The apparent validity of the theory rises and falls on the basis of the magnitude and consistency across studies of the difference in likelihood, between depressed versus nondepressed individuals, of displaying the hypothesized cognitive diathesis (hypothesized depressogenic attributional style).* That in one case attributional style and depression are measured at the same point in time (cross-sectional method) whereas in the other case attributional styles are measured prior to the development of depression (prospective method) has no relevance for our critique.

FUNDAMENTAL PROBLEMS IN RESEARCH STRATEGIES

This critique does not provide an exhaustive discussion of all of the conceptual and methodological problems associated with work designed to test the hopelessness theory (e.g., the use of measures of unknown reliability and validity; see Peterson & Seligman, 1984, and Raps *et al.*, 1982, for this criticism). Instead, the critique focuses on basic flaws in research strategy and design that make it difficult to assess meaningfully the validity of the theory. The essence of the critique is that it is possible to obtain strong, modest, weak, or no differences in attributional styles between depressed versus nondepressed (or future depressed versus future nondepressed) subjects in the typical research designs, if the hopelessness theory is correct. Therefore, contrary to the assumptions of recent reviewers (e.g., Coyne & Gotlib, 1983), the magnitude and consistency across studies of results from these research strategies do not provide an appropriate criterion against which to evaluate the validity of the theroy. In fact, assuming error-free measurement, with the possible exception of the finding that nondepressives (or future nondepressives) are more likely to exhibit the hypothesized depressogenic attributional style than are depressives (or future depressives), no set of results from the typical cross-sectional or prospective research strategies can "disconfirm" or challenge the theory. Moreover, inconsistency in results across studies utilizing these research strategies does not embarrass the theory. If one's preferred mode of testing theories is to subject them to "grave danger of refutation" (Meehl, 1978; Popper, 1959, 1962, 1972), then these research strategies are wholly inadequate, and a most unsatisfactory state of affairs exists in work on the hopelessness theory. A central theme in our critique is that the basic problems in research strategy associated with work designed to test the theory result, in part, from a failure to appreciate the full methodological implications of the kinds of causal relationships among variables specified in the theory, as well as the heterogeneity that may exist among the depressive disorders.

ASSESSING THE VALIDITY OF A PROXIMAL SUFFICIENT CAUSE

The methodological implications of a theory with a proximal sufficient cause component and a distal diathesis-stress component require consideration. We will examine each component separately. It is inappropriate to assess the validity of the statement of the proximal sufficient cause in the hopelessness theory on the basis of the magnitude and consistency across studies of the difference in the likelihood of displaying hopelessness between depressed versus nondepressed (or future depressed versus future nondepressed) subjects. Because the theory specifies a sufficient, but not necessary, proximal cause of depression, the existence of subtypes of depression not associated with hopelessness (e.g., biochemical depressions) does not challenge the validity of the proximal sufficient cause component of the theory. However, the existence of such other subtypes of depression would weaken the magnitude of difference in the likelihood of displaying hopelessness between depressed versus nondepressed (or future depressed versus future nondepressed) subjects. Moreover, if the proportion of individuals displaying other subtypes of depression varied across the subject samples used in different studies, then the magnitude of difference in likelihood of displaying hopelessness between depressed versus nondepressed (or future depressed versus future nondepressed) subjects also would vary if the theory were correct.

Of course, the finding that nondepressed (or future nondepressed) subjects display hopelessness would challenge the theory. Thus, if depression is, in fact, a heterogeneous disorder with many subtypes, then it is inappropriate to simply lump all depressives together and examine their expectations about the future to test the theory. That is, this theory may be correct in hypothesizing the existence of the subtype of hopelessness depression, but the subtype would go undetected with current research methods unless a sufficiently large number of depressives suffered from hopelessness depression (see also Buchsbaum & Rieder, 1979; Craighead, 1980; Depue & Monroe, 1983; Hamilton & Abramson, 1983).

ASSESSING THE VALIDITY OF A DIATHESIS-STRESS COMPONENT

Given the kinds of causal relations specified in the hopelessness theory, it would be inappropriate for the apparent validity of the theory to rise or fall on the basis of the magnitude and consistency across studies of the difference in likelihood of displaying the hypothesized depressogenic attributional style between depressed versus nondepressed (or future depressed versus future nondepressed) subjects. Of course, two conditions must be met in order to actually obtain "big empirical effects" with these typically used research strategies: (1) A high proportion of depressed (or future depressed) subjects in the sample must display the hypothesized depressogenic attributional style, and (2) a high proportion of the nondepressed (or future nondepressed) subjects in the sample must not display the hypothesized depressogenic attributional style. However, neither of these conditions needs to be met for the diathesis-stress component of the theory to be correct.

1. The hopelessness theory's validity does not require that the first condition be met for two reasons. First, because the theory involves a proximal sufficient, but not necessary, cause component (i.e., hopelessness), other subtypes of depression may exist that do not involve the hypothesized attributional style in their causation. Second, because the theory involves a diathesis-stress component, in cases in which there is a low base rate of negative life events in a given sample, few cases of hopelessness depression will exist that involve the hypothesized depressogenic attributional style in their causation.

2. The hopelessness theory's validity does not require that the second condition be met because when the base rate of negative life events is low in a given sample, a relatively large proportion of nondepressed (or future nondepressed) subjects may display the hypothesized depressogenic attributional style. In the limiting case of a 0 percent base rate of negative life events, the nondepressed (or future nondepressed) subjects will be just as likely as the depressed (or future depressed) subjects to display the hypothesized depressogenic attributional style. Clearly, then, it is inappropriate, and even misleading, to evaluate the validity of the hopelessness theory on the basis of the magnitude and consistency across studies of the difference in likelihood of displaying the hypothesized depressogenic attributional style between depressed versus nondepressed (or future depressed versus future nondepressed) subjects in the absence of additional information about the base rates of negative life events and other subtypes of depression.

At this point it is useful to note that not all studies attempting to evaluate the hopelessness theory conform exactly to our description of the "typically used" research strategies. In particular, some recent studies (e.g., Cutrona, 1983; Kayne *et al.*, 1988; Metalsky *et al.*, 1982, 1987) have attempted to test the diathesis-stress component of the hopelessness theory. However, although these studies are an important advance over previous strategies in this area, they suffer from the problems, discussed above, arising from not taking into account the methodological and logical implications of a theory featuring a proximal sufficient cause. In addition, some of these studies do not provide completely adequate tests of the diathesis-stress component of the hopelessness theory (see Kayne *et al.*, 1988; Metalsky *et al.*, 1987). For example, although Cutrona (1983) examined both attributional style and life events as predictors of depression, she did not report the results for the interaction term involving number of stresses and causal attributions in her hierarchical regression analyses. This interaction term, of course, is the piece of information in her study most pertinent to testing the diathesis-stress component of the hopelessness theory (cf. Kayne *et al.*, 1988; Metalsky *et al.*, 1987). Thus, although the trend in research on the hopelessness theory is toward more adequate tests of this theory, we believe that as of yet the hopelessness theory has not been subjected to tests allowing for the possibility of "grave danger of refutation" (cf. Popper, 1959, 1962, 1972).

This discussion highlights an oddity in the progression of research on the hopelessness theory. From the order in which studies have been conducted, one might infer that investigators believe that it is necessary for the hopelessness theory to survive the kinds of tests presented by the typically used research strategies in order to qualify as worthy of more fine-grained tests involving examination of the diathesis-stress component, and so on. Our discussion shows that such an approach is wrong-headed: The hopelessness theory could be entirely correct and still not pass the kinds of tests presented by the typical strategies. A moment's reflection reveals that, ironically, those factors most likely to pass with flying colors the tests presented by the typically used cross-sectional research strategies (e.g., consistent high magnitude relationship to depression) are the symptoms, rather than the causes, of depression!

RATIONALE FOR THE HOPELESSNESS THEORY

Perhaps the reader is wondering about the clinical or scientific significance of a theory that posits a vulnerability factor that may not explain a large amount of variance in depression or depression-proneness or qualify as a necessary and sufficient antecedent of depression. Would the hopelessness theory qualify as an important theory of depression if it only provided an account of a specific subtype? Maybe it would be wiser for us to spend our time formulating a theory of depression that does attempt to account for the majority of variance in this disorder, rather than working toward more adequate tests of the hopelessness theory.

The history of medicine provides a useful analogy, which suggests that it probably would be a mistake to attempt to formulate a theory that features a hypothesized necessary and sufficient cause of depression and thereby treats depression as a unitary disorder. In medicine, scientific and clinical progress usually has come from delineating meaningful etiological or functional subtypes within large heterogeneous disorders rather than from formulating theories that attempt to provide exhaustive accounts of apparently heterogeneous disorders.

A PROPOSAL FOR A RESEARCH STRATEGY

As the preceding logical analysis has revealed, neither the cross-sectional nor the prospective research strategies typically used to test the hopelessness theory of depression provide an adequate test of it. In this section, we describe the general outline of a new research strategy that would provide a more adequate evaluation of the validity of the causal relations specified in the hopelessness theory. In addition, our suggested methodological approach places this theory more explicitly in the context of work in descriptive psychiatry investigating the heterogeneity of the depressive disorders.

We note at the outset that taking into account the kinds of causal relations specified in the hopelessness theory and the heterogeneity that may exist among the depressive disorders is a tough problem and, in fact, raises some of the most challenging and difficult questions facing any psychopathologist, such as: What is a useful category of psychopathology? How can one determine whether or not a hypothesized psychopathological entity exists in nature? How can one most meaningfully subdivide a heterogeneous disorder into its constituent subtypes? (cf. Meehl & Golden, 1982). Although there are a number of possible approaches one may take in attempting to address these basic issues in a given research context, a discussion of all possible approaches would take us far afield (see Skinner, 1981, for a recent discussion). Thus, we do not provide a "cookbook" of all possible approaches and specific procedures one conceivably might take to evaluate the validity of the hopelessness theory. Instead, we develop a general strategic framework that we believe may be most suitable for testing it and discuss some of the difficult methodological issues that will arise in conducting such tests.

We believe that a more adequate test of the hopelessness theory involves four components: (1) a test of the diathesis-stress component of the theory; (2) a test of the mediational processes specified by the theory to culminate in hopelessness; (3) a test of the symptoms hypothesized to constitute the hopelessness subtype of depression; and (4) delineation of the place of this subtype of in the context of descriptive psychiatry. In describing what would comprise a more adequate test of each of these components of the hopelessness theory, we distinguish between tests that are *necessary* to evaluate the empirical validity of theoretical statements that must be true in order for the hopelessness theory to be true and tests that *elaborate* the nomological network relevant to each component of the theory, but about which the theory currently makes no explicit predictions.

Our goal is to provide a brief outline of a research strategy, not a complete research program, which would include an adequate conceptualization of each component of the hopelessness theory, a set of assessment strategies for translating these conceptualizations into measured variables, and so on. Unfortunately, these extremely important considerations are beyond the scope of this chapter (see Abramson & Alloy, 1986a, 1986b, and Alloy & Abramson, 1986a, 1986b for discussions of these issues).

DIATHESIS-STRESS COMPONENT: NECESSARY TEST

The hopelessness theory of depression explicitly predicts that a style of attributing negative life events to internal, stable, and global causes and viewing these events as important (the hypothesized depressogenic attributional diathesis) *interacts* with the occurrence of negative life events (stress) to increase the probability of onset of depression, specifically the hopelessness subtype. An adequate test of this component of the theory involves a demonstration that the *interaction* between the hypothesized depressogenic attributional style and negative life events (1) provides better prediction of future depression, specifically hopelessness depression, than either the hypothesized depressogenic attributional style or negative life events alone (cf. Kayne *et al.*, 1988; Metalsky *et al.*, 1987), and (2) predicts the complete constellation of features hypothesized to constitute the *hopelessness subtype of depression*, as opposed to only a subset of these features or ones that constitute other subtypes.

In addition, the logic of the etiological sequence postulated by the hopelessness theory implies that a depressogenic attributional style in a particular content domain (e.g., for interpersonal-related events) provides "specific vulnerability" (cf. Beck, 1967) to hopelessness depression when an individual is confronted with negative life events in that same content domain (e.g., social rejection). This specific vulnerability hypothesis requires that there be a *match* between the content areas of an individual's depressogenic attributional style and the negative life events he or she encounters for the attributional diathesis-stress interaction to predict future hopelessness depression (cf. Alloy & Abramson, 1986a; Alloy *et al.*, 1985; Hammen, Marks, Mayol, & deMayo, 1985; Kayne *et al.*, 1988; Metalsky *et al.*, 1987).

DIATHESIS-STRESS COMPONENT: ELABORATIVE TEST

One issue relevant to elaborating the hopelessness theory of depression, but for which the theory currently makes no explicit predictions, is the relative stability of the hypothesized depressogenic attributional style. Although it often is assumed that the hopelessness theory predicts that the depressogenic attributional style is trait-like, in fact, nothing in the logic of the theory requires that the attributional diathesis be enduring. For example, even if the hypothesized depressogenic attributional style is relatively state-like, as long as the interaction of this style and negative events increases risk for depression, specifically hopelessness depression, the hopelessness theory would be corroborated. Questions that need to be addressed in examining the stability of the depressogenic attributional style include the following: (1) In the natural course of depression, specifically hopelessness depression, does a depressogenic attributional style persist beyond remission of a current depressive episode (cf. Eaves & Rush, 1984; Hamilton & Abramson, 1983; Persons & Rao, 1985)? (2) In the presence of formal treatments for depression (e.g., pharmacotherapy), does a depressogenic attributional diathesis persist beyond remission of a current depressive episode? and (3) to what degree does depressogenic attributional style fluctuate over time in synchrony with environmental circumstances? That is, do challenges to an individual's cognitive system by environmental stressors (negative life events) "activate" or "prime" a depressogenic attributional style (cf. Alloy *et al.*, 1985; Riskind & Rholes, 1984)?

A second elaborative issue concerns the specific kinds of negative life events that contribute to hopelessness-depression-proneness in interaction with the hypothesized depressogenic atrributional style. Although the hopelessness theory makes no explicit predictions, some kinds of negative events may be especially likely to induce hopelessness in cognitively vulnerable individuals (e.g., uncontrollable events, exits from the social field, chronic stressors) (cf. Alloy *et al.*, 1985; Kayne *et al.*, 1988). Finally, an examination of whether or not there is a feedback loop among the hypothesized depressogenic attributional style, negative life events, and depression (specifically, hopelessness depression), such that current depression alone or current depression in interaction with stress predicts the development of a depressogenic attributional style as well as the depressogenic attributional style–stress interaction predicting the development of depression would increase significantly our understanding of the interplay among these factors in hopelessness depression (cf. Beck, 1967; Hamilton & Abramson, 1983).

MEDIATIONAL PROCESSES COMPONENT: NECESSARY TEST

The hopelessness theory of depression not only postulates a distal diathesis-stress component and a proximal sufficient cause component but also specifies a causal chain of events hypothesized to mediate between these components. Thus, it is necessary to determine whether the *probability linkages* delineated in the theory actually obtain in nature. Is the likelihood of each causal component in the hypothesized etiological chain increased by the occurrence of the next most distal causal component? Specifically, an investigation of the empirical status of three probability linkages is required for a more adequate test of the mediational processes component of the hopelessness theory. (1) Individuals who exhibit the hypothesized depressogenic attributional style should be more likely than individuals who do not exhibit this style to attribute a particular negative life event (stress) to an internal, stable, and global cause and view this event as important. Because attributional style contributes to, but is not sufficient for, the particular attribution a person makes, this probability linkage should be greater than 0 but less than 1.0 (cf. Metalsky *et al.*, 1987). (2) A stable, global attribution for a particular negative life event and viewing the event as important should increase the likelihood of forming hopelessness. Again, because the particular attribution an individual makes for a negative event is hypothesized to contribute to, but not be sufficient for, the formation of hopelessness, this probability linkage also should be greater than 0 but less than 1.0 (cf. Alloy, 1982). (3) The occurrence of hopelessness should increase the likelihood of the development of depression (particularly hopelessness depression). Because hopelessness is hypothesized to be a sufficient cause of depression, this probability linkage should equal 1.0 in the case of error-free measurement.

MEDIATIONAL PROCESS COMPONENT: ELABORATIVE TEST

Although the hopelessness theory clearly specifies the probability linkages among the hypothesized causal components in the etiological chain culminating in hopelessness depression, the theory is silent about the temporal intervals between pairs of causal components (Cochran & Hammen, 1985; Metalsky *et al.*, 1987). For instance, if the hopelessness theory is correct, what is the time lag between when an individual exhibiting the hypothesized depressogenic attributional style is confronted with a negative life event and when this individual attributes the particular event to an internal, stable, and global cause? Does it take milliseconds, seconds, minutes, hours, days, weeks, or even months for the person to select his or her final explanation for the event? Consideration of this temporal issue is important because investigators who attempt to test the probability linkages predicted by the theory could conclude mistakenly that the theory is invalid if the relevant causal components are assessed with inappropriate time lags (Kayne *et al.*, 1988; Metalsky *et al.*, 1987).

SYMPTOM COMPONENT: NECESSARY TEST

The hopelessness theory predicts that the hopelessness subtype of depression will be characterized by at least three major symptoms, including retarded initiation of voluntary responses (motivational symptom), difficulty in seeing that one's responses control outcomes related or similar to the outcome about which one feels hopeless (cognitive symptom), and sad affect (emotional symptom) as well as by a fourth symptom, low self-esteem when individuals expect that other people can attain the outcomes about which they feel hopeless. Thus, a necessary condition for the validity of the symptom component of the hopelessness theory is that these three (or four) symptoms should be *intercorrelated* with one another and not as highly correlated with other symptoms found both in depression and in other psychopathologies. A second necessary condition is that this constellation of symptoms must be correlated with *hopelessness*, the hypothesized proximal sufficient cause of these symptoms. Moreover, hopelessness not only should be correlated with the motivational, cognitive, and affective symptom complex, it also must *temporally precede* the formation of this symptom constellation.

SYMPTOM COMPONENT: ELABORATIVE TEST

Because the concept of hopelessness depression is open, exploratory work is needed to further characterize this subtype. The following issues need examination: (1) other symptoms and clinical characteristics that may cohere with the predicted constellation of symptoms of hopelessness depression (e.g., suicidal potential; see the discussion in the section "Hypothesized cause, symptoms, course, and variants"); (2) demographic and family history correlates of the symptoms of hopelessness depression; (3) predictors of course, duration, and recurrence of the symptoms of hopelessness depression; (4) whether or not individuals experiencing a current episode of hopelessness depression also exhibit an increased number of past or future episodes of hopelessness depression; and (5) whether individuals exhibiting the symptoms of hopelessness depression show a better or worse outcome than individuals exhibiting other subtypes of depression.

DESCRIPTIVE PSYCHIATRY CONTEXT

Before laying out our research suggestions for determining the relationship between hopelessness depression and other subtypes of depression, it is important to note that the former consists of at least two components: (1) the constellation of symptoms postulated by the hopelessness theory and (2) the causal chain of events postulated by the theory to culminate in this symptom complex. For example, the hypothesized symptom constellation may, in fact, cohere in nature but not be caused by the chain of events specified in the theory. Alternatively, the etiological sequence described by the theory may produce a depressive outcome, but not specifically the aggregate of symptoms hypothesized to comprise the hopelessness subtype of depression. Consequently, in delineating the issues involved in determining hopelessness depression's place in descriptive psychiatry, we distinguish between its symptom component and causal chain component.

The descriptive psychiatric questions that need to be addressed include the following.

1. Does the concept of hopelessness depression *map onto* any nosological category of affective disorders that currently is diagnosed (e.g., dysthymic disorder, unipolar major depression, intermittent depression)? In particular, does the constellation of symptoms hypothesized to constitute hopelessness depression map onto the symptoms featured in any currently diagnosed nosological category of affective disorders? Further, does the causal chain specified by the hopelessness theory produce an outcome (other than the constellation of symptoms hypothesized to constitute hopelessness depression) that maps onto the symptoms featured in any currently diagnosed nosological category of affective disorders?

2. Does the concept of hopelessness depression *cut across* the various nosological categories of affective disorders or even nonaffective disorders that currently are diagnosed (cf. Halberstadt *et al.*, 1988; Seligman, 1978)? Specifically, does the constellation of symptoms hypothesized to comprise hopelessness depression cut across the symptoms featured in currently diagnosed nosological categories of affective or nonaffective disorders? That is, is the constellation of symptoms hypothesized to constitute hopelessness depression a feature of a subset of a number of currently diagnosed nosological categories of affective disorders? For example, is this constellation of symptoms exhibited by a subset of individuals currently diagnosed as suffering from DSM-III major depressive disorder as well as a subset of individuals currently diagnosed as DSM-III dysthymic disorder? In addition, does the causal chain described by the hopelessness theory produce an outcome (other than the constellation of symptoms hypothesized to constitute hopelessness depression) that cuts across currently diagnosed affective or nonaffective disorder categories?

As Seligman (1978) speculated, the category of hopelessness depression may not map directly in a one-to-one fashion onto any existing nosological category of depression. Instead, the category of hopelessness depression may cut across traditional diagnostic categories of depression and perhaps even include psychological phenomena not previously covered by the existing nosologies of depression. If this speculation is correct, then an integration of the hopelessness theory with descriptive psychiatry would not simply involve designating the current nosological categories of depression to which the hopelessness theory is applicable. Instead, such an integration would require a reorganization of the existing classification systems to accommodate the inclusion of the category of hopelessness depression.

IMPORTANCE OF AN ADEQUATE TEST OF THE THEORY

We believe that for at least five reasons it is crucial to provide an adequate test of the hopelessness theory of depression. First, although depression long has been recognized as a major form of psychopathology, investigators only are just beginning to amass cumulative knowledge about its cause (Klerman, 1978). Despite the flurry of experimental studies designed to test the hopelessness theory of depression, our critique suggests that, as of yet, this theory remains untested in very important respects. Thus, adequately testing *causal theories* of depression, such as the hopelessness theory, may increase significantly our scientific understanding of this not-yet-well-understood form of psychopathology.

Second, from the standpoint of clinical description, one of the most intriguing speculations of Abramson and colleagues (1978) is their proposal of a hopelessness subtype of depression. Insofar as *causal processes* figure prominently in the definition of the hopelessness subtype(s), from the perspective of both clinical description of depression and scientific understanding of this disorder, a search for the hopelessness subtype(s) may prove very fruitful.

A third reason for adequately testing the hopelessness theory of depression is that it has clear-cut *therapeutic and preventive implications* for depression (see the section "Cure and Prevention of Hopelessness Depression") (Alloy *et al.*, 1985; Beach *et al.*, 1981; Halberstadt *et al.*, 1984). In addition, an adequate test of the theory may aid in understanding the causal mechanisms responsible for the success of cognitive therapy for depression.

A fourth reason for adequately testing the hopelessness theory is that it explicitly specifies *invulnerability* factors for depression. For instance, a clear-cut prediction of the theory is that individuals who exhibit a style of attributing negative life events to unstable, specific causes should be relatively unvulnerable to depression, specifically hopelessness depression. We believe that an accurate understanding of factors that protect against depression is crucial for a comprehensive theory of depression. Yet little work has been conducted to uncover invulnerability factors (see Brown & Harris, 1978, for an exception).

A final reason for providing a more adequate test of the hopelessness theory is that increases in understanding depression and nondepression from a cognitive perspective will help build a *bridge between clinical and experimental psychology*. Although researchers in several areas of psychology (e.g., neuropsychology and visual perception) have utilized the strategy of studying abnormal individuals as a means of developing principles of normal psychological functioning, clinical psychologists rarely have pursued this line of inquiry. Clinical investigators typically conduct research on depression simply in order to understand this disorder. We believe that such research also can illuminate the functions of pervasive optimistic biases in normal cognition. These biases may be highly robust and have adaptive and/or evolutionary significance (e.g., Abramson & Alloy, 1981; Alloy & Abramson, 1979; Freud, 1917/1957; Greenwald, 1980; Martin, Abramson, & Alloy, 1984; Tiger, 1979).

GENERAL IMPLICATIONS

Our discussion of basic inadequacies in prior research strategies used to test the hopelessness theory of depression and our suggestions for future research strategies in this area have implications for other work in the field of depression.

1. We believe that another possible example of investigators relying on inappropriate criteria to evaluate the validity of a current theory of depression is Coyne and Gotlib's (1983) recent critique of Beck's (1967, 1976) cognitive theory of depression. In the abstract of their critique of cognitive theories of depression, Coyne and Gotlib state, "The review of the literature suggests that neither Beck's nor the learned helplessness model of depression has a strong empirical base. Depressed persons present themselves negatively on a variety of measures, but less consistently than either model suggests" (p. 472). Apparently Coyne and Gotlib (1983) believe that the magnitude and consistency of differences between depressed and nondepressed people in negative cognitive patterns are important criteria against which to evaluate the validity of Beck's theory of depression. In contrast, we suggest that reliance on these criteria may mislead investigators about the validity of Beck's theory.

Although Beck never has presented an explicit statement about the precise nature of the causal relations among variables in his theory of depression, it seems to us that at a formal level, his theory of depression is very similar to the hopelessness theory (cf. Alloy *et al.*, 1985). In brief, Beck's theory appears to feature a proximal sufficient cause component (the negative cognitive triad) with a more distal contributory diathesis-stress component (the negative self-schema is the diathesis and specific life events are the stress) as well as mediating contributory causes of the proximal sufficient cause (cognitive distortions) (see Figure 2-2). If our characterization of Beck's theory is correct, then by the logic of our prior analysis of research strategies inadequate for testing such theories (i.e., theories featuring a proximal sufficient cause component and a relatively more distal diathesis-stress component), it is inappropriate to evaluate the validity of Beck's theory on the basis of the magnitude and consistency of cognitive differences between depressed and nondepressed people. Furthermore, if Beck's theory of depression is characterized appropriately as similar to the hopelessness theory of depression in its formal aspects, then our critique of the research designed to test the hopelessness theory of depression suggests that no study to date has tested adequately Beck's theory and that his theory remains fundamentally untested.

A second implication of our discussion for the field of depression is that many so-called competing theories of this disorder may not be competing at all (see Akiskal & McKinney, 1975). These theories simply may be describing different points along a particular causal pathway to depression, with some theories focusing on more distal causes than others. In this vein, Brown and Harris (1978) have integrated their work on the social origins of depression

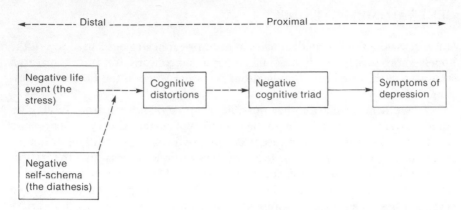

FIGURE 2-2. Causal chain implied in Beck's cognitive theory of depression. (Arrows with solid lines indicate sufficient causes. Arrows with broken lines indicate contributory causes.)

with the cognitive theories of depression by suggesting that the presence of particular social factors modulates the likelihood that an individual will become hopeless when confronted with a negative life event. Alternatively, various theories of depression may be describing equally proximal complementary contributory causes in a particular causal pathway culminating in depression. For example, as we argued earlier, inferred consequences of negative life events may have such a status in relation to causal attributions for negative life events. Of course, we do not mean to imply that all current or future theories of depression can be reconciled with one another. Some of these theories indeed may compete with one another.

Historically, work on depression conducted by psychologists has had little or no influence on formal nosological systems such as DSM-III. No doubt there are many reasons for this disappointing state of affairs. We suspect that one cause is the apparent lack of cumulative progress in psychopathology research. If theories simply come and go in clinical psychology (cf. Meehl, 1978), why incorporate them into formal nosological systems? A second cause may be that research on psychopathology by psychologists has not had clearcut therapeutic and preventive implications. Perhaps when psychopathologists propose theories of depression that specify clearly the formal and sequential relationships between causes and symptoms, and heed the methodological implications of the specified causal relations in testing the theories, their work will significantly influence formal nosological systems.

ACKNOWLEDGMENT

Preparation of this chapter was supported by a grant from the MacArthur Foundation.

REFERENCES

Abramson, L. Y., & Alloy, L. B. (1981). Depression, nondepression, and cognitive illusions: A reply to Schwartz. *Journal of Experimental Psychology: General, 110,* 436–447.

Abramson, L. Y., & Alloy L. B. (1988a). *Conceptualization and assessment of the components of the cognitive theories of depression: II. Stress.* Manuscript in preparation.

Abramson, L. Y., & Alloy, L. B. (1988b). *Conceptualization and assessment of the components of the cognitive theories of depression: IV. The cognitive subtype of depression.* Manuscript in preparation.

Abramson, L. Y., & Martin, D. (1981). Depression and the causal inference process. In J. Harvey, W. Ickes, & R. Kidd (Eds.), *New directions in attribution research.* Hillsdale, NJ: Erlbaum.

Abramson, L. Y., Seligman, M. E. P., & Teasdale, J. (1978). Learned helplessness in humans: Critique and reformulation. *Journal of Abnormal Psychology, 87,* 49–74.

Ariskal, H. S. (1983). Dysthymic disorder: Psychopathology of proposed chronic depressive subtypes. *American Journal of Psychiatry, 140,* 11–20.

Ariskal, H. S., & McKinney, W. T. (1975). Overview of recent research in depression: Integration of ten conceptual models into a comprehensive clinical frame. *Archives of General Psychiatry, 32,* 285–305.

Alloy, L. B. (1982). The role of perceptions and attributions for response-outcome noncontingency in learned helplessness: A commentary and discussion. *Journal of Personality, 50,* 443–479.

Alloy, L. B., & Abramson, L. Y. (1979). Judgment of contingency in depressed and nondepressed students: Sadder but wiser? *Journal of Experimental Psychology: General, 108,* 441–485.

Alloy, L. B., & Abramson, L. Y. (1988a). *Conceptualization and assessment of the components of the cognitive theories of depression: I. Cognitive diatheses.* Manuscript in preparation.

Alloy, L. B., & Abramson, L. Y. (1988b). *Conceptualization and assessment of the components of the cognitive theories of depression: III. Pragmatic inferences and biases.* Manuscript in preparation.

Alloy, L. B., Clements, C., & Kolden, G. (1985). The cognitive diathesis-stress theories of depression: Therapeutic implications. In S. Reiss & R. Bootzin (Eds.), *Theoretical issues in behavior therapy.* New York: Academic Press.

Alloy, L. B., & Tabachnik, N. (1984). The assessment of covariation by humans and animals: The joint influence of prior expectations and current situational information. *Psychological Review, 91,* 112–149.

Barthé, D., & Hammen, C. (1981). A naturalistic extension of the attributional model of depression. *Personality and Social Psychology Bulletin, 7,* 53–58.

Beach, S. R. H., Abramson, L. Y., & Levine, F. M. (1981). Attributional reformulation of learned helplessness and depression: Therapeutic implications. In J. F. Clarkin & H. I. Glazer (Eds.), *Depression: Behavioral and directive intervention strategies.* New York: Garland.

Beck, A. T. (1967). *Depression: Clinical, experimental, and theoretical aspects.* New York: Harper & Row.

Beck, A. T. (1976). *Cognitive therapy and the emotional disorders.* New York: International Universities Press.

Beck, A. T., Kovacs, M., & Weissman, A. (1975). Hopelessness and suicidal behavior: An overview. *Journal of the American Medical Association, 234,* 1146–1149.

Beck, A. T., Rush, A. J., Shaw, B. F., & Emery, G. (1979). *Cognitive therapy of depression.* New York: Guilford.

Blackburn, I. M., Bishop, S., Glen, A., Whalley, L. J., & Christie, J. E. (1981). The efficacy of cognitive therapy in depression: A treatment trial using cognitive therapy and pharmacotherapy, each alone and in combination. *British Journal of Psychiatry, 139,* 181–189.

Blaney, P. H., Behar, V., & Head, R. (1980). Two measures of depressive cognitions: Their association with depression and with each other. *Journal of Abnormal Psychology, 89,* 678–682.

Bradley, G. W. (1978). Self-serving biases in the attribution process: A reexamination of the fact or fiction question. *Journal of Personality and Social Psychology, 36*, 56–71.

Brown, G. W., & Harris, T. (1978). *Social origins of depression.* New York: Free Press.

Buchsbaum, M. S., & Rieder, R. (1979). Biologic heterogeneity and psychiatric research. *Archives of General Psychiatry, 36*, 1163–1169.

Cochran, S. D., & Hammen, C. L. (1985). Perceptions of stressful life events and depression: A test of attributional models. *Journal of Personality and Social Psychology, 48*, 1562–1571.

Costello, C. G. (1972). Depression: Loss of reinforcers or loss of reinforcer effectiveness? *Behavior Therapy, 3*, 240–247.

Coyne, J. C., & Gotlib, I. H. (1983). The role of cognition in depression: A critical appraisal. *Psychological Bulletin, 94*, 472–505.

Craighead, W. E. (1980). Away from a unitary model of depression. *Behavior Therapy, 11*, 122–128.

Cronbach, L. J., & Meehl, P. E. (1955). Construct validity in psychological tests. *Psychological Bulletin, 52*, 281–302.

Cutrona, C. E. (1983). Causal attributions and perinatal depression. *Journal of Abnormal Psychology, 92*, 161–192.

Depue, R. A., & Monroe, S. M. (1978). Learned helplessness in the perspective of the depressive disorders. *Journal of Abnormal Psychology, 87*, 3–20.

Depue, R. A., & Monroe, S. M. (1983). Psychopathology research. In M. Hersen, A. E. Kazdin, & A. S. Bellack (Eds.), *The clinical psychology handbook.* Elmsford, NY: Pergamon.

Derry, P. A., & Kuiper, N. A. (1981). Schematic processing and self-reference in clinical depression. *Journal of Abnormal Psychology, 90*, 286–297.

Eaves, G., & Rush, A. J. (1984). Cognitive patterns in symptomatic and remitted unipolar major depression. *Journal of Abnormal Psychology, 93*, 31–40.

Enzle, M. E., & Schopflocher, D. (1978). Instigation of attribution processes by attributional questions. *Personality and Social Psychology Bulletin, 4*, 595–599.

Epstein, S. (1979). The stability of behavior: I. On predicting most of the people much of the time. *Journal of Personality and Social Psychology, 37*, 1097–1126.

Epstein, S. (1980). The stability of behavior: II. Implications for psychological research. *American Psychologist, 35*, 790–806.

Feather, N. T., & Barber, J. G. (1983). Depressive reactions and unemployment. *Journal of Abnormal Psychology, 92*, 185–195.

Freud, S. (1957). Mourning and melancholia. In J. Strachey (Ed. and Trans.), *Standard edition of the complete psychological works of Sigmund Freud.* (Vol. 14). London: Hogarth. (Original work published 1917.)

Gillespie, R. D. (1929). Clinical differentiation of types of depression. *Guy Hospital Reports, 79*, 306–344.

Golin, S., Sweeney, P. D., & Shaeffer, D. E. (1981). The causality of causal attributions in depression: A cross-lagged panel correlational analysis. *Journal of Abnormal Psychology, 90*, 14–22.

Gong-Guy, E., & Hammen, C. (1980). Causal perceptions of stressful life events in depressed and nondepressed clinic outpatients. *Journal of Abnormal Psychology, 89*, 662–669.

Greenwald, A. G. (1980). The totalitarian ego: Fabrication and revision of personal history. *American Psychologist, 35*, 603–618.

Halberstadt, L. J., Andrews, D., Metalsky, G. I., & Abramson, L. Y. (1984). Helplessness, hopelessness, and depression: A review of progress and future directions. In N. S. Endler & J. Hunt (Eds.), *Personality and behavior disorders.* New York: Wiley.

Halberstadt, L. J., Mukherji, B. R., & Abramson, L. Y. (1988). *Cognitive styles among college students: Toward an integration of the cognitive theories of depression with cognitive psychology and descriptive psychiatry.* Manuscript submitted for publication.

Hamilton, E. W., & Abramson, L. Y. (1983). Cognitive patterns in major depressive disorder: A longitudinal study in a hospital setting. *Journal of Abnormal Psychology, 92*, 173–184.

Hammen, C., & Cochran, S. (1981). Cognitive correlates of life stress and depression in college students. *Journal of Abnormal Psychology, 90*, 23–27.

Hammen, C., & deMayo, R. (1982). Cognitive correlates of teacher stress and depressive symptoms: Implications for attributional models of depression. *Journal of Abnormal Psychology, 91*, 96–101.

Hammen, C., Krantz, S., & Cochran, S. (1981). Relationships between depression and causal attributions about stressful life events. *Cognitive Therapy and Research, 5*, 351–358.

Hammen, C., Marks, T., Mayol, A., & deMayo, R. (1985). Depressive self-schemas, life stress, and vulnerability to depression. *Journal of Abnormal Psychology, 94*, 308–319.

Hammen, C., & Mayol, A. (1982). Depression and cognitive characteristics of stressful life-event types. *Journal of Abnormal Psychology, 91*, 165–174.

Harvey, D. (1981). Depression and attributional style: Interpretations of important personal events. *Journal of Abnormal Psychology, 90*, 134–142.

Harvey, J. H., Ickes, W. J., & Kidd, R. F., (Eds.). (1976, 1978, 1981). *New directions in attribution research*. (Vols. 1–3). Hillsdale, NJ: Erlbaum.

Harvey, J. H., & Weary, G. (1981). *Perspectives on attributional processes*. Dubuque, IA: William C. Brown.

Heider, F. (1958). *The psychology of interpersonal relations*. New York: Wiley.

Hempel, C. G. (1952). *Fundamentals of concept formation in empirical science*. Chicago: University of Chicago Press.

Hempel, C. G. (1965). *Aspects of scientific explanation*. New York: Free Press.

Ickes, W., & Layden, M. A. (1978). Attributional styles. In J. Harvey, W. Ickes, & R. Kidd (Eds.), *New directions in attribution research* (Vol. 2). Hillsdale, NJ: Erlbaum.

Kayne, N. T., Alloy, L. B., Romer, D., & Crocker, J. (1988). *Predicting depressive reactions in the classroom: A test of a cognitive diathesis-stress theory of depression with causal modeling techniques*. Manuscript submitted for publication.

Kazdin, A. E., French, N. H., Unis, A. S., Esveldt-Dawson, K., & Sherick, R. B. (1983). Hopelessness, depression, and suicidal intent among psychiatrically disturbed inpatient children. *Journal of Consulting and Clinical Psychology, 51*, 504–510.

Kelley, H. H. (1967). Attribution theory in social psychology. In D. Levine (Ed.), *Nebraska symposium on motivation* (Vol. 15). Lincoln, NE: University of Nebraska Press.

Kendell, R. E. (1968). *The classification of depression illness*. London: Oxford University Press.

Klein, D. F. (1974). Endogenomorphic depression: Conceptual and terminological revision. *Archives of General Psychiatry, 31*, 447–454.

Klerman, G. L. (1978). The evolution of a scientific nosology. In J. C. Shershow (Ed.), *Schizophrenia: Science and practice*. Cambridge, MA: Harvard University Press.

Klinger, E. (1975). Consequences of commitment to and disengagement from incentives. *Psychological Review, 82*, 1–25.

Kovacs, M., Rush, A. J., Beck, A. T., & Hollon, S. D. (1981). Depressed outpatients treated with cognitive therapy or pharmacotherapy. *Archives of General Psychiatry, 38*, 33–39.

Kraepelin, E. (1913). Manic-depressive insanity and paranoia. In *Textbook of psychiatry* (R. M. Barclay, Trans.). Edinburgh: Livingstone.

Krantz, S., & Hammen, C. (1979). Assessment of cognitive bias in depression. *Journal of Abnormal Psychology, 88*, 611–619.

Lewinsohn, P. M., Steinmetz, J. L., Larson, D. W., & Franklin, J. (1981). Depression-related cognitions: Antecedent or consequence? *Journal of Abnormal Psychology, 90*, 213–219.

Martin, D., Abramson, L. Y., & Alloy, L. B. (1984). The illusion of control for self and others in depressed and nondepressed college students. *Journal of Personality and Social Psychology, 46*, 125–136.

McArthur, L. A. (1972). The how and what of why: Some determinants and consequences of causal attributions. *Journal of Personality and Social Psychology, 22*, 171–193.

Meehl, P. E. (1972). Specific genetic etiology, psychodynamics and therapeutic nihilism. *International Journal of Mental Health, 1*, 10–27.

Meehl, P. E. (1978). Theoretical risks and tabular asterisks: Sir Karl, Sir Ronald, and the slow progress of soft psychology. *Journal of Consulting and Clinical Psychology, 46*, 806–834.

Meehl, P. E., & Golden, R. R. (1982). Taxometric methods. In P. C. Kendall & J. N. Butcher (Eds.), *Handbook of research methods in clinical psychology*. New York: Wiley.

Melges, F. T., & Bowlby, J. (1969). Types of hopelessness in psychopathological process. *Archives of General Psychiatry, 20*, 690–699.

Metalsky, G. I., & Abramson, L. Y. (1981). Attributional styles: Toward a framework for conceptualization and assessment. In P. C. Kendall & S. D. Hollon (Eds.), *Cognitive-behavioral interventions: Assessment methods*. New York: Academic.

Metalsky, G. I., Abramson, L. Y., Seligman, M. E. P., Semmel, A., & Peterson, C. (1982). Attributional styles and life events in the classroom: Vulnerability and invulnerability to depressive mood reactions. *Journal of Personality and Social Psychology, 43*, 612–617.

Metalsky, G. E., Halberstadt, L. J., & Abramson, L. Y. (1987). Vulnerability to depressive mood reactions: Toward a more powerful test of the diathesis-stress and causal mediation components of the reformulated theory of depression. *Journal of Personality and Social Psychology, 52*, 386–393.

Miller, D. T. (1976). Ego involvement and attributions for success and failure. *Journal of Personality and Social Psychology, 34*, 901–906.

Miller, D. T., & Ross, M. (1975). Self-serving biases in the attribution of causality: Fact or fiction? *Psychological Bulletin, 82*, 213–225.

Miller, I. W., Klee, S. H., & Norman, W. H. (1982). Depressed and nondepressed inpatients' cognitions of hypothetical events, experimental tasks, and stressful life events. *Journal of Abnormal Psychology, 91*, 78–81.

Minkoff, K., Bergman E., Beck, A. T., & Beck, R. (1973). Hopelessness, depression and attempted suicide. *American Journal of Psychiatry, 130*, 455–459.

Nisbett, R., & Ross, L. (1980). *Human inference: Strategies and shortcomings of social judgment*. Englewood Cliffs, NJ: Prentice-Hall.

Pap, A. (1953). Reduction-sentences and open concepts. *Methods, 5*, 3–30.

Paykel, E. S. (1979). Recent life events in the development of the depressive disorders. In R. A. Depue (Ed.), *The psychobiology of the depressive disorders: Implications for the effects of stress*. New York: Academic.

Persons, J. B., & Rao, P. A. (1985). Longitudinal study of cognitions, life events, and depression in psychiatric inpatients. *Journal of Abnormal Psychology, 94*, 51–63.

Peterson, C., Schwartz, S. M., & Seligman, M. E. P. (1981). Self-blame and depressive symptoms. *Journal of Personality and Social Psychology, 41*, 253–259.

Peterson, C., & Seligman, M. E. P. (1984). Causal explanations as a risk factor for depression: Theory and evidence. *Psychological Review, 91*, 347–374.

Petrie, K., & Chamberlain, K. (1983). Hopelessness and social desirability as moderator variables in predicting suicidal behavior. *Journal of Consulting and Clinical Psychology, 51*, 485–487.

Pittman, T. S., & Pittman, N. L. (1980). Deprivation of control and the attribution process. *Journal of Personality and Social Psychology, 39*, 377–389.

Popper, K. R. (1959). *The logic of scientific discovery*. New York: Basic Books.

Popper, K. R. (1962). *Conjectures and refutations*. New York: Basic Books.

Popper, K. R. (1972). *Objective knowledge*. Oxford: Oxford University Press.

Pyszczynski, T. A., & Greenberg, J. (1981). Role of disconfirmed expectancies in the instigation of attributional processing. *Journal of Personality and Social Psychology, 40*, 31–38.

Raps, C. S., Peterson, C. Reinhard, K. E., Abramson, L. Y., & Seligman, M. E. P. (1982). Attributional style among depressed patients. *Journal of Abnormal Psychology, 91*, 102–108.

Riskind, J. H., & Rholes, W. S. (1984). Cognitive accessibility and the capacity of cognitions to predict future depression: A theoretical note. *Cognitive Therapy and Research, 8*, 1–12.

Sarason, I. G., Johnson, J. H., & Siegel, J. M. (1978). Assessing the impact of life changes: Development of the Life Experiences Survey. *Journal of Consulting and Clinical Psychology, 46,* 932–946.

Secunda, S., Katz, M. M., & Friedman, R. (1973). The depressive disorders in 1973. National Institute of Mental Health. Washington, DC: U.S. Government Printing Office.

Seligman, M. E. P. (1975). *Helplessness: On depression, development, and death.* San Francisco: Freeman.

Seligman, M. E. P. (1978). Comment and integration. *Journal of Abnormal Psychology, 87,* 165–179.

Seligman, M. E. P., Abramson, L. Y., Semmel, A., & von Baeyer, C. (1979). Depressive attributional style. *Journal of Abnormal Psychology, 88,* 242–247.

Seligman, M. E. P., Peterson, C., Kaslow, N. J., Tanenbaum, R. L., Alloy, L. B., & Abramson, L. Y. (1984). Attributional style and depressive symptoms among children. *Journal of Abnormal Psychology, 93,* 235–238.

Skinner, H. A. (1981). Toward the intergration of classification theory and methods. *Journal of Abnormal Psychology, 90,* 68–87.

Snyder, M. L., Stephan, W. G., & Rosenfield, D. (1978). Attributional egotism. In J. H. Harvey, W. J. Ickes, & R. F. Kidd (Eds.), *New directions in attribution research.* (Vol. 2). Hillsdale, NJ: Erlbaum.

Stevens, L., & Jones, E. E. (1976). Defensive attribution and the Kelley cube. *Journal of Personality and Social Psychology, 34,* 809–820.

Tiger, L. (1979). *Optimism: The biology of hope.* New York: Simon & Schuster.

Trope, Y. (1975). Seeking information about one's own ability as a determinant of choice among tasks. *Journal of Personality and Social Psychology, 32,* 1004–1013.

Trope, Y., & Brickman, P. (1975). Difficulty and diagnosticity as determinants of choice among tasks. *Journal of Personality and Social Psychology, 31,* 918–925.

Weary, G. (1979). Self-serving attributional biases: Perceptual or response distortions? *Journal of Personality and Social Psycholgoy, 37,* 1418–1420.

Weiner, B. (1972). *Theories of motivation: From mechanism to cognition.* Chicago: Rand McNally.

Weiner, B. (1974). *Achievement motivation and attribution theory.* Morristown, NJ: General Learning Press.

Williams, T. A., Friedman, R. J., & Secunda, S. K. (1970. The depressive illness. National Institute of Mental Health. Washington, DC: U.S. Government Printing Office.

Wong, P. T. P., & Weiner, B. (1981). When people ask "why" questions, and the heuristics of attributional search. *Journal of Personality and Social Psychology, 40,* 650–663.

Wortman, C. B., & Dintzer, L. (1978). Is an attributional analysis of the learned helplessness phenomenon viable? A critique of the Abramson-Seligman-Teasdale reformulation. *Journal of Abnormal Psychology, 87,* 75–90.

Zuckerman, M. (1979). Attribution of success and failure revisited, or: The motivational bias is alive and well in attribution theory. *Journal of Personality, 47,* 245–287.

3

Attributional Styles and the Self-concept

WILLIAM ICKES

"Causal conspirators" (A Melodrama in Three Acts). Everis Wright, a self-made man (played by E. G. Otis), marries Totie Lee Wrong, a self-unmade woman (played by Mia Culp). Their relationship is based on a curious symbiosis: He takes credit for all the positive outcomes they experience, but denies responsibility for any negative ones; she does just the opposite. By the end of the play, Everis's regard for himself is so high that he has declared himself to be completely self-actualized; Totie's self-esteem is so low that she has checked herself into a mental hospital for treatment of depression.

A playwright, trying to portray people's different styles of explaining the causes and relative importance of events in everyday life, might attempt to dramatize these differences in a play such as the imaginary one outlined above. A psychologist, not having a similar license to fabricate the data he or she presents, must proceed in a different manner. In a previous publication (Ickes & Layden, 1978), Mary Anne Layden and I reported the various steps by which we attempted to demonstrate the existence of "attributional styles" and explore their relationship to the self-concept. Coming from a clinical perspective, Abramson, Seligman, and Teasdale (1978) similarly speculated that individual differences exist in attributional styles and hypothesized that certain attributional styles are vulnerability factors for "hopelessness depression" (Abramson, Alloy, & Metalsky, 1988; Abramson, Metalsky, & Alloy, 1987, Abramson, Metalsky, & Alloy, Chapter 2, this volume).

In this chapter, I propose that attributional style is dynamically related to other aspects of the self-concept, with important implications for mental health and psychological adjustment. After first reviewing the conceptualization and measurement of attributional styles, I will describe their relationship to the self-concept and consider their implications for a number of clinical problem areas.

ATTRIBUTIONAL STYLES: CONCEPTUALIZATION
AND MEASUREMENT

The notion that individuals may display characteristic styles of attribution is not a new one. Although the term "attribution" was not used much prior to Heider's (1944) paper, and although most of the theoretical and empirical work in attribution has been done within the last 20 years (see edited sourcebooks by Jones *et al.*, 1972; and by Harvey, Ickes, & Kidd, 1976, 1978, 1981), the phenomena that fall within the domain of the various attributional formulations have been of interest to psychologists since the field was first established. A lengthy examination of the historical antecedents of the attributional styles construct is beyond the scope of this paper; however, a few of the more obvious ones should at least be noted. These include Sigmund Freud's (1920) analysis of ego defense mechanisms, George Kelly's (1955) theory of personal constructs, Fritz Heider's (1958) psychology of interpersonal relations, and Julian Rotter's (1966) conception of locus of control.

If one attempts to extract some common themes from these diverse works, a general conception of attributional styles begins to emerge, based on the assumption that there are relatively stable, individual differences in the kinds of causal attributions people are predisposed to make in accounting for the personal outcomes that they and others experience (Cutrona, Russell, & Jones, 1985; Metalsky & Abramson, 1981). Although the possible sources of these differences are not well defined and are a matter of some debate, there is at least some consensus that these differences in attributional style are closely and dynamically related to corresponding differences in self-conception. Indeed, most theorists would probably have little difficulty endorsing Heider's (1958) assertion that a given attribution will be "acceptable" to a person only if it satisfies both of the following two criteria: (1) that it is plausible (i.e., the attributed cause could reasonably have produced the outcome), and (2) that it is consistent with the person's needs, wishes, and "cognitive expectations about connections between motives, attitudes, and behavior, etc." (pp. 172–173). In other words, a given attribution does not stand alone, in isolation; rather, it is embedded in a system of interrelated attributions and cognitions that collectively constitute the person's view of himself or herself, other people, the outcomes they respectively experience, and the physical and psychological worlds they inhabit. If it is further assumed that this system of attributions and cognitions has evolved in order to provide the person with a viable and internally consistent representation of "reality," then it follows that any attribution that would disrupt the internal consistency of this system should be less acceptable to the person than one that would not.

The primary question raised by this conception is how a person's outcome attributions are related to his or her more general view of "reality," including his or her self-conception. Addressing this issue will be my major concern in this chapter, but a number of more immediate, related questions will, of necessity, be discussed as well. First, what types of attributions for personal outcomes do people typically make and on what dimensions can these attributions be classified (cf. Weiner, 1985)? Second, what evidence is there from past research that individual differences in attributional preference really do exist (cf. Cutrona *et al.*, 1985)? Third, what individual difference variables are related to attributional styles and what is the nature of these relationships?

IDENTIFICATION AND CLASSIFICATION OF OUTCOME ATTRIBUTIONS

A wide variety of studies have attempted to catalogue the kinds of attributions people make to account for personal outcomes (for a review, see Weiner, 1985). In a prototypical study, Frieze (1973, cited by Weiner, 1974) asked college students to assume that an individual had succeeded or failed at either an academic or a nonacademic task and then to specify why that particular outcome had occurred. She found that 86 percent of her subjects' responses across both tasks could be classified reliably into nine causal categories. "The categories, listed in order of their frequency of usage, were ability, immediate effort, task difficulty, luck, . . . [causal influence due] to other people (such as teacher bias), mood, stable effort expenditure, fatigue, and other unclassifiable causes," (Weiner, 1974, p. 7).

It is worth noting that Frieze's list of empirically derived causes of personal outcomes incorporates all of those causal factors previously identified as important by Heider (1958). Heider suggested that the causes of personal outcomes could be classified on a *causal locus* dimension—a dimension most contemporary researchers regard as fundamental. Causes are classified on this dimension as internal (having a "self" origin, or "locus") or as external (having an "other" or environmental origin, or locus). According to Heider, the four major causal determinants of an individual's personal outcomes are ability and effort (internal factors) and task difficulty and luck (external factors). In calling the fourth factor "luck," Heider intended no mystical connotations; rather, he considered this word to be the best colloquial term available for summarizing the entire array of adventitious environmental influences that can affect a person's outcome on a given task.

A second attributional dimension—*stability*—was later proposed by Weiner and his colleagues (Weiner, 1972; Weiner *et al.*, 1971) as orthogonal to (statistically independent of) the causal locus dimension. In Weiner's 2×2 taxonomic scheme, Heider's four major causal factors are reclassified. Ability is seen as a stable, internal cause; task difficulty is stable and external; effort is unstable and internal; and luck is unstable and external. The identification of the stability dimension proved to be an important theoretical step in the analysis of outcome attributions, because it led to the discovery that stability and causal locus effects had been confounded in some earlier work on expectancy shifts and affective reactions following success and failure (see Weiner, 1974, 1985, for reviews).

More recently, two additional attributional dimensions have been proposed. The first of these was originally conceptualized by Rosenbaum (1972) as the "intentionality" dimension. However, it is likely that the term *controllability* provides a more precise and operationally defensible label for this dimension, on which controllable and uncontrollable causal factors are contrasted (Weiner, 1979, 1985; Wortman & Dintzer, 1978). The second dimension, initially proposed by Abramson *et al.*, (1978), contrasts *global versus specific* causal factors. On this dimension some factors are classified as affecting many, if not all, of an individual's outcomes, whereas other factors are classified as affecting only some outcomes and not others. Although the conceptual utility of these last two dimensions has been questioned (e.g., Buchwald, Coyne, & Cole, 1978; Wortman & Dintzer, 1978), empirical support for these distinctions has been provided by recent research (for reviews, see Abramson, Alloy, & Metalsky, 1988, Abramson *et al.*, 1987, Chapter 2, this volume; Peterson & Seligman, 1984; Sweeney, Anderson, & Bailey, 1986).

A curious aspect of this accelerating search for dimensions on which to classify the causes of personal outcomes (see also Wortman & Dintzer, 1978, regarding a proposed "foreseeability" dimension) is that theorists within the psychological tradition have made almost no attempt to identify dimensions on which to classify the outcomes themselves. This emphasis on causes rather than outcomes is naive in two respects, but understandable in a third. It is naive, first, in its implicit assumption that perceived causes are more important than perceived outcomes in determining emotions and behavior—an assumption most reinforcement theorists would certainly question. Even as cognitively oriented a theorist as Weiner (1985) recently suggested that following the outcome of an event, there is a general positive or negative reaction based on the perceived success or failure of the outcome; Weiner dubbed these "primitive" emotions as outcome dependent–attribution independent (see also Metalsky, Halberstadt, & Abramson, 1987).

Second, the emphasis on causes neglects the possibility that the effects on behavior of causal perceptions and outcome perceptions may be interactive, such that the same causal attribution may have different behavioral implications given one type of outcome than given another. Because it is reasonable to expect that causal perceptions and outcome perceptions will *both* affect behavior, not only as main effects but also in interaction, the lack of theoretical attention given to outcome perceptions would seem to reflect a surprising lack of insight. Fortunately, a number of investigators examining the role of stress in physical and psychological disorders have begun to specify on what dimensions it might be useful to classify events (e.g., Alloy, Hartlage, & Abramson, 1988; Folkman, 1984; Kanner, Coyne, Schaefer, & Lazarus, 1981; Monroe, 1983a, 1983b; Monroe, Imhoff, Wise, & Harris, 1983; Paykel, 1979; Zimmerman, 1983).

The apparent reluctance of most theorists to classify outcomes may be understandable when one considers that outcomes are typically differentiated in rather subjective terms. Thus, whereas causes can be classified on relatively "objective" dimensions such as causal locus and stability, outcomes must be distinguished on the basis of relatively "subjective" dimensions such as their perceived relevance–irrelevance to the self, their perceived positive or negative valence, perceived consequentiality, and so forth. Although most scientists are trained to avoid the use of any theoretical constructs that must be subjectively defined, such constructs may nevertheless prove to be essential to a detailed understanding of the attributional determinants of human behavior (see Wortman & Dintzer, 1978, for a related discussion).

To the extent that outcomes have been classified at all, the primary dimension employed has been the positive–negative *valence* dimension (e.g., Fitch, 1970; Ickes & Layden, 1978; Weiner, 1985). There is considerable evidence that this outcome dimension is a fundamental and important one, and I will review a portion of this evidence below.

EVIDENCE FOR INDIVIDUAL DIFFERENCES IN ATTRIBUTION

The importance of correctly identifying the fundamental causal and outcome dimensions becomes apparent when one considers the results of previous attempts to identify and measure attributional styles. Perhaps the earliest and most influential measures of attributional styles have been the various versions of Rotter's (1966) locus of control scale. Although the locus of control dimension presumably tapped by these measures is not identical to the locus of causality dimension in attribution, the overlap is sufficiently great that the similarities as well as the differences between the two are worth exploring.

Locus of control scales are intended to measure the degree to which individuals believe that the outcomes they experience are under their own control as opposed to control by other people or by the environment. Individuals whose responses reflect a strong belief that their outcomes are internally controlled are assessed as "internals," whereas those whose responses reflect a strong belief that their outcomes are externally controlled are assessed as "externals."

The extreme "internal" and "external" types are also represented (as minor characters) in the play "Causal Conspirators." In the second act of the play, prior to checking into the mental hospital, Totie seeks some relief by becoming a client of Dr. Otto Cozl, founder of Cozl Obfuscation and Servility Training (COST). Cozl believes in and promotes the theory that people are completely responsible for everything that ever happens to them—good and bad. Ironically, however, his preferred mode of treatment is to keep his clients in a chronic state of confusion by telling them that (1) they are totally in charge of their own lives, but (2) they can't even go to the bathroom without his permission. Cozl's assistant, Faye Tullis, is a former society debutante who was kidnapped and brainwashed by the Roonies (the members of a religious organization dedicated to the worship of a short, hypersexed comedy actor). Having been first deprogrammed and then reprogrammed by Cozl, Faye is now under his enlightened control. In her off-hours, she falls under the influence of anyone she happens to meet and "goes with the flow."

The use of a trait approach is based on the explicit assumption that individuals' locus of control orientations are relatively stable and invariant over time. However, some additional, more implicit assumptions can be inferred from the kinds of items typically included in locus of control measures. These assumptions highlight a number of important differences between the locus of control and the locus of causality dimensions.

First, locus of control scales often confound locus of control with locus of causality by using (1) items that imply causality but no control of an event (e.g., Rotter, 1966), (2) items that imply control but no causality of an event, (e.g., Mischel, Zeiss, & Zeiss, 1974), or (3) items that imply both (Crandall, Katkovsky, & Crandall, 1965). Second, the confusion between control and causality is particularly evident in the research that deals with negative events. It is not clear whether internal control of negative outcomes means that the subjects *caused* the negative event (Mischel *et al.*, 1974), or whether it means that a negative outcome can be escaped or avoided and therefore "controlled" (see Glass & Singer, 1972; Wortman, Panciera, Shusterman, & Hibscher, 1976. See also Abramson *et al.*, 1978, and Weiner, 1985, for similar critiques of work on locus of control). Third, Rotter's (1966) scale, the one most widely used, suffers from additional problems. The scale collapses over positive and negative outcomes, reflecting an implicit assumption that subjects would perceive a similar degree of internal versus external control for both. Moreover, some items are written in the first person and others in the third person, reflecting a second implicit assumption that whatever subjects see as the locus of control for other people's outcomes will also be seen as the locus of control of their own. Studies I will cite below tend to invalidate the first of these assumptions, and findings relevant to actor–observer differences in attribution (see Monson & Snyder, 1977) and attributional style and depression (Sweeney, Shaeffer, & Golin, 1982) tend to invalidate the second.

Fortunately, the locus of control literature does not provide the only evidence of individual differences in attributional style. A review of a number of converging literatures suggests that individual differences in attributional preference are systematically linked to individual differences in self-esteem, gender, sex-role identification, depression, and loneliness. Layden and I (1978) discovered some striking similarities in the patterns of these relationships that suggested to us that attributional preferences might be integrally related to the individual's self-concept.

For example, individual differences in self-esteem have consistently been related to attributional differences in reactions to negative or "failure" outcomes (Tennen & Herzberger, 1987). In a study published in 1956, Solley and Stagner recorded the spontaneous remarks of subjects working on unsolvable anagrams. They found that high self-valuing subjects made more comments such as "Is this a word?" or "Is this English?", whereas low self-valuing subjects made more comments such as "I must be stupid." Although the authors did not discuss these results in attributional terms, it seems likely that the high self-esteem subjects were attributing their failure to external causes, whereas the low self-esteem subjects were attributing their failure to some internal deficiency.

In conceptually related studies, Fitch (1970) and Gilmore and Minton (1974) reported additional evidence that high self-esteem (or high task-confident) subjects tend to attribute success more internally but failure more externally than low self-esteem (or low task-confident) subjects. Moreover, data from studies employing measures of actual and expected performance reveal that high self-esteem subjects appear to accept the validity of success feedback but reject the validity of failure feedback; thus, success feedback affects both their expected and actual performance ratings (Ryckman & Rodda, 1972; Shrauger & Rosenberg, 1970), whereas failure feedback does not. Conversely, low self-esteem subjects appear to accept the validity of failure feedback but reject the validity of success feedback. Although success feedback may have some impact on the expectations and subsequent performance of low self-esteem subjects if it is not inconsistent with their self-concept (Maracek & Mettee, 1972), the effects of failure feedback are probably more likely to be reflected in their behavior (Cruz Perez, 1973).

Gender differences have also been related to attribution and performance in a pattern of data that is generally correspondent with that obtained for self-esteem (see Deaux, 1976, for a review). In general, the actual performance, expected performance, and causal attributions of males tend to resemble those of high self-esteem subjects, whereas the responses of females on the same measures resemble those of low self-esteem subjects. Males not only have a higher expectancy of success than females over a wide range of skill and achievement tasks (e.g., Crandall, 1969; Deaux, White, & Farris, 1975; Feather, 1969; Montanelli & Hill, 1969), but are also more likely to attribute their successes to the internal–stable factor of ability (Deaux & Emswiller, 1974; Deaux & Farris, 1974).

The reason for this intriguing parallel between gender and self-esteem in their relationship to attribution and performance becomes more evident when one examines the correlations between self-esteem and sex-role measures of masculinity and femininity (e.g., Ickes & Layden, 1975, unpublished data; Wetter, 1975). These data reveal that self-esteem is positively correlated with assessed masculinity (rs ranged from .32 to .49) but is uncorrelated with assessed femininity (rs ranged from −.11 to .13). Thus, self-esteem in our culture appears to be defined primarily by the presence of those traits and behaviors that are stereotypically associated with a masculine sex-role identification—a finding that helps to account for the parallel relationships of gender and self-esteem to measures of attribution and performance.

INDIVIDUAL DIFFERENCE VARIABLES AND ATTRIBUTIONAL STYLES

To further explore the interrelation of self-esteem, sex, and attributional preference, Mary Anne Layden and I conducted a series of studies in which we employed our own measures of attributional style (Ickes & Layden, 1978). In the first two studies we examined the differences in attributional preference exhibited by groups differing in gender and level of self-esteem. In the third study we attempted to determine whether changes in attributional preferences are associated with corresponding changes in self-esteem. In the fourth study we assessed the independent effects of self-esteem, gender, and attributional style on behavioral reactions to experimentally induced "failure" in a standard performance situation.

STUDIES 1 AND 2: GENDER AND SELF-ESTEEM DIFFERENCES

Our first two studies were designed to examine the specific differences in attributional style exhibited by groups differing in gender and level of self-esteem. The subjects in these studies were male and female undergraduates who were tested in large groups, in hour-long sessions. During each session the subjects completed a number of pencil-and-paper measures that included a self-esteem inventory designed for use with a college population (Morse & Gergen, 1970) and our measure of attributional style. The two measures were separated by a number of other scales so that subjects would not be likely to see them as being related.

The attributional style measure used in the first study consisted of 12 items. Each item contained a brief description of the outcome of a hypothetical event (for example, "You got an 'A' on a class project") followed by four possible causes of the outcome ("You worked hard to prepare this project," "The project was relatively easy," "The project is one in which you have considerable skill," or "You were lucky and happened to do a project that corresponded to the professor's interest"). The subjects' task was to read each item, imagine that they had experienced the outcome described, and then choose what they would consider to be the single most probable cause of the outcome. The items were written to minimize potential gender bias in the subjects' responses, and were designed to represent a wide range of conceptually distinct situations. Within each type of situation, the outcomes of the events were counterbalanced so that half were positive and half were negative.

The four possible causes provided for each outcome corresponded (in a random order) to the four types of causes in the two-dimensional taxonomy proposed by Weiner *et al.* (1971). Thus, for each outcome described, an example of a cause in each of the following (causal locus × stability) categories was offered as an alternative: internal–stable, internal–unstable, external–stable, external–unstable. Because of a number of practical considerations, we did not attempt to incorporate either the "controllability" or "global–specific" causal dimensions into the response alternatives.

The original attribution measure was scored by summing the number of times the subject chose each of the four types of causes for the two separate categories of positive and negative outcomes. This response format proved to be problematic because of the nonindependence of the four scores within the positive- and negative-outcome categories. The nonindependence of these scores made it necessary to analyze the data "in pieces," by means of a series of multivariate analyses in which only three of the four scores within each outcome category were analyzed. It also suggested to us the desirability of conducting a second study in order to replicate our initial results with an extensively revised version of the attributional style measure that was free of the problems inherent in the first.

To avoid the nonindependence problem inherent in the first version, the response format of the second was changed so that instead of choosing the most probable of the four alternative causes, the subjects rated the probability of each of the causes on a 5-point scale ranging from "not at all probable" (1) to "extremely probable" (5). To minimize the chances that some of the initial results might be due to the influence of a particular item or items rather than to more general attributional preferences, items on the first version for which response variance was low were either discarded or rewritten. In addition, new items were added to expand the revised measure from 12 to 24 descriptions of hypothetical event outcomes. Care was again taken in the writing or revising of the items to ensure that potential gender biases were not built into the items' content. A replication study employing this revised measure was then conducted in the same manner as the first, with large groups of male and female undergraduates serving as subjects.

Taken collectively, the results of the second study were very similar to those of the first, and both sets of data were consistent with the results of studies I have reviewed earlier. The findings that were significant across both studies may be summarized as follows:

1. With respect to self-esteem differences, the data indicated that high self-esteem subjects were inclined to take credit for positive outcomes by ascribing them to internal causes. In contrast, low self-esteem subjects tended to take less credit for positive outcomes by attributing them relatively more often to external causes. For negative outcomes, high self-esteem subjects either made external attributions or else rated all causal factors (and, by implication, the outcomes themselves) as improbable, whereas low self-esteem subjects tended to "blame" themselves for such outcomes by making relatively more internal attributions to explain them.

2. With respect to sex differences, the data indicated that males at each level of self-esteem exhibited attributional tendencies resembling those of high self-esteem subjects, whereas the attributional tendencies of females at each level resembled those of low self-esteem subjects. These relationships were relatively weak, however, in comparison to those obtained for self-esteem.

3. With respect to the stability variable, the data indicated a general tendency for subjects in all groups to choose unstable causes more often than stable causes for the outcomes described, and this tendency was especially pronounced for outcomes that were negative and/or perceived as internally caused.

Interpretations

There are essentially two major theoretical interpretations that could account for the three patterns of results listed. First, some or all of these results may be valid representations of the typical kinds of cause–outcome relationships that the subjects have experienced. Second, some or all may reflect relatively invalid, reality-distorting "biases" in the attribution process (see Rizley, 1978, for a similar separation of these two interpretations). These "biases" may be either (1) learned biases that have been acquired through socialization, or (2) motivated biases that derive either from the need to maintain a stable self-conception (Heider, 1958) or from the need to maintain a feeling of control over one's outcomes (Kelley, 1971).

Looking, for example, at the self-esteem differences, the difficulty of deciding between the two alternative interpretations becomes apparent. On the one hand, it is possible that the typical cause–outcome relationships experienced by high self-esteem subjects are *genuinely different* from those experienced by low self-esteem subjects. Thus, if high self-esteem subjects possess—in addition to their high self-esteem—other socially desirable traits, skills, and abilities that low self-esteem subjects do not possess, their positive outcomes may in fact be more generally attributable to internal factors, whereas the positive outcomes of low self-esteem subjects may not. By the same reasoning, negative outcomes may in fact not be as probable for high as for low self-esteem subjects, especially to the degree that they are internally caused (see Orvis, cited in Weiner, 1974, p. 19).

On the other hand, it is possible that the typical cause–outcome relationships experienced by high and low self-esteem subjects are not really different but are *merely perceived differently* because of biases affecting the attributions of subjects in one or both groups. Given this type of explanation, however, there are still two viable possibilities: (1) that these attributional biases have been acquired by subjects—through instruction, imitation, or other means—as a product of the socialization process, or (2) that these biases have emerged psychodynamically as defense mechanisms by means of which subjects attempt to maintain a stable self-conception or a feeling of control over their outcomes.

Of these two forms of attributional bias, the hypothetical processes involved in the first are fairly straightforward: The individual is taught (either explicitly or implicitly) by parents, teachers, peers, and other socializing agents that he or she is causally responsible for good outcomes but not for bad ones, or vice versa. Presumably, this learning eventually becomes internalized as a general predisposition or attributional style that then influences a wide range of attributions the person makes. The continued use of this attributional style may be the direct cause of corresponding changes in the person's level of self-esteem, or the two variables may be dynamically related such that a change in either variable may effect a parallel change in the other.

The hypothetical processes involved in the second form of attributional bias are based on Heider's (1958) assertion that an attribution will not be acceptable to the person unless it not only provides a plausible cause of the outcome to be explained but is also congruent with the person's view of himself or herself and the "cognitive expectations about connections between motives, attitudes, and behavior, etc.," that he or she holds (pp. 172–173). This reasoning suggests that the entire "naive psychology" of the person may have to be taken into account, and that the organizing principles of balance and attribution should not be seen as divorced from each other, but should instead be regarded as dynamically related within the person's life space (Heider, 1975). A person's attributions must tend, therefore, to be consistent with the self-concept, and vice versa, if a relatively stable view of the self and its relation to the world is to be maintained.

A detailed analysis of the dynamics of this consistency between the person's attributions and his or her self-concept is unfortunately beyond the scope of this chapter. For the present, it is probably sufficient to note that the attributional differences obtained in these first two studies reveal a consistent and predictable relationship to the individual difference variables of sex and self-esteem, even if the source and meaning of these differences are not altogether clear.

STUDY 3: CHANGES IN ATTRIBUTIONAL STYLE AND SELF-ESTEEM

Despite this acknowledged ambiguity regarding the source of attributional styles, the fairly unequivocal relationship of self-esteem to attributional preferences suggested that it might be possible to effect positive changes in self-esteem by inducing individuals to adopt the attributional style most characteristic of high self-esteem subjects. It is useful to examine this "attributional style therapy" in the larger context of cognitive theory and therapy for depression.

Insofar as both Beck's (1967, 1976, 1984; Beck, Rush, Shaw, & Emery, 1979) cognitive theory of depression and the hopelessness theory of depression (Abramson, Alloy, & Metalsky, 1988; Abramson *et al.*, 1987, Chapter 2, this volume; previously referred to as the reformulated theory of helplessness and depression, Abramson *et al.*, 1978) postulate that the attributional style observed in low self-esteem subjects is a vulnerability factor for depression, it is important to determine how to modify this attributional style. Although cognitive theorists (e.g., Alloy, Clements, & Kolden, 1985; Beach, Abramson, & Levine, 1981; Beck *et al.*, 1979; Halberstadt, Andrews, Metalsky, & Abramson, 1984; Hollon & Garber, Chapter 8, this volume) have begun to suggest therapeutic strategies and techniques to modify depressive attributional styles, no published studies provide explicit tests of these suggestions.

In an attempt to test this notion, Mary Anne Layden and I designed an experiment for which 60 subjects were selected on the basis of pretest data indicating that they were not only low in self-esteem but also showed the attributional style most characteristic of low self-esteem subjects—internalizing negative outcomes but not positive ones. Of these 60 subjects, 45 were randomly assigned to one of three experimental conditions to receive attributional retraining. The remaining 15 subjects were employed as nonretrained controls. The subjects in all four conditions were roughly counterbalanced according to gender.

The 45 subjects in the experimental conditions were contacted by telephone and asked to participate in a project that would extend over a 5-week period. As a cover story for the experiment, each subject was told that the project in which he or she had been enlisted was designed to help refine and improve an "attribution questionnaire" that the authors were developing. Because of some dissatisfaction with the current version of the questionnaire, a group of students was being asked to help generate some new items for a revised version. These new items would potentially be more credible and meaningful to a college population because they would be based on real situations that students had experienced.

Using response forms provided by the experimenter, each subject was instructed to record—for each of the 5 weeks—three positive outcome events and three negative outcome events that he or she had actually experienced during that week, along with a list of possible causes for each event. Subjects were instructed to list as many plausible causes as they could think of for the events described, but the *types* of causes they could list were restricted according to their experimental condition. Subjects in Group 1 were asked to list only internal causes for their positive outcome events and only external causes for their negative outcome events. Subjects in Group 2 were allowed to list any types of causes for their positive outcomes but were required to list only external causes for their negative ones. Subjects in Group 3 were given instructions the reverse of those given to subjects in Group 2: They were asked to provide only internal causes for their positive outcomes but could list any types of causes for their negative ones. The intent of these manipulations was to give the experimental subjects practice in making attributions that were somewhat inconsistent with their own attributional style but that either partially (Groups 2 and 3) or totally (Group 1) resembled the attributional style most characteristic of high self-esteem subjects.

Unfortunately, our subjects' original attributional styles proved surprisingly resistant to change, as evidenced by the results of a disguised self-esteem posttest, a retest measure of attributional style, and an extensive open-ended debriefing. Although subjects whose attributional style changed in the direction of the typical high self-esteem pattern did show a greater increase in self-esteem ($\bar{X} = 6.1$ scale points) than those whose attributional style showed no or reverse change relative to this pattern ($\bar{X} = 2.3$ scale points; $p < .03$, one-tailed test), the experimental manipulations were not a significant factor in producing these changes. Moreover, during the open-ended debriefing sessions, a majority of the subjects appeared quite resistant to the notion that their attributional style may have been (or should, in principle, be) altered. Many saw their own style as appropriate and "modest," in contrast to the style characteristic of high self-esteem subjects, which these low self-esteem subjects often referred to disparagingly as "immodest" or "egotistical." In short, their own attributional style appeared to be a relatively stable and important aspect of their overall personality structure. Lacking the belief that the new attributions were more appropriate than the old ones (see Valle & Frieze, 1976), and having little or no motivation to change, they would not be easily induced to adopt a new style.

Work in experimental social psychology also suggests that attributional styles might be resistant to change. A number of social psychologists (e.g., Ajzen, 1977; Ross, 1977, 1978) have suggested that in making causal attributions, people not only rely on current relevant information but also on their prior beliefs or schemas. A major therapeutic implication of the view that causal attributions are schema-driven is that people's attributional styles may not be easily changed through mere exposure to contradictory information (Ross, 1977). The logic of this implication is straightforward. Because the information is interpreted selectively in accordance with the person's beliefs or schemas, it is unlikely to provide strong disconfirmation of those schemas that are guiding the causal attributions the person makes. Thus, simply exposing low self-esteem subjects to information suggesting they attribute outcomes to the causes typically invoked by high self-esteem subjects may produce attributional style changes only very slowly.

Contemporary work in social psychology may provide some useful insight about how to produce more powerful and rapid changes in attributional style. Although it is only suggestive at this point, a study by Ross, Lepper, and Hubbard (1975) on the effects of debriefing provides some reason to believe that personal insight concerning one's attributional biases may facilitate changes in these attributional tendencies. An implication of this study is that informing low self-esteem subjects that they exhibit a particular attributional style and that its operation may lead them to experience lower self-esteem than high self-esteem subjects might facilitate modification of this style. In this regard, it is noteworthy that in their cognitive therapy for depression, Beck and his colleagues (e.g., Beck *et al.*, 1979) have reported that they devote a considerable portion of the initial therapy sessions to developing a common conceptualization of cognitive therapy with the depressed patient. The patient is effectively "socialized" into the system of cognitive therapy.

Study 4: Attributional Style, Gender, and Reactions to Failure

If attributional styles were indeed as integral to the self-concept as the results of Study 3 suggested, would they influence not only subjects' beliefs about their present outcomes but the nature of their future outcomes as well? In a fourth study, we sought to determine whether subjects with different attributional styles would respond differently to an experimentally induced "failure" experience. Because, in earlier studies of reactions to failure, differences in gender and self-esteem were presumably confounded with differences in attributional style, a further goal of this fourth study was to determine whether self-esteem or gender would have any effect on behavioral reactions to failure when attributional style was varied independently.

Forty subjects, preselected on the basis of individual difference data collected earlier, were assigned to eight groups that represented a complete factorial design comprised of three 2-level factors: self-esteem (high vs. low, based upon a median split), gender (male vs. female), and attributional style for failure (internal vs. external). To assess the independent effects of self-esteem, sex, and attributional style, care was taken to block the groups on the three variables so that the means and standard deviations of the blocked variable(s) were comparable for each of the test-variable groups.

As a pretest, baseline measure of performance, subjects completed 4 "practice" anagrams that were solvable and of moderate difficulty. They were then presented with a "test" series of 13 anagrams, of which only the last 4 were solvable. The presentation of the preceding 9 unsolvable anagrams was designed as an experimentally induced "failure" experience that the subjects would have to overcome in order to do well on the final set of four. Performance measures of speed and accuracy were taken for all of the pretest (first four) and posttest (last four) trials.

A pretest–posttest analysis of the speed (average time to completion) and error (total number incorrect) data revealed no significant differences for self-esteem on either measure ($Fs < 1$). However, as Figure 3-1 indicates, there were pronounced differences for groups separated on the basis of attributional style. The performance of subjects who were predisposed to internalize their

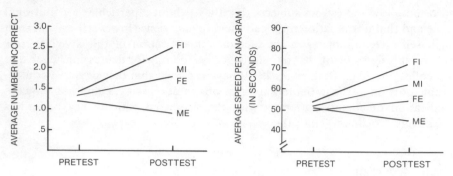

FIGURE 3-1. Measures of performance on a standard anagram task prior to (pretest) and following (posttest) an experimentally induced "failure" experience (Study 4). ME = males who externalize failure; MI = males who internalize failure; FE = females who externalize failure; FI = females who internalize failure.

negative or "failure" outcomes became significantly less accurate ($p < .005$) and slower ($p < .025$) following their unsuccessful attempt to solve the unsolvable anagrams. No impairment of performance was noted for subjects predisposed to externalize their negative outcomes ($Fs < 1$). This finding suggests that performance deficits that previously were attributed to self-esteem may really be due to attributional style. Thus, a crucial element underlying these deficits is apparently *not* low self-esteem per se, but the attributional tendency to internalize one's failures.

Given this pattern of results, we might expect that attributional style would also account for the variations in performance that have previously been attributed to sex, especially in light of the findings of our first two studies. This, however, was clearly *not* the case. The obtained sex differences were of the same magnitude as those obtained for attributional style and were in the direction predicted by previous research: The performance of the female subjects was definitely impaired by the failure experience, becoming significantly less accurate ($p < .005$) and slower ($p < .05$), whereas the performance of the male subjects was essentially unimpaired by failure ($Fs < 1$).

An examination of Figure 3-1 reveals that the independent effects of attributional style and sex were additive in nature. In other words, there was a performance deficit associated with internalizing failure and a separate performance deficit associated with being female. Thus, the disruption of performance by a failure experience was least evident for males who externalize failure and most evident for females who internalize it. Apparently females, in general, and subjects of both sexes who internalize failure, in particular, are disposed to react to failure or frustration in an achievement situation by essentially giving up. Through their socialization (Dweck & Goetz, 1978) or by some other means, these individuals have acquired some beliefs about the causes of their negative outcomes that are particularly debilitating. Because such individuals should be at high risk for "hopelessness depression" (Abramson *et al.*, 1987, in press, Chapter 2 in this volume), it is important to determine if the key element(s) in these beliefs can be identified more precisely.

STUDY 5: ABILITY ATTRIBUTIONS AND SELF-CONCEPTIONS

A study based on data collected by the author and subsequently analyzed at the University of Rochester by Yasmin Haddad and Harry Reis (Haddad, Reis, & Ickes, 1980) suggests that the key element in subjects' attributional styles may be the degree to which ability (or its lack) is seen as the cause of their positive and negative outcomes.

In this study, which resembled Studies 1 and 2 in most respects, large groups of male and female undergraduates completed Bem's (1974) Sex Role Inventory (BSRI) and provided self-report ratings of elation and depression in addition to completing the 24-item version of the attributional style measure and Morse and Gergen's (1970) measure of self-esteem. The resulting data were then subjected to several forms of statistical analysis at a level much more fine-grained than that attempted in Studies 1 and 2. The most meaningful and informative distillation of these results takes the form of the correlation matrix represented in Table 3-1. Subjects' outcome attributions to internal–stable ("ability"), internal–unstable ("effort"), external–stable ("task difficulty"), and external–unstable ("luck") factors are correlated with the criterion variables of assessed masculinity, femininity, self-esteem, elation, and depression, and these correlations are presented separately for males and for females.

The major findings and some suggested interpretations are summarized as follows:

1. Attribution of positive outcomes to ability was positively correlated with assessed masculinity in both sexes, and with assessed femininity in males. Follow-up ANOVAs revealed that androgynous males (those with high levels of *both* masculinity and femininity) were particularly likely to attribute positive outcomes to their ability.

2. Attribution of positive outcomes to ability was positively correlated with self-esteem and reported elation in both sexes, whereas attribution of negative outcomes to a lack of ability was negatively correlated with self-esteem and positively correlated with reported depression. In general, ability attributions were the best predictors of self-reported masculinity, self-esteem, and elation–depression.

3. The pattern of correlations for effort attributions was similar to that for ability attributions, but the magnitude of these correlations was generally less.

4. Although attribution of positive outcomes to effort was correlated with elation in both sexes, attribution of negative outcomes to a lack of effort was not correlated with depression. This finding, which contrasts with the ability

TABLE 3-1. Correlations of Attributional Factors with Criterion Variables for Males and Females (Study 5)

Attribution/Outcome	Masculinity		Femininity		Self-esteem		Elation		Depression	
	M	F	M	F	M	F	M	F	M	F
Ability/Positive	.34*	.44*	.50*	.13	.42*	.54*	.21*	.22*	-.17	-.16
Ability/Negative	-.20	-.10	-.09	-.05	-.60*	-.35*	-.13	.02	.35*	.43*
Effort/Positive	.20	.23*	.44*	.22*	.13	.25*	.20*	.28*	-.18	-.12
Effort/Negative	.00	.13	.12	.10	-.32*	-.11	.01	-.08	.06	.01
Task difficulty/Positive	.05	.24*	.30*	.12	.17	.15	.09	.18	-.17	-.10
Task difficulty/Negative	-.16	.33*	.03	-.03	-.26*	-.04	-.16	-.01	.21*	.11
Luck/Positive	.01	.09	.38*	.15	-.14	.07	.09	.23*	.03	-.07
Luck/Negative	-.09	.27*	.19	-.05	-.04	.00	-.07	.04	.04	.01

*$p < .05$ (*df*s for individual correlations vary somewhat due to missing data).

attribution data, suggests that whereas people may feel good about having ability and bad about lacking it, they can feel good about trying without necessarily feeling bad about *not* trying. A causally speculative corollary of this finding is that people are depressed primarily because of a perceived lack of ability and not because of a perceived lack of effort. This speculation is consistent with Halberstadt, Mukherji, and Abramson's (1988) finding that whereas an internal, stable, global attributional style for failures (e.g., lack of ability) was associated with depression, an internal, unstable, specific attributional style for failures (e.g., lack of effort) is associated with nondepression (see also Peterson, Schwartz, & Seligman, 1981). More generally, Janoff-Bulman (1979) has distinguished between characterological self-blame (e.g., lack of ability) and behavioral self-blame (e.g., lack of effort) and hypothesized that the former is maladaptive whereas the latter is adaptive.

5. Attribution of negative outcomes to task difficulty was negatively correlated with self-esteem and positively correlated with depression in males. This finding may mean either (a) that males disparage themselves for their failures to cope with difficult tasks, or (b) that males who attribute their failures to task difficulty have lower self-esteem and are more depressed to begin with.

6. Regardless of the type of outcome (positive or negative), the more masculine sex-typed the females were, the more likely they were to emphasize task demands as causal in influencing outcomes.

7. Attribution of positive outcomes to good "luck" (i.e., unstable environmental factors) was positively correlated with assessed femininity in males, whereas attribution of negative outcomes of bad "luck" was negatively correlated with assessed masculinity in females. These data seem to be congruent with the bulk of the sex-difference data in suggesting that externalizing success is a typically feminine response, whereas externalizing failure is a typically masculine one.

In the more general context of this discussion, the data from Study 5 suggest that the internal–stable factor of perceived ability may be the specific component of attributional styles that connects them to sex, sex-role identification, self-esteem, and elation–depression. Intuitively, this "common link" relationship makes sense, since ability (or lack-of-ability) attributions are probably central not only to individuals' characteristic perceptions of the causes of their personal outcomes but to their gender identity, sex-role identity, level of self-esteem, and characteristic affective states as well.

The conclusions to be drawn from this and the other four studies I have just described are profoundly simple and straightforward. The data indicate that the types of outcomes people envision themselves experiencing across a variety of situations are directly related to their perceptions of what they are *able* or *unable* to do. These same ability attributions are also directly related to their conceptions of themselves as individuals across a variety of dimensions that include their gender, sex role, self-esteem, and characteristic affective states. We will now consider some of the implications of the attributional style data for clinical psychology.

ATTRIBUTIONAL STYLES: IMPLICATIONS FOR CLINICAL PSYCHOLOGY

DEPRESSION AND LEARNED HELPLESSNESS

The centrality of ability attributions to various aspects of the individual's experience—his or her self-concept, self-esteem, characteristic affective states, and reactions to personal outcomes—has direct bearing on the phenomena of depression and learned helplessness. The simplest and most parsimonious explanation to be inferred from the data is that these phenomena have their basis in individuals' beliefs that a lack of ability is responsible for their unsatisfactory outcomes.[1]

Not surprisingly, the role of ability attributions in clinical depression and learned helplessness is already well-documented in the literature. For example, in early writings, Lichtenberg (1957) and Melges and Bowlby (1969) stress that depressed patients' feelings of hopelessness typically stem from their belief that they will be incapable of attaining goals because of their incompetence. Their depression appears to deepen when the self-blame engendered by such thoughts becomes generalized from a limited number of specific situations to create a pervasive cognitive style. Similarly, Beck (1967) has hypothesized that the cognitive elements of depression are really more central to the disorder than the emotional factors. He contends that the patients' low self-esteem and thoughts of hopelessness generate their negative moods, in contrast to the generally held notion that the reverse is true. In his study of the verbalizations of depressed patients, Beck found frequently recurring themes of negative self-evaluation, self-blame, expectations of future incompetence, and hopelessness about themselves, their world, and their future. Finally, the hopelessness theory of depression (Abramson *et al.*, 1987, 1988, and Chapter 2, this volume) depicts the style of making internal, stable, global attributions (e.g., lack of ability) for negative life events as a cognitive vulnerability factor for depression.

The covert verbalizations or "self-talk" of depressed patients also suggest that they have developed a general predisposition or bias to interpret situations as providing evidence of their inadequacy, even when this response would seem to be totally inappropriate. In general, they appear to base their self-appraisals

1. To what degree depressed individuals are consciously aware of such beliefs (e.g., Wortman & Dintzer, 1978) is an issue that I will not attempt to resolve here. However, it seems likely that the representation of such beliefs in conscious awareness is not a necessary condition for their influence on behavior (e.g., Ellis & Griegen, 1977; Langer, 1978), although it may be a sufficient one.

upon a magnification of any failures (or supposed failures) and a minimization of favorable outcomes or attributes. They also make unfavorable social comparisons that contribute heavily to their feelings of inferiority. When comparing themselves to other members of their reference group, depressed patients consistently rate themselves as inferior in such ability-relevant attributes as intelligence, status, productivity, attractiveness, or financial security (see also Ahrens, in press; Alloy & Ahrens, in press). Taken together, a wide variety of cross-sectional and prospective studies have shown that compared to nondepressives, depressives make internal, stable, global attributions for negative life events and, to a lesser extent, external, unstable, specific attributions for positive life events (see Abramson *et al.*, 1987, 1988, and Chapter 2, this volume; Brewin, 1985; Coyne & Gotlib, 1983; Peterson & Seligman, 1984; Sweeney, Anderson, & Bailey, 1986, for reviews).

As all of these perceptions are typically associated with the inability or unwillingness to consider alternative interpretations that may be more reality-based, depressed patients may exhibit a consistent attributional distortion that Beck (1967) refers to as "a bias against themselves" (p. 234) (see also Abramson & Sackeim, 1977, and Rizley, 1978). This attributional bias appears to be associated with their low self-esteem, as evidenced in a study by Laxer (1964). He found that hospitalized patients who exhibited a depressed mood but high other-blame expressed less negative self-evaluation than patients whose depressed mood was combined with a high degree of self-blame.

We should remember, however, that this cognitive aspect of depression is part of a more general syndrome that has affective and behavioral aspects as well. Data on the behavioral aspects of the syndrome indicate that depressives tend to have slower reaction times and less consistency in their responses than normals and neurotics (Friedman, 1964; Hall & Stride, 1954; Huston & Senf, 1952; Martin & Rees, 1966). They also tend to underestimate their performance on a number of tasks and/or overestimate their degree of debilitation and may do so even when they are performing adequately (Colbert & Harrow, 1968; Friedman, 1964; Loeb, Beck, & Diggory, 1971). In general, the behavioral aspects of the syndrome are essentially those characteristic of the "learned helplessness" syndrome and include lessened response initiation and slower learning of appropriate instrumental responses after conditions of uncontrollable aversive stimulation (Seligman, Klein, & Miller, 1976; Seligman & Maier, 1967).

Recent work with human subjects has connected such "learned helplessness" responses to the kinds of attributions subjects make to account for some aversive outcome or event (e.g., Abramson *et al.*, 1978; Alloy, Peterson, Abramson, & Seligman, 1984; Chapin & Dyck, 1976; Cohen, Rothbart, & Phillips, 1976; Dollinger & Taub, 1977; DuCette & Wolk, 1973; Dweck, 1975; Dweck & Reppucci, 1973; Feather, 1968; Gregory, Chartier, & Wright, 1979; Hiroto, 1974; Houston, 1972; Klein, Fencil-Morse, & Seligman, 1976; Klein & Seligman, 1976; Maracek & Mettee, 1972; Rizley, 1978; Sacco & Hokanson,

1978; Seligman, 1978; Tennen & Eller, 1977; Watson & Baumal, 1967; Weiner & Sierad, 1975; Wortman, Panciera, Shusterman, & Hibscher, 1976). Taken in sum, the results of these and other studies indicate that lack-of-ability attributions probably underlie the learned helplessness syndrome. They also indicate that supplying learned helplessness subjects with a new attribution can have a pronounced effect on their subsequent motivation and performance, but *only* if the new attribution is acceptable to the subject in terms of the two criteria for acceptability specified by Heider (1958): constituting a plausible causal explanation of an outcome, and being congruent with an individual's view of himself or herself.

The difficulties posed by Heider's two criteria for attribution change would appear to be rather formidable in the clinical setting. Although changing the client's ability attributions should have the most direct impact on the symptoms of depression and learned helplessness, these internal–stable attributions are probably the most resistant to change because of their centrality to the self-concept. Clients may therefore be likely to reject the new and contrasting attributions provided by the therapist as being both implausible and inconsistent with their conception of self. Despite Dweck's (1975) demonstration that grade-school-age children can be persuaded that they really do have the ability they think they lack and thus be induced to reattribute their prior failures to a simple lack of effort, it is doubtful that the internal–stable attributions of adults can be so easily modified (Beach *et al.*, 1981; Wortman & Dintzer, 1978).

These anticipated difficulties in changing ability attributions can probably be ameliorated if the assessed validity of the client's self-limiting attributions can be used to determine the optimal kind of therapy to employ in a given case (Metalsky & Abramson, 1981). For clients whose attributions are clearly nonveridical or "biased," a cognitive restructuring approach may be the most appropriate. The nature and origin of the client's biased perceptions—whether acquired through socialization or motivated psychodynamically—could be explored, and the perceptions could subsequently be changed by the therapist's forceful and persistent presentation of demonstratively veridical counterevidence. Attacks on the irrationality or invalidity of the client's own attributions and the beliefs that support them could also be employed, as in Ellis's rational–emotive psychotherapy (Ellis & Griegen, 1977). Exposure to other clients who have already experienced attributional change and surmounted their depression may be even more effective than exposure to a therapist, as Wortman and Dintzer (1978) have suggested. Finally, the conception of lay epistemology developed by Kruglanski and his colleagues (Kruglanski, 1980; Kruglanski & Ajzen, 1983; Kruglanski & Freund, 1983; Kruglanski & Jaffe, Chapter 9, this volume) suggests that motivational techniques can also be helpful in altering cognitive biases.

On the other hand, for clients whose self-attributions of incompetence and inadequacy are apparently accurate and well-founded, a skills-training approach would obviously be more appropriate, realistic, and credible than a potentially disorienting cognitive restructuring approach. As clients in a skills-training program acquire the specific abilities needed to change their aversive outcomes, corresponding changes in their attributional style and self-concept could be facilitated by suggestions and reinforcements provided by the therapist at appropriate points.[2]

It should probably be noted that the data from our own studies, particularly Studies 1, 2, and 4, are consistent with the results of surveys by Cannon and Redick (1973) and Weissman and Klerman (1977) in indicating that females are likely to be more susceptible to depression than males (roughly a 2:1 ratio in several different countries over the past 40–50 years). Collectively, all of the relevant evidence appears to implicate a cognitive–motivational syndrome of performance deficit, learned helplessness, and depression—a syndrome to which individuals with low self-esteem, and females in general, are most likely to be susceptible. This syndrome appears to correspond closely to the concept of hopelessness depression proposed by Abramson *et al.* (1987, 1988, and Chapter 2, this volume).

Having now considered the relationship between attributional preference and depression, let us briefly consider the relationship between the former and a number of other clinical problems. Investigators have just begun to examine the relationship between attributional patterns and other disorders and personality types.

"DEVIANT" PERSONALITIES

Intuition suggests that extreme attributional styles may be associated with extreme or "deviant" personalities. The imagined characters in "Causal Conspirators" are rather fanciful embodiments of these extremes, but there is little doubt that they have their real-world counterparts. Everis Wright, the self-serving braggart who takes undeserved credit but refuses to accept deserved blame, is characterized by an extreme use of the +I−E attributional style (internalizing positive outcomes but externalizing negative ones). For such a person, the attributional style most characteristic of high self-esteem subjects has been pushed far past its healthy, nonneurotic limit. Perhaps narcissistic, Machiavellian, or even psychopathic personality types may be shown to exhibit in extremity one or both elements of this projective and ego-enhancing attributional style. In this regard, Pearce-McCall and Newman (1983) recently

---

2. In many cases, the client's depression may stem from some kind of loss experience (due to the death of a spouse or loss of job, wealth, or status, for example). In such cases, the client's perceived lack of ability to have foreseen the loss, to have averted it, or to cope successfully with its consequences may be the crucial attributional element(s) the therapist wishes to address during treatment.

speculated that individuals suffering from "syndromes of disinhibition" (e.g., psychopathy, extraversion) may exhibit a "paradoxical" reaction to punishment involving response facilitation as opposed to response inhibition. Ego-enhancing attributional styles may be one component of such paradoxical reactions. Consistent with this hypothesis, Pearce-McCall and Newman reported that following an experience of noncontingent punishment, extraverts reported higher levels of perceived control and placed larger wagers on their ability to succeed than did introverts. Interestingly, extraverts exposed to noncontingent punishment increased their expectation for success whereas introverts decreased their performance expectations.

Totie Lee Wrong, the depressed self-punisher who accepts all blame but refuses to take any credit, is characterized by an extreme use of the +E−I attributional style (externalizing positive outcomes but internalizing negative ones). As we have seen, such a person is likely to have low self-esteem and depressed affect, and is statistically twice as likely to be a female as a male. The rather masochistic orientation of this self-punishing attributional style contrasts sharply with the projective, other-blaming orientation of the +I−E style.[3]

Otto Cozl, the hypercontroller who perceives all personal outcomes—both positive and negative—as being self-caused, is characterized by an extreme +I−I attributional style. One might expect such a person to be obsessive–compulsive or manic–depressive in orientation. This individual's intense ego involvement with and sense of responsibility for all personal outcomes should result in an elated or "manic" affective state when these outcomes are predominantly positive, but a depressed affective state when these outcomes are predominantly negative. The extreme +I−I style also suggests the Type A, coronary-stress-prone personality (Friedman & Rosenman, 1974; Glass, 1977), whose attributional style investigators recently have begun to examine. Strube (1985) reported that Type A individuals tended to exhibit a more self-serving attributional style (i.e., making more internal, stable, and global attributions for positive than negative outcomes) than Type B individuals. Thus, the attributional preferences of the Type A personality may resemble more closely those associated with high self-esteem and hypothesized to be associated, in extreme form, with narcissistic, Machiavellian, or psychopathic types than those hypothesized to be associated with the obsessive–compulsive personality.

In direct contrast to Cozl, the overly involved hypercontroller, there is Faye Tullis, the overly detached fatalist—a person who denies responsibility for any personal outcomes, good or bad. Some individuals displaying extreme forms of this +E−E attributional style may be classified as schizophrenic,

---

3. The relatively deviant, pathological nature of the +E−I style is reflected by its low incidence in a "normal" population. For example, in the first of the studies employing our attributional style measure, this extreme +E−I style was found in 11 percent of the low self-esteem subjects, 4 percent of the moderate self-esteem subjects, and less than 1 percent of the subjects with high self-esteem. Although these percentages differed significantly across self-esteem levels by chi-square test ($p < .001$), it is apparent that the extreme +E−I style is not common in a normal population.

either because of their lack of affective response to and involvement in everyday life activities or because of their extreme belief that their lives are externally controlled (e.g., delusions of persecution). The extreme +E−E style, with its marked emphasis on external control, may also be associated with hyperdependency and a relatively nondepressive form of learned helplessness.

Beyond these differences in personality suggested by attributional style differences on the causal locus dimension, it is possible that differences in personality may be mediated by attributional style differences on other dimensions as well. For example, attributional styles may also differ on the stable–unstable dimension, with dogmatic-authoritarian individuals characterized by extreme stability and rigidity in their attributions and flexible-egalitarian individuals characterized by greater lability in theirs.

All of these suggested relationships between extreme attributional preferences and extreme personalities must be regarded as speculative, of course. These suggested relationships are by no means proposed as definitive, but instead are offered for their heuristic value in encouraging future research on the links between "deviant" personalities and attributional styles. At the least, the attributional style construct could enrich our understanding of "deviant" or extreme personalities; at the most, it could provide a basis for conceptually redefining them.

NEUROTIC EGO DEFENSE

It is intriguing that the two elements comprising the "high self-esteem attributional style"—internalizing positive outcomes and externalizing negative ones—are, in their more biased and extreme forms, probably also the bases of most neurotic ego defense. The second of these elements is essentially equivalent to Freud's (1920) concept of projection, and the combination of both elements has been described as "attributional egotism" by Snyder, Stephan, and Rosenfield (1978). In a review of their own and others' work, these authors found evidence for attributional egotism in a variety of experimental and nonexperimental contexts (see also Weary-Bradley, 1978). More recently, Snyder and Wicklund (1981) have proposed a more general theory of attributional ambiguity that promises to provide a viable framework for the analysis of other forms of ego defense, particularly those characterized as self- or other-deceptive (see also Weary & Arkin, 1981).

INTERPERSONAL CONFLICT AND MISUNDERSTANDING

A substantial literature is beginning to develop on the attributional mediation of interpersonal conflict and misunderstanding. Examples include Orvis, Kelley, and Butler's (1976) study of attribution-based conflict in young heterosexual couples; Harvey, Wells, and Alvarez's (1978) study of attributional differences in couples who had divorced or separated; Shields and Hanneke's (1983) study of the perceived attributions of battered wives and their husbands; and the studies by Fincham and his colleagues (e.g., Fincham, 1985; Fincham & O'Leary, 1983, Fincham, Beach, & Baucom, 1987, Fincham & Bradbury, in press-*a*) of causal attributions in distressed and nondistressed couples (see also Holtzworth-Munroe & Jacobson, 1985). Broader theoretical statements about the attributional mediation of interpersonal conflict have been proposed by Sillars (1981, 1985) and by Fincham & Bradbury (in press-*b*).

At this stage, attributional styles have not been directly implicated in this work, but there is reason to believe they eventually will be. The scenario described at the beginning of this chapter involving Mr. and Mrs. Everis Wright may be played out all too frequently in the real world. If, as in the scenario, the two dyad members' attributional styles are congruent and mutually supportive, their effects on subsequent perceptions and behavior may continue unchecked in the form of "exacerbation syndromes" (Storms & McCaul, 1976) that drive both individuals farther and farther away from an objective view of themselves and each other. On the other hand, although incongruent attributional styles should ideally precipitate discussion and reality-testing (even if these processes take the form of argument and conflict), Sillars's (1981) data indicate somewhat pessimistically that the most common response to the perception of such differences is to avoid even mentioning them.

In any event, it already seems clear that attributional approaches will have much to say about the dynamics of interpersonal conflict and conflict resolution. These topics will undoubtedly provide the focus for much research.

OTHER EXACERBATION SYNDROMES

A variety of other "exacerbation syndromes" having an attributional basis have been proposed, most notably by Valins and Nisbett (1971) and by Storms and McCaul (1976). These authors suggest that a range of clinical problems may be amenable to attributional analysis and treatment, particularly those in which anxiety is a key factor, such as impotence, insomnia, or stuttering. Again, however, the role of attributional styles in these anxiety-related syndromes remains to be explored.

CONCLUSION

In summary, the kinds of personal outcome attributions individuals are predisposed to make are integrally related to various aspects of their experience—to their self-concepts, self-esteem, characteristic affective states, and their reactions to personal outcomes. These attributional preferences, whether considered in the specific case or in the context of more general attributional styles, appear to underlie much of the "normal" and "nonnormal" behavior that individuals display. The data I have reviewed in this chapter suggest that the links interrelating attributional styles, self-conceptions and behavior may have implications for a number of problem areas within clinical psychology. These areas include depression and learned helplessness, "deviant" personalities, neurotic ego defense, interpersonal conflict and misunderstanding, and anxiety-related exacerbation syndromes.

ACKNOWLEDGMENTS

I would like to express my appreciation to Mary Anne Layden, whose ideas, abilities, and efforts contributed greatly to a number of the studies described in this chapter. Gratitude is also expressed to Yasmin Haddad and Harry Reis for their patient and expert analyses of a disconcertingly large mass of self-report data collected in another of the studies.

REFERENCES

Abramson, L. Y., Alloy, L. B., & Metalsky, G. I. (1988). The cognitive diathesis-stress theories of depression: Toward an adequate evaluation of the theories' validities. In L. B. Alloy (Ed.), *Cognitive processes in depression.* New York: Guilford.

Abramson, L. Y., Metalsky, G. I., & Alloy, L. B. (1987). *The hopelessness theory of depression: A metatheoretical analysis with implications for psychopathology research.* Manuscript submitted for publication.

Abramson, L. Y., & Sackeim, H. A. (1977). A paradox in depression: Uncontrollability and self-blame. *Psychological Bulletin, 84,* 838–851.

Abramson, L. Y., Seligman, M. E. P., & Teasdale, J. D. (1978). Learned helplessness in humans: Critique and reformulation. *Journal of Abnormal Psychology, 87,* 49–74.

Ahrens, A. H. (in press). Theories of depression: The role of goals and the self-evaluation process. *Cognitive Therapy and Research.*

Ajzen, I. (1977). Intuitive theories of events and the effects of base-rate information on prediction. *Journal of Personality and Social Psychology, 35,* 303–324.

Alloy, L. B., & Ahrens, A. H. (in press). Depression and pessimism for the future: Biased use of statistically relevant information in predictions for self versus others. *Journal of Personality and Social Psychology.*

Alloy, L. B., Clements, C., & Kolden, G. (1985). The cognitive diathesis-stress theories of depression: Therapeutic implications. In S. Reiss & R. Bootzin (Eds.), *Theoretical issues in behavior therapy.* New York: Academic Press.

Alloy, L. B., Hartlage, S., & Abramson, L. Y. (1988). Testing the cognitive diathesis-stress theories of depression: Issues of research design, conceptualization, and assessment. In L. B. Alloy (Ed.), *Cognitive processes in depression.* New York: Guilford.

Alloy, L. B., Peterson, C., Abramson, L. Y., & Seligman, M. E. P. (1984). Attributional style and the generality of learned helplessness. *Journal of Personality and Social Psychology, 46,* 681–687.

Beach, S. R. H., Abramson, L. Y., & Levine, F. M. (1981). Attributional reformulation of learned helplessness and depression: Therapeutic implications. In J. F. Clarkin & H. I. Glazer (Eds.), *Depression: Behavioral and directive intervention strategies*. New York: Garland.

Beck, A. T. (1967). *Depression: Clinical, experimental, and theoretical aspects*. New York: Hoeber.

Beck, A. T. (1976). *Cognitive therapy and the emotional disorders*. New York: International Universities Press.

Beck, A. T. (1984). Cognitive therapy, behavior therapy, psychoanalysis, and pharmacotherapy: The cognitive continuum. In J. B. W. Williams & R. L. Spitzer (Eds.), *Psychotherapy research: Where are we and where should we go?* New York: Guilford.

Beck, A. T., Rush, A. J., Shaw, B. F., & Emery, G. (1979). *Cognitive therapy of depression*. New York: Guilford.

Bem, S. L. (1974). The measurement of psychological androgyny. *Journal of Consulting and Clinical Psychology, 42*, 155–162.

Brewin, C. R. (1985). Depression and causal attributions: What is their relation? *Psychological Bulletin, 98*, 297–309.

Buchwald, A. M., Coyne, J. C., & Cole, C. S. (1978). A critical evaluation of the learned helplessness model of depression. *Journal of Abnormal Psychology, 87*, 180–183.

Cannon, M. S., & Redick, R. W. (1973). *Differential utilization of psychiatric facilities by men and women: United States, 1970*. (Statistical note #81, Biometry Branch, Survey and Reports Section. Rockville, MD: National Institutes of Mental Health. (1976).

Chapin, M., & Dyck, D. G. (1976). Persistence in children's reading behavior as a function of N length and attribution retraining. *Journal of Abnormal Psychology, 85*, 511–515.

Cohen, S., Rothbart, M., & Phillips, S. (1976). Locus of control and the generalizability of learned helplessness in humans. *Journal of Personality and Social Psychology, 34*, 1049–1056.

Colbert, J., & Harrow, M. (1968). Psychomotor retardation in depressive syndromes. *Journal of Nervous and Mental Disease, 145*, 405–419.

Coyne, J. C., & Gotlib, I. H. (1983). The role of cognition in depression: A critical appraisal. *Psychological Bulletin, 94*, 472–505.

Crandall, V. (1969). Sex differences in expectancy of intellectual and academic reinforcement. In C. P. Smith (Ed.), *Achievement-related motives in children*. New York: Russell Sage.

Crandall, V., Katkovsky, W., & Crandall, V. (1965). Children's beliefs in their own control of reinforcements in intellectual–academic achievement situations. *Child Development, 36*, 91–109.

Cruz Perez, R. (1973). The effects of experimentally induced failure, self-esteem and sex on cognitive differentiation. *Journal of Abnormal Psychology, 81*, 74–79.

Cutrona, C. E., Russell, D., & Jones, R. D. (1985). Cross-situational consistency in causal attributions: Does attributional style exist? *Journal of Personality and Social Psychology, 47*, 1043–1058.

Deaux, K. (1976). Sex: A perspective on the attribution process. In J. H. Harvey, W. Ickes, & R. F. Kidd (Eds.), *New directions in attribution research* (Vol. 1). Hillsdale, NJ: Erlbaum.

Deaux, K., & Emswiller, T. (1974). Explanations of successful performance on sex-linked tasks: What is skill for the male is luck for the female. *Journal of Personality and Social Psychology, 29*, 80–85.

Deaux, K., & Farris, E. (1974). *Attributing causes for one's own performance: The effects of sex, norms and outcomes*. Unpublished manuscript, Purdue University, Lafayette, IN.

Deaux, K., White, L., & Farris, E. (1975). Skill vs. luck: Field and laboratory studies of male and female preferences. *Journal of Personality and Social Psychology, 32*, 629–636.

Dollinger, S., & Taub, S. (1977). The interaction of locus of control expectancies in providing purpose on children's motivation. *Journal of Research in Personality, 11*, 118–127.

DuCette, J., & Wolk, S. (1973). Cognitive and motivational correlates of generalized expectancies for control. *Journal of Personality and Social Psychology, 23*, 420–426.

Dweck, C. S. (1975). The role of expectations and attributions in the alleviation of learned helplessness. *Journal of Personality and Social Psychology, 31*, 674–685.

Dweck, C. S., & Goetz, T. E. (1978). Attributions and learned helplessness. In J. H. Harvey, W. Ickes, & R. F. Kidd (Eds.), *New directions in attribution research* (Vol. 2). Hillsdale, NJ: Erlbaum.

Dweck, C. S., & Reppucci, N. D. (1973). Learned helplessness and reinforcement responsibility in children. *Journal of Personality and Social Psychology, 25*, 109–116.

Ellis, A., & Griegen, R. (Eds.). (1977). *Handbook of rational-emotive therapy*. New York: Springer.

Feather, N. T. (1968). Change in confidence following success or failure as a predictor of subsequent performance. *Journal of Personality and Social Psychology, 9*, 38–46.

Feather, N. T. (1969). Attribution of responsibility and valence of success and failure in relation to initial confidence and task performance. *Journal of Personality and Social Psychology, 13*, 129–144.

Fincham, F. (1985). Attributional processes in distressed and nondistressed couples: 2. Responsibility for marital problems. *Journal of Abnormal Psychology, 94*, 183–190.

Fincham, F., Beach, S., & Baucon, D. (1987). Attribution processes in distressed and nondistressed couples: 4. Self–partner attribution differences. *Journal of Personality and Social Psychology, 52*, 739–748.

Fincham, F., & Bradbury, T. (in press-a). The impact of attributions in marriage: A longitudinal analysis. *Journal of Personality and Social Psychology*.

Fincham, F., & Bradbury, T. (in press-b). The impact of attributions in marriage: Empirical and conceptual foundation. *British Journal of Clinical Psychology*.

Fincham, F., & O'Leary, K. D. (1983). Causal inferences for spouse behavior in maritally distressed and nondistressed couples. *Journal of Social and Clinical Psychology, 1*, 42–57.

Fitch, G. (1970). Effects of self-esteem, perceived performance and choice on causal attributions. *Journal of Personality and Social Psychology, 16*, 311–315.

Folkman, S. (1984). Personal control and stress and coping processes: A theoretical analysis. *Journal of Personality and Social Psychology, 46*, 839–852.

Freud, S. (1920). *A general introduction to psychoanalysis*. New York: Liveright.

Friedman, A. S. (1964). Minimal effects of severe depression on cognitive functioning. *Journal of Abnormal and Social Psychology, 69*, 237–243.

Friedman, M., & Rosenman, R. H. (1974). *Type A behavior and your heart*. New York: Knopf.

Gilmore, T., & Minton, H. (1974). Internal vs. external attribution of task performance as a function of locus of control, initial confidence and success–failure outcome. *Journal of Personality, 42*, 159–174.

Glass, D. C. (1977). *Behavior patterns, stress, and coronary disease*. Hillsdale, NJ: Erlbaum.

Glass, D. C., & Singer, J. E. (1972). *Urban stress*. New York: Academic Press.

Gregory, W., Chartier, G., & Wright, M. (1979). Learned helplessness and learned effectiveness: Effects of explicit response cues on individuals differing in personal control expectancies. *Journal of Personality and Social Psychology, 37*, 1982–1992.

Haddad, Y., Reiss, H., & Ickes, W. (1980, September). *Sex-role orientation and attributional styles*. Paper presented at the annual convention of the American Psychological Association, Montreal.

Halberstadt, L. J., Mukherji, B. R., & Abramson, L. Y. (1988). *Cognitive styles among college students: Toward an integration of the cognitive theories of depression with cognitive psychology and descriptive psychiatry*. Manuscript submitted for publication.

Halberstadt, L. J., Andrews, D., Metalsky, G. I., & Abramson, L. Y. (1984). Helplessness, hopelessness, and depression: A review of progress and future directions. In N. S. Endler & J. Hunt (Eds.), *Personality and behavior disorders*. New York: Wiley.

Hall, K. R. L., & Stride, E. (1954). Some factors affecting reaction times to auditory stimuli in mental patients. *Journal of Mental Science, 100*, 462–477.

Harvey, J. H., Ickes, W., & Kidd, R. F. (Eds.). (1976). *New directions in attribution research* (Vol. 1). Hillsdale, NJ: Erlbaum.

Harvey, J. H., Ickes, W., & Kidd, R. F. (Eds.). (1978). *New directions in attribution research* (Vol. 2). Hillsdale, NJ: Erlbaum.

Harvey, J. H., Ickes, W., & Kidd, R. F. (Eds.). (1981) *New directions in attribution research* (Vol. 3). Hillsdale, NJ: Erlbaum.

Harvey, J. H., Wells, G., & Alvarez, M. (1978). Attribution in the context of conflict and separation in close relationships. In J. H. Harvey, W. Ickes, & R. F. Kidd (Eds.), *New directions in attribution research* (Vol. 2). Hillsdale, NJ: Erlbaum.

Heider, F. (1944). Social perception and phenomenal causality. *Psychological Review, 51*, 358–374.

Heider, F. (1958). *The psychology of interpersonal relations.* New York: Wiley.

Heider, F. (1975). *On balance and attribution.* Paper presented at the Symposium on Social Networks, Dartmouth University, Hanover, NH.

Hiroto, D. S. (1974). Locus of control and learned helplessness. *Journal of Experimental Psychology, 102*, 187–193.

Holtzworth-Munroe, A., & Jacobson, N. S. (1985). Causal attributions of married couples: When do they search for causes? What do they conclude when they do? *Journal of Personality and Social Psychology, 48*, 1398–1412.

Houston, B. K. (1972). Control over stress, locus of control, and response to stress. *Journal of Personality and Social Psychology, 31*, 311–327.

Huston, P. E., & Senf, R. (1952). Psychopathology of schizophrenia and depression: I. Effect of amytal and amphetamine sulfate on level and maintenance of attention. *American Journal of Psychiatry, 109*, 131–138.

Ickes, W., & Layden, M. A. (1975). Correlations between self-esteem and sex-role measures of masculinity and femininity. Unpublished data, University of Wisconsin—Madison, WI.

Ickes, W., & Layden, M. A. (1978). Attributional styles. In J. H. Harvey, W. Ickes, & R. F. Kidd (Eds.), *New directions in attribution research* (Vol. 2). Hillsdale, NJ: Erlbaum.

Janoff-Bulman, R. (1979). Characterological versus behavioral self-blame: Inquiries into depression and rape. *Journal of Personality and Social Psychology, 37*, 1798–1809.

Jones, E. E., Kanouse, D., Kelley, H. H., Nisbett, R., Valins, S., & Weiner, B. (1972). *Attribution: Perceiving the causes of behavior.* Morristown, NJ: General Learning Press.

Kanner, A. D., Coyne, J. C., Schaefer, C., & Lazarus, R. S. (1981). Comparison of two modes of stress measurement: Daily hassles and uplifts versus major life events. *Journal of Behavioral Medicine, 4*, 1–39.

Kelley, H. H. (1971). *Attribution in social interaction.* Morristown, NJ: General Learning Press.

Kelly, G. (1955). *The psychology of personal constructs.* New York: Norton.

Klein, D. C., Fencil-Morse, E., & Seligman, M. E. P. (1976). Learned helplessness, depression and the attribution of failure. *Journal of Personality and Social Psychology, 33*, 508–516.

Klein, D. C., & Seligman, M. E. P. (1976). Reversal of performance deficits in learned helplessness and depression. *Journal of Abnormal Psychology, 85*, 11–26.

Kruglanski, A. W. (1980). Lay epistemologic process and contents. *Psychological Review, 87*, 70–87.

Kruglanski, A. W., & Ajzen, I. (1983). Bias and error in human judgment. *European Journal of Social Psychology, 13*, 1–44.

Kruglanski, A. W., & Freund, T. (1983). The freezing and unfreezing of lay inferences: Effects on impressional primacy, ethnic stereotyping and numerical anchoring. *Journal of Experimental Social Psychology, 19*, 448–468.

Langer, E. J. (1978). Rethinking the role of thought in social interaction. In J. H. Harvey, W. Ickes, & R. F. Kidd (Eds.), *New directions in attribution research* (Vol. 2). Hillsdale, NJ: Erlbaum.

Laxer, R. M. (1964). Relation of real self-rating to mood and blame and their interaction in depression. *Journal of Consulting Psychology, 28*, 214–219.

Lichtenberg, P. (1957). A definition and analysis of depression. *Archives of Neurology and Psychiatry, 77*, 519–527.

Loeb, A., Beck, A. T., & Diggory, J. (1971). Differential effects of success and failure on depressed and nondepressed patients. *Journal of Nervous and Mental Disease, 152*, 106–114.

Maracek, J., & Mettee, D. (1972). Avoidance of continued success as a function of self-esteem, level of esteem certainty and responsibility for success. *Journal of Personality and Social Psychology, 22*, 98–107.

Martin, I., & Rees, L. (1966). Reaction times and somatic reactivity in depressed patients. *Journal of Psychosomatic Research, 9*, 375–382.

Melges, F. T., & Bowlby, J. (1969). Types of hopelessness in psychopathological process. *Archives of General Psychiatry, 20*, 1313–1320.

Metalsky, G. I., & Abramson, L. Y. (1981). Attributional styles: Toward a framework for conceptualization and assessment. In P. C. Kendall & S. D. Hollon (Eds.), *Cognitive-behavioral interventions: Assessment methods.* New York: Academic Press.

Metalsky, G. I., Halberstadt, L. J., & Abramson, L. Y. (1987). Vulnerability to depressive mood reactions: Toward a more powerful test of the diathesis-stress and causal mediation components of the reformulated theory of depression. *Journal of Personality and Social Psychology, 52*, 386–393.

Mischel, W., Zeiss, R., & Zeiss, A. (1974). Internal and external control and persistence. *Journal of Personality and Social Psychology, 29*, 265–278.

Monroe, S. M. (1983a). Major and minor life events as predictors of disorder: Further issues and findings. *Journal of Behavioral Medicine, 6*, 189–205.

Monroe, S. M. (1983b). Social support and disorder: Toward an untangling of cause and effect. *American Journal of Community Psychology, 11*, 81–97.

Monroe, S. M., Imhoff, D., Wise, B. D., & Harris, J. E. (1983). Prediction of psychological symptoms under high-risk psychosocial circumstances: Life events, social support, and symptom specificity. *Journal of Abnormal Psychology, 92*, 338–350.

Monson, T. C., & Snyder, M. K. (1977). Actors, observers, and the attribution process: Toward a reconceptualization. *Journal of Experimental Social Psychology, 13*, 89–111.

Montanelli, D. S., & Hill, K. T. (1969). Children's achievement expectations and performance as a function of two consecutive reinforcement experiences, sex of subject, and sex of experimenter. *Journal of Personality and Social Psychology, 13*, 115–128.

Morse, S., & Gergen, K. (1970). Social comparison, self-consistency and the concept of self. *Journal of Personality and Social Psychology, 16*, 148–156.

Orvis, B. K., Kelley, H. H., & Butler, D. (1976). Attributional conflict in young couples. In J. H. Harvey, W. Ickes, & R. F. Kidd (Eds.), *New directions in attribution research* (Vol. 1). Hillsdale, NJ: Erlbaum.

Paykel, E. S. (1979). Recent life events in the development of the depressive disorders. In R. A. Depue (Ed.), *The psychobiology of the depressive disorders: Implications for the effects of stress.* New York: Academic Press.

Pearce-McCall, D., & Newman, J. P. (1986). Expectation of success following noncontingent punishment in introverts and extraverts. *Journal of Personality and Social Psychology, 50*, 439–446.

Peterson, C., Schwartz, S. M., & Seligman, M. E. P. (1981). Self-blame and depressive symptoms. *Journal of Personality and Social Psychology, 41*, 253–259.

Peterson, C., & Seligman, M. E. P. (1984). Causal explanations as a risk factor for depression: Theory and evidence. *Psychological Review, 91*, 347–374.

Rizley, R. (1978). Depression and distortion in the attribution of causality. *Journal of Abnormal Psychology, 87*, 32–48.

Rosenbaum, R. M. (1972). *A dimensional analysis of the perceived causes of success and failure.* Unpublished doctoral dissertation, University of California, Los Angeles.

Ross, L. (1977). The intuitive psychologist and his shortcomings. In L. Berkowitz (Ed.), *Advances in experimental social psychology* (Vol. 10). New York: Academic Press.

Ross, L. (1978). Some after-thoughts on the intuitive psychologist. In L. Berkowitz (Ed.), *Cognitive theories in social psychology*. New York: Academic Press.

Ross, L., Lepper, M., & Hubbard, M. (1975). Perseverance in self-perception and social perception: Biased attributional processes in the debriefing paradigm. *Journal of Personality and Social Psychology, 32,* 880–892.

Rotter, J. B. (1966). Generalized expectancies for internal vs. external control of reinforcement. *Psychological Monographs, 80,* 1–28.

Ryckman, R., & Rodda, W. (1972). Confidence maintenance and performance as function of chronic self-esteem and initial task experience. *Psychological Record, 22,* 241–247.

Sacco, W. P., & Hokanson, J. E. (1978). Expectations of success and anagram performance of depressives in a public and private setting. *Journal of Abnormal Psychology, 87,* 122–130.

Seligman, M. E. P. (1978). Comment and integration. *Journal of Abnormal Psychology, 87,* 165–179.

Seligman, M. E. P., Klein, D. C., & Miller, W. R. (1976). Depression. In H. Leitenberg (Ed.), *Handbook of behavior modification and behavior therapy*. Englewood Cliffs, NJ: Prentice-Hall.

Seligman, M. E. P., & Maier, S. F. (1967). Failure to escape traumatic shock. *Journal of Experimental Psychology, 74,* 1–9.

Shields, N. M., & Hanneke (1983). Attribution processes in violent relationships. Perceptions of violent husbands and their wives. *Journal of Applied Social Psychology, 13,* 515–527.

Shrauger, J., & Rosenberg, S. (1970). Self-esteem and the effects of success and failure feedback on performance. *Journal of Personality, 38,* 404–417.

Sillars, A. (1981). Applications of attribution theory to problems in interpersonal conflict resolution. In J. H. Harvey, W. Ickes, & R. F. Kidd (Eds.), *New directions in attribution research* (Vol. 3). Hillsdale, NJ: Erlbaum.

Sillars, A. (1985). Interpersonal perception in relationships. In W. Ickes (Ed.), *Compatible and incompatible relationships*. New York: Springer.

Snyder, M. L., & Wicklund, R. A. (1981). Attribute ambiguity. In J. Harvey, W. Ickes, & R. F. Kidd (Eds.), *New directions in attribution research* (Vol. 3). Hillsdale, NJ: Erlbaum.

Snyder, M. L., Stephan, W., & Rosenfield, D. (1978). Attributional egotism. In J. H. Harvey, W. Ickes, & R. F. Kidd (Eds.), *New directions in attribution research* (Vol. 2). Hillsdale, NJ: Erlbaum.

Solley, C. M., & Stagner, R. (1956). Effects of magnitude of temporal barriers, type of goal and perception of self. *Journal of Experimental Psychology, 51,* 62–70.

Storms, M. D., & McCaul, K. D. (1976). Attribution processes and emotional exacerbation of dysfunctional behavior. In J. H. Harvey, W. Ickes, & R. F. Kidd (Eds.), *New directions in attribution research* (Vol. 1). Hillsdale, NJ: Erlbaum.

Strube, M. J. (1985). Attributional style and the type A coronary-prone behavior pattern. *Journal of Personality and Social Psychology, 49,* 500–509.

Sweeney, P. D., Anderson, K., & Bailey, S. (1986). Attributional style in depression: A meta-analytic review. *Journal of Personality and Social Psychology, 50,* 974–991.

Sweeney, P. D., Shaeffer, D., & Golin, S. (1982). Attributions about self and others in depression. *Personality and Social Psychology Bulletin, 8,* 37–42.

Tennen, H., & Eller, S. J. (1977). Attributional components of learned helplessness and facilitation. *Journal of Personality and Social Psychology, 35,* 265–271.

Tennen, H., & Herzberger, S. (1987). Depression, self-esteem, and the absence of self-protective attributional biases. *Journal of Personality and Social Psychology, 52,* 72–80.

Valins, S., & Nisbett, R. E. (1971). *Attribution processes in the development and treatment of emotional disorders*. Morristown, NJ: General Learning Press.

Valle, V. A., & Frieze, I. H. (1976). Stability of causal attributions as a mediator in changing expectations for success. *Journal of Personality and Social Psychology, 33,* 579–387.

Watson, D., & Baumal, E. (1967). Effects of locus of control and expectation of future control upon present performance. *Journal of Personality and Social Psychology, 6*, 212–215.

Weary, G., & Arkin, R. (1981). Attributional self-presentation and the regulation of self-evaluation. In J. H. Harvey, W. Ickes, & R. F. Kidd (Eds.), *New directions in attribution research* (Vol. 3). Hillsdale, NJ: Erlbaum.

Weary-Bradley, G. (1978). Self-serving biases in the attribution process: A re-examination of the fact or fiction question. *Journal of Personality and Social Psychology, 36*, 56–71.

Weiner, B. (1972). *Theories of motivation: From mechanism to cognition.* New York: Markham.

Weiner, B. (1974). *Achievement motivation and attribution theory.* Morristown, NJ: General Learning Press.

Weiner, B. (1979). A theory of motivation for some classroom experiences. *Journal of Educational Psychology, 71*, 3–25.

Weiner, B. (1985). An attributional theory of achievement motivation and emotion. *Psychological Review, 92*, 548–573.

Weiner, B., Frieze, I., Kukla, A., Reed, L., Rest, S., & Rosenbaum, R. M. (1971). *Perceiving the causes of success and failure.* Morristown, NJ: General Learning Press.

Weiner, B., & Sierad, J. (1975). Misattribution for failure and enhancement of achievement strivings. *Journal of Personality and Social Psychology, 31*, 415–421.

Weissman, M. M., & Klerman, G. L. (1977). Sex differences and the epidemiology of depression. *Archives of General Psychiatry, 34*, 98–111.

Wetter, R. (1975, August 30). *Levels of self-esteem associated with four sex role categories.* Paper presented at the 83rd annual meeting of the American Psychological Association, Chicago.

Wortman, C., & Dintzer, L. (1978). Is an attribution analysis of learned helplessness phenomenon viable? A critique of the Abramson–Seligman–Teasdale reformulation. *Journal of Abnormal Psychology, 87*, 75–90.

Wortman, C., Panciera, L., Shusterman, L., & Hibscher, J. (1976). Attributions of causality and reactions to uncontrollable outcomes. *Journal of Experimental Social Psychology, 12*, 301–316.

Zimmerman, M. (1983). Methodological issues in the assessment of life events: A review of issues and research. *Clinical Psychology Review, 3*, 339–370.

4

Information-seeking, Self-esteem, and Helplessness

RICHARD SCHULZ

BARBARA HARTMAN HANUSA

Since the original learned helplessness hypothesis was first proposed (Maier, Seligman, & Solomon, 1969; Seligman, 1975; Seligman & Maier, 1967; Seligman, Maier, & Solomon, 1971) investigators have placed increasing emphasis on cognitive processes as mediators of noncontingency experiences (e.g., Abramson, Alloy, & Metalsky, 1988; Abramson, Metalsky, & Alloy, 1987; Abramson, Metalsky, & Alloy, Chapter 2, this volume; Abramson, Seligman, & Teasdale, 1978; Alloy, 1982; Miller & Norman, 1979). The reformulation of the original learned helplessness model to incorporate attributional processes (Abramson *et al.*, 1978; currently referred to as the hopelessness theory: Abramson, Alloy, & Metalsky, 1988; Abramson *et al.*, 1987, and Chapter 2, this volume) is a good example of this trend. According to the reformulated model, people generate reasons for their success or failure to control outcomes, and these reasons can be classified along three orthogonal dimensions. Two of these dimensions (internal–external, stable–unstable) have been used by attribution theorists (e.g., Weiner, 1974), while the third (global–specific) was introduced as a new dimension by Abramson *et al.* (1978). Thus, internal causes stem from the individual, and external causes from the environment; stable factors are long-lived and recurrent, whereas unstable factors are short-lived and intermittent. Finally, global factors occur across situations, whereas specific factors are unique to a particular context. Abramson *et al.* (1978) further suggest that each type of attribution has specific consequences for the individual: Attributions to internal–external factors should affect self-esteem; attributions to stable–unstable factors should determine the long-term consequences of a particular experience; and attributions to global–specific factors should determine the extent to which individuals will generalize a particular experience to other situations.

   Although a wide variety of cross-sectional and prospective studies have been conducted to examine the relationship between attributional style and depression (see Abramson, Alloy, & Metalsky, 1988; Abramson *et al.*, 1987, and Chapter 2, this volume; Brewin, 1985; Coyne & Gotlib, 1983; Peterson & Seligman, 1984; Sweeney, Anderson, & Bailey, 1986, for reviews), relatively few laboratory studies explicitly testing attributional models of learned helplessness have been conducted (e.g., Alloy, Peterson, Abramson, & Seligman, 1984; Danker-Brown & Baucom, 1982; Hanusa & Schulz, 1977; Klein, Fencil-Morse, & Seligman, 1976; Pasahow, 1980; Wortman, Panciera, Shusterman, & Hibscher, 1976). Taken together, these studies have yielded mixed results. Contrary to predictions derived from the reformulated helplessness model, studies by Wortman *et al.* (1976) and by Hanusa and Schulz (1977) showed that subjects induced to make a lack-of-ability attribution for their inability to control aversive outcomes performed *better* during testing than subjects induced to make situational attributions, such as the difficulty of the task. These data are theoretically important. Although a number of investigators (e.g., Brockner *et al.*, 1983; Pittman & Pittman, 1979, 1980) have reported "facilitation effects" produced by exposure to uncontrollable events, the reformulated theory cannot account for such effects (Zuroff, 1980).

Attempting to explain the results obtained by Wortman *et al.* (1976) and Hanusa and Schulz (1977), Abramson *et al.* (1978) noted that these inconsistent data may indicate that the helplessness training in these studies was not extensive enough to elicit the predicted effects. On the other hand, Wortman and Dintzer (1978) suggested that subjects may have used the testing phase of the experiment to gain information to dispute the lack-of-ability attribution generated during the training phase. According to the latter view, persons who have received ability information inconsistent with expectation based on past performance may be especially eager to perform in new settings where they might attain additional information about their abilities. Wortman and Dintzer label this process "hypothesis testing" and maintain that "when confronted with an uncontrollable outcome, individuals develop one or more hypotheses about its cause and about the likelihood of future uncontrollability. They may then attempt to test these hypotheses by seeking out information about their own behavior in other settings and/or information about the behavior of others" (p. 78).

Wortman and Dintzer's (1978) hypothesis-testing conceptualization points to a gap in the reformulated theory which has not yet been filled satisfactorily: What processes determine which causal attribution a person selects to explain the occurrence of an uncontrollable event (cf. Abramson, Alloy, & Metalsky, 1988; Abramson *et al.*, 1987, and Chapter 2, this volume)? One important implication of this view is that not only the deficits exhibited but also the information-seeking strategies used by persons exposed to uncontrollable outcomes should be examined (see also Swann, Stephenson, & Pittman, 1981). Perhaps the first and more important question to ask is, What kind of information is sought? The present study was carried out to answer this question by giving subjects an opportunity to choose among testing tasks varying in their informational value about the subjects' ability.

DESIGN OF THE STUDY

Three different groups of subjects were asked to work on a computer-administered concept formation task identical to the one used in an earlier study by Hanusa and Schulz (1977). One of these groups received contingent feedback and successfully solved the problems, while the remaining two groups were given noncontingent feedback. The two noncontingent feedback groups were given either no attribution or an ability attribution for their failure at the task. A no-treatment group which participated only in the second phase of the experiment was also included. In the second phase of the experiment, all subjects were given the opportunity to choose anagrams, which they were to solve, from six different lists, each varying in informational value about one's ability (diagnosticity, either high or low) and difficulty (easy, medium, hard). The selection procedure was modeled after one used by Trope (1975) and Trope and Brickman (1975).

HYPOTHESIS-TESTING PREDICTIONS

The hypothesis-testing view predicts that persons exposed to uncontrollable outcomes develop one or more hypotheses about the cause and attempt to test these hypotheses in subsequent settings. In the context of this learned helplessness experiment, such persons should be most eager to obtain information about their ability and should, therefore, choose higher diagnostic items than groups exposed to controllable outcomes.

Implicit in the hypothesis-testing view is Bandura's (1977) notion that "discrepancies between performance and standards create dissatisfactions that motivate corrective changes in behavior" (p. 193). This formulation would explain why the lack-of-ability attribution groups in both the Hanusa and Schulz (1977) and the Wortman *et al.* (1976) studies exhibited facilitation effects. Presumably, individuals in this condition were motivated to test out and demonstrate to themselves that it was their current performance that was poor rather than their standard that was incorrect. Because the method for inducing the lack-of-ability attribution in this study was identical to the one used by Hanusa and Schulz, it was expected that the subjects in this condition should be similarly motivated to test out their standing on the ability dimension. Hence, it was predicted that preference for high diagnostic items should be strongest in the lack-of-ability attribution condition.

LEARNED HELPLESSNESS PREDICTIONS

The learned helplessness theory makes no clear predictions about an individual's information search after helplessness training, but a reasonable extension of the theory would suggest that subjects induced to make a lack-of-ability attribution for their failure should desire diagnostic information less than other groups. These subjects may feel they already know their ability level and, consequently, they may not desire any more information. In an area similar to learned helplessness research, Trope (1975) found that subjects with low achievement motivation chose significantly fewer high diagnostic items than subjects with high achievement motivation. Inasmuch as helplessness training is said to cause general motivational deficits,[1] one might also predict helpless individuals would behave more like those with low achievement motivation than those with high achievement motivation.

Previous researchers (Trope, 1975; Trope & Brickman, 1975) have found that diagnostic value was the major determinant of task choice, so it is difficult to make predictions regarding choice of difficulty level. However, in order to draw conclusions about the effects of diagnosticity unconfounded by difficulty it was necessary to include the latter dimension in the study as well.

METHOD

OVERVIEW

The experimental design included four groups: a no-training group, a contingent reinforcement training group, a noncontingent reinforcement training group given no attributional information, and a noncontingent reinforcement training group provided with a lack-of-ability attribution. The training session was modeled after Hanusa and Schulz (1977) and consisted of three computerized concept formation problems. The second phase of the study, in which subjects completed questionnaires and selected anagrams varying in difficulty and diagnosticity, took place in a separate room with a different experimenter who was blind to the subjects' condition.

SUBJECTS

Fifty-four subjects from the undergraduate subject pool at Carnegie-Mellon University (C-MU) participated in the experiment. Data from five subjects—one from the no-training condition, three from the contingent reinforcement condition, and one from the no-attribution condition—were discarded because they were acquainted with the undergraduate who carried out the second phase of the experiment. Data obtained from four additional subjects—two from the

---

1. The meaning here given to the term "motivational deficits" differs from the definition used in most learned helplessness experiments, where measures of passivity or intellectual slowness are employed as indicators of motivational deficits.

no-training and two from the contingent reinforcement condition—were discarded because they did not follow instructions in the second phase of the experiment. The resulting 45 subjects were distributed proportionately among the four cells. All cells contained eight male and three female subjects, except for the ability-attribution group which contained eight male and four female subjects.

STIMULI

Training Task

The training task was identical to the one used by Hanusa and Schulz (1977) and consisted of three concept formation problems presented by a PDP-11 computer on a Telterm terminal. The patterns of stimuli for the three problems were randomly chosen (without replacement) from the set of all possible patterns with three levels of three dimensions. The three dimensions were position, color, and letter. The three levels for each were, respectively, left, middle, right; red, black, green; and X, Y, Z.

The terminal displayed a pattern of three stimuli and prompted the subject for a response. The subject was given 30 seconds to respond Yes (1), the concept is there, or No (0), the concept is not there. If the subject did not respond within 30 seconds, the computer displayed "Enter 1 or 0" every 5 seconds until the subject did respond. After the subject's response, the computer provided feedback, either "Correct" or "Wrong," and then displayed another pattern. All subjects, except the no-training subjects, had 25 such trials on the first problem, 22 on the second problem, and 18 on the third.

In the contingent training condition the concepts being tested were (1) patterns with a green–red–black sequence of colors, (2) patterns with an X–Y–Z letter sequence, and (3) the presence of a black Z in any position. Pilot testing indicated that most subjects could solve these problems. In the noncontingent training conditions the computer's response was preset by a schedule of random numbers. The sequence of random Correct and Wrong responses was different for each of the three problems.

Testing Task

Subjects selected 25 anagrams from six larger pools of anagrams that varied on two dimensions, diagnosticity (high–low) and difficulty (high–moderate–low). This task was modeled after Trope (1975) and Trope and Brickman (1975). Information about diagnosticity and difficulty was presented in the form of a large bar graph.

The graph consisted of two bars—one red and the other green—for each of the six lists. One bar of each pair depicted the probability of success for students low in ability. The first three lists varied in difficulty and were of low diagnosticity. The second three lists also varied in difficulty but had high diagnostic value because they clearly differentiated between students of low and high ability. The percentages of success of high and low ability groups for each of the six lists were identical to those used by Trope (1975).

All subjects were given the same anagrams selected from lists prepared by Tresselt and Mayzner (1966). The anagrams used had mean solution times between 140 to 240 seconds and are considered difficult anagrams.

PROCEDURE

Subjects signed up to participate in two experiments. The first was labeled a computerized concept formation experiment and the second a problem-solving experiment. Subjects were told that the experiments were run consecutively because the second experimenter needed subjects with the same experience prior to participating in the problem-solving task. All subjects were run individually.

Training Session

When subjects started the first experiment (the training task) they were told that it involved a computer-administered test. The test was described as an indicator of ability to integrate information; furthermore, it was claimed that this ability was a very good indicator of academic potential. All subjects then read a bogus newspaper article supporting this claim. After reading the article, subjects were asked if they wanted to continue and were given a consent form to sign. (No subject refused to participate). Once the subject gave his or her consent, the experimenter elaborated further on the importance and validity of the test. For example, the experimenter pointed out that the test was excellent not only for engineering and science students but also for humanities or fine arts majors.

Next, the subjects were randomly assigned to one of three conditions. The computer program was then started, and subjects were told that the remainder of the instructions would be delivered via the Telterm. The computer printed out the instructions for the task along with further embellishments about the importance of the test. Before the concept formation problems were presented, the experimenter demonstrated one sample problem and delivered the first attribution manipulation to subjects in the ability-attribution group. Subjects assigned to this condition were told, "It looks as if this test is a really good indicator of academic potential—so far I've really been impressed with how well everyone has done."

After the subject has unsuccessfully attempted to solve the problems, the computer printed out bogus results and additional ability-attribution information for subjects assigned to that condition. The subject was informed that only 2 of the 89 others who had taken the test failed to solve any problems. He or she also read a bogus case history of a female psychology major who had been able to solve the same problems that the subject had received. Finally, the attribution was restated by the first experimenter before taking the subject to the second experimental room, in comments such as "I don't know what to say, everyone else did so well. I guess you weren't able to use information that was given to you."

Subjects in both the contingent and noncontingent no-attribution conditions were given no information other than the number of problems they were able to solve. If subjects in the no-attribution conditions asked for information about their performance relative to others, they were told that not enough data were available from C-MU students to evaluate their performance.

Testing Session

The first experimenter escorted all subjects to a new room and introduced the subject to the second experimenter. The first experimenter asked the subject to complete a questionnaire regarding the first experiment and asked the second experimenter to collect the questionnaire, explaining as she left that she needed time to get ready for the next subject.

Subjects were told that the second experiment involved selecting a list of anagrams to solve and then solving their chosen anagrams. At this point, a prerecorded message was played, explaining the anagram task and the selection process. The message informed subjects how to solve anagrams, that the anagrams they were selecting were part of the Michigan Integrative Orientation Survey, that this survey had been used many times with students at C-MU and other universities, and that roughly half of the students at C-MU have high ability on this test while the other half have low ability. They were then referred to the bar graph and informed that the test consisted of six lists of anagrams from which they were to choose 25 anagrams. Each of the six lists was explained as follows:

> Let me tell you something about each of the six lists. Looking at the top of the chart you will notice that there is an easy, moderate, and difficult list, followed by another three lists which are also easy, moderate, and difficult. For each of the six lists we have the percentage of correct responses for individuals of high and low ability. For example, looking at list A, an easy list, on the left-hand side of the chart, you will find that individuals of high ability scored 73.4 percent correct, whereas individuals of low ability scored 66.6 percent correct. The total percentage correct for list A was 70 percent. As you would expect, the total percentage for the moderate difficulty list was lower. It is 51.5 percent, indicated above the letter B. And finally, the percentage correct for individuals doing the difficult list is 30.5 percent. Looking at list C, you will note that individuals of high ability scored approximately 33.4 percent on list C, whereas individuals of low ability had 26.6 percent correct.

List D is also an easy list. The total percentage correct is the same as it was for list A, that is, 70 percent. However, list D differs in its ability to distinguish between individuals of high and low ability. Individuals of high ability on list D scored 90.2 percent correct, whereas individuals of low ability scored 49.9 percent correct. Thus, although the total percentage correct for list D is the same as it is for list A, you will note that the difference between high and low ability persons is much greater on list D. A similar effect is found when comparing the two moderate difficulty lists. For both the moderate difficulty lists, that is, list B and list E, the total percentage correct was 51.5 percent. However, for list E, individuals of high ability scored 75.2 percent, whereas individuals of low ability scored only 27.8 percent correct. Again, list E is much better at discriminating between individuals of high and low ability. Finally, list F, a difficult list, is good at discriminating between individuals of high and low ability. High ability subjects scored 50.8 percent correct, whereas low ability subjects scored only 10.1 percent correct. The overall percentage correct for list F, however, is 30.5 percent, the same percentage correct obtained by individuals doing list C, also a difficult list. Again, the only difference between list C and list F is that list F is much better at discriminating between high and low ability persons, whereas list C is not as good at discriminating between such persons.

In summary, you will note that we have three levels of difficulty available to you. That is, we have easy lists, moderately difficult lists, and difficult lists. And we also have two levels of discriminability. We have lists that are very good at discriminating between high and low ability subjects—lists D, E, and F—and lists that are not good at this—lists A, B, and C.

At the end of the tape, the experimenter stated that subjects could select as many anagrams as they desired from each of the six lists and that the choice was totally theirs. They were also told that they would be given 45 seconds to solve each anagram.

After questions had been answered, subjects were presented with a form on which they indicated how many anagrams from each of the six lists they wanted to solve. The experimenter timed the selection. Subjects were also asked to indicate how many of the 25 they expected to solve, what their most preferred list was, and how strong their preference for their selected list was.

While the experimenter "selected" the anagrams the subjects had chosen, the subjects completed a questionnaire asking about their performance expectations, and whether they thought the previous experiment had affected their choices.

All subjects were then given the same 12 anagrams to solve. The experimenter timed their solutions and stopped their work on any particular anagram after 45 seconds. After attempting all the anagrams, subjects were asked to complete a final questionnaire. This questionnaire assessed subjects' performance evaluations and their evaluations of the anagrams. Subjects were then intensively debriefed by the first experimenter or one of the authors. The debriefing procedure used has been shown to be effective in eliminating any potential long-term effects (Hanusa & Schulz, 1979).

RESULTS

EFFECTIVENESS OF TRAINING

Subjects' responses to the posttraining questionnaire were analyzed using 1×3 analyses of variance. Significant experimental treatment effects were found in responses to questions regarding the difficulty of the task $(F(2,31) = 5.26, \quad p < .05)$, assessments of performance on the task $(F(2,31) = 35.24, p < .001)$, the solvability of the problems $(F(2,31) = 9.66, p < .005)$, how competent subjects felt $(F(2,31) = 15.84, p < .001)$, how helpless subjects felt $(F(2,31) = 5.65, p < .01)$, and how much control subjects felt they had over the test $(F(2,31) = 6.68, p < .01)$. Post hoc tests (Tukey a) indicated that the significant differences were primarily attributable to differences between the contingent reinforcement condition and the two noncontingent reinforcement conditions. Subjects in the contingent reinforcement condition thought the problems were easier and more solvable. They thought their performance was better and they felt more competent, less helpless, and in more control of the situation than subjects in either of the noncontingent groups $(p < .01$ for all comparisons). Additionally, subjects in the ability-attribution group felt less competent than subjects in the no-attribution condition $(F(1,31) = 4.05, p < .06)$. In summary, there is strong evidence that the contingency manipulation and ability information had their intended effects.

ANAGRAM SELECTION RESULTS

The major dependent variable in this study was the number of anagrams selected from lists that varied in diagnosticity and difficulty. These data were analyzed with a 4 (Experimental Treatment, a between-subjects factor) $\times$ 2 (Level of Diagnosticity, a within-subjects factor) $\times$ 3 (Level of Difficulty, a within-subjects factor) analysis of variance.[2] A significant main effect for diagnosticity was found: Subjects preferred high diagnostic items to low diagnostic items $(X_{high} = 14.78$ vs. $X_{low} = 10.22, F(1,123^3) = 14.44, p < .01)$. There was also an experimental treatment $\times$ diagnosticity interaction $F(3,123^3) = 3.67, p < .05)$. All other main effects and interactions were not significant.

Closer inspection of the experimental treatment $\times$ diagnosticity interaction depicted in Figure 4-1 revealed that subjects in the contingent reinforce-

---

2. This analysis is analogous to the one reported in Trope (1975) and Trope and Brickman (1975), thereby allowing for comparisons among the three studies.

3. The error term used in these calculations is a pooled error term derived from the combination of the Subjects $\times$ Diagnosticity interaction and Subjects $\times$ Diagnosticity $\times$ Difficulty interaction. This pooling procedure is recommended by Winer (1962, pp. 321–323) when the higher order interactions are not statistically significant.

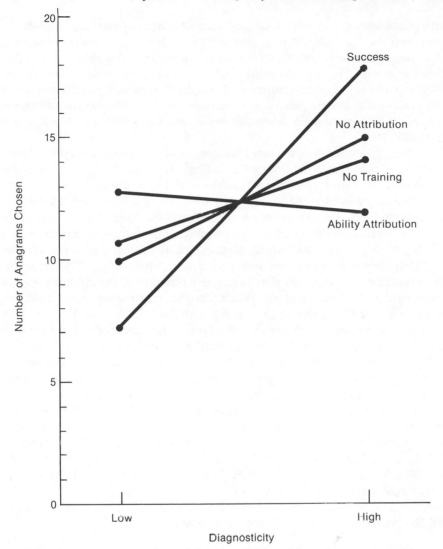

FIGURE 4-1. Anagram choices as a function of diagnosticity and treatment conditions.

ment training and no-attribution noncontingent reinforcement conditions preferred significantly more high diagnostic anagrams than low diagnostic anagrams ($p < .05$, for contingent, $p < .06$ for no-attribution) while the ability-attribution subjects exhibited no difference in preference. Subjects in the no-training condition also preferred high diagnostic ($X_{low} = 10.73$, $X_{high} = 14.28$) to low diagnostic items, but this difference was not significant.

When comparisons (Tukey a) were made between the experimental treatment groups on the number of high diagnostic items chosen, the following differences were found to be statistically significant: The contingent reinforcement training (success) group selected more high diagnostic items than subjects in all other conditions ($p < .05$ for all comparisons); the ability-attribution group selected fewer high diagnostic items than all other groups ($p < .05$ for all comparisons). The no-training and no-attribution subjects did not differ from each other but did select fewer high diagnostic items than the contingent groups ($p < .05$) and more diagnostic items than the ability-attribution group ($p < .05$).

These differences in preference for diagnostic anagrams are also reflected in subjects' most preferred lists. When asked, "If you had to choose only one list, which list would you choose?" subjects in the contingent reinforcement and no-attribution noncontingent reinforcement conditions overwhelmingly chose high diagnostic lists (only 1 subject out of 22 selected a low diagnostic list). In contrast, subjects in the no-training and ability-attribution groups selected both high (14) and low (9) diagnostic lists as their most preferred list.

Consistent with earlier research (e.g., Trope & Brickman, 1975), no statistically significant differences were found as a function of the difficulty level of the anagrams. Subjects in all conditions selected approximately equal number of easy ($\bar{X} = 9.07$), moderate ($\bar{X} = 8.78$), and difficult ($\bar{X} = 7.15$) items. Subjects were also asked the reasons for their preference, and their responses were coded by two raters, blind to the subjects' experimental condition, into the following five categories: diagnostic, difficulty, variety, random, and uncodable. The only pattern to emerge from these data was that the contingent group mentioned diagnosticity more frequently than any other group.

After making their selection, subjects were also asked how they would do compared to others who selected the same list. A 1×4 analysis of variance revealed that subjects in the ability-attribution condition predicted they would not do as well as others would ($F(3,40) = 5.20$, $p < .005$); ($F(1,40) = 14.56$, $p < .01$), for the comparison of ability against all other groups). No statistically significant differences were found for questions assessing the difficulty or diagnosticity of the selected list, how hard subjects would try, or whether they felt the previous experience affected their choice of lists.

ANAGRAM PERFORMANCE

After obtaining subjects' assessment of the selected anagrams, experimenters gave them the same 12 anagrams to solve. An analysis of the number of anagrams solved and elapsed time to solution yielded no differences between groups. This lack of significant differences is not surprising, for at least three reasons. First, a relatively long period of time had elapsed since the training phase of the experiment. Subjects took approximately 20 minutes to complete the two lengthy questionnaires and approximately 10 minutes to make the anagram selections. Whether or not the impact of the training task would persist after the interim tasks is questionable. Second, it is possible that performance was confounded by choice of lists. Finally, performance may have been affected because only difficult anagrams were given to all subjects independent of their choices.

DISCUSSION

The results of this study proved to be inconsistent with predictions derived from the hypothesis-testing view. Subjects who were induced to attribute their performance at the computer task to lack of ability were less interested in obtaining information about their ability than all other groups. Subjects induced to make a lack-of-ability attribution chose equal numbers of high and low diagnostic anagrams, whereas subjects in all other groups selected more high than low diagnostic anagrams. In fact, contrary to our predictions, persons who succeeded at the computer task—who were most confident about their ability—desired self-evaluative feedback more than any other group. They selected the most high diagnostic items. At the least, the data suggest some modifications of the hypothesis-testing view are necessary, and these are presented later in this discussion.

INFORMATION SEARCH AND LEARNED HELPLESSNESS

While Abramson and colleagues have not specifically addressed the issue of information search after helplessness training, the obtained data for the lack-of-ability attribution group appear to be consistent with the revised model. The pattern of low diagnostic choices for this group is virtually identical to the data obtained by Trope (1975) for people with low achievement motivation. Trope found that the lower the achievement motive, as measured by Mehrabian's Achievement Scale (Mehrabian, 1969), the weaker the preference for high diagnostic items over low diagnostic items. Low achievement motivated persons selected approximately equal numbers of each. Trope also found that level of achievement motive was not related to the difficulty level of the items chosen.

The motivational deficits associated with learned helplessness in humans consist of retarded initiation of voluntary responses and are typically reflected in measures of passivity and intellectual slowness. Dependent measures used as indicators of motivational deficits have included initiation of avoidance behavior in the presence of aversive noise (Hiroto, 1974), measures of persistence (Hanusa & Schulz, 1977; Roth & Kubal, 1975), and measures of failure to generate complex hypotheses (Abramson, Alloy, & Rosoff, 1981).

The index of motivational state used in the present study was very different from existing measures. The findings suggest there may be important similarities between a helpless individual and one who is low in achievement motivation and between learned helplessness and achievement motivation in general. While it would be inappropriate to carry out a detailed comparative analysis of achievement motivation and learned helplessness theories here, some obvious similarities immediately come to mind. Both theories emphasize the importance of contingency experiences for optimal development of the organism and both have produced elaborate rehabilitation therapies based in part on providing subjects with contingency experiences and appropriate attributional labels (see Abramson *et al.*, 1978, and McClelland, 1965, 1978, for the respective treatment strategies). Further comparative analysis of these theories is warranted and should increase our understanding of both phenomena.

INFORMATION-SEEKING AS AN EXPLANATION FOR FACILITATION EFFECTS

This study was carried out in an effort to understand the facilitation effects found for subjects persuaded to attribute their failures to their lack of ability (Hanusa & Schulz, 1977; Wortman *et al.*, 1976). One explanation of the facilitation effects has been that the subjects have not experienced sufficient helplessness training to produce performance deficits (e.g., Abramson *et al.*, 1978). However, this explanation implies that subjects are uncertain about their ability to control outcomes in the first situation and consequently try harder in the second. This reasoning suggests that information-search strategies following inadequate helplessness training should be reflected in a greater desire for diagnostic information. This result was not obtained in this study.

On the other hand, if the results of this experiment lead to the conclusion that subjects induced to attribute their failure to lack of ability are certain about their lack of ability and consequently desire less information, then the facilitation effects found in Hanusa and Schulz (1977) and Wortman *et al.* (1976) remain unexplained. Recent work by Frankel and Snyder (1978) and Berglas and Jones (1978) may help account for the choices of both the ability-attribution subjects and the contingency training subjects, as well as the facilitation effect.

Frankel and Snyder (1978) argue that the reduced motivation and impaired performance observed after helplessness training may not be the result of expectations that outcomes are independent of responses. They suggest instead that they are strategic behaviors designed to protect a subject's image of self-competence in the face of poor performance. According to this view, after a failure experience individuals expect to do poorly and, in effect, do poorly on purpose in order to downplay the significance of their anticipated poor showing. By not trying, subjects have a readily available unstable attribution for poor performance and therefore avoid any further threats to self-esteem.

This explanation was tested by presenting subjects with either solvable or unsolvable discrimination learning problems and then with a number of solvable anagrams that were alleged to be either extremely or moderately difficult. When poor performance would have threatened self-esteem, that is, when anagrams were described as only moderately difficult, subjects exhibited the deficits predicted by learned helplessness theory. They solved fewer anagrams following experience with unsolvable problems than with solvable problems. However, when poor performance was not as likely to threaten self-esteem, that is, when the anagrams were ostensibly very difficult, no such performance decrement was found. Contrary to a learned helplessness theory prediction, helpless individuals did better when they thought the anagrams were extremely difficult rather than moderately difficult.

A similar notion is proposed by Berglas and Jones (1978) in their research on self-handicapping as a strategy used in response to noncontingent outcomes. They propose that people select the available environment best designed to protect their image of self-competence in the event of poor performance. In their study they found that after a noncontingent success experience, males chose a performance-inhibiting drug (placebo) rather than a performance-enhancing drug (placebo) before attempting similar problems, presumably because they wished to externalize probable failure on the retest. The authors conclude that diagnostic information will be avoided when the chances are good that such information will indicate inferior performance.

The behavior of the lack-of-ability attribution group in the present study is consistent with the Frankel and Snyder and the Berglas and Jones analyses. Given their recent failure experience, along with the attributional information indicating lack of ability as the cause, it is not surprising these subjects were reluctant to acquire any further diagnostic information regarding their ability. The probabilities were high that such information would only further threaten their already reduced level of self-esteem.

On the other hand, subjects who failed but had the opportunity to attribute their failure to external or unstable factors (the no-attribution group) had no reason to avoid diagnostic information. Presumably, the explanation that enabled subjects to externalize the first failure would serve the same purpose should they fail again. Finally, the contingent response group had nothing to lose and much to gain by selecting the highly diagnostic items. These subjects already had a success experience which they may have attributed to internal causes—they did perceive themselves as significantly more competent than did either the no-attribution or lack-of-ability attribution groups. Failure on the second task could always be attributed to unstable factors such as fatigue without threatening the significance of the earlier success experience. In sum, the choice of self-evaluative feedback on the testing task for all three groups is consistent with the notion that "people arrange their environments to influence the dispositions that can be attributed to them—by themselves as well as by others" (Berglas & Jones, 1978, p. 416).

HYPOTHESIS TESTING REVISITED

As discussed earlier, the data were inconsistent with the hypothesis-testing view presented by Wortman and Dintzer (1978). However, we believe a hypothesis-testing perspective is a viable explanation of these data if we add to it an assumption underlying the self-esteem analysis—that people are motivated to protect and enhance existing levels of self-esteem (see Zuckerman, 1979). Thus, individuals engage in hypothesis-testing behaviors, but only to the extent that such tests are likely to yield positive self-relevant information. This bias for positive feedback should be strongest for attributes that are important to the individuals, such as intellectual ability, and weaker for attributes the individual cares little about. For example, someone who does not consider himself or herself an extraordinary athlete may use very unbiased testing strategies to discover his or her ability at various sports, whereas almost everyone, especially college students, is likely to use biased strategies to obtain information about his or her intellectual abilities.

CONCLUSION

The data presented here and the studies reviewed earlier suggest that biasing processes may operate at any one of the following three states: *information-seeking, performance*, and *interpretation*. Biasing processes can be distinguished from helplessness in that they serve to enhance or overestimate the contingency between individuals' responses and outcomes; helplessness usually serves to diminish or underestimate contingencies between responses and outcomes.

First, the individual can select environments or tasks to minimize diagnostic feedback when poor performance is anticipated. The desire for minimal diagnostic feedback by the lack-of-ability attribution group and the desire for highly diagnostic feedback by the success group are examples of the use of this mechanism. Some of the behaviors associated with social comparison processes (Festinger, 1954) also fall within this category. The individual who selects a comparison other similar to or slightly inferior to himself or herself obviously maximizes the possibility of positive self-evaluations (Ahrens, in press; Taylor, 1983). Thus, for example, the institutionalized elderly individual who compares his or her cognitive and physical abilities to other institutionalized individuals is likely to reach very different conclusions about ability level than one who uses younger or noninstitutionalized individuals as comparison others.

Second, one can bias performance so that failures can be externalized and successes internalized. An example of this is found in Frankel and Snyder's (1979) study, where subjects working on moderately difficult anagrams did not try as hard as subjects working on difficult anagrams. The subject who fails at solving difficult problems can attribute his or her failure to the difficulty of the task. Success can be attributed to high ability. The individual who tries hard and fails at a moderately difficult task must confront the possibility that failure is due to lack of ability. The tendency of older individuals to avoid responding on problem-solving tasks may be another example of this phenomenon. (Botwinick, 1978). It is generally accepted that the elderly are less likely to respond in ambiguous situations and more likely to avoid decision situations altogether because they wish to minimize the possibility of being wrong. Cautiousness is thus viewed as a defense for ego-saving purposes (Botwinick, 1978).

Third, and finally, individuals may reinterpret performance feedback after the fact. That is, they may decide that a poor outcome is attributable to unstable factors such as lack of effort, while a good outcome is attributable to stable internal factors such as ability. The large variety of such biases is described and documented in a number of reviews of the attribution literature (e.g., Miller & Porter, Chapter 1, this volume; Zuckerman, 1979).

There may be other biasing mechanisms not captured by the three generic categories presented above. However, even without any additions to this list, the available arsenal appears to us quite powerful. The three processes identified can be used individually under circumstances where the options are limited, or they may be used in tandem. For example, the individual who seeks positive diagnostic information, but receives negative information instead, can still fall back on interpretive processes to maintain or enhance self-esteem.

In summary, our analysis suggests that at least some of the behaviors that have been identified as "helpless" are not due to expectations of noncontingency between responses and outcomes but are instead varieties of strategic behaviors aimed at preserving or enhancing self-esteem. Under certain circumstances, identical behaviors may be serving diametrically opposed motivations.

ACKNOWLEDGMENTS

We wish to thank Phil Brickman, Susan Fiske, and Michael Scheier for comments and suggestions on this chapter. Our appreciation is also extended to Steve Ciampi, Sara Dittman, Elizabeth Nagy, Debra Rubenstein, and Pamela Silmore for serving as experimenters. This research was supported in part by Grant No. AG 00525 from the National Institute on Aging.

REFERENCES

Abramson, L. Y., Alloy, L. B., & Metalsky, G. I. (1988). The cognitive diathesis-stress theories of depression: Toward an adequate evaluation of the theories' validities. In L. B. Alloy (Ed.), *Cognitive processes in depression*. New York: Guilford.
Abramson, L. Y., Alloy, L. B., & Rosoff, R. (1981). Depression and the generation of complex hypotheses in the judgment of contingency. *Behavior Research and Therapy, 19*, 35–45.

Abramson, L. Y., Metalsky, G. I., & Alloy, L. B. (1987). The hopelessness theory of depression: A metatheoretical analysis with implications for psychopathology research. Manuscript submitted for publication.

Abramson, L. Y., Seligman, M. E. P., & Teasdale, J. D. (1978). Learned helplessness in humans: Critique and reformulation. *Journal of Abnormal Psychology, 87*, 49–74.

Ahrens, A. H. (in press). Theories of depression: The role of goals and the self-evaluation process. *Cognitive Therapy and Research.*

Alloy, L. B. (1982). The role of perceptions and attributions for response-outcome noncontingency in learned helplessness: A commentary and discussion. *Journal of Personality, 50*, 443–479.

Alloy, L. B., Peterson, C., Abramson, L. Y., & Seligman, M. E. P. (1984). Attributional style and the generality of learned helplessness. *Journal of Personality and Social Psychology, 46*, 681–687.

Bandura, A. (1977). Self-efficacy: Toward a unifying theory of behavioral change. *Psychological Review, 84*, 191–215.

Berglas, S., & Jones. E. E. (1978). Drug choice as an externalization strategy in response to noncontingent success. *Journal of Personality and Social Psychology, 36*, 405–417.

Botwinick, J. (1978). *Aging and behavior* (2nd ed.). New York: Springer.

Brewin, C. R. (1985). Depression and causal attributions: What is their relation? *Psychological Bulletin, 98*, 297–309.

Brockner, J., Gardner, M., Bierman, J., Mahan, T., Thomas, B., Weiss, W., Winters, L., & Mitchell, A. (1983). The roles of self-esteem and self-consciousness in the Wortman–Brehm model of reactance and learned helplessness. *Journal of Personality and Social Psychology, 45*, 199–209.

Coyne, J. C., & Gotlib, I. H. (1983). The role of cognition in depression: A critical appraisal. *Psychological Bulletin, 94*, 472–505.

Danker-Brown, P., & Baucom, D. H. (1982). Cognitive influences on the development of learned helplessness. *Journal of Personality and Social Psychology, 43*, 793–801.

Festinger, L. (1954). A theory of social comparison processes. *Human Relations, 7*, 117–140.

Frankel, A., & Snyder, M. L. (1978). Poor performance following unsolvable problems: Learned helplessness or egotism? *Journal of Personality and Social Psychology, 36*, 1415–1423.

Hanusa, B. H., & Schulz, R. (1977). Attributional mediators of learned helplessness. *Journal of Personality and Social Psychology, 35*, 602–611.

Hanusa, B. H., & Schulz, R. (1979). *Long-term effects of participating in a learned helplessness experiment.* Unpublished manuscript, Carnegie-Mellon University, New York.

Hiroto, D. S. (1974). Locus of control and learned helplessness. *Journal of Experimental Psychology, 102*, 187–193.

Klein, D. C., Fencil-Morse, E., & Seligman, M. E. P. (1976). Learned helplessness, depression, and the attribution of failure. *Journal of Personality and Social Psychology, 33*, 508–516.

Maier, S. F., Seligman, M. E. P., & Solomon, R. L. (1969). Pavlovian fear conditioning and learned helplessness. In B. A. Campbell & R. M. Church (Eds.), *Punishment.* New York: Appleton–Century–Crofts.

McClelland, D. C. (1965). Toward a theory of motive acquisition. *American Psychologist, 20*, 321–333.

McClelland, D. C. (1978). Managing motivation to expand human freedom. *American Psychologist, 33*, 201–210.

Mehrabian, A. (1969). Measures of achieving tendency. *Educational and Psychological Measurement, 20*, 445–451.

Miller, I. W., III, & Norman, W. H. (1979). Learned helplessness in humans: A review and attribution-theory model. *Psychological Bulletin, 86*, 93–118.

Pasahow, R. J. (1980). The relation between an attributional dimension and learned helplessness. *Journal of Abnormal Psychology, 89*, 358–367.

Peterson, C., & Seligman, M. E. P. (1984). Causal explanations as a risk factor for depression: Theory and evidence. *Psychological Review, 91,* 347–374.

Pittman, N. L., & Pittman, T. S. (1979). Effects of amount of helplessness training and internal-external locus of control on mood and performance. *Journal of Personality and Social Psychology, 37,* 39–47.

Pittman, T. S., & Pittman, N. L. (1980). Deprivation of control and the attribution process. *Journal of Personality and Social Psychology, 39,* 377–389.

Roth, S., & Kubal, L. (1975). Effects of noncontingent reinforcement on tasks of differing importance: Facilitation and learned helplessness. *Journal of Personality and Social Psychology, 32,* 680–691.

Seligman, M. E. P. (1975). Helplessness: On depression, development, and death. San Francisco: Freeman.

Seligman, M. E. P., & Maier, S. F. (1967). Failure to escape traumatic shock. *Journal of Experimental Psychology, 74,* 1–9.

Seligman, M. E. P., Maier, S. F., & Solomon, R. L. (1971). Unpredictable and uncontrollable aversive events. In F. R. Brush (Ed.), *Aversive conditioning and learning.* New York: Academic Press.

Swann, W. B., Stephenson, B., & Pittman, T. S. (1981). Curiosity and control: On the determinants of the search for social knowledge. *Journal of Personality and Social Psychology, 40,* 635–642.

Sweeney, P. D., Anderson, K., & Bailey, S. (1986). Attributional style in depression: A meta-analytic review. *Journal of Personality and Social Psychology, 50,* 974–991.

Taylor, S. E. (1983). Adjustment to threatening events: A theory of cognitive adaptation. *American Psychologist, 38,* 1161–1173.

Tresselt, M. E., & Mayzner, M. S. (1966). Normative solution times for a sample of 134 solution words and 378 associated anagrams. *Psychonomic Monograph Supplements, 1,* 293–298.

Trope, Y. (1975). Seeking information about one's own ability as a determinant of choice among tasks. *Journal of Personality and Social Psychology, 32,* 1004–1013.

Trope, Y., & Brickman, P. (1975). Difficulty and diagnosticity as determinants of choice among tasks. *Journal of Personality and Social Psychology, 32,* 918–925.

Weiner, B. (1974). *Achievement motivation and attribution theory.* Morristown, N.J.: General Learning.

Winer, B. J. (1962). *Statistical principles in experimental design.* New York: McGraw-Hill.

Wortman, C. B., & Dintzer, L. (1978). Is an attributional analysis of the learned helplessness phenomenon viable?: A critique of the Abramson–Seligman–Teasdale reformulation. *Journal of Abnormal Psychology, 87,* 75–90.

Wortman, C. B., Panciera, L., Shusterman, L., & Hibscher, J. (1976). Attributions of causality and reactions to uncontrollable outcomes. *Journal of Experimental Social Psychology, 12,* 301–316.

Zuckerman, M. (1979). Attribution of success and failure revisited, or: The motivational bias is alive and well in attribution theory. *Journal of Personality, 47,* 245–287.

Zuroff, D. C. (1980). Learned helplessness in humans: An analysis of learning processes and the roles of individual and situational differences. *Journal of Personality and Social Psychology, 39,* 130–146.

5

Coping with Disease, Crime, and Accidents: The Role of Self-blame Attributions

RONNIE JANOFF-BULMAN
LINDA LANG-GUNN

Victims' attributions for disease, crime, and accidents represent cognitive attempts to understand and explain these highly stressful, undesirable events. Serious illness or injury highlights the unpredictable and uncontrollable nature of life events and underscores the vulnerability of the individual. Given the popular conception of self-blame as psychologically damaging, it is surprising that self-blame attributions are common reactions to disease, crime and accidents. This chapter will document the extent of self-blame attributions and analyze why such seemingly negative attributions occur. Central to the analysis is the proposition that not all self-blame is maladaptive.

ATTRIBUTIONS AND THE NEED FOR MEANING

An attributional perspective on coping with serious illness or injury emphasizes the role of cognitive processes in determining reactions to these negative events (cf. Lazarus, 1966, 1974). Disease, accidents, and criminal victimizations may severely violate an individual's customary self-view or worldview and pose a serious threat to the person's "assumptive world" (Epstein, 1973; Janoff-Bulman, 1985; Janoff-Bulman & Frieze, 1983; Parkes, 1971). The coping demands placed on individuals (or significant others) as a result of a serious violation of their basic assumptions may be at least as formidable as regaining their physical and social adjustment. People have a need for meaning, for a world in which events are comprehensible and orderly (Antonovsky, 1979; Silver & Wortman, 1980). Making sense of the event, finding a "general purpose or pattern of meaning" in it, is a critical task of the person confronted with serious illness or injury (Moos & Tsu, 1977). It is the need for meaning that is primarily addressed by the attributional question, "Why?"

While psychologists have cautioned against assuming that people make attributions without being cued by researchers' questions (Wortman & Dintzer, 1978; cf. Langer, 1978), there is reason to believe that attributions are particularly likely to be made following undesirable personal outcomes such as accidents and diseases. These life events are of great intensity and personal significance (Wortman & Dintzer, 1978). Further, as Brickman and his colleagues (Brickman *et al.*, 1980) propose, the attributional question is strategic; individuals should more readily make attributions for negative events than positive ones, because they want to change the former outcomes. In a series of studies, Wong and Weiner (1981) found that people do in fact make spontaneous attributions in response to failure and unexpected outcomes; these researchers point to events that are stressful and of great personal importance as instigators of the attributional process. Diseases, accidents, and criminal victimizations should satisfy the conditions required for spontaneous attributions, for they are outcomes that are negative, intense, personally important, stressful, and unexpected. These are apparently conditions that challenge working assumptions and trigger a search to satisfy one's need for meaning.

While the need for meaning increases the probability that individuals will make an attribution, it is minimally constraining in terms of the kinds of attributions people will make. Although they may explain the negative outcome in terms of their own contributions (i.e., make an internal attribution), external attributions, such as a belief in God's will or predestination, are an alternative means of satisfying the need for meaning. In fact, the sole causal explanation that appears to be ruled out is an attribution to chance alone, because it entails a view of life outcomes as randomly distributed and of one's world as arbitrary and indiscriminate. As psychological experiments have demonstrated, people tend not to recognize randomness even when it occurs (see Jenkins & Ward, 1965). Like the friar in *The Bridge of San Luis Rey*, who investigated the lives of those who died in the bridge collapse in order to make sense of their seemingly arbitrary deaths, we perceive our world as meaningful and impose meaning even in those instances when randomness may operate.

The need for meaning has been particularly noted by individuals who have studied intense group victimizations. Based on his experiences in and emergence from Auschwitz, Victor Frankl (1963) posited the need for meaning as a fundamental motivation, more basic than the need to maximize pleasure and avoid pain. According to Frankl's analysis, surviving the German concentration camps required the perception of meaning and purpose in one's suffering. Kaplan (1965), in his record of the Warsaw Ghetto, similarly wrote, "The worst part of this ugly kind of death is that you don't know the reason for it . . . We feel compelled to find some sort of system to explain these nightmare murders" (p. 52). And Lifton (1967), in his studies of the survivors of Hiroshima, wrote, "The dropping of the atomic bomb in Hiroshima annihilated a general sense of life's coherence as much as it did human bodies" (p. 525). The survivors of

Hiroshima intently sought a sense of world order and were at a loss to find a spiritual or ideological explanation for the disaster. Victims of accidents, crimes, and diseases engage in a similar search for meaning.

"WHY ME?": THE PROBLEM OF SELECTIVE INCIDENCE

Those who have suffered through such extreme situations as concentration camps, bombings, and natural disasters have been involved in group experiences (cf. Bettelheim, 1943), unlike the victims of many accidents, crimes, and diseases. An individual in the latter category may feel "singled out" by the misfortune, and is left to explain why the event happened to him or her, in particular. Thus, although the rape victim can account for the general occurrence or incidence of rape by pointing a finger at society and its socialization of men and women, this does not provide a satisfactory response to the question, "Why me?" The automobile passenger who is paralyzed when another car jumps the median and hits her automobile can understand the mechanics of the collision, but not why it happened to her. The man who is beaten and robbed on a city street can account for the thief's actions by noting the socioeconomic inequalities in this country, but is at a loss to explain why the thief picked him as a target. A woman may understand the biology of cancer in terms of cell growth, but is at a loss to explain why she, in particular, developed breast cancer. It is the selective incidence of the victimization that is especially troublesome for these victims.

Anthropologist Max Gluckman (1944) explains the belief in witchcraft among the Azande of the Sudan in terms of a need to explain the selective incidence of events, the need to answer "Why misfortune to me and not others?" Discussing the reactions of a father whose son died when his boat was overturned by a hippopotamus, Gluckman (1944) wrote, "The African is fully aware that his son drowned because his lungs filled with water; but he argues that it was a witch, or a sorcerer by his medicines, who brought together the paths of dugout and an angry mother hippo to kill the son" (p. 65). Witchcraft explains the why; science can explain the how, but not the why. The Azande hold that witchcraft does not harm people arbitrarily and haphazardly, which allows them to maintain a belief in a meaningful, orderly world (Gluckman, 1944).

Religion can provide a similar answer to the selective incidence of events. In our relatively secular world, it is often difficult for individuals to turn to religion for meaning, but science cannot provide an explanation of the why of victimizations. As Zola (1972) has noted, when an individual is asked what caused his or her illness (e.g., heart disease or diabetes), the scientific terminology, if not the content, of the response is often quite accurate. If, however, such inquiries into the perceived cause of illness are followed by probes such as "Of all the people in your community (family, etc.) who were exposed to X, why did you get . . . ?" then "the rational scientific veneer is pierced and concern with personal and moral responsibility emerges quite strikingly. Indeed the issue 'Why me?' becomes of great concern and is generally expressed in quite moral terms of what they did wrong" (p. 491). Further, as Bulman and Wortman's (1977) study of accident victims makes apparent, the question of "Why me?" need not be precipitated by the inquiries of others; all respondents in their study had spontaneously asked themselves this personally disturbing question.

We suggest that victims turn to themselves and their role in the victimizing event in order to provide a personally satisfying response to the question, "Why me?" Attributions are attempts to explain events, and self-blame attributions seem to satisfactorily explain why the event occurred to the victim *in particular*. Before discussing whether such attributions are ultimately adaptive or maladaptive, it seemes appropriate to question whether or not people actually blame themselves for events such as accidents, crimes, and diseases. Is there any evidence to suggest that self-blame is, in fact, a common response to such victimizations? The following section is an attempt to address this question.

REVIEW OF DESCRIPTIVE STUDIES OF SELF-BLAME

It should be noted at the outset that there are very few reported studies of the attributions and explanations of people who have been victimized by accidents, crimes, or diseases. Even when such questions have been asked, the responses are frequently reported in an offhand, anecdotal manner. However, the available "evidence" should suffice to demonstrate that self-blame, albeit not the only reaction, is a common reaction to victimization (cf. Wortman, 1976).

Accidents and Criminal Victimizations

In a study of accident victims, Bulman and Wortman (1977) intensively interviewed 29 individuals who were paralyzed (from the neck or waist down) as a result of seemingly "freak" accidents—car accidents, diving accidents, shootings on city streets, falls, hang gliding, severe football-playing injuries. From an observer's perspective, a strong element of chance seemed to define the accidents. For example, the victim was frequently the passenger, and not the driver, of the auto; or the individuals who were paralyzed from diving had dived in the same pool many times prior to the accident. Yet when asked to attribute blame for the accidents (to oneself, other people, the environment, and/or chance), the victims engaged in a considerable amount of self-blame: 63 percent of the respondents blamed themselves at least in part for the accident, and 35 percent blamed themselves more than any other factor for the accident.

Bard and Sangrey (1979), in their work with victims of crime, suggested that victims often seem eager to take responsibility. A burglary victim, for example, blamed himself for having left a window open. A woman whose purse was snatched blamed herself because she realized the neighborhood in which she was walking was dangerous, but she didn't have the money for a taxi. Some victims blamed themselves because they felt they were being justly punished; for example, a robbery victim explained that he was being punished for having had a fight with his wife the morning of the robbery, and a rape victim felt she was being punished for having been sexually active.

Self-blame attributions by victims of rape appear to be well documented (Bryant & Cirel, 1977; Burgess & Holmstrom, 1974a; Medea & Thompson, 1974; Weis & Weis, 1975). Self-blame is second only to fear as a psychological reaction to rape (Bryant & Cirel, 1977). It appears to be the most common attribution in which rape victims engage. "Interestingly, *anger* does not seem to be a main component of the victim's initial reaction. She appears to feel responsible in spite of her feelings of helplessness and fear" (Calhoun, Selby, & King, 1976, p. 123). Burgess and Holmstrom (1974b) illustrated the apparent inappropriateness of such a response in the case of a woman who was assaulted outside of her apartment one afternoon, while searching through her purse for her keys. Although the woman fought back, even managing to take the assailant's knife, the man forced his way into her apartment and beat and raped her. Surprisingly, the woman later said that she should have acted differently when she first saw the man; then neither she nor the rapist "would be in trouble" (p. 983). Hursch (1977) was referring to self-blame when she wrote, "If you have been raped and are still alive, you will forever ask yourself why you didn't fight harder, why you didn't think of some trick to break away, or why you didn't engage in some other act—obvious to you now—which would have prevented the rape" (p. 95). In a survey of workers at rape crisis centers across the country, respondents reported that 74 percent of the women they see at their centers blame themselves at least in part for the rape (Janoff-Bulman, 1979). The rape literature does seem to attest to the phenomenon of self-blame on the part of women who are raped; while the precise nature of this blame differs with each author's perspective and experience, self-blame as a major component of rape victims' reactions does appear to be well substantiated.[1]

In a related vein, another victimized population—battered women—has been found to exhibit a considerable amount of self-blame. Frieze (1979) compared battered women's attributions for the first violent incident that had occurred in their relationship with their attributions for a hypothetical case of

1. The National Commission on the Causes and Prevention of Violence (1969) reported that only 4.4 percent of all rapes are victim-precipitated, suggesting that the frequency of self-blame by victims does not at all reflect an accurate appraisal of the woman's causal role in rape.

wife-battering. She concluded that "although many of the battered women blamed their husbands for their own beatings, they saw themselves as more responsible than they felt other women were—suggesting a relatively high level of self-blame" (Frieze, 1979, p. 101). Similarly high levels of self-blame have also been reported by other researchers working with this population (e.g., Hilberman & Munson, 1978; Walker, 1979).

DISEASE

Unlike accidents and criminal victimizations, serious illness does not often occur suddenly, clearly, and without warning. Because of the insidious and ambiguous onset of many illnesses, the attribution process has an especially important role in reactions to illness, because the individual must make sense of both the initial symptoms and the illness, once diagnosed. Depending on how symptoms are interpreted and explained, individuals may take or delay action. Physical symptoms are commonly experienced (Mechanic, 1972; Pennebaker & Skelton, 1978) and are often quite vague; the individual thus has considerable latitude in interpreting and reacting to them. Based on knowledge and prior experience, many symptoms may be considered normal and may become a part of the person's expectations. When symptoms depart from an individual's expectations, however, the person may attempt to "normalize" the symptoms by interpreting them within a minimally threatening explanatory framework (Davis, 1963; Mechanic, 1972). The person may, for example, attribute unusual symptoms to a common virus or overexertion. Attempts at normalization may persist until the symptoms subside, or until the symptoms can no longer be explained within a conventional framework and the individual is forced to acknowledge the possibility of serious illness and seek help.

Efforts to make sense of unusual symptoms and to "test hypotheses" about the causes and the seriousness of symptoms may contribute to delays in seeking medical attention and care. In other cases, the initial ambiguity and attributional latitude may provide individuals with the time necessary to anticipate and cope with the possibility of a serious illness. For other people, the fear and uncertainty of "not knowing" may lead to prompt action.

Once diagnosed, illness threatens an indivdual's psychological and social, as well as physical, well-being. The seriously ill individual must deal with pain, changes in life-style, physiological imbalance, fear of getting worse or dying, and disruption of the domestic, social, and professional spheres; further, in most cases the person must leave his or her future up to "experts" (Gruen, 1975). For the victims of some diseases (most notably cancer), even medical experts cannot explain *why* the illness occurred. When the etiology of an illness is known, and a medical explanation is provided and accepted, the person may still seek to understand why he or she, in particular, developed the illness—"Why me'?" Thus, patients may supplement (or even supplant) an impersonal, clinical explanation of a disease with their own personal attributions about why they developed the illness.

If a disease were to strike a whole community at a time, it would seem less likely to evoke spontaneously the question "Why me?"; in this respect, diseases resemble such terrifying group experiences as natural disasters, concentration camps, and wartime bombings (e.g., Hiroshima). Most serious diseases, however, appear to single out individuals, and it is in these instances that this question becomes important. Davis (1963), in discussing the reactions of the families of polio victims commented, "This shift in the family's self-image, from a group more or less like other families . . . to one that had been 'singled out' for misfortune, constituted one of the most alienative features of the crisis experience" (p. 40). In her discussion of the popular mythology of tuberculosis and cancer, Sontag (1978) also noted that the "singling out" of victims is a profoundly significant element of these diseases, leading to the question "Why me?" Although much of the evidence derives from unsystematic observations, the available data suggest that the answer to this question often takes the form of self-blaming attributions.

Bard and Dyk (1956) intensively interviewed 100 patients who had undergone one of three surgical procedures: gastrectomy, colostomy, or radical mastectomy. Of the 100 patients, approximately half expressed spontaneous, unsolicited beliefs regarding the cause of their illness, including self-blame beliefs. The self-blame attributions generally identified the illness as punishment for wrongdoing in the past (generalized wrongdoing or a specific act) or as evidence of personal failure. Bard and Dyk (1956) argued that the individual confronted with serious illness *must* establish a belief explaining the event.

Abrams and Finesinger (1953) also reported a marked tendency of cancer patients to explain the cause of their disease in terms of their own role in the occurrence of the illness. Fully half of their sample (30 of 60 patients) blamed their own past actions for their illness, citing actions ranging from a fall to sins. Moses and Cividali (1966) observed that 8 of their cancer patients blamed themselves, while 30 of their patients blamed others. Similarly, Taylor and Levin (1976) reported that many women attribute their breast cancer to premarital sex or other guilt-provoking acts.

Disease victims have been found to blame themselves for acts they believe brought about the disease, such as eating "inferior" food, working too hard, or engaging in irregular or rapid eating habits (e.g., Bard & Dyk, 1956; Kubler-Ross, 1969), and for failure to have prevented the disease. For example, breast cancer patients have been found to blame themselves for having delayed seeking medical help (Abrams & Finesinger, 1953). Similarly, in a study of 46 parents of children with leukemia, Friedman, Chodoff, Mason, and Hamburg (1977) noted that once the cancer diagnosis was made, the parents would, almost without exception, initially blame themselves for not having paid more attention to the early nonspecific manifestations of the disease. They wondered whether the child would not have had a better chance of responding to therapy if the diagnosis had been made sooner. (p. 355)

Concerns about possible blameworthiness or negligence were also observed by Davis (1963) in his study of families of polio victims. The child's illness appeared to challenge the parents' conceptions of themselves as responsible and devoted parents, and they worried that they could have done something to have prevented the illness or to have lessened its severity.

People may perceive their illness as punishment for prior deeds or misdeeds, rather than as the result of specific acts of commission or omission. Evidence of beliefs that illness represents some sort of divine retribution for prior transgressions has been reported by several researchers (Abrams & Finesinger, 1953; Bard & Dyk, 1956; Chodoff, Friedman, & Hamburg, 1964; Davis, 1963; Friedman *et al.*, 1977; Schoenberg & Senescu, 1970).

Self-blame attributions are certainly not the only, nor necessarily the most common, category of causal explanations made by disease victims, but self-blame does appear repeatedly in clinical reports of individuals' reactions to their illnesses. Apparently, the sick person (or the parent of a terminally ill child) often prefers to feel responsible for the illness, than to believe that the event was arbitrary and beyond control. In fact, self-blame attributions seem to occur with sufficient frequency to challenge the conclusion that such a reaction is irrational and pathological. To an observer, an individual's character or behavior may often seem to be an irrational and medically inaccurate explanation of why an illness occurred, but it does appear to provide a personally satisfying response to the question "Why me?" Very often, what is taken as a causal explanation—a response to the question "Why?"—may, implicitly, be a response to the more personally significant question, "Why me?"

SURVIVOR GUILT

Victimizations experienced by a group, such as epidemics, natural disasters, concentration camps, and bombings, generally do not raise the question "Why me?" (Wolfenstein, 1957), but the survival of a group misfortune by an individual may evoke this question. When an individual has shared victimization with others, but has survived while others have lost their lives, he or she is likely to ask "Why me?" ("Why have I lived while others have not?") and to engage in self-blame. Such documented instances of self-blame by survivors have been labeled "survivor guilt." Although survivor guilt is not a phenomenon that is directly related to attributions for disease, crime, and accidents, both are reactions to events that single out the individual. Several examples of the phenomenon will be discussed briefly in order to describe another instance in which self-blame occurs, despite the fact that such an attributional pattern appears entirely unwarranted from the perspective of an observer.

Discussions of survivor guilt have appeared in newspapers and magazines in response to the reactions of survivors of huge air crashes ("Facing the fear of flying: Grief counseling for victims of postcrash syndrome," 1979). Reporters and psychologists have been struck by the frequency with which survivors blame themselves for "not having done enough for those who perished . . . the survivor feels guilty for not having died instead of his loved ones, or in an effort to save them" (Wolfenstein, 1957, p. 216).

The bombing of Hiroshima resulted in a great deal of survivor guilt, involving what Lifton (1967) regards as guilt over "survival priority," the belief that one's survival was achieved at the expense of another's life. Lifton (1971) reported that many survivors felt guilty about the deaths of specific family members whom they were unable to help, whereas others felt guilty about the deaths of the "anonymous" dead. Survivors related how they would walk through the city and feel the eyes of the dead looking up to them for help. Most survivors, according to Lifton (1971), focused upon a single incident or sight that left them with a feeling of profound guilt. Nagai (1951), a Hiroshima survivor himself, also documented the pervasiveness of self-blame relating to personal survival, and described numerous cases of individuals engaging in self-reproach. He summarized his observations by stating, "Those who survived the atomic bomb were people who ignored their friends crying out *in extremis*; or who shook off wounded neighbors who clung to them, pleading to be saved . . . . Those who survived the bomb were, if not merely lucky, in a greater or lesser degree selfish, self-centered, guided by instinct more than by civilization . . . and we know it, we who have survived. Knowing it is a dull ache without surcease" (cited in Wolfenstein, 1957, pp. 217–218).

A similar sense of survivor guilt existed among concentration camp victims. Chodoff (1970) stated that this pervasive guilt is, in some cases, attributable to specific episodes in which survivors felt they had done something to save their own life at increased risk to others. Lifton (1967) contended that the concentration camp experience was particularly conducive to self-accusations for survival, because competition for survival was, in a sense, built into the experience. The epitome of such competition was the "selections," in which prisoners were brought before an official to have their fate decided by the point of a finger. Chodoff (1970) emphasized, however, that in a large number of cases, the guilt is "attached to nothing more than the very fact that they survived when so many were lost" (p. 348). This is not unlike the reactions of the friends and relatives of a sick person, who sometimes feel that they should not enjoy themselves while the patient is suffering (Kubler-Ross, 1969).

The extreme scale of survival guilt by individuals who themselves experienced so much suffering is not immediately comprehensible. It is interesting to note, however, that guilt is an expected phase in the normal course of grieving. Lindemann (1977), drawing from his classic work on grief reactions, states that mourners have a strong preoccupation with feelings of guilt. "The bereaved searches the time before the death for evidence of failure to do right by the lost one. He accuses himself of negligence and exaggerates minor omissions. After the [Cocoanut Grove] fire disaster the central topic of discussion for a young married woman was the fact that her husband died after he left her following a quarrel, and a young man whose wife died was preoccupied with having fainted too soon to save her" (p. 336). It appears that when victimization is defined in terms of the loss of others (especially those close to oneself), then self-blame and self-accusations are common features of one's psychological reaction to the loss.

Like the victims of accidents, crimes, and diseases, the survivors of personal or large-scale disasters appear to engage in self-blame attributions. Although the relative frequency of self-blame attributions (compared with other causal explanations for accidents, crimes, disease, and disaster) is virtually impossible to ascertain, sufficient evidence seems to exist to suggest that self-blame is at least not àn uncommon response to misfortune. Pointing an accusatory finger at oneself enables an individual to explain why he or she, in particular, was singled out for misfortune. The adaptiveness of self-blame attributions in terms of coping success or failure will be examined as a separate issue in the following section, in terms of the individual's perceptions of vulnerability or invulnerability.

THE PERCEPTION OF PERSONAL INVULNERABILITY

The daily assumption that the world is meaningful and orderly is congruent with the widely held assumption, on the part of each individual, that he or she is relatively invulnerable ("It won't happen to me"). This belief in personal safety and freedom from misfortune may be responsible for the difficulty involved in getting people to heed warnings about serious risks such as lung cancer or nuclear accidents (cf. Janis, 1974). People underestimate the extent to which they are vulnerable to misfortunes such as accidents or diseases. In a study by Lang (1980), experimental subjects rated themselves as far less likely than the "average person" to develop any of a number of diseases (including pneumonia, diabetes, and leukemia). More recently, work by Weinstein (1980; Weinstein & Lachendro, 1982) has consistently shown that people overestimate the likelihood of positive events happening to them and underestimate the likelihood of negative events. Such "unrealistic optimism" (Weinstein, 1980) has also been discussed by Perloff (1983). In general, we operate on the basis of an "illusion of invulnerability." We may recognize that bad things happen, but we do not believe they will happen to us. When such a primary postulate as personal invulnerability is rudely shaken by the experience of a personal disaster such as a serious illness or injury, the victim is psychologically forced to contend not only with the question of meaning and order in the world, but also with the related issue of personal vulnerability.

The disaster literature attests to the difficulty people have in dealing with a new and unwelcome sense of vulnerability. Janis (1974), for example, concluded that "narrowly escaping from danger, losing close friends or relatives, and witnessing maimed bodies appear to have the effect of shattering the entire set of psychological defenses involved in maintaining expectations of personal invulnerability" (p. 162). Mechanic (1972, 1978) similarly argues that such "near-miss" experiences severely undermine a sense of invulnerability that is necessary for "psychological survival." Lifton (1967, 1971), in his study of the survivors of Hiroshima, declared,

> What needs to be emphasized is the survivor's having experienced a *jarring awareness of the fact of death*, as well as its extent and violence. Not only has any pre-existing illusion of invulnerability been shattered, but he has been confronted with his own mortality . . . . This sense of heightened vulnerability strongly affects the survivor's overall sense of the world around him. (Lifton, 1967, p. 481)

According to Wolfenstein (1957), disaster victims feel that anything may now happen to them. Bard and Sangrey (1979) discussed the problem of vulnerability experienced by the victim of crime. Even when a wallet or purse is taken without physical injury, the victim is rudely reminded of his or her vulnerability in a world that was heretofore perceived as safe.

Social psychological formulations regarding individuals' reactions to victims of misfortune provide some interesting insights into the significance of maintaining a sense of relative invulnerability. Research on the just world hypothesis (e.g., Lerner, 1970, 1971; Lerner & Miller, 1978; Lerner & Simmons, 1966), for example, has demonstrated that observers blame innocent victims for their plight. According to just world theorists, this derogation of victims derives from a fundamental need of the individual to believe in a just world, a world in which people get what they deserve, and deserve what they get. In this manner, it appears, people can operate in their world with a quasi-guarantee that if they are good people and do good deeds, desirable outcomes will be theirs. A perception of invulnerability is implicit in the theory and its findings, for in blaming innocent victims, an observer is able to maintain a belief that he or she, by virtue of good character or acts, will not be vulnerable to a similar misfortune. Walster (1966) addressed the vulnerability issue in stating that people blame victims in an effort to believe that a similar misfortune will not befall them. In Walster's formulation, blaming derives from a need to believe in a controllable rather than a just world; individuals want to believe that serious misfortune is avoidable.

Sociological studies of people's reactions to disasters also lend some support to the contention that a state of vulnerability is undesirable. Bucher (1957), in her studies of individuals who experienced community disasters (e.g., communities in which several plane crashes had occurred), found that the tendency to place responsibility for the disasters was primarily dictated by where people saw the power to remedy the situation. "It was not instrumentality in causing the crashes which determined responsibility but ability to do something to prevent their recurrence" (Bucher, 1957, p. 471; cf. Drabeck & Quarantelli, 1967, on the effects of personalizing blame). From this perspective, the assessment of blame and responsibility appears directly linked to people's desire to minimize their own vulnerability in the future; they are less concerned with who/what caused the disaster, than with who/what can prevent it from occurring again.

Symptoms of psychological distress are frequently manifested by an individual whose sense of personal invulnerability has been shattered. For example, Wolfenstein (1957) stated that subjective near-miss situations are associated with subsequent emotional disturbances as a result of a lost sense of safety. According to Janis (1974), among the symptoms displayed are excessive fear, acute anxiety, and maladaptive hypervigilance, symptoms similar to those described in investigations of acute war neurosis. In a series of studies of traumatized soldiers and flyers, for example, Grinker and Spiegel (1945) have demonstrated that individuals who have lost a sense of personal invulnerability tend to severely overreact to mild threats. While these men generally had high morale and great confidence about their survival abilities at the beginning of their service, they gradually began to lose this sense of personal safety. This loss was especially apparent after missions involving narrow escapes, and after seeing their friends shot down. The authors reported that the individuals they studied experienced a basic change in self-confidence and an unnerving sense of helplessness; their ability to fly deteriorated dramatically and their attitudes changed from "nothing terrible will happen to me" to "something terrible is bound to happen to me" (Grinker & Spiegel, 1945). Similarly, in a questionnaire study of 544 flyers (officers) who had completed their tour of combat duty, Grinker, Willerman, Bradley, and Fastovsky (1946) found evidence of a direct relationship between loss of a sense of personal invulnerability and "acute neurotic symptoms."

While the relationship between perceptions of personal vulnerability and psychological symptoms such as acute anxiety has been examined in studies of war neurosis, the relationship between the loss of invulnerability and poor coping has more recently been recognized by Weisman (1979) in his work with cancer patients. For Weisman, vulnerability is associated with emotional distress:

> Distress is difficult to measure and evaluate. Like pain, it is vivid, private, and almost impossible to describe adequately. The concept of "vulnerability" is intended to designate different types, degrees, and fluctuations of distress over time. Because it is inversely related to coping, vulnerability is also an implicit measure of noncoping . . . The central core of vulnerability is a condition of helpless uncertainty. I call it *existential despair*. (pp. 56, 63)

Depression may in part be a psychological reaction to feelings of vulnerability. The "illusion of control" (Langer, 1975), which is generally observed among nondepressives, implicitly involves a perception of invulnerability. One is safe and will obtain positive outcomes because one has control over these outcomes. A number of investigators (Alloy & Abramson, 1979; Golin, Terrell, & Johnson, 1977; Golin, Terrell, Weitz, & Drost, 1979) have documented that depressives are less likely to manifest this "illusion of control" than nondepressives; the latter are more likely to believe they have control when in fact they do not. Despite what may be greater accuracy in perception, depressives appear to be defined by a decreased sense of personal control (see Seligman, 1975) and a markedly increased sense of vulnerability.

There appears to be some evidence, then, that an individual's loss of his or her sense of invulnerability entails a difficult psychological adjustment. Although some feeling of vulnerability may be important in dealing effectively with realistic dangers or risks, a heightened sense of vulnerability seems to have negative psychological effects. Whether the loss of a sense of invulnerability results in acute anxiety, hypervigilance, distress, depression, or despair, there appear to be maladaptive emotional concomitants of regarding oneself as vulnerable to misfortune. While attributions may arise as a response to "Why?" or "Why me?" queries following personal misfortunes, the extent to which one's attributions enable an individual to maintain a sense of invulnerability may provide a clue to the relative adaptiveness of particular attributional responses. Thus, we would argue that to the extent that an attribution for a personal misfortune or disaster (e.g., accidents, criminal victimizations, disease) enables an individual to believe in his or her relative invulnerability in the future, the attribution will be associated with positive coping and an adpative response in the aftermath of the accident or disease; to the extent that an attribution increases a sense of vulnerability, the attribution will be associated with maladaptive coping.

THE ADAPTIVE/MALADAPTIVE NATURE OF SELF-BLAME

Although self-blame is a common reaction to personal disaster, it is not necessarily a psychologically adaptive response to misfortune. Self-blame attributions do appear to play a functional role in allowing individuals to account for the selective incidence of personal misfortune, the problem of meaning implicit in the question "Why me?" However, while self-blame attributions may help victims "solve" the problem of meaning and order in the world, they must still contend with the problem of personal vulnerability. The victims' former sense of safety and invulnerability has been threatened, perhaps severely, and they must attempt to rebuild a world view that promotes a perception of their own safety and relative invulnerability. The question at hand, then, is the extent to which self-blame fosters or hinders the individuals' efforts to recover a sense of relative safety and invulnerability; in other words, is self-blame adaptive or maladaptive?

In their study of paralyzed accident victims, Bulman and Wortman (1977) investigated the relationship between victims' attributions and coping. The respondents were asked a number of questions designed to probe their attributions for the accidents. Assessments of victims' coping were made independently by both a nurse and a social worker who worked with each accident victim. For present purposes, the importance of the study lies in its findings regarding self-blame. Multivariate analyses indicated that blaming other people was a very strong predictor of poor coping and that self-blame was a strong predictor of good coping. This study of accident victims, though exploratory, suggested that those who cope well with a misfortune tend to be individuals who blame themselves and not others.

Bulman and Wortman's (1977) study thus provided some evidence for the adaptive value of self-blame. Their results are consistent with the conclusions of Chodoff, Friedman, and Hamburg (1964), in their study of the coping behavior of the parents of children with leukemia. These authors concluded that parents' self-blame—the belief that the disease was caused by something they did or failed to do—facilitated coping, by denying the painful conclusions that nothing could affect the disease and no one was responsible.

However, these results directly contradict the conclusions of Abrams and Finesinger (1953), who suggested that the self-blame attributions of many cancer patients lead to debilitating feelings of guilt and inferiority, which impair the coping process. The view of self-blame as an adaptive mechanism also appears to contradict both the popular conception of self-blame and the view held by depression theorists such as Beck (1967), who regard self-blame as a symptom of depression. Beck (1967) has found that the depressive manifests "perseverating self-blame" and is

> particularly prone to ascribe adverse occurrences to some deficiency in himself. . . . In the more severe cases, the patient may blame himself for happenings that are in no way connected with him, and abuse himself in a savage manner. . . . In mild cases, the patient is prone to blame and criticize himself when he falls short of his rigid perfectionistic standards. (p. 24)

Given the strong association between self-blame and depression, how can the results of Bulman and Wortman (1977) and the conclusions drawn by Chodoff, Friedman, and Hamburg (1964) be explained?

Two Types of Self-blame

Janoff-Bulman (1979) attempted to reconcile these apparent inconsistencies by positing that there are, in fact, two distinct types of self-blame, one representing an adaptive response, the other a maladaptive one. *Behavioral* self-blame consists of blaming one's own behaviors for the occurrence of negative outcomes. In contrast, *characterological* self-blame consists of blaming one's own character or enduring qualities for the occurrence of negative outcomes. Reactions to rape illustrate the difference between these two types of self-blame. A rape victim may blame herself for having walked alone at night, for having hitchhiked, or for having let a particular man into her apartment; in these instances, the woman is engaging in behavioral self-blame. A woman who blames herself characterologically might blame herself for being too trusting, a bad person, or the "type of person who attracts rapists."

An important distinction between behavioral and characterological self-blame concerns the perceived *controllability* (i.e., modifiability through one's own efforts) of the factor(s) blamed. This difference in controllability suggests that the two types of self-blame may have very different implications for victims' perceptions of their future vulnerability to or control over events. Individuals who blame themselves behaviorally can believe that by altering their behavior in the future, they will be able to avoid a recurrence of the misfortune. Those who blame themselves characterologically are apt to focus on some personal deficiency that they regard as relatively nonmodifiable and uncontrollable. In fact, Janoff-Bulman (1979) suggested that individuals who blame their behavior are concerned with the future avoidability of the negative outcome, whereas individuals who blame their character are more concerned with the issue of deservingness for past outcomes.[2]

Janoff-Bulman (1979) noted that the future-oriented concerns of behavioral self-blamers need not focus exclusively on the future avoidability of the negative outcomes for which the attributor is blaming himself or herself; rather behavioral self-blame may promote a general belief in one's ability to avoid negative outcomes in the future. For example, the paralyzed victims in the Bulman and Wortman (1977) study were apt to be better copers if they blamed themselves. However, self-blame was more likely to be in the service of a general belief in future control (e.g., I'll be able to improve my physical condition through physical therapy) rather than a more specific belief in the future avoidability of their own paralysis, which was medically regarded as irreversible in all cases.

The distinction between behavioral and characterological self-blame may resolve the controversy about whether or not self-blame is adaptive (cf. Miller & Porter, 1983). Behavioral self-blame is adaptive, for it enables an individual

---

2. It is interesting to note a parallel in the orientations of helpless versus mastery-oriented children as observed by Diener and Dweck (1978). These researchers investigated a number of achievement-related cognitions of these two groups and concluded that helpless children focus on the cause of their failure, while mastery-oriented children focus on possible remedies. These differences correspond to the hypothesized differences between individuals who engage in characterological versus behavioral self-blame; it is proposed that the former focus on the past and their deservingness, whereas the latter focus on the future and what they can do to avoid a recurrence of the misfortune.

to reestablish a sense of invulnerability and perceived control (see, e.g., Bowers, 1968; Glass & Singer, 1972; Langer & Rodin, 1976; Schulz, 1976, for evidence of the advantages of perceived control). In contrast, characterological self-blame is "maladaptive"; it not only precludes a sense of invulnerability and control, but is associated with harsh self-criticism, low self-esteem, and perceptions of helplessness (Abramson, Seligman, & Teasdale, 1978).

Research on attributions for achievement-related outcomes supports the conceptual analysis of the differential adaptiveness of the two types of self-blame. The distinction between characterological and behavioral self-blame corresponds to a distinction drawn by Weiner and his colleagues (Weiner *et al.*, 1971) in their attributional schema for achievement outcomes. In the case of failure, for example, individuals who make internal attributions (i.e., attributions to themselves) can point to their own lack of effort (regarded as an unstable cause) or to their own lack of ability (regarded as a stable cause). Individuals who make an effort attribution can believe that as long as they try harder, they will be able to alter their outcomes in a positive manner and succeed; those who make an ability attribution, however, are not likely to believe that there is much they can do to change the achievement situation and thereby succeed (see Dweck, 1975). Moreover, individuals who engage in ability attributions are likely to give up in the face of failure, whereas those who make effort attributions are likely to persist (Weiner *et al.*, 1971). Effort attributions for failure correspond to behavioral self-blame for misfortune, in that both attributions foster a perception of outcomes as personally controllable and modifiable. In contrast, ability attributions resemble characterological self-blame, in that they imply that outcomes are uncontrollable and nonmodifiable.

The taxonomic scheme developed by Abramson *et al.* (1978) in their reformulation of learned helplessness can further inform the distinction between behavioral and characterological self-blame. Using their schema, behavioral self-blame is an internal, unstable, specific attribution, whereas characterological self-blame is an internal, stable, global attribution. While Abramson *et al.* (1978) implied that external, unstable, specific attributions are most adaptive by suggesting that therapy for depressives should involve changes toward these attributions, the present analysis suggests that such attributions will be most adaptive only in those cases in which individuals can simultaneously maintain a belief in future invulnerability; people could believe they are protected from misfortune without suffering the slightest feelings of regret or self-censure. Because people's expectations for the future, however, are likely to be strongly associated with their attributions for past misfortunes (e.g., attributions that imply control in the past will imply control in the future), internal, unstable, specific attributions (i.e., behavioral self-blame) rather than external, unstable, specific attributions may be most adaptive in many cases. In fact, in their most recent reformulation of the "hopelessness theory of depression," Abramson, Metalsky, and Alloy (1987, and Chapter 2, this volume) present behavioral self-blame as adaptive and predict that it will protect against depression in the face of negative events. Characterological self-blame (internal, stable, and global), not behavioral self-blame, should be the type of attribution manifested by depressives.[3]

EMPIRICAL SUPPORT: STUDIES ON DEPRESSION AND RAPE

Janoff-Bulman (1979) conducted a study to determine whether characterological, rather than behavioral, self-blame is a distinguishing characteristic of depressed individuals. The participants were 120 university women who were divided into depressed and nondepressed groups based on their responses to the Zung Self-Rating Depression Scale (Zung, 1965). The participants read four scenarios describing various negative outcomes and were asked to imagine that they had actually experienced each of the outcomes. The situations, in which the role of the target person was intentionally ambiguous, involved a car accident, rejection by a friend, rejection by a lover, and letting a friend down. After reading each scenario, participants indicated the extent to which they blamed themselves, other people, the environment (i.e., impersonal world), and chance, for each of the situations described; they also indicated how much they blamed themselves for the kind of person they are (characterological blame) and for what they did (behavioral blame). A summed score for each dependent measure was calculated across the four scenarios.

The results supported Janoff-Bulman's (1979) distinction between the two types of self-blame. The depressed and nondepressed groups did not differ in the amount of blame they attributed to themselves in general, nor did they differ in the amount of behavioral self-blame reported. However, the two groups did differ significantly in the amount of characterological self-blame reported, with the depressed women reporting more characterological self-blame than the nondepressed women. The depressed group also blamed chance significantly more than did the nondepressed group, and a marginally significant difference emerged for deservingness, with the depressed group reporting greater deservingness than the nondepressed group. Additional analyses indicated that those who engaged in low characterological self-blame reported

3. Abramson and Sackeim (1977) presented the "paradox in depression" in discussing the theories of Beck (1967) and Seligman (1975). The paradox involves the conjunction of both helplessness and self-blaming symptom patterns on the part of depressed individuals—that is, how can individuals blame themselves for outcomes over which they have no control? According to Janoff-Bulman (1979), this paradox is resolved if depressed individuals blame themselves characterologically. In such instances, depressed individuals blame themselves for negative outcomes because of the kind of people they perceive themselves to be; such an attribution entails a belief in the nonmodifiability of the factor blamed (i.e., their character) and thus in the uncontrollability of negative outcomes. It is as if they are being punished for who they are.

significantly less deservingness than those who engaged in high characterological self-blame; conversely, those who engaged in low behavioral self-blame believed less in the future avoidability of the outcomes than did those who engaged in high behavioral self-blame. This study revealed that when self-blame was regarded as a single entity, no differences were found between depressed and nondepressed groups. When self-blame was distinguished in terms of its focus on character or behavior, however, differences emerged, such that the depressed and nondepressed groups differed in terms of characterological self-blame, but not behavioral self-blame.[4] Some support was also found for the relationship between characterological self-blame and perceived deservingness, and between behavioral self-blame and perceived avoidability.

Further empirical support for the usefulness of the self-blame distinctions in differentiating depressed and nondepressed groups was provided in a study by Peterson, Schwartz, and Seligman (1981). Using the Beck Depression Inventory (Beck, Ward, Mendelson, Mock, & Erbaugh, 1961) to classify subjects, these researchers presented 87 university women with a questionnaire that briefly described 6 good events and 18 bad events (e.g., "You do a project which is highly praised"; "You meet a friend who acts hostilely to you"). The subjects were asked to imagine themselves in the situations and to write the major cause of the event in the space provided. The subjects also rated the perceived internality, stability, and globality of the attributed cause, and the helplessness and guilt they would feel if the event happened to them. Judges blind to subjects' depression scores coded the open-ended attributions as external, behavioral, or characterological.

The results of the study indicated that while behavioral and external attributions for bad events were negatively correlated with depression scores, characterological attributions for negative events were positively correlated with depression scores. Moreover, additional analyses revealed that characterological attributions for bad events were perceived as more stable and global than behavioral attributions, and events attributed to behavioral factors were perceived as more controllable (as determined from the helplessness ratings) than events attributed to either characterological or external factors. These

---

4. The results of this study would have been more compelling if the nondepressed group had been observed to engage in more behavioral self-blame than the depressed group. It can be argued, however, that the behavioral self-blame exhibited by the depressed and nondepressed groups differed in an important way; for the depressed group, behavioral self-blame was manifested in conjunction with characterological self-blame. When behavioral self-blame occurs with characterological self-blame, it may represent an extension of characterological self-blame (e.g., "I am a stupid person and therefore do stupid things"), whereas when behavioral self-blame occurs alone, it does not reflect decreased self-esteem, but rather the belief that one's behavior is modifiable. In the former case, the individual may be less likely to regard the behavior as controllable and modifiable. Thus, it may not be possible to blame oneself characterologically without also blaming oneself behaviorally, whereas it is likely that people can blame themselves behaviorally without blaming themselves characterologically.

results provide further support for the contention that characterological self-blame is maladaptive and associated with depression; behavioral self-blame, on the other hand, does not appear to be associated with depession, and does not seem to fit the popular view of self-blame as a maladaptive psychological state.

Given two types of self-blame, one adaptive and one maladaptive, is the self-blame expressed by the victims of misfortune largely of a characterological or a behavioral nature? Rape, a victimizing event for which self-blame reactions have been well-documented, may provide a useful area in which to examine this question. The concept of masochism has been invoked frequently in an effort to account for the pervasiveness of self-blame following rape (see, e.g., Brownmiller, 1975). The image of women as helpless and masochistic may serve to account for the phenomenon of self-blame, but it entirely overlooks the possibility that self-blame by victims of rape may represent an adaptive response, an attempt to reestablish control following the traumatic experience. Researchers have found that a feeling of vulnerability and loss of control over one's life is a common reaction to rape (Bard & Ellison, 1974; Bryant & Cirel, 1977). Perhaps in blaming herself the rape victim is engaging in a type of self-blame that maximizes a belief in personal control—behavioral rather than characterological self-blame.

In an effort to determine which type of self-blame is more frequently exhibited by rape victims, Janoff-Bulman (1979) surveyed rape crisis centers across the United States. Questionnaires were mailed to 120 centers; 30 questionnaires were returned "addressee unknown," and of the remaining 90 centers, 48 completed and returned the questionnaire. Recipients of the questionnaire were asked to base their responses on their experiences as counselors of rape victims. Aside from some general questions about their center, the questions dealt primarily with the issue of self-blame. The respondents were asked to indicate the total percentage of women they counsel who blame themselves, at least in part, for the rape, the percentage who blame themselves behaviorally ("Of the rape victims you see, what percentage blame themselves for the rape because of some behavior [act or omission] they engaged in at the time of or immediately prior to the rape?"), and the percentage who blame themselves characterologically ("Of the rape victims you see, what percentage blame themselves for the rape because of some character trait or personality 'flaw' they believe they have?"). A few examples of each type of blame were provided, and the respondents were asked to cite examples from their counseling experiences of each type of self-blame.

While the rape crisis centers that responded varied markedly in size, the mean number of victims counseled by the centers was 335. In general, self-blame was reported as quite common; an average of 74 percent of the rape victims seen by the centers were reported to have blamed themselves, at least in part, for the rape. Of those who blamed themselves, however, behavioral self-blame was far more frequently expressed than characterological self-blame; an average of 69 percent blamed themselves behaviorally, whereas an average of 19 percent blamed themselves characterologically. While many respondents indicated that they had never considered distinguishing between self-blame focusing on character and behavior, respectively, the examples provided by the rape crisis centers confirmed that they were readily able to distinguish between them. Frequently mentioned examples of behavioral self-blame included the following statements: I should not have hitchhiked; I should not have walked alone; I should not have gone up to his apartment; I should have locked my car; I should not have left my window open; I should not have let someone I didn't know into my apartment. Frequently cited examples of characterological self-blame included these comments: I'm too naive and gullible; I'm the kind of person who attracts trouble; I'm not a very aware person; I'm immature and can't take care of myself; I'm not a good judge of character; I'm a bad person. It is worth noting that examples of behavioral self-blame were, without exception, reported in the past tense (i.e., I should/should not have), whereas examples of characterological self-blame were reported in the present tense (I am/am not), perhaps implicitly indicating the presumed modifiability of factors associated with the two types of self-blame.

The results of this survey of rape crisis centers indicate that while the majority of rape victims blame themselves following the rape, the focus of this blame is generally a behavioral act of omission occurring at the time of (or immediately prior to) the rape. Fewer than one-fifth of the women were reported to have blamed themselves characterologically, a finding that raises serious questions about the "popular" view of the rape victim as masochistic.[5] One type of self-blame—behavioral self-blame—is most characteristic of the rape victim following her victimization. Apart from evidence that it is not associated with depression, is there support for the proposition that behavioral self-blame is associated with effective coping?

The results of a study conducted by Burgess and Holmstrom (1979) and reported in *The New York Times* (Bennets, 1978) provides evidence pertinent to this question, despite the fact that these researchers did not themselves

---

5. An important criticism that could be raised about this survey is that a self-selected population of behavioral self-blamers may be served by rape crisis centers. While this may be true, it should be recognized that the research literature on reactions to rape is based almost exclusively on the reactions of women who seek help after rape (at crisis centers or women's centers) or consent to be interviewed (also a self-selected group), and not on those who attempt to keep their reactions to themselves. The documented pervasiveness of self-blame in the rape literature is therefore based on a population likely to be very similar to the sample in this study. The negative image of the masochistic rape victim who blames herself for the rape thus derives from a population similar to that served by the rape crisis centers surveyed. Further, it is conceivable that those who have had the least difficulty coping (and who are apt to blame themselves behaviorally) are also underrepresented in the rape crisis center population. Perhaps it is sufficient to point out that within the population of women served by rape crisis centers, self-blame has improperly been interpreted as self-derogating and masochistic rather than as a potentially positive attempt to reestablish control.

distinguish between types of self-blame. They interviewed 146 rape victims over a 5-year period and concluded that one important determinant of the coping success of the victim was the style of the rape attack. Burgess and Holmstrom (1974a) classified rapes into two types: The "blitz" attack in which the woman is raped without warning by an individual she does not know, and the "confidence" rape, in which the victim has had at least some prior interaction with the rapist. According to their findings, a high percentage of the women who have not recovered from the attack after 5 years had experienced a blitz attack; women who were surprised and raped in their own bedrooms, in fact, had the most difficulty recovering.

> Such an experience haunts a woman with the feeling, "If I'm not safe in my own bed, then where am I safe in this world?" She had not done anything to deserve the attack, couldn't have done anything to prevent it, and the random meaninglessness of such an experience proved extremely difficult for the woman to accept." (Bennets, 1978, p. A16)

For women who were involved in confidence rapes, coping seemed to be an easier process. Burgess and Holmstrom provide the example of a woman who was walking and was pulled into a man's car when she stopped to give him directions. "She could tell herself later, 'that was a dumb thing to do, I shouldn't have done that.' When a woman can make some rational explanation for what happened to her, she seems to recover better" (cited in Bennets, 1978, p. A16). The findings of Burgess and Holmstrom (1979) illustrate the victim's strong sense of vulnerability and need for meaning following rape, and also suggest that the woman who believes she should have acted differently is the woman who has the least difficulty in coping. This is the woman who engages in behavioral self-blame.

These conclusions are further supported by the findings of Scheppele and Bart (1983), in their study of women's recovery following rape. Based on in-depth interviews with 94 women who had been raped, these researchers concluded that the women's perceptions of the safety of the situation in which the attack took place dramatically influenced the women's coping responses. Those women who were raped in situations that they had defined as safe were those who were most likely to have severe, negative reactions to the rape. These women were most apt to manifest a "total fear reaction," which involved considerable psychological distress and disruption. Citing Janoff-Bulman's (1979) work on behavioral self-blame, Scheppele and Bart (1983) concluded,

> Perhaps one of the reasons why being attacked in safe circumstances leads to such a greatly altered perception is that it is harder to use "behavioral self-blame" as a way of reestablishing control . . . . If women are attacked in situations where they thought they were safe (where their conduct was "blameless"), then there may seem to be little else the women can do to prevent the event from happening in the future . . . . Blaming one's own behavior by understanding that the situation posed a risk may be an adaptive response to a bad circumstance. (Scheppele & Bart, 1983, p. 79)

Behavioral self-blame attributions not only provide an explanation for the rape (as does characterological self-blame), but allow the women to minimize their perceptions of personal vulnerability by permitting them to maintain a belief in control over their world and, specifically, over the possible recurrence of rape. Certainly, situations vary in the extent to which they allow for behavioral self-blame attributions, but the woman who engages in behavioral self-blame is likely to cope more effectively than the woman who engages in characterological self-blame.

In general, behavioral self-blame seems to be positively associated with improved adjustment following rape (cf. Meyer & Taylor, 1986) and is not the type of self-blame that is symptomatic of depression. Recent empirical research conducted with victims of diseases and accidents has also found that behavioral self-blame is, in fact, an adaptive response to these victimizations, in that it is associated with positive coping outcomes (e.g., Affleck, Allen, Tennen, McGrade, & Ratzan, 1985; Affleck, McGrade, Allen, & McQueeney, 1985; Baum, Flemming, & Singer, 1983; Tennen, Affleck, & Gershman, 1986; Tennen, Affleck, Allen, McGrade, & Ratzan, 1984; Timko & Janoff-Bulman, 1985; cf. Kiecolt-Glaser & Williams, in press).

In considering the adaptive nature of behavioral self-blame, one might question whether behavioral self-blame is related to self-esteem and locus of control. Is behavioral self-blame associated with individuals who have high self-esteem and beliefs in internal control, or rather with individuals who have low self-esteem and external control beliefs? The former finding would suggest an association between positive coping and behavioral self-blame, whereas the latter would suggest that this type of blame is maladaptive.

To study the personality correlates of the two types of self-blame, Janoff-Bulman (1982) conducted an analogue study in which 168 women first completed the Janis–Field Feelings of Inadequacy Scale (Eagly, 1967) and the Rotter Internal–External Locus of Control Scale (Rotter, 1966), and then read one of two lengthy, detailed accounts of a rape, which were first-person accounts derived from actual rapes as reported by rape victims (Russell, 1975). Following their reading of the account, the respondents indicated the extent of their agreement with 12 statements, 6 of which were specifically designed to measure behavioral self-blame (e.g., I shouldn't have gone back to his apartment with him), and 6 specifically designed to assess characterological self-blame (e.g., I'm the kind of person who attracts trouble), and also indicated their perceptions of the future avoidability of a rape recurrence. Each respondent read the scenario and dependent measures either as the victim or as an observer. Overall, those in the victim condition engaged in more behavioral self-blame and less characterological self-blame than observers; further, behavioral self-blame was directly related to perceptions of future avoidability. Most important, in the victim condition respondents who were high in self-esteem and internal control beliefs engaged in the most behavioral self-blame, whereas those with low self-esteem and low internal control (i.e., external control) beliefs engaged in the most characterological self-blame.

This study provided some support for a view of behavioral self-blame as adaptive in comparison with characterological self-blame. It should be noted that the relationship between the personality measures and the two types of self-blame indicates that the type of self-blame in which an individual engages may actually be part of the larger personality cluster defining an individual. However, even if an individual's attributions and coping are more or less independently determined by personality characteristics, this would not preclude the possibility that therapeutic attempts to alter attributions from characterological to behavioral self-blame may be clinically adaptive for the individual (cf. Dweck, 1975). Certainly, self-blame attributions may be more malleable and directly modifiable than self-esteem or internal–external control beliefs, and may thus be an important preliminary step in helping victims to cope with the feeling of vulnerability arising from their traumatic experiences.

THE ISSUE OF "OBJECTIVE" VULNERABILITY

The prevalence of self-blame attributions following accidents, disease, and criminal victimizations becomes comprehensible as one recognizes the adaptive value of behavioral self-blame. While the need for meaning maximizes the probability that a victim will make an attribution, the attempt to answer "Why me?" will bias the given attribution to be internal. The adaptive nature of behavioral self-blame may, in turn, bias the given internal attribution to be behavioral rather than characterological. The adaptiveness of behavioral self-blame lies in the positive implications of this attribution for a perception of future invulnerability. In hypothesizing a relationship between perceived vulnerability and behavioral self-blame, however, it is important to consider the distinction between *perceived* vulnerability and a more "objective" sense of vulnerability; that is, the difference between individuals' perceptions of the likelihood that negative events will happen to them, and the actual likelihood. From the perspective of "objective" vulnerability, behavioral self-blame may not be very adaptive if, in fact, the individual is quite likely to experience the misfortune again, regardless of his or her attributions. An important question to consider, then, is whether attributions (particularly behavioral self-blame) can positively affect the actual course of future personal outcomes, so that the person who engages in behavioral self-blame is, in fact, less vulnerable and less susceptible to future victimizations.

It is possible that the advantages of behavioral self-blame are not limited to decreased perceptions of vulnerability by the victim, but include a decrease in actual vulnerability. While this link between attributions and vulnerability is certainly a tenuous one, there are at least two ways in which attributions could positively affect personal outcomes by reducing an individual's vulnerability:

One way involves a behavioral route to victimization avoidance, the other involves a psychological–biological route.

The behavioral route to decreased vulnerability is straightforward: If individuals blame themselves for behaviors believed to have brought about their initial misfortune, they will, presumably, alter their behavior to be consistent with safer prospects in the future. This behavior change option is particularly appropriate when the misfortune was a discrete event, with a relatively clear-cut beginning and end, such as a criminal victimization. Certain diseases also lend themselves to behavior change; heart disease, usually dramatically manifested in the relatively discrete event of the heart attack, is a case in point. Following a heart attack, individuals who blame themselves for having engaged in specific behaviors (e.g., overeating to obesity, eating high cholesterol foods) or for having failed to engage in specific behaviors (e.g., not exercising, not spending enough time away from an office and occupational pressures) may alter their behavior to be consistent with better health. Because there is empirical evidence, based on prospective studies, that factors such as obesity, lack of physical activity, life stresses, and a diet high in cholesterol do contribute to coronary risk status (Henderson, Hall, & Lipton, 1979), such behavior change on the part of the heart attack victim would presumably be adaptive and reduce the future risk of recurrence.

In the case of criminal victimizations, behavior change is also apt to be effective in reducing the risks of recurrence. A man who is mugged when walking through a particular neighborhood alone at night might blame himself for having done so, and is likely to attempt to alter his behavior so that in the future he walks with others, uses other means of transportation, or changes his route. Newcomers to cities who are mugged or robbed, frequently adopt new behaviors consistent with "city survival tactics." The woman who is raped while hitchhiking may be less likely to engage in this behavior in the future. Certainly, however, victimizations are never entirely avoidable by the victim, although the probability may be reduced. Unfortunately for the victims of crime, changing behavior to reduce the risk of victimization often involves a curtailment of their personal freedom, with no guarantee of safety. An individual may decide that the cost of changing his or her behavior may not be worth the reduction in risk.

The behavior change route to victimization avoidance thus involves a direct link between causal attributions for the past victimization and consequent changes in behavior. In general, the individual seeks to alter the probability of a future recurrence of the same victimization. It is conceivable that even when a repetition of the misfortune is not a possibility because the negative effects are irreversible (e.g., paralysis), behavioral self-blame may still serve a positive adaptive function via behavioral change. For example, in the study of paralyzed accident victims, it was found that those who engaged in self-blame were more likely to be actively involved in attempts to ameliorate their situation; they appeared to work hardest in physical therapy to improve their chances of moving from wheelchairs to crutches and braces (Bulman & Wortman, 1977). Perhaps blaming one's behavior for a past misfortune enables an individual to believe not only in his or her instrumentality in avoiding the same misfortune in the future but also in improving his or her future situation in general.

The second way in which behavioral self-blame attributions may affect actual, as well as perceived, vulnerability—via a psychological–biological route—is far less direct than the link from attributions to behavior change to decreased vulnerability. The basis for this second perspective is the assumption that an individual's psychological state plays a role in the etiology and course of disease and thereby affects actual vulnerability. An individual who engages in behavioral self-blame is apt to continue to believe in a world in which outcomes, at least in part, are determined by one's own efforts. By evoking beliefs in relative invulnerability and personal control, behavioral self-blame contributes to a healthier psychological state which, in turn, may lead to a decrease in the actual vulnerability of the individual. While behavior change operates most satisfactorily in the case of discrete victimizing events, the psychological–biological route is more likely to play a significant role when the misfortune involves less discrete, long-term, and generally health-related outcomes.

The significance of an optimistic outlook and a positive state of mind in curing and/or avoiding disease is becoming increasingly recognized. Frank (1975), a Johns Hopkins physician, has written that the psychological state of the patient is related to recovery and that a destructive mental state will keep an individual from recovering. Such a perspective has recently been popularized by Norman Cousins (1979) in his best-selling book about his recovery from a presumably fatal disease. In addition to massive doses of Vitamin C, Cousins's therapy involved attempts to maintain a positive emotional state. Work by medical researchers such as Engel (1968) and Schmale (1972) emphasized the significance of psychological state in disease onset. These researchers proposed that if feelings of helplessness and hopelessness develop in individuals following an actual or threatened loss, disease is likely to result. Thus, the "giving-up–given-up complex," as it has been labeled, is a psychological state of mind which is believed to mediate the onset of disease. Recent studies on the course of cancer offer additional suggestive evidence that "giving up" may be a destructive mental state with regard to physical health; there is some evidence that emotional expressiveness, perhaps indicating a willingness to "fight" rather than give up, is associated with a longer survival rate from cancer (Cohen, 1979).

Despite the increasing medical and anecdotal evidence suggesting a relationship between psychological state and physical health (i.e., disease onset or recovery), the precise manner in which psychological states are translated biologically into a physical state of health remains largely an open question. Models linking psychology, biology, and disease have often involved stress as an important factor. Thus, Selye (1956) argued that psychological and physical stressors bring about a "general adaptation syndrome" (which includes increased output of adrenal cortical hormones); this in turn lowers bodily resistance, which, if prolonged, leads to illness. To Schmale (1972), the psychological–biological link entails a "conservation-withdrawal reaction," involving the repulsion of nutritive substances by organic cells, which in turn leads to increased somatic vulnerability. Other models more generally postulate increased output of hormones, which leads to decreased immunological response, which in turn lower body resistance and leads to the development of disease or its further progress (Cohen, 1979).

Although much additional research is necessary before the psychological–biological links regarding disease onset and progress are fully understood, there appears at this point to be growing acceptance of the notion that such a link may exist. If it is the case, then, that an individual's psychological state is an important mediator of physical health, there is reason to believe that attributions for misfortune that allow an individual to hold an optimistic outlook and positive emotional orientation are likely to be physically as well as psychologically adaptive. Rather than manifesting depression and "giving up," people who engage in behavioral self-blame are more likely to have a greater sense of personal control, leading, in turn, to increased optimism for future outcomes and maintaining a psychological state that protects them from the future onset of disease or from further progress of a current disease state. Thus, the decreased vulnerability perceived by individuals who blame their own behavior for illness may translate into an actual decrease in vulnerability to disease.

Clearly, much research is needed to clarify the relationships between self-blame and coping; for example, it is likely that behavioral self-blame can be taken to a maladaptive extreme (Janoff-Bulman & Brickman, 1982). However, self-blame should not be regarded as a monolithic concept, but rather as a label for two very distinct types of response. While characterological self-blame is consistent with the negative view of self-blame expressed both popularly and by depression theorists, a second type of self-blame—behavioral self-blame— appears to reflect a more positive psychological orientation. An individual who engages in characterological self-blame requires therapeutic interventions that emphasize the reestablishment of self-esteem and feelings of personal worth. An individual who expresses behavioral self-blame, on the other hand, is more apt to profit from interventions that emphasize the reestablishment of perceived personal control.

Behavioral self-blame represents an adaptive response following misfortune; in addition to satisfying the questions of meaning and selective incidence, it allows the individual to regain a sense of relative invulnerability, a psychological perception that is usually taken for granted, but which is generally shattered by a victimizing experience. Further, behavioral self-blame may not be adaptive only in terms of perceived vulnerability but may affect the actual future vulnerability of the individual, either through direct behavior change, or through psychological–biological links that are as yet not fully understood. Those who blame their own behavior following misfortunes such as accidents, crime, and disease should not be regarded as individuals who are engaging in a maladaptive psychological reaction; rather, their reactions may represent adaptive responses to highly stressful, negative events.

EPILOGUE

This chapter was originally written in June 1980. An attempt has been made to update references so that recent relevant work is cited. Although the authors still agree with the ideas presented in the chapter, we nevertheless now regard this analysis of behavioral self-blame as somewhat incomplete. A more thorough analysis, yet one which still maintains that behavioral self-blame is an adaptive response following victimization, involves an understanding of the role of behavioral self-blame in maintaining people's basic assumptions about themselves and the world, including assumptions about the benevolence and meaningfulness of the world and about one's self-worth. Central to such an analysis is the importance of maintaining or rebuilding a viable conceptual system, one that incorporates the "data" of the victimization, following a traumatic negative event. Discussions of the adaptive role of behavioral self-blame in light of people's basic conceptual systems can be found in Janoff-Bulman and Thomas (in press) and, briefly, in Janoff-Bulman (1985). The treatment of behavioral self-blame in this chapter is completely consistent with the newer perspective and is incorporated as a part of this newer analysis.

REFERENCES

Abrams, R. D., & Finesinger, J. E. (1953). Guilt reactions in patients with cancer. *Cancer, 6*, 474–482.
Abramson, L. Y., Metalsky, G. I., & Alloy, L. B. (1987). *The hopelessness theory of depression: A metatheoretical analysis with implications for psychopathology research.* Manuscript submitted for publication.
Abramson, L. Y., & Sackeim, H. A. (1977). A paradox in depression: Uncontrollability and self-blame. *Psychological Bulletin, 84*, 838–851.
Abramson, L. Y., Seligman, M. E. P., & Teasdale, J. D. (1978). Learned helplessness in humans: Critique and reformulation. *Journal of Abnormal Psychology, 87*, 49–74.
Affleck, G., Allen, D. A., Tennen, H., McGrade, B. J., & Ratzan, S. (1985). Causal and control cognitions in parent coping with a chronically ill child. *Journal of Social and Clinical Psychology, 3*, 369–379.

Affleck, G., McGrade, B. J., Allen D. A., & McQueeney, M. (1985). Mothers' beliefs about behavioral causes for their developmentally disabled infant's condition: What do they signify? *Journal of Pediatric Psychology, 10,* 193–303.

Alloy, L. B., & Abramson, L. Y. (1979). Judgment of contingency in depressed and nondepressed students: Sadder but wiser? *Journal of Experimental Psychology: General, 108,* 441–485.

Antonovsky, A. *Health, stress, and coping.* (1979). San Francisco: Jossey-Bass.

Bard, M., & Dyk, R. B. (1956). The psychodynamic significance of beliefs regarding the cause of serious illness. *Psychoanalytic Review, 43,* 146–162.

Bard, M., & Ellison, K. (1974). Crisis intervention and investigation of forcible rape. *The Police Chief, 41,* 68–73.

Bard, M., & Sangrey, D. (1979). *The crime victim's book.* New York: Basic.

Baum, A., Flemming, R., & Singer, J. E. (1983). Coping with victimization by technological disaster. *Journal of Social Issues, 39,* 119–140.

Beck, A. T. (1967). *Depression: Clinical, experimental, and theoretical aspects.* New York: Harper & Row.

Beck, A. T., Ward, C. H., Mendelson, M., Mock, J., & Erbaugh, J. (1961). An inventory for measuring depression. *Archives of General Psychiatry, 4,* 561–571.

Bennets, L. (1978, April 14). The type of attack affects rape victims' speed of recovery, study shows. *The New York Times,* p. A16.

Bettelheim, B. (1943). Individual and mass behavior in extreme situations. *Journal of Abnormal and Social Psychology, 38,* 417–452.

Bowers, K. (1968). Pain, anxiety, and perceived control. *Journal of Consulting and Clinical Psychology, 32,* 596–602.

Brickman, P., Rabinowitz, V. C., Karuza, J., Coates, D., Cohn, E., & Kidder, L. (1980). *Models of helping and coping.* Unpublished manuscript, University of Michigan, Ann Arbor, Michigan.

Brownmiller, S. (1975). *Against our will: Men, women, and rape.* New York: Simon & Schuster.

Bryant, G., & Cirel, P. (1977). *A community response to rape: An exemplary project (Polk County Rape/Sexual Assault Care Center).* Washington, DC: National Institute of Law Enforcement and Criminal Justice.

Bucher, R. (1957). Blame and hostility in disaster. *American Journal of Sociology, 62,* 467–475.

Bulman, R. J., & Wortman, C. B. (1977). Attributions of blame and coping in the "real world": Severe accident victims react to their lot. *Journal of Personality and Social Psychology, 35,* 351–363.

Burgess, A. W., & Holmstrom, L. L. (1979). Adaptive Strategies and recovery from rape. *American Journal of Psychiatry, 136,* 1278–1282.

Burgess, A. W., & Holmstrom, L. L. (1974a). *Rape: Victims of crisis.* Bowie, MD: Robert J. Brady.

Burgess, A. W., & Holmstrom, L. L. (1974b). Rape trauma syndrome. *American Journal of Psychiatry, 131,* 981–985.

Calhoun, L. G., Selby, J. W., & King, H. E. (1976). Abortion and rape: Problems unique to women. In L. G. Calhoun, J. W. Selby, & H. E. King (Eds.), *Dealing with crisis: A guide to critical life problems.* Englewood Cliffs, NJ: Prentice-Hall.

Chodoff, P. (1970). The German concentration camp as a psychological stress. *Archives of General Psychiatry, 22,* 78–87.

Chodoff, P., Friedman, S. B., & Hamburg, D. A. (1964). Stress, defenses, and coping behavior: Observations in parents of children with malignant diseases. *American Journal of Psychiatry, 120,* 743–749.

Cohen, F. (1979). Personality, stress, and the development of physical illness. In G. C. Stone, F. Cohen, & N. E. Adler (Eds.), *Health psychology.* San Francisco: Jossey-Bass.

Cousins, N. (1979). *Anatomy of an illness as perceived by the patient.* New York: Norton.

Davis, F. (1963). *Passage through crisis: Polio victims and their families.* Indianapolis: Bobbs-Merrill.

Diener, C. I., & Dweck, C. S. (1978). An analysis of learned helplessness: Continuous changes in performance, strategy, and achievement conditions following failure. *Journal of Personality and Social Psychology, 36,* 451–462.

Drabeck, T., & Quarantelli, E. L. (1967). Scapegoats, villains, and disasters. *Trans-Action, 4,* 12–17.

Dweck, C. S. (1975). The role of expectations and attributions in the alleviation of learned helplessness. *Journal of Personality and Social Psychology, 31,* 674–685.

Eagly, A. H. (1967). Involvement as a determinant of response to favorable and unfavorable information. *Journal of Personality and Social Psychology Monographs, 7*(Whole No. 643), 1–15.

Engel, G. L. (1968). A life setting conducive to illness: The giving up–given up complex. *Bulletin of the Menninger Clinic, 32,* 355–365.

Epstein, S. (1973). The self concept revisited: Or a theory of a theory. *American Psychologist, 28,* 404–416.

Facing the fear of flying: Grief counseling for victims of postcrash syndrome. (1979, November 19). *Time,* p. 60.

Frank, J. D. (1975). The faith that heals. *Johns Hopkins Medical Journal, 137,* 127–131.

Frankl, V. E. (1963). *Man's search for meaning: An introduction to logotherapy.* New York: Washington Square Press.

Friedman, S. B., Chodoff, P., Mason, J. E., & Hamburg, D. A. (1977). Behavioral observations on parents anticipating the death of a child. In A. Monat & R. S. Lazarus (Eds.), *Stress and coping.* New York: Columbia University Press.

Frieze, I. H. (1979). Perceptions of battered wives. In I. H. Frieze, D. Bar-Tal, & J. S. Carroll (Eds.), *New approaches to social problems.* San Francisco: Jossey-Bass.

Glass, D. C., & Singer, J. E. (1972). *Urban stress: Experiments on noise and social stressors.* New York: Academic Press.

Gluckman, M. (1944, June). The logic of African science and witchcraft: An appreciation of Evans-Pritchard's "witchcraft oracles and magic among the Azande" of the Sudan. *The Rhodes-Livingstone Institute Journal,* pp. 64–71.

Golin, S., Terrell, T., & Johnson, B. (1977). Depression and the illusion of control. *Journal of Abnormal Psychology, 86,* 440–442.

Golin, S., Terrell, T., Weitz, J., & Drost, P. L. (1979). The illusion of control among depressed patients. *Journal of Abnormal Psychology, 88,* 454–457.

Grinker, R. R., & Spiegel, J. P. (1945). *Men under stress.* Philadelphia: Blakiston.

Grinker, R. R., Willerman, B., Bradley, A., & Fastovsky, A. (1946). A study of psychological predisposition to the development of operational fatigue, sections 1 and 2. *American Journal of Orthopsychiatry, 16,* 191–214.

Gruen, W. (1975). Effects of brief psychotherapy during the hospitalization period on the recovery process in heart attacks. *Journal of Consulting and Clinical Psychology, 43,* 223–232.

Henderson, J. B., Hall, S. M., & Lipton, H. L. (1979). Changing self-destructive behaviors. In G. S. Stone, F. Cohen, & S. N. E. Adler (Eds.), *Health psychology.* San Francisco: Jossey-Bass.

Hilberman, E., & Munson, K. (1978). Sixty battered women. *Victimology, 2,* 460–471.

Hursch, C. H. (1977). *The trouble with rape.* Chicago: Nelson-Hall.

Janis, I. L. (1974). Vigilance and decision making in personal crises. In G. V. Coelho, D. A. Hamburg, & J. E. Adams (Eds.), *Coping and adaption.* New York: Basic.

Janoff-Bulman, R. (1979). Characterological versus behavioral self-blame: Inquiries into depression and rape. *Journal of Personality and Social Psychology, 37,* 1798–1809.

Janoff-Bulman, R. (1982). Esteem and control bases of blame: Adaptive strategies for victims versus observers. *Journal of Personality, 50,* 180–191.

Janoff-Bulman, R. (1985). The aftermath of victimization: Rebuilding shattered assumptions. In C. R. Figley (Ed.), *Trauma and its wake.* New York: Brunner/Mazel.

Janoff-Bulman, R., & Brickman, P. (1982). Expectations and what people learn from failure. In. N. Feather (Ed.), *Expectations and actions: Expectancy-value models in psychology*. Hillsdale, NJ: Erlbaum.

Janoff-Bulman, R., & Frieze, I. H. (1983). A theoretical perspective for understanding reactions to victimization. *Journal of Social Issues, 39*, 1–17.

Janoff-Bulman, R., & Thomas, C. E. (in press). Towards an understanding of self-defeating responses following victimization. In R. C. Curtis (Ed.), *Self-defeating behaviors: Experimental research and practical implications*. New York: Plenum.

Jenkins, H. M., & Ward, W. C. (1965). Judgment of contingency between responses and outcomes. *Psychological Monographs, 79*(Whole No. 594).

Kaplan, C. (1965, November). A journal of the Warsaw ghetto. *Commentary*, pp. 43–58, 52.

Kiecolt-Glaser, J. K., & Williams, D. (in press). Self-blame, compliance, and distress among burn patients. *Journal of Personality and Social Psychology*.

Kubler-Ross, E. (1969). *On death and dying*. New York: Macmillan.

Lang, L. (1980). Sickness as sin: Observers' perceptions of the physically ill. Unpublished manuscript, University of Massachusetts, Amherst.

Langer, E. (1975). The illusion of control. *Journal of Personality and Social Psychology, 32*, 311–328.

Langer, E. (1978). Rethinking the role of thought in social interaction. In J. Harvey, W. Ickes, & R. Kidd (Eds.), *New directions in attribution research*. (Vol. 2). Hillsdale, NJ: Erlbaum.

Langer, E. J., & Rodin, J. (1976). The effects of choice and enhanced responsibility for the aged: A field experiment in an institutional setting. *Journal of Personality and Social Psychology, 33*, 951–955.

Lazarus, R. S. (1966). *Psychological stress and the coping process*. New York: McGraw-Hill.

Lazarus, R. S. (1974). Psychological stress and coping in adaptation and illness. *International Journal of Psychiatry in Medicine, 5*, 321–333.

Lerner, M. J. (1970). The desire for justice and reactions to victims. In J. Macauley & L. Berkowitz (Eds.), *Altruism and helping behavior*. New York: Academic Press.

Lerner, M. J. (1971). Observer's evaluation of a victim: Justice, guilt, and veridical perception. *Journal of Personality and Social Psychology, 20*, 127–135.

Lerner, M. J., & Miller, D. T. (1978). Just world research and the attribution process: Looking back and ahead. *Psychological Bulletin, 85*, 1030–1051.

Lerner, M. J., & Simmons, C. H. (1966). Observers' reactions to the "innocent victim": Compassion or rejection? *Journal of Personality and Social Psychology, 4*, 403–410.

Lifton, R. J. (1967). *Death in life: Survivors of Hiroshima*. New York: Simon & Schuster.

Lifton, R. J. (1971). *History and human survival*. New York: Vintage Books.

Lindemann, E. (1977). Symptomatology and management of acute grief. In A. Monat & R. S. Lazarus (Eds.), *Stress and coping*. New York: Columbia University Press.

Mechanic, D. (1972). Social psychologic factors affecting the presentation of bodily complaints. *New England Journal of Medicine, 286*, 1132–1139.

Mechanic, D. (1978). *Medical sociology: A comprehensive text* (2nd ed.). New York: Free Press.

Medea, A., & Thompson, K. (1974). *Against rape*. New York: Farrar, Straus, & Giroux.

Meyer, C. B., & Taylor, S. E. (1986). Adjustment to rape. *Journal of Personality and Social Psychology, 50*, 1226–1234.

Miller, D. T., & Porter, C. A. (1983). Self-blame in victims of violence. *Journal of Social Issues, 39*, 141–154.

Moos, R. H., & Tsu, V. D. (1977). The crisis of physical illness: An overview. In R. H. Moos (Ed.), *Coping with physical illness*. New York: Plenum.

Moses, R., & Cividali, M. (1966). Differential levels of awareness of illness: Their relation to some salient features in cancer patients. *Annals of the New York Academy of Science, 125*, 984–999.

Nagai, T. (1951). *We of Nagasaki*. New York: Duell, Sloan & Pearce.

National Commission on the Causes and Prevention of Violence. (1969). *Crimes of Violence.* (Vol. 2). Washington, DC: U.S. Government Printing Office.

Parkes, C. M. (1971). Psycho-social transitions: A field for study. *Social Science and Medicine, 5,* 101–115.

Pennebaker, J. W., & Skelton, J. A. (1978). Psychological parameters of physical symptoms. *Personality and Social Psychology Bulletin, 4,* 524–530.

Perloff, L. S. (1983). Perceptions of vulnerability to victimization. *Journal of Social Issues, 39*(2), 41–62.

Peterson, C., Schwartz, S. M., & Seligman, M. E. P. (1981). Self-blame and depressive symptoms. *Journal of Personality and Social Psychology, 41,* 253–259.

Rotter, J. B. (1966). Generalized expectancies for internal versus exernal control of reinforcement. *Psychological Monographs, 80,* (1, Whole No. 609).

Russell, D. E. H. (1975). *The politics of rape: The victim's perspective.* New York: Stein & Day.

Scheppele, K. L., & Bart, P. B. (1983). Through women's eyes: Defining danger in the wake of sexual asssault. *Journal of Social Issues, 39,* 63–81.

Schmale, A. H., Jr. (1972). Giving up as a final common pathway to changes in health. *Advances in Psychosomatic Medicine, 8,* 20–40.

Schoenberg, B., & Senescu, R. A. (1970). The patient's reaction to a fatal illness. In B. Schoenberg, A. C. Carr, D. Peretz, & A. H. Kutscher (Eds.), *Loss and grief: Psychological management in medical practice.* New York: Columbia University Press.

Schulz, R. (1976). Effects of control and predictability on the physical and psychological well-being of the institutionalized aged. *Journal of Personality and Social Psychology, 33,* 563–573.

Seligman, M. E. P. (1975). *Helplessness: On depression, development and death.* San Francisco: Freeman.

Selye, H. (1956). *The stress of life.* New York: McGraw-Hill.

Silver, R. L., & Wortman, C. B. (1980). Coping with undesirable life events. In J. Garber & M. E. P. Seligman (Eds.), *Human helplessness: Theory and application.* New York: Academic Press.

Sontag, S. (1978). *Illness as metaphor.* New York: Farrar, Straus, & Giroux.

Taylor, S., & Levin, S. (1976). The psychological impact of breast cancer: Theory and practice. In A. Enelow (Ed.), *Psychological aspects of breast cancer.* San Francisco: West Coast Cancer Foundation.

Tennen, H., Affleck, G., & Gershman, K. (1986). Self-blame among parents of infants with perinatal complications: The role of self-protective motives. *Journal of Personality and Social Psychology, 50,* 690–696.

Tennen, H., Affleck, G., Allen, D. A., McGrade, B. J., & Ratzan, S. (1984). Causal attributions and coping with insulin-dependent diabetes. *Basic and Applied Social Psychology, 5,* 131–142.

Timko, C., & Janoff-Bulman, R. (1985). Attributions, vulnerability, and psychological adjustment: The case of breast cancer. *Health Psychology, 4,* 521–544.

Walker, L. E. (1979). *The battered woman.* New York: Harper & Row.

Walster, E. (1966). Assignment of responsibility for an accident. *Journal of Personality and Social Psychology, 3,* 73–79.

Weiner, B., Frieze, I. H., Kukla, A., Reed, L., Rest, S., & Rosenbaum, R. M. (1971). *Perceiving the causes of success and failure.* Morristown, NJ: General Learning Press.

Weinstein, N. D. (1980). Unrealistic optimism about future life events. *Journal of Personality and Social Psychology, 39,* 806–820.

Weinstein, N. D., & Lachendro, E. (1982). Egocentrism as a source of unrealistic optimism. *Personality and Social Psychology Bulletin, 8,* 195–200.

Weis, K., & Weis, S. (1975). Victimology and the justification of rape. In I. Drapkin & E. Viano (Eds.), *Victimology: A new focus: Exploiters and exploited* (Vol. 5). Lexington, MA: Lexington Books.

Weisman, A. D. (1979). *Coping with cancer.* New York: McGraw-Hill.

Wolfenstein, M. (1957). *Disaster: A psychological essay.* Glencoe, IL: The Free Press.

Wong, P., & Weiner, B. (1981). When people ask "why" questions, and the heuristics of attributional search. *Journal of Personality and Social Psychology, 40,* 650–663.

Wortman, C. B. (1976). Causal attributions and personal control. In J. H. Harvey, W. J. Ickes, & R. F. Kidd (Eds.), *New directions in attribution research* (Vol. 1). Hillsdale, NJ: Erlbaum.

Wortman, C. B., & Dintzer, L. (1978). Is an attributional analysis of the learned helplessness phenomenon viable?: A critique of the Abramson–Seligman–Teasdale reformulation. *Journal of Abnormal Psychology, 87,* 75–90.

Zola, I. K. (1972). Medicine as an institution of social control. *The Sociological Review, 20,* 487–504.

Zung, W. K. (1965). A self-rating depression scale. *Archives of General Psychiatry, 12,* 63–70.

6

Investigating the Development and Courses of Intimate Relationships

HELEN M. NEWMAN
ELLEN J. LANGER

This chapter consitutes an attempt to explore particular intrapersonal and interpersonal phenomena that characterize intimate interpersonal relationships, and to suggest various clinical implications that follow from analysis of these phenomena. The major unifying focus of the discussion, however, centers upon the role of cognitive processes in reflecting, as well as shaping, various aspects of relationship development over time.

Intimate relating is an extremely complex process, one that cannot be sufficiently understood without consideration of an array of emotional, cognitive, behavioral, and social variables as they interact over time. However, investigation of attributions and mindfulness/mindlessness might provide a reference point for understanding and predicting better how intimate relationships are experienced over time, how dysfunctional patterns of interaction develop, why interpersonal conflict is so often perpetuated, and why relationships break down. For example, we suggest that the amount and kind of information individuals attend to at given stages of their relationships influence the formation of stable perceptions, expectations, and patterns of communication. The manner in which individuals think about their partners, evaluate partners' behaviors, and provide attributions for interpersonal events has great impact upon emotional and communicative relatedness as well as general relationship well-being. And to the extent that individuals predominantly employ particular kinds of attributions and interpretations, they actively construct, without fully realizing it, distinct kinds of psychological and emotional relationships vis-à-vis their partners.

Various phases of interpersonal relatedness might be differentiated on the basis of the degree of mindfulness and styles of interpretation and attribution-making that characterize them. Similarly, changes in attributional activity and mindfulness/mindlessness might reciprocally interact with changes in emotional relatedness to bring about new, or renewed, interpersonal and intrapersonal awareness.

ATTRIBUTION-MAKING AND LEVELS OF MINDFULNESS

Various researchers have already illustrated the important role of attributions within the context of ongoing intimate relationships (e.g., Harvey, Wells, & Alvarez, 1978; Kelly, 1979; Newman, 1981a; Newman & Langer, 1981; Orvis, Kelley, & Butler, 1976; Peplau, Rubin, & Hill, 1977). Although references have been made to a number of different styles of attribution-making (cf. Kruglanski, 1975), certain kinds of attributions appear to more strongly influence, and stem from, those patterns of interpersonal relatedness experienced within intimate dyads.

Much recent research, for example, has revealed that distressed and nondistressed couples differ in their styles of attribution-making (e.g., Doherty, 1982; Fincham & O'Leary, 1983; Holtzworth-Monroe & Jacobson, 1985; Jacobson, McDonald, Follette, & Berley, 1985) and that particular types of cognitive processing are associated with marital conflict and marital satisfaction (e.g., Berley & Jacobson, 1984; Fincham & Bradbury, 1987; Jacobson, Follette, & McDonald, 1982).

In the following discussion, attempts are made to primarily address the implications of the use of both *dispositional* and *interpersonal* attributions as categories of interpretation within intimate relationships. The dispositional versus situational dichotomy, pertaining both to actors and observers within social interactions, has been elucidated by Jones and Nisbett (1972). By dispositional attributions, we mean those explanations for intrapersonal and interpersonal reactions that point primarily to perceived, stable characteristics of either self or partner. Thus, individuals using dispositional attributions will often assign causality in the form of a statement that describes, categorizes, or labels a person in a specific manner (e.g., She is gentle; He is inconsiderate). Such attributions differ from situational attributions, which explain events by pointing to external circumstances or situational influences residing outside of self, partner, and the communication system itself. The interpersonal attribution category has been proposed by Newman (1981a) to be a style of attribution-making relevant to intimate relating over time. It takes into account those developing interactive patterns of communication that are jointly perceived to exist *between* the two relationship partners. By interpersonal attributions, we mean those explanations pointing, for the most part, to how the self is in regard to the other and how the other is in regard to the self (e.g., She wants to dominate me; He is always competing with me; I was trying to please him; We communicate well); thus, they consider features of the communicative relationship, as created and sustained by *both* partners interactively. The interpersonal attribution category, along with dispositional and situational attribution categories, might coexist or overlap in an explanation of various interpersonal phenomena. For example, an individual might view his or her relationship dissatisfaction to be basically caused by a "partner's lack of interest" in him or her. However, the individual, at other times, might explain the same dissatisfaction with reference to related factors; such as "My partner is basically withholding and undemonstrative," or "My partner is preoccupied with work pressures right now."

In addition to considering the content of cognitive inferences that individuals make, there are various questions to consider regarding individuals' degree of cognitive activity. For example, just how "mindful" are individuals within various phases and stages of their intimate relationships? The implications of varying degrees of mindfulness versus mindlessness for behavior have already been explored (e.g., Chanowitz & Langer, 1980; Langer, 1978, 1980; Langer, Blank, & Chanowitz, 1978; Langer & Imber, 1980; Langer & Newman, 1979). As proposed by Langer and her colleagues, "mindlessness" constitutes the relative absence of active, ongoing information-processing; when "mindless," individuals are not utilizing the available relevant information; their behavior is overdetermined by the past. When "mindful," on the other hand, individuals are actively engaged in making distinctions within interpersonal situations, rather than in using preformed categories of meaning.

For the purposes of this discussion, we will be using the term "mindfulness" in two related ways. The first way is to view mindfulness as active cognitive activity in which relationship partners actually make use of past and present communicative information that is available to them; in line with this view, the notion of mindlessness would characterize those patterns of perceiving, interpreting, interacting, and responding wherein individuals rely upon preestablished styles, or patterns, of intrapersonal and interpersonal response. The second view of mindfulness considers more generally the propensity individuals have toward active consideraton of the motives and reasons behind interpersonal events (especially those involving a partner). In this regard, mindfulness might connote the cognitive tendency to consider the question "Why?" and to engage in extensive attributional analysis of behavior.

In intimate relating, as in all other forms of human activity, individuals are prone to move among various amounts of mindfulness in response to a wide array of variable circumstances. Certain specific phases of intimate relationship development might characteristically serve to promote or elicit greater or lesser mindfulness.

RELATIONSHIP FORMATION

The initial formation of a relationship marks a time characterized by a great deal of novelty, uncertainty, and lack of predictability—factors that often contribute to the sense of excitement and stimulation individuals report during relationship beginnings (Berlyne, 1960). However, during this time, individuals are confronted with a high level of information and ambiguity. They have not yet learned what to expect from their prospective partners or, for that matter, what is expected of them; they do not yet have the comfort that comes with the establishment of stable and familiar patterns of interaction; they have the task of making meaningful sense out of a vast array of new and complex interpersonal behaviors presented by an unfamiliar person; and, all the while, the decision of whether or not to become intimately involved with this other person is bound to exact a great deal of information-seeking coupled with careful thought and evaluation. For this reason, the demand for mindful cognitive activity, especially in the form of attribution-making, might be particularly strong during the beginning of relationship development (see Newman, 1981a, 1982). In addition, there are certain processes characterizing relationship beginnings that are especially significant, as they potentially form the basis for various patterns of functional and dysfunctional communication that may emerge later on in the relationship. We propose that, within many relationships, the stages of ambiguity-reduction, attribution-making, and idealization might even foreshadow the stages of conflict and dissolution that sometimes occur after relationship stabilization has been reached.

AMBIGUITY-REDUCTION

In efforts to reduce the demand for a high level of cognitive activity, or overload (Langer, 1978), and to make information-processing more orderly and manageable (e.g., Heider, 1958), people will inevitably construct stable cognitions regarding what their partners are like and what they can expect from their relationships. These cognitions, or assumptions, contribute to the formation of a stable set of "relational premises" that enable individuals to make incoming information more comprehensible and predictable (e.g., Bannister & Fransella, 1971; Duck, 1973; Wegner & Vallacher, 1977). During initial stages of communicative exchange, individuals have the opportunity to formulate, test, modify, validate, and reinforce their relational premises. Eventually, whether the premises are correct or incorrect "objectively," individuals will assign meaning to communicative messages through the filters of "what they believe to be true" about the other person and the nature of the larger relationship (Berger & Kellner, 1971; Newman, 1982).

From an interpersonal perspective, individuals are reducing ambiguity and uncertainty by establishing stable patterns of communication and implicit relationship rules (of interaction) that limit the array of alternatives open to them in relating to each other (Morton, Alexander, & Altman, 1976; Watzlawick, Beavin, & Jackson, 1967). The development of such patterns serves to shape and, in turn, is shaped by those intrapersonal relationship premises that are also emerging (cf. Newman, 1981b). The encoding and decoding of interpersonal messages is soon accomplished with a greater degree of certainty. Interpretations assigned to ongoing messages will often be derived from those meanings and definitions implicit to the larger relational context (see, for example, Cronen, Pearce, & Harris, 1979; Harris, 1980) created by both individuals.

ATTRIBUTION-MAKING AND "RELATIONAL PREMISES"

In an effort to determine what another person is like and whether or not an intimate relationship with that person is desirable (e.g., Berkowitz & Walster, 1976; Thibaut & Kelley, 1959) individuals are bound to engage in mindful information-processing characterized by careful evaluation and categorization. To facilitate this implicit goal, they will most likely employ both dispositional and interpersonal attributions to explain various interpersonal events.

By thinking in terms of distinct attributes that label and define partners along stable dimensions, individuals can formulate a clearer understanding of their partners' behaviors and also accrue data upon which to make evaluative judgments. The use of dispositional attributions, in particular, enables individuals to depict their partners as conglomerates of discrete attributes, some desirable and others undesirable (Taguiri & Petrullo, 1958). Dispositional attributions also increase levels of predictability concerning partners' range of behaviors (e.g., Berger & Calabrese, 1975; Crockett & Friedman, 1980; Jones & Davis, 1965). The labeling and categorizing system facilitated by the use of dispositional attributions serves as the basis for the refinement of those relational premises that will be referred to as "dispositional premises." Dispositional premises include evaluative assumptions concerning partners' traits (e.g., She is sloppy; She is competent; He is energetic) as well as related assumptions (cf. Kelley, 1979) concerning partners' motives, feelings, likes, and dislikes (e.g., He likes to be the center of attention; She wants to make a lot of money; He hates fancy restaurants). Dispositional premises are important cognitive constructs because they mediate interpretations of, and responses to, ongoing interpersonal messages.

Besides dispositional attribution-making, individuals are likely to search for explanations for interpersonal communicative behaviors that enable them to predict what their partners are like *in regard to them*, and what a relationship with this partner will be like. The use of interpersonal attributions enables individuals to infer, from immediate exchanges, the styles of relating that might characterize their interactions over time: for example, what their partners feel about them, what their partners want from them, what intentions their partners have in regard to the relationship, what responses their partners elicit from them, etc. (see Newman, 1981a, 1982). Interpersonal attribution-making thereby aids in the formulation of ongoing expectations and "interpersonal premises" that influence subsequent interpretations of ongoing communicative behaviors. These interpersonal premises might include negative perceptions of the relationship (e.g., We can't seem to get along; He wants to control me; She is always nagging me) as well as more positive perceptions of the partner (e.g., He wants to make me happy; She tries to help me; He shares feelings with me). It is important to note, too, that the interpersonal premises a person formulates (i.e., wants to see) need not necessarily be congruent or consistent with the dispositional premises that have also been established. However, a contradiction among assumptions and expectations can contribute to relationship problems, as will be shown later in this chapter.

Given that individuals formulate relational premises, partly in order to help move their relationships to a more comfortable, stable, and predictable level, two additional considerations arise:

1. What kinds of expectations are implicitly established through the selective employment of particular attributions?
2. In developing a set of relational premises and expectations, how much of the information available to them do individuals actually utilize?

During relationship beginnings, individuals may selectively utilize dispositional and interpersonal attributions in order to formulate, and sustain, a positive set of perceptions concerning partner, self, and relationships. For example, by consciously relying upon particular attributions to the exclusion of others, an individual's cognitive activity can serve to reinforce the choice of a partner as a good one as well as sustain desired feelings and perceptions. In this way, cognitive activity during relationship beginnings may work in the service of emotional needs, by promoting favorable perceptions of partner and relationship, and by helping remove negative perceptions from awareness so that the relationship can develop smoothly (cf. Stevens & Jones, 1976). Partners may also help individuals to arrive at such favorable perceptions by decribing themselves and their past relationships in positive ways (Newman, 1982).

The notion that reliance upon positively versus negatively toned dispositional and interpersonal attributions mediates feelings of closeness versus distance has been argued elsewhere (Berley & Jacobson, 1984; Fincham & Bradbury, 1987; Jacobson, Follette, & McDonald, 1982; Newman, 1981a). Other data, collected from individuals in relationships for a period averaging from 2 to 5 years (Newman, 1978), reflects the relationship between selective awareness along with the use of relational premises and subsequent satisfaction versus dissatisfaction. These data partly validate the significance of interpersonal premises to intimate relating (see Table 6-1).

Once individuals formulate a stable repertoire of relationship premises and attributions, they may fail to consciously consider alternative explanations for their partners' behavior (both positive and negative) and to establish a wide range of evaluative categories that more realistically reflect the information available to them. According to Berley & Jacobson (1984), individuals come to expect behavior consistent with established causal attributions. They argue that "biased cognitions process data in ways that bolster those expectations and discount alternative explanations" (p. 33). This problem is exacerbated to the degree that individuals engage in idealization of their partners.

TABLE 6-1. Salience of Positive and Negative Interpersonal Premises in Individuals Who Are Satisfied versus Dissatisfied in their Relationships

	Average degree of interpersonal premise validation[a]	
Interpersonal premises	Happy in relationship ($n = 30$)	Unhappy in relationship ($n = 20$)
"My partner . . .		
1. disapproves of things I say or do."	3.1	5.4
2. knows what I'm feeling when I'm upset."	6.93	6.8
3. tries to make me jealous."	1.26	3.2
4. tries to make me feel guilty."	2.10	5.15
5. tries to dominate me."	2.30	4.45
6. shows interest in what I have to say."	8.1	5.0
7. gets defensive or angry when criticized."	3.83	5.95
8. tries to lie to me or deceive me."	1.06	3.15
9. gets annoyed when I give attention to others."	1.96	5.0
10. respects my judgment and my opinions."	7.98	4.9

[a]A 10-point scale was used, with 1 = very low degree of reported validation of interpersonal premises, and 10 = very high degree of validation. Data represents the average scale value corresponding to the degree to which subjects report that an interpersonal premise is valid for their relationships.

IDEALIZATION

By idealization, we are referring to two important and distinct processes, both of which are influenced by emotional and cognitive factors. One is the tendency to selectively attend to particular information (i.e., about one's partner) to the exclusion of other data. To the extent that perceptions of "undesirable" characteristics cause discomfort and anxiety, people might opt to close out particular information from awareness; thus, they eliminate certain negative attributes from mindful discrimination and evaluation processes and attend more exclusively to various positive attributes and behaviors. This process of idealization (Dicks, 1953) has been shown to contribute to the highly positive evaluations and feelings characterizing many love relationships.

The second characteristic of idealization is that people often perceive their partners as they want to see them, rather than as they "actually" exist (i.e., as others might see them). Therefore, to the extent that perceptions are influenced by the strong needs, wishes, and fantasies of each perceiver, a good amount of distortion and unconscious projection will inevitably take place (e.g., Dicks, 1967; Klein, 1932; Willi, 1982). Thus, one might view one's partner in light of certain relational premises (often formulated as expectancies from interpersonal experiences with previous partners) that have little or no connection to those "real" attributes of the partner or relationship. Alternatively, an individual might perceive a trait that the partner possesses (i.e., domineering) but then choose to consider only the desirable, as opposed to undesirable, interpersonal implications of this characteristic (e.g., He will protect me vs. He will try to dominate me).

To the extent that idealization, in general, serves to promote favorable evaluations of a partner, heighten positive expectations, and facilitate a stable, although perhaps illusory, picture of a partner, it aids in the process of relationship formation and the choice to continue on an intimate path. However, in a mindlessness framework, idealization means the loss of another kind of cognitive activity—that in which individuals use the information available to them when making discriminations and forming a thoughtful understanding of their partners. There is the danger, in idealization, of unrealistic expectations for continuity and consistency in particular styles of behaving, relating, and feeling. There is also the danger that expectancies bred from idealized perceptions will preclude preparation for those later stages of relationship development in which a partner often turns out to be other than what one wanted him or her to be.

Clinical observations offered by Dicks (1953) and Willi (1982) suggest that tensions and misunderstandings between partners result from disappointments which one or both of them feel when the other fails to play the role of spouse in accordance with some preconceived figure in their fantasy world. An idealized image of what a partner should be may result cognitively rather than motivationally from a premature cognitive commitment. Such a mindset is often formed in childhood from a child's selective exposure to parental or other adult relationships (cf. Chanowitz & Langer, 1981). Deviation from this mindlessly held image may lead to disappointment.

RELATIONSHIP STABILIZATION

As implied in the preceding discussion, it is during the total period of relationship formation that certain important cognitive adjustments are facilitated. Most significantly, the degree of mindfulness initially demanded of each individual is greatly reduced. Through the use of dispositional and interpersonal attributions, the validation of relational premises, the formation of evaluative sets and expectations, the establishment of interactive rules and patterns, and the removal of discomforting cognitions and uncertainty—all more mindful cognitive activity—information-processing is made more predictable and there is less need to think about and evaluate the relationship. Instead, individuals are able to filter information through preset categories and interpret novel events in line with established expectancies and assumptions.

Once novelty and ambiguity are exchanged for a greater sense of certainty, once the need for active evaluation diminishes, once behavior is more predictable, once a relationship is well defined and under way, and once implicit rules of interaction have been established, *relationship stabilization* has been effected. Such stabilization is an adaptive and rewarding stage of relationship development; individuals usually experience a sense of comfort, security, and familiarity with their partners, all of which make thought about the relationship, reevaluation, and attribution-making much less necessary. For many couples, relationship stabilization might mark a sort of "comfort zone" within which they operate a good deal of the time and which enables them to experience an optimal level of stimulation (cf. Berlyne, 1960). Many individuals no doubt sustain periods of relationship stabilization as the most prevalent, and recurring, stage of their total relationship development.

However desirable the achievement of relationship stabilization might be, for certain individuals it will inevitably provide the transition point into and out of periods of relationship dissatisfaction and conflict. This is most likely if the individuals are not equipped with the means by which to integrate new and different categories of evaluation, perceptual discriminations, expectations, and styles of relating into preestablished cognitive and behavioral sets (cf. Langer, 1978). What are the effects of the move from the more *mindful*, cognitively and emotionally arousing states of relationship formation to those more *mindless* stabilized states of intimate relating, wherein individuals are no longer considering much of the information initially available to them? For most individuals, it is likely that the stage of relationship stabilization brings with it changes in intrapersonal and interpersonal involvement that might set the stage for feelings of betrayal and relationship dissatisfaction.

The rest of this chapter will examine various emotional and relational phenomena that follow from, and might be influenced by, the overall process of relationship stabilization. Some of these phenomena have been observed in relationships where one or both partners experience dissatisfaction and conflict. Others are general styles of cognitive activity, common to most intimate relationships, which interact with the kinds of relational premises individuals might have constructed during early periods of their interaction. Most of the stages, however, reflect a move from relationship stabilization to relationship conflict, accompanied by renewed mindfulness and evaluation.

RELATIONSHIP DISSATISFACTION AND CONFLICT

LOSS OF INTERPERSONAL AROUSAL

When interpersonal communication patterns have become more redundant and therefore more predictable, individuals may come to experience a proportionate loss in the cognitive and emotional arousal originally provided during relationship beginnings. This condition is most likely to occur when communicative messages are "overpredicted" and when interactions are devoid of sufficient novelty to maintain interest and involvement. The need to engage in a greater degree of cognitive/emotional arousal may be satisfied by attention to sources of interest outside of one's relationship (e.g., other people, children, work) as well as by increased attention to one's intrapersonal feelings and awarenesses. However, where these sources of input are unacceptable, individuals may demand that a greater level of cognitive and emotional involvement be provided by their partners or through the relationship. They may also demand that their partners provide more of what they need or want from the relationship. These demands may more likely be the case if individuals have idealized their relationships and have looked to them as the sole source of emotional well-being; it may also be more likely for individuals who desire distraction from those intrapersonal awarenesses or negative feelings that they encounter within themselves when given the increased opportunity to experience them (e.g., Feldman, 1979). In either case, individuals might react to the insufficient or unsatisfying interpersonal stimulation with various negative feelings, such as boredom, anxiety, and dissatisfaction. Furthermore, although these negative emotions might have nothing to do with what one's partner is "really" like, they may still be attributed to something about the relationship. In this way, negative *intrapersonal* experiences promote a search for what is wrong *interpersonally*, and a reevaluation process concerning partner and relationship ensues.

While reevaluating a relationship, individuals enter, once again, a period of mindfulness similar to that characterizing their relationship beginnings. However, this time they will no doubt observe things they had not perceived before, attend to previously ignored characteristics of their partners' behaviors, and explore new sources of information. In each case this information should be highly negative, because the more positive was mindfully and then mindlessly addressed in the first stage of the relationship.

When looking for information to explain either a loss of arousal or a change in interpersonal feeling, individuals may (1) focus upon routine and redundant behaviors performed by their partners or themselves (because redundancy is commonly associated with boredom), and (2) generate interpersonal explanations for a reduced level of involvement. For many individuals, both of these mindful activities potentially can generate an escalation in negative feeling as well as mediate in the formation of active interpersonal conflict. For example, focusing on redundant or overpracticed behaviors often causes them to "grate on the nerves." In this regard, individuals can blame their dissatisfaction on negative things about a partner's habits (i.e., dispositional attributions) or a lack of variety in role performance. Similarly, in a search for more interpersonal arousal, individuals might monitor their interpersonal communication, give more thought to motives and intentions of a partner, and unwittingly seek out evidence for negative interpersonal premises (e.g., He doesn't pay enough attention to me; She is always undermining my progress).

To the extent that individuals explain dissatisfaction with the aid of negative dispositional and interpersonal premises, they inevitably promote emotional distance and may trigger arguments and conflicts when they verbalize to their partners the attributions for their dissatisfaction. Thus, a reciprocal relationship develops between loss of interpersonal arousal/involvement and negative evaluations (of relationship and partner)—leading to the establishment of stable patterns of interpersonal *conflict* (e.g., Fincham & Bradbury, 1987). These patterns of interpersonal conflict can be rewarding to individuals because they sustain a needed relational connectedness that makes attending to self and seeking alternative explanations for dissatisfaction practically unnecessary.

More empirical research is needed to discover what constitutes "loss of arousal" "redundancy," and "overpredictability" for different types of individuals. It may be the case that dissatisfaction rooted in feelings of loss of arousal might be exacerbated by too high a level of ambiguity-reduction during earlier states of a relationship. For example, individuals who have formulated a narrow and unrealistic set of interpersonal relationship premises, selectively employed particular dispositional and interpersonal attributions, or relied upon distorted and idealized conceptions of partner, and so forth, might be more likely candidates for feelings of disillusionment and loss of arousal than individuals who have been using more of the information available to them (e.g., thinking in terms of multifaceted interpersonal and situational influences, making more refined categorical distinctions and discriminations, and accepting negative characteristics of the partner and relationship). On the other hand, as relationships develop over time, it is quite possible that—for all individuals—new sources of (negative) information will become apparent and changes in interpersonal relatedness will occur. Perhaps what then becomes most significant are the attributions and interpretations individuals have available to them for understanding and explaining these relationship changes.

Discrepancy Evaluation and Interpersonal Conflict

Aside from the experienced loss of interpersonal arousal, another potential source of relationship dissatisfaction is the "discrepancy evaluation process," related to the perception of relational *changes*. There are several reasons why changes are bound to occur in the course of relationship development over time (Huston & Burgess, 1979; Levinger, 1980). People inevitably change, and styles of relating are bound to vary over time in response to variable intrapersonal, interpersonal, situational, and circumstantial influences. On the other hand, there are perceptions of changes in a partner that follow from a new awareness of certain traits and characteristics that had not been mindfully processed during earlier stages of relationship formation and idealization. In this case, even though their partners have *not* changed in certain respects, individuals are interpreting seemingly novel or discrepant behaviors as signs that their partners "must have changed." Thus, as we have observed in clinical work, it is not uncommon for distressed partners, after years of relating to individuals who display set, stable behavior patterns, to begin complaining, for example, "She is so unemotional; He doesn't clean up enough; or She is too preoccupied with business."

From a cognitive perspective, it is suggested that the awareness of change or discrepancy within a relationship is one of the conditions that triggers renewed mindfulness in the form of attribution-making and evaluation (for discussion of other conditions, see Langer, 1978, and Newman, 1981a). Insofar as people use interpersonal attributions and interpersonal premises in order to monitor the quality of their relationships (Newman, 1981a), they have already made implicit evaluations concerning various characteristics of their relationships: for example, levels of emotional relatedness, success of communication, compatibility, and amount of sexual interest. Now, however, to the extent that these characteristics can be viewed in relation to prior trends, they represent not only positive or negative phenomena in their own right, but also escalations and deescalations in former styles of relating. When evaluated in a developmental time framework, interpersonal experiences take on additional connotative meanings that often fuel more powerful emotional reactions. For example, negative reactions to emerging patterns of communication (i.e., arguments) might be exacerbated given the perception that frequent arguing had not characterized earlier stages of a relationship.

This phenomenon is similar to the negative effects of renewed mindfulness that Langer and Imber (1980) have demonstrated at the intrapersonal level in their study of deviance. Deviance by definition provokes mindfulness. In this study, when evaluating a deviant, the increased mindfulness led subjects to notice more of the target's physical characteristics than when they thought they were evaluating a normal target. Because the individuals are too often mindless in their interactions with normals, quite typical characteristics seemed rather atypical and hence erroneously supported their negative evaluations of the deviants.

The fact that people mindfully evaluate and respond negatively to discrepancies within their relationships has been documented by Harvey *et al.* (1978). Of the various explanations their subjects provided for the breakups of their relationships, several included implicit references to some sort of emergent change: a decline in love and emotional giving, a growing apart, the desire for a new life-style, or the escalation of discontent, loneliness, and control battles. This reasearch suggests that the ways in which individuals construe and integrate changes occurring within their relationships might have important implications for relational satisfaction versus dissatisfaction. Newman (1978) collected some data that included perceptions of relationship discrepancies. The data revealed that individuals who defined their relationships as *rocky*, and in need of improvement, reported *more* causes of relational changes and evaluated those changes more *negatively* than did those individuals who defined their relationships as *smooth*, strong, and harmonious. Apparently people do not always respond to perceived change positively (see Table 6-2).

TABLE 6-2. Perception and Evaluation of Discrepancies on the Part of Satisfied versus Dissatisfied Subjects

Examples of relationship changes	Percentage of Ss perceiving the change		Percentage of Ss providing *negative* interpretations of the change		Percentage of Ss providing *positive* interpretations for the change	
	Satisfied[a] ($n = 43$)	Dissatisfied[b] ($n = 33$)	Satisfied ($n = 43$)	Dissatisfied ($n = 33$)	Satisfied ($n = 43$)	Dissatisfied ($n = 33$)
1. Amount of sexual activity	56	82	20	54	23	6
2. Amount of fighting	53	64	9	51	30	3
3. Amount of excitement at being together	49	79	6	64	35	9
4. Other	49	67	9	61	44	0

Examples of relationship changes	Examples of *negative* interpretations for perceived changes	Examples of *positive* interpretations for perceived changes
1. Sexual activity	"Loss of interest, different drives; difficulty communicating; not enough sex"	"Even though less, it's more intense; more closeness and affection; we feel more comfortable"
2. Fighting	"Too much conflict; loss of compatibility; dissatisfaction; can't communicate"	"More honesty now; the honeymoon is over; see each other realistically"
3. Excitement	"We're drifting apart; we're not as attractive to each other any more"	"We're more stable; more comfort and closeness; we're coming alive"
4. Other changes	"Partner too dependent, competitive, possessive; loss of interest"	"Partner more trusting; relationship growing; more stability/closeness"

[a]Satisfied = Define relationship as smooth, harmonious, and selves as happy in it.
[b]Dissatisfied = Define relationship as rocky, in trouble, and in need of help.

Particular relationship changes, such as those changes subjects reported in this study (e.g., partner seems less attractive, loss of interest, less communication, more competition, partner more possessive, or partner less understanding) might be interpreted as interpersonal betrayal (Dicks, 1967), as violations of preestablished relationship rules (Watzlawick *et al.*, 1967), or as violations to one's own self-discrepancy system (Higgins, 1987). They might lead individuals to infer, rightly or wrongly, that their relationships must be "in trouble" or "over." Willi (1987) notes that people mindlessly cling to their original definitions of a relationship as well as bind their partners to that definition. Therefore, when the original definition inevitably changes, they will experience such reactions as disappointment, fear, and anger.

The notion of discrepancy evaluation offers a construct that reflects a particular kind of attributional analysis important to intimate relating and to the potential development of negative interpersonal and dispositional premises. It also implicitly suggests that dissatisfaction is often *intrapersonally* generated (based upon unrealistic expectations, evaluation, emotional investments) yet then might manifest itself *interpersonally* in the form of efforts to change a partner or restore desired interpersonal experiences. Efforts to promote change at the interpersonal level (e.g., place unrealistic demands on the partner or criticize him or her) will often only result in increased fighting and defensiveness. Thus, the feedback loop is ultimately established between negative intrapersonal premises regarding partner/relationship and dysfunctional styles of interpersonal relating.

How an individual engages in discrepancy-evaluation within an interpersonal framework might be influenced by those types of discrepancies he or she experiences between self-state representations (Higgins, 1987). Higgins's self-discrepancy theory states that different types of self-discrepancies represent negative psychological situations which, in turn, are associated with various kinds of discomfort. He suggests that people's emotions in relationships may be influenced by the role their partners play in their self-discrepancy system. Also, if individuals use their own self-guides when evaluating their partners, self-discrepancy theory could predict both the nature of their judgments (positive versus negative) as well as what their emotional responses to their partners' behaviors are likely to be. For example, "a target's behavior that was discrepant from a perceiver's ideal standards could cause the perceiver to feel dissatisfied and disappointed with the target . . . whereas a target's behavior that was discrepant from a perceiver's ought standards could cause the perceiver to feel resentful or critical toward the target" (p. 336).

It is important to note that awareness of discrepancies, per se, does not inevitably lead to dissatisfaction. Some individuals might not interpret discrepancies to mean that something has gone wrong, partly because they might be better able to integrate changes into existing sets of relationship premises and expectations. Furthermore, in resolving discrepancies, dissatisfaction might well be rationalized or denied if acknowledgment of relational difficulty comes into conflict with other interpersonal expectations or if prospects of separation are too threatening. Discovery of those changes that individuals are less or more likely to accept awaits future research.

ATTRIBUTION-MAKING AND INTERPERSONAL CONFLICT

As implied above, attributions (and misattributions) often mediate interpersonal responses and serve to promote or sustain interpersonal conflicts (i.e., Kelley, 1979). Once conflicts have been created by relationship partners, differing styles of interpretation and attribution-making may, themselves, provide a basis for ongoing disagreement and dissatisfaction (e.g., Harvey *et al.*, 1978; Orvis *et al.*, 1976). This idea is supported by research highlighting differences in attributional styles between distressed and nondistressed couples. For example, Jacobson *et al.* (1985) found that whereas nondistressed couples attributed their partners' positive behaviors to internal factors, distressed couples more often attributed their partners' positive behaviors to external factors and their negative behaviors to internal factors. Distressed spouses not only appear to make more dispositional attributions for negative behaviors but also view them as intentional, stable, and global. The use of particular attributions (which serve to close out alternative ways of construing events) can also help to create and sustain dysfunctional patterns of relating. For example, Watzlawick *et al.* (1967) report on a relational problem called "faulty punctuation." It occurs when an interlocking pattern of responses has been established (e.g., husband withdrawn . . . wife nags . . . husband withdraws . . . wife nags . . .) wherein each partner justifies his or her own contribution as a response to the other partner's behavior. It appears that in order to change this type of dysfunctional cycle it might be necessary for each partner to change the attributional set, or underlying logic (Harris, 1980), accompanying his or her own ongoing response (cf. Newman, 1981b).

Attribution errors, along with inappropriate choices of attribution, constitute another possible basis for the development of relationship dissatisfaction and conflict. For example, making dispositional attributions for interpersonal events could prove to be maladaptive in cases where interpersonal or situational attributions would be more realistic (e.g., Altmaier, Leary, Forsyth, & Ansel, 1979; Valins & Nisbett, 1979). This is particularly true in regard to explanations individuals provide for their own relationship problems, conflicts, and other symptoms of distress. Individuals who use dispositional premises to sustain the simplistic picture that "it is my partner who is to blame" or "if only my partner were different these problems would disappear" are usually those individuals who encounter greater difficulty in attempts to deescalate interpersonal patterns of anger and conflict.

It seems of little surprise that data collected by Newman (1978) reveal that 59 percent of the individuals who defined their relationships to be "in trouble" provided dispositional attributions to explain the shakiness. Although questioned about problems with their *relationship*, only 30 percent of subjects' responses suggested recognition of the contribution of interpersonal factors to their interpersonal difficulties. On the other hand, 62 percent of the people who perceived their relationships to be strong and smooth supported their evaluations with interpersonal premises and attributions. Recent research cited earlier (Berley & Jacobson, 1984; Fincham & O'Leary, 1983; Holtzworth-Munroe & Jacobson, 1985) corroborates the notion that individuals in more conflict-free relationships engage in less blame and have more recognition of the contribution both partners (and outside influences) make to relationship stability versus instability (Bernal & Baker, 1979; Watzlawick *et al.*, 1967).

Besides the danger inherent in overreliance upon dispositional attributions (cf. Altman *et al.*, 1979; Valins & Nisbett, 1979), extensive use of interpersonal attributions may also be problematic. This would be the case when individuals "read themselves into" the causes of their partners' behavior. For example, consider the following illustration: Mrs. Smith, in response to Mr. Smith's request that they spend more time socializing with other couples, concludes that "he doesn't like being alone with me any more." Such an attribution would clearly create a different emotional response from consideration of the explanation that "he is basically an extrovert who seeks social contact" (e.g., Ellis, 1977). It has also been observed in our clinical work that people tend to view their partner's traits through the filters of interpersonal attributions and then react negatively to their own interpersonal premises. For example, the fact that one's partner is a controlling person does not become subject for thought; instead, individuals experience feelings of indignation, anger, and betrayal in response to their perception that "my partner is trying to control *me*."

By relying upon interpersonal attributions, individuals overestimate their own contribution to their partner's behaviors or their partner's contribution to theirs. The interpretation of certain verbal and nonverbal messages of emotion could lead individuals to question, "What did I (or he or she) do to make my partner (me) feel this way," when the more appropriate question might be "Did I do anything to upset him or her?" The latter would allow an answer that extracts the individual from the situation.

This phenomenon, which we have labeled "interpersonal embeddedness," is endemic to intimate relating. Interpersonal embeddedness can be defined as the tendency to (1) perceive a partner's (or one's own) behavior as movement toward or away from self (other), rather than as an event unto itself, and (2) interpret a partner's (one's own) emotional and behavioral expression as, in some way, a function of self (partner). To the extent that interpersonal embeddedness is a problem, individuals will overattribute events to interpersonal factors, assign blame to a partner, and assume personal responsibility for a partner's feelings or problems (e.g., I should take away her anxiety, or I made him angry). These attributions might not only constitute misinterpretations of behavior, emotion, and intention but also promote negative premises regarding oneself, one's partner, or the nature of one's relationship.

Therefore, although psychologists have defined the "fundamental attribution error" (cf. Heider, 1958; Jones, 1979; Ross, 1977) to be an exaggerated awareness of *dispositional* factors over situational ones, within the context of *intimate* relating a second "attribution error" might be to exaggerate the interpersonal significance of random behaviors (those motivated by dispositional or situational factors and not necessarily *intended* as relational messages). This form of attribution error—perceiving one's own or one's partner's behaviors as an interactive response, rather than as an expression of dispositional or idiosyncratic influences—might be more prevalent within those relationships that are characterized by (1) needs for a high level of interpersonal arousal and involvement, (2) a high level of intrapersonal and interpersonal conflict, and (3) a high degree of mutual interdependence. Certain conflicts, misunderstandings, and dissatisfactions that plague intimate relationships might derive from interpersonal premises that individuals read into seemingly innocent behavior. This is particulary likely to occur since the processes of transference and projection inevitably characterize intimate relating and contribute to the distortion of incoming information.

COGNITIVE ACTIVITY AND VERBALIZATION OF ATTRIBUTIONS

The preceding analysis suggests that, to the extent individuals engage in active interpretation of interpersonal events, they create new perspectives on each other's behavior that mediate the establishment of emotional and behavioral response patterns. This sort of mindful cognitive activity could prove problematic if a partner's behavior is overly analyzed and viewed too extensively in connection with the self or in connection with a limited set of explanations. While mindfulness is an adaptive state (Langer, 1980), a high degree of mindfulness about one's relationship may seem to be quite maladaptive because one is potentially drawing more and more negative distinctions regarding the partner and the ongoing interactions.

For example, when emotional conflict or relationship dissatisfaction arises, there follows renewed mindfulness in the form of evaluation, and much of this evaluation reinforces negative interpersonal and dispositional premises. Whereas several recurring periods of extreme mindfulness (e.g., evaluation and attributional analysis) are bound to occur in most relationships, and whereas renewed mindfulness represents a functional, temporary departure from the less mindful stage of relationship stabilization, persisting and high degrees of relationship mindfulness might preclude the ability of partners to regain the comfort and harmony that characterize relationship stabilization. This is especially so if partners are used to a more mindless mode of experience in regard to their relationships (Langer & Imber, 1980).

However, mindful consideration of negative content is potentially more adaptive than mindless acceptance of negative content in that when mindful (1) the process itself is rewarding from an individual's perspective, (2) positive content is more likely to arise for consideration, and (3) more categories become available for subsequent relationship evaluation (Langer, in press). Thus, if during a period of increased mindfulness, an individual latches on to a few negative interpretations of his or her partner's behavior and then proceeds to reduce thought at this point, dissatisfaction and dysfunctional responses might follow. This is more likely to occur when negative evaluations produce anxiety and, in efforts to reduce anxiety, an individual returns to a more mindless state without seeking clarification regarding his or her attributions. On the other hand, if increased mindfulness results in more open and sustained thought about a partner (or a relationship) and an individual can be mindful of *multiple* interpretations for behavior rather than routinizing thought at this level, he or she might ultimately be better able to generate positive interpretations, alternative patterns of response, and resolutions to interpersonal conflict (Berley & Jacobson, 1984). Once an individual can perceive and analyze communication in several different ways, he or she may also seek clarification regarding which are the correct perceptions. One means of seeking such clarification is by verbalizing interpretations and feelings to one's partner.

In the case of verbalizing negative attributions to a partner, the potential for interpersonal conflict may be renewed. This is especially true when individuals either rarely verbalize their feelings and perceptions or verbalize their feelings and perceptions too frequently. It has already been noted that verbalized attributions often serve as important "intercommunications" in their own right (Orvis *et al.*, 1976), and that unverbalized attributions might constitute a more insidious basis for attributional and emotional conflict (Newman, 1981a). For example, suppose *X* interprets *Y*'s bad mood to mean "She's angry at me for staying out so late last night." Suppose, too, that *X*'s interpretation causes feelings of anger and defensiveness in turn. Were *X* to have verbalized his attribution to *Y* in the form of a question ("Why are you angry?") he would have had a chance to validate or disconfirm the hypothesis. Disconfirmation of inaccurate attributions theoretically could decrease the chances for a subsequent eruption of interpersonal conflict. On the other hand, excessive verbalization of perceptions and attributions—such as "Why are you being so cold?; Why can't you be less defensive?; or You're always criticizing me"—may lead a partner to feel intruded upon, criticized, or blamed. These reactions would, in turn, only escalate emotional and communicative conflicts.

Attempts to validate attributions and explore with a partner the reasons behind interpersonal responses might contribute to the process of "metacommunication" (Watzlawick *et al.*, 1967), also referred to as "intentional metacommunication" (Perlmutter & Hatfield, 1980) and as "metatalk." The process of metacommunication—referring to two partners' communication about their relationship (and their communication)—has generally been regarded as a *potentially* adaptive communication effort (e.g., Bernal & Baker, 1979; Perlmutter & Hatfield, 1980; Wilmot, 1975) that often facilitates awareness and resolution of interpersonal problems. However, too much metacommunication, possibly arising from excessive and routinized thought about one's relationship, might exacerbate the likelihood of dysfunctional interaction and prohibit individuals from independently addressing their own contributions to relationship dissatisfaction or conflict. Also there is the danger that dysfunctional patterns of interaction will only be repeated and reinforced on the metacommunicative level (Watzlawick *et al.*, 1967). Furthermore, ongoing emotional experiences and the description or discussion of such experiences might not only constitute quite distinct phenomena, but the latter might serve to reduce, alter, or obscure the former (see Chanowitz & Langer, 1980; Schacter & Singer, 1962; Zajonc, 1980).

On the other hand, a lack of metacommunication, possibly rooted in the reluctance to share those dispositional and interpersonal premises that sustain dissatisfaction, can also be damaging to relationship progress (e.g., Altman & Taylor, 1973; Jourard, 1964). Insufficient metacommunication may preclude the opportunity for individuals to acknowledge, accept, or change existing relationship problems. As with an open, adaptive state of mindfulness, a flexible and open process of metacommunication is necessary for individuals attempting to deescalate negative patterns of relating. It might facilitate a shift, for partners, from a phase of interpersonal conflict to a phase of relationship stabilization. The elucidation of the complex relationships among verbalized and unverbalized attributions, metacommunication, levels of relationship mindfulness, and relationship dissatisfaction still awaits empirical investigation. However, it would seem that whereas metacommunication (with or without the aid of therapeutic intervention) often forestalls or prevents decisions to terminate a relationship, some of the factors described above might contribute to severe emotional changes that make steps to end a relationship inevitable.

RELATIONSHIP ENDINGS

As a stage of relationship development, relationship endings often result from partners' inability to restore (at the interpersonal level) those styles of relating that they depend upon for attaining personal "relationship satisfaction." Although primarily a consequence of *emotional* dissatisfaction and conflict, relationship endings necessitate certain cognitive processes aimed at reducing discomfort and uncertainty. The decision to terminate a relationship will most likely promote a great deal of ambivalence and discomfort; once it is apparent that relationship stabilization cannot be restored, individuals are still faced with the task of justifying their decisions and generating the motivation to break off from their partners (Albrecht & Kunz, 1980). To some extent these tasks will be facilitated not only insofar as other alternatives to the relationship present themselves (Levinger, 1976) but also insofar as individuals can ascribe their own dissatisfaction, and their relational problems, to negative attributes of their partner. As stated earlier, individuals who blame their partners might be more prone to distance themselves emotionally as well as to justify their actions. Unfortunately, in the long run, a reliance upon dispositional attributions could prove maladaptive—especially during the period in which individuals try to adapt to their relationship breakups (e.g., Newman & Langer, 1981).

DEIDEALIZATION, SELF-COLLUSION,
AND INTERPERSONAL DISTANCING

The decision to end a relationship, once made, represents a period in which mindfulness becomes necessary once again. How can one support a decision to dissolve a union that has extracted so much emotional energy and that still provides at least some degree of comfort and familiarity? How can one reject a partner for whom feelings were once so positive? And how can one mobilize energies to make actual movement away from a (familiar) partner and style of life? To aid in efforts at breaking out of relational bonds, people rely upon mindful supports that facilitate detachment and distance. Two of these supports are deidealization and self-collusion.

Through deidealization, as through idealization, people selectively perceive particular attributes that reinforce the evaluation they wish to foster (in this case, a negative one). A heightened attention to what is most undesirable about the other person will take place, and the idealized, positive perceptions that were originally fostered will correspondingly diminish. In addition, individuals will selectively attend to characteristics of their relationships of which they were mindless during relationship beginnings and look to evidence that reinforces whatever negative interpersonal and dispositional premises they have stored within their relationship theories over time. The deidealization process enables people to view their partners from a stance of greater objectivity and more negative emotional involvement; from this removed stance a different picture emerges, one characterized by an emphasis on both the more negative and the more unfamiliar features, which, though perhaps recognized from the beginning, were temporarily excluded from view. This detached mindful stance might explain anecdotal evidence that many individuals perceive an actual change in their partners' physical appearances, usually described as a less attractive look, during relationship endings. This is also quite consistent with the evidence presented earlier from the study on deviance, where mindfulness resulted in erroneous judgments of atypicality (Langer & Imber, 1980).

In addition to the perceptual and emotional changes that characterize deidealization, individuals increase their intrapersonal evaluative statements, further distancing them from their partners. "Self-collusion" is suggested as a label for that private, intrapersonal communication process through which people preoccupy themselves with negative thoughts about their partners and their relationships. We observed, in clinical settings, that self-collusion appears to be a kind of conspiracy process, in that individuals ally or collude with the self against the other person (cf. Willi, 1987). They actively search for data that will provide cognitive support for a desired movement away from their partners or for negative feelings. Furthermore, these negative evaluations are rarely disclosed to partners; therefore, they heighten interpersonal distance and preclude the opportunity for a partner to either disprove them or work to help to change them. During phases of self-collusion, as during deidealization phases, individuals display difficulties in generating and reexperiencing whatever *positive* interpersonal premises they have developed overtime. Self-collusion might be one tool that provides individuals with the leverage and momentum they need in order to deal with the ending process and reduce ambivalence.

ATTRIBUTION-MAKING AND RELATIONSHIP TERMINATION

There is one final cognitive/attributional task that people must attend to when they terminate a relationship. Other people will ask them why their relationships have ended, and they will want to provide clear explanations to others, as well as to themselves, for this event. Once a relationship is over, the manner by which individuals explain, and come to understand, the actual causes of their relationship dissolution might very well affect their personal well-being and self-esteem as well as their feelings about entering a new relationship. In this regard, reliance upon negatively toned dispositional attributions—which point to undesirable characteristics of self and partner—may prove significantly more harmful than interpersonal attributions. For example, Newman and Langer (1981) found that women who made situational and interpersonal attributions for their divorces were more likely to be happy, socially active, generally optimistic, and more confident than those who made dispositional attributions. Situational and interpersonal explanations rather than dispositional attributions more realistically address the issue that the ending of a relationship has resulted from contributing behaviors on the part of *both* partners (e.g., Berley & Jacobson, 1984; Watzlawick *et al.*, 1967) as well as from the contribution of external influences. Dispositional attributions, on the other hand, suggest that stable, personal deficiencies are at the heart of relationship problems and that partners can "fail" at relationships and/or cause each other's total satisfaction or dissatisfaction. Hence they more readily lead to feelings of helplessness.

It is also important to note that simple, unidimensional explanations for relationship endings might prove more maladaptive than consideration of a complex set of interrelated explanations. The Newman and Langer (1981) study, along with other research (e.g., Albrecht & Kunz, 1980), reveals that individuals often offer *one* basic reason why their relationships ended. While this might allow for ease of explaining breakups to other people, it seems to diminish opportunities for individuals to learn from their relational experiences and to better understand relational processes. It also fosters mindlessness for the individual, as he or she is not viewing the complexity of the information which is potentially available about the relationship.

Another phenomenon that this same data revealed was the following: Individuals appear to more easily and readily provide attributions for their relationship endings than they can for their initial choices of a partner. Perhaps people are more aware of the reasons why they leave their relationships than they are of the reasons (often unconscious) why they are getting involved in them in the first place. Indeed, to the extent that individuals are eager at the outset of the relationship to reduce the unpredictability of the new relationship, continued mindful evaluation becomes unlikely. However, to the extent that individuals are in fact mindless in their *choices* of relationship partners, the resulting pattern of relationship conflict and dissatisfaction becomes all the more understandable. It would be interesting to discover whether the divorce rate would be quite as high as it is today if individuals were better equipped to think about and evaluate those reasons *why* they seek out intimate relationships with particular intimate partners in the first place.

SUMMARY AND CLINICAL APPLICATIONS

The preceding discussion offers one framework within which particular relationship processes and problems of communication might be viewed. The ideas presented are suggestive of ways to understand and alleviate relationship distress. We have attempted to highlight various concerns regarding mindful cognitive processes (e.g., interpretation, inference-making, attribution-making) and some basic characteristics of developing intimate relationships. Clinical implications associated with these complex concerns were suggested. A summary of the central ideas we proposed follows.

1. Styles of information-reduction during relationship beginnings (e.g., what information people are open to versus what they close out, or how people interpret behavior and formulate expectations) will predict patterns of communication and interpersonal conflict experienced in later relationship stages.

2. To the extent that individuals are mindless with regard to aspects of a partner's behavior pattern or personality, information that has not been utilized during relationship beginnings might become a source of dissatisfaction later on.

3. Individuals reduce uncertainty by formulating a set of relationship premises. These often include conflicting assumptions. For example, individuals can move through their relationships with certain cognitive "mismatches" between formulated dispositional premises (He is timid; She is controlling) and formulated interpersonal premises (He will protect me; She will share decision-making responsibility democratically), or between formulated dispositional premises (She is too emotional) and other dispositional premises (She is too rational). Efforts to resolve cognitive mismatches and effect ambiguity-reduction can lead to selective interpretation and rationalization for (partners') behaviors facilitated by particular styles of attribution-making. (For example, ambiguity-reduction is facilitated by the use of attributions that promote a basically positive evaluation of one's partner and sustain interpersonal closeness.)

4. The stage of relationship stabilization is characterized by increased comfort and predictability and a reduction in cognitive demands; more opportunity for intrapersonal involvement is facilitated during this stage.

5. Relationship conflict may be prompted by the attribution of the cause of feelings of loss of arousal, dissatisfaction, or unhappiness to the partner and/or relationship. This conflict promotes renewed mindful cognitive activity.

> a. Relationship conflict will be more likely to occur to the extent that people have relied too much upon particular interpersonal and dispositional attributions, have been unable to integrate and explain changes occurring within their relationships, and have been "overly explaining" behaviors with the aid of dispositional or interpersonal attributions.
>
> b. Relationship conflict is exacerbated by heightened attention to negative events and negative discrepancies without mindful exploration of the potentially multifaceted nature of those events or discrepancies. It is also exacerbated by attempts to change one's partner rather than explore intrapersonal conflict and dissatisfaction.
>
> c. Conflict as "form" rather than "content," allows for attempts to enact intrapersonal feelings of anger and dissatisfaction in an interpersonal realm as well as attempts to sustain a desired level of interpersonal arousal or involvement. Interpersonal conflict is often intrapersonally rather than interpersonally generated—yet then is sustained through patterns of interpersonal responding.
>
> d. *Interpersonal embeddedness*, possibly a symptom of excessive mutual interdependence, can cause individuals to perceive random behavior through the lens of a "communicative set," thereby promoting inappropriate explanations and reactions to much behavior that warrants no reaction at all. As part of this process, individuals may project their own feelings and anxieties onto partners, thereby locating within patterns of interpersonal relating that which is actually a function of intrapersonal experience.

6. Relationship endings are characterized by high levels of cognitive activity brought about by reevaluation and uncertainty. Once decisions to terminate a relationship are made, interpretations and attributions are selectively employed and, with the aid of self-collusion, effect overall negative evaluations of partner and interpersonal distancing.

7. The degree to which individuals remain open or closed to communicative information when explaining their relationship endings might influence the nature of their postbreakup adjustment. The attributions and interpretations made during this time may, in turn, influence subsequent relationship beginnings.

REFERENCES

Albrecht, S. L., & Kunz, P. R. (1980). The decision to divorce: A social exchange perspective. *Journal of Divorce, 3*(4), 319–337.

Altmaier, E., Leary, M., Forsyth, D., & Ansel, J. Attribution therapy: Effects of locus of control and timing of treatment. (1979). *Journal of Counseling Psychology, 26*, 481–486.

Altman, I., & Taylor, D. (1973). *Social penetration: The development of interpersonal relationships.* New York: Holt.

Bannister, D., & Fransella, F. (1971). *Inquiring man: The theory of personal constructs.* Harmondsworth, England: Penguin.

Berger, C., & Calabrese, R. (1975). Some explorations in initial intervention and beyond: Toward a developmental theory of interpersonal communication. *Human Communication Research, 1*, 99–112.

Berger, P., & Kellner, H. (1971). Marriage and the construction of reality: An exercise in the microsociology of knowledge. In B. Casin, I. Dale, G. Esland, & D. Swift (Eds.), *School and society: A sociological reader.* Cambridge, MA: MIT Press.

Berkowtiz, L., & Walster, E. (Eds.) (1976). *Equity theory: Toward a general theory of social interaction.* New York: Academic Press.

Berley, R. A., & Jacobson, N. S. (1984). Causal attributions in intimate relationships: Toward a model of cognitive-behavioral marital therapy. In P. Kendall (Ed.), *Advances in cognitive-behavioral research and therapy* (Vol. 3). New York: Academic Press.

Berlyne, D. (1960). *Conflict, arousal and curiosity.* New York: McGraw-Hill.

Bernal, G., & Baker, J. (1979). Toward a metacommunicational framework of couple interactions. *Family Process, 18*, 293–302.

Chanowitz, B., & Langer, E. (1980). Knowing more (or less) than you can show: Understanding control through the mindlessness/mindfulness distinction. In M. E. P. Seligman & J. Garber (Eds.), *Human helplessness.* New York: Academic Press.

Chanowitz, B., & Langer, E. (1981). Premature cognitive commitment. *Journal of Personality & Social Psychology, 41*, 1051–1063.

Crockett, W., & Friedman, P. (1980). Theoretical explorations of the processes of initial interactions. *Western Journal of Speech Communication, 44*, 86–92.

Cronen, V., Pearce, W., & Harris, L. (1979). The logic of coordinated meaning: A rules-based approach to the first course in interpersonal communication. *Communication Education, 28*, 22–38.

Dicks, H. (1953). Experiences with marital tensions seen in the psychological clinic in "Clinical studies in marriage and the family: A symposium on methods." *British Journal of Medical Psychology, 26*, 181–196.

Dicks, H. (1967). *Marital tensions.* New York: Basic.

Doherty, W. J. (1982). Attributional style and negative problem-solving in marriage. *Family Relations, 31*, 23–27.

Duck, S. (1973). *Personal relationships and personal constructs: A study of friendship formation.* London: Wiley.

Ellis, A. (1977). Rational–emotive therapy: Research data that suggest the clinical and personality hypotheses of RET and other modes of cognitive-behavior therapy. *The Counseling Psychologist, 7*, 2–42.

Feldman, L. (1979). Marital conflict and marital intimacy: An integrative psychodynamic–behavioral–systemic model. *Family Process, 18*(1), 69–78.

Fincham, F. D., & Bradbury, T. N. (1987). The impact of attributions in marriage: A longitudinal analysis. *Journal of Personality and Social Psychology, 53*(3), 510–517.

Fincham, F. D., & O'Leary, K. D. (1983). Causal inferences for spouse behavior in maritally distressed and nondistressed couples. *Journal of Social and Clinical Psychology, 1*, 42–57.

Harris, L. (1980). Analysis of a paradoxical logic: A case study. *Family Process, 19*, 19–33.

Harvey, J., Wells, G., & Alvarez, M. (1978). Attribution in the context of conflict and separation in close relationship. In J. Harvey, W. Ickes, & R. Kidd (Eds.), *New directions in attribution research*, (Vol. 2). Hillsdale, NJ: Erlbaum.

Heider, F. (1958). *The psychology of interpersonal relations.* New York: Wiley.

Higgins, E. T. (1987). Self-discrepancy: A theory relating self and affect. *Psychological Review, 94*(3), 319–340.

Holtzworth-Monroe, A., & Jacobson, N. S. (1985). Causal attributions of married couples: When do they search for causes? What do they conclude when they do? *Journal of Personality and Social Psychology, 48*,1398–1412.

Huston, T., & Burgess, R. (1979). The analysis of social exchange in developing relationships. In R. Burgess & T. Huston (Eds.), *Social exchange in developing relationships.* New York: Academic Press.

Jacobson, N. S., Follette, W. C., & McDonald, D. W. (1982). Reactivity to positive and negative behavior in distressed and nondistressed married couples. *Journal of Consulting and Clinical Psychology, 50*, 706–714.

Jacobson, N. S., McDonald, D. W., Follette, W. C., and Berley, R. A. (1985). Attribution processes in distressed and nondistressed married couples. *Cognitive Therapy and Research, 9*, 35–50.

Jones, E. (1979). The rocky road from acts to dispositions. *American Psychologist, 34*, 107–119.

Jones, E., & Davis, K. (1965). From acts to dispositions: The attribution process in person perceptions. In L. Berkowitz (Ed.), *Advances in experimental social psychology* (Vol. 2). New York: Academic Press.

Jones, E., & Nisbett, R. (1972). The actor and the observer: Divergent perceptions of the causes of behavior. In E. Jones, D. Kanouse, H. Kelley, R. Nisbett, S. Valins, & B. Wiener (Eds.), *Attribution: Perceiving the causes of behavior.* Morristown, NJ: General Learning Press.

Jourard, S. (1964). *The transparent self.* Princeton, NJ: Van Nostrand.

Kelley, H. (1979). *Personal relationships: Their structures and processes.* Hillsdale, NJ: Erlbaum.

Klein, M. (1932). *The psychoanalysis of children.* London: Hogarth.

Kruglanski, A. (1975). The endogenous–exogenous partition in attribution theory. *Psychological Review, 82*, 387–406.

Langer, E. (in press). *Mindfulness.* Reading, MA: Addison-Wesley.

Langer, E. (1978). Rethinking the role of thought in social interaction. In J. Harvey, W. Ickes, & R. Kidd (Eds.), *New directions in attribution research* (Vol. 2). Hillsdale, NJ: Erlbaum.

Langer, E. (1980). Old age: An artifact? In S. Kiesler & J. McGaugh (Eds.), *Biology, behavior and aging.* New York: Academic Press.

Langer, E., Blank, A., & Chanowitz, B. (1978). The mindlessness of ostensibly thoughtful action: The role of placebic information in interpersonal interaction. *Journal of Personality and Social Psychology, 36*, 635–642.

Langer, E., & Imber, L. (1980). The role of mindlessness in the perception of deviance. *Journal of Personality and Social Psychology, 39*, 360–367.

Langer, E., & Newman, H. (1979). The role of mindlessness in a typical social psychological experiment. *Personality and Social Psychology Bulletin, 5*, 295–299.

Levinger, G. (1976). A social psychological perspective on marital dissolution. *Journal of Social Issues, 32*, 21–47.

Levinger, S. (1980). Toward the analysis of close relationships. *Journal of Experimental Social Psychology, 16*, 510–544.

Morton, T., Alexander, J., & Altman, I. (1976). Communication and relationship definition. In G. Miller (Ed.), *Explorations in interpersonal communication*. Beverly Hills, CA: Sage.

Newman, H. (1981a). Communication within ongoing intimate relationships: An attributional perspective. *Personality and Social Psychology Bulletin, 7*, 59–70.

Newman, H. (1981b). Interpretation and explanation: Influences on communicative exchanges within intimate relationships. *Communication Quarterly, 29*(2), 123–131.

Newman, H. (1982). Talk about a past relationship partner: Metacommunicative implications. *American Journal of Family Therapy, 10*(3), 24–32.

Newman, H. (1978). A discrepancy-evaluation model of relationship satisfaction versus dissatisfaction. Unpublished manuscript, City University of New York, New York.

Newman, H., & Langer, E. (1981). Post divorce attribution as a function of the attribution of responsibility. *Sex roles, 7*, 223–232.

Orvis, B., Kelley, H., & Butler, D. (1976). Attributional conflict in young couples. In J. Harvey, W. Ickes,, & R. Kidd (Eds.), *New directions in attribution research* (Vol. 1). Hillsdale, NJ: Erlbaum.

Peplau, L., Rubin, Z., & Hill, C. (1977). Sexual intimacy in dating relationships. *Journal of Social Issues, 33*, 86–109.

Perlmutter, M., & Hatfield, E. (1980). Intimacy, intentional metacommunication and second order change. *American Journal of Family Therapy, 8*, 17–23.

Ross, L. (1977). The intuitive psychologist and his shortcomings: Distortions in the attribution process. In L. Berkowitz (Ed.), *Advances in experimental social psychology* (Vol. 10). New York: Academic Press.

Schacter, S., & Singer, J. (1962). Cognitive, social and physiological determinants of emotional state. *Psychological Review, 69*, 379–399.

Stevens, L., & Jones, E. (1976). Defensive attribution and the Kelley cube. *Journal of Personality and Social Psychology, 34*, 809–820.

Taguiri, R., & Petrullo, L. (Eds.). (1958). *Person perception and interpersonal behavior*. Stanford, CA: Stanford University Press.

Thibaut, J., & Kelley, H. (1959). *The social psychology of groups*. New York: Wiley.

Valins, D., & Nisbett, R. (1979). Attribution processes in the developmental treatment of emotional disorders. In E. Jones, D. Kanouse, H. Kelley, R. Nisbett, S. Valins, & B. Wiener (Eds.), *Attribution: Perceiving the causes of behavior*. Morristown, NJ: General Learning Press.

Watzlawick, P., Beavin, J., & Jackson, D. (1967). *Pragmatics of human communication: A study of interactional patterns, pathologies and paradoxes*. New York: Norton.

Wegner, D., & Vallacher, R. (1977). *Implicit psychology: An introduction to social cognition*. New York: Oxford University Press.

Wilmot, W. (1975). *Dyadic communication: A transactional perspective*. Reading, MA: Addison-Wesley.

Willi, J. (1982). *Couples in collusion*. New York: Aronson.

Zajonc, R. (1980). Feeling and thinking: Preferences need no inferences. *American Psychologist, 35*, 151–175.

III

A Social Cognition Perspective on Psychotherapy

7

Psychotherapy as Helping: An Attributional Analysis

VITA C. RABINOWITZ

MICHAEL A. ZEVON

JURGIS KARUZA, JR.

The purpose of this chapter is to consider various psychotherapeutic systems as *helping* interventions and to examine the role of the therapist's attributional judgments on the process of therapy. Construing different psychotherapies as special cases of the broad category of helping allows us to describe them in terms of four basic helping models proposed by Brickman *et al.* (1982). We view psychotherapeutic approaches as differing importantly in the therapist's attributional judgments about the client's responsibility for the origin of his or her problem as well as for the solution to it. The implicit or explicit attributional assumptions of particular psychotherapies may cause each therapy to be more or less appropriate in treating various psychological disorders. In contrast to existing psychotherapies that rely on a single attributional perspective throughout the course of treatment, we suggest that at times it may be useful to shift perspectives in viewing the causes of and solutions to the client's problems as therapy progresses.

PSYCHOTHERAPY AS HELP

In its early form, psychotherapy consisted primarily of a single therapeutic approach employed in the treatment of a narrow range of specific and debilitating disorders (Freud, 1912/1958). Since this beginning, however, psychotherapy has evolved and expanded to encompass a vast number and diversity of therapeutic systems. In their contemporary form, these systems address a wide range of human problems, from specific behavioral disorders to the fostering of optimal human development and growth. As a number of reviews have noted (Corsini, 1973; Goldstein & Simonson, 1971; Urban & Ford, 1971), the days of psychotherapy *qua* psychotherapy are long past.

Despite the multiplicity of modern day therapeutic approaches, it is important not to overlook the fact that psychotherapy remains a helping process (Wills, 1982; Wolman, 1976). As Weiner (1975) has stated, psychotherapy "is an interpersonal process in which one person communicates to another that he understands him, respects him, and wants to be of help to him" (p. 3). From within this framework, we view therapists as help givers who use their skills and training to bring about improvement in their clients' functioning. Clients are seen as recipients of help, individuals who experience and acknowledge, in some sense, an inability to resolve a particular problem or set of problems. We view this helping process as basic to psychotherapy, and see it operating across the theoretical boundaries of particular psychotherapeutic systems.

It is becoming apparent through recent empirical work, however, that the psychotherapeutic process is determined and influenced by a wide variety of factors. These elements range from nonspecific therapeutic ingredients (Goldstein & Stein, 1976), such as the interpersonal relationship between client and therapist (Fehrenbach & O'Leary, 1982; Schofield, 1964), to specific factors, such as the mediating goals and procedures inherent in a particular therapeutic orientation (Parloff, Waskow, & Wolfe, 1978). Together, these components structure the therapeutic process and determine its effectiveness. Given this multidimensional and multidetermined view of psychotherapy, no simple model of the therapeutic process is readily apparent.

Contemporary approaches to the analysis of the therapeutic process (e.g., Howard, Orlinsky, & Perilstein, 1976) have attempted to deal with this complexity by determining the relative contribution of various therapeutic components to the process and outcome of therapy. Taking their lead, we will focus on the therapists and how they translate the mediating goals and procedures of the therapeutic school they embody. Specifically, we will propose an attributional analysis of various therapeutic orientations and consider the attributional foundation of the clinical decisions made by the therapist in psychotherapy.

JUDGMENTS IN PSYCHOTHERAPY

Despite the admitted complexity of psychotherapeutic processes, we will focus here on the clinical decision-making basis from which the therapist makes critical decisions about the client and structures the process and pace of therapy. (Urban & Ford, 1971). On the basis of experience and training in psychotherapeutic systems, the therapist makes, implicitly or explicitly, decisions directed at issues such as whether to accept a client for therapy, the etiology of the presenting complaint, the appropriate interventions, and the criteria for judging the success of the treatment. The therapist must process information about the client and his or her complaint; in other words, the therapist must make a series of evaluations and judgments about the client.

A complicating factor in this view of psychotherapy is the variation of the therapist's role as dictated by the numerous schools of psychotherapy. For example, Gestalt, rational–emotive, and psychoanalytic therapies stress the evaluative and interpretive role of the therapist. On the other hand, therapies such as Rogers's client-centered approach stress a nondirective, evaluation-free orientation. Indeed, client-centered practitioners pride themselves on their nonjudgmental approach to therapy and would perhaps bridle at any intimation that the therapist makes judgments concerning the client. It can be argued, however, on both empirical and logical grounds, that therapists of all persuasions do make judgments about clients and, further, that these judgments either implicitly or explicitly play an important role in psychotherapy. Strupp and colleagues (Strupp, 1978; Strupp & Wallach, 1973; Strupp & Williams, 1973) cogently make the point when they state that whatever the therapist's background or level of training, he or she cannot escape the necessity of (1) forming some notions or hypotheses about the patient's "problem" or difficulty, and (2) deciding what needs to be done to bring about an improvement in the patient's condition. In order to address this issue, a consideration of "judgment" is in order.

Judgments come in a variety of forms. On the one hand a judgment can involve an opinion held about another and, as such, possesses an evaluative or critical component. More pertinent to our analysis, however, is the sense of judgment that refers to an assessment or appraisal that is nonevaluative and instrumental. Judgments of this nature would seem to be endemic to psychotherapy, and, indeed, at the heart of each school of psychotherapy is a theory that defines a particular view of human nature. In attempting to explain behavior, each theory more or less explicitly guides therapists in their attempts to understand clients and their presenting problems. This guidance, in turn, sets up expectancies about clients' potentials and their ability to control their behavior. Implicitly, the theory serves as a prescriptive framework from which the therapist makes instrumental judgments and attributions about the nature of the presenting complaint and how to solve it.

While the proper role of evaluative judgments in psychotherapy may be moot, we view it as unrealistic to contend that instrumental judgments are not or should not be made. While psychotherapies may differ in the form, overtness, and centrality of these instrumental judgments, we view them as basic to the psychotherapeutic process and guided by the theoretical orientation of the therapist.

ATTRIBUTIONAL PROCESSES IN PSYCHOTHERAPEUTIC JUDGMENTS

With the goal in mind of ameliorating the client's presenting complaint, the therapist must make two instrumental judgments; he or she must determine the nature of the presenting complaint and its solution. Using the analysis of

Brickman *et al.* (1982), these judgments may be seen as reflecting two strategic concerns: who or what is to blame for the cause of the presenting complaint and who or what is to have control over its solution. These concerns can best be defined in terms of two distinct attributions about the client: (1) the extent to which the client is responsible for the cause of the presenting complaint, and (2) the extent to which the client is to be held responsible for the solution to the presenting complaint.

Although several researchers and theoreticians (e.g., Ross, Rodin, & Zimbardo, 1969; Storms & McCauly, 1976; Wills, 1978) have applied attributional analysis to clinical issues, they have, in the main, avoided the consideration of the attributional dynamics that define and shape the mediating goals and procedures of therapy. We view this, at least in part, as the result of an inadequate mapping of the instrumental judgments that underlie psychotherapy (as well as other helping interventions, see Karuza, Zevon, Rabinowitz, & Brickman, 1982). As Brickman *et al.* (1982) point out, traditional attributional analyses are predicated on a view of individuals as generally objective scientists who seek to determine the causes of events in order to achieve an accurate understanding of the world. Therapists, however, may be less interested in objectively defining causes of events than with acting on the presenting complaint.

Further, traditional attributional analyses (e.g., Jones & Davis, 1965; Kelley, 1967; Weiner *et al.*, 1971) tend to emphasize how causality is assigned for past or current events. What is typically overlooked is how attributions are made about the cause and control of future behavior, an issue that is critical in setting the goals and direction of therapy. Because of the orientation of existing attributional theories and their language (e.g., internal or external locus of control; stable or unstable, global or specific causes) they do not clearly define the interrelationship of the strategic attributions about the client's responsibility for the cause of the presenting complaint, a past-focused attribution, and the client's responsibility for the solution of the presenting complaint, a future-focused attribution.

In the section that follows we will review the existing theoretical and empirical clinical literature that shows the impact of the attributions about the cause of and solution to the client's presenting complaint on the therapeutic enterprise.

ATTRIBUTIONS ABOUT THE CLIENT'S RESPONSIBILITY

A number of historical trends and ongoing debates in clinical psychology are concerned with determining the most useful attributional perspective for conceptualizing and understanding patients' presenting problems. In a historical vein, the treatment advocated by, among others, Phillipe Pinel and William H. Tuke proposed that mental patients be treated with kindness, understanding, and the belief that they (given the required environmental support) possessed the necessary capacity to effect change and experience a "cure." The decline of moral treatment and the ascendence of medical forms of treatment represented a shift in attributional perspective: The "cure" was now the responsibility of the psychiatric expert, and the patient's responsibility was reduced to a "passive, submissive, quiet, untroublesome waiting for the discovery of a cure" (Ullman & Krasner, 1975, p. 138). In a related vein, the essence of the behaviorists' challenge of psychoanalytic theory is to a large extent the question of whether deviant behavior is caused by factors in the person (an internal attribution—the psychoanalytic approach) or factors in the environment (an external attribution—the behavioral approach). We contend that therapists, as a result of their training and allegiance to a particular theory of abnormal behavior and psychotherapy, operationalize these attributions in terms of assigning responsibility for the causes of and solutions to the patient's problems. In his discussion of the difficulties in understanding abnormal behavior, Price (1972) states:

> What passes for theory in the study of abnormal behavior is often mixed with large doses of ideology. Whether this is a beneficial effect is arguable. In any event, theory and ideology are often mistaken for one another, and it is sometimes unclear whether the intent of a particular viewpoint is descriptive or prescriptive. (p. 5)

Past-focused Attributions

Evidence supporting our contention that therapists make attributions about the client's responsibility for the cause of problems can be found in examinations of the theoretical language of various psychotherapeutic schools. Therapeutic systems such as rational–emotive therapy (Ellis, 1962) and client-centered therapy (Rogers, 1951) adopt a view that stresses personal responsibility for one's actions, while the behavioristic therapies focus on the environment and see the causes of behavior as externally based. The psychoanalytic perspective has, likewise, implicit views on the causes of and responsibility for the client's difficulties. The major thrust of the psychoanalytic approach is a historical analysis of the client in which his or her present dysfunction is seen as caused by a past trauma. The salience of attributions for understanding psychological disturbance is more directly addressed in recent formulations of the learned hopelessness theory, formerly the learned helplessness theory, of depression, which emphasizes an attributional analysis of the causes for negative life events as key to understanding the dynamics of depression (Abramson, Metalsky, & Alloy, Chapter 2, this volume; Abramson, Seligman, & Teasdale, 1978). Increasingly, clinical researchers are recognizing the role of attributions in the development and maintenance of psychological problems, as well as the attributional aspects of psychotherapy (e.g., Harvey & Galvin, 1984; Leary & Maddux, 1987).

Further support for the prevalence of therapist-based attributions about client responsibility for the cause of problems can be inferred from investigations that illustrate the personalistic attributions made by observers for the causes of a client's problems (see Wills, 1978, for a review). An example is the study by Snyder, Shenkel, and Schmidt (1976) in which subjects were instructed to adopt the perspective of a counselor when listening to a therapy interview. Results showed that subjects under these instructions made more personalistic attributions of the cause of the client's problems as compared to subjects instructed to adopt the perspective of the client and subjects in a control group given no instructions. This tendency is echoed in Rosenhan's (1973) well-known study, which reported hospital psychiatric staff as more likely to ascribe the behavior of patients to personalistic, rather than situational, factors. As this discussion suggests, attributions regarding the cause of, and responsibility for, the client's problems are a component of all forms of psychotherapy.

Future-focused Attributions

The question of who should be responsible for solving the presenting complaint is an often overlooked but central one in psychotherapy. Only by making judgments about the client's future potentials, and the extent to which clients can be seen as responsible agents in seeking solutions to their problems, can the therapist rationally design and implement interventions.

Evidence for the salience of attributions of the client's responsibility for the solution to the presenting problem can again be found by examining the theory underlying the activity of the psychotherapist. Each theory of psychotherapy proposes intervention styles or techniques that involve a set of expectations about the client's role in, and potential for, change. Client-centered therapy, for example, sees the client as the ultimately responsible agent. The therapist's role as a change agent is minimized and consists of developing a relationship with the client based on congruence, positive regard, and empathic understanding (Rogers, 1959). Cognitively based behavioral therapies also stress the responsibility of the client for achieving a solution to the problem. The therapist's role is primarily that of a teacher who instructs the client. The client, however, is responsible for the mastery and employment of these techniques.

On the other hand, a number of therapeutic approaches exist that see the client as having little or no responsibility for the solution to the problem. Psychoanalysis is the premier example of a psychotherapy where clients are assumed to have little future responsibility for directly solving their problems. The psychoanalytic approach stresses the unconscious motivation that underlies behavior, a motivation the unanalyzed client can have little hope of controlling or even understanding directly. A further example can be found by examining the approach of therapeutic groups such as Alcoholics Anonymous. Within these therapeutic systems the client is seen as having little individual control over his or her problem. The group, its support system, and a spiritual force are held to be important regulators of behavior and the ultimate "cause" for the future adjustment of the client. Most pronounced, perhaps, is the orientation of pharmacological treatments; their practitioners assume that behavioral change and future effective functioning is largely beyond the ability of the individual. The solution to the problem and the subsequent adjustment of the client result from the administration of the external chemical intervention.

Considerable empirical evidence for the presence, in therapy, of attributions about client responsibility solutions can be found in the clinical literature. For example, Saltzman, Luetgert, Roth, Creaser, and Howard (1976) had therapists and clients rate each other on a variety of dimensions, including the perceived responsibility of the client and the therapist for solving the client's problem. The therapists' assessment of the degree of resolution of the presenting problem was found to be significantly correlated with their perceptions of the clients' acceptance of responsibility. In addition, clients' reported resolution of presenting problems was significantly correlated with their perceptions of their own responsibility for their behavior and with their therapists' perceptions of their responsibility. The fact that judgments of client responsibility were made, and that they were related to therapeutic outcome, shows the importance of considering attributions of the client's future responsibility for the solution to the problem.

As our review suggests, the therapist's attributions about responsibility for the cause of and solution to the client's problems, whether explicit or implicit, combine to affect the entire course of psychotherapy. First, these attributional judgments help define the presenting problem and its scope and therefore allow the therapist to understand the nature of the problem. Second, in assessing the cause of the problem and the potential of the client, the therapist is able to judge when, how, and where to intervene in order to ameliorate the problem. Finally, knowledge of the client's potentials and his or her responsibility for the cause of the problem provides the therapist with indications of where to look for improvement and furnishes guidelines for gauging the effectiveness of therapy.

Ideally speaking, by applying our attributional analysis to psychotherapy, a client can be viewed as having high or low responsibility for the cause of the presenting problem and at the same time be expected to have either high or low responsibility for the resolution of the problem. Thus, by crossing the two attributional dimensions, four distinct attributional combinations in psychotherapy can be derived.

ATTRIBUTIONS OF RESPONSIBILITY AND FOUR MODELS OF HELPING

Both theoretical (Brickman *et al.*, 1982) and empirical (Rabinowitz, 1979) investigations have argued that each of four attributional combinations defines a particular approach to helping. The attributional combinations for presenting problems are high causal responsibility–high solution responsibility, low causal responsibility–high solution responsibility, low causal responsibility–low solution responsibility, and high causal responsibility–low solution responsibility. Each model embodies a specific helping ideology that in turn determines: (1) the characterization of clients, (2) the essential agents of change, and (3) the intervention strategy. Each of these models appears to be internally consistent and incompatible with the others. The models are described most fully in Brickman *et al.* (1982) and are summarized here in Table 7-1. We will first briefly describe the general characteristics of each model.

MORAL MODEL

Attributing responsibility for both the cause and solution of the problem to potential clients characterizes the moral model of treatment. At the beginning of the century, treatment of alcoholics and mental patients was guided by this model. These groups were generally viewed as responsible for their problems and for getting better. When help is given under moral model assumptions, it is the kind of help that motivates or reminds the person to accept responsibility

TABLE 7-1. Consequences of Attribution of Responsibility in Four Models of Helping and Coping

Attribution to self of responsibility for problem	Attribution to self of responsibility for solution	
High	High (Moral model)	Low (Enlightenment model)
Perception of self	Lazy	Guilty
Actions expected of self	Striving	Submission
Others besides self who must act	Peers	Authorities
Actions expected of others	Exhortation	Discipline
Implicit view of human nature	Strong	Bad
Pathology	Loneliness	Fanaticism
Low	(Compensatory model)	(Medical model)
Perception of self	Deprived	Ill
Actions expected of self	Assertion	Acceptance
Others besides self who must act	Subordinates	Experts
Actions expected of others	Mobilization	Treatment
Implicit view of human nature	Good	Weak
Pathology	Alienation	Dependency

Note. Adapted from Brickman *et al.* (1982).

for getting in and out of trouble and to take control of his or her life. Potential clients are considered to be unaware that their own actions or perceptions are at the heart of the problem, or stubborn in their refusal to relinquish these self-defeating actions or perceptions. Helpers' interventions can best be described as motivating or exhorting clients to change themselves.

The moral model is presently exemplified in the vast array of popular "how to" books, newspaper advice columns, and radio phone-in shows. Readers and listeners are generally shown how they have caused or compounded their problems and what they can do to solve or improve the problem. But the most dramatic illustration of the moral model of helping is the formerly fashionable program of Erhard Seminars Training, or est (Brewer, 1975; Frederick, 1974). The primary message to est participants is that they are "deficient" for not having realized that they are totally responsible for everything they ever have been or will be.

COMPENSATORY MODEL

The compensatory model of helping does not attribute responsibility to people for the cause of their problem, but expects them, after help is delivered, to take responsibility for the solution to it. The help is compensatory in the sense that it requires clients to take steps to compensate for their problems. Unlike the moral model, these problems are not seen as caused by the client. Thus, in the compensatory model, clients are seen as deprived or victimized by circumstances beyond their control, yet fully responsible for finding a solution. Helpers are expected to provide resources, training and opportunities to the client, who is expected, in turn, to use them to craft a solution to the problem. Because this kind of help is goal-directed and targeted at specific deficits, it is fixed and temporary in duration.

Examples of help in this model abound in community-action programs and government-sponsored aid to underprivileged minorities. Among psychotherapies, cognitive-behavioral treatments that incorporate such elements as self-observation, cognitive restructuring, contingency contracting, and skills training, are based on this model.

MEDICAL MODEL

The case in which recipients of help are not responsible for either the cause of their problem or the solution to it has come to be known as the medical model of treatment. Problems are viewed as disorders and clients as ill and unable to find solutions. The essential agents of change in this model are expert helpers, who are specially trained to solve a particular set of problems. The intervention requires skilled individuals who provide the needed treatment or service to clients who could not provide for themselves. Help in hospitals is the most familiar embodiment of the medical model.

There are now numerous biological treatments that attempt to relieve psychological disorders by altering some aspect of physiology, particularly the central nervous system. These include psychoactive drugs, electroconvulsive therapy, and the most radical of all biological treatments, psychosurgery.

ENLIGHTENMENT MODEL

In this model, clients are held responsible for the cause of their problem, but not for the solution of their problem. The name is derived from the essential feature of help given under this model: Clients must come to see themselves as the source of their problems, but someone or something outside of themselves as their salvation.

The agent of change in this model is a "force" or authority, often found in a select community of fellow and former sufferers. This group is uniquely suited to provide the critical resources of discipline and understanding. Having or having had the same problem as the client, the group members can sympathize with the client's distress. At the same time, their own experience with the problem gives them the knowledge and legitimacy to impose the strict rules regarded as necessary to contain and manage the problem.

Because the solution to the problem lies outside the individual, it can be maintained only so long as the relationship with the group is maintained. Thus, the treatment is relatively permanent. Past recipients of help in this model often maintain their ties to the community and thus continue to receive help and reaffirm their commitment to improvement by helping others with the same problem. With no help, individuals are seen as likely to continue their troubled behavior.

Some peer support groups for problems like alcoholism, drug addiction, and overeating are examples of enlightenment model helping. In each case, only when participants put their trust and their futures in the therapeutic community can the problem be managed.

UNIQUE ADVANTAGES OF THE HELPING MODEL

These moral, compensatory, medical, and enlightenment models of help represent distinct orientations. While it is ostensibly true that any of the four approaches could be applied to any presenting problem, each of the models occupies a particular domain in which it is uniquely valid and instrumental. In this section, the unique advantages associated with each model will be discussed.

MORAL MODEL

There is probably no model in which greater overall potency is attributed to clients than in the moral one. Within this framework, clients are held responsible for their pasts and futures, successes and failures. By attributing this potency to clients, therapists reflect a belief in the client's capacity to improve, a belief which in itself may cause an amelioration of the presenting complaint. The extensive literature on self-fulfilling prophecy lends further credence to this premise (Rosenthal & Jacobson, 1968). Research further suggests that when clients are induced to view themselves as responsible causal agents, it is more likely that any improvement they do exhibit will be attributed to internal rather than external forces, and thereby be more enduring (Davison & Valins, 1969; Miller, Brickman, and Bolen, 1975).

In a related vein, when clients see themselves as both the source of and solution to their problems, they may avoid the tendency to adopt a "sick role" with its attendant manifestations of dependency and malingering. They may also be less likely to rely unduly on external excuses and supports. As Brickman *et al.* (1982) have contended, holding individuals responsible for solutions (and, often times unfairly, for the causes of problems as well) may be the most effective way to motivate them to make positive changes that they may not otherwise be inclined to make. If, as in the case of a rape victim, a certain measure of personal responsibility is assigned, the victim may be more disposed to install better locks on doors, travel with a companion at night, or move out of a dangerous neighborhood than those victims who view themselves as powerless to prevent future rapes. As Janoff-Bulman (1979) indicated, a majority of women who present themselves for rape counseling do in fact assign some responsibility to themselves for the rape, often for imprudent or unwise behavior.

According to existential philosophers, accepting full responsibility for one's acts affords an individual not only a personal dignity, but also the opportunity to discover the deepest meaning of existence. Viktor Frankl, an existentially oriented psychiatrist and founder of logotherapy, has stated (1959):

> Ultimately, man should not ask what the meaning of his life is, but rather must recognize that it is *he* who is asked. In a word, each man is questioned by life, and he can only answer to life by answering for his own life; to life he can only respond by being responsible. Thus, logotherapy sees in responsibleness the very essence of human existence. (p. 172)

The moral model orientation offers many advantages to therapists as well as clients. If help is given, but is insufficient or fails, the failure cannot be attributed to the therapy. Further, when help does occur in this model, it tends to be offered at the discretion of the therapist, to be limited in scope and duration, and to be symbolic rather than material. The moral model is expected to achieve greatest results when applied to those clients who already possess the resources, talent, support, and opportunities to better themselves, but who require a new perspective on their problems or a motivational boost.

COMPENSATORY MODEL

No model takes a more auspicious view of the client's blameworthiness or prospects than the compensatory model. While clients are not seen as the sources of their own problems, they are perceived as being able to effect necessary changes in their lives. Implicit in this model is a particularly optimistic view of the client's potential: If just given the skills, resources, or opportunities, the client will be successful and self-reliant (Karuza, Zevon, Rabinowitz, & Brickman, 1982).

The attributional pattern of the compensatory model (along with the enlightenment model) asks something of both clients and therapists, and involves the two in a mutually responsive relationship. Therapists are requested to contribute some combination of time, resources, and opportunities to deserving clients in a manner that unites the therapist's feelings of competence with the fate of the clients. While the therapist is active in this form of treatment, the duration of the therapy is expected to be fixed and temporary, because it is the client's role to implement the solution.

Because this model appears to have so much to recommend it, we would expect it to work well with a large variety of clients who can play a significant role in their treatment and whose need is primarily to acquire skills.

MEDICAL MODEL

As with the compensatory model, the medical model orientation does not hold clients responsible for the causes of their problem and thus relieves them of the guilt and anxiety that come from wondering what they have done to bring on their difficulties. Medical ideology specifies that help is to be given to all, regardless of the circumstances surrounding the illness or injury, the personal or social characteristics of the needy, or even how effective the help is likely to be. But because in the medical model clients are also not held responsible for the solutions to their problems, there is probably no model in which clients are seen as more passive and helpless, and more needy of indefinite amounts of help.

The passivity on the part of clients, which is a natural consequence of this model's assumptions, can make it easier to treat certain disorders. If the solution to a problem requires treatment aimed at specific organs or processes rather than at the "whole person," medical model assumptions may be ideal. Passivity on the part of the patients also makes it easier to treat large numbers of patients in a relatively short period of time, and to treat patients in institutional settings. Thus, the medical model may constitute a highly cost-effective type of treatment. The features that make patients easier to treat are, of course, advantageous to helpers in this model.

ENLIGHTENMENT MODEL

How can holding people responsible for problems which they are deemed incapable of solving be advantageous? For one thing, attributing responsibility to clients implies a view of them as effective and willful, if misguided, actors, a view which, we have argued, has its merits. On the other hand, denying clients responsibility for improvement encourages a perception of them as really needing, if not deserving, help. Its historic popularity and current appeal may derive from the fact that, unlike the compensatory model, the assumptions of the enlightenment model call for interventions that keep clients under tight social control.

For another, admitting one's guilt may initially be quite painful, but may ultimately bring a tremendous relief as one relaxes one's pretenses. In addition, the realization that one cannot overcome one's problems by oneself may further reduce discomfort. Encouraging clients to relinquish notions of being able to solve their problems while at the same time holding them responsible for the causes of the problem discourages clients from adopting a "sick role."

Perhaps the greatest advantage of this model lies in the special relationship of the client to the therapeutic community. In no other model is the investment of helpers in the success of the client so large. Indeed, when recipients in this model succeed, it is as if the helper's own solution (and way of life) is vindicated.

When solutions require discipline on the part of recipients, the difficult question of who has the right to impose this discipline must be addressed. When problems require empathy or understanding, the question of who can best empathize with recipients is a delicate one. Clearly, individuals who have overcome the problem seem uniquely suited to provide both discipline and understanding. In this connection, two of the most robust findings in the helping literature are that people who have close personal relationships with others cope better with their problems than those who do not (e.g., Lowenthal & Haven, 1968; Moos & Mitchell, 1982) and that similar others provide troubled people with special validation and support (cf. Gottlieb, 1983). Individuals who would be expected to profit most from the enlightenment model assumptions are those whose solutions require sustained discipline and continued support from concerned others.

THE MODELS AND MODES OF PSYCHOTHERAPY: AN ATTRIBUTIONAL ANALYSIS

The models discussed are seen as relatively pure and general types, strongly determined by specific attributional patterns. As such, we would not expect them to be neatly embodied in any existing form of psychotherapy. Nonetheless, as previously noted, in all modes of psychotherapy implicit and explicit assumptions about the client's responsibility for the causes and solution to the presenting problem are made. Further, these attributions seem to underlie and justify the intervention strategy.

Although there are hundreds of different types of psychotherapies, we can isolate a few dominant modes that illustrate each of the four models. First, however, a few caveats are in order. The mapping of psychotherapies onto models is bound to be somewhat imprecise because, in many cases, attributions of responsibility must be inferred from the therapy's theoretical framework. Further, many of the dominant modes of therapy have significant variations. At the very least, each type of psychotherapy may be interpreted differently by its advocates, and each therapist's unique style and approach to therapy may further contribute to variations within modes. Despite these reservations, we feel that an understanding of psychotherapies may be enhanced by considering the underlying attributional assumptions they make. For heuristic purposes, then, we will consider four ideologically distinct therapeutic approaches: rational-emotive therapy, behavior modification, psychoanalysis, and therapeutic communities.

RATIONAL-EMOTIVE THERAPY AS A MORAL MODEL TREATMENT

Rational-emotive therapy (RET), like several existential therapies, appears to be a clear embodiment of the moral model. Ellis (1962, 1973) rejected the medically toned term "psychotherapy" to describe his approach in favor of descriptors such as "emotional education."

This form of therapy sees clients as stubbornly fixed in their self-defeating perceptions. Their cognitive errors and irrational thoughts are seen as needing "vigorous and persistent attacks" by the therapist (Ellis, 1973). RET is usually conducted in face-to-face settings in as "efficient and rapid-fire a manner as the client can tolerate" (Ellis, 1973).

As we would expect in the case of a moral model treatment, the notion of responsibility is central to Ellis's perception of the causes and solutions to psychological problems. Ellis lays the responsibility for the client's problems squarely on the client's shoulders. He states that "It follows that feelings of worthlessness do not stem from the attitudes that an individual's parents take toward him, but from his one tendency to take these attitudes too seriously, to internalize them, then perpetuate them through the years" (Ellis, 1973, p. 34).

Ellis is just as clear on the locus of the solution to people's problems as he is on their cause. He writes:

> To argue a better solution to the problem of his own worth, the individual had better see his own propensities to exaggerate the significance of others' attitudes toward him, and see clearly that he can vigorously question, challenge, change, and minimize these tendencies toward distorted thinking about himself and others.

Because, in moral model fashion, clients are seen as completely responsible for their problems, treatment is didactic, consisting mainly of persuasion attempts and candid feedback on the client's attempts at change.

BEHAVIOR MODIFICATION AS A COMPENSATORY MODEL TREATMENT

We regard the recently developed self-control and social and cognitive learning therapies as examples of compensatory model treatments. The following is just a sampling of the therapies that have been called self-control or cognitive learning therapies (cf. Mahoney & Arnkoff, 1978): self-monitoring, the strategy of recording one's habits; self-reinforcement, the self-presentation of rewards contingent on performance of some desired response; thought stopping, the procedure designed to terminate unwanted cognitions; and coping skills therapy, a combination of procedures such as relaxation training, meditation, and preperformance rehearsal. The therapies that come under this umbrella are varied in their underlying assumptions and their intervention strategies. What they share, however, is the belief that maladaptive behavior and cognitive processes, no matter how developed, can be treated by teaching the clients skills and techniques for rearranging the environmental contingencies that affect their behavior.

Unlike radical behaviorists, who adopt the view that the individual is but a pawn of external influences (Skinner, 1972), utterly incapable of influencing his or her own actions, let alone being responsible for them, cognitively oriented behavior therapists generally advocate a position of "reciprocal determinism." This is the notion that people are, in fact, partially free because environmental contingencies are partly of their own making (Bandura, 1977). But whether a behavorist supports the position of environmental determinism or of a reciprocal relationship between environment and behavior, virtually all behavior therapy techniques look to faulty environmental contingencies as the source of the problem.

Consistent with this attribution, solutions are believed to follow a simple rearrangement of the contingencies. The role of the behavior modifier is critical, but limited to that of a "diagnostician–educator" (Mahoney & Arnkoff, 1978). He or she assesses the maladaptive cognitive processes and teaches the client how to alter the cognitions, behaviors, and patterns of affect that are troublesome. Once taught how to recognize and control maladaptive thoughts and behaviors, however, the client is often expected not only to monitor his or her own behavior and to compare monitored performance to goals or standards, but also to self-reward or self-criticize (Kanter, 1970).

PSYCHOANALYSIS AS A MEDICAL MODEL TREATMENT

Psychoanalysis is the process by which unconscious conflicts are brought into consciousness, that is, abreaction. There they can be examined, "understood," and accepted, and the effects of events and experiences of the past can be interpreted in the light of these conflicts. The therapist's interpretations of the patient's dreams, free associations, malapropisms, and humor are traced to the influence of unconscious repressed instinctual drives and defenses. The transference of the client's beliefs and feelings from significant others in his or her life to the therapist is believed to be a necessary component of this process.

Traditional psychoanalysis holds that individuals are at the mercy of forces which they cannot identify or understand, let alone control. Human nature, the fallibility of parents, and the rigid demands of civilized society all combine to create neurotic patterns in the individual. More specifically, neuroses are seen as forced upon individuals by the peculiar circumstances of their lives; too much or too little gratification, frustration, condemnation, and so forth. It is one purpose of psychoanalysis to relieve patients of their guilt and responsibility for their past. Discussing psychoanalysis, Dollard and Miller (1950) point out:

> From the patient's standpoint, the novelty of the therapeutic situation lies in its permissiveness. The therapist is understanding and friendly. He is willing, so far as he can, to look at matters from the patient's side and make the best case for the patient's view of things. (p. 243)

> The therapist takes the view that what is past had to happen. The patient understands this acceptance as forgiveness, which in a sense, it is. . . . If the recital is followed by condemnation and punishment, we would not expect the effect of the confession to be therapeutic. (pp. 245–246)

It has been noted that simply being accepted for psychoanalytic treatment is so reassuring to clients that it is immediately followed by a decrease in symptomatology.

The solutions to the client's problems, like the causes, are seen as lying entirely outside the patient. Learning, or any real change in personality, comes about only through psychoanalysis. Since the dynamics of behavior lie hidden in the unconscious, the unanalyzed client cannot possibly know the real truth about himself or herself, despite his or her best efforts and those of significant others. In fact, the analyst generally takes the position that the client cannot and should not discuss his or her problems with anyone else, as that would weaken the transference. Talking freely with the analyst is regarded as therapeutically sufficient. Because they do not adequately understand their motives, new clients are warned that they should not, at least in the short run, make any major decisions or changes in their lives without consulting their analyst.

Psychoanalysis may be distinguished from other psychotherapies primarily by the therapist's interpretations of the client's statements, and on the presumed necessity for the therapist to uncover the client's drives and motives. Of course, the asymmetrical relationship between analyst and patient facilitates this general relinquishing of responsibility by the client. In typical medical model fashion, the therapist is viewed as an expert in an esoteric area poorly understood by the uninitiated. The behaviors of the client are viewed as "symptoms" of an underlying disorder.

THERAPEUTIC COMMUNITIES AS ENLIGHTENMENT MODEL TREATMENTS

As we noted earlier, we see many group therapeutic treatments as examples of help based on enlightenment model grounds. Obviously, this form of treatment appears to be much more narrow and focused than the other examples reviewed in this section. However, the model on which these groups are based can be and appears to have been applied to a variety of specific problems, including drug addiction (e.g., Daytop Village), obesity (e.g., Overeaters Anonymous), and compulsive gambling (e.g., Gamblers Anonymous), and to general problems in living. Two central features of all of these treatments can be identified: (1) the existence of a special community of former or current sufferers as the agents of change, specifically of emotional support and discipline, and (2) the client's acceptance of and strict adherence to enlightenment model assumptions about the causes of and solutions to the problem.

People who join group therapeutic treatments are either predisposed or socialized to accept full responsibility for their problem. Any confession by a newcomer that attempts to share the blame with family or friends is roundly denounced. At the same time that clients are required to acknowledge their responsibility for the problem, they are also required to admit that the problem is beyond their ability to solve or control. They are compelled to acknowledge that forces beyond their control determine their futures—the power embodied in the community of repentent and reformed peers. It is only with the help of the community that group members' desire to drink (or overeat or gamble, and so forth) can be overcome. The closely knit community, with its rituals of confessions and testimonials, serves to reinforce the notions of accepting responsibility for the solution.

IMPLICATIONS OF AN ATTRIBUTIONAL ANALYSIS
OF PSYCHOTHERAPY

We have detailed an attributional analysis of the decision-making component in psychotherapy. In doing so, we have proposed that various psychotherapeutic schools and their intervention strategies are describable in terms of their underlying attributional assumptions. In this section we will consider some of the implications our attributional analysis has for the psychotherapy.

Specific psychotherapies may be differentially efficient and effective for certain subsets of clients and disorders. We would further maintain that as an alternative to arguing for the supremacy of one psychotherapy over another, closer attention should be paid to considering the attributional assumptions of the therapeutic school and how they are translated into the activity of the therapist.

While at this juncture it is tempting to offer a series of prescriptions of which therapy would be optimally effective for particular disorders, we feel we must resist at present. Several factors lead us to this position. For one, several attempts have been made at offering prescriptive framworks (e.g. Goldstein & Stein, 1976). In general, a mixed picture has emerged. This lack of clarity is due, in a large measure, to a realization of the complexity of the therapeutic effort. As was pointed out previously, a host of factors, ranging from client and therapist characteristics to the mediating goals of a particular therapeutic system, interact to produce the structure and pace of therapy. In this context, a therapy's attributional assumptions may be only one factor, albeit a potentially important one, that governs the efficacy of the therapeutic intervention.

A second difficulty in offering prescriptive statements is the possibility of slippage between the therapist's ideological orientation and his or her actual practice of therapy. The therapist's expectancies and approaches may not directly mirror the formal school he or she represents. In a real sense, the therapist's experiences and worldview may dilute and distort the "pure" orientation of the formal therapeutic system. Indeed, research by Fiedler (1950) and Strupp (1955; Strupp & Wallach, 1973; Strupp & Williams, 1973) has shown that the distinction among therapists of different schools blurs when one investigates therapists who have been practicing for an extended period. These therapist factors, such as their worldview or expectations about clients and the presenting complaints, may affect the attributional process and color the instrumental judgments guiding the therapy. Any attempts to offer a convincing prescriptive framework should consider these therapist factors in conjunction with the formal tenets of the psychotherapeutic system. While such a full-blown analysis is beyond the scope of this chapter, it is our hope that research that considers both the formal and informal attributional processes in therapy (especially on the consequences of having an accurate mapping of the client's responsibility for the cause of the presenting complaint and for its solution) can offer the basis for prescriptive statements about therapeutic effectiveness.

PROBLEMS IN ADOPTING
AN ADEQUATE ATTRIBUTIONAL PERSPECTIVE

One important issue in this research is an adequate definition of a "proper attribution" of the client's responsibility. Should the client's beliefs about causality, the results of diagnostic instruments, or the therapist's understanding of the situation serve as the criterion? Further, the existence of causal chaining (Brickman, Ryan, & Wortman, 1975) may compound the questions of finding an adequate attributional framework. As these authors point out, there is no logical reason why attributions about the causes of events should stop at any one point. For example, an internal cause for a disorder (a disposition or trait) may itself be attributed to an external cause, (for example, the child-rearing practices of an individual's family). In a certain sense, it may be a matter of personal preference as to where to look for the causes of particular behaviors or how far one is willing to go before the "true" cause is found. The assumptions of the therapeutic school and the helping model it embodies may artificially direct the search for the causes and solutions of the problem. In practice, though, the stopping point in the causal chain may be operationally determined as the intervention strategy based on the set of attributions that first lead to a desirable change in the client. We see these questions, however, as empirical in their scope. Research exploring the relationship of client, therapist, and "objectively" based attributions to the effectiveness of the therapy is needed. On a theoretical level, however, we can specify certain factors that may cloud the true attributional picture.

First, the therapist's allegiance to a particular psychotherapeutic model may bias attributions about the cause of the client's presenting complaint and the solution for that complaint. Acting upon these attributional assumptions, the therapist may incorrectly define the etiology of the client's problem. The resulting interventions may be inappropriately related to the problem and, in the worst possible case, work against the client.

A related and complicating factor is the inherent complexity of causal analysis. Nisbett and Ross (1980) address this issue in the context of human inference; their arguments, however, directly apply to the activity of the psychotherapist. Particularly relevant is the principle of misguided parsimony, otherwise known as the "hydraulic" model of causation. Drawing upon Mill (1843/1974) and Kanouse (1972), the authors state:

> The pronounced availability effects on causal attribution would appear to depend on the individual's willingness to be content when a single sufficient cause has been adduced and to forego exhaustive searches for further, potentially influential antecedents. That is, by manipulating the causal factors that the person will notice or ponder first, one can manipulate the person's ultimately preferred explanation for the event in question. (p. 128)

Our contention is that, in psychotherapy, the causal factors that are perceived first will be those most congruent with the attributional perspective of the therapist.

A further source of attributional bias in therapy may be the tendency of therapists to view their clients in a negative light (Wills, 1978). A number of studies have shown that therapists and professional help givers view clients as less adjusted (Wills, 1978), less capable of improvement (Batson, O'Quin, & Pych, 1982), and more in need of help as contrasted with individuals not seeking treatment and with the perceptions of the clients themselves. This negative bias may shape and direct the therapist's attributional judgments and lead him or her to see the client as less responsible both for the cause of the presenting complaint and for its solution. In terms of the analysis presented above, this lack of responsibility for cause and solution is characteristic of the medical model orientation. In other words, the negativity bias may cause the therapeutic endeavor to regress toward this medical model orientation, which views the client as sick and dependent on the therapist for amelioration of the problem. This negativity bias is a therapist-specific factor that operates independently of any formal theoretical orientation.

Wills suggests several causes for this bias. Of particular importance is the fact that the clinician's training and experiences may lead to a selective focus on the weakness and deficiencies of clients. Large caseloads and their resulting time pressures may force the therapist to concentrate on the problematic aspects of the client's behavior "because these are most immediately relevant for ameliorating the client's presenting problem" (Wills, 1978, p. 987). Certain personal or social characteristics of clients, such as advanced age, appear to elicit among professional helpers and observers alike unfavorable assumptions about the clients' prospects for solving their problems or controlling their futures (Karuza, Zevon, & Rabinowitz, 1986; Zevon, Karuza, & Brickman, 1982). In addition, the therapist's training may predispose him or her to identify negative or unpleasant facts in the client's background as playing an important etiological role (Meehl, 1973).

This negativity bias may be particularly deleterious when one considers that it may work against psychotherapies that reflect the moral, compensatory, or enlightenment models. The therapist may be caught between the attributional assumptions reflected in the therapeutic orientation and his or her personal attributional bias in regard to the client's responsibility. The negative bias may become prepotent for the therapist and result in the therapy drifting toward medical model attributional assumptions and associated intervention strategies.

Also contributing toward this drift is a corresponding therapist "burnout" effect. The initial image of the client as a troubled and overwhelmed individual stands in contrast to the image of the therapist as a responsible, competent expert. If the therapist were not perceived in this way, the client would presumably not seek his or her help, and the therapist would not inspire the confidence needed for a successful therapeutic interaction (Frank 1973). At least relative to the clients, then, therapists may initially view themselves as being in control of their lives, responsible for their problems and solutions. With competence attributed to them and deficits attributed to clients, they may also view themselves as responsible for clients and the course of therapy.

However, all of the factors that make it difficult for clients in psychotherapy to improve, including the simple intractability of some problems, make it easy for therapists to change their perceptions of themselves as well as their clients. When help is wholly or partly unsuccessful, there is some evidence to suggest that therapists tend to minimize their own responsibility for clients and heighten their sense of client's responsibility for themselves (Maslach, 1978; Wills, 1978). The therapist who has devoted much time and effort to an unsuccessful case may come to believe that the client is at fault for the failure to help because he or she is stubborn, uncooperative, irresponsible, or incorrigible. At the same time, the therapist may come to feel frustrated and helpless for being ineffective (Maslach, 1978). In the end, especially with unsuccessful cases, the attributional orientation of the therapist is likely to be the reverse of what it was at the start of therapy. Therapists may see clients as responsible for the causes of their problems and their failure to improve. On the other hand, they may see themselves as not responsible for their client's problems or for solving those problems.

PROCESS REDEFINED

In the beginning, we viewed psychotherapy as a problem-solving process in which the therapist's attributional judgements played an important role in the dynamic process of defining the client's presenting complaint, setting the goals of therapy, and crafting a solution for the client's problem. In our considerations of the attributional bases of various psychotherapeutic systems, much of this process view was absent. For the sake of expediency, we intentionally adopted a static compartmentalized view of these components of psychotherapy. We did so for two reasons: first, to isolate and highlight the particular attributional orientation of each therapy, and, second, to illustrate how the attributional orientation defines and is mirrored in the actual intervention strategy of the therapist. *In vivo*, psychotherapy is an ongoing process that ideally leads the client through a series of cognitive/emotional changes. As therapy progresses, changes occur in the client–therapist relationship, the client's self-disclosure (Jourard, 1964), self-perceptions, self examination, and behavior. For each psychotherapeutic school, the attributional assumptions not only define the nature of the presenting complaint, but offer the therapist a criterion, or definition of a fully functioning, adjusted client. The thrust of the therapeutic endeavor is to lead the client to this goal. In this traditional sense, the process of therapy is theoretically canalized.

At this point, we would like to reconsider the process notion in therapy from an admittedly speculative perspective. As the therapy progresses and interventions are implemented, changes may occur in the client's behavior and his or her verbal reports, changes that may be indicative of a shift in the client's view of his or her responsibility for past, present, and future actions. The ability and tendency of the therapist to recognize these changes and reevaluate the client's responsibility for his or her actions may be limited by the directional momentum of the therapy. As indicated above, the therapist may adhere to a specific set of attributions about the client that are dictated by the therapist's theoretical orientation. Thus, the therapist may fail to recognize change in the client, incorrectly attribute causes for a particular behavior of the client, distort the potentials of the client, or continue with interventions that are ineffective or irrelevant. When clients do not fit the attributional profile dictated by the therapeutic system, therapists may label the client as uncooperative or incompetent, or the therapists may start to feel that they are failing. This may set the stage for the negativity bias in viewing clients or, in the long run, to therapist "burn-out."

Conversely, if the client is initially "cooperative" and responds to the therapy early on with an alleviation of symptoms, the therapist may be seduced into accepting the attributional assumption of the therapy as an absolute. Thus, the therapist may set up expectancies for the client that mirror the attributional ideology of the therapeutic system, expectancies that may be unrealistically accepted and embodied by the client. Further, the therapist, upon seeing the preliminary success of the treatment, may be tempted to continue treating the client with the same intervention strategy that brought about the initial change, even though it is based on erroneous assumptions and is unlikely to be helpful in the long run.

Erroneous attributions about the client's ability to take responsibility for solving a problem may underlie some current approaches to the treatment of alcoholism. A controversial issue in the treatment of alcohol abuse is whether alcoholics can learn to control their drinking so that they can drink in moderation. The prospect of being able to "drink socially" is appealing to many alcoholics and attracts them to treatment (Pomerleau, Pertschuk, Adkins, Brady, 1978). Several multimodal cognitive-behavior therapies have been developed to promote controlled drinking among alcoholics. These therapies embody the characteristically optimistic compensatory model assumptions that once clients acquire the knowledge, skills, and resources to control their drinking, they can become responsible "social drinkers." To this end, clients receive education about the effects of alcohol and how to discriminate their blood alcohol level, group therapy, self-management skills, job-seeking and interpersonal skills training, social drinking practice sessions and relaxation training. Despite reports of short-term success with such programs, there is no evidence to suggest that they have any long-term success (Armor, Polich, & Stambu, 1976; Foy, Nunn, & Rychtarik, 1984) or that their orientation to alcoholism is valid over time.

In redefining the "process" in psychotherapy, we are contending that therapy naturally affects the client's and therapist's view of the client's responsibility. We propose that this fluidity of attributional perspective may be adaptive, and offer it as an alternative to the more intransient attributional stance associated with existing theories of psychotherapy. Specifically, we see that each of the four attributional views of the client may be valid at various steps in the course of therapy. As clients change, the old set of attributions guiding the therapist's activities may no longer be relevant, while new assumptions of the cause of the client's present and future behavior may become valid. Instead of locking the client into a fixed set of attributions, we are arguing that therapists should be flexible, reevaluating clients periodically and implementing interventions that are in keeping with the changes in the clients' perceived responsibility for their behavior and in their newly developing potentials. In other words, we are proposing a guided eclecticism in which the attributional orientations and interventions of each therapeutic model are employed. As therapy progresses, instead of approaching the client from a particular therapeutic vantage point, a shifting perspective may better serve the goals of psychotherapy.

To illustrate this point, let us consider a rational–emotive approach, which reflects the moral model of helping. A client, when he or she first approaches the therapist, may indeed feel helpless and dependent, more typical of someone who fits a medical model orientation. The first task of the therapist, rather than preaching self-reliance, might be to help organize the client's life, offering suggestions and directions on how to take care of some of the pressing problems of the client (e.g., "Whom should I see for a divorce?" or "How can I avoid confronting my mother?"). As the client gets on firmer footing, the therapist may then shift to a compensatory approach, training the client in skills needed to cope with the demands of life (e.g., assertiveness training) and reinforcing the client's sense of responsibility for his or her future. After these skills have been acquired, the therapist may be better able to implement the rational–emotive approach, that is, to encourage and motivate the client to take control over his or her life.

An example of this can be found by considering the "paradox of depression." According to Abramson and Sackeim (1977), depressed people blame themselves for their own unhappiness and that which they inflict on others, yet feel helpless to do anything about the situation. From the vantage point of the models, the paradox disappears. Feelings of responsibility for problems and solutions, for pasts and futures, need not be correlated. It seems entirely possible that people might feel responsible for the origin of the problem, but not for the solution.

When people become stuck in this attributional set, relief may come simply by moving them out of this set—to any of the others. If it is recognized that a central problem with depression is precisely this pattern of attributions, then helping might take the form of changing people's attitudes about the origin or the solution to the problem. The recent popularity of cognitively oriented therapies such as Beck's (1976) for problems like depression may indicate the virtues of demanding more active and responsible behavior on the part of the client.

Increasingly, it is becoming clear that more than half of all visits to physicians are for conditions with no known physical basis (Cummings & Follette, 1976). Many of the complaints brought to medical doctors are stress-related illnesses or physical symptoms caused by psychological problems. Doctors and patients who pursue biological explanations for what are essentially emotional problems and look to a pill, a shot, or an operation to cure the malady may be incorrectly applying the medical model to the presenting problem. Mounting evidence suggests that simply inducing these patients to discuss their problems and feelings and enter short- or long-term psychotherapy can have lasting positive effects on their physical health (Cummings & Follette, 1976; Jones & Vischi, 1979). One of the most commonly offered explanations for this consistent finding is that the psychotherapeutic and behavioral treatments make patients more active and responsible participants in their own care. Again, it appears that guiding clients to adopt a new orientation to long-standing problems can be quite beneficial.

By following a more fluid or cyclic approach, the advantages of each therapy can be used to build a more comprehensive and effective therapeutic effort. At the same time, the problems associated with a unidirectional attributional approach may be avoided. What we are proposing is theoretical in nature, and perhaps anathema to theoretical purists. However, we hope that a consideration of the attributional foundations of psychotherapy and the dynamic changes in attributions inherent in therapy will stimulate research in social and clinical psychology that, in the long run, will inform and improve the therapeutic process.

REFERENCES

Abramson, L. Y., & Sackeim, H. A. (1977). A paradox in depression: Uncontrollability and self-blame. *Psychological Bulletin, 84*(5), 838–851.
Abramson, L. Y., Seligman, M. E. D., & Teasdale, J. (1978). Learned helplessness in humans: Critique and reformulation. *Journal of Abnormal Psychology, 87*, 49–74.
Armor, D. J., Polich, J. M., & Stambul, H. B. (1976). *Alcoholism and treatment.* Santa Monica, CA: Rand Corporation.
Bandura, A. (1977). Self-efficacy: Toward a unifying theory of behavioral change. *Psychological Review, 84*, 191–215.
Batson, C. D., O'Quin, K., & Pych, V. (1982). An attribution theory analysis of trained helpers' inferences about clients' needs. In T. A. Wills (Ed.), *Basic processes in helping relationships.* New York: Academic Press.
Beck, A. T. (1976). *Cognitive therapy and emotional disorders.* New York: International Universities Press.
Brewer, M. (1975, August). Erhard seminars training: "We're gonna tear you down and put you back together." *Psychology Today*, pp. 35–40, 82, 88–89.

Brickman, P., Rabinowitz, V. C., Karuza, J., Jr., Coates, D., Cohn, E., & Kidder, L. (1982). Models of helping and coping. *American Psychologist, 37*(4), 368–384.

Brickman, P., Ryan, K., & Wortman, C. B. (1975). Causal chains: Attribution of responsibility as a function of immediate and prior causes. *Journal of Personality and Social Psychology, 32*, 1060–1067.

Corsini, R. J. (1973). *Current psychotherapies.* Itasca, IL: F. E. Peacock.

Cummings, N. A., & Follette, W. T. (1976). Brief psychotherapy and medical utilization: An eight-year follow-up. In H. Sörken & Associates (Eds.), *The professional psychologist today: New developments in law, health insurance, and health practice.* San Francisco, CA: Jossey-Bass.

Davison, G. C., & Valins, S. (1969). Maintenance of self-attributed and drug-attributed behavior change. *Journal of Personality and Social Psychology, 11*, 25–33.

Dollard, J., & Miller, N. E. (1950). *Personality and psychotherapy: An analysis in terms of learning, thinking, and culture.* Toronto: McGraw-Hill.

Ellis, A. (1962). *Reason and emotion in psychotherapy.* New York: Lyle Stuart.

Ellis, A. (1973). *Humanistic psychotherapy: The rational-emotive approach.* New York: McGraw-Hill.

Fehrenbach, P. A., & O'Leary, M. R. (1982). Interpersonal attraction and treatment decisions in inpatient and outpatient psychiatric settings. In T. A. Wills (Ed.), *Basic processes in helping relationships.* New York: Academic.

Fiedler, F. (1950). A comparison of therapeutic relationships in psychoanalytic, non-directive and Adlerian therapy. *Journal of Consulting Psychology, 14*, 436–445.

Foy, D. W., Nunn, L. B., & Rychtarik, R. G. (1984). Broad-spectrum behavioral treatment for chronic alcoholics: Effects of training controlled drinking skills. *Journal of Consulting and Clinical Psychology, 52*, 218–230.

Frank, J. D. (1973). *Persuasion and healing: A comparative study of psychotherapy.* Baltimore: Johns Hopkins University Press.

Frankl, V. (1959). *From death camp to existentialism.* Boston: Beacon.

Frederick, C. (1974). *EST: Playing the game the new way.* New York: Dell.

Freud, S. (1958). [Recommendations to physicians practicing psycho-analysis]. In J. Strachey (Ed. & trans.) *The standard edition of the complete psychological works of Sigmund Freud* (Vol. 12). London: Hogarth Press. (Originally published, 1912.)

Goldstein, A. P., & Simonson, N. R. (1971). Social psychological approaches to psychotherapy research. In A. E. Bergin & S. L. Garfield (Eds.), *Handbook of psychotherapy and behavior change.* New York: Wiley.

Goldstein, A. P., & Stein, N. (1976). *Prescriptive psychotherapies.* New York: Pergamon.

Gottlieb, B. H. (1983). Social support as a focus for integrative research in psychology. *American Psychologist, 38*, 278–287.

Harvey, J. H., & Galvin, K. S. (1984). Clinical implications of attribution, theory and research. *Clinical Psychology Review, 4*, 15–33.

Howard, K. I., Orlinsky, D. E., & Perilstein, J. (1976). Contribution of therapists to patients' experiences in psychotherapy: A components of variance model for analyzing process data. *Journal of Consulting and Clinical Psychology, 44*, 250–256.

Janoff-Bulman, R. (1979). Characterologic versus behavioral self-blame: Inquiries into depression and rape. *Journal of Personality and Social Psychology, 37*, 1798–1809.

Jones, E. E., & Davis, K. E. (1965). From acts to dispositions. In L. Berkowitz (Ed.), *Advances in experimental social psychology.* New York: Academic.

Jones, K., & Vischi, J. (1979). Impact of alcohol, drug abuse, and mental health treatment on medical care utilization: A review of the research literature. *Medical Care, 17*(12), 1–82.

Jourard, S. M. (1964). *The transparent self: Self-disclosure and well-being.* New York: Van Nostrand.

Kanouse, D. E. (1972). Language, labeling, and attribution. In E. E. Jones, D. E. Kanouse, H. H. Kelley, R. E. Nisbett, S. Valins, & B. Weiner (Eds.), *Attribution: Perceiving the causes of behavior.* Morristown, NJ: General Learning Press.

Kanter, F. H. (1970). Self-monitoring: Methodological limitations and clinical applications. *Journal of Consulting and Clinical Psychology, 35,* 148–152.

Karuza, J., Jr., Rabinowitz, V. C., & Zevon, M. A. (1986). Implications of control and responsibility on helping the aged. In M. M. Baltes & P. B. Baltes, *The psychology of control and aging.* Hillsdale, NJ: Erlbaum.

Karuza, J., Jr., Zevon, M. A., Rabinowitz, V. C., & Brickman, P. (1982). Attribution of responsibility by helpers and recipients. In T. A. Wills (Ed.), *Basic processes in helping relationships.* New York: Academic.

Kelley, H. H. (1967). Attribution theory in social psychology. *Nebraska Symposium of Motivation, 15,* 192–228.

Leary, M. R., & Maddux, J. E. (1987). Progress toward a viable interface between social and clinical-counseling psychology. *American Psychologist, 42,* 904–914.

Lowenthal, M. F., & Haven, C. (1968). Interaction and adaptation: Intimacy as a critical variable. *American Sociological Review, 33,* 20–30.

Mahoney, M. J., & Arnkoff, D. B. (1978). Cognitive and self-control therapies. In S. L. Garfield & A. E. Bergin (Eds.), *Handbook of psychotherapy and behavior change: An empirical analysis* (2nd ed.). New York: Wiley.

Maslach, C. (1978). The client role in staff burn-out. *Journal of Social Issues, 34*(4), 111–124.

Meehl, P. E. (1973). Why I do not attend case conferences. In P. E. Meehl (Ed.), *Psychodiagnosis: Selected papers.* New York: Norton.

Mill, J. S. (1974). *A system of logic ratiocinative and inductive: Being a connected view of the principles of evidence and the methods of scientific investigation.* Toronto: University of Toronto Press. (Original work published 1843)

Miller, R. L., Brickman, P., & Bolen, D. (1975). Attribution versus persuasion as a means of modifying behavior. *Journal of Personality and Social Psychology, 31,* 430–441.

Moos, R. H., & Mitchell, R. E. (1982). Social network resources and adaptation: A conceptual framework. In T. A. Wills (Ed.), *Basic Processes in Helping Relationships.* New York: Academic.

Nisbett, R., & Ross, L. (1980). Human inference: Strategies and shortcomings of social judgment. Englewood Cliffs, NJ: Prentice-Hall.

Parloff, M. B., Waskow, I. E., & Wolfe, B. E. (1978). Research on therapist variables in relation to process and outcome. In S. L. Garfield & A. E. Bergin (Eds.), *Handbook of psychotherapy and behavior change: An empirical analysis* (2nd ed.). New York: Wiley.

Pomerleau, O. F., Pertschuk, M., Adkins, D., & Brady, J. A. (1978). A comparison of behavioral and traditional treatment of middle-income problem drinkers. *Journal of Behavioral Medicine, 1,* 187–200.

Price, R. H. (1972). *Abnormal behavior: Perspectives in conflict.* New York: Holt, Rinehart and Winston.

Rabinowitz, V. C. (1979). Orientations to help in four natural settings. (Doctoral dissertation, Northwestern University, 1978). *Dissertation Abstracts International.* (University Microfilms No. 79-07, 928.)

Rogers, C. R. (1951). *Client-centered therapy.* Boston: Houghton Mifflin.

Rogers, C. R. (1959). A theory of therapy, personality and interpersonal relationships as developed in the client-centered framework. In S. Koch (Ed.), *Psychology: A study of a science* (Vol. 3). New York: McGraw-Hill.

Rosenhan, D. L. (1973). On being sane in insane places. *Science, 179,* 250–258.

Rosenthal, R., & Jacobson, L. (1968). *Pygmalion in the classroom.* New York: Holt, Rinehart and Winston.

Ross, L. D., Rodin, J., & Zimbardo, P. G. (1969). Toward an attribution therapy: The reduction of fear through induced cognitive-emotional misattribution. *Journal of Personality and Social Psychology, 12,* 279–288.

Saltzman, C., Luetgert, M. J., Roth, C. H., Creaser, J., & Howard, L. (1976). Formation of a therapeutic relationship: Experiences during the initial phase of psychotherapy as predictors of treatment duration and outcome. *Journal of Consulting and Clinical Psychology, 44*, 546–555.

Schofield, W. (1964). *Psychotherapy: The purchase of friendship.* Englewood Cliffs, NJ: Prentice-Hall.

Skinner, B. F. (1972). *Beyond freedom and dignity.* New York: Knopf.

Snyder, C. R., Shenkel, R. J., & Schmidt, A. (1976). The effects of role perspective and client psychiatric history on locus of problem. *Journal of Consulting and Clinical Psychology, 44*, 467–472.

Storms, M. D., & McCauly, K. D. (1976). Attribution processes and emotional exacerbation of dysfunctional behavior. In J. H. Harvey, W. J. Ickes, & R. F. Kidd (Eds.), *New directions in attribution research* (Vol. 1), pp. 143–164. Hillsdale, NJ: Erlbaum.

Strupp, H. (1955). Psychotherapeutic technique, professional affiliation and experience level. *Journal of Consulting Psychology, 19*, 97–102.

Strupp, H. H., & Wallach, M. S. (1973). Psychotherapists' clinical judgments and attitudes toward patients. In H. H. Strupp (Ed.), *Psychotherapy: Clinical, research, and theoretical issues.* New York: Aronson.

Strupp, H. H., & Williams, J. V. (1973). Some determinants of clinical evaluations. In H. H. Strupp (Ed.), *Psychotherapy: Clinical, research, and theoretical issues.* New York: Aronson.

Ullman, L. P., & Krasner, L. (1975). *A psychological approach to abnormal behavior* (2nd ed.). Englewood Cliffs, NJ: Prentice-Hall.

Urban, H. B., & Ford, D. H. (1971). Some historical and conceptual perspectives on psychotherapy and behavioral change. In A. E. Bergin & S. L. Garfield (Eds.), *Handbook of psychotherapy and behavior change.* New York: Wiley.

Weiner, I. B. (1975). *Principles of psychotherapy.* New York: Wiley.

Weiner, B., Frieze, I., Kukla, A., Reed, L., Rest, S., & Rosenbaum, R. (1971). Perceiving the causes of success and failure. In E. E. Jones, D. E. Kanouse, H. H. Kelley, R. E. Nisbett, S. Valinis, & B. Weiner (Eds.), *Attribution: Perceiving the causes of behavior.* Morristown, NJ: General Learning Press.

Wills, T. A. (1978). Perceptions of clients by professional helpers. *Psychological Bulletin, 85*, 968–1000.

Wills, T. A. (1982). The study of helping relationships. In T.A. Wills (Ed.), *Basic Processes in Helping Relationships.* New York: Academic.

Wolman, B. (1976). The process of treatment. In B. Wolman (Ed.), *The therapist's handbook.* New York: Van Nostrand.

Zevon, M. A., Karuza, J., Jr., & Brickman, P. (1982). Responsibility and the elderly: Implications for psychotherapy. *Psychotherapy: Theory, Research, and Practice, 19*, 405–411.

8

Cognitive Therapy

STEVEN D. HOLLON

JUDY GARBER

In this chapter, we attempt to analyze one cognitive-behavioral approach to psychotherapy, cognitive therapy, from the perspective of recent advances in attribution theory and social cognition. The approach has emerged as an important psychological intervention for the treatment of depression, typically matching the tricyclic pharmacotherapies in the generation of acute response and providing evidence of long-term prophylaxis against relapse or recurrence (see Hollon & Beck, 1986, or Hollon & Najavits, 1988, for reviews). Our emphasis is on how the procedures utilized in cognitive therapy can be understood in terms of principles identified in social-cognitive and basic cognitive research. In some instances, such an analysis will point to areas of overlap between clinical interventions and basic research; in other instances, areas already explored in one domain may provide a guide to innovation in the other.

First, we will briefly review some of the main themes emerging from the social-cognitive and cognitive psychological literatures. In general, this literature has been largely descriptive and explanatory in nature; its focus has been on exploring how people think and on identifying the processes that mediate cognitive activities. Only recently has this literature shifted toward the issues of *what* people believe and *how* they process information (see, for example, Kahneman, Slovic, & Tversky, 1982, or Nisbett & Ross, 1980).

In the second section of this chapter, we present a detailed analysis of the major techniques and strategies involved in cognitive therapy (Beck, 1970; Beck, Rush, Shaw, & Emery, 1979; Emery, Hollon, & Bedrosian, 1981). Despite its formal name, cognitive therapy is actually a cognitive-behavioral approach to treatment, only one of several such approaches that have been articulated (See Mahoney & Arnkoff, 1978, or Hollon & Beck, 1986, for a discussion of the diverse array of cognitive-behavioral approaches). Cognitive therapy is an explicitly *metacognitive* approach to treatment (using metacognitive in Flavell's [1979] sense of the term), which means that it not only attempts to produce change by altering clients' beliefs and information-processing strategies, but that it also seeks to do so, in part, by teaching clients to think about and act upon their own belief systems.

Cognitive therapy is predicated upon a cognitive theory of psychopathology (Abramson, Seligman, & Teasdale, 1978; Beck, 1963, 1976; Ellis, 1962; Mahoney, 1977). In general, such theories suggest that the beliefs that people hold and the ways they process information play a major role in determining negative affective states and maladaptive behavior patterns. In short, many types of psychopathology are attributed to the adherence to inaccurate beliefs, the absence of adaptive mediating cognitions, or distortions in information-processing.

Cognitive psychopathologists have long looked to basic research for inspiration and support. For example, both Beck and Ellis have regarded Schacter and colleagues' work on the role of cognition in determining affective experience (Schacter, 1959, 1964; Schacter & Singer, 1962; Schacter & Wheeler, 1962) to be central to their own clinical observations. Seligman, Abramson, and colleagues have drawn heavily on basic research by Irwin on expectancy formation (Irwin, 1971) and by Weiner and colleagues on the role of attributions in determining the affective and behavioral consequences of success–failure in achievement settings (Weiner *et al.*, 1971) in their development of the original learned helplessness theory of depression (Seligman, 1975) and the later reformulated attributional helplessness theory (Abramson, Garber, & Seligman, 1980; Abramson *et al.*, 1978). In addition, Meichenbaum (1977) has drawn upon the work of Vygotsky (1962) to explain the failure of impulsive individuals to develop appropriate mediating cognitions.

There has been less explicit attention paid to grounding theories of change in basic research, however. The one notable exception is the work of Bandura and colleagues (Bandura, 1977; Bandura & Adams, 1977) on the role of expectations in the change process. Earlier reviews by Kopel and Arkowitz (1975) and Strong (1970, 1978) attempted to relate various theories of change to social psychological principles. The present chapter will examine the basic social-cognitive and cognitive principles relevant to a particular form of intervention—cognitive therapy.

In an earlier chapter (Hollon & Garber, 1980), we attempted to speculate about the central processes involved in the treatment of depression in particular. Similarly, Seligman (1981) and Beach, Abramson, and Levine (1981) have described a therapeutic approach whose foundation was based upon principles elucidated in the experimental laboratory. In general, the basic cognitive research literature has been less concerned with explicating the principles underlying the production of *change*, and more focused on describing the typical operations of cognitive systems. It is the goal of this chapter to identify and examine principles and variables from attribution theory, social cognition, and cognitive research that are most relevant to the therapeutic change process.

COGNITIVE CONTENT AND INFORMATION-PROCESSING

Preliminary to our analysis of cognitive-behavioral therapy from a social cognitive perspective will be a brief review and clarification of the terms and concepts central to the basic cognitive and social-cognitive literatures. The critical distinction for our present discussion is between cognitive contents and cognitive processes (see Hollon & Bemis, 1981; Hollon & Garber, 1980; Hollon & Kriss, 1984; or Ingram & Hollon, 1986, for an extended discussion). *Content* will be defined here as information stored within the central nervous system. This comprises the raw data of information-processing. *Process* refers to the rules by which this information is perceived, encoded, stored, retrieved, and combined during cognitive activities.

If we adopt a computer analogy, recognizing the limitations inherent in such a metaphor (Kihlstrom & Hasby, 1981; Neisser, 1976), we would consider the raw input data to be analogous to the cognitive *content*. *Organizing structures* are the principles that dictate the internal relationships among these data and fall under the rubric of *schemata* (to be discussed below). The *processes*, on the other hand, are analogous to the rules by which these data are manipulated, be they reasonable approximations to optimal logical principles, as in Kelley's (1967) covariation principle, or suboptimal, nonnormative strategies, such as Kelley's *discounting* or *augmentation* principles (Kelley, 1972a, 1973) or Kahneman and Tversky's intuitive heuristics (Kahneman & Tversky, 1972, 1973; Tversky & Kahneman, 1974). The *products* of the application of those processes to basic information are analogous to the outputs. These various products are the inferences, judgments, and beliefs that are the major concern (dependent variables) of attribution theory and social-cognitive research.

These distinctions are critical to our later discussions of cognitive therapy and form the basis for the central premise of this chapter. We will suggest that although there appears to be considerable empirical evidence that many psychopathological groups systematically differ from normals with respect to both cognitive contents and products (e.g., Hollon & Kendall, 1980; Hollon, Kendall, & Lumry, 1986; Seligman, Abramson, Semmel, & von Baeyer, 1979) and structures (e.g., Derry & Kuiper, 1981; Kuiper & Derry, 1980; Landau, 1980; Landau & Goldfried, 1981; see Ruchlman, West, & Pasahow, 1985, for a review), there is little evidence that these populations differ with respect to process (see Cook & Peterson, 1986, for the sole exception). That is, it may be that normal and psychopathological populations differ from one another more in terms of their cognitive content than in the ways they process information.

A recent study by Dykman, Abramson, Alloy, and Hartlage (1987), which was conducted since the writing of this chapter, found empirical support for this perspective. Basically, Dykman *et al.* found that depressed and nondepressed individuals did, indeed, show "content" differences rather than "process" differences. Specifically, both depressed and nondepressed individuals relied on schematic processing in order to encode information, although the outcome of such processing differed between the groups depending upon the match between the valence or content of their original schema and the nature of the informational feedback provided.

The implications of this distinction for cognitive therapy are profound. Because cognitive therapy seeks to induce clients to utilize more nearly normative information-processing strategies as a means of altering existing beliefs, it becomes important to ascertain, first, whether people can readily adopt such strategies, and, second, whether doing so really proves to be beneficial. Thus, it seems that a major goal of cognitive therapy is to teach clients to utilize processes different than or at least only infrequently used by individuals not in therapy as a means of ultimately altering their cognitive content. In other words, cognitive therapy essentially may seek to induce clients to believe what others believe by virtue of thinking in ways that few people think (see Evans & Hollon, 1988, for an extended discussion of this point).

The remainder of this section will briefly review the various components of cognitive content and processes relevant to our later discussion of cognitive therapy. The central components of cognitive content included here are cognitive products (e.g., attributions and expectations) and cognitive structures (schemata). The cognitive processes of interest here include heuristics, biases and distortions, and automatic versus deliberate information-processing.

TAXONOMY OF COGNITIVE PRODUCTS

Because both attribution theory and cognitive theories of psychopathology and therapy deal with many types of cognitions, it is important to define some of these different types of cognitive contents or products. Attribution theory attempts to explicate how individuals use information about both the social and nonsocial environment to generate inferences about the causes of events and the behaviors of people. Issues regarding attributional processes were first raised systematically by Heider (1958), and extended by Kelley (1967, 1972a), among others. Ross (1977) has suggested that attribution theory has three main tasks: to explain (1) *causal* judgments—the factors determining how an individual attributes effect to cause, (2) *social inference*—the processes through which individuals ascribe characteristics to persons or situations, and (3) the *prediction of outcomes and behaviors*. Thus, according to Ross, attribution theory has traditionally been concerned with more than just how people generate causal statements; it also encompasses the characteristics people ascribe to organisms and situations, one's cognitive representation of those things, and the predictions people make about various events, including their own and other's behavior and its consequences.

Major areas of research have developed around the relationship of attributional processes to the experience of affect (Schacter, 1959; Schacter & Singer, 1962; Schacter & Wheeler, 1962), subsequent motivation, behavior, and affect in achievement situations (Weiner, 1972, 1974, 1979; Weiner et al., 1971; Weiner & Litman-Adizes, 1980), and psychopathology (Abramson et al., 1978, 1980; Abramson, Metalsky, & Alloy, 1987). The ascription of characteristics appears to play a major role in person perception, both of the self (Markus, 1977) and of others (Cantor, 1980a, 1980b; Cantor & Mischel, 1977, 1979), and in psychopathological states such as depression (Derry & Kuiper 1981; Hammen, Marks, & deMayo, & Mayol, 1985; Hammen, Marks, Mayol, & deMayo, 1985; Kuiper & Derry, 1980) and phobias (Landau, 1980; Landau & Goldfried, 1981), Finally, the generation of expectations and their modification has been explicitly linked to the therapy process (Abramson *et al.*, 1987; Bandura, 1977; Hollon & Garber, 1980).

In our present discussion, we will adopt the following definitions of relevant terms:

1. *Causal attributions* are beliefs ascribing an effect to some one or more presumed causes. Causal attributions take the form of "Some event (Y) was caused by some one or more antecedent events (Xs)."
2. *Attributes or ascriptions* refer to the characteristics of a person, situation, or thing. Attributes or ascriptions take the form of "Some characteristic (x) belongs to some object (X) and is descriptive of that object."
3. *Expectations* are beliefs regarding the probability of occurrence of one or more events, given one's current state of knowledge. Expectations take the form of "Some event (Y) has a given likelihood of occurrence (P), given various antecedent conditions (Xs)." The antecedent events (the Xs) may be seen as either being causes or merely incidental correlates of the consequent events (Ys).

These three types of specific cognitive contents or products can be seen to match the three areas of inquiry targeted by Ross (1977) as representing the domains of interest to attribution theory: (1) causal inferences, (2) person or situation perceptions, and (3) the prediction of outcomes or behaviors. In essence, attribution theory is clearly concerned with more than attributions of causality, per se, as evidence by the attention to the characteristics ascribed to objects and the events predicted to follow from various antecedent cues.

Other types of cognitive contents of interest include the following:

4. *Perceptions of contingency*, or the perception of relationship between two or more stimuli. These perceptions take the form of "The occurrence of some event (X) is related in some fashion to the occurrence of some other event (Y)."
5. *Perceptions of control*, or the perception that some individual or agency exerts a causal influence over the occurrence of some event
6. *Perceptions of responsibility*, or the ascription of accountability for an event to some individual or agency
7. *Perceptions of value*, or the attribution of worth or hedonic relevance to some event or object

Other relevant classes of cognitive contents or products doubtlessly could be enumerated. The key aspect for our present purpose is that different types of specific cognitive contents or products can be defined, which may obey different processes and heuristics in their formulation and which may affect differentially other phenomena of interest, such as behavior, emotions, or subsequent cognitions. For example, we have argued elsewhere that although negative causal attributions for undesirable events may play a critical role in initiating an episode of depression, the empirical disconfirmation of negative expectations may provide the most efficient point of entry for reversing that episode once initiated (Hollon & Garber, 1980; see also the recent articulation of "hopelessness theory" by Abramson *et al.*, 1987, a major theoretical advance specifying distal attributional causes and proximal expectational causes). Both types of contents (products) are of concern to attribution theory, although only the former are explicitly attributions of causality.

COGNITIVE STRUCTURES: SCHEMATA

Cognitive schemata are postulated to be naive theories regarding some stimulus domain; they represent organizations or structurings of information regarding some area of knowledge. Neisser (1976), the primary exponent of the schema construct in contemporary psychology, has described schemata as

> that portion of the entire perceptual cycle which is internal to the perceiver, modifiable by experience, and somehow specific to what is being perceived. The schema accepts information as it becomes available at sensory surfaces and is changed by that information; it directs movements and exploratory activities that make more information available by which it is further modified. (p. 54)

Kihlstrom and Nasby (1981), in a succinct review of the schema construct, note that different theorists use the construct in subtly different ways. Markus (1977) has done a particularly thoughtful job of assessing schematic operations in a nontautological fashion.

Thorndyke and Hayes-Roth (1979) have extracted several properties across the various definitions of schema, including the following ones:

1. A schema represents a prototypical abstraction of the complex concept it represents; only reasonable approximations of a schema may be necessary to trigger its operation.
2. Schemata are induced from past examples of the concept it represents; that is, we abstract schemata after repeated experiences to relevant examples.

3. Schemata guide the organization of incoming information into clusters of knowledge that are instantiations (i.e., specific examples) of the schema. This represents the goal-directed focusing of processing by active memory schemata.

Thus, schemata organize the structure of information in memory, determine the acceptable form that information must take in order to be perceived accurately, and suggest where and how to search for this information. Finally, operating schemata appear to contain procedures for dealing with "missing values"; if sufficient information is present in a specific instance to fit a schema, missing aspects may be inferred to be present despite their actual absence.

According to Hastie (1980) schema-incongruent information may fare differently at different points in information-processing. Specifically, schema-incongruent information appears to receive greater attention when it is first encountered, increasing the likelihood that it is *encoded* into a richer, better articulated memory trace (or, as we will see later, discounted, discredited, or modified to fit with the schema). Conversely, schema-congruent information appears to be more easily retrieved from memory than schema-incongruent information. Thus, schemata not only guide perception and organize knowledge, but they also direct the processing of new information and the retrieval of information stored in memory.

Kelley (1972b, 1973) and Tversky and Kahneman (1980) have described the operation of schematic organizations in the causal attribution process. Markus (1977) has described the nature and operation of schematic processes in self-perception, while Cantor has done the same for person and situation perception (Cantor, 1980a, 1980b; Cantor & Mischel, 1977, 1979). Beck (1963, 1967, 1976) has long described the operation of maladaptive cognitive schemata in various psychopathological groups, an argument supported by work by Derry and Kuiper (1981), among others, with self-schemata for depressives, and Landau and Goldfried (Landau, 1980; Landau & Goldfried, 1981) with regard to phobic object perception for phobics.

Overall, schemata appear to be ubiquitous, operating in all populations, both psychopathological and normal. They appear to play an important role in information-processing at several stages: perception, encoding, retrieval, judgment formation, and information search. There are several additional questions concerning schemata that need to be addressed.

1. How do schemata develop?
2. How are schemata engaged, or activated?
3. How are schemata modified or replaced?
4. How do schemata influence information-processing, affect, and behavior?

Indeed, Fiske and Linville (1980) similarly have noted that an important direction for future research concerns schema development and change.

Moreover, a central question for our present discussion, relevant to the content-process distinction noted earlier, is whether schemata obey different rules in different populations (e.g., nonpathological versus pathological) or whether such populations differ only in the content and organization of their schemata, rather than in the rules those schemata observe. Kihlstrom and Nasby (1981) have argued persuasively that any consideration of schematic operations must first specify the content domain of interest. Once that is done, however, it may prove interesting to see if major differences remain in operating principles across populations.

HEURISTICS, BIASES, AND DISTORTIONS

There are three related terms appearing in the literature that refer to various nonnormative information-processing strategies; these are heuristics, biases, and distortions. Tversky and Kahneman (1974) have defined intuitive *heuristic* principles as information-processing strategies that reduce complex judgmental tasks to a set of simpler operations. Typically, these simpler operations process information in a manner not fully consistent with careful, normative strategies. An example is Tversky and Kahneman's *availability heuristic* (1973), under which judges tend to estimate the probability of occurrence of an event on the basis of the ease with which similar instances are retrieved from memory, rather than actuarial base-rates for prior occurrence.

These heuristics are seen as "shortcut" strategies which, under typical circumstances, facilitate efficient information processing. However, their operation can produce *biases*, that is, particular tendencies or inclinations in judgmental processes leading to inferences at variance with what would be produced under normative processing strategies. Tversky and Kahneman note that the biases resulting from the operation of intuitive heuristics need not be attributed to motivational processes or distortions of judgments related to payoffs and penalties. Biases are typically defined more generally, including any particular tendency or inclination preventing an unprejudiced consideration of a position, whether that tendency stems from the operation of heuristics of motivational considerations.

Distortions are best defined as misrepresentations, and distorting processes as those processes leading to a misrepresentation of reality. Beck (1963, 1967, 1976) has described various distortions in information-processing that occur in psychopathology, including *selective abstraction, magnification, all-or-none thinking*, and *arbitrary inference*. In general, Beck considers these distortions to be unmotivated biases. That is, they are tendencies in information-processing reflecting nonnormative processing strategies heavily influenced by currently operating schemata. Thus, Beck's notion of selective abstraction refers to the tendency of depressed individuals to base a judgment (e.g., "I never do anything right") on only those pieces of evidence (e.g., one instance of nonsuccess embedded in a series of successes) consistent with prior beliefs (e.g., "I'm a loser").

The important points for our current discussion are that heuristics, biases, and distortions appear to operate in the information-processing of all individuals, whether psychopathological or not (see also Evans & Hollon, 1988). These processes may be influenced by motivational factors, but they need not be. In some instances, biased and/or distorted judgmental products may be produced by the operation of schema-driven heuristics. If there is any consolation to be found in the fact that intuitive scientists frequently do not process information as lay scientists should, it is that similar intuitive heuristics often guide the thinking of trained scientists, leading, at times, to similar biases and distortions in judgment (Einhorn, 1982; Kahneman & Tversky, 1982; Ross & Sicoly, 1979; Tversky & Kahneman, 1971).

The key question to which we return again is whether various psychopathological groups differ from normals in the heuristics they utilize as well as their cognitive contents, products, and structures per se. For example, Tversky and Kahneman (1974) have described the operation of an *adjustment and anchoring* heuristic, in which providing new information discrepant from an initial belief (anchor) typically produces an underadjustment (relative to normative expectations) in subsequent inferences away from that initial anchor. Assuming that two individuals enter the same situation with different beliefs— for example, one maintains a belief in personal competence whereas the other maintains a belief in personal incompetence—comparable new information, such as failure and success, respectively, will tend to have less impact in shifting either self-perception than strictly normative calculations would predict. Thus, although there is evidence that various psychopathological groups differ from nonpsychopathological groups with respect to both the beliefs they construct (products) and the schematic organizations they hold (structures), it is not yet clear that they utilize different heuristics. The precise implications of this point for cognitive therapy will be discussed in a later section.

Intuitive Scientist versus Fallible Information-Processor

An important issue relevant to the concept of cognitive processes concerns whether humans behave like intuitive scientists or use fallible strategies when processing information. Whereas Kelley (1967, 1972a) has asserted that the lay person making attributions "generally acts like a good scientist, examining covariation between cause and effect" (1972a, p. 2), social psychologists researching basic cognitive processes (e.g., Jones & Davis, 1965; Kahneman *et al.*, 1982; Kahneman & Tversky, 1972, 1973, 1982; Nisbett & Ross, 1980; Ross, 1977; Taylor & Fiske, 1975, 1978; Tversky & Kahneman, 1971, 1973, 1974, 1980) have found that lay persons frequently utilize nonnormative heuristics in arriving at judgments, and respond more to the saliency, availability, or recency of information than actual occurrence. Recent volumes by Nisbett and Ross (1980), *Human inference: Strategies and shortcomings of social judgment,* and Kahneman *et al.* (1982), *Judgment under uncertainty: Heuristics and biases,* provide particularly succinct reviews of work in this area.

The real issue is not whether people process information normatively or nonnormatively; clearly, they frequently do the latter and, occasionally, the former. Rather, the issue involves specifying when they do each and which is more useful under given conditions. Kelley (1973) has suggested that information-processing is likely to be dominated by nonnormative heuristics and biases under conditions of minimum available information and inadequate processing time. According to Kelley, naive attributions begin to approximate more normative information processes when multiple sources of information are available. As we shall describe in the section to follow, cognitive therapy operates under the assumption that many psychopathological populations would benefit from operating more like Kelley's naive scientist in generating inferences and organizing knowledge. Whether that assumption is correct remains an empirical question (see Alloy & Abramson, 1979), as does the hypothesis that cognitive therapy increases the likelihood that clients function like naive scientists.

In the study by Alloy and Abramson (1979), depressed college students were consistently more accurate in judging the degree of contingency between their own actions and outcomes than were nondepressed students, who frequently overestimated the degree of control they exerted over events. Similarly, Lewinsohn, Mischel, Chaplin, and Barton (1980) reported that depressed patients were more likely to concur with independent observers when evaluating their own low level of social skills than were nondepressed individuals, who tended to rate their own level of social skills more favorably than did the outside observers. These findings raise important questions concerning precisely what are the goals and methods of cognitive therapy. What cognitive changes actually are being produced via cognitive therapy? In general, cognitive therapists have presumed that they were teaching clients to think more accurately, adaptively, and like "normals." As Alloy and Abramson (1979) and Lewinsohn *et al.* (1980) have suggested, however, accuracy may not be synonomous with adaptivity, and, as Kahneman, Tversky, and colleagues (Kahneman *et al.*, 1982) and Nisbett and Ross (1980) and others have suggested, "normals" may think in highly fallible fashions.

Recently, Evans and Hollon (1988) addressed this issue by hypothesizing three competing models of depressed and nondepressed patterns of causal inferences, relative accuracy, and mechanisms of change produced in cognitive therapy. They argued that cognitive therapy works through the process of training depressed clients to be *more* systematic and normative in their processing of information than are most nondepressives. Moreover, they suggested that the differences between depressed and nondepressed individuals is not a matter of one group being more accurate than the other or one group distorting their information-processing more than the other, but, rather, that both types of individuals show systematic errors in the processing of information that sometimes makes one group appear to be more accurate than the other in a given context (see also Dykman *et al.*, 1987).

If this is indeed so, then we are still left with three important questions: (1) What differentiates depressed and nondepressed individuals if it is not distortions in cognitive processing? (2) What is it that we are trying to change through cognitive therapy? And (3) what is the best procedure for bringing about these changes? Consistent with the conclusions of Evans and Hollon (1988) we suggest here that depressed and nondepressed individuals differ primarily in their cognitive content (products and schemata) rather than their cognitive processes, and that the goal of cognitive therapy is to alter these cognitive contents. The procedures for bringing about these changes, however, lie in altering the depressed individuals' typical methods of processing information toward a more normative and less biased fashion, and, thus, to cause them to process information in a way not typically used by nonpsychopathological individuals. The specific procedures of cognitive therapy used to produce these changes will be discussed in a later section.

AUTOMATIC VERSUS DELIBERATE INFORMATION-PROCESSING

Recent research in human cognition has suggested an important distinction between automatic versus deliberate (controlled) information-processing (Keele, 1973; Neely, 1977; Posner & Snyder, 1975; Schneider & Shiffrin, 1977; Shiffrin & Schneider, 1977). Schneider and Shiffrin (1977) provide a representative definition.

> Automatic processing is activation of a learned sequence of elements in long-term memory that is initiated by appropriate inputs and then proceeds automatically— without subject control, without exceeding the capacity limitations of the system, and without necessarily demanding attention. Controlled processing is a temporary activation of a sequence of elements that can be set up quickly and easily but requires attention, is capacity-limited (usually serial in nature), and is controlled by the subject. (p. 1)

In essence, automatic processing appears to represent an overlearned processing strategy, probably closely tied to currently operating schemata, and relying heavily on intuitive heuristics. Controlled, or deliberate, processing appears to represent a more painstaking and effortful examination of input information and the steps through which it is transformed.

Both processes probably occur in all individuals at various times, and it is unlikely that there are many differences between various pathological and nonpathological groups in the tendency to operate in one mode as opposed to another. It is more likely, however, that there would be major differences in the

contents of those "learned sequences of elements" between those two populations. Our experience suggests that most of the clients' belief systems that are
of initial concern to cognitive therapists operate in a largely automatic fashion.
Often, the first task of therapy is to move the client out of an automatic
information-processing mode into a deliberate mode of processing. Richard
Lazarus's (1966) classic distinction between appraisal and reappraisal may map
onto this automatic–deliberate dichotomy. As a consequence of the structure
application of hypothesis-testing principles in a deliberate mode during the
course of therapy, the client may be able to modify the content of his or her
processing in the automatic mode. At the very least, we might expect the client
to develop "learned sequences of elements" related to therapeutic reality-
testing procedures available through automatic mode processes.

ASSIMILATION VERSUS ACCOMMODATION

A final distinction worth noting is between the two modes of functioning
available to the developing organism: assimilation and accommodation
(Piaget, 1954). *Assimilation* refers to the tendency to construe environmental
inputs in ways that make them comprehensible and usable. *Accommodation*
refers to the tendency to alter one's schema in response to environmental
realities. Although Piaget's concepts involve more than cognitive functioning,
following Nisbett and Ross (1980), we will restrict our attention to their
cognitive referents only.

When an individual encounters new information inconsistent with an
existing theory or schema, one of two events may occur: (1) The information
can be altered such that it is assimilated into the existing schema, or (2) the
existing schema can be altered so as to accommodate the discrepant information. The majority of the recent work in cognitive psychology appears to
suggest that the assimilation process is more likely, but not inevitable.

We might speculate that a third outcome is also possible. If we presume
that at different times it is possible for individuals to operate in accordance
with relatively incompatible (or at least distinct) schemata, then exposure to
schema-discrepant or inconsistent information might well trigger a switch from
one operating schema to another. For example, consider the change that
comes over many self-sufficient adults when returning home for a visit with
their parents. Moreover, our work with depressed clients suggests that when
depressives experience a clinical relapse, they do not so much redevelop a
depressive schema, but rather they "switch" rapidly and fully into the same
schema that dominated earlier depressive episodes. (see Hollon, Evans, &
DeRubeis, 1988; or Ingram & Hollon, 1986, for further discussions of this
issue).

If these distinctions accurately reflect the state of nature, then cognitive
therapists might well find themselves in an interesting position vis-à-vis maxi-

mizing short-term changes versus long-term stability. Clearly, assimilation is the least desirable fate for disconfirming evidence, because that evidence would be distorted in such a way that it was consistent with the operating schema (see Ross, 1977). Fostering a "switch" from, say, a depressive schema to a nondepressive schema may prove to be the most efficient way to interrupt an ongoing depression. However, such a rapid "switch," assuming that we know how to produce it, might leave the depressive schema relatively intact, ready to reemerge during future episodes. In contrast, a therapist might prefer that the depressive schema remain in force during an ongoing process of evidential disconfirmation, thus invoking an accommodation process that modifies the basic nature of the schema itself.

Ross (1977) has proposed three approaches for changing beliefs, including evidential disconfirmation, discrediting existing beliefs and replacing them with new ones, and altering the ways information is processed. If the goal of therapy is for long-term change in the clients' underlying cognitive organization, then this would argue in favor of using evidence to disconfirm an intact depressive schema (Ross's first approach) over simply overwhelming and wholesale replacement of the belief system (Ross's second approach). The former approach seems to be the cognitive version of the psychoanalytic concept of "flight into health," in which the therapist pushes for a more gradual approach to symptom reduction in service of long-term stability.

CONCLUSIONS ABOUT INFORMATION-PROCESSING

In general, recent work in the area of social cognition and cognitive psychology has suggested that the intuitive scientist is frequently quite fallible. Schema-dominated information-processing and a reliance on inferential heuristics leading to biases or distortions dominate thinking even in the absence of motivational anomalies. Although nonpsychopathological and psychopathological populations appear to differ in what they have come to believe, it is not yet clear that they differ in the ways they process information, beyond the extent to which initial beliefs influence processing.

As we shall describe in the sections to follow, cognitive therapy generally attempts to move clients' from reliance on

1. simple attributional processes to more complex, multicausal models;
2. unstructured (i.e., schema-governed) information search and data retrieval to structured information-gathering;
3. heuristic-dominated to more strictly normative inference-generating strategies;
4. automatic information-processing to more deliberate strategies; and
5. assimilation of schema-disconfirming data to the accommodation of existing schemata to external realities.

In the sections that follow, we analyze the ways in which cognitive therapy attempts to meet these goals.

CHANGING COGNITIVE CONTENTS AND PROCESSES CLINICALLY

In this section, we address the issue of how to produce changes in cognitive contents and processes. In general, we focus on causal ascriptions, person perceptions, and expectational processes. Central to this discussion will be the role played by cognitive schemata and heuristics in information-processing. The focus of attention will be primarily on Beck's cognitive therapy (Beck *et al.*, 1979)), with some secondary attention to other cognitive-behavioral approaches, and minimal coverage of other approaches to therapy.

ESSENTIALS OF COGNITIVE THERAPY

Cognitive therapy consists of a systematic application of empirical procedures to the cognitive, behavioral, and affective processes of various client types (see Beck *et al.*, 1979, or Hollon & Beck, 1979, for detailed summaries of treatment procedures). The practice of cognitive therapy can be likened to the conduct of any scientific inquiry. Beliefs, assumptions, and expectations are treated as "hypotheses" to be tested. Emphasis is placed on formulating rigorous tests of these beliefs based on sound methodological principles. The main strategy that underlies the interactions between the client and therapist is one of *collaborative empiricism*. The client and therapist are active collaborators in the identification of problem areas and in the design and execution of tests of the various beliefs. The data generated by these tests, rather than therapist credibility or authority, are relied upon to provide understanding and, ideally, to produce change. Thus, the client is not persuaded to change by the therapist, but, rather, the evidence generated by the client in unbiased experiments is allowed to speak for itself.

How compatible are the procedures utilized in cognitive therapy with the principles for changing belief systems and information-processing heuristics that have been identified in the social-cognitive and cognitive psychological literatures? As noted earlier, Ross (1977) has outlined three methods for producing changes in beliefs that are particularly relevant to cognitive therapy, including, (1) "brute" force of consistently disconfirming data, (2) wholesale assaults on entire existing belief systems, targeted at discrediting those beliefs and replacing them with an entirely new explanatory system, and (3) "process"-centered discussions that focus on the ways the individual collects, stores, retrieves, and combines information, that is, on the heuristics utilized. Cognitive therapy attempts to incorporate all three. Great emphasis is placed on formulating and testing hypotheses, that is, on articulating expectations consistent with the client's current belief systems and subjecting these hypotheses to both retrospective and prospective tests. Repetition is considered to be a necessity and empiricism a virtue. Moreover, given the propensity of individuals to distort earlier predictions after the evidence is collected (Fischhoff, 1975, 1976, 1982; Fischhoff & Beyth, 1975), it is also important to ensure that the client generates a written record of his or her earlier predictions.

Principles from the social-cognitive and cognitive literatures may be particularly useful in contrasting cognitive-behavioral therapy with its "first-cousin," rational–emotive therapy (RET) (Ellis, 1962). For example, in keeping with Nisbett and colleagues' observation that concrete, vivid instances typically have a greater impact than abstract, pallid generalizations (Nisbett & Borgida, 1975; Nisbett, Borgida, Crandall, & Reed, 1976), cognitive therapy pays great attention to engaging the client in explicit, specific, action–outcome sequences. Emphasis is placed on multiple, concrete, experiential tests rather than a primary reliance on discussions of abstract beliefs and principles, as is typically done in RET.

A second important distinction concerns that between inductive and deductive reasoning. Tversky and Kahneman (1980) have suggested that people are more likely to draw causal rather than diagnostic inferences given equally informative feedback. Thus, individuals are more willing to infer effects given that a purported cause has occurred than they are to infer a cause given that they observe an effect. Closely associated is the tendency for people to feel more confident in inductive reasoning (inducing general rules from specific examples) than they are in deductive reasoning (deducing specific examples from general rules).

Beck's version of cognitive-behavior therapy (CB) advocates an inductive progression, emphasizing the accumulation of specific, concrete confirmation/disconfirmations of specific hypotheses, dealing with larger themes or underlying assumptions only later in therapy (Beck *et al.*, 1979; Hollon & Beck, 1979). In contrast, Ellis (1962) favors the early identification of general abstract principles, or irrational assumptions. Ellis and colleagues have enumerated a finite list of what they consider to be the major irrational assumptions. Early in the course of therapy, preferably the initial session, the therapist attempts to identify the client's irrational assumption(s) organizing his or her problems. The client is informed as to the nature of this (these) belief(s), and the therapist then proceeds to present logical arguments designed to persuade the client to abandon these beliefs. The rational–emotive therapist is ready to *supply* a more rational set of beliefs and does so at the earliest opportunity, encouraging the client to abandon his or her irrational, upsetting beliefs in favor of a more "sane" worldview. In contrast, the cognitive-behavior therapist helps the client to design empirical tests that presumably will lead to a more accurate set of beliefs (Hollon & Beck, 1979, 1986).

In a sense, RET appears to emphasize the second of Ross's two mechanisms, a wholesale assault on the client's existing explanatory system with the intent of replacing that system with a new one. Both RET and CB mix inductive, evidential disconfirmation and deductive belief system replacement, although in different proportions. In CB, the therapist also attempts to draw out the client with regard to his or her current belief system, articulating both the client's existing system and alternative ways of interpreting experiences. In a sense, CB is most similar to RET in its efforts to elucidate the existing belief system and to propose an alternative.

Both approaches are explicitly metacognitive (Flavell, 1979); that is, both not only try to change cognition, but also explicitly teach clients to think about their thought processes. In this respect, both differ from another therapy approach—participant modeling, advocated by Bandura (1977). Bandura essentially has suggested that whereas the most powerful processes mediating change (in phobias) are cognitive, the most efficient procedures for producing these changes are enactive. Thus, beliefs (in particular, expectations) are presumed to mediate phobic avoidance and anxiety arousal. Changing those beliefs is hypothesized to mediate change in symptoms, and expectancy disconfirmation via enactive experience is seen as the optimal strategy for producing that disconfirmation. What is not utilized, however, are explicit discussions of those expectations, the evidence supporting their efficacy, the effects they have on information-processing, and the implication that their disconfirmation would have. In effect, participant modeling can be considered cognitively targeted but not metacognitive in nature.

These comments are not intended as a critique of Bandura's masterful analysis of the relationship between process and procedure, his powerful articulation of a model for the change norm, nor his final recommendations. Although we agree that experience or evidential disconfirmation through enactive behavior (Ross's first method), is vitally important, we suggest that pursuing such enactive, evidential disconfirmations of existing beliefs in a metacognitive fashion, with the antecedent articulation of at least two different explanatory models—the client's current model and an alternative one—(Ross's second prescription) provides an even more powerful treatment package. There is not yet available, however, any direct evidence to support this latter proposition.

Ross's third prescription, that of attempting to identify the processes engaged in by the client when evaluating information, is also consistent with the recommendations of Beck and colleagues (Beck *et al.*, 1979; Hollon & Beck, 1979). Beck (1964), for example, has long been impressed by the systematic distortions in depressed patients' evaluations of stimulus information. Examples of such distortions include *selective abstraction*, in which the individual forms a conclusion regarding a particular event based on only a single isolated detail, while ignoring contradictory and more salient data; *arbitrary inference*, in which the individual draws a conclusion in the absence of any supporting evidence; *overgeneralization*, in which beliefs or rules are extracted on the basis of a particular event and are applied in an unjustifiable fashion to other dissimilar situations; *magnification*, in which the individual overestimates the significance or magnitude of the undesirable consequences of an event; and *all-or-none thinking*, a tendency to think in extreme, absolute terms.

Two points are relevant to the present discussion. First, procedurally CB has always emphasized the desirability of describing the operation of such information-processing strategies, recognizing and collecting examples of their operation, and attempting to assist the client in developing compensatory strategies. In essence, cognitive therapy is in part (at least in theory) "process"-oriented. From the initial reading material assigned to the patient, Beck and Greenberg's *Coping with Depression* (1974), efforts are made to educate clients about, determine the occurrence of, and compensate for such pathology-related biases and distortions.

The second point to be made here, however, as discussed previously, is that these distorting processes are in no way specific to psychopathological groups. Clearly, the work of Kahneman and Tversky (1972, 1973; Kahneman *et al.*, 1982; Tversky & Kahneman, 1971, 1973, 1974) has amply documented the operation of nonnormative processing heuristics among normals. In general, it seems fair to say that human beings appear to be relatively nonnormative in their processing of information. That is, when processing information, individuals appear to rely more on various heuristics that facilitate their arriving rapidly at judgments under conditions of uncertainty but that can lead to systematic errors, than they do on normative information-processing (Kahneman & Tversky, 1972, 1973; Tversky & Kahneman, 1971, 1973, 1974).

Thus, what Beck (1964) refers to as selective abstraction may prove to be analogous to the tendency of nondepressives to attend to evidence consistent with existing beliefs, while discounting evidence inconsistent with those beliefs (Ross's [1977] distortion mechanism). Arbitrary inference may prove to be mediated by the operation of Tversky and Kahneman's causal schemas, whereby individuals' assume the occurrence of purported causal factors based upon the observation of events believed to be caused by those factors; this tendency is clearly found in normals. Overgeneralization may well prove to be analogous to those same *causal schema* processes through which normals have been observed to be strikingly willing to generate general rules on the basis of specific, but limited, data that are then generalized in an uncritical and unjustified fashion. Tversky and Kahneman (1971) have demonstrated convincingly that the tendency to overgeneralize those specific data is not limited to the "intuitive psychologist" or layperson, be they normal or otherwise, but also exists in scientists who supposedly are trained to know better.

In short, although Beck may have been correct about the operation of various heuristics and biases in depressed (and other) psychopathological populations, these heuristics seem remarkably similar to the heuristics utilized by nonpsychopathological populations. Thus, when cognitive therapy focuses on altering "distortions in information-processing" in a metacognitive fashion, it does not appear to be teaching the target psychopathological populations to think like normals. Rather, it may be training clients to think in a very "atypical" fashion, replacing everyday heuristics with alternative strategies that, ideally, more closely approximate optimal normative or statistical decision rules. This is doubtless the sequence involved in training scientists, statisticians, and mathematicians. If Tversky and Kahneman's work with these populations is accurate, then it probably is the case that new strategies are added rather than simply replacing existing heuristics, and that some degree of vigilance and intention continues to be necessary in mediating the differential selection of strategies. Thus, one important way CB teaches clients to think in an other than "normal" way is to be more deliberate and less automatic in their processing of information. Although this is a somewhat less efficient strategy, it tends to be more accurate.

The foregoing discussion highlights an interesting set of issues in need of further discussion and research. The majority of the empirical data describing the operation of biases and heuristics as well as the mechanisms for changing beliefs has been based on research with nonpsychopathological populations. Whether or not these findings can be generalized to various psychopathological populations remains an important and intriguing empirical question. Nevertheless, the procedures used in cognitive therapy advocated by Beck and colleagues (Beck, 1967; Beck *et al.*, 1979) appear to closely approximate the procedures for changing beliefs emerging from the social-cognitive literature. This raises an interesting dilemma. If the procedures involved in CB for dealing with psychopathological distortions approximate the best procedures currently recognized in the cognitive and social-cognitive literatures for dealing with nonpsychopathological biases and heuristics, then either the distortions in information-processing must be common between the two populations or the procedures adopted by CB may actually be better suited for nonpsychopathological populations than pathological ones. Moreover, if psychopathological and normal populations make similar information-processing erors, what then differentiates these groups?

An interesting study by Lord, Lepper, and Ross (1979) provides a good example of how the same heuristics can lead to different products, given the same stimulus input but different prior beliefs. In that investigation, two groups of nonpathological subjects were exposed to information from two different empirical studies, both purported to be actual studies. One study supported the efficacy of capital punishment as a deterrent to crime; the second did not. One group of subjects initially endorsed capital punishment; the second did not. After each group of subjects had read both studies (in counterbalanced fashion), both groups became even more polarized in their views. That is, people who believed in the efficacy of capital punishment before reading the mixed evidence believed in it more strongly afterward, and people who did not believe in its efficacy adhered even more strongly to that negative position. Moreover, the more detail provided about the studies, the more polarized the attitudes became.

This demonstration suggested that the operation of the same heuristic in which disconfirming evidence was discounted in a way that increased the strength of the subject's initial belief system may have been operating for both sets of subjects. Both groups were exposed to identical sets of information, but because each had different initial beliefs, they ended up with very different conclusions. In short, it may well prove that the same heuristic applied to the same new data by individuals differing in preexisting beliefs may produce very different cognitive products.

This conceptualization may, in part, help to explain how it is that psychopathological groups and normals may share similar biases and heuristics in their information-processing, yet end up with very different cognitive products (Hollon & Kendall, 1980; Seligman *et al.*, 1979). It may be that these groups start out with different beliefs or cognitive schema, and then, when faced with new information, apply similar heuristics yet end up with very different products because of the initially different schema.

The implications for cognitive therapy are the following: (1) The ultimate goal of cognitive therapy is to alter the beliefs and cognitive schema presumably maintaining the psychopathology, and (2) the means by which cognitive therapy changes these beliefs is by altering clients' processing of information to a more normative (albeit less "normal") inference-generating rather than heuristic-dominated processing mode. The key to this strategy is that it is deliberate rather than automatic, and it involves structured information-gathering in the context of empirical hypothesis testing rather than unstructured, schema-governed interpretations of events. Through this more deliberate, albeit less efficient, information-processing strategy, it is presumed that more accurate data will be obtained that then will produce changes in the original beliefs. Thus, ideally, the client's existing schemata will accommodate to the external realities rather than assimilating the schema-disconfirming data.

This is viewed as an ongoing process that only begins in therapy. It is not considered to be a "quick cure," or something that the client only does during the therapy session. Cognitive therapy essentially teaches clients a new skill involving a new way of thinking that they are not used to, and that most people do not use. The hope is that ultimately the "depressive" schema will be altered, lay dormant, or be replaced with less depressive schema. Should the depressive schema reemerge, however, the cognitive therapy client is now presumed to have in his or her cognitive armamentarium a means for dealing with it, including the return to more deliberate, structured information-gathering strategies. The specific techniques used in CB to bring about these changes will be discussed from a social-cognitive perspective in the following sections.

SELF-MONITORING SKILLS

Clients in Beck's cognitive therapy (Beck *et al.*, 1979) and, indeed, most other cognitive-behavioral approaches (see Hollon & Kendall, 1981), are explicitly trained in systematic self-monitoring procedures. The specific targets and techniques vary, but, within the context of these approaches, all attempt to structure event monitoring so as to reduce the operation of belief-linked biases in perception and recall (see, for example, work by Bower, 1981, or Clark & Teasdale, 1982, for the effects of mood on information-processing).

A typical system may involve asking the client to keep track of what happened to him or her (the events) and what he or she did (the behavior), and his or her mood levels (the affect) on an hourly basis between sessions. Examples of precisely such systems are given for a depressed client in Hollon and Beck (1979, reprinted in Hollon & Kendall, 1981) and for a pansituationally anxious client in Hollon (1981). Cognitive self-monitoring is also frequently utilized, although clinical experience suggests that most clients have greater trouble understanding and executing such requests, at least early in therapy. Therefore, therapists in CB frequently begin by teaching the client to systematically monitor events, actions, and moods, expanding to cognitive self-monitoring only after several sessions, but reviewing with the client in the sessions cognitions associated with key events, actions, or shifts in affect noted in these early attempts at self-monitoring.

Such systems serve at least two main purposes from an information-processing perspective. First, they provide the therapist with a clearer picture of what the client's life is currently like than typically can be obtained from retrospective summaries. Second, they provide one source of evidential data drawn from specific, concrete events experienced and noted by the client himself or herself, for testing the client's beliefs. Both purposes are subsumed by the following principle: *The more abstract, asynchronous, and inferential the cognitive task requested of an individual, the more heavily influenced the product of that task will be by heuristics, biases, and idiosyncratic beliefs.* Whenever the therapist wants the most accurate statement of events possible, he or she should ask the client to *describe* what occurred. Whenever the therapist wants to sample the operation of biasing processes, he or she should ask the client to *evaluate* or *summarize* what has occurred.

BEHAVIORAL TECHNIQUES

Numerous specific behavioral techniques are frequently employed in cognitive therapy, especially with more severely impaired clients. These can include, but are not limited to, *activity scheduling*, in which therapist and client plan some or all of the client's activities over some period of time; *graded task assignment*, in which a given task is decomposed into its various parts ("chunking") and structured such that the client begins with the components most likely to be initiated and accomplished; *scheduling* specific types of activities (e.g., pleasurable, masterful, assertive, and so forth), in which selected categories of events or activities are targeted so as to increase the probability of their occurrence; and "*success therapy*," in which some unrelated, but easily accomplishable, task is used to get the individual moving prior to attempting some more difficult or onerous task. Any of these and other related specific maneuvers can be executed and interpreted in the context of other noncognitive theoretical systems (e.g., Lewinsohn, 1974, 1975). What makes them relevant for our present purposes are efforts to target these manipulations at producing changes in beliefs as well as in behavior, whether in a metacognitive manner or not.

One example of utilizing such behavioral techniques in a metacognitive fashion can be drawn from the treatment of "J.," described by Hollon and Beck (1979). The client was a middle-aged former academic who had lost his job as a consequence of financial retrenchment. When first seen for cognitive therapy, he had been out of work in his chosen profession for 3 years, was depressed episodically throughout that time, and was convinced that his was a "reality-based" depression that would remit only when he found more suitable employment. Despite his extreme dissatisfaction with his current status as a menial day laborer, he was making only desultory efforts at securing more suitable employment, largely because he believed that no one would hire him at his age, especially after his 3-year absence from academic employment. Compounding these beliefs were his convictions that his mental and interpersonal capacities had deteriorated such that he could no longer execute the behaviors necessary to find another job (in Bandura's [1977] terms, a negative self-efficacy expectation). Finally, he fully believed, with some justification, that the job market itself was barren. Even if someone had the right skills and attributes, J. believed that no suitable employment would be available (in Bandura's [1977] terms, a negative outcome expectation).

These beliefs, all of which were *predictions* related to his current views about himself, his world, and his future, were duly noted and discussed. A larger target, the initiation of job-seeking behavior, was agreed upon (fatalistically by the client, who foresaw little prospect of success) and broken down ("chunked") into various component steps in accordance with a *graded task assignment* approach. The first task selected was the preparation of a résumé (which the client further predicted he would not be able to accomplish, based on his observation that he had tried to do so on several occasions over the past 3 years without success). The task was further decomposed into smaller units, such as gathering the necessary materials and selecting a spot for work, and the client was encouraged to approach the tasks as a series of experiments. If he made progress toward his goals, he was to check off each step he completed. If not, he was to carefully record what thoughts he had experienced during the process of attempting the task.

The client found himself readily able to begin and to complete the generation of his résumé, and was so pleased with himself that he pushed beyond his scheduled task and prepared several other letters to accompany the applications (such "success" is by no means the rule; quite often clients return with lists of "problematic beliefs" generated, rather than success experiences). At the next session, the therapist carefully reviewed the clients's prior predictions with him, going over his prior certainty of failure and discussing the implications of this specific instance of negative self-efficacy expectational disconfirmation for other, equally strongly held, negative predictions (e.g., "I could never get through a job interview"). In effect, the specific behavioral procedure of graded task assignment was utilized not only to alter the client's behavior but also to provide a concrete test of the specific predictions generated by the client in that situation. Further, this interaction provided a basis for a metacognitive exploration of the client's currrent expectancy-formation tendencies (his expectations were consistently negative and frequently incorrect), in a manner analogous to Ross's (1977) third recommendation, attention to inferential processes.

A nonmetacognitive approach (e.g., enactive exposure alone) might readily have produced behavior change, but it would have left explicit expectancy disconfirmation to chance. Any of a number of heuristic-based processes could have intervened to undermine the power and generality of the behavioral manipulation. As Tversky and Kahneman (1980) have described, evidence disconfirming strongly held beliefs frequently gets reinterpreted (e.g., "The task was easier than I had anticipated; if I could do it, it must not have been very difficult"). Similarly, Fischhoff (1976, 1982) has described individuals' propensity for recalling a wholly different expectation after the fact than they had generated before (e.g., "Well, I figured all along that I could complete a résumé; it's going to the job interview that really scares me"). Our experience has been that even the careful recording of predictions and discussions of these "processes,"; both before and after task engagement, will not totally forestall such occurrences, but may reduce their likelihood. Thus, although we strongly concur with Bandura's (1977) observation that enactive behavioral methods provide the strongest procedures for producing cognitive change, we think such enactive approaches can be enhanced even further if they are embedded in a metacognitive framework.

J. also believed that he really was, at best, a mediocre talent (a dispositional attribution or self-perception) and that although the earlier loss of his academic position may have been triggered by larger economic forces, it had been facilitated by others' recognition of his mediocrity (a causal attribution); further, he believed this mediocrity would be perceived, sooner or later, by any prospective employer (expectation). Had we (Hollon & Beck) been approaching therapy from a more deductive, rational perspective, such as that favored by RET, we would have spent more time early in therapy disputing the logical premises upon which these beliefs were based. In particular, we would have relied heavily on persuasion and logic to disabuse the client of the irrational assumption that he could only be happy if he were seen as being competent, in both his own and others' eyes. Such an approach would have emphasized Ross's second approach, pitting one integrated belief system against another, largely by attacking the logical basis of the former. We did lay out an alternative model (i.e., that the client might be reasonably competent, but that bad luck followed by belief-mediated behavioral ineffectiveness, a self-fulfilling prophecy, had largely accounted for his recent misfortune and distress), but we did not insist upon its logical superiority or its greater accuracy. Rather, we simply suggested that any of several possible models (professional mediocrity versus the combination of bad luck, misattribution, and self-fulfilling prophecy or other potential models yet to be specified) might provide adequate explanations of his current status.

Rather than relying solely on persuasion and logic, our tactic was to suggest an open-minded, empirical test pitting hypotheses generated from each model against one another in the form of specific predictions. Tasks such as résumé construction would serve as the experiments. Expectations generated from the competing explanatory models (i.e., "I can't possibly do it," from the "personal mediocrity" model, versus "I can probably do it if I don't let myself get overwhelmed by my self-doubts," from the "bad-luck/self-fulfilling prophecy" model) were compared, with the client's own observation of consequences ("Did I succeed or did I not") providing the evidential outcome. Consistent with Ross's second suggestion, alternative explanatory models were formulated, but, as opposed to RET, were presented only as potential alternatives to be evaluated empirically, not as foregone conclusions.

There are two rationales for this emphasis. First, it is not that unusual to find that parts or whole segments of a client's belief system may be very accurate indeed, although sometimes for the wrong reason. Clients may lack specific skills or may tend to behave in ways likely to bring external retribution, and an inductive, empirical approach is as much a check on the therapist's tendency to overestimate the client's capacities and opportunities as it is a test of the client's underestimations. If, for example, the client really doesn't know how to construct a résumé, he or she needs to acquire skills, not simply change beliefs. Second, such an inductive, empirically based approach is more likely to have a powerful impact than is a deductive, nonevidential debate. Just as the empirical sciences have emerged from philosophy because of their greater credibility (when they can be applied), so too will empirically based approaches prove to be more credible than rationally based ones. We do recognize, however, that our own beliefs in this regard may simply reflect "egocentric attribution bias" (or "attributional projection"; see Heider, 1958; Holmes, 1968; Jones & Nisbett, 1972) on our part. Because we purport to be empiricists, extolling the virtues of hard data, we presume that everyone else is as well. We have had clients who have been singularly unimpressed by the slow unfolding of carefully constructed empirical trials, just as we have known friends who prefer philosophy to science. One potentially interesting direction for future research might well be to determine whether individual differences exist with regard to what type of information people find most compelling.

COGNITIVE TECHNIQUES

There are several meaningful divisions that can be made with regard to the cognitive phenomena targeted by cognitive therapy. The first, the distinction between automatic thoughts and underlying assumptions, has long been recognized by Beck and colleagues (Beck, 1970, 1976; Beck *et al.*, 1979; Hollon & Beck, 1979). Automatic thoughts are defined as specific cognitive products (either ruminative or imaginal) that occur in the spontaneous trains of thought that people have. An example might be the client J. thinking to himself, "I'll never be able to get a job" when encouraged to generate a résumé. Although many people are not particularly adept at introspection, with training and practice even the most concrete individual can usually learn to attend to such moment-to-moment cognitive products.

Underlying, or silent, assumptions are typically more abstract, refer to more situations, and may rarely occur spontaneously in the client's moment-to-moment train of thought, and thus are more difficult to identify and change. An example is our client's general prescription that "unless I'm competent at all times in all situations, no one will love me, myself included." Typically, such propositions are inferred by a therapist and client in CB from repeated instances. Our experience has been that clients rarely report experiencing such thoughts and not infrequently deny believing them, even when they seem to feel and act as if they do. An important difference between an inductive metacognitive approach such as CB and a deductive metacognitive approach such as RET is that the former typically begins by emphasizing the identification and evaluation of specific situations-linked automatic thoughts earlier in therapy, inferring the nature of underlying assumptions only later in treatment from the repeated invocation of particular patterns of specific beliefs, whereas the latter emphasizes the early identification and disputation of those more general beliefs.

A second meaningful distinction concerns the nature of the relationships conveyed by different cognitions (e.g., Hollon & Garber, 1980). According to the taxonomy of cognitive contents discussed earlier, causal attributions refer to ascriptions of effect to cause and are distinguished from expectations or predictions, that infer consequences from indicator or cause (Tversky & Kahneman, 1980). There are various other distinctions that can be made as well; for example, *attributes* (as distinct from attributions of causality) can be seen as ascriptions of characteristic belongingness, as when ascribing a trait to a person or a characteristic to a situation. In line with Ross (1977), we recognize that modern attribution theory is concerned with all three types of processes/products, but, in keeping with Tversky and Kahneman (1980), we suggest that different inferential processes follow different rules (heuristics) and may have different consequences. Thus, elsewhere (Hollon & Garber, 1980; see also Abramson *et al.*, 1987) we have argued that expectational processes lend themselves more readily to empirical confirmation/disconfirmation than do causal attributions, because of the inherent temporal asymmetry between them, as well as the tendency for people to prefer and to feel more confident when inferring the general from the specific (Tversky & Kahneman, 1980).

The third distinction, described earlier, lies between process and product (or content). It may seem useful to distinguish between the types of cognitive distortions identified by Beck (1970, 1976)—such as all-or-none thinking, selective abstraction, and so forth—and the heuristics, identified by Tversky and Kahneman (1974, 1980), versus the products of those processes—that is, the specific attributions of causality, dispositional ascriptions, and expectations, among others. As mentioned previously, an important issue for future research is precisely how and why various psychopathological groups differ from nonpsychopathological populations with respect to these processes and products. If two people arrive at different products (attributions, ascriptions, predictions, and so forth) is that because of differences in their original beliefs, processing heuristics, newly received input information, or some combination of these? With the recent advances in the fields of cognitive psychology (Kahneman *et al.*, 1982), and social cognition (Kelley, 1973; Nisbett & Ross, 1980), the technologies for exploring these issues appear to exist. The recent work by Alloy and Abramson (1979, 1982) on the process and products of the perception of contingency appears to represent one such promising example.

Specific cognitive change techniques are generally metacognitive in nature. In the sections that follow, we describe several of these procedures, examining them from the perspective of change in social cognition (Nisbett & Ross, 1980; Ross, 1977, 1978) and cognitive heuristics (Kahneman *et al.*, 1982).

Presentation of a Cognitive Model

One of the earliest steps typically undertaken in cognitive therapy, usually in the first session and sometimes prior to the first session via a recommended reading entitled "Coping with Depression" (Beck & Greenberg, 1974), is the presentation of a cognitive theory of affect and behavior. This usually is presented in an "A-B-C" format, in which the "As" are the antecedent events, the "Bs," the purportedly mediating cognitions, and the "Cs," the consequences, either affective or behavioral. Thus, the model is described as a general statement as to how beliefs influence feelings and actions. Ellis (1957) first articulated the "A-B-C" model in this format, and it is quite compatible with Schacter's two-process theory of emotions (Schacter, 1964; Schacter & Singer, 1962; Schacter & Wheeler, 1962), and cognitively mediated theories of achievement motivation (Atkinson, 1964; Feather, 1967; Feather & Simon, 1971; Weiner, 1972, 1974; Weiner *et al.*, 1971).

The initial presentation of this model is largely didactic. A general discussion is provided, accompanied by examples drawn from other individuals' experiences. In addition, efforts are made to contrast this cognitive model with various possible alternative models that relegate cognition solely to epiphenomenon status. Chief among these are the views that clients are passive recipients, either responding only in an invariant and reactive fashion to environmental events (a peripheral behaviorist model, similar to a strict "life-events" model), or controlled by purely biochemical processes. The therapist's efforts in presenting the cognitive model appears to be a reasonable approximation of Ross's second change procedure—the articulation of a preferred explanatory model in contrast to less favored alternative models. In general, cognitive therapists typically do not explicitly discredit other potential factors (e.g., the role of life events, biochemical processes, early childhood experiences). Rather, cognitive factors are emphasized, and general evidence supporting their validity is presented.

After the didactic initial presentation, the therapist rapidly pursues the generation of more personally relevant evidence supportive of the role of cognitive mediation. Typically, he or she invites the client to provide instances that either fit or do not fit such a cognitive model by asking, for example, "Can you think of any recent experiences when your mood shifted rapidly? Let's examine that instance and see if there were any beliefs associated with that shift."

Similarly, the therapist may inquire about whether or not variance in response by the client to the same situation over time was cognitively mediated. For example, with our client, J., it became evident in the first session that his affect varied from hour to hour and day to day while he was at his place of employment. In effect, the therapist utilized this *inconsistency* across time in the same situation (Kelley, 1967, 1972a, 1973) to stimulate doubt as to the accuracy of the client's attribution of negative affect to his work situation.

Typically, this hypothesis-testing strategy, analogous to Ross's first principle for inducing cognitive change, is rapidly worked into a prospective test format by being defined as a rationale for the event/affect self-monitoring described earlier. Although clients are typically not asked to record specific cognitions this early in therapy (our clinical experience has taught us that clients are too easily overwhelmed by such complex tasks early in treatment, and most people find monitoring ongoing thought processes far more difficult than monitoring events and feelings), they are instructed to attend to instances of such possible mediation. Further, at the ensuring session, the therapist reviews the self-monitored records with the client, and inquires about the presence of possible cognitive mediators.

Our impression is that cognitive therapists may well capitalize on a nonnormative tendency (heuristic) in human information-processing when testing the evidence concerning cognitive mediation. As has been frequently described (Einhorn, 1982; Jenkins & Ward, 1965; Smedslund, 1963; Ward & Jenkins, 1965; Wason, 1960; Wason & Johnson-Laird, 1972), individuals have a tendency to overlook the information value of nonoccurrence when judging contingency between two classes of events. Thus, therapists attend most avidly to instances in which plausible cognitive mediators can be supplied for interesting shifts in affect or important behavior. A more powerful test would be to collect a representative sample of target affects and behavior, as well as their nonoccurrence, and simultaneously catalogue the occurrence and nonoccurrence of purported cognitive mediators. It might prove instructive to examine (1) whether our impression of current practice in cognitive therapy is really accurate (for example, it would be a simple matter to have independent raters listen to archived therapy samples to determine what actually occurs), and (2) whether clients' beliefs are as powerfully influenced by "shortcut" procedures as by the more logically defensible, but more time consuming, four-cell contingency evaluation.

Finally, attention is paid to the way in which individuals process information, Ross's third procedure for producing change, albeit this aspect plays only a minor role at this stage. Such attention takes the form of emphasizing that most people are not very adept at monitoring their own thinking, whether concerning the *processes* involved in arriving at various judgments, perceptions, or beliefs, or those *products* (*contents*) themselves (see Hollon & Bemis, 1981, or Turk & Speers, 1983, for a discussion of the process–products distinction). In this attempt at providing an understanding of how the individual client processes information, the therapist typically points out that people seem to be more adept at monitoring events, actions, and affects than they are at monitoring cognitions. The therapist frequently suggests that this relative proclivity in attending to noncognitive aspects of a sequence of events contributes to the client's initial adherence to a noncognitive explanatory model. The clear implication is that greater sensitivity to cognition, combined with training in cognitive self-monitoring, will likely provide evidence at least partially supportive of cognitive models of distress.

From social-cognitive and cognitive psychological perspectives, several interesting processes may be operating here. First, it has been fairly well established that, when explaining the causes of events, "actors" are more likely to attribute consequent outcomes or actions to various aspects of the situation in which those consequences arise than are outside "observers," whereas those observers are more likely to attribute outcomes to stable dispositions in the actor (Jones & Davis, 1965; Jones & Nisbett, 1972). Current theorists have tended to attribute this phenomenon to "perceptual focusing," in which the attributor tends to make attributions to those objects most salient in the stimulus field. (Arkin & Duval, 1975; Duval & Wicklund, 1972; Regan & Totten, 1975; Storms, 1973; Taylor & Fiske, 1975). For an actor, attention is typically focused on the surrounding environment, hence, an external attribution to events, rather than an internal attribution to beliefs to explain such consequent processes as behavior, affects, or outcomes. In a sense, such "perceptual focusing" may represent a special case of Tversky and Kahneman's (1973) availability heuristic, in which the phenomena most likely to be selected as causal mediators are those phenomena most salient in the attributor's immediate perceptual field.

These musing are, of course, highly speculative. Nonetheless, it may provide a guide for some interesting research. For example, do individuals become more introspective when their attention is explicitly focused on themselves? There appears already to be evidence that this is precisely what occurs (Duval & Wicklund, 1972). Does increasing the salience of cognitive phenomena increase the likelihood of individuals' ascribing to them a role in the causal chain mediating actions, affects, and outcomes? Do people have an easier time ascribing a causal role to thinking in the experience of others than for themselves? We know of no strong evidence for these latter hypotheses, but it does conform to our experience with group cognitive therapy (Hollon & Evans, 1983; Hollon & Shaw, 1979).

Identifying Automatic Thoughts

The process of training clients to be more facile in identifying the operation of cognitive processes and their end products begins, as has already been described, as an extension of efforts to communicate a cognitive model of psychopathology and a cognitive theory of change. Additional efforts typically include *in vivo* (in-session) efforts by the therapist to target instances in which nonverbal cues are used to signal the possible occurrence of affective changes. The therapist then asks the client to describe what just passed through his or her train-of-consciousness. The therapist frequently models describing multiple trains-of-thought (e.g., "Even as I'm sitting here listening to what you're telling me, I'm also thinking ahead to other aspects that I want to ask you about or what things I want you to consider doing between sessions"). Further, therapists will often explicitly attempt to disinhibit the client from describing potentially embarrassing or seemingly irrelevant cognitive content (e.g., "Not only do I sometimes think task-relevant thoughts that I don't speak out loud, such as 'What shall I ask next,' but I also sometimes think things that might be a little embarrassing if you knew I was thinking about them, for example, 'Am I any good as a therapist? Can I help this client?'"). These efforts at modeling and disinhibition are designed to increase the client's capacity to identify and willingness to report accessible cognitive content. Although important to cognitive therapy in general, they appear to have little direct relevance to the type of cognitive change processes we have been describing. The same can probably be said about additional therapist maneuvers, such as encouraging the client to picture (and verbalize) the situation in which thoughts occurred before attempting to recall those thoughts, training in self-monitoring, and systematic record keeping.

Identifying Cognitive Distortions

Closely related to the efforts to identify automatic thoughts are efforts to train clients to recognize systematic distortions in information-processing. As we described earlier, attention to such distortion processes as "all-or-none thinking," selective abstraction, arbitrary inference, and so forth, represents the closest approximation to Ross's third procedure (education about cognitive processes). Such processes appear to represent almost direct analogues to Tversky and Kahneman's concept of heuristics (Kahneman & Tversky, 1972, 1973; Tversky & Kahneman, 1971, 1973, 1974).

Specific procedures involve a combination of didactic training and attention to specific instances of the operation of such processes in the material reported during sessions or monitored between sessions. Frequently, the therapist relies on the client's adherence to a normative model in an effort to produce change. For example, in the case of the client J., one clear example came from his understanding of his marital problems with his wife. He inferred, based on feedback that he received from her, that she was dissatisfied with him as a sexual partner. During a conjoint session, she expressed amazement not only that he believed that to be a valid representation of her beliefs but that he believed that to be an accurate rendition of her comments to him. What she had recalled saying to him was that she was dissatisfied that since he had been depressed, he rarely demonstrated any affection toward her, referring to his aversion to talking, hugging, taking walks, and other forms of nonsexual interactions. He had inferred from this that she was dissatisfied with him as a sexual partner, leading him to become even more cautious in engaging in any type of interaction that might lead to sexual demands. In the ensuing discussions, J. was readily able to recognize the arbitrariness of the inference he had drawn, in which he had not only attributed his concerns to his wife, but had misrecalled her precise words to him on the subject.

In cognitive therapy, teaching clients about such systematic information-processing errors and then identifying specific instances as they occur represent the procedures utilized to alter those distortions. We suspect that these are sufficient procedures, although we have no firm evidence in that regard. If we attend to the cognitive psychological literature, these procedures appear to be consistent with the techniques suggested there to alter operating heuristics (Fischhoff, 1982; Kahneman & Tversky, 1982; Nisbett, Krantz, Jepson, & Fong, 1982). In general, these steps include basic *education* about the nature of the operating heuristics, buttressed by specific examples of their operation, discussion of more accurate or appropriate *normative baselines*, and training in recognizing *specific instances* in the client's own information-processing.

Within nonpsychopathological domains, individuals such as scientists, statisticians, and mathematicians clearly must overcome the operation of nonnormative intuitive heuristics in order to operate within their respective areas of expertise. Such professionals increase their capacity to do so through extended professional training consisting largely of education about common errors, the working through of normative solutions, and specific practice in applying those normative models. Typically, change occurs, relative to the nonprofessional intuitive scientist, although frequently it is insufficient (Einhorn, 1982; Ross, 1977; Tversky & Kahneman, 1971). Efforts to increase our understanding of the factors that maintain such operating heuristics remain a primary target of inquiry, with regard to both nonpsychopathological and psychopathological populations. We fully recognize, and emphasize again, that there may be few distinctions between the heuristics that operate in these two populations.

Evaluating Belief Validity

Assessing Schemata

The heart of cognitive therapy involves the examination of belief validity on a moment-to-moment basis (Hollon & Beck, 1979). To a somewhat lesser extent, thoughts may be examined for their adaptiveness (e.g., for a client whose job it was to handle poisonous snakes at the city zoo, worrying about being bitten was maladaptive when handling the snakes, although the fear itself was not invalid.) In general, however, attention is devoted to testing the validity of the client's beliefs.

We have argued elsewhere (Hollon & Garber, 1980; see also Abramson *et al.*, 1987) that the specific cognitive products that should be the focus of the hypothesis-testing procedure are the client's *expectations*, rather than his or her attributions. We have suggested that cognitive change is most powerfully produced through a process of empirical hypothesis testing that utilizes prospective experiments. The goal of these prospective tests is to collect evidence that may confirm or disconfirm the client's expectations.

In contrast, we have been particularly pessimistic about the utility in the change process of focusing on the client's existing causal attributions, largely because such attributions are typically made for events that have already occurred, thus necessitating efforts at post hoc reinterpretation. In contrast, the disconfirmation of expectations in the context of a prospective experiment may provide the more powerful procedure for change, because the outcome actually experienced by the client cannot be explained away as reflecting nothing more than the therapist's persuasiveness. Thus, in effect, we are pitting Ross's first procedure, evidential disconfirmation, against his second procedure, rational critiques of the existing explanatory system, and endorsing the former.

Although we still suspect that expectancy disconfirmation (Ross's "brute" evidence) provides the single most powerful approach to cognitive change, recently we have become convinced that the incorporation of Ross's other two strategies—articulation of the opposing explanatory systems and identification of nonoptimal information-processing heuristics—may provide the best *combination* of belief-change procedures. In any science, a procedure that articulates competing models, generates specific differential hypotheses unique to each, self-consciously compensates for highly probable errors of inference, and relies on empirical observation to test the respective hypotheses provides the optimal package for the advancement of knowledge. In essence, this is precisely what cognitive therapy attempts to do and precisely the way it is supposed to be done (Beck *et al.*, 1979; Hollon & Beck, 1979). These suggestions lead to the formulation of the following hypotheses: (1) expectancy disconfirmation should produce greater change in existing beliefs than either the articulation of existing beliefs or the identification of nonoptimal heuristics, and (2) the combination of all three components should prove superior to any one alone.

The specific techniques in cognitive therapy most relevant to these belief-change procedures involve several steps. The first and perhaps most critical although least well-understood step in the larger cognitive evaluation process is labeled "distancing" (Beck, 1970). This involves the clients learning that any belief, no matter how compelling, is essentially a hypothesis rather than a fact, until carefully tested. A variety of strategies can be utilized to facilitate this process, such as discussions and practice during therapy, adopting alternative perspectives (e.g., responding to one's own beliefs as one might respond to a student's, trainee's, or child's), or routinizing standardized cognitions to serve as reminders (e.g., "That's just a prediction," or "That's a belief, not a fact"). This is one area in which self-instructional training (Kendall & Finch, 1979; Meichenbaum, 1977), with its emphasis on utilizing overt verbalizations as a means of increasing the probability of the occurrence of similar covert cognitions, may be particularly useful as a technique for reminding oneself of compensatory strategies for dealing with suboptimal intuitive heuristics.

Once a belief has been targeted for evaluation, clients in cognitive therapy next are encouraged to pursue two lines of inquiry. The first, sometimes referred to as the "downward arrow" technique (Burns, 1979), involves mapping out the additional meanings associated with a given belief. For example, if a client indicates that he or she fears going for a job interview, the therapist might first inquire what the client thinks might happen, that is, what the client's expectations are. If, for example, the client didn't think he or she would get the job, the therapist would then inquire what that would mean to the client. If depressed, the client might respond that that would mean that he or she was a failure (a global, stable, internal attribution in the terminology of Abramson *et al.*, 1978). The therapist might continue to explore for further meaning by asking again, "And what would that mean?"; the client might respond that that would mean that he or she was inept and incompetent, and would never get what he or she wanted from life. The essence of the procedure is that the therapist coaxes the client to explicate his or her construct system, or, in Beck's term, the client's cognitive schema, by continually asking about the specific meaning of a belief to him or her.

Not infrequently, the initial beliefs or cognitions that the client reports in association with an affect or troublesome situation do not seem to fully explain the degree of affect reported or the action undertaken. In such instances, it is especially important to map out the meaning system in the manner described above. This procedure appears to be a partial variation of Ross's second procedure, the explication of the client's existing belief system and the articulation of a competing model, with the emphasis on the former.

There are several additional points to be considered with respect to the concept of cognitive schemata and the procedures used to identify and change them. First, although there is considerable evidence that various psychopathological groups exhibit different cognitive organizations, or schemata, than do nonpsychopathological groups (e.g., Derry & Kuiper, 1981, Kuiper & Derry, 1980; Landau, 1980; Landau & Goldfried, 1981), there is considerably less clarity concerning precisely what schemata are, how they are organized, or what rules they obey (see Kihlstrom & Nasby, 1981, for a particularly salient review).

Given that there exists a fair amount of controversy among experimentalists with regard to precisely what schemata are, it is hardly surprising that even less is known about how they operate. As described earlier, Hastie (1980) has suggested that congruent versus incongruent information may fare differently at different points in the processing sequence. Specifically, schemata-incongruent information appears to receive greater attention when encountered, leading to a higher probability of being *encoded* and to a richer, better articulated memory trace. Conversely, schematic-congruent information appears to be more easily *retrieved* from memory. If true, these observations would have the following implications for therapy: (1) When the therapist wants to facilitate change, he or she should avoid relaying solely on retrospective, memorial processes, because such processes are most likely to retrieve information supportive of existing schemata, but (2) when the therapist is attempting to explore operating schemata, procedures that ask for context-free recall (such as asking what successive thoughts suggest, mean, or imply, as is done in the "downward arrow" technique) appear to be quite serviceable. Although this appears to be close to what is done in cognitive therapy, we can only wonder if a metacognitive explication of these processes might not further accelerate the client's capacity to change.

Second, although the mapping out of meaning is largely assessment-focused, inadequate determination of the client's underlying schematic organization can lead to impoverished and ineffectual hypothesis testing. Cognitively oriented social psychologists have long talked about the distinction between "hot" and "cold" cognitions (Abelson, 1968; Nisbett & Ross, 1980), with the former denoting beliefs closely linked to affective experiences, and the latter denoting passionless, usually rational, information-processing. Although we do not ascribe to a theory that divorces cognition from affective processes, we are quite impressed by Zajonc's (1980) work suggesting that affective responses frequently occur more rapidly than sequential higher order cognitive processes can operate. We suspect that these various distinctions are all encompassed by the distinction between automatic versus deliberate information-processing (Keele, 1973; Neely, 1977; Posner & Snyder, 1975; Schneider & Shiffrin, 1977;

Shiffrin & Schneider, 1977). Whereas "hot" or affect-related cognitions are most likely to be processed automatically and rapidly, and to conform most closely with dominant schematic principles, "cold" or dispassionate cognitions are most likely to flow from deliberate, sequential information-processing. Closely related is Lazarus' (1966) classic distinction between appraisal and reappraisal processes. The essential points here are that (1) a truly *meaningful* assessment of the individual's construct system is a necessary precursor to efforts to produce change in that system, and (2) that assessment may prove to be best pursued if the client is asked to respond to rapid, briefly phrased prompts relying largely on automatic, appraisal-related reactions, rather than a more deliberate, analytic approach.

Finally, our experience in training and supervision has suggested to us that the orientation and prior training of therapists retrained in cognitive-behavioral therapy may significantly influence the process of identifying schemata and testing beliefs. Although we are unaware of any empirical data in this regard, our impression has been that cognitive-behaviorists originally trained as staunch behaviorists (see Hollon & Kendall, 1979; Kendall & Hollon, 1979a) tend to err on the side of acting without fully understanding what they are trying to change, whereas retrained "traditional dynamic-eclectic therapists" tend to err in the direction of not being active enough in attempting to alter belief systems that have been nicely explicated.

Testing Beliefs

Once a belief or set of beliefs has been identified, it can be subjected to critical scrutiny. We have come to value an approach that emphasizes the application of several standard questions to most explicit examples of construct systems. These questions are intended solely to serve as the beginning of cognitive evaluation and are a heuristic device that facilitates the recall of therapeutic maneuvers by both therapist and client.

1. "What is the evidence for that belief?"—the *evidence* question.
2. "Is there any other way of looking at this?"—the *alternative explanations* question.
3. "Even if it is true, is it as bad as it seems?"—the *implications* question.

The therapist typically begins raising these questions and guiding the ensuing discussion as early as the first therapy session. Therapists appear to vary in the degree to which they concretize and routinize their efforts to evaluate the validity of the client's beliefs (DeRubeis, Hollon, Evans, & Bemis, 1982; Evans, Hollon, DeRubeis, Auerbach, 1983; Tuason, & Wiemer, 1983; Hollon, Evans, Elkin, & Lowery, 1984). Although we have not formally tested this view, we hypothesize that, all things being equal, greater routinization, perhaps using self-instructional training procedures (Kendall & Finch, 1979; Meichenbaum, 1977) should facilitate greater recall and utilization of these techniques by the client later.

The *evidence* question typically leads to several related lines of inquiry: intensive reviews of unstructured prior experience, intensive reviews of systematically garnered evidence (e.g., self-monitored materials), and prospective hypothesis testing. Unstructured retrospective information retrieval is typically the most convenient but the least reliable vehicle. As Hastie (1980) has described, reliance on such a methodology allows existing schemata the greatest latitude to determine the material recovered. Nonetheless, it is frequently a useful point of departure.

Examination of systematically gathered information is typically more fruitful, since it does not depend on the vagaries of recall. For example, in working with our exemplar client J., we were able to test his belief that his depression was directly related to his "dead-end" job as a menial laborer and would lift only when he found more suitable employment. On reviewing his own event–affect self-monitoring records over the first 4 weeks of treatment, the client discovered that his lowest average moods occurred on the weekends, particularly Sunday, while his highest average moods occurred during work, and particularly on Mondays. Based on this evidence, although it was not gathered specifically to test his hypothesis but rather was generated following systematic self-observation principles, he rejected his original hypothesis that his job produced his depression.

Prospective hypothesis testing appears to provide the most powerful vehicle for producing change, although it is invariably the most difficult type of evidence to collect, and frequently elicits the greatest arousal from both client and therapist. In J.'s case, for example, after observing that his self-monitored mood did not conform to his belief-generated expectations, he and the therapist speculated about what other factors might more accurately describe his affective variation (see the discussion of the *alternative explanations* questions below). It became apparent from a review of his self-monitoring materials that J. tended to "relax" on the weekends, which meant that he kept his time unstructured and typically spent it laying in front of the television for hours at a time. His primary activity involved ruminating about how desolate his life had become. Therapist and client agreed upon an experiment in which J. would alternately "relax" in an unstructured fashion on one given weekend day or evening and actively schedule tasks (some potentially pleasurable, some potentially masterful) on the alternate day, self-monitoring his mood on each of the successive days. After a period of such "experimentation," it became abundantly clear that his mood was far more elevated (as was his wife's) during the periods in which he was actively scheduling activities for himself. Through this prospective-hypothesis-testing procedure, which fully incorporated behavior change techniques as the "experimental manipulations," the client further disconfirmed his original hypothesis that "bad job produces bad mood" and began to replace it with a recognition that unstructured periods of inactivity filled with ruminations about his miserable plight produced (or at least maintained) his negative affective states.

Some investigators (Nisbett & Ross, 1980; Ross, 1977, 1978; Ross & Lepper, 1980) have cautioned that existing beliefs, once established, can be remarkably resistant to change. Beliefs appear to survive the disconfirmation of the original data upon which they were based (Lau, Lepper, & Ross, 1976; Lepper, Ross, & Lau, 1979), especially when causal inferences were generated for those initial data (Ross, Lepper, Strack, & Steinmetz, 1977). Moreover, evidence-based efforts to disconfirm existing belief systems may, at times, actually produce stronger adherence to those beliefs. In at least one instance, providing disconfirming evidence (in association with confirmatory evidence) appeared to produce even stronger adherence to initial beliefs (Lord et al., 1979). Ross (1977) has commented on this literature, stating that

> Erroneous impressions, theories, and data processing strategies, therefore, may not be changed through mere exposure to samples of new evidence. It is not intended, of course, that new evidence can never produce change—only that new evidence will produce less change than would be demanded by any logical or rational information-processing model. Thus, new evidence that is strongly and consistently contrary to one's impressions or theories can, and frequently does, produce change, albeit at a slower rate than would result from an unbiased or dispassionate view of the evidence. (p. 211)

Although in some instances it is possible that disconfirming evidence may actually strengthen adherence to one's original beliefs, we suspect that this concern is overstated. The majority of evidence cited for such an assertion actually comes from two related types of studies. First are the "debriefing" studies (Anderson, Lepper, & Ross, 1980; Jennings, Lepper, & Ross, 1980; Lau et al., 1976; Lepper et al., 1979; Ross, Lepper, & Hubbard, 1975) in which subjects first have a perception induced via presentation of a contrived situation, then are provided with a "debriefing" that attempts to discredit the veracity of the original perception. Typically, subjects continue to maintain some belief in their original perception, even after the debriefing procedure. Although this phenomenon has been quite appropriately interpreted as indicating an unjustified perseverance of beliefs in the face of disconfirmatory evidence, it speaks only to the inefficacy of evidence-based disconfirmation procedures *relative* to a normative model, but not in *absolute* terms. That is, the degree of belief does appear to change as a consequence of debriefing; it simply doesn't change as much as an observer might expect if the subjects were operating in accordance with a fully logical, normative model. As such, these experiments may well represent examples of the operation of one of Tversky and Kahneman's (1974) original heuristics, insufficient *adjustment* away from an existing conceptual *anchorpoint* in the face of new information.

The second line of evidence, one which indicates that being confronted with disconfirming evidence strengthens the preexistent beliefs, comes from a single study conducted by Lord et al. (1979). We have discussed that study in greater detail earlier, so we will sketch only the relevant aspects here. In brief, subjects differing in their initial beliefs concerning capital punishment were presented with two ostensibly real studies, one supportive and the other not supportive of capital punishment. Both sets of subjects indicated an even stronger adherence to their original beliefs after exposure. Moreover, belief-consistent studies were rated as more convincing than belief-incongruent studies, and subjects given greater details in the description of the methodologies utilized evidence an *enhanced* polarization effect.

Several comments are in order here. First, we regard this as an extremely important study. Although no one would want to base major statements on a single study, should those findings prove reliable, the implications for such evidential-based approaches such as cognitive therapy are striking. Clearly one would have to shift away from our earlier targeting of evidential-based procedures, Ross's first procedure, as the "first among equals" of means of producing change.

There are, however, several additional points that lead us to question the interpretation of the findings of this study. For example, although subjects were presented with disconfirmatory evidence, they were also presented with a relatively equivalent amount of confirmatory data. Thus the Lord *et al.* findings do not speak so much to polarization in the face of disconfirmation as they speak of polarization in the face of equally mixed confirmation-disconfirmation. Future studies building on the Lord *et al.* paradigm might profitably investigate the effect of various levels of mixed feedback in cognitive change.

Second, beliefs regarding issues such as capital punishment may well be adopted and maintained on the basis of both dispassionate utilitarian grounds (e.g., evidence of efficacy in controlling crime) and passionate values (e.g., adherence to an "eye-for-an-eye" philosophy versus a moral abhorrence of taking any human life). We wonder whether the nature of the factors related to the maintenance of any given belief (i.e., informational versus motivational) may not interact in determining the impact of disconfirmatory evidence on existing beliefs. Although dynamic formulations would not concur, most cognitive theories of psychopathology are predicated on the notion that individuals would prefer to believe other than they do (i.e., they are not motivated by anything other than a desire to accurately assess reality when they adopt and maintain their beliefs).

Third, the design itself provided no control for the effect of attending to one's beliefs on a topic in the absence of new information presentation. It may well be that attention alone produced a polarization of attitudes that is actually mitigated by exposure to counterattitudinal evidence.

Finally, our experience in cognitive therapy is nicely described by Ross's (1977) phrase "the sheer force of 'brute' evidence." What was understandably not addressed in the Lord *et al.* design were the effects of repeated efforts at evidential-based disconfirmation. Stated explicitly, the consequences of repeated exposure to disconfirmatory evidence may be very different from the consequences of the initial exposure. By way of analogy, we can point to the effects of repeated nonreinforcement in previously reinforced behavior. Initially, most organisms show increased effort and behavioral persistance (facilitation), eventually lapsing into striking behavioral reductions (cf. Klinger, 1975; Roth & Kubal, 1975).

Ross (1977) has speculated about the processes that serve to influence what a person does with disconfirmatory information. He has identified three processes: (1) *distortion*, in which the weight assigned to additional evidence depends upon its consistency with existing beliefs; (2) *autonomy*, in which initial impressions are not only enhanced by distortion of subsequent evidence, but are also maintained by it; and (3) *explanation*, in which after inferring a cause for an observed event, the subsequent occurrence of that purported cause is taken to imply the occurrence of the presumed consequence. It should be noted that each of these processes was abstracted by Ross from work with largely nonpathological populations. Although we are unaware of any evidence that they operate in clinical populations in a similar or altered form, it would be surprising if they did not.

Kihlstrom and Nasby's (1981) distinction between cognitive "hardware"—the structural integrity of the brain and its processes—and cognitive "software"—the cognitions pertaining to some specific domain of content, the information it contains, and the rules by which it operates—seems relevant here. When we deal with nonpsychotic populations, we appear to be dealing largely with "software" issues. Ross's three processes appear to be "software" rules applied to new information processed in the context of existing beliefs. Although it seems clear that those existing beliefs may differ between various pathological groups and the larger nonpathological population, it is not clear that the "software" rules necessarily differ between these groups. The *alternative explanations* question used in cognitive therapy (i.e., "Is there any other way of looking at this?") is intended to stimulate the client to consider other possible causal attributions for a given event. For example, our client J. had shown a fairly early response to therapy, becoming mostly asymptomatic after the first four sessions held during the first 2 weeks of treatment. When he then began becoming progressively more symptomatic over the following week, he became convinced that he was untreatable and that therapy didn't really work for him. He had made a dispositional attribution, that he was a "loser" who was incapable of profiting from therapy, and he verbalized an intent to drop out of therapy. Fortunately, he had described similar experiences in other forms of treatment over the past several years during the initial pretreatment interview, and the therapist had cautioned him even then against overinterpreting a "placebo" response to initiating a new therapy. During the first few weeks of treatment, the therapist had been far more cautious than the client in attributing observed change to the specific therapy procedures being utilized. When reminded of these predictions, especially with the aid of audiotapes from the earlier sessions, the client was able to acknowledge that perhaps he had made two erroneous causal attributions: the first in attributing early change to the acquisition of specific, nontransistory skills, and the second in attributing his returning symptoms to the combination of a pernicious depressive disposition and the inefficacy of the specific therapy techniques. He did not substitute one explanation for the other (such a wholesale "conversion" would be viewed with considerable suspicion by a metacognitive methodologist), but he was at least willing to entertain multiple plausible explanations and to consider testing between the two by conducting further "experiments."

Although we have minimized the role of Ross's second change procedure, providing competing explanatory models for prior observations, in our earlier writing (cf. Hollon & Garber, 1980), a minimization not shared by Beck and colleagues (Beck, 1967, 1970, 1976; Beck *et al.*, 1979), we did note that this process has an important role to play. We are not sure, however, precisely how that role is best played. On the one hand, being able to articulate competing theories should produce more powerful and wide-ranging change across a full belief system in response to evidential-based disconfirmation than should the same evidential-based diconfirmation treated as a single isolated occurrence. On the other hand, drawing out fully the implications of any given piece of evidential disconfirmation may decrease the probability of its acceptance, because the procedure may serve to mobilize powerful heuristics supportive of the existing beliefs. We regard the delineation of optimal combinations of evidential and explanatory techniques in producing (and maintaining) cognitive change to be a prime area for subsequent research.

Reattribution therapy is a specialized vignette in cognitive therapy that represents an expansion of the *explanation* question. Typically, it is utilized when some major event is interpreted in a particularly maladaptive fashion. Examples might include the loss of an important case by a lawyer, the ending of a relationship, or the loss of a job. Typically, the client generates a schema-consistent attribution for the event; for example, a depression-prone individual might be inclined to explain the loss of a job by concluding that he or she is really an incompetent loser, or a chronically angry client might attribute the ending of a relationship to the basic untrustworthiness and immorality of members of the opposite sex (Novaco, 1979).

As Beck and colleagues describe it (Beck *et al.*, 1979), reattribution therapy might proceed by having the client draw a large circle representing 100 percent of the causal variance for the event. The therapist might first ask the client what he or she thinks caused the outcome. In the case of a depressed client, for example, the client would probably attribute the event (e.g., the loss of an important legal case) to his or her own incompetence—a global, stable, internal attribution (see Eaves & Rush, 1984; Hamilton & Abramson, 1983; Kuiper, 1978; Metalsky & Abramson, 1981; Miller, Klee, & Norman, 1982; Persons & Rau, 1985; Peterson & Seligman, 1984; Raps, Peterson, Reinhard, Abramson, & Seligman, 1982; Rizley, 1978; and Seligman *et al.*, 1979, for discussions of depressive attributional patterns, and Sweeney, Anderson, & Bailey, 1986, for a meta-analytic review, but also see Barthe & Hammen, 1981;

Gong-Guy & Hammen, 1980; Hammen & Cochran, 1981; Hammen & de-Mayo, 1982; Hammen, Krantz, & Cochran, 1981; Hammen & Mayol, 1982; and Harvey, 1981, for studies not wholly supportive of this formulation, and Coyne & Gotlib, 1983, for a conceptual critique). The therapist would then inquire about other potential causal factors. Did the composition of the jury make a difference? Did the selection of the judge play a role in the outcome? What were the objective merits of the case? As each factor is raised, the client is asked to rate the amount of variance he or she would attribute to that factor, usually in percentage terms. Not infrequently, depressed clients move from attributing 100 percent of the "blame" for some undesirable outcome to themselves to a far smaller percentage of the causal variance, often in the space of minutes.

In a sense, this procedure appears analogous to encouraging the client to shift from a single-sufficient-factor causal schema to a multiple-factor causal schema (Kelley, 1972b). In our experience, the therapist rarely needs to attempt to persuade the client. It is usually necessary only to help the client to enumerate additional possible causal factors. Typically we have not found Kelley's *discounting* or *augmentation principles* to operate or be obvious impediments during this process, but we may have failed to recognize their occurrence. What does appear to be critical is encouraging the client to enumerate other possible factors. It is almost as if clients are invited to *reappraise* (in Lazarus's [1966] sense of the term) their initial attribution, doubtless made in a relatively automatic (as opposed to deliberate) fashion (Schneider & Shiffrin, 1977; Shiffrin & Schneider, 1977). This elicits the consideration of potential causes not available (Kahneman & Tversky, 1973) during the initial attributional formulation. With regard to the interaction of automaticity–deliberateness and the availability heuristic, we have frequently seen clients provide and incorporate possible causal processes that the therapist could never have foreseen. For example, we have worked with clients who operated in social or professional roles with which we, as therapists, were only dimly familiar. When encouraged to do so, these clients frequently could enumerate possible causal processes that we had not known were possible.

Two additional maneuvers have proven helpful to us in the past, both potentially interpretable in social-cognitive terms. First, we have observed instances in which asking the client to describe the causal processes operating in other relevant instances of the same situations or for other relevant individuals in the same situation have proved helpful. The first instance is essentially a call for an evaluation of the *consistency* with which a given factor has occurred across instances, whereas the latter is a call for the evaluation of the *consensuality* of those factors across actors (Kelley, 1967, 1972a, 1973). The key is that we have asked clients to shift from the single-observation case, in which causal schemata are believed to operate the most strongly, to a multiple-observation case, in which we might expect the *covariation principle* to operate more powerfully (Kelley, 1967, 1972b, 1973).

Second, we have utilized induced changes in role perspective to assess additional causal processes. In this procedure, clients are asked to imagine that they are someone else, such as a therapist, an employer, or a teacher, and then to ascribe and evaluate causal factors from the perspective of this social role. Ross and colleagues (Ross, 1977; Ross, Amabile, & Steinmetz, 1977) have observed that attributors typically fail to take into account the role-prescribed nature of interactional behavior when making dispositional attributions. The other side of this phenomenon appears to be the individual's ability to view situations differently when asked to take on other social roles. This procedure has proved clinically useful in eliciting additional causal attributions, evaluating the strength of those factors, generating expectations, and eliciting descriptions of coping behavior.

Finally, the *implications* question ("Even if it is true, is it as bad as it seems?") is adapted from Ellis's (1962) more bluntly phrased "So what?" question. In essence, it asks the client to evaluate the realistic probabilities associated with the perceived implications of his or her beliefs. Frequently, these implications lend themselves nicely to prospective hypothesis testing (e.g., "If I don't get this job, I'll never get another opportunity"), although just as frequently one is dealing not only with events but with the accuracy of ascriptions (e.g., "If I'm really a loser, how do I account for my various successes?"). In actuality, the *implications* question leads directly to additional applications of the *evidence* and the *explanation* questions to those beliefs.

All of these cognitive change techniques incorporate enactive behavioral procedures to a greater or lesser extent, in keeping with Bandura's (1977) dictum that enactive procedures provide the single most powerful procedures for producing cognitive change. Moreover, all of these procedures are explicitly metacognitive in nature (Flavell, 1979). We suggest that such a metacognitive approach enhances the extent and nature of the enactive procedures. Each of these hypotheses, however, will require testing before their validity can be determined.

Identifying Underlying Assumptions

Cognitive therapists typically wait until later in therapy to attempt to articulate the underlying assumptions that organize the client's belief systems. In some respects, these underlying assumptions may represent generic constructs in the schematic system. As we noted earlier, Ellis's RET typically encourages identifying those beliefs earlier in therapy than does Beck's cognitive therapy. This reflects a preference in the former for a deductive approach, with a greater reliance on Ross's second principle, in contrast to Beck's inductive approach, with a greater emphasis on Ross's first principle.

Hollon and Beck (1979) have provided an example of eliciting an underlying assumption from a client. In brief, a basic chaining of beliefs culminating in the end point notion that he was a "bad person" whom "no one could love" seemed to underline numerous reactions by our client J. across disparate situations. By the time we had clearly formulated that cluster of beliefs, along with its trigger (any situation in which the client failed to pursue things which he valued, regardless of whether it was possible or convenient to do so), we had already elicited multiple instances of its operation, examined the validity of the client's dispositional attribution "bad person," and tested the validity of its implication (that no one would love him).

Moreover, we were able to introduce another procedure often utilized in cognitive therapy but typically reserved until later in its course (after the client is mostly asymptomatic), that of exploring the early learning experiences that contributed to the acquisition of the underlying assumption. In the case of our client J., it turned out that he could first recall experiencing the operation of a phenomenologically similar construct when, as a preadolescent, he and his younger brother would compete with one another for their father's approval by helping the father in his mail-order business. J. was less skilled and less interested than his brother, although a year older than him, and he frequently failed to meet the levels of production achieved by his younger sibling. He became aware that he may have acquired his understanding of how the world worked in a highly artificial situation, one not totally representative of subsequent situations or relationships encountered in adult life. In a sense, this exercise in historical reconstruction served two purposes: (1) It provided a normalizing explanation for long-standing sources of emotional distress, and (2) it facilitated the reexamination and discarding of those beliefs by pointing up their context-specific nature and the relative immaturity of the client's reality-testing capacities at the time those beliefs were adopted.

CONCLUSIONS

In our clinical teaching, we often have been confronted by students and workshop participants who state, "We are not sure that you really can produce clinical change *simply* by getting people to change their beliefs." Although we concur that it is worth questioning whether clinical change follows cognitive change, we must emphasize that producing the cognitive change is by no means *simple*. Both our clinical experience as well as the social-cognitive and cognitive literatures suggest that changing attitudes and beliefs is a complex and somewhat slow process.

Our review of the relevant literatures seems to suggest that all humans, both psychopathological and normal, are quite fallible information-processors. A major task for cognitive psychopathologists is to delineate precisely how and why people think what they think and how pathological and nonpathological populations differ. We have suggested here that these populations may differ more with respect to their cognitive contents, products, and schemata than they do in the ways they process information. We further suggested that the major goal in cognitive therapy is to alter the beliefs and cognitive schemata that are presumably maintaining the psychopathology, this may be achieved by altering the client's information-processing to a more normative (although less "typical") inference-generating rather than heuristic-dominated processing mode. Thus, cognitive therapy teaches clients to hold beliefs more like "normals" by using processes rarely utilized by those "normals."

It further appears that the processes and procedures of cognitive therapy are quite compatible with the major principles of change emerging from the social-cognitive and cognitive psychological literatures. Consistent with Ross's (1977) formulation, these approaches seek to systematically generate disconfirming evidence, explicate and evaluate existing belief systems, and generate "insight" into information-processing. Given that the theory and procedures of cognitive therapy developed relatively independently of the basic research tradition summarized by Ross (at least over the last 2 decades), this convergence is particularly striking.

There are points of divergence, however. For one, most of the basic research has been conducted with nonpsychopathological populations. We clearly need to determine whether the processes and procedures leading to cognitive change differ as a function of psychopathological status. Second, in clinical settings, therapists typically have repeated access to their clients, whereas most of the cognitive change literature has been based on briefer exposures. Whether or not duration and repetition influences the probability of change remains to be determined, but we suspect that it does. Finally, cognitive therapists, at least those who remember that the approach is cognitive-behavioral in nature, can work with their clients to generate enactive behavioral tests of existing beliefs; that is, they can "short-circuit" self-fulfilling prophecies by encouraging clients to execute alternative behavior at variance with their expectations. Such enactive hypothesis testing is not easy to achieve, but it is one of the most powerful tools in the therapeutic armamentarium when it can be implemented successfully.

We close by observing that a more systematic integration of basic cognitive research and clinical change theory and procedure is not only desirable but highly possible. The paucity of explicit *change* research can be easily rectified, building on work such as that of Ross and colleagues, and adapting those paradigms to more clinically focused inquiries. We regard such efforts as being both quite exciting and highly feasible.

ACKNOWLEDGMENTS

Preparation of this chapter was supported, in part, by PHS Grant 1-R01-MH32209-03 to the senior author; the University of Minnesota; and the Medical Education and Research Foundation Grant #6287, Department of Psychiatry, St. Paul-Ramsey Medical Center, St. Paul, Minnesota. We would like to thank Kelly M. Bemis, Robert J. DeRubeis, Mark D. Evans, and Margaret Kriss for their comments on an earlier version of this manuscript. We would also like to thank Jane Gendron for secretarial assistance in the preparation of the manuscript.

REFERENCES

Abelson, R. P. (1968). In R. P. Abelson, E. Aronson, W. J. McGuire, T. M. Newcomb, M. J. Rosenberg, & P. H. Tannenbaum (Eds.), *Theories of cognitive consistency: A sourcebook.* Chicago: Rand McNally.

Abramson, L. Y., Garber, J., & Seligman, M. E. P. (1980). Learned helplessness in humans: An attributional analysis. In J. Garber & M. E. P. Seligman (Eds.), *Human helplessness: Theory and applications.* New York: Guilford.

Abramson, L. Y., Metalsky, G. I., & Alloy, L. B. (1987). *The hopelessness theory of depression: A metatheoretical analysis with implications for psychotherapy research.* Manuscript submitted for publication, University of Wisconsin, Madison.

Abramson, L. Y., Seligman, M. E. P., & Teasdale, J. (1978). Learned helplessness in humans: Critique and reformulation. *Journal of Abnormal Psychology, 87,* 49–74.

Alloy, L. B., & Abramson, L. Y. (1979). Judgment of contingency in depressed and nondepressed students: Sadder but wiser? *Journal of Experimental Psychology: General, 108,* 441–485.

Anderson, C. A., Lepper, M. R., & Ross, L. (1980). The perseverance of social theories: The role of explanation in the persistence of discredited information. *Journal of Personality and Social Psychology, 39,* 1037–1049.

Arkin, R. M., & Duval, S. (1975). Focus of attention and causal attributions of actors and observers. *Journal of Experimental Social Psychology, 11,* 427–438.

Atkinson, J. W. (1964). *An introduction to motivation.* Princeton, NJ: Van Nostrand.

Bandura, A. (1977). Self-efficacy: Toward a unifying theory of behavioral change. *Psychological Review, 84,* 191–215.

Bandura, A., & Adams, N. E. (1977). Analysis of self-efficacy theory of behavioral change. *Cognitive Therapy and Research, 1,* 287–310.

Barnhart, C. L. (Ed.). (1947). *The American College Dictionary.* New York: Random House.

Barthe, D., & Hammen, C. (1981). A naturalistic extension of the attributional model of depression. *Personality and Social Psychology Bulletin, 7,* 53–58.

Beach, S. R. H., Abramson, L. Y., & Levine, F. M. (1981). The attributional reformulation of learned helplessness and depression: Therapeutic implications. In J. Clarkin & H. Glazer (Eds.), *Depression: Behavioral and directive intervention strategies.* New York: Garland.

Beck, A. T. (1963). Thinking and depression: 1. Idiosyncratic content and cognitive distortions. *Archives of General Psychiatry, 9,* 324–333.

Beck, A. T. (1964). Thinking and depression: 2. Theory and therapy. *Archives of General Psychiatry, 10,* 561–571.

Beck, A. T. (1967). *Depression: Clinical, experimental, and theoretical aspects.* New York: Hoeber.

Beck, A. T. (1970). Cognitive therapy: Nature and relation to behavior therapy. *Behavior Therapy, 1,* 184–200.

Beck, A. T. (1976). *Cognitive therapy and the emotional disorders.* New York: International Universities Press.

Beck, A. T., & Greenberg, R. L. (1974). *Coping with depression* [booklet]. New York: Institute for Rational Living.

Beck, A. T., Rush, A. J., Shaw, B. F., & Emery, G. (1979). *Cognitive therapy of depression: A treatment manual.* New York: Guilford.

Bower, G. H. (1981). Mood and memory. *American Psychologist, 2,* 129–148.

Burns, D. (1979). *Feeling good: The new mood therapy.* New York: Simon & Schuster.

Cantor, N. A. (1980a). A cognitive-social analysis of personality. In N. A. Cantor & J. F. Kihlstrom (Eds.), *Personality, cognition, and social interaction.* Hillsdale, NJ: Erlbaum.

Cantor, N. A. (1980b). Perceptions of situations: Situation prototypes and person-situation prototypes. In D. Magnuson (Ed.), *The situation: An interactional perspective.* Hillsdale, NJ: Erlbaum.

Cantor, N. A., & Mischel, W. (1977). Traits as prototypes: Effects on recognition memory. *Journal of Personality and Social Psychology, 35*, 38–48.

Cantor, N. A., & Mischel, W. (1979). Prototypes in person perception. In L. Berkowitz (Ed.), *Advances in experimental social psychology* (Vol. 12). New York: Academic.

Clark, D. M., & Teasdale, J. D. (1982). Diurnal variation in clinical depression and accessibility of memories of positive and negative experiences. *Journal of Abnormal Psychology, 91*, 87–95.

Cook, M. L., & Peterson, C. (1986). Depressive irrationality. *Cognitive Therapy and Research, 10*, 293–298.

Coyne, J. C., & Gotlib, I. H. (1983). The role of cognition in depression: A critical appraisal. *Psychological Bulletin, 93*, 472–505.

Derry, P. A., & Kuiper, N. A. (1981). Schematic processing and self-reference in clinical depression. *Journal of Abnormal Psychology, 90*, 286–297.

DeRubeis, R. J., Hollon, S. D., Evans, M. D., & Bemis, K. M. (1982). Can psychotherapies for depression be discriminated? A systematic investigation of cognitive therapy and interpersonal therapy. *Journal of Consulting and Clinical Psychology, 50*, 744–756.

Duval, S., & Wicklund, R. A. (1972). *A theory of objective self-awareness.* New York: Academic.

Dykman, B. M., Abramson, L. Y., Alloy, B., & Hartlage, S. (1987). *Processing of ambiguous and unambiguous feedback by depressed and nondepressed college students: Schematic biases and their implications for depressive realism.* Manuscript submitted for publication, University of Wisconsin, Madison.

Eaves, G., & Rush, A. J. (1984). Cognitive patterns in symptomatic and remitted unipolar major depression. *Journal of Abnormal Psychology, 93*, 31–40.

Einhorn, H. J. (1982). Learning from experience and suboptimal rules in decision making. In D. Kahneman, P. Slovic, & A. Tversky (Eds.), *Judgment under uncertainty: Heuristics and biases.* Cambridge: Cambridge University Press.

Ellis, A. (1957). Outcome of employing three techniques of psychotherapy. *Journal of Clinical Psychology, 13*, 344–350.

Ellis, A. (1962). *Reason and emotion in psychotherapy.* New York: Lyle Stuart.

Emery, G., Hollon, S. D., & Bedrosian, R. C. (Eds.). (1981). *New directions in cognitive therapy: A casebook.* New York: Guilford.

Evans, M. D., & Hollon, S. D. (1988). Patterns of personal and causal influence: Implications for the cognitive therapy of depression. In L. B. Alloy (Ed.), *Cognitive processes in depression.* New York: Guilford.

Evans, M. D., Hollon, S. D., DeRubeis, R. J., Auerbach, A., Tuason, V. B., Wiemer, M. J. (1983, July). *Development of a system for rating psychotherapies for depression.* Paper presented at the Annual Meeting of the Society for Psychotherapy Research, Sheffield, England.

Feather, N. T. (1967). Valence of outcome and expectation of success in relation to task difficulty and perceived locus of control. *Journal of Personality and Social Psychology, 7*, 552–561.

Feather, N. T., & Simon, J. G. (1971). Causal attributions for success and failure in relation to expectations of success based upon selective or manipulant control. *Journal of Personality, 39*, 527–554.

Fischhoff, B. (1975). Hindsight-foresight: The effect of outcome knowledge on judgment under uncertainty. *Journal of Experimental Psychology: Human perception and performance, 1*, 288–299.

Fischhoff, B. (1976). Attribution theory and judgment under uncertainty. In J. H. Harvey, E. J. Ickes, & R. F. Kidd (Eds.), *New directions in attribution research* (Vol. 1). Hillsdale, NJ: Erlbaum.

Fischhoff, B. (1982). Debiasing. In D. Kahneman, P. Slovic, & A. Tversky (Eds.), *Judgment under uncertainty: Heuristics and biases.* Cambridge: Cambridge University Press.

Fischhoff, B., & Beyth, R. (1975). "I knew it would happen"—Remembered probabilities of once-future things. *Organizational Behavior and Human Performance, 13*, 1–16.

Fiske, S. T., & Linville, P. W. (1980). What does the schema concept buy us? *Personality and Social Psychology Bulletin, 6,* 543–557.

Flavell, J. H. (1979). Metacognition and cognitive monitoring: A new area of cognitive development inquiry. *American Psychologist, 34,* 906–911.

Gong-Guy, E., & Hammen, C. (1980). Causal perceptions of stressful life events in depressed and nondepressed clinic outpatients. *Journal of Abnormal Psychology, 89,* 662–669.

Hamilton, E. W., & Abramson, L. Y. (1983). Cognitive patterns and major depressive disorders: A longitudinal study in a hospital setting. *Journal of Abnormal Psychology, 92,* 173–184.

Hammen, C., & Cochran, S. (1981). Cognitive correlates of life stress and depression in college students. *Journal of Abnormal Psychology, 90,* 23–27.

Hammen, C., & deMayo, R. (1982). Cognitive correlates of teacher stress and depressive symptoms: Implications for attributional models of depression. *Journal of Abnormal Psychology, 91,* 96–101.

Hammen, C., Krantz, S., & Cochran, S. (1981). Relationships between depression and causal attributions about stressful life events. *Cognitive Therapy and Research, 5,* 351–358.

Hammen, C., Marks, T., deMayo, R., & Mayol, A. (1985). Self-schemas and risk for depression: A prospective study. *Journal of Personality and Social Psychology, 49,* 1147–1159.

Hammen, C., Marks, T., Mayol, A., & deMayo, R. (1985). Depressive self-schemas, life stress, and vulnerability to depression. *Journal of Abnormal Psychology, 94,* 308–319.

Hammen, C., & Mayol, A. (1982). Depression and cognitive characteristics of stressful life-event types. *Journal of Abnormal Psychology, 91,* 165–174.

Harvey, D. M. (1981). Depression and attributional style: Interpretations of important personal events. *Journal of Abnormal Psychology, 90,* 134–142.

Hastie, R. (1980). Schematic principles in human memory. In E. T. Higgins, P. Herman, & M. P. Zanna (Eds.), *Social cognition: The Ontario symposium.* Hillsdale, NJ: Erlbaum.

Heider, F. (1958). *The psychology of interpersonal relations.* New York: Wiley.

Hollon, S. D. (1981). Cognitive-behavioral treatment of drug-induced pansituational anxiety states. In G. Emery, S. D. Hollon, & R. C. Bedrosian (Eds.), *New directions in cognitive therapy: A casebook.* New York: Guilford.

Hollon, S. D., & Beck, A. T. (1979). Cognitive therapy of depression. In P. C. Kendall & S. D. Hollon (Eds.), *Cognitive-behavioral interventions: Theory, research, and procedures.* New York: Academic.

Hollon, S. D., & Beck, A. T. (1986). Cognitive and cognitive-behavioral therapies. In S. L. Garfield & A. E. Bergin (Eds.), *Handbook of psychotherapy and behavior change* (3rd ed.). New York: Wiley.

Hollon, S. D., & Bemis, K. M. (1981). Self-report and the assessment of cognitive functions. In M. Hersen & A. S. Bellack (Eds.), *Behavioral assessment: A practical handbook* (2nd ed.). Elmsford, NY: Pergamon.

Hollon, S. D., DeRubeis, R. J., & Evans, M. D. (1987). Causal mediation of change in treatment for depression: Discriminating between nonspecificity and noncausality. *Psychological Bulletin, 102,* 139–149.

Hollon, S. D., & Evans, M. D. (1983). Clinical issues in group cognitive therapy for depression. In A. Freeman (Ed.), *Group therapy: A clinical perspective.* New York: Plenum.

Hollon, S. D., Evans, M. D., & DeRubeis, R. J. (1988). Preventing relapse following treatment for depression: The Cognitive Pharmacotherapy Project. In T. Field, P. McCabe, & N. Schneiderman (Eds.), *Stress and coping across development.* Hillsdale, NJ: Erlbaum.

Hollon, S. D., Evans, M. M., Elkin, I., & Lowery, A. (1984, May). *System for rating therapies for depression.* Paper presented at the Annual Meeting of the American Psychiatric Association, Los Angeles, CA.

Hollon, S. D., & Garber, J. (1980). A cognitive-expectancy theory of therapy for helplessness and depression. In J. Garber & M. E. Seligman (Eds.), *Human helplessness: Theory and applications.* New York: Guilford.

Hollon, S. D., & Kendall, P. C. (1979). *Cognitive-behavioral interventions: Theory, research, and procedures.* New York: Academic.

Hollon, S. D., & Kendall, P. C. (1980). Cognitive self-statements in depression: Development of an automatic thoughts questionnaire. *Cognitive Therapy and Research, 4,* 383–396.

Hollon, S. D., & Kendall, P. C. (1981). *In vivo* assessment techniques for cognitive-behavioral processes. In P. C. Kendall & S. D. Hollon (Eds.), *Assessment strategies for cognitive-behavioral interventions.* New York: Academic.

Hollon, S. D., Kendall, P. C., & Lumry, A. (1986). Specificity of depressotypic cognitions in clinical depression. *Journal of Abnormal Psychology, 95,* 52–59.

Hollon, S. D., & Kriss, M. R. (1984). Cognitive factors in clinical research and practice. *Clinical Psychology Review, 3,* 35–76.

Hollon, S. D., & Najavits, L. (1988). Review of empirical studies on cognitive therapy. In A. J. Frances & R. E. Hales (Eds.), *American Psychiatric Press Review of Psychiatry* (Vol. 7). Washington, DC: American Psychiatric Press.

Hollon, S. D., & Shaw, B. F. (1979). Group cognitive therapy for depressed patients. In A. T. Beck, A. J. Rush, & B. F. Shaw, & G. Emery. *Cognitive therapy of depression.* New York: Guilford.

Holmes, D. S. (1968). Dimensions of projection. *Psychological Bulletin, 69,* 248–268.

Ingram, R. E., & Hollon, S. D. (1986). Cognitive therapy for depression from an information processing perspective. In R. E. Ingram (Ed.), *Information processing approaches to clinical psychology.* New York: Academic.

Irwin, F. W. (1971). *Intentional behavior and motivation: A cognitive theory.* Philadelphia: Lippincott.

Jenkins, H. M., & Ward, W. C. (1965). Judgment of contingency between response and outcomes. *Psychological Monographs, 79.*

Jennings, D. L., Lepper, M. N., & Ross, L. (1980). *Persistence of impressions of personal persuasiveness: Perseverance of self-assessments outside the debriefing paradigm.* Unpublished manuscript, Stanford University, Palo Alto, CA.

Jones, E. E., & Davis, K. E. (1965). From acts to dispositions: The attributional process in person perception. In L. Berkowitz (Ed.), *Advances in experimental social psychology* (Vol. 2). New York: Academic.

Jones, E. E., & Nisbett, R. E. (1972). The actor and the observer: Divergent perceptions of the causes of behavior. In E. E. Jones, D. E. Kanouse, H. H. Kelley, R. E. Nisbett, S. Valins, & B. Weiner (Eds.), *Attribution: Perceiving the causes of behavior.* Morristown, NJ: General Learning Press.

Kahneman, D., Slovic, P., & Tversky, A. (Eds.). (1982). *Judgment under certainty: Heuristics and biases.* Cambridge: Cambridge University Press.

Kahneman, D., & Tversky, A. (1972). Subjective probability: A judgment representativeness. *Cognitive Psychology, 3,* 430–454. (Reprinted in D. Kahneman, P. Slovic, & A. Tversky [Eds.], *Judgment under uncertainty: Heuristics and biases.* Cambridge: Cambridge University Press, 1982)

Kahneman, D., & Tversky, A. (1973). On the psychology of prediction. *Psychological Review, 80,* 237–251. (Reprinted in D. Kahneman, P. Slovic, & A. Tversky [Eds.], *Judgment under uncertainty: Heuristics and biases.* Cambridge: Cambridge University Press, 1982)

Kahneman, D., & Tversky, A. (1982). Intuitive prediction: Biases and corrective procedures. In D. Kahneman, P. Slovic, & A. Tversky (Eds.), *Judgment under uncertainty: Heuristics and biases.* Cambridge: Cambridge University Press.

Keele, S. W. (1973). *Attention and human performance.* Pacific Palisades, CA: Goodyear.

Kelley, H. H. (1967). Attribution theory in social psychology. In D. Levine (Ed.), *Nebraska symposium in motivation* (Vol. 15). Lincoln, NE: University of Nebraska Press.

Kelley, H. H. (1972a). Attribution in social interaction. In E. E. Jones, D. E. Jones, D. E. Kanouse, H. H. Kelley, R. E. Nisbett, S. Valins, & B. Weiner (Eds.), *Attribution: Perceiving the causes of behavior.* Morristown, NJ: General Learning Press.

Kelley, H. H. (1972b). Causal schemata and the attribution process. In E. E. Jones, D. E. Kanouse, H. H. Kelley, R. E. Nisbett, S. Valins, & B. Weiner (Eds.), *Attribution: Perceiving the causes of behavior*. Morristown, NJ: General Learning Press.

Kelley, H. H. (1973). The processes of causal attribution. *American Psychologist, 28*, 107–128.

Kendall, P. C., & Finch, A. J., Jr. (1979). Developing nonimpulsive behavior in children: Cognitive-behavioral strategies for self-control. In P. C. Kendall & S. D. Hollon (Eds.), *Cognitive-behavioral interventions: Theory, research, and procedures*. New York: Academic.

Kendall, P. C., & Hollon, S. D. (1979). Cognitive-behavioral interventions: Overview and current status. In P. C. Kendall & S. D. Hollon (Eds.), *Cognitive-behavioral interventions: Theory, research, and procedures*. New York: Academic.

Kihlstrom, J. F., & Nasby, W. (1981). Cognitive tasks in clinical assessment: An exercise in applied psychology. In P. C. Kendall & S. D. Hollon (Eds.), *Assessment strategies in cognitive-behavioral interventions*. New York: Academic.

Klinger, E. (1975). Consequences of commitment to and disengagement from incentives. *Psychological Review, 85*, 1–25.

Kopel, S., & Arkowitz, H. (1975). The role of attribution and self-perception in behavior change: Implications for behavior change. *Genetic Psychology Monographs, 92*, 175–212.

Kuiper, N. A. (1978). Depression and causal attributions for success and failure. *Journal of Personality and Social Psychology, 36*, 236–246.

Kuiper, N. A., & Derry, P. A. (1980). The self as a cognitive prototype: An application to person perception and depression. In N. Cantor & J. F. Kihlstrom (Eds.), *Personality, cognition, and social interaction*. Hillsdale, NJ: Erlbaum.

Landau, R. J. (1980). The role of semantic schemata in phobic word interpretation. *Cognitive Therapy and Research, 4*, 427–434.

Landau, R. J., & Goldfried, M. R. (1981). The assessment of schemata: A unifying framework for cognitive, behavioral, and traditional assessment. In P. C. Kendall & S. D. Hollon (Eds.), *Assessment strategies for cognitive-behavioral interventions*. New York: Academic.

Lau, R., Lepper, M. R., & Ross, L. (1976). *Persistence of inaccurate and discredited personal impressions: A field demonstration of attributional perseverance*. Unpublished manuscript, Stanford University. (Cited in Ross, 1977)

Lazarus, R. S. (1966). *Psychological stress and the coping process*. New York: McGraw-Hill.

Lepper, M. R., Ross, L., & Lau, R. (1979). *Persistance of inaccurate and discredited personal impressions: A field demonstration of attributional perserverance*. Unpublished manuscript, Stanford University.

Lewinsohn, P. M. (1974). A behavioral approach to depression. In R. J. Friedman & M. M. Katz (Eds.), *The psychology of depression: Contemporary theory and research*. Washington, DC: V. H. Winston.

Lewinsohn, P. M. (1975). The behavioral study and treatment of depression. In M. Hersen, R. Eisler, & P. Miller (Eds.), *Progress in behavior modification*. New York: Academic.

Lewinsohn, P. M., Mischel, W., Chaplin, W., & Barton, R. (1980). Social competence and depression: The role of illusory self-perceptions. *Journal of Abnormal Psychology, 89*, 203–212.

Lord, C. G., Lepper, M. R., & Ross, L. (1979). Biased assimilation and attitude polarization: The effects of prior theories on subsequently considered evidence. *Journal of Personality and Social Psychology, 37*, 2098–2109.

Mahoney, M. J. (1977). Reflection on the cognitive learning trend in psychotherapy. *American Psychologist, 32*, 5–13.

Mahoney, M. J., & Arnkoff, D. (1978). Cognitive and self-control therapies. In S. L. Garfield & A. E. Bergin (Eds.), *Handbook of psychotherapy and behavior change: An empirical analysis* (2nd ed.). New York: Wiley.

Markus, H. (1977). Self-schemas and processing information about the self. *Journal of Personality and Social Psychology, 35*, 63–78.

Meichenbaum, D. (1977). *Cognitive-behavior modification: An integrative approach.* New York: Plenum.

Metalsky, G. I., & Abramson, L. Y. (1981). Attributional styles: Toward a framework for conceptualization and assessment. In P. C. Kendall & S. D. Hollon (Eds.), *Assessment strategies for cognitive-behavioral interventions.* New York: Academic.

Miller, I. W., Klee, S. H., & Norman, W. H. (1982). Depressed and nondepressed inpatients' cognitions of hypothetical events, experimental tasks, and stressful life events. *Journal of Abnormal Psychology, 91,* 78-81.

Neely, J. H. (1977). Semantic printing and retrieval from lexical memory: Roles of inhibitionless spreading activation and limited-capacity attention. *Journal of Experimental Psychology: General, 84,* 226-254.

Neisser, U. (1976). *Cognition and reality: Principles and implications of cognitive psychology.* San Francisco: Freeman.

Nisbett, R. E., & Borgida, E. (1975). Attribution and the psychology of prediction. *Journal of Personality and Social Psychology, 32,* 932-943.

Nisbett, R. E., Borgida, E., Crandall, R., & Reed, H. (1976). Popular induction: Information is not necessarily informative. In J. S. Carroll & J. W. Payne (Eds.), *Cognition and social behavior.* Hillsdale, NJ: Erlbaum, (Reprinted in D. Kahneman, P. Slovic, & A. Tversky [Eds.] *Judgment under uncertainty: Heuristics and biases.* Cambridge: Cambridge University Press, 1982)

Nisbett, R. E., Krantz, D. H., Jepson, C., & Fong, G. J. (1982). Improving inductive inference. In D. Kahneman, P. Slovic, & A. Tversky (Eds.), *Judgement under uncertainty: Heuristics and bias.* Cambridge: Cambridge University Press.

Nisbett, R. E., & Ross, L. (1980). *Human inference: Strategies and shortcomings of social judgment.* Englewood Cliffs, NJ: Prentice-Hall.

Novaco, R. W. (1979). The cognitive regulation of anger and stress. In P. C. Kendall & S. D. Hollon (Eds.). *Cognitive-behavioral interventions: Theory, research and procedures.* New York, Academic.

Persons, J. B., & Rao, P. A. (1985). Longitudinal studies of cognitions, life events, and depression in psychiatric inpatients. *Journal of Abnormal Psychology, 94,* 51-63.

Peterson, C., & Seligman, M. E. P. (1984). Explanatory style and depression: Theory and evidence. *Psychological Review, 91,* 188-204.

Piaget, J. (1954). *The construction of reality in the child.* New York: Basic Books.

Posner, M. L., & Snyder, C. R. (1975). Attention and cognitive control. In R. L. Solso (Ed.), *Information processing and cognition: The Loyola Symposium.* Hillsdale, NJ: Erlbaum.

Raps, C. S., Reinhard, K. E., Peterson, C., Abramson, L. Y., & Seligman, M. E. P. (1982). Attributional style among depressed patients. *Journal of Abnormal Psychology, 91,* 102-108.

Regan, D. T., & Totten, J. (1975). Empathy and attribution: Turning observers into actors. *Journal of Personality and Social Psychology, 32,* 850-856.

Rizley, R. (1978). Depression and distortion in the attribution of causality. *Journal of Abnormal Psychology, 87,* 32-48.

Ross, L. (1977). The intuitive psychologist and his shortcomings: Distortions in the attribution process. In L. Berkowitz (Ed.), *Advance in experimental social psychology* (Vol. 10). New York: Academic.

Ross, L. (1978). Some afterthoughts on the intuitive psychologist. In L. Berkowitz (Ed.), *Cognitive theories in social psychology.* New York: Academic.

Ross, L., Amabile, T. M., & Steinmetz, J. L. (1977). Social roles, social control, and biases in social perceptive processes. *Journal of Personality and Social Psychology, 35,* 485-494.

Ross, L., & Lepper, M. R. (1980). The perseverance of beliefs: Empirical and normative considerations. In R. A. Schweder (Ed.), *New directions for methodology of behavioral science: Fallible judgments in behavioral research.* San Francisco: Jossey-Bass.

Ross, L., Lepper, M., & Hubbard, M. (1975). Perseverance in self-perception and social perception: Biased attributional processes in the debriefing paradigm. *Journal of Personality and Social Psychology, 32*, 880–892.

Ross, L., Lepper, M. R., Strack, F., & Steinmetz, J. L. (1977). Social explanation and social expectation: The effects of real and hypothetical explanations upon subjective likelihood. *Journal of Personality and Social Psychology, 35*, 817–829.

Ross, M., & Sicoly, F. (1979). Egocentric biases in availability and attribution. *Journal of Personality and Social Psychology, 37*, 322–336. (Reprinted in D. Kahneman, P. Slovic, & A. Tversky [Eds.], *Judgment under uncertainty: Heuristics and biases.* Cambridge: Cambridge University Press, 1982)

Roth, S., & Kubal, L. (1975). Effects of noncontingent reinforcement on tasks of differing importance: Facilitation and learned helplessness. *Journal of Personality and Social Psychology, 32*, 680–691.

Ruehlman, L. S., West, S. G., & Pasahow, R. J. (1985). Depression and evaluative schemata. *Journal of Personality, 53*, 46–92.

Schacter, S. (1959). *The psychology of affiliation.* Stanford University Press.

Schacter, S. (1964). The interaction of cognitive and physiological determinants of emotional state. In L. Berkowitz (Ed.), *Advances in experimental social psychology* (Vol. 1). New York: Academic.

Schacter, S., & Singer, J. E. (1962). Cognitive, social, and physiological determinants of emotional state. *Psychological Review, 69*, 379–399.

Schacter, S., & Wheeler, L. (1962). Epinephrine, chlorpromazine, and amusement. *Journal of Abnormal and Social Psychology, 65*, 121–128.

Schneider, W., & Shiffrin, R. M. (1977). Controlled and automatic human information processing: I. Detection, search, and attention. *Psychological Review, 84*, 1–66.

Seligman, M. E. P. (1975). *Helplessness.* San Francisco: Freeman.

Seligman, M. E. P. (1981). Behavioral and cognitive therapy for depression from a learned helplessness point of view. In L. P. Rehm (Ed.), *Behavior therapy for depression: Present status and future direction.* New York: Academic.

Seligman, M. E. P., Abramson, L. Y., Semmel, A., & von Baeyer, C. (1979). Depressive attributional style. *Journal of Abnormal Psychology, 88*, 242–247.

Shiffrin, R. M., & Schneider, W. (1977). Controlled and automatic human information processing: II. Perceptual learning, automatic attending, and a general theory. *Psychological Review, 84*, 127–190.

Smedslund, J. (1963). The concept of correlation in adults. *Scandinavian Journal of Psychology, 4*, 165–173.

Storms, M. D. (1973). Videotape and the attribution process: Reversing actors' and observers' points of view. *Journal of Personality and Social Psychology, 27*, 165–175.

Strong, S. R. (1970). Causal attribution in counseling and psychology. *Journal of Counseling Psychology, 17*, 388–389.

Strong, S. R. (1978). Social psychological approach to psychotherapy research. In S. L. Garfield & A. E. Bergen (Eds.), *Handbook of psychotherapy and behavior change: An empirical analysis* (2nd ed.). New York: Wiley.

Sweeney, P. D., Anderson, K., & Bailey, S. (1986). Attributional style in depression: A meta-analytic review. *Journal of Personality and Social Psychology, 50*, 974–991.

Taylor, S. E., & Fiske, S. T. (1975). Point of view and perceptions of causality. *Journal of Personality and Social Psychology, 32*, 439–445.

Taylor, S. E., & Fiske, S. T. (1978). Salience, attention, and attribution: Top of the head phenomena. In L. Berkowitz (Ed.), *Advance in experimental social psychology* (Vol. 2). New York: Academic.

Thorndyke, P. W., & Hayes-Roth, B. (1979). The use of schemata in the acquisition and transfer of knowledge. *Cognitive Psychology, 11*, 82–106.

Turk, D. C., & Speers, M. A. (1983) Cognitive schemata and cognitive processes in cognitive behavior modification: Going beyond the information given. In P. C. Kendall (Ed.), *Advances in cognitive-behavioral research and therapy* (Vol. 2). New York: Academic.

Tversky, A., & Kahneman, D. (1971). The belief in the law of small numbers. *Psychological Bulletin, 76,* 105–110. (Reprinted in D. Kahneman, P. Slovic, & A. Tversky [Eds.], *Judgment under uncertainty: Heuristics and biases.* Cambridge: Cambridge University Press, 1982)

Tversky, A., & Kahneman, D. (1973). Availability: A heuristic for judging frequency and probability. *Cognitive Psychology, 5,* 207–232.

Tversky, A., & Kahneman, D. (1974). Judgment under uncertainty: Heuristics and biases. *Science, 185,* 1124–1131. (Reprinted in D. Kahneman, P. Slovic, & A. Tversky [Eds.], *Judgment under uncertainty: Heuristics and biases.* Cambridge: Cambridge University Press, 1982)

Tversky, A., & Kahneman, D. (1980). Causal schemata in judgments under uncertainty. In M. Fishbein (Ed.), *Progress in social psychology,* Hillsdale, NJ: Erlbaum. (Reprinted in D. Kahneman, P. Slovic, & A. Tversky, [Eds.], *Judgment under uncertainty: Heuristics and biases.* Cambridge: Cambridge University Press, 1982)

Vygotsky, L. S. (1962). *Thought and language.* E. Hanfmann & G. Vakan (Eds. and Trans.). Cambridge, MA: M.I.T. Press.

Ward, W. C., & Jenkins, H. M. (1965). The display of information and the judgment of contingency. *Canadian Journal of Psychology, 19,* 231–241.

Wason, P. C. (1960). On the failure to eliminate hypotheses in a conceptual task. *Quarterly Journal of Experimental Psychology, 12,* 129–140.

Wason, P. C., & Johnson-Laird, P. N. (1972). *Psychology of reasoning: Structure and content.* London: Batsford.

Weiner, B. (1972). *Theories of motivation: From mechanism to cognition.* Chicago: Rand McNally.

Weiner, B. (Ed.) (1974). *Achievement motivation and attribution theory.* Morristown, NJ: General Learning Press.

Weiner, B. (1979). A theory of motivation for some classroom experiences. *Journal of Educational Psychology, 71,* 3–25.

Weiner, B., Frieze, I., Kukla, A., Reed, L., Rest, S., & Rosenbaum, R. M. (1971). *Perceiving the causes of success and failure.* Morristown, NJ: General Learning Press.

Weiner, B., & Litman-Adizes, T. (1980). An attributional, expectancy-value analysis of learned helplessness and depression. In J. Garber & M. E. P. Seligman (Eds.), *Human helplessness: Theory and applications.* New York: Academic.

Zajonc, R. (1980). Feeling and thinking: Preferences need no inferences. *American Psychologist, 35,* 151–175.

9

Curing by Knowing: The Epistemic Approach to Cognitive Therapy

ARIE W. KRUGLANSKI

YORAM JAFFE

The purpose of the present chapter is to present a new approach to the theory and practice of cognitive therapy. The approach is based on a conception of lay epistemology developed recently by Kruglanski and his colleagues (Kruglanski, 1980; Kruglanski & Ajzen, 1983; Kruglanski & Freund, 1983; Kruglanski and Klar, 1987). The theory of lay epistemology addresses several fundamental issues in the area of social cognition. It considers the role of logic and motivation in the formation and modification of beliefs, the determinants of judgmental biases and errors, conditions affecting the formation of cognitive sets and belief-perseverance phenomena, and related topics. The theory of lay epistemology was originally proposed as an integrative alternative to the variety of attributional models constructed by social psychologists (Heider, 1958; Jones & Davis, 1965; Kelley, 1967, 1971, 1978; Kruglanski, 1975; Weiner *et al.*, 1971). Further extensions of the theory (Kruglanski & Klar, 1987) demonstrate how the lay epistemic framework subsumes as its special cases the various cognitive-consistency theories: for example, balance (Heider, 1958) or dissonance (Festinger, 1957), and notions of social comparison (Kruglanski & Mayseless, 1987) and of judgmental heuristics (Kruglanski, Friedland & Farkash, 1984).

Thus, the theory of lay epistemology constitutes a broad conceptual framework addressing the *general* process of cognitive change. By contrast, cognitive therapy deals with a *specific* type of cognitive change: the substitution of functional or adaptive cognitive elements for dysfunctional or maladaptive ones. In those terms, cognitive therapy may be conceived of as a case in which general epistemic principles are applied to specific cognitive contents characterized as dysfunctional for the individual.

It is worth noting at the outset that the lay epistemic approach to cognitive therapy is at odds with several assumptions prevalent in the field today.

Departing from a post-Popperian philosophical tradition, the following widely popular cognitive therapeutic conceptions are challenged: (1) that "veridical," "undistorted," or "realistic" conceptions are functional for the individual and contribute to his or her sense of well-being, (2) that "normals" are generally more accurate in their judgments than neurotics, and (3) that veridical judgments are more likely to be rendered if one adopts the appropriate method of inference based on logical and empirical principles. In contrast, the lay epistemic approach holds that the functionality or adaptability of a belief derives from its particular content rather than from its truth value.

This chapter has the following major objectives: (1) to introduce the lay epistemic theory, highlighting aspects particularly relevant to cognitive therapy; (2) to provide a general conception of the functional–dysfunctional dimension of belief contents; (3) to show how the principles of lay epistemology can be fruitfully applied to the modification of dysfunctional cognitions and their replacement by functional ones; and (4) to analyze the similarities and differences of the lay epistemic approach and some major current schools of cognitive therapy.

A THEORY OF LAY EPISTEMOLOGY: THE HOW OF COGNITIVE THERAPY

The theory of lay epistemology rests on several notions usually identified with a modern philosophical position called nonjustificationism (Bartley, 1962). The nonjustificationist approach was initiated by Karl Popper (e.g., 1959, 1966, 1973) and has since become a major alternative to the problematic inductivist interpretations of scientific knowledge still popular among many scientific practitioners. A detailed summary of the nonjustificationist viewpoint is well beyond the scope of the present essay (for an excellent summary, see Weimer, 1976). Instead, the concepts underlying this approach will be introduced whenever relevant to an adequate communication of the present epistemic theory. The following exposition will consider the following issues: (1) the properties of knowledge, (2) the sequence of knowledge-seeking (epistemic) behavior, and (3) the braking mechanisms of such behavior.

THE PROPERTIES OF KNOWLEDGE: STRUCTURES AND THEIR VALIDITY

Definite knowledge is made of propositions assumed to be valid. A (subjectively) valid proposition is a cognitive structure. It constrains the individual's reality in a given way; it says that something rather than something else is the case; it dispels ambiguity. Propositions may vary in their contents and the confidence with which they are held (the degree of subjective validity). For example, a content of a proposition might be that "Mary had a little lamb." A person might believe this strongly, know it for a fact, or regard it as a hypothesis—that is, varying degrees of confidence in the proposition's validity are possible.

The contents of a proposition are composed of concepts. Each concept is a universal term (Popper, 1959, pp. 94–95), divisible into an endless number of particular instances. The distinction between universal and particular terms is relative rather than absolute. Each particular term is, in turn, infinitely divisible into its own special instances, and so on. Even such a seemingly specific term as "Mary Jones" is potentially divisible into Mary Jones at an endless number of temporal or spatial points: Mary Jones observed by an endless number of persons, or from an endless number of visual angles, and so forth. Each of these is a special case of the Mary Jones concept.

That propositions are made of universals and that each of these is infinitely divisible has this significant implication: For each proposition there exist an infinity of relevant items of evidence, each bearing on a single particular instance of the proposition at issue. For example, if what Mary had indeed was a little lamb, it would follow that the animal in question had all the properties of a lamb, was recognized as such by all expert zoologists, and was never known to exhibit un-lamb-like qualities such as talking, flying, egg laying, barking, and so on.

That there exist endless items of evidence pertinent to each and any proposition suggests the impossibility of ever surveying a complete set of such evidence. This means that *in principle* our inferences are basd on incomplete arrays of evidence with no *objective basis* for certainty about the truth of any of our propositions. The thesis that all our knowledge, lay and scientific alike, is uncertain and conjectual is a cornerstone of the nonjustificationist philosophy of knowledge elaborated by Popper (e.g., 1959, 1966, 1973), Kuhn (1962, 1970), and their followers. This thesis implies that all our knowledge is potentially erroneous, for any of it could be contradicted by the very first item of relevant evidence that we have not previously examined.

Another significant characteristic of knowledge is that it is inevitably *biased*. In contrast to *error*, the case in which a proposition is contradicted by a firmly believed-in item of relevant evidence (see Kruglanski, in press–b), *bias* is assumed to represent a subjectively based preference for a given conclusion over possible alternative conclusions. However, any amount of evidence is compatible with a vast (in fact, an infinite) number of alternative interpretations or conclusions. Suppose that everyone who saw X concluded that she was Mary; this would be definitely compatible with the hypothesis that X is Mary, but it would also be compatible with the hypothesis that X is Mary's similar looking twin sister, a skillful imposter, and so on. The decision to believe the first hypothesis and not the second or the third is thus a subjectively based preference or bias that cannot claim objectively valid reasons in its support.

To sum up, all of our knowledge constitutes a bias and may potentially contain an error. The foregoing characteristics of knowledge, emphasized by leading nonjustificationist philosophers of science, have some intriguing implications for major, current systems of cognitive therapy in which the notions of bias and error have been presumed to uniquely characterize the thinking of disturbed individuals. We will discuss this point more fully later in this chapter.

THE EPISTEMIC SEQUENCE

Hypothesis Validation

According to the theory of lay epistemology (see, e.g., Kruglanski & Ajzen, 1983; Kruglanski, in press-a) the process whereby all knowledge is formed or modified involves a two-phase sequence in which hypotheses are generated and validated. The hypothesis validation stage is assumed to be accomplished deductively. The individual departs from a premise that links (in an if-then fashion) a given category of evidence with a given hypothesis, and proceeds to infer the hypothesis upon affirming the evidence. For instance, a knower may believe that "if the alarm rings the time is 7:00 AM." This person may then "know" on hearing the alarm go off that it is 7 o'clock. More generally, the individual would tend to believe a hypothesis if it were consistent with (or deducible from) the relevant evidence. To the contrary, if the evidence was inconsistent with the hypothesis the person's confidence in the hypothesis may wane. In case of a contradiction between two cognitions the less strongly believed of the two would tend to be rejected, thus eliminating the inconsistency. As implied earlier, a cognition labeled as mere "hypothesis" would usually give way if contradicted by a cognition labeled as "fact," because the latter term implies the individual's stronger degree of belief than the former (for discussion, see Kruglanski & Klar, 1987).

The process of hypothesis generation and validation may govern emotional behavior as well as intellectual belief. Pertinent here are findings revealing the conditions under which false feedback about one's level of autonomic arousal would affect the intensity of emotional behavior. Research (reviewed in Kopel & Arkowitz, 1975) suggests that when the initial intensity of arousal evoked by the presence of a phobic object is moderate, false feedback indicating a low level of arousal would lower the intensity of emotional behavior. But "when the individual's actual and perceived level of arousal is high and is salient to the individual then false feedback manipulations which attempt to reduce fearfulness may not be effective" (Kopel & Arkowitz, 1975, p. 183). This observation may be restated in lay epistemologic terms. When the individual's "actual and perceived" level of arousal is high, the individual is highly confident of being aroused. Similarly, the case in which the individual's "actual" arousal is moderate represents the individual's lower confidence regarding his or her arousal. In line with this analysis, the confidently held arousal hypothesis characterizing the high arousal subjects is less likely to be offset by the inconsistent feedback regarding low arousal than is the less confidently held arousal hypothesis characterizing the moderate arousal subjects.

At this juncture it will be helpful to relate our discussion of hypothesis testing to the issue of falsifying versus corroborating a hypothesis. Although Popper's early position was that hypotheses may be falsified but not verified, modern nonjustificationism (Weimer, 1979) maintains that hypotheses may not be securely falsified either. Consider that the falsifying bit of evidence is itself a hypothesis that might be falsified in turn. A hypothesis falsified via a "false" bit of evidence could therefore be restored to the status of a subjectively true proposition. Thus, not only may we not be (objectively) sure which of our hypotheses are true, but we may not be sure which are objectively false, either. For example, suppose one attempts to falsify a depressive's negative view of himself or herself by exposing this person to a striking success experience. The depressive may question the authenticity of the experience, suspecting it to have been deliberately contrived by the therapist.

Subjective Relevance of Evidence and the Notion of Epistemic Authority

The relevance of evidence to hypotheses is assumed to be adjudged subjectively, hence, to be "in the eye of the beholder," as it were. This means that persons may vary in what they consider "good" or compelling evidence for a given proposition: What is convincing to one individual may fail to be so for another individual. For a qualified physician, a specific set of symptoms may be clearly indicative of a particular illness, whereas for the lay person the very same syndrome may have little meaning. Often the source from which a given piece of information originates is treated as relevant evidence for its validity. For example, a person might believe in a given item of information because it was printed in a reputable newspaper. A source whose pronouncements are assumed to be valid is said to have high epistemic authority for the individual. It is possible to distinguish between positive and negative epistemic authorities, that is, sources whose attributes are respectively considered supportive or refuting evidence for the validity of the information. What may constitute an epistemic authority (positive or negative) for a given person would vary across individuals as well as within individuals across circumstances. For example, some people may have high regard for the epistemic authority of a religious priest or the tribal shaman (Frank, 1973), others may place particular trust in the judgments of a skilled professional, and still others may find their "safety in numbers" and trust in particular opinions based on a wide consensus. Similarly, some people may have low regard for the epistemic authority of children, women, or members of various cultural or ethnic groups. Finally, a person may trust or distruct his or her own epistemic authority, that is, have a high or low confidence in his or her own judgments; this might vary widely across topics and circumstances. A business executive might be highly confident in his or her opinions on economic matters but not as confident in personal judgments on aesthetics or public relations. Social and counseling psychologists have generated a vast research literature on variables affecting the credibility, or epistemic authority, of a communication source (e.g., Hovland, Janis, & Kelley, 1953; McGuire, 1969; Strong, 1978).

Hypothesis Generation: Notions of Capability and Motivation

The deductive process of hypothesis validation has no unique or natural point of termination. In principle, it should be always possible to generate further alternative hypotheses compatible with the same body of evidence (cf. Campbell, 1969; Weimer, 1979). As at most times we possess definite knowledge on various topics, the epistemic sequence must come to a halt somehow. Hence, we need to identify the mechanisms that affect the cessation (or conversely, the initiation or continuation) of the epistemic sequence. The lay epistemic model recognizes two broad categories of such mechanisms, respectively related to notions of cognitive *capability* and epistemic *motivation.*

Cognitive Capability

Two broad capability notions, long-term and momentary, are sometimes discerned in the social cognitive literature. Long-term capability to generate hypotheses on a given topic has to do with the concept of availability (cf. Higgins, King, & Mavin, 1982). This refers to the individual's general repertory of social knowledge stored in long-term memory. Short-term capacity to generate hypotheses on a topic has to do with the concept of accessibility (cf. Bruner, 1957; Higgins & King, 1981; Higgins, Rholes, & Jones, 1977).

Research by Higgins, Bargh, and Lombardi (1985) has demonstrated that the accessibility of an idea is, among other factors, a function of the recency and frequency with which it has been activated. This means that following prolonged lack of activation an idea would become less accessible. Furthermore, after prolonged inactivity an idea may become partially dissociated from its evidential base (Cook, Gruder, Hennigan, & Flay, 1979; Greenwald, Baumgardner, & Leipper, 1979; Hovland, Lumsdaine, & Sheffield, 1954). As discussed in a later section, those properties of the cognitive system may be used advantageously in the course of therapy.

Epistemic Motivations

The second category of braking (starting) mechanisms for the epistemic sequence relates to the person's epistemic needs. Three such needs are presently discerned: (1) the need for cognitive closure, (2) the need for preferential closure, and (3) the need for cognitive openness (for fuller exposition, see Kruglanski, in press–b).

The *need for cognitive closure* represents the desire for a definite answer on some issue, *any* answer as opposed to confusion and ambiguity. Such need thus represents a quest for assured knowledge that affords predictability and a base for action. A heightened need for closure is likely to trigger intense epistemic activity where no initial knowledge existed and to bring such activity to a halt once some plausible hypothesis was advanced and supported by extant evidence. In this sense, the need for closure is said to promote epistemic "freezing" (see Freund, Kruglanski, & Schpitzajzen, 1985; Kruglanski & Ajzen, 1983; Kruglanski & Freund, 1983).

The need for closure could arise out of two general categories of conditions: (1) perceived benefits of having closure, such as comforting predictability or a guide for action, and/or (2) perceived costs of *not* having closure, such as the time and effort required for further information-processing. Relevant to the latter factors, several recent studies have manipulated the need for closure via *time pressure* assumed to render judgmental indecision rather costly (Bechtold, Naccarato, & Zanna, 1986; Freund, Kruglanski, & Schpitzajzen, 1985; Jamieson & Zanna, in press; Kruglanski & Freund, 1983; Kruglanski & Mayseless, 1987; Sanbomatsu & Fazio, 1987).

The "need for closure" construct denotes a desire for a definite answer to a question without prejudice as to the answer's special properties. Often, however, individuals are partial toward specific answers to their questions. Those predilections represent *needs for preferential closure*. A need for preferential closure could relate to any of the answer's properties, for instance, to its particular contents that may be flattering or otherwise desirable, to its novelty, apparent creativity, or complexity, in short, to any contentual, structural, or formal feature of a closure that might appear attractive in given circumstances.

If the need for closure may generally promote epistemic "freezing," that for a preferential closure might promote either "freezing" or "unfreezing," depending on whether current knowledge was congruent with one's particular desires. For instance, someone who entertains the possibility that (he or she contracted a dangerous illness or is about to lose an attractive job might seek out new evidence possibly contrary to such undesirable conclusions, and/or be ready to accept alternative, less negative interpretations of extant evidence. In contrast, a person who surmises that he or she is about to receive a desirable job offer, or that he or she will do well on an exam, might often be refractory to contrary evidence and be quick to dismiss alternative, less sanguine interpretations of available information.

Thus, the term "need for preferential closure" refers to a directionally biased influence on the epistemic process. Such influence may steer the proces away from undesirable knowledge structures and direct it towards desirable ones. Furthermore, needs for preferential closures are assumed to be topic-bound in accordance with individuals' particular interests and inclinations. A high school student who aspires to become an actor might care little whether he passed or failed a mathemathics exam, whereas a fellow student who hopes to become a physicist may entertain definite preferences between the two outcomes.

The above analysis suggests that a person would be more likely to reach conclusions congruent with his or her wishes than ones incongruent with them. This idea is hardly novel. The thesis that people may often engage in "wishful thinking" has long been a central theme in psychological theorizing, from psychoanalysis to the experimental study of perception (e.g., the "new look" approach of the 1950s). In social psychology this theme has been the cornerstone of the several cognitive-consistency theories that exerted enormous influence on research in this area during the 1960s (Festinger, 1957; Heider, 1958; Osgood & Tannenbaum, 1955; Rosenberg, 1960). For a discussion of recent social psychological research relevant to the "wishful thinking" hypothesis see Zuckerman (1979) or Harvey and Weary (1984).

A third motivational force assumed relevant to the epistemic process is the *need for openness*. The need for openness pertains to situations where judgmental noncommitment is valued or desired. Under some circumstances this might be occasioned by a person's fear of invalidity, stemming from the appreciable expected costs of mistaken judgments (cf. Mayseless & Kruglanski, 1987). Where the erroneous commitment to a judgment threatens to prove costly, persons might value cognitive openness, such as that occasioned by indecision among multiple competing hypotheses and/or inconsistent items of information.

A need for openness may also arise from the unwanted restriction of potential imposed by a definite judgment. Occasionally, definite self-knowledge might connote unattractive predictability and dullness. In such instances persons might well prefer to maintain cognitive openness and eschew closure. Furthermore, mystery occasionally might be compatible with a cherished, romantic worldview. For instance, many persons might not actually wish to find out "what is this thing called love" if the answers could be as banal as "attitude similarity," "proximity," or "the mediation of rewards." The need for openness may instigate intense epistemic activity where closure was in the danger of forming. This might induce increased sensitivity to new information possibly inconsistent with the current hypothesis and/or an increased tendency to generate competing alternatives to the hypothesis. Furthermore, where openness existed to start with, a need for openness might suppress further epistemic activity that "threatens" to bring about unwanted closure. Generally then, the need for openness may promote epistemic "unfreezing."

In summary, the present theory of knowledge acquisition stresses the following major points:

1. All knowledge is propositional, and it contains the twin aspects of structure and validity. Propositions are constituted of concepts, which are universal terms. Each universal term is divisible into an infinite number of particular instances, all representing relevant items of evidence for the concept in question. As one can only check a finite sample of evidential items, one has no objective basis for concluding that an inference is definitely true. Each proposition thus inevitably contains the potentiality of error and, in principle, constitutes a bias, that is, a subjectively based preference for a given hypothesis over its possible alternatives.

2. Knowledge-seeking behavior may be conceived of as an interwoven sequence of hypothesis generation and validation. Hypothesis validation is assumed to be governed by the principle of deducibility from subjectively relevant evidence. However, deducibility from evidence is assumed to be a necessary but not a sufficient condition for accepting a given hypothesis as true. In addition, a mechanism needs to be activated to inhibit the generation of alternative hypotheses similarly consistent with the evidence. Two major categories of such mechanisms have been identified: cognitive capability and epistemic motivation. The major capability notions pertinent to the hypothesis generation process are those of mental availability and accessibility of relevant constructs. The major epistemic motivations that may impact upon this process are the *need for closure*, assumed to facilitate epistemic "freezing," the *need for preferential closure*, assumed to promote either "freezing" or "unfreezing," and the *need for openness*, assumed to facilitate "unfreezing."

THE FRUSTRATIVE HYPOTHESIS: THE WHAT OF COGNITIVE THERAPY

The present analysis applies the principles of lay epistemology to a specific *content dimension* of beliefs. This is the dysfunctional–functional dimension on which beliefs are classified into those that evoke in the individual the sense of dissatisfaction and ill-being and those that elicit feelings of satisfaction and well-being. In the forthcoming section we further analyze the particular content characteristics of beliefs that underlie their functional or dysfunctional properties. According to the lay epistemologic view, suffering and displeasure result simply from the perceived thwarting of one's goals, needs, or desires. Cast in cognitive terminology, suffering results from *the belief* that one has failed or will fail to attain an important objective. As the popular saying goes, "Ignorance is [or can be] bliss"; in short, *belief* in (or knowledge of) a past or a future frustration is assumed critical to the experiencing of unhappiness or demoralization (Frank, 1973). Henceforth, we will refer to this type of belief as the *frustrative hypothesis*.

It is important to note that "frustration" is used here in a broad sense to include states of deprivation and loss as well as the blocking of goal-directed actions. For example, if a person's objective was to excel in absolutely everything, he or she would be likely to suffer upon failing at a given task. Similarly, if an individual's objective was to be well liked and adored by all, he or she would be likely to suffer upon being rejected by at least some people. The foregoing are examples of beliefs or types of knowledge pertaining to what Aaron Beck *et al.* (1980) has described as the states of loss leading to the depression syndrome. "Depression" may be conceptualized as evolving from past frustration, or a "loss" already experienced.

In contrast, an anticipatory frustration could lead to what Beck has termed a "danger to domain," experienced as anxiety or fear. For example, a person might fear situations in which the delivery of a public speech is required because of a belief that in those particular situations he or she is likely to be ridiculed by members of the audience. The anticipatory fear in this example represents the belief that at some future time the person's objective of maintaining positive esteem would be thwarted. It is possible to extend this analysis to other cases of psychological disorders dealt with by cognitive therapists (e.g., to the variety of phobias) and to show that in all those instances the disorder refers to a sense of pain and ill-being attendant upon a belief that some important personal objectives have been or will be frustrated. Therefore, the object of cognitive therapy is to persuade the patient to modify his or her frustrative hypotheses. Different possible types of such modification will be discussed in the following section.

MODIFYING THE FRUSTRATIVE HYPOTHESIS

The therapeutically relevant changes that one could perform on the frustrative hypothesis can be naturally classified according to the conceptual structure of such a hypothesis. A frustrative hypothesis contains the elements of a *goal*, a *means* to that goal, and a relation of *inefficiency* connecting the two (by which is indicated that the means is an inefficient way of getting to the goal). Accordingly, the frustrative hypothesis could be profitably modified *via* (1) an *assessment shift*, that is, a change in the perceived relation of inefficiency between the current means and goal to one of perceivd efficiency; (2) a *goal shift*, that is, a change in the person's goal to a more readily attainable objective, given the individual's resources; or (3) a *means shift*, that is, a change in the person's means of getting to the goal to a more efficient one.

An assessment shift concerns the case in which it may be possible to effect the required change in the frustrative hypothesis by getting the client to take a new look at the relevant evidence, including "facts" not sufficiently attended to heretofore. In such a case no attempt is made to change the person's goal or his or her particular means of reaching it; instead, an attempt is made to help the person perceive that, contrary to former assessment, the current means is an effective (rather than ineffective) way of attaining a goal in question. Just as an erstwhile ugly duckling may discover that it is actually a beautiful swan, a person whose suffering stems from believing that he or she is disrespected by other people or is failing at his or her job may be introduced to evidence suggesting the contrary to be the case.

But sometimes all evidence available to the client as well as the therapist may unequivocally support the client's frustrative belief. It may appear that this person indeed is failing to earn the approval of important others, is ignored, disliked, or ridiculed, or is poorly endowed to cope with a given category of tasks. Under those circumstances it would seem futile, besides being unethical, to convince the client of the opposite or to induce him or her to execute an assessment shift. In such a case there are two principal approaches for inducing the individual to abandon dysfunctional beliefs that produce suffering: they are a means shift and a goal shift. To reiterate, a means shift refers to the substitution of a new, efficient means to the desired goal for the old, inefficient one. A means shift could promote the belief that the end may indeed be attained, and thereby eliminate the suffering founded on the contrary belief. Unlike an assessment shift, in which the client is encouraged to operate in the *cognitive* mode—that is, to *think* about evidence and arguments presented by the therapist, in a means shift he or she must enter the *active mode*—that is, engage in novel actions presumed to ultimately yield evidence inconsistent with the frustrative hypothesis. For example, a person who fails to attain his or her goals because of a lack of assertiveness may be induced to undergo an assertiveness training course to improve interpersonal relations; a person with frustrations in the sexual domain may be induced to attend a Masters and Johnson's course in sexual techniques and ultimately abandon the negative beliefs about his or her sexual inadequacies.

However, a means shift may not always be an appropriate way of changing a person's frustrative belief. First, regardless of the attempted means, some goals may appear unrealistic or unattainable by almost anyone. For example, the goal of succeeding at every task, or of being admired by every person seem to belong in that category. Second, some goals may seem unattainable for particular individuals who lack the unique qualities necessary for their attainment. Many people could not hope to become successful writers, musicians, or businessmen because of a lack of talent in those areas. In cases in which the goal seems to lie beyond a person's reasonable means, an efficient way of dealing with frustration and suffering might be to induce the individual to abandon the goal in question and substitute for it a new, more readily achievable objective. The task of facilitating a *goal shift* may require (1) a criticism of the original goal (e.g., that it is unworthy of pursuit, wholly unrealistic, and so forth) and (2) advocacy aimed at "selling" the new goal to the individual. Any goal seems capable of being shifted, even such an apparently inborn goal as staying alive. The kamikaze pilot or historic Moslem warrior, for example, regarded honorable death as a highly desirable objective. Indeed, such persons have been reported to experience relatively little fear when exposed to a life danger, that is, little anticipatory frustration of a valued goal. In these cases, the goal of living may have been relinquished as a result of social or normative pressures. In more common cases of suicide, however, the individual may rely on his or her own analysis of the situation (that is, on his or her own epistemic authority) to conclude that life is not worth living.

In summary, we propose that negative affect may stem from a person's frustrative belief, that is, a belief that he or she is or will be failing to attain an important objective. To alleviate the pain attendant on such a belief it seems necessary to modify it, which may be accomplished in one of three general ways. (1) Leaving constant the goal and the means employed toward its accomplishment, a person may execute an *assessment shift* that is, a reassessment in the light of new evidence and, ultimately, abandonment of the frustrative hypothesis. (2) One may execute a *means shift*, that is, substitute a new, more efficient means of getting to the goal for the old, inefficient means. (3) One may execute a *goal shift*, that is, abandon the goal being hopelessly frustrated and substitute for it a more realistically attainable objective. Each of these approaches is assumed to be potentially helpful in appropriately modifying the patient's frustrative belief, and in this sense each is considered to constitute a mode of cognitive therapy. Which of the three approaches should be used in a given case will depend upon its cost effectiveness or the ease with which it may produce the desired results under the specific circumstances. Regardless of the approach finally selected, the way in which therapy is actually implemented will depend upon the persuasion techniques available to the therapist. It is in this context that the principles of lay epistemology become especially useful as the following sections will attempt to illustrate.

THE HOW OF THERAPEUTIC CHANGE: APPLYING LAY EPISTEMIC PRINCIPLES

In an earlier section we have outlined a set of epistemic principles assumed to affect the process of cognitive change. Here we will examine how those principles may be employed in the course of cognitive therapy.

STRUCTURES AND THEIR VALIDITY

Through cognitive therapy, dysfunctional structures (frustrative hypotheses) are replaced by functional ones. Frequently this may be accomplished by criticizing the dysfunctional structures as invalid and by establishing the validity of the functional structures. As noted earlier, validity arguments are based upon the principle of logical consistency. To attack the validity of a given proposition it is necessary to show that it is inconsistent with other beliefs held by the individual, and to establish the validity of an alternative proposition it is incumbent to show that it is consistent with those beliefs. Such uses of the consistency principle are frequent among practitioners of cognitive therapy.

For instance, therapists such as Albert Ellis or Aaron Beck typically pinpoint logical contradictions in the patient's belief systems and use this as leverage to effect the desired cognitive change. In almost all schools of cognitive therapy the client is induced to engage in a kind of hypothesis testing in which the evidence obtained favors the substitute, functional hypothesis over the original, dysfunctional one. For example, success experienced at some task in the course of therapy (Bandura, 1977) is inconsistent with a client's notion that he or she is a hopeless failure. Acceptance of the client by the therapist or members of a therapeutic group (Carl Rogers's "unconditional positive regard") is inconsistent with the client's belief that he or she is objectionable to everyone.

For therapy to be successful, the cognitive structures imparted to the client in the course of treatment should not encounter logically inconsistent (hence invalidating) evidence outside the therapeutic setting. No matter how functional or pleasing a given belief might be for the client, it would hardly last if contradicted by easily discoverable "facts." Even if the therapist succeeded, in sheltered sessions, in persuading the client of his or her considerable charms or talents or of the desirability of a given behavioral norm (e.g., openness and frankness in interpersonal relations), those beliefs might be quickly shattered by inconsistent evidence in the "outside" world.

Thus, a frequent criticism leveled at the variety of group therapies has been that subcultures created in group sessions contained norms or beliefs inconsistent with those outside the group. In such cases, possible beneficial effects achieved in the group atmosphere may quickly dissipate when the individual is reexposed to his or her routine surroundings and activities. The idea that the (cognitive) change that the client undergoes in the course of therapy should be compatible (that is, consistent) with, and constantly checked against, events and opinions in the outside world has been stressed by Strong (1970). It also seems implicit in the "open" or ambulatory treatment of psychotic disorders (Raush & Raush, 1968).

Epistemic Authority

In supporting the functional beliefs the therapist may wish to impart to the client, he or she may make extensive use of this individual's revered epistemic authorities. In the following section the generic construct of epistemic authority is illustrated by three exemplary subclasses: expert authority, group authority, and self authority.

Expert Authority

An "expert authority" approach involves the therapist invoking his or her professional expertise, scientific status, or presumptively superior intellect in order to influence the client in the direction of a desired change (for a thorough discussion of this point, see Strong, 1978, pp. 106–111). Reliance on the therapist's personal authority is prominent in certain major systems of cognitive treatment. Meichenbaum (1977b), for example, comments on the forceful, authoritative manner in which Albert Ellis conducts therapy. In Meichenbaum's word's, Dr. Ellis's approach "is forceful, so forceful that on one occasion I was moved to suggest rather tongue in cheek the RET [rational-emotive therapy] as conducted by Ellis would only be successful with New Yorkers" (p. 190). Beck (1976) explicitly recognizes that psychotherapy can have the greatest impact on the resoluton of emotional problems because of the considerable authority attributed to the therapist. Such authority also figures prominently in Victor Raimy's (1975) method "of explanation," in which the therapist presents an alternative account of the evidence" which is more valid than that upon which the [patient's] misconception is based" (p. 44).

Finally, although not usually discussed in these terms, the therapist's personal authority probably plays an important role in therapy as practiced by the cognitive behavior modifiers (e.g., see Mahoney, 1974, and Meichenbaum, 1977a, for reviews of the literature). Thus, in teaching the client to talk to himself or herself or to self-instruct (Meichenbaum, 1977a), the therapist suggests the content of things to be said to oneself in specific circumstances. These statements are clearly more than just behavioral acts of a verbal nature. They are better regarded as *hypotheses* that the therapist is proposing to the client, the *credibility* of which has a great deal to do with the therapist's epistemic authority in the client's eyes. For example, in inducing a child to be creative, the therapist might suggest that he or she utter self-directions such as the following: "If you push yourself you can be creative" or "Think of something no one else will think of." Both statements are intended as credible or valid hypotheses regarding efficient means to the end of creativity. Undoubtedly, the client's readiness to believe in such hypotheses has much to do with the therapist's perceived authority.

Group Authority

In addition to the therapist's personal authority, the collective authority of a therapeutic group can be employed to persuade a client to make desired changes. A respected reference group might induce the individual to attempt various new means of attaining the desired goal (that is, to excecute a means shift). For example, a feminist group might lend legitimacy to a woman's initiative in striking up an acquaintance with a male, or a gay group might lend legitimacy to public openness about one's gay identity. Alternatively, an individual might substitute one set of goals for another (execute a goal shift), based on the influence of a respected reference group. For example, after having joined a commune or the Moonies' organization, a person might quickly adjust his or her life objectives to the prevailing group norms.

Indeed, the use of groups is a frequent weapon in the arsenal of many cognitive therapists. Ellis's RET frequently employs groups in which the collective authority of an individual's peers, appropriately led by the therapist, is utilized to weed out maladaptive beliefs. Beck (1976) also recommends that persuasion be accomplished via interaction with other people in certain organized situations, that is, through the collective authority of one's peers. Finally, cognitive therapists with a more behavioral bent (e.g., Meichenbaum, 1977a) frequently utilize groups in order to facilitate the desired cognitive change. For instance, in some cases the therapist might make a behavioral contract with the group as a whole. The group's acceptance of the contract as worthwhile and desirable could serve as an important influence on the individual members (i.e., If everyone else thinks it is a good idea to do the behavioral homework assignments proposed by the therapist, maybe it is a good idea after all).

Self as Authority

The client's own perceived authority can be fruitfully employed to modify dysfunctional beliefs in the desired ways. Frequently a person's own experiences may constitute a powerful epistemic authority whereby beliefs may be induced or modified. "Seeing it with one's own eyes" may sometimes be a more efficient means of communication and persuasion than receiving it on expert or collective (group) authority. According to a Chinese saying, A picture is worth a thousand words. For example, a success experience at some task may go a long way, in an individual's eyes, toward refuting the failure hypothesis or toward recognizing the inherent potential of a new means of coping with a particular task.

Reliance on the client's perceived authority is prominently featured in many schools of cognitive therapy. Ellis, for example, makes frequent use of behavioral homework assignments such as asking a member of the opposite sex for a date. This exercise is intended to demonstrate to the client that such an experience, even if unsuccessful, does not have the devastating consequences that might have been feared. In terms of the concepts discussed here, the homework assignment technique represents a reliance on the client's own perceived authority as means of persuasion: The client experiences the events, he or she "sees them with his or her own eyes," so to speak. This can be very convincing, providing the client trusts his or her own eyes, that is, considers himself or herself a reliable epistemic authority for interpreting the events experienced. Beck's mode of cognitive therapy also frequently utilizes the client's self-ascribed authority in situations where his or her hypotheses are experientially tested, for example, in situations where a client, "in response to his psychotherapist's warmth and acceptance . . . modifies his stereotyped conception of authority figures" (Beck, 1976, p. 215).

Finally, the cognitive-behavioral approach to psychotherapy often relies on the patient's self-ascribed authority as means of effecting the desired cognitive change. For example, in the technique of modeling (Rosenthal & Bandura, 1978), the client, by observing role models, tests the hypothesis that people like himself or herself can reach a desired end by following a certain route. The frequent use of imagination in cognitive behavioral therapy may be viewed as representing personal hypothesis testing. For instance, in the technique of desensitization (see, e.g., Murray & Jacobson, 1978; Yates, 1975), the client discovers he or she can think of a given object or situation (e.g., snakes, water, or high places) without necessarily getting upset. Whatever else this particular procedure might accomplish, it certainly refutes the hypothesis that a mere thought about the phobic objects necessarily brings about considerable tension and disturbance.

In a study relevant to the notion of self as perceived authority, Ellis and Kruglanski (1987) hypothesized that persons whose self-ascribed epistemic authority in a domain is high would benefit more from *experiential learning* than persons whose ascribed epistemic authority is low. In one experiment, the domain investigated was that of mathemathics, whereas in the second experiment the domain was empathy. Subjects' perception of own epistemic authority in each domain was measured *via* appropriate questionnaires. It was found that in the mathemathics study, highs on epistemic authority outperformed the lows in the experiential learning condition, whereas the two groups did not differ in a condition where the same material was conveyed via a frontal lecture. In the empathy study, the highs again outperformed the lows in the experiential learning condition and they actually performed more poorly than the lows in the frontal lecture condition, where the lows (versus the highs) also perceived the instructor's epistemic authority as higher. This pattern of findings supports the notion that a person's ability to form confident knowledge may depend in part on perceived epistemic authority of the source (self or another person) of the information.

FREEZING AND UNFREEZING MECHANISMS: COGNITIVE CAPABILITY EFFECTS

The replacement of dysfuntional cognitions by functional ones through cognitive therapy requires that the former be "unfrozen" and the latter "refrozen" in their stead. To accomplish this, one might use some of the "unfreezing" mechanisms discussed earlier under the labels of cognitive capability and epistemic motivation factors. Thus, the therapist may impart to the client useful ways of thinking about his or her problem that may have been otherwise either unavailable or inaccessible to this person. The client may be surprised to learn that his or her "glass" can be considered half full rather than half empty, that a goal (e.g., of making it in the corporate "rat race") is not as sacrosanct as he or she has previously supposed, or that a relatively brief course of study may effectively rid him or her of what heretofore were considered unalterable personal attributes, such as social awkwardness, nonassertiveness, or shyness. Therapist-engendered accessibility of functional notions may constitute an important precondition to the client's ability to "unfreeze" his or her maladaptive conceptions.

Instead of (or in addition to) attempting to increase the accessibility of functional notions the therapist might try to decrease the accessibility of dysfunctional ones. Occasionally, this may mean a recommendation to avoid contexts or persons in whose presence such maladaptive notions are likely to be activated. For instance, the client may be advised to limit his or her participation in activities of an elitist country club that invoke in him or her notions of inadequacy or personal failure. A client may be advised to avoid violent films if those activate severe fears and anxieties or to shun the company of cynical friends whose company may strongly activate dysfunctional notions about life's futility and purposelessness. As noted earlier, following prolonged inactivity the dysfunctional notions may become dissociated in the person's mind from their evidential basis, and hence become less securely entrenched and possibly more tractable or amenable to alteration.

Motivational Influences

Preferred Closure Needs and Persuasive Efficacy

To enhance persuasive efficacy a therapist might make use of the idea that an individual's needs and desires may exert a selective influence on this person's inferences, leading him or her to engage in wishful thinking. Two complementary therapeutic strategies derive from this notion. (1) The therapist may aim to demonstrate that the dysfunctional belief (the frustrative hypothesis) is incongruent with the person's specific needs and desires and/or that this belief has consequences contributing to the frustration of other needs or desires. Alternatively, (2) the therapist may aim to convince the client that a given substitute belief is indeed congruent with a need or a desire, and so enhance the likelihood of it being accepted. For example, the therapist might suspect that a client's depressive belief that he or she is an utter failure is prompted by this person's need to elicit compassion and sympathy from other people. Under those circumstances the therapist could attempt to persuade the client that far from soliciting compassion, presentation of self as a failure invites instead disdain and rejection; the therapist could further suggest that a self-presentation as an average person with a share of failures and successes is most conducive to widespread sympathy.

Typically, cognitive therapists eschew explicit references to motivational variables. However, occasionally they seem to utilize such variables in the course of therapy. For example, in one case reported by Beck (1976), the client's content-bound needs were enlisted in the aid of therapeutic persuasion. The case concerns modification of an elderly man's belief that "his elderly wife was carrying on an affair with his young physician" (p. 225) by pointing out to him the negative consequences of such a belief, including the possibility of his wife ultimately ceasing to care for him and leaving him. As a result, the client stopped making accusations and "the delusion of infidelity may have become attenuated" (p. 225). In this particular instance, a demonstration that the content of a given belief may ultimately lead to the frustration of an important need (of continuing to be taken care of by one's wife) may have discouraged the client from adhering to the belief.

Needs for Closure and Openness

A heightened need for cognitive closure (e.g., aroused by an impending decision) could facilitate the adoption of any plausible conception relevant to such a decision. For example, a person might be more readily persuaded by the therapist's argument extolling a training course in social skills if this person expected to soon have to decide whether or not to enroll in the course at issue. The need for cognitive closure may thus be conceived of and appropriately utilized as a consolidating influence that may "freeze" the individual's belief on a given hypothesis (ideally the one proposed by the therapist) and suppress the client's tendency to generate rival alternative hypotheses.

The use of homework assignments (Shelton & Ackerman, 1976) may capitalize on the client's closure needs. A belief proposed by the therapist (e.g., "I will not be devastated by social rejection") is likely to be accepted by the client more readily if he or she is about to commit himself or herself to some definite action or homework assignment in the immediate future (like striking up a conversation with an attractive stranger), whose rationality derives from the belief in question. The contracts and commitments typical of more behaviorally oriented brands of cognitive therapy (Kanfer, 1975) make efficient use of the closure need in order to consolidate ("refreeze") in the client's mind the new, desired belief. The pressure on the client to make a firm commitment or contract regarding a course of action renders it likely that he or she will quickly formulate a conception relevant to such action. Typically this would be the conception provided by the therapist. If the client might have been hesitant about believing in the conception at issue, the pressure of a commitment to action congruent with it would enhance the probability of its acceptance.

Mobilization of the client's need for closure may be useful at the stage of consolidating new beliefs assumed therapeutic in their consequences. In contrast, enlistment of the need for openness may be useful at the stage of uprooting the old, dysfunctional beliefs assumed responsible for pain and suffering. The need for openness is particularly likely to arise when the price of making a mistake is adjudged severe. In this situation the individual may be more than ordinarily ready to question and reassess extant beliefs and sympathetically consider the alternatives offered. For example, a person might be inclinced to abandon a belief about his or her need to be approved of by everyone if that belief was ridiculed by the therapist and/or by members of a therapy group. As a useful persuasive technique, the therapist might therefore question the validity of dysfunctional beliefs while making salient the price that must be paid for such invalidity.

Ellis's therapeutic system frequently invokes the client's fear of invalidity in order to unfreeze his or her maladaptive beliefs and refreeze their more adaptive substitutes. We refer here to the somewhat aggressive mode of questioning typical of RET in which the client's dysfunctional ideas are challenged and ridiculed. According to Ellis (1977) himself, "RET largely consists of the use of [the] logical-empirical method of scientific questioning[,] challenging and debating. . . . This kind of debating really consists of rhetorical questions designed to dispute and rip up the false belief" (p. 20). Under those circumstances the client may indeed become quite motivated to be rid of the beliefs in question and accept in their stead the more "rational, scientifically provable, empirically validatable" notions proposed by the therapist. Invocation of the client's need for openness through intellectual challenge, questioning of his or her dysfunctional ideas, and the judicious use of humor is a prominent feature of the therapeutic procedures developed by Beck (1976; Beck, Rush, Shaw, & Emery, 1979) but is less frequently used by cognitive therapists of the behavioral tradition (such as Bandura, 1977, or Meichenbaum, 1977a).

THE WHAT OF THERAPEUTIC CHANGE

The foregoing sections demonstrated how numerous elements of cognitive therapy can be explicated in terms of the present analysis of the epistemic *process*. This section will show that the *content* of change striven for in the course of cognitive therapy represents a change in the client's frustrative beliefs and is accomplished via shifts in his or her assessments, goals, or means.

In Bandura's conception (1977), for example, the aim of cognitive therapy is enhancement of the client's sense of self-efficacy; this is the belief in one's ability to attain (through one's own efforts) one's important objectives (i.e., the obverse of the frustrative belief). In Ellis's or Beck's system a similar change is striven for. Thus, Ellis (1978) describes a hypothetical case of an individual fired from his job, who considers this loss unfortunate and disadvantageous. Ellis comments that had the individual believed that it really did not matter whether he kept or lost the job he would hardly feel depressed or sad on the occasion. This is an instance in which a shift in the person's goals would have a suffering-reducing effect. Clearly such a shift would eliminate the person's frustrative belief—that he is failing to attain his desired ends. Indeed, Ellis mentions among possible objectives of rational-emotive therapy a change in the client's core values: a shift in the ultimate goals that the individual deems worth pursuing.

Ellis's therapeutic techniques frequently include attempts to bring about a means shift in the client. In Ellis's RET, the client may be shown how to stay on a long-term diet, given training in assertiveness without hostility, and, in general, taught various new means of getting to the desired ends. Finally, Ellis's techniques sometimes include inducing an assessment shift regarding the relation of the means to the desired goal. For example, Ellis views full acceptance or tolerance of the client by the therapist as a way of demonstrating that the client "is acceptable even with his unfortunate present traits," (p. 12). In terms of the present analysis, the client's goal of being acceptable remains constant, as does this person's means of attaining acceptability (through a set of personality traits, including the ones the client considers unworthy of acceptance by others). Instead of encouraging the client to modify his or her goals or means, the therapist presents in this case new evidence for the client's essential acceptability; this invites a reassessment and revision of the individual's former beliefs on that topic.

The categories of goal, means, or assessment shifts are readily applicable to the kinds of therapeutic techniques utilized by Aaron Beck. Thus, in one reported instance Beck (1976) portrays as ridiculous a client's concern about strangers' opinions of him. This represents the therapist's attempt to dissuade the client from considering social acceptance by strangers a worthwhile goal (hence, to facilitate a goal shift). Encouragement of a means shift is apparent in Beck's (1976) reference to techniques such as "assertiveness-training . . . that may enhance the patient's self confidence[,] and other behavioral methods" (p. 214). An assessment shift in the perceived means–ends relation is also frequently referred to in Beck's reports about psychotherapy. Thus, in one example, "a patient in response to his therapist's warmth and acceptance often modifies his stereotyped conception of authority figures" (Beck, 1976, p. 214). In present terms, this signifies a shift in the client's erstwhile assessment that his or her goal of being accepted by authority figures was frustrated.

The elements of means, goal, or assessment shifts are apparent also in the works of cognitive therapists of a behavioral orientation. Thus, Meichenbaum (1977a) reviews various skills-training programs offering the client *new means* of coping with difficulties in areas such as speech anxiety, test anxiety, social incompetence, social withdrawal (in children), and other problems (Meichenbaum, 1977a). In other cases the self-instructional techniques practiced by behaviorally oriented cognitive therapists include elements of *goal* shifting. For example, a client feeling anxious about being interrogated by a date on a topic about which he knows very little may be encouraged to say to himself a statement such as "It is not such a big deal to admit I don't know something. There are probably lots of things I know that she doesn't" (Meichenabaum, 1977a, p. 132). In this case the individual is clearly encouraged to abandon the goal of appearing all-knowledgeable; the possible failure to attain this objective appears now not nearly as devastating as might have been originally feared by the client.

Finally, therapists who employ self-instructional methods occasionally incorporate elements of assessment shift techniques. For example, in a study on the control of obesity, Mahoney and Mahoney (1976) viewed as therapeutically appropriate statements such as "Eating does not satisfy psychological problems, it creates them" or "my [eating] schedule is not worse than anyone else's," that is, statements asserting relations between behavioral means and desired ends not heretofore apparent to (or salient for) the client.

LAY EPISTEMOLOGY AND COGNITIVE THERAPIES: A COMPARATIVE APPRAISAL

So far we have seen that the various approaches to cognitive therapy have included techniques of inducing cognitive change that are explicable in terms of the theory of lay epistemology presented here. Thus, the lay epistemic framework provides an integrative scheme for discussing the heretofore isolated and disparate methods employed by cognitive therapists of various persuasions. It is of interest to point out that in descriptions of cognitive therapy, the techniques singled out in this chapter as important are presented in an offhand manner and appear to constitute the "ground" rather than the "figure" of cognitive therapy. For instance, major contemporary systems of cognitive therapy treat as obvious and undeserving of special comment the logical-consistency criterion of belief assessment, the use of epistemic authorities, or the reliance on epistemically relevant needs. Instead, such systems highlight as conceptually critical several notions and hypotheses with which the present epistemic analysis is sharply at odds. We might say that the lay epistemic framework can account for the kind of things that cognitive therapists *actually do* while differing with respect to what they *say* they do. In the following sections we explore some of the differences and consider their implications for the practice of cognitive therapy.

The Dysfunctional Misconception (Distortion) Hypothesis

To the question of why one should attempt to change, in the course of therapy, the client's conceptions and beliefs, many cognitive therapists would probably reply that those particular ideas are dysfunctional, that is, maladaptive or irrational, and that they ultimately cause pain and suffering for the individual. The following passage from Ellis (1977) indicates this viewpoint clearly: "By irrationality I mean any thought, emotion, or behavior that leads to self-defeating or self-destructive consequences that significantly interfere with the survival and happiness of the organism" (p. 15). Thus far we would agree. In the lay epistemic framework too, dysfunctional thoughts are defined as pain-inducing and are further characterized by the frustrative hypothesis.

Where we do not agree with several major schools of cognitive therapy is in the confounding of dysfunctional ideation with misconceptions about reality. Such an identification is, for example, a cornerstone of Ellis's (1973) approach to therapy: "RET holds that virtually all serious emotional problems with which humans are beset directly stem from their magical, superstitious, empirically invalidatable thinking" (p. 172). Ellis's list of "irrational" attributes, includes "senseless," "illogical," "unreasonable," "unrealistic," and/or "absolutistic," "overgeneralizations" that "distort reality." Hence, an essential rhetorical question that Ellis would pose to his client in order to "dispute and to rip up the false belief is: "In which way does it have truth—or falseness?" (Ellis, 1977, p. 20).

In Beck's system of cognitive therapy dysfunction and distortion are similarly equated. In Beck's (1976) terms, "psychological problems may result from . . . making incorrect inferences, and not distinguishing between imagination and reality . . ." (p. 19); thus "a profound or chronic discrepancy between the internal and external systems may culminate in psychological disorders" (p. 24). Further, "problems are derived from certain distortions of reality based on erroneous premises and misconceptions" (p. 20). Accordingly, the pivotal endeavor in Beck's therapy aims at a rectification of departures from reality. A cognitive therapy manual by Beck and his associates (Beck, Rush, Shaw, & Emery, 1979) asserts this in the following terms:

> The therapeutic techniques are designed to identify, reality-test, and correct distorted conceptualizations and the dysfunctional beliefs (schemas) underlying these conditions. . . . The cognitive therapist helps the patient to think and act more realistically and adaptively about his psychological problems and thus reduces symptoms.

The identification of dysfunctionality with cognitive distortion has been especially salient in Raimy's (1975) writings, where this issue is extensively treated under the heading of the "misconception hypothesis." Raimy claims that "successful psychological treatment occurs when faulty ideas or beliefs are modified or eliminated" (p. 4). In summary, as Arnold Lazarus (1971) asserted "the bulk of psychotherapeutic endeavors may be said to center around the correction of misconceptions" (p. 165).

In contrast to these views, typical of several major approaches to cognitive therapy, our analysis takes issue with the dysfunctional misconception hypothesis, that is, with the notion that erroneous thoughts are pain inflicting. Life seems replete with examples in which uncompromising "truth" is anything but salutary in its consequences for the individual: the betrayed lover, the bankrupt businessman, or the terminally ill patient may not only suffer terribly upon the discovery of "truth" about their condition but may sometimes be driven to self-destruction in such circumstances. This is not to say that "truthful" ideas or beliefs may not be beneficial and false ones pernicious in their consequences. But, in general, there seems little basis for concluding that a (deterministic or statistical) relation exists between the veridicality of a belief or an inference and the happiness or unhappiness that it may promote.

Buttressing this argument are the commentary and data presented by personality researchers such as Richard Lazarus and Walter Mischel. Lazarus (1980) suggests that cognitive therapists conceptualize pertinent cognitive processes in terms of faulty conceptions or irrationalities because of their use of psychopathology as a reference framework for the understanding of human functioning in general. Reminding us that mental health professionals have for long been "monogamously wedded to reality testing as the main hallmark of psychological well-being" Lazarus particularly objects to the prevailing cognitive therapy view that "only accurate perceptions of reality (or correct assumptions about life) can be adaptationally effective and desirable" (p. 3).

Based on his own, long-standing research on stress and coping, Lazarus (1979) argues that well-functioning people may sometimes have to improve their lot by "bending reality a bit to maintain certain illusions" (p. 3). In fact, there are stress conditions (e.g., terminal illness, incapacitation, aging) that essentially preclude the direct action, problem-solving mode of coping, leaving accessible primarily the intrapsychic (cognitive), palliative mode, which is not necessarily second-best. This palliative function "regulates the distressing emotion itself which arises from a harm or threat appraisal," and includes "minimizing . . . avoiding, denying, or detaching" (p. 4)—all representing what many cognitive therapists have downgraded as maladaptive conceptions about reality. Lazarus aptly concudes that

> although people often can be helped by getting them to see the hard realities and the illusory and irrational nature of their assumptions about living, we often also need the luxury of some illusions, and therapy in some instances might better revolve around helping the person to think more positively about his or her plight rather than fixating on the painful truth. So much of life is ambiguous that there is much room for variation in appraisal. One's cup can be half full rather than half empty. (p. 5)

Difficulties with a reliance on cognitive distortion in explanations of affective disorders have been highlighted in recent self-perception studies conducted with depressed patients. Lewinsohn, Mischel, Chaplin, and Barton (1980) found that for these individuals, initial self-evaluations of performance in group interaction, as well as evaluations of such performance by independent observers, were more negative as compared to self-evaluations rendered by nondepressed psychiatric controls and by normal controls. Of particular pertinence is the finding that the self-evaluations of depressed patients coincided more closely with the observers' evaluations than did evaluations of subjects in both control groups; the latter subjects' self-perceptions were more positive than the observers' evaluations. In other words, the depressives were more "realistic" than were the controls in evaluating their own social competencies: They were closer to the "social reality" as defined by the judgment of objective observers.

As Mischel (1979) points out, the findings of Lewinsohn *et al.* (1980) are inconsistent with Beck's (1976) view regarding the etiological importance in depression of an "unrealistically negative view of self." Also inconsistent with this view are the findings that depressed individuals were surprisingly accurate in their recall of feedback (Nelson & Craighead, 1977) and in their judgments of the degree of contingency between their own responses and the outcomes obtained (Alloy & Abramson, 1979, 1988). It is particularly interesting to note that in the Lewinsohn *et al.* (1980) study, a second assessment of social competence, made at a later point in treatment, revealed that self-perception of the depressed patients became more positive and so more similar to that of the controls, who didn't change much over time; that is, with treatment the depressed patients had become increasingly *less* rather than more "realistic." Mischel's (1979) concludes:

> It is tempting to conjecture that a key to avoiding depression is to see oneself less stringently and more favorably than others see one. If so, the beliefs that unrealistic self-appraisals are a basic ingredient of depression and that realism is the crux of appropriate affect may have to be seriously questioned. To feel good about ourselves we may have to judge ourselves more kindly than we are judged. Self-enhancing information processing and biased self-encoding may be both a requirement for positive affect and the price for achieving it. (p. 752)

Finally, the hypothesized positive relation between "realism" and well-being is belied by several misattribution studies demonstrating that negative emotional behavior can be reduced if the subject is "falsely" led to believe that his autonomic arousal was caused by an emotionally irrelevant stimulus (Nisbett & Schachter, 1966; Ross, Rodin, & Zimbardo, 1969; Storms & Nisbett, 1970; Valins, 1966).

ARE DEPRESSIVES WISER?

The preceding discussion suggests that alleviation of the depressed client's suffering may depend on his or her success in relinquishing the frustrative hypothesis rather than on the realism of his or her inferences. Moreover, such realism can not be satisfactorily established anyway. In this sense, the presumptive realism of the depressives in the Lewinsohn *et al.* (1980) study is to be seriously questioned. After all, it appears less plausible to assume that truth was given to depressives than that they may have incidentally shared the biases of the external observers, whereas the normals might have possessed a different set of biases. For example, the normals may have had strong self-esteem needs disposing them to believe in their considerable competence. Depressives might lack such a need for some reason and in this sense be closer in vantage point to an impartial observer. Alternatively, the depressives' self-esteem needs might be equally forceful as the normals', yet the effects of these needs might be counteracted by highly negative beliefs about themselves to which the depressives subscribe. The net judgmental effect would be the same as for an external observer lacking both the negative beliefs and the preferential closure (esteem) needs.

Thus, according to our analysis, to agree with outside observers, a prevailing consensus, or an expert opinion is merely to adopt a different bias rather than to avoid bias or to attain ultimate realism. Essentially, the therapist may never be certain that the cognitive change which he or she advocates is any closer to the truth than the client's original inferences. At the very best, the therapist may hope to demonstrate that the beliefs that he or she advocates, besides being consistent with all past evidence, are also consistent with new evidence contrary to the client's original ideas. This does not mean that the advocated beliefs are immune to the possibility of being in turn contradicted by further, as yet unexamined evidence. But the client's original beliefs might also have been consistent with past evidence, so that the client's and therapist's inferences are exactly on par as far as their ultimate truth status is concerned.

For example, consider a young male client whose depression is apparently founded on the belief that "all women despise him." Assume further that this particular belief was prompted by two consecutive experiences in which he was rejected by a woman. A therapist may quickly challenge the client's belief on grounds of *overgeneralization*; one is not really justified in concluding that all women have a certain attitude if only two women have exhibited it. But while possibly incorrect, the client's conclusion is at least consistent with the available evidence: If it were true that all women despise him, any woman would tend to reject him, including the two who actually did.

Now, suppose that in an effort to overthrow this dysfunctional generalization, the therapist arranged for a situation in which some female members of the therapy group admitted to finding this man attractive. Also suppose that based on those pleasant experiences the client was persuaded to abandon his original, depressing conclusion regarding his sex appeal and exchange it for the more optimistic view that at least some women are not repelled by him. The latter conclusion is certainly more pleasing and therefore more functional for the client than the former one. But is it therefore "truer"? Not necessarily. This individual may encounter several successive rejections outside of the therapeutic group, that might lead him to question the sincerity of the apparent acceptances. Under those circumstances he may feel justified in reverting to the gloomy outlook with which he first came to therapy.

In other words, any interpretation (including that offered by a therapist) may at best be consistent with past evidence but could be overthrown by future evidence. Thus, it does not seem justifiable to consider the inferences that the therapist imparts to the client as in any *objective sense* truer or more veridical than the client's original ruminations.

The indeterminacy of the truth status of any (nontautological) proposition is particularly striking when contrasting the views of a paranoid psychotic and those of a therapist. Both belief systems may be equally consistent or internally coherent, and equally grounded in subjective evidence whose objective veridicality is in principle indeterminate. Admittedly, the belief system of the paranoid is private, while that of the therapist may be shared by numerous other persons. But consensus does not determine truth, and, on occasion, vast numbers of persons have been known to err (believing that the Earth is flat, for example). The internal consistency of the paranoid's belief system is illuminated by the following anecdote in which a therapist attempts to undermine a patient's belief that he is dead. "You would agree that dead persons do not have blood in their veins," begins the therapist. "Of course I do," replies the patient. At this point the therapist makes a small incision in the patient's forearm until some blood is showing. "Do you still believe you are dead?" asks the therapist, triumphantly. "Indeed I do," retorts the patient, "but I admit to having been wrong, dead people do appear to have blood in their veins!" For a thorough discussion of the undecidability problem in comparing normal and psychotic views see Fried and Agassi's (1976) work on paranoia.

According to the present analysis, no conception, theory, or hypothesis can be proven true or even partially true, that is, can be said to represent a portion of objective reality. This applies even to the most carefully and extensively corroborated scientific theories, let alone to a therapist's impressions of a client's life events, which may be occasionally at odds with the client's interpretations. To reiterate, according to the lay epistemic view (based on a nonjustificationist philosophy of knowledge), any statement is a generalization, and any generalization is potentially an overgeneralization. Therefore, the claim that a client's ideas contain numerous overgeneralizations, while undeniably valid, hardly sets those ideas apart from their possible alternatives, including those favored by the therapist.

From this perspective it would not be efficient to characterize a client's conceptions as *selective abstractions* (Beck, 1976); because any abstraction is selective in that the same pattern of evidence is compatible with a vast number of alternative interpretations (Campbell, 1969) whose relative validity cannot be assessed with any demonstrable degree of objectivity. Nor would it be efficient to characterize the patient's inferences as *arbitrary*, as in jumping "to a conclusion when evidence is lacking or is actually contrary to the conclusion" (Beck, 1963, p. 94). Any inference is in a sense arbitrary: It cannot claim in its support a basis of objective proof, or a definitive exclusion of all alternative inferences (potentially infinite in number) consistent with a given data pattern. As we have seen, any inference or hypothesis is composed of universal terms, each having no less than an infinity of possible implications. No matter how hard we try, we can only check a finite number of such implications; hence, any inference that we may make is forever deemed to be based on an incomplete array of relevant evidence.

Furthermore, according to the present framework, the objective-sounding term "evidence" actually refers to conceptions and hypotheses whose objective truth status is in principle the same as that of inferences. For that very reason, instances in which an individual might seem to reach an inference contrary to a given bit of evidence might be ones in which he or she dismissed, doubted, or did not even entertain the "evidential" propositions assumed as obvious by the therapist. All of this is perfectly in keeping with the rational epistemic process, if by "rational" is meant the process whereby any scientist, however carefully trained, is arriving at his or her inferences.

In short, the client's conceptions, dysfunctional though they might be, cannot be distinguished from those of the therapist in terms of their objective validity, or truth status. However, this does not imply that in attempting to effect cognitive change the therapist should not depict the client's beliefs as invalid and his or her own substitute propositions as more valid. To imply this would be to deny that people evaluate or validate their hypotheses, whereas the present theory accords a central place to the validational process. But while at a given moment the therapist's interpretation or hypothesis might indeed appear to be more valid than the client's, this does not mean that this particular interpretation really is a true and unalterable one. Such an assumption might only render the therapist closed-minded and impervious to various alternative suggestions and possibilities, some of which might be potentially very useful in solving the client's problem.

Further, a therapist's belief in the infallibility of the scientific method or the necessarily erroneous nature of the client's dysfunctional thoughts might heavily load the therapeutic process toward an induction of cognitive change via arousing the fear of invalidity. As we have seen, however, such a mode of induction is merely one possible approach open to the therapist. In at least some circumstances it may not be the best tack available, for the client's adherence to a belief might stem from its correspondence with his or her wishes, for example. In such circumstances, frontal attack on the validity of the client's notions might fail or boomerang. Persuasive attempts at weakening the linkage between the belief and the wish, might work more efficiently.

THE CONTENTS OF IRRATIONAL BELIEFS

As we have discussed, a dysfunctional belief represents the perceived frustration of an important goal. This means that the contents of dysfunctional beliefs can vary considerably in accordance with the diversity of possible personal goals as well as individuals' perceived ability to attain the particular goals. At the same time it should be possible to identify within a given cultural context a set of relatively common yet impossible-to-attain goals. Those goals are likely to represent prevalent frustrative hypotheses shared by large numbers of people. Their identification may profitably guide the activities of a cognitive therapist. Indeed, several influential approaches to cognitive therapy, such as those of Ellis (1978), Beck (1976), and Raimy (1975) specify lists of "irrational beliefs" or "themes" assumed to underlie the suffering of numerous patients. "I must be loved by absolutely everybody," or "I must succeed at every task I attempt" are widely cited examples of such irrational beliefs. Contrary to common assumption, the dysfunctionality of such beliefs does not reside in their falsity (which is ultimately indeterminate) but rather in their signification of impossible goals, likely to give rise to frustrative hypotheses.

In this connection it is important to note that personal goals may shift, as may individual's capacities to attain those goals. Thus an irrational and/or a dysfunctional goal may, with a shift in context, cease representing a goal or come to represent a readily attainable goal. In other words, it is important to recognize the relative status of dysfunctional themes. Unlike truth or falsity, which are absolute and constant, goals and relevant capacities can change in the course of time. According to this analysis, no belief is *inherently* dysfunctional; it is dysfunctional only to the extent that it represents an unattainable goal. This idea is generally unrecognized in the cognitive therapy literature.

For example, Albert Bandura's (1977) claims for the central role played in individuals' psychological welfare by the belief in self-efficacy can be looked at as an absolutistic emphasis on the *content* of a belief per se without explicit recognition of its relation to an important cultural goal. But while self-efficacy undoubtedly represents an important goal in Western cultures committed to the value of individualism, it may be less important in alternative, communal cultures (e.g., for India's Buddhist communities). At any rate, even in Western cultures self-efficacy is not the only goal that people might have, and a belief in the frustration of any goal should be aversive or suffering-inducing. For example, a belief that every inhabitant of a given place is an intellectually inferior dullard with whom there can be no meaningful contact might frustrate one's need for fulfilling social relationships. A belief in an impending pain or danger to one's survival represents the frustration of one's need for physical welfare. None of the latter needs or goals seem to properly belong in the self-efficacy category (unless this is interpreted so broadly as to include all possible goals), yet a belief in their frustration would seem capable of engendering considerable pain and, in this sense, would be a proper target for cognitive therapy.

Finally, approaches to cognitive therapy with conceptual roots in attribution theory (Heider, 1958; Kelley, 1967) often deal with specific contents of hypotheses (Kruglanski, 1979) without concern about how these relate to important goals. For instance, the considerable preoccupation of attributional researchers with "internal" and "external" ascriptions of causality represents an intrinsic interest in specific cognitive contents classified as generically functional or dysfunctional without regard to the relation of such contents to individuals' goals. Thus, "internal" ascription of behavioral changes is usually considered beneficial for a person, because it is assumed to suggest persistence and stability of the changes, parallelling the assumed stability of the (internal) self. But according to the lay epistemic viewpoint, internal attribution should be considered beneficial only if the changes represent attainment of formerly frustrated goals. In time, those goals could shift, in which case behavioral persistence as such could become irrelevant or even contrary to the individual's well-being. For example, behavioral toughness and violence could serve well the member of a street gang, yet their persistence would be counterproductive if this individual aspired to acceptance in middle-class society. Ultimately then, whether a content of a given attribution or inference (like the internal attribution just referred to) would be beneficial to the individual should depend on whether or not it represented an abandonment of the frustrative hypothesis. The latter thus remains the essential content category of relevance to cognitive therapy.

To summarize, while the lay epistemic approach acknowledges the utility of constructing *a priori* lists of pervasive dysfunctional themes, it stresses that (1) the dysfunctionality of the themes derives from their signification of impossible goals rather than from their falseness, and (2) a pervasive cultural goal may shift in time, and an *impossible* goal may cease to be so in course of time. Thus, we recommend a cautiously relativistic approach to lists of dysfunctional themes, as opposed to an absolutistic approach based on their identification as "false."

PRIMACY OF EXPERIENCE AS THE MEDIATOR OF COGNITIVE CHANGE

The present epistemic approach differs from those analyses that regard personal experience of performance outcomes as a uniquely effective mediator of cognitive change. For example, Kopel and Arkowitz (1975) commented that "The therapeutic effects brought about by observing one's own behavior may be more powerful than the effects obtained from a verbal interchange which conveys the basic information to the client" (p. 195). Bandura (1977) similarly implied that expectancies or inferences arrived at via actual performance are superior to those based on alternative modes of persuasion (e.g., verbal) or on vicarious experience, because the latter methods "do not provide an authentic experiential base . . . for them" (p. 198). Therefore, "it is performance-based procedures that are proving to be most powerful for effecting psychological changes . . . [and] cognitive events are induced and altered most readily by experiences of mastery arising from effective performance" (p. 191).

Within the present theoretical framework, personal experience is tantamount to the case in which the knower must rely on his or her own epistemic authority in evaluating the validity of an inference. Whether or not such a reliance would be an effective mediator of cognitive change should depend on whether or not in specific circumstances the knower adjudged his or her own authority as sufficient for clearly interpreting the experience. For example, a "success experience" at some task is unlikely to uplift feelings of self-efficacy if one seriously doubted one's own qualifications for pronouncing the "experienced outcomes" a success. Bandura (1977) does note that the efficacy of experiential methods is constrained by the interpretations imposed on the experiences. In the present scheme, we propose to abolish the distinction between "experience" and "interpretation" and to regard both as equally conceptual or interpretative (Popper, 1973; Weimer, 1979).

According to our analysis, the knower's self-ascribed authority is merely one among several factors affecting his or her tendency to accept a given hypothesis. Other factors are alternative authorities linked with this particular hypothesis, authorities associated with possible alternative hypotheses, the motivational significance of the hypothesis, and so on. From our perspective, the question of which of these factors is the most effective mediator of cognitive change cannot be settled a priori. The answer would depend on the relative strengths (or levels) of those various factors in a particular set of circumstances; this may not be known in advance of specifying these circumstances.

Thus, the lay epistemic scheme, while capable of accounting for many of the activities actually constituting cognitive therapy, differs from major extant schools in the interpretation it imposes on those activities. Lay epistemology does not assume that in the course of cognitive therapy warped and distorted beliefs are replaced by more veridical or realistic ones, but rather than suffering-promoting beliefs are replaced by satisfaction-promoting ones. The present scheme does not assume that teaching an individual the scientific way of reasoning is an effective avenue of curing his or her ills. The lay and scientific modes of reasoning are fundamentally similar, and neither guarantees the content of beliefs ultimately arrived at. Therefore, application of the scientific way of reasoning cannot, in itself, have therapeutic effects. Unlike some major systems of cognitive therapy, the lay epistemic approach stays relatively uncommitted regarding the contents of beliefs in need of changing. Its only emphasis is that cognitive therapy should concern itself with beliefs whose content is frustrative in the sense elaborated above. Finally, unlike some behaviorally oriented approaches, the present analysis does not assume the primacy of behavior or personal experience as the mediators of cognitive change. Both are assumed to represent the case in which the knower's self-ascribed authority is brought to bear on the inference process. The extent to which this facilitates the arrival at confident inferences should depend on the degree to which such self-ascribed authority is high or low in a specific situation.

Interpretative Innovations of the Epistemic Analysis

It might be said that the innovation of the present analysis lies more in the interpretation it imposes on the activities of cognitive therapists than in suggestions for modifying such activities. And insofar as what really matters in therapy are actions rather than interpretations, the question might be raised whether the new analysis can be expected to have any practical consequences whatsoever. The answer to this question seems clearly affirmative. After all, it is interpretation that guides action, and different interpretations can be expected to have different action implications.

More specifically, if the present epistemic analysis is accepted, current practices of cognitive therapy would be likely to succeed only in those cases where they operationalized the present theoretical constructs, and not in alternative cases. For example, the therapist's critique of the client's dysfunctional thoughts on the grounds of their being "unprovable generalizations" might successfully "unfreeze" such thoughts to the extent that it aroused the person's fear of invalidity, which may enhance the need for openness. But in some cases the same critique might fail to arouse such a fear: The individual could be a philosopher of science firmly convinced that no beliefs are provable and that all generalizations are overgeneralizations anyway. It is highly doubtful whether the therapist's approach would have the expected curative effect on this client. Under these circumstances, fear of invalidity might be aroused by alternative means, such as by pointing out to this individual that his or her dysfunctional views are at sharp variance with a philosophical authority that he or she admires.

Similarly, a therapist's attempt to uproot a client's belief on the grounds of it being included in an a priori roster of "irrational contents" would fail to have a therapeutic effect if the belief in question did not in fact represent a frustrative hypothesis. For example, an individual might believe that unless all women adored him he would undergo a nervous breakdown, but fortunately also believe that all women did in fact adore him. A modification of his beliefs is unlikely to enhance his satisfaction and well-being. In the same vein, the use of group therapy would fail or boomerang if a client regarded groups as "thoughtless mobs," that is, if he or she held a negative view of groups as epistemic authorities. Similarly, exposure to "actual" experiences would fail in instances where an individual distrusted his or her ability to make sense of the experiences in question, and so on.

Therefore, it appears that while current practices of cognitive therapy might often be effective, often they might not be. Which would be the case would depend on the degree to which they "operationally defined," or represented, the constructs of the present epistemic analysis. These constructs are conceived of as generative principles from which it should be possible to derive a variety of operational techniques. In some instances those might be the techniques currently in use, but in other cases they might be as yet untried techniques. For instance, the construct of epistemic authority suggests that in administering cognitive therapy to a member of a street gang one might do better to enlist the assistance of the gang's leader, rather than relying on the therapist's professional status.

A METACOGNITIVE GOAL FOR COGNITIVE THERAPY

According to an old Mexican proverb, "He who catches a fish may eat for a day, while he who learns how to fish may eat for a lifetime." Figuratively speaking, thus far we have dealt with the former, more specific activity of "catching" a single "therapeutic fish," or inducing a singular change in a particular set of dysfunctional beliefs. But therapy could aim at a higher, metacognitive objective of imparting to the client (via a set of lectures, drills, and structured experiences) an "epistemic ideology," or life philosophy based on a nonjustificationist conception of truth, including a set of principles whereby cognitive change could be brought about. In this sense, the aim of therapy could be "teaching clients how to fish" by instructing them in a set of metacognitive skills helpful in conducting self-therapeutic activities in accordance with the principles of lay epistemology. In broad outline, such "epistemic ideology" could involve the following notions.

1. Truth is objectively unprovable and is therefore indeed in "the eye of the beholder."
2. One's most staunchly believed facts could be conceived of as hypotheses held with high degrees of conviction.
3. Despite the strength of initial conviction, all of one's beliefs could be modified or abandoned under the appropriate conditions.

Using the construct of "preferred closure," for example, one could attempt to rid oneself of a highly negative attitude toward a given person or topic by deliberately recalling objectives or desires with which the attitude in question was at variance. A person holding a negative attitude toward his or her spouse, for instance, might think of a goal whose attainment requires the spouse's close cooperation. Or the emotional upheaval occasioned by an unexpected disruption of one's life plans and routines might be mitigated via deliberate attenuation of one's need for closure, by counterarguing its importance.

IMPLICATIONS FOR RESEARCH AND PRACTICE

The lay epistemic analysis not only provides a new perspective for viewing the process of cognitive therapy, it has numerous implications for research aimed at providing empirical evidence for its various propositions, as well as for novel ways of doing cognitive therapy if such supportive evidence were indeed obtained. Turning first to possible research that could be fruitfully conducted under the present framework, questions such as the following come to mind.

1. Can one establish for every client a hierarchy of epistemic authorities to whom this person might be differentially responsive? Would such a hierarchy correlate positively with the efficacy of change accomplished via the various authorities?

2. How can one employ the person's needs for closure and openness in order to appropriately unfreeze dysfunctional beliefs and refreeze more functional alternatives in their stead?

3. How does the client's view of himself or herself as an epistemic authority affect his or her differential responsiveness to personal experience? (Would a person with a positive view of self as epistemic authority be particularly prone to accept hypotheses if he or she personally experienced their implications? Similarly, would a person with a negative view of self as an epistemic authority be relatively unresponsive to personal experiences?)

4. Would a person's deductive powers determine the mode of cognitive influence to which he or she is most likely to respond? For example, someone with weak deductive powers might have difficulty in deriving much information from personal experiences, insofar as these assume an ability to deduce specific implications from a given hypothesis before comparing them with the experiential evidence.

5. Would certain characteristics of beliefs determine the most efficient mode of their induction? For example, relatively vague concepts, whose implications are not entirely clear, might be imparted more efficiently via the influence of external authority or motivational factors than via personal experiences that might be ambiguous.

These research questions are merely a sample of those implied by the present epistemic framework and relevant to the topic of cognitive therapy. Some such research is already underway at Tel Aviv University and we hope that more will soon be initiated. But even before all the data are in it is possible to adumbrate the image of therapy emerging from the present analysis. First and foremost, this would be a highly contingent kind of therapy that derives particular treatment procedures from the client's specific circumstances. This implies an extensive diagnostic stage in which such circumstances are carefully delineated. There would be no a priori commitment to focusing on specific "irrational" beliefs or to an invariant sequence of treatment techniques to which all clients are undifferentially exposed. The diagnostic stage just referred to would aim to tailor the *what* and the *how* of the indicated cognitive change uniquely for each individual.

Thus, the therapist would aim to establish (1) *what* frustrated goal apparently is responsible for a particular person's distress and (2) *why* the individual perceives this goal as frustrated. In light of the information available to him or her, the therapist would determine whether the client's goal does appear to be frustrated and why. Is it because the goal seems unrealistic given the person's specific capabilities, or because he or she has failed to apply the appropriate means of attaining the goal? Answers to these questions would furnish the necessary base for choosing the appropriate direction in which the process of therapeutic persuasion should aim in a given instance. The therapist would decide whether the client's goals might best be shifted, whether the client might best be induced to try a new means of getting to those goals, or whether he or she might best reassess and consequently abandon his or her frustrative belief in the light of new evidence and arguments.

The diagnostic stage recommended by the present analysis should also aim to characterize the client's unique epistemic sensitivities and predispositions. An attempt should be made to identify his or her positive and negative epistemic authorities and to ascertain how positive is his or her self-view as an epistemic authority. The strength of the client's needs for closure and openness should be assessed, and alternative salient needs possibly pertinent to the dysfunctional beliefs should be identified.

Subsequent treatment would be closely tailored to the person's epistemic style and the kind of cognitive shift that seems most indicated. For example, a client with a particular respect for expert authority might be profitably exposed to individual sessions with the therapist, whereas an individual with high regard for group authority might be more profitably exposed to therapy in group settings, and a person with high confidence in his or her own expertise or authority in a given area might be exposed to relevant personal experiences. Dysfunctional beliefs would be addressed from the viewpoint of the needs they might be tacitly serving. An attempt might be made to convince the client that those very beliefs may lead to the frustration of other important needs and/or that the needs implicitly assumed to be served by the dysfunctional beliefs can be fulfilled more efficiently otherwise. An appropriate use would be made of the client's openness and closure needs at the respective stages of unfreezing and refreezing the appropriate beliefs.

To summarize, this chapter presented a new framework for viewing the enterprise of cognitive therapy, based on an analysis of lay epistemology. While sharing with several alternative approaches the assumption that cognitions are the critical mediators of suffering and distress, the present framework differs in important theoretical respects from major cognitive therapy approaches. At the same time, it provides a general conceptual scheme within which therapeutic procedures and techniques conducted within the alternative approaches could be interpreted in common language. Last but not least in importance, the present theoretical framework was shown to be of heuristic value for guiding future research on cognitive therapy and to have specific implications for ways in which the practice of cognitive therapy could be rendered more efficient.

ACKNOWLEDGMENTS

Support was provided to Dr. Kruglanski by the Ford Foundation Grant 9404, received through the Israel Foundations Trustees, and by the Israel Academy of Science Grant 9693.

The authors are indebted to Dr. Azy Barak for insighful comments on an earlier draft of this chapter.

REFERENCES

Alloy, L. B., & Abramson, L. Y. (1979). Judgment of contingency in depressed and nondepressed students: Sadder but wiser? *Journal of Experimental Psychology: General, 108*, 441–485.

Alloy, L. B., & Abramson, L. Y. (1988). Depressive realism: Four theoretical perspectives. In L. B. Alloy (Ed.), *Cognitive processes in depression*. New York: Guilford.

Asch, S. E. (1952). *Social psychology*. Englewood Cliffs, NJ: Prentice-Hall.

Bandura, A. (1977). Self-efficacy: Toward a unifying theory of behavioral change. *Psychological Review, 84,* 191–215.

Barber, B. (1952). *Sciences and the social order.* New York: Collier.

Bartley, W. W., III. (1962). *The retreat of knowledge.* New York: Knopf.

Beck, A. T. (1963). Thinking and depression. *Archives of General Psychiatry, 9,* 324–333.

Beck, A. T. (1976). *Cognitive therapy and the emotional disorders.* New York: International Universities Press.

Bechtold, A., Naccarator, M. E., & Zanna, M. P. (1986). *Need for structure and the prejudice-discrimination link.* Paper presented at the annual meeting of the Canadian Psychological Association, Toronto, Ontario.

Beck, A. T., Rush, A. J., Shaw, B. F., & Emery, G. (1979). *Cognitive therapy of depression.* New York: Guilford.

Bruner, J. S. (1957). On perceptual readiness. *Psychological Review, 64,* 123–152.

Campbell, C. T. (1969). Prospective: Artifact and control. In R. Rosenthal & R. C. Rosnow (Eds.), *Artifact in behavioral research.* San Diego, CA: Academic.

Cook, T. D., Gruder, C. L., Hennigan, K. M., & Flay, B. R. (1979). History of the sleeper effect: Some logical pitfalls in accepting the null hypothesis. *Psychological Bulletin, 86,* 662–679.

Ellis, A. (1973). *Humanistic psychotherapy: The rational-emotive approach.* New York: Julian Press.

Ellis, A. (1977). The basic clinical theory of rational-emotive therapy. In A. Ellis & R. Grieger (Eds.), *Handbook of rational emotive therapy.* New York: Springer.

Ellis, A. (1978). The rational emotive approach to counselling. In A. M. Buck's (Ed.), *Theories of counseling.* New York: McGraw-Hill.

Ellis, S., & Kruglanski, A. W. (1987). *On learning from experience: The role of our epistemic authority.* Unpublished manuscript. University of Maryland.

Festinger, L. (1957). *A theory of cognitive dissonance.* Evanston, IL: Row, Peterson.

Frank, J. D. (1973). *Persuasion and healing.* Baltimore, MD: John Hopkins University Press.

Frenkel-Brunswik, E. (1949). Intolerance of ambiguity as emotional and perceptual personality variable. *Journal of Personality, 18,* 108–143.

Fried, Y., & Agassi, J. (1976). *Paranoia: A study in diagnosis.* Boston, MA: D. Reidel.

Freund, T., Kruglanski, A. W., & Schpitzajzen, A. (1985). The freezing and unfreezing of impressional primary: Effects of the need for structure and the fear of invalidity. *Personalty and Social Psychology Bulletin, 11,* 479–487.

Greenwald, A. G., Baumgardner, M. H., & Leippe, M. R. (1979). *In search of reliable persuasion effects: III. The sleeper effect is dead: Long live the sleeper affect.* Unpublished manuscript, Ohio State University.

Harvey, J. H., & Weary, G. (1984). Current issues in attribution theory and research. *Annual Review of Psychology, 35,* 427–459.

Heider, F. (1958). *The psychology of interpersonal relations.* New York: Wiley.

Higgins, E. T., King, G. D., & Mavin, G. (1982). Individual construct accessibility and subjective impressions and recall. *Journal of Personality and Social Psychology, 43,* 35–47.

Higgins, E. T., Rholes, S., & Jones, C. R. (1977). Category accessibility and impression formation. *Journal of Experimental Social Psychology, 13,* 141–154.

Higgins, E. T., & King. G. (1981). Accessibility of social constructs: Information processing consequences of individual and contextual variability. In N. Cantor & J. Kihlstrom (Eds.), *Personality, cognition and social interaction.* Hillsdale, NJ: Erlbaum.

Higgins, E. T., Bargh, J. A., & Lombardi, W. (1985). The nature of priming effects on categorization. *Journal of Experimental Psychology: Learning, Memory and Cognition, 11,* 69–99.

Hoveland, C. I., Lumsdaine, A. A., & Sheffield, F. D. (1949). *Experiments on mass communication*. Princeton, NJ: Princeton University Press.

Hoveland, C. I., Janis, I. L., & Kelley, H. H. (1953). *Communication and persuasion: Psychological studies of opinion change*. New Haven, CT: Yale University Press.

James, W. (1890). *Principles of psychology*. New York: Holt.

Jamieson, D. W., & Zanna, M. P. (in press). Need for structure in attitude formation and expression. In A. R. Pratkanis, S. J. Breckler, & A. G. Greenwald (Eds.) *Attitude structure and function*. Hillsdale, NJ: Erlbaum.

Jones, E. E., & Davis, K. E. (1965). From acts to dispositions. In L. Berkowitz (Ed.), *Advances in experimental social psychology*. (Vol. 2). New York: Academic.

Kanfer, F. H. (1975). Self-management methods. In F. H. Kanter & A. P. Goldstein (Eds.), *Helping people change*. Elmsford, NY: Pergamon.

Kelley, H. H. (1967). Attribution theory in social psychology. In D. Levine (Ed.), *Nebraska symposium on motivation*. Lincoln, NE: University of Nebraska Press.

Kelley, H. H. (1971). *Attribution in social interaction*. Morristown, NJ: General Learning Press.

Kelley, H. H. (1973). The process of causal attribution. *American Psychologist, 28*, 107–128.

Kopel, S., & Arkowitz, H. (1975). The role of attribution and self-perception in behavior change: Implications for behavior therapy. *Genetic Psychology Monographs, 92*, 178–212.

Kruglanski, A. W. (1975). The endogenous–exogenous partition in attribution theory. *Psychological Review, 82*, 387–406.

Kruglanski, A. W. (1979). Causal explanation, teleological explanation: On radical particularism in attribution theory. *Journal of Personality and Social Psychology, 37*, 1447–1457.

Kruglanski, A. W. (1980). Lay epistemo-logic process and contents. *Psychological Review, 87*, 70–87.

Kruglanski, A. W., & Ajzen, I. (1983). Bias and error in human judgment. *European Journal of Social Psychology, 13*, 1–44.

Kruglanski, A. W., & Freund, T. (1983). The freezing and unfreezing of lay inferences: Effects on impressional primacy, ethnic stereotyping and numerical anchoring. *Journal of Experimental Social Psychology, 19*, 448–468.

Kruglanski, A. W., Friedland, N., & Farkash, E. (1984). Layperson's sensitivity to statistical information: The case of high perceived applicability. *Journal of Personality and Social Psychology, 46*, 503–518.

Kruglanski, A. W., & Klar, I. (1987). A view from a bridge: Synthesizing the attribution and cognitive consistency paradigm from a lay-epistemic perspective. *European Journal of Social Psychology, 17*, 211–241.

Kruglanski, A. W. (in press–a). The cognitive-motivational bases of human knowledge: A theory of lay-epistemics. New York: Plenum.

Kruglanski, A. W. (in press–b). Motivations for judging and knowing: Implications for causal attribution. In E. T. Higgins & R. M. Sorrentino (Eds.), *Handbook of motivation and cognition: Foundations of social behavior* (2nd ed.). New York: Guilford.

Kruglanski, A. W., & Mayseless, O. (1987). Motivational effects in the social comparison of opinions. *Journal of Personality and Social Psychology, 53*, 834–842.

Kuhn, T. S. (1962). *The structure of scientific revolutions*. Chicago: University of Chicago Press.

Kuhn, T. S. (1970). Logic of discovery or psychology of research? In I. Lakatos & A. Musgrave (Eds.), *Criticism and the growth of knowledge*. Cambridge: Cambridge University Press, 1–23.

Lazarus, A. A. (1971). *Behavior therapy and beyond*. New York: McGraw-Hill.

Lazarus, R. S. (1980). Cognitive behavior therapy as psychodynamics revisited. In M. J. Mahoney (Ed.), *Psychotherapy process: Current issues and future directions*. New York: Plenum.

Lewinsohn, P. N., Mischel, W., Chaplin, W., & Barton, R. (1980). Social competence and depression: The role of illusory self-perceptions? *Journal of Abnormal Psychology, 89*, 203–212.

Mahoney, M. J. (1974). *Cognitive and behavior modification*. Cambridge, MA: Ballinger.

Mahoney, M J. (1976). *Scientist as subject: The psychological imperative.* Cambridge, MA: Hallinger.

Mahoney, M. J. (1977a). Publication prejudices: An empirical study of confirmatory biases in the peer review system. *Cognitive Therapy and Research, 1,* 161–175.

Mahoncy, M., & Mahoney, K. (1976). *Permanent weight control.* New York: Norton.

Mayseless, O., & Kruglanski, A. W. (1987). What makes you so sure? Effects of epistemic motivations on judgmental confidence. *Organizational Behavior and Human Decision Processes, 39,* 162–183.

McGuire, W. J. (1969). The nature of attitudes and attitude change. In G. Lindzey & E. Aronson (Eds.), *The Handbook of social psychology* (Vol. 3, 2nd ed.). Reading, MA: Addison-Wesley.

Meichenbaum, D. (1977a). *Cognitive-behavior modification.* New York: Plenum.

Meichenbaum, C. (1977b). Dr. Ellis, please stand up. *The Counseling Psychologist, 7,* 43–44.

Mischel, W. (1979). On the interface of cognition and personality: Beyond the person–situation debate. *American Psychologist, 34,* 740–754.

Murray, E. J., & Jacobson, L. I. (1978). Cognition and learning in traditional and behavioral therapy. In S. L. Garfield & A. E. Bergin (Eds.), *Handbook of psychotherapy and behavior change: An empirical analysis.* New York: Wiley.

Nelson, R. E., & Craighead, W. E. (1977). Selective recall of positive and negative feedback, self-control behaviors, and depression. *Journal of Abnormal Psychology, 86,* 379–388.

Nisbett, R. E., & Schachter, S. (1966). Cognitive manipulation of pain. *Journal of Experimental Social Psychology, 2,* 227–236.

Osgood, I. E., & Tannenbaum, P. H. (1955). The principles of congruity in the prediction of attitude change. *Psychological Review, 62,* 42–55.

Popper, K. R. (1959). *The logic of scientific discovery.* New York: Harper & Row.

Popper, K. R. (1966). *Conjectures and refutations.* New York: Basic Books.

Popper, K. R. (1973). *Objective knowledge: An evolutionary approach.* Oxford: Clarendon.

Raimy, V. (1975). *Misunderstandings of the self.* San Francisco: Jossey-Bass.

Raush, H. S., & Raush, C. L. (1968). *The half-way house movement: A Search for sanity.* New York: Appleton–Century–Crofts.

Rosenberg, M. J. (1960). Cognitive reorganization in response to the hypnotic reversal of attitudinal effect. *Journal of Personality, 28,* 39–63.

Rosenthal, T., & Bandura, A. (1978). Psychological modeling: Theory and practice. In S. L. Garfield & A. E. Bergin (Eds.), *Handbook of psychotherapy and behavior change: An empirical analysis.* New York: Wiley.

Ross, L., Rodin, J., & Zimbardo, P. G. (1969). Toward an attribution therapy: The reduction of fear through induced cognitive-emotional misattribution. *Journal of Personality and Social Psychology, 12,* 279–288.

Sanbomatsu, D. M., & Fazio, R. H. (1987). Unpublished data, University of Indiana.

Shelton, J. L., & Ackerman, J. M. (1976). *Homework in counseling and psychotherapy.* Springfield, IL: Charles C Thomas.

Smock, C. D. (1955). The influence of psychological stress on the "intolerance of ambiguity." *Journal of Abnormal and Social Psychology, 50,* 177–182.

Storms, M. D., & Nisbett, R. E. (1970). Insomnia and the attribution process. *Journal of Personality and Social Psychology, 16,* 319–328.

Strong, S. R. (1970). Causal attribution in counseling and psychotherapy. *Journal of Counseling Psychology, 17,* 388–399.

Strong, S. R. (1978). Social psychological approach to psychotherapy research. In S. I. Garfield & A. E. Bergin (Eds.), *Handbook of psychotherapy and behavior change: An empirical analysis.* New York: Wiley.

Tversky, A., & Kahneman, D. (1974). Judgment under uncertainty: Heuristics and biases. *Science, 188,* 1124–1131.

Valins, S. (1966). Cognitive effects of false heart-rate feedback. *Journal of Personality and Social Psychology, 4*, 400–408.

Weimer, W. E. (1979). *Psychology and the conceptual foundations of science.* Hillsdale, NJ: Erlbaum.

Weiner, B., Frieze, I., Kukla, A., Reed, L., Rest, S., & Rosenbaum, R. M. (1971). *Perceiving the causes of success and failure.* Morristown, NJ: General Learning Press.

Yates, A. J. (1975). *Theory and practice in behavior therapy.* New York: Wiley.

Zuckerman, M. (1979). Attribution of success and failure revisited, or: The motivational bias is alive and well in attribution theory. *Journal of Personality, 47*, 245–287.

IV

*Interaction of Clinicians'
and Patients' Cognitive Biases*

10

Clinician and Patient as Aberrant Actuaries: Expectation-based Distortions in Assessment of Covariation

NAOMI TABACHNIK KAYNE
LAUREN B. ALLOY

ASSESSMENT OF COVARIATION IN THE CLINIC

Consider the following clinical phenomena:

1. Many clinicians continue to use and report great confidence in certain psychodiagnostic tests as an aid to classifying patients, despite the fact that the validity of these instruments has consistently been demonstrated to be low or nonexistent (Chapman & Chapman, 1967, 1969). Treatment programs are often based on the diagnoses derived, in part, from these tests.

2. Psychiatrists, clinical psychologists, and graduate students in clinical psychology who listened to a tape-recorded interview of a normal man tended to diagnose this man as psychotic if told that a prestigious person in their field had said "the patient looked neurotic but actually was quite psychotic" (Temerlin, 1968, p. 350).

3. Eight "sane" people successfully gained admission to 12 different psychiatric institutions with a diagnosis, in all but one case, of schizophrenia. The mean length of hospitalization for these "pseudopatients" was 19 days. Not one was discharged as "normal"; instead, all were given discharge diagnoses of schizophrenia in "remission" (Rosenhan, 1973).

4. Psychotherapy outcome studies in which the assessment of therapeutic outcome is likely to be biased (e.g., is conducted by raters who are not blind to treatment condition) tend to find that the favored therapy works best. In contrast, those studies with unbiased assessment of outcome are likely to show no differences between the therapies compared.

5. A depressed man claims, "I'm responsible for the violence and suffering in the world" (Beck, 1967, p. 24), whereas another states "What's the use. I had tried so hard to make something of myself, but the struggle seemed useless. Life seemed utterly futile" (Reid, 1910, p. 613).

6. In Freud's (1909/1950) famous case study of Little Hans, psychoanalytic therapy proceeded by attempting to induce Hans to perceive the connection between his phobia of horses and an underlying fear of his father. The cure of Hans's phobia was thought by Freud to depend upon Hans's insight into the symbolic meaning of his symptom. Similarly, in Mary Cover Jones's (1924) famous case of Little Peter (the precursor to systematic desensitization), Peter's phobia of rabbits was treated by pairing a rabbit with an unconditioned stimulus (food) that elicited positive emotional reactions. The success of treatment was attributed to Peter's formation of a new association between the rabbit and food.

Each of these phenomena is probably quite familiar to the clinically knowledgeable reader. The first is an example of what Chapman and Chapman (1967, 1969) have termed "illusory correlation": the report by clinicians and naive observers of a correlation between psychodiagnostic test signs and patients' symptoms which, in reality, are not correlated or are correlated to a smaller degree than that reported. The succeeding two examples are instances of "labeling bias." Exposure to the general label "patient" (or to more specific diagnostic labels such as "psychotic" or "schizophrenic") tends to influence the clinician's interaction with a patient in such a way as to confirm the original label in the clinician's ultimate diagnosis. The fourth example illustrates what might be called "therapy outcome bias." Practicing clinicians generally believe that therapeutic techniques toward which they are favorably predisposed are more effective in remediating patients' symptoms than are alternative treatment strategies. Moreover, their beliefs are often confirmed when they carry out empirical outcome studies. Yet when well-controlled comparison experiments are conducted, their favored strategies often show no advantage over alternative therapies. The fifth instance describes the perceptions of two depressed patients with regard to their control over environmental events. One appears to show an exaggerated estimate of his impact on the world while the other believes that his actions are futile. Finally, the last item describes prototypical examples of psychoanalytic and behavioral therapies for eliminating phobias. Both treatments appear to involve the formation of a new connection on the part of the patient.

What does this myriad assortment of clinical phenomena have in common? We believe they are all instances of covariation assessment in the clinic. A covariation refers to the relationship between two events and may be defined in terms of their cooccurrence, that is, the degree to which one event occurs more often in the presence than in the absence of the other event. Information about the relationships or covariations between events in the world provides people with a means of explaining the past, controlling the present, and predicting the future, thereby maximizing the likelihood that they can obtain desired outcomes and avoid aversive ones. For example, the young child who comes to associate fighting with her brother with a spanking from her father may infer that the cause of her father's anger is her naughtiness. Knowledge about this causal relationship would allow the child to predict in future situations what behaviors make her father angry, thus enabling her to avoid aversive spankings altogether. In addition, she may be able to learn to control her father's anger, perhaps by crying, in order to escape spankings once they have begun.

Assessments of covariation comprise an important component of many of the clinician's tasks, much of patients' psychopathology, and much of the therapeutic process itself. In diagnosing a patient, the clinician must be able to accurately detect which symptoms covary together, which symptoms are associated with which diagnostic categories and, if using psychological tests, which test responses are related to which pathologies. Consideration of the illusory correlation and labeling biases indicates that such judgments are often in error and can lead to interventions for psychiatric patients based on faulty or incomplete diagnoses. As a psychotherapist, the clinician must judge the covariation between various treatment strategies and therapeutic outcome. The phenomenon of therapy outcome bias suggests that clinicians' assessments of therapeutic effectiveness are not based solely on objective data but are also influenced by their general expectations or theories about psychopathology and psychotherapy.

Recent work in social and clinical psychology attests to the importance of causal explanation and perceived contingencies for people's physical and psychological well-being. Attribution theorists (e.g., Heider, 1958; Jones & Davis, 1965; Jones & Nisbett, 1971; Kelley, 1967, 1972, 1973; Weiner, 1972, 1974, 1979) as well as many "insight-oriented" clinicians (e.g., Adler, 1927; Ellis, 1962; A. Freud, 1946; S. Freud, 1920/1966; Jung, 1953) have consistently emphasized the role of understanding the causes of one's own and other's behavior in coping with the demands of everyday life. In addition, a growing body of empirical research has shown that the belief, even if nonveridical, that one can predict and/or control aversive outcomes decreases subjective pain and stress, reduces subjective and objective components of anxiety and depression, reverses problem-solving and performance deficits associated with lack of control, reduces the negative impact of institutionalization on the aged, decreases the susceptibility to heart disease, cancer, and other illnesses and finally, may even postpone death (see Alloy, Kelly, Mineka, & Clements, in press; Averill, 1973; Baum & Singer, 1980; Folkman, 1984; Garber & Seligman, 1980; Scheier & Carver, in press; Seligman, 1975; Sklar & Anisman, 1981; Taylor & Brown, in press; Thompson, 1981, for reviews of this work).

A unique characteristic of the clinical setting is that it provides a particularly rich source of data for examining individual differences in such covariation judgments. Across a number of theoretical perspectives (e.g., Arieti, 1970; Beck, 1967, 1976; Bruch, 1973; Ellis, 1962; Rogers, 1961; Seligman, 1975), both psychotic and neurotic symptoms have been attributed to faulty or inappropriate cognitions that are deficient or divergent from the norm. It is probably safe to assume that most people seeking (or being sent for) clinical assistance are there because some aspect of their adaptive behavior has gone awry. An analysis of adaptive behavior as consisting, in part, of the ability to detect covariations in one's environment suggests that some of the maladaptive behavior of psychopathological individuals may be rooted in an inability to accurately detect covariations. For example, manic individuals have often been characterized as suffering from exaggerated beliefs about their degree of personal control over life events (Beck, 1976; Langer, 1975), while paranoid individuals may be viewed as suffering from equally irrational beliefs about other people's control over life events. Similarly, both of the depressed individuals in our examples appeared to hold unrealistic beliefs concerning their impact on life events. In this context, we might expect that psychopathological individuals' judgments of contingency would be especially subject to bias from distorted generalized beliefs about the self and the world.

A covariation perspective for the clinic would not be complete without an exploration of the way in which clinicians' and patients' assessments of covariation interact. As do all people, both clinicians and patients must make judgments of covariation to explain, predict, and control their own environments. Within the context of a therapeutic relationship (i.e., the points at which clinicians' and patients' environments intersect), however, clinicians and patients both engage in explanation, prediction, and control of the patient's world. Because each of these individuals may be expected to bring a different set of expectations about event relationships into therapy sessions, their assessments of covariations in the patient's environment may be highly discrepant.

Regardless of whether the therapist's or the patient's judgments of the significant contingencies in the patient's environment are more accurate, a critical component of successful therapy is that it entails a change in patients' beliefs about the covariations between events in their lives. For example, orthodox psychoanalytic therapy involves inducing patients to reassess covariations and perceive the relationship between "crazy" symptoms and underlying conflicts or wishes that they do not initially perceive (e.g., the case of Little Hans). Through the appropriate timing of interpretations and working through of the transference relationship, patients in psychoanalytic treatment can come to recognize heretofore unacknowledged symptom–conflict contingencies. Similarly, behavioral therapists attempt to aid patients to form associations between adaptive behaviors and environmental reinforcements and to break already established contingencies between dysfunctional behaviors and environmental reinforcements (e.g., the case of Little Peter). Cognitive therapists, too, through the use of techniques such as reattribution training and correction of cognitive distortions (Beck, Rush, Shaw, & Emery, 1979) encourage patients to reappraise their inaccurate and maladaptive assessments of covariation.

While there has been a recent upsurge of interest in attributional accounts of psychopathology and psychotherapy (see, for example, the contributions to this volume), relatively little work has been devoted to the role of covariation assessment in the clinical setting. This state of affairs is rather surprising given the theoretical importance assigned to the use of covariation information by social perceivers during the causal attribution process (Heider, 1958; Kelley, 1967, 1972, 1973). In this chapter, we apply a recent theoretical model of people's and animals' covariation assessments in general (Alloy & Tabachnik, 1984) to clinicians' and patients' covariation assessments in particular, in an attempt to formulate a covariation perspective for the clinic. In so doing, we pose an important question as the focus of our chapter: To what extent are clinicians' and patients' judgments of the relationships between clinically significant events based on objective covariation information encountered in their everyday experience versus their preconceptions or beliefs about the relationships between events in the world? In other words, in an attempt to understand the therapeutic (or countertherapeutic) interaction, we examine the extent to which clinicians and patients make sense of or impose sense upon the world. The characterization of humankind as imposing sense upon the world carries with it the implication of lesser accuracy than the alternative view of humans as making sense of their world. In this chapter, however, we will present evidence from the experimental laboratory and the clinic demonstrating that both processes are involved and that clinicians' and patients' assessments of covariation are influenced jointly by expectations and data. We will see, though, that when covariation judgments go awry (as in our examples at the beginning of this chapter), it is usually because they have been biased by a priori expectations or beliefs.

AN EXPECTATION BY SITUATIONAL INFORMATION INTERACTIONAL FRAMEWORK

Recently, Alloy and Tabachnik (1984) proposed a theoretical framework for understanding and integrating people's and animals' covariation assessments (see also Goddard & Allan, 1988, for a critique of this theory and Alloy, 1988b, for a reply). According to Alloy and Tabachnik, two sources of information jointly determine the perception of covariation between two events: the situational information about the objective contingency between the events provided by the current environment and the organism's prior expectations or beliefs about the event covariation in question. The degree to which any particular subjective perception of contingency matches the objective contingency between events represented in the environment (i.e., is accurate) depends on the relative strength of prior expectations and current situational information. The concept of expectation strength refers to the degree to which the organism holds extant beliefs about the nature of the event covariation in question. Such expectations may arise either from prior direct experience with the events in similar situations or from other indirect sources (e.g., cultural transmission, biological predispositions). The concept of strength of situational information refers to the relative availability to the organism of information about event relationships in the present environment. Current situational information can be unavailable or weak because it is insufficient in quantity to support a covariation perception (e.g., the organism has had little experience with the events in the current situation) or because it is ambiguous (e.g., it is not very diagnostic).

Table 10-1 summarizes the interaction between prior expectations and current situational information in determining covariation perception and provides the theoretical framework we will use to organize and explain clinicians' and patients' covariation assessments. The cells of Table 10-1 (see Alloy & Tabachnik, 1984) are formed by considering the four possible combinations of low versus high strength of prior expectations and low versus high strength of current situational information.[1]

In Cell 1 of Table 10-1, both situational information and prior expectations regarding the covariation between two events are weak. Under such conditions, people and other animals should have great difficulty forming a perception of covariation. Thus, they will forgo making a covariation inference at all or will make an inference with low confidence.

In Cell 2 of the table, the strength of prior expectations about an event covariation is high, although as in Cell 1, situational information is weak and provides relatively little support for any particular covariation perception. Under these conditions, covariation judgments are predicted to be direct reflections of a priori expectations. People and animals will be likely to form strong covariation perceptions in the face of weak evidence. The relative accuracy of such perceptions will depend on the accuracy or appropriateness of the individual's extant beliefs.

In Cell 3, available situational information about the covariation between two events is stronger than are prior expectations. In the absence of strong beliefs about the covariation in question, humans' or animals' perceptions should accurately reflect the objective contingency between the events represented in the environment.

Finally, Cell 4 is of particular interest for understanding the nature of the interaction between data-based and expectation-based processing in covariation inference. Cell 4 represents the situation in which both expectations and situational information strongly and independently suggest a particular covariation perception. If a priori expectations and situational information are congruent (Case 1 of Cell 4), the organism is in a fortunate position. With a minimal amount of cognitive effort, he or she could make a covariation judgment with accuracy and extreme confidence. If, however, generalized beliefs and situational information are incongruent and imply different percep-

---

1. Although we view strength of expectations and situational information as continua, for ease of exposition, we present these two dimensions as dichotomies in Table 10-1.

TABLE 10-1. The Role of Prior Expectations and Situational Information in the Covariation Assessment Process

	The strength of current situational information about the covariation between two events	
	Low	High
The strength of prior expectations about the covariation between two events Low	CELL 1 A person or animal will refrain from making any causal attribution or covariation inference at all or will make a judgment with low confidence.	CELL 3 A person or animal will make a causal attribution or perceive covariation in line with the available situational information.
High	CELL 2 A person or animal will make a causal attribution or perceive covariation in line with his or her or its prior expectancies.	CELL 4 *Case 1.* Prior expectations and situational information imply the same causal attribution or covariation perception. A person or animal will make an attribution or perceive covariation with extreme confidence. *Case 2.* Prior expectations and situational information imply different causal attributions or covariation perceptions. A person or animal is in a cognitive dilemma (see text for ways in which a person or animal might solve this dilemma).

Note. From "Assessment of covariation by humans and animals: The joint influence of prior expectations and current situational information" by L. B. Alloy and N. Tabachnik, 1984, *Psychological Review, 91,* 112–149. Copyright 1984 by the American Psychological Association. Reprinted by permission of the author.

tions of contingency (Case 2 of Cell 4), the perceiver is faced with a "cognitive dilemma" (Metalsky & Abramson, 1981). The person or animal could distort, misremember, or disregard current situational information and make a covariation judgment in line with prior expectations or ignore or reinterpret strongly held beliefs about the covariation in question in favor of the situational information instead. Empirical evidence suggests that people and animals faced with this dilemma generally make covariation assessments biased in the direction of their initial expectations (see Alloy & Tabachnik, 1984). However, a substantial amount of belief-contradictory evidence or particularly salient contradictory evidence can lead to covariation assessments pulled in the direction of current situational information. In other words, the relative strength of the two sources of information determine the nature and accuracy of the covariation perception.

Alloy and Tabachnik (1984) reviewed four lines of research that provided support for this model of covariation assessment. Of most relevance to this chapter is their review of work on people's use of covariation information in making causal attributions and people's abilities to actually detect covariations when allowed to directly observe event co-occurrences.

ASSESSMENT OF COVARIATION: LABORATORY INVESTIGATIONS

Researchers have examined people's use and detection of relationships between events in two general types of laboratory tasks. In attribution studies, subjects are typically presented with real or hypothetical behaviors or events for which they must determine the cause. Investigators in this tradition are interested in the manner in which people make use of available information about the covariation between the behavior or event in question and possible causes of this behavior or event in arriving at causal attributions. It is interesting to note that in this line of research, subjects are provided with "prepackaged" covariation information; no attempt is made to examine the processes by which subjects actually perceive contingencies. In judgment-of-contingency or -covariation studies, however, subjects are given the opportunity to observe cooccurrences between events and are required to determine the objective degree of contingency between these events. The focal concern in this line of research is with the degree of correspondence between subjective judgments of covariation and the objective contingencies presented.

THE USE OF COVARIATION INFORMATION IN CAUSAL ATTRIBUTION

Data-based Processing

Beginning with Kelley's (1967) seminal paper on attribution theory, social psychologists have viewed the layperson as a "naive scientist" who rationally seeks out covariation information in order to draw inferences about the causes of events. According to Kelley, three kinds of covariation information are relevant to making causal attributions: *consensus*, *consistency*, and *distinctiveness*. Consensus information refers to the degree to which an event covaries across people. Consistency information refers to the degree to which an event covaries over time. Distinctiveness information refers to the degree to which an event covaries across stimuli in the environment.

Similar to a scientist conducting a statistical analysis of variance, an individual utilizes the available consensus, consistency, and distinctiveness information to arrive at the most plausible cause for the event or behavior in question. Kelley and his colleagues (Kelley, 1967, 1972, 1973; Orvis, Cunningham, & Kelley, 1975) have delineated the particular patterns of situational information that lead people to make specific attributions. If consensus, consistency, and distinctiveness are all high, Kelley argues that the event will be explained in terms of some property of the environmental stimulus. In contrast, if the pattern of information about an event points to low distinctiveness, low consensus, and high consistency, the event will be attributed to some property of the person who engaged in the event. Finally, a pattern of high distinctiveness but low consensus and consistency, is associated with an attribution to some special property of the situation in which a behavior or event occurred.

McArthur (1972, 1976) provided empirical support for Kelley's characterization of the layperson as a data-based processor, who makes attributions by utilizing available configurations of situational information. Subjects in an experimental group were presented with consensus, consistency, and distinctiveness information with which to disambiguate the cause of several hypothetical responses; control subjects were given no situational information. McArthur found that those subjects who were provided with information about the degree of covariation of a response across actions, time, and stimuli, systematically employed this information in making statistically based causal inferences.

Expectation-based Processing

In many situations, however, immediately available data are insufficient for making an assessment of the covariation between an event and its possible causes. How do people make causal attributions in situations in which consensus, consistency, and distinctiveness are insufficient for making statistically based inferences? Kelley (1972, 1973) suggested that in such situations people invoke causal schemata. A causal schema can be conceptualized as an assumed pattern of data about covariation between an event and its possible causes. In other words, a causal schema represents a person's theories or beliefs about the way in which causes and effects in the world covary with each other.

Orvis *et al.* (1975) provided direct support for the notion that people expect certain configurations of consensus, consistency, and distinctiveness information to correspond to particular causal attributions. In a paradigm similar to McArthur's (1972), subjects were presented with a number of descriptions of behavioral events. In their study, however, Orvis *et al.* presented subjects with incomplete patterns of consensus, consistency, and distinctiveness information and required them to make causal attributions. In addition, some subjects were also asked to judge the level of missing information. Both attributions and completions reflected the tendency of subjects to associate certain patterns of consensus, consistency, and distinctiveness (i.e., those a priori predicted by Kelley's theory) with particular attributions.

Joint Influence of Expectation- and Data-based Processing

Kelley's characterization of people as naive scientists emphasizes that people are more likely to make rational or data-based attributions when situational information is sufficient to make a statistically based inference, but are more likely to make expectation-based attributions when such situational information is unavailable. However, attribution theorists have provided evidence for the biasing influence of generalized expectations on causal attributions even in situations in which there is *sufficient* information to conduct a complete causal analysis. Ross (1977), for example, pointed out a number of ways in which the lay attributor distorts systematically his or her interpretation of behavioral events in the direction of implicit theories about human nature and situational forces.

First, Ross (1977) cited the ubiquity of the fundamental attribution error, or the tendency of the "intuitive psychologist" to overestimate the importance of personal or dispositional factors relative to environmental factors as causes of behavior (Heider, 1958; Jones & Nisbett, 1971; Kelley, 1972). In this sense, the intuitive psychologist is a personality theorist who gathers and interprets data in light of the theory that human behavior is in large part a function of individual differences. Both the personality theorist and intuitive psychologist seem to hold generalized beliefs that behaviors tend to be highly stable over time and generalizable across situations (see Nisbett & Ross, 1980, for a discussion of how such beliefs in temporal stability and cross-situational consistency of behavior might form). In Kelley's (1972, 1973) causal schema terms, these generalized beliefs would consist of an assumed pattern of high consistency and low distinctiveness information. Even when situational information pointing to the importance of environmental factors as a cause of behavior is encountered, this situational information is interpreted only in light of the attributor's assumed pattern of covariation data. Such inconsistent situational information may be given relatively little weight in the judgment process because it represents only one instance of contrary evidence against a large background of experiential data summarized by the causal schema (see also Nisbett & Ross, 1980).

Another source of error that Ross postulates for the intuitive psychologist is the behaviorist bias: the tendency to attend only to actions and occurrences when making inferences, seriously disregarding information conveyed in nonoccurrences of behaviors or events. It may be that occurrences of behaviors or events are more vivid or salient, and therefore command more attention than do nonoccurrences of behaviors or events, analogous to the manner in which "figure" stands out from "ground" in perceptual phenomena. Indeed, evidence from cognitive and social psychology on concept learning and hypothesis testing attests to the tendency of people to overlook and underutilize negative instances relative to positive instances (Bruner, Goodnow, & Austin, 1956; Hovland & Weiss, 1953; Levine, 1969; Mynatt, Doherty, & Tweeney, 1977, 1978; Schustack & Sternberg, 1981; Smoke, 1933; Snyder & Cantor, 1979; Snyder & Swann, 1978a, 1978b; Wason & Johnson-Laird, 1972). Interestingly enough, by psychologically eliminating statistically relevant data about nonoccurrences, the intuitive psychologist's behaviorist bias might actually transform situations in which covariation information is sufficient to make accurate causal inferences into situations in which information is insufficient to do so.

McArthur (1972) noted an additional bias in the data-based attribution process. People consistently underutilize consensus information (i.e., base-rates) relative to consistency and distinctiveness information (see also Ajzen, 1977; Hansen & Donoghue, 1977; Hansen & Lowe, 1976; Kahneman & Tversky, 1973; Nisbett & Borgida, 1975; Nisbett, Borgida, Crandall, & Reed, 1976; Wells & Harvey, 1977).

Kassin (1979b) introduced a distinction between explicit base-rates, or consensus information, and implicit base-rates, or normative expectancies, as a means of explaining the underutilization of consensus effect. Implicit base-rates consist of knowledge or beliefs about the behavior of others that may be derived from everyday experiences as well as cultural transmission. According to Kassin, such implicit base-rates serve as the initial basis for prediction and causal attribution, in light of which explicit situational information is examined and assimilated. If explicitly presented consensus information is either highly redundant with or highly inconsistent with an individual's schema about consensus, the explicit consensus information will tend to be underutilized. Kassin (1979b) suggests several cognitive strategies by which this might occur. Explicit consensus that is highly redundant with an individual's normative expectancies may be underutilizied because it provides little or no information over and above that provided by no explicit consensus (Nisbett *et al.*, 1976; Wells & Harvey, 1977). On the other hand, an individual may discount explicit consensus that is highly inconsistent with his or her normative expectancies by assuming that this situational information is derived from either a biased or small, and therefore unrepresentative, sample (Kassin, 1979a; Wells & Harvey, 1977). To the extent that implicit base-rates presuppose a particular pattern of consensus information, so will corresponding causal inferences about situational information be biased in their direction (see Ajzen, 1977, and Tversky & Kahneman, 1978, for a demonstration of the manner in which causal theories influence the use of base-rate information in prediction).

Apparently, the causal attribution process is neither purely data-based nor purely expectation-based. Instead, the research and theory on people's use of covariation information in causal inference indicates that consistent with the Alloy and Tabachnik (1984) model, there is an interaction between data and expectations with preconceptions serving to bias or distort presumably more rational or data-based processing (see also Metalsky & Abramson, 1981).

DETECTION OF COVARIATION

In the previous section we reviewed people's use of covariation information in making causal attributions. In these tasks, as already noted, subjects are presented with configurations of information about covarying cues, rather than having to detect the covariation between potential causes and effects themselves. Rarely, in the real world, does covariation information come in such prepackaged form. Below, we discuss basic laboratory research on the covariation judgment process itself. Surprisingly, although people appear to be accurate detectors under certain circumstances, much of the time they misjudge event relationships systematically.

To account both for the accuracies and inaccuracies of people's covariation detection, the Alloy and Tabachnik (1984) model emphasizes the nature of the interaction between currently available covariation data and prior expectations or beliefs. Consistent with the model, a concise summary of the empirical work on people's covariation detection is that judgments of covariation are relatively accurate when people lack strong beliefs or expectations about the relationship between the events in question (Cell 3 of Table 10-1) or when the situational information concerning the objective degree of correlation between the events is congruent with people's preconceptions about the event relationship (Case 1 of Cell 4, Table 10-1). When objective data and preconceptions are incongruent (Case 2 of Cell 4, Table 10-1), judgments of covariation are frequently erroneous and biased in the direction of initial expectations.

Experiments that examine people's judgments of correlation for non-binary or continuous events (Beach & Scopp, 1966; Erlick, 1966; Erlick & Mills, 1967) find that people are quite sensitive to the actual degree of correlation between the events and do not make systematic errors. These studies have in common the fact that they used stimulus events (e.g., pairs of numbers or locations on dials) for which subjects presumably have no relevant expectations (i.e., Cell 3 of Table 10-1). In the absence of strong biasing preconceptions about the event relationships, subjects rely on the available situational information in making their judgments and thus, subjective judgments of correlation mirror objective correlations.

In contrast, studies that examine people's covariation judgments for dichotomous stimulus events (e.g., Alloy & Abramson, 1979; Jenkins & Ward, 1965; Peterson, 1980; Ward & Jenkins, 1965) have involved situations for which subjects can reasonably be expected to have relevant preconceptions. The results of these studies are mixed, supporting the appropriateness of subjective judgments under some circumstances and the inappropriateness of such judgments under other circumstances. Ward and Jenkins (1965), for instance, had subjects estimate the degree of covariation between cloud seeding and rainfall and found that subjects relied on the frequency of cases in which cloud seeding was followed by rain; and possibly those cases in which absence of cloud seeding was followed by no rain. It is common knowledge that cloud seeding is at least partially effective in producing rain, so it is reasonable to assume that Ward and Jenkins's subjects expected cloud seeding to be followed by rain and absence of cloud seeding to be followed by no rain. Thus, the use of expectation-confirming cases offers a plausible account of the Ward and Jenkins data. Note that subjects' judgments were relatively accurate when the programmed experimental contingencies were consistent with a priori expectations. Similarly, Peterson (1980) argued that people do not expect events within psychology experiments to be random and, thus, he found that subjects only detected a noncontingent relationship between two stimulus events if the hypothesis of noncontingency was introduced into the experimental setting.

Finally, a large number of covariation detection studies have investigated people's ability to detect the relationship and lack of relationship between their own responses and environmental outcomes (e.g., Alloy & Abramson, 1979; Bruner & Revusky, 1961; Catania & Cutts, 1963; Jenkins & Ward, 1965; Langer, 1975; Langer & Roth, 1975; Wortman, 1975; Wright, 1962). Abramson and Alloy (1980) and Langer (1975) have argued that the use of responses and outcomes as the events in judgment-of-contingency studies is likely to bring into play strong, well-articulated schemata about personal control over events. According to Abramson and Alloy (1980), such control schemata are based on a substantial amount of prior experience suggesting that one's own behavior produces outcomes when outcomes follow responses closely in time, when features such as practice, choice, and foreknowledge of the goal are associated with responding, and when outcomes are frequent and desirable. Such control schemata may also include expectations that one's own behavior does *not* control outcomes when responses are *not* followed closely in time by outcomes, when elements such as practice, choice, and foreknowledge of the goal are *not* associated with responding, and when outcomes are infrequent and undesirable.

In their review, Alloy and Tabachnik found that the presence of these control-relevant factors influenced the level of accuracy of subjects' judgments in this group of covariation-detection studies. The presence of these factors was associated with accurate judgments when the objective contingencies presented by the experimenters happened to match expectations about personal control (Case 1 of Cell 4, Table 10-1) as well as with distorted judgments when the objective experimental contingencies were inconsistent with expectations of personal control (Case 2 of Cell 4, Table 10-1). For example, Alloy and Abramson (1979) found that nondepressed subjects detected a zero response-outcome contingency accurately if the outcome occurred infrequently and/or was a negative event (control schema-consistent) but overestimated the degree of contingency if the experimental outcome occurred frequently and/or was a positive event (control schema-inconsistent). In addition, when the experimental outcome was negative but subjects actually exerted control over the outcome (control schema-inconsistent), nondepressed subjects underestimated the degree of contingency (see the section "Depression: An example?" in this chapter, for a discussion of depressed people's failure to succumb to such biases). Similar arguments regarding the joint influence of objective covariation data and biasing control expectations can be advanced to explain the results of other response–outcome covariation detection studies (e.g., Bruner & Revusky, 1961; Catania & Cutts, 1963; Jenkins & Ward, 1965; Langer, 1975; Langer & Roth, 1975; Wortman, 1975; Wright, 1962).

Several more recent covariation detection studies have explicitly measured or manipulated subjects' expectations about event relationships and current situational data and provide more direct support for the Alloy and Tabachnik interactional model of covariation assessment (e.g., Benassi, Knoth & Mahler, 1985, Experiment 1; Chatlosh, Neunaber, & Wasserman, 1985, Experiment 2; Coppel & Smith, 1980; Crocker & Taylor, 1978; Dickinson, Shanks, & Evenden, 1983; Hoch, 1985; Jennings, Amabile, & Ross, 1982; John, Scott, & Bettman, 1986; Kameda, 1985; Neunaber & Wasserman, 1986, Experiment 2; Shanks, 1985a, 1985b; Spears, van der Pligt, & Eiser, 1986; Strube, Lott, Heilizer, & Gregg, 1986; Trolier & Hamilton, 1986; Yates & Curley, in press).

For example, Strube *et al.* (1986) found that in line with the interactional prediction of the theory, observers' expectations about the amount of control different actors would exert over an experimental outcome interacted with the objective contingency between the actors' responses and the outcome in determining the observers' control judgments for the actors. Similarly, in a video game, Dickinson *et al.* (1983) asked subjects to judge the contingency between the firing of a shell and tank destruction when the two events were either unrelated (Experiment 2) or positively related (Experiment 3). Half of the subjects observed a positive covariation between another event, mine explosions, and the occurrence of tank destruction prior to observing the shell–tank destruction contingency. This prior exposure to the mine–tank destruction contingency blocked subjects' detection of the shell–tank destruction contingency, leading to lower judgments of control by these subjects than by subjects who were not exposed to the first covariation. Dickinson *et al.* suggested that subjects' expectations that the mines were an effective cause of destruction interfered with their perceptions of the shell's effectiveness. That is, prior mine-destruction expectations biased interpretation of subsequent situational information indicating shell-destruction covariation.

Alloy, Crocker, and Tabachnik (1980) explicitly measured depressed and nondepressed students' expectations about the relationships between various kinds of events and examined the influence of these expectations on subsequent data-based covariation judgments. They reasoned that the previous work (Alloy & Abramson, 1979, 1982; Alloy, Abramson, & Viscusi, 1981) demonstrating that nondepressed people are often less accurate in judging the degree of contingency between their responses and outcomes than are depressed people might be partially due to the distorting effect of strong schemata regarding personal control over positive outcomes and lack of control over negative outcomes characteristic of nondepressed but not depressed people (see the section "Depression: An Example?" in this chapter, for a discussion of this work). The fact that nondepressives' judgments of contingency are as accurate as those of depressives when such control schemata are likely to be absent (Alloy, Abramson, & Kossman, 1985) is consistent with this idea.

The results of the Alloy *et al.* (1980) studies were rather surprising. First, subjects' judgments of covariation were highly correlated with the actual correlation between the events, although subjects did show a general bias to perceive events as more positively related then they actually were. However, the significant correlation between covariation judgments and objective contingency indicates that experiential data does, indeed, influence the covariation judgment process. A second general finding was that consistent with previous work (Abramson & Alloy, 1981; Alloy & Abramson, 1979, 1982; Alloy *et al.*, 1981), depressives' judgments of covariation were more accurate overall than were nondepressives' judgments. However, the general tendency of nondepressives' judgments to be less accurate than those of depressives depended upon experimental condition. Nondepressives' judgments were especially biased in cases where they had strong preconceptions about the event relationships presented.

The Normative Model of Assessment of Covariation

By what mechanisms do preconceptions about event relationships exert their influence on covariation judgments? Alloy and Tabachnik (1984) reviewed some of the cognitive processes by which strong expectations about event relationships could bias or distort covariation judgments based on Crocker's (1981) description of five steps in the normative model of covariation assessment (see also Nisbett & Ross, 1980).

Step 1. Data Relevant to the Covariation Judgment

The first step in making a covariation judgment involves deciding what information (how much and what kinds of data) one needs to make the estimate. The normative model prescribes that in order to determine the degree of covariation between two binary events one must know the number of cases that fall into each cell of a 2 × 2 contingency table (see Table 10-2). For example, if an individual wishes to know whether there is a covariation between gender and personality such that women tend to be sociable, he or she would need to know how many women are sociable (Cell A of Table 10-2), how many women are not sociable (Cell B), how many men are sociable

TABLE 10-2. Four Types of Evidence Relevant to Judging the Covariation between Gender and Sociability

		Sociability	
		Sociable	Unsociable
Gender	Female	A	B
	Male	C	D

(Cell C) and how many men are not sociable (Cell D). Cells A and D constitute *confirming cases* (i.e., cases that confirm there is a relationship between being a woman and being sociable because when one of these conditions is absent, the other is also absent). Cells B and C constitute *disconfirming cases* (i.e., cases in which the relationship does not hold).

Research from concept formation (e.g., Bruner *et al.*, 1956; Hovland & Weiss, 1953; Levine, 1969; Smoke, 1933) and hypothesis-testing tasks (Mynatt, Doherty, & Tweeney, 1977, 1978; Schustack & Sternberg, 1981; Snyder & Cantor, 1979; Snyder & Swann, 1978a, 1978b; Wason & Johnson-Laird, 1972) suggests that people may regard information that can confirm, rather than disconfirm, their expectations as more relevant to covariation judgments. In particular, Crocker (1982) and Schustack and Sternberg (1981) have found that people overwhelmingly regard positive confirming cases (Cell A cases) as most relevant to answering a covariation question or evaluating the causal relationship between a target cause and outcome (see also Arkes & Harkness, 1983) while negative confirming cases (Cell D cases) are regarded as least relevant (see the section "The Use of Covariation Information in Causal Attribution" in this chapter, for an explanation of the reduced salience of negative instances). In addition, it is reasonable to assume that individuals will be likely to seek out less information relevant to making a covariation judgment when they have strong preconceptions about the relationship between two events than when they have weak preconceptions because less information is needed to confirm strong preconceptions (Metalsky & Abramson, 1981). Thus, expectations may be likely to exert a biasing influence early in the covariation judgment process by affecting the amount and kinds of data people seek.

Step 2. Sampling Cases

Once an individual has decided what instances are relevant to making a covariation judgment, he or she must sample instances from the total population of potential instances. For most covariation questions, not every relevant instance can be observed and used as data in the covariation judgment. According to the normative model, the instances one samples should be representative of the population of instances as a whole.

Crocker (1981) has noted two sources of bias likely to occur in people's sampling of evidence. First, whether one recalls relevant instances from past experiences or seeks out new instances, the people and/or events which serve as a database for a covariation judgment are likely to be a nonrandom sample because the people and events any individual is exposed to are not a random sample. Second, research from other judgment tasks has shown that people seem to be unaware that the smaller one's sample, the more likely it is to be atypical of the general population from which it is drawn (Kahneman & Tversky, 1972; Tversky & Kahneman, 1971; but see Kassin, 1979a, for an exception to this finding). People's ignorance of the "law of large numbers" may lead them to sample fewer cases than is statistically necessary for making an accurate covariation estimate. People may be especially likely to sample only a few cases if they have strong preconceptions about the nature of the covariation in question.

In most covariation-detection studies, possible biases in information search (Step 1) and the sampling of cases (Step 2) are eliminated because subjects are presented with a sample of relevant cases selected by the experimenter. However, in their studies examining the influence of expectations on covariation judgments, Alloy *et al.* (1980) also investigated whether biases in people's judgments result from the kinds and amount of information they seek when making a covariation estimate (see also John *et al.*, 1986). They found that information-search strategies accounted, in large part, for the patterns of errors in subjects' covariation judgments. In general, subjects requested more information regarding occurrences of causes and outcomes than nonoccurrences across all experimental conditions. This tendency, however, was less strong for depressed subjects than for nondepressed subjects. That is, depressives' information search was more balanced than that of nondepressives. Because of their tendency to ask for more occurrences than nonoccurrences, subjects received more confirming cases (Cells A and D of Table 10-2) than disconfirming cases (Cells B and C of Table 10-2), although again, this was less true for depressives. These findings regarding information search may explain both subjects' general bias toward perceiving events as more positively related than they actually were and depressed subjects' greater accuracy overall than nondepressed subjects.

Step 3. Classifying Instances

Once instances have been sampled, they must be interpreted and classified as confirming or disconfirming cases. Crocker (1981) has described the role of the perceiver's initial preconceptions in introducing systematic bias into the process of classifying instances, and thus ultimately, in covariation judgments.

Initial expectations may influence the interpretation of ambiguous events as well as the credibility of evidence that disconfirms these expectations. It has been widely demonstrated that ambiguous instances are usually perceived to be congruent with a priori beliefs (e.g., Allport, 1954; Bower, Black, & Turner, 1979; Bruner & Postman, 1949; Bugelski & Alampay, 1961; Leeper, 1935; Nisbett & Ross, 1980; Owens, Bower, & Black, 1979; Posner, & Keele, 1968). In addition, instances that contradict one's expectations may be discredited either by attributing their occurrence to unstable or external factors (e.g., Bell, Wicklund, Manko, & Larkin, 1976; Deaux, 1976; Deaux & Emswiller, 1974; Feldman-Summers, & Kiesler, 1974; Hayden & Mischel, 1976; D. Taylor & Jaggi, 1974) or by regarding the sample from which they were drawn as unrepresentative of the general population (e.g., Hansen & Donoghue, 1977; Kassin, 1979a, 1979b; Wells & Harvey, 1977). Finally, Crocker (1981) has pointed out that negative confirming cases (Cell D of Table 10-2) may not be recognized as such and instead may be coded as irrelevant to the covariation in question. This result is attributed to people coding instances on the basis of what they are rather than on the basis of what they are not.

Step 4. Recalling the Evidence and Estimating Frequencies

Once relevant evidence has been sampled and interpreted, it must be recalled and the totals of confirming and disconfirming cases that have been observed must be estimated. Many studies in cognitive and social psychology have demonstrated that information that is consistent with an individual's schemata or expectations is more likely to be recalled than information that is irrelevant to or inconsistent with the individual's schemata (e.g., Bartlett, 1932; Bower *et al.*, 1979; Bransford & Johnson, 1973; Cantor & Mischel, 1979; Cohen, 1977; Frederiksen, 1975; Hamilton, 1977; Hamilton & Rose, 1980; Owens *et al.*, 1979; Rothbart, Evans, & Fulero, 1979; Sulin & Dooling, 1974; Thorndyke, 1977; Zadny & Gerard, 1974; but see also Hastie, 1981; Hastie & Kumar, 1979). In addition, studies of recognition memory have often found that people go beyond the information given and intrude events that are consistent with their schemata but were never actually observed (e.g., Bartlett, 1932; Bransford, Barclay, & Franks, 1972; Bower *et al.*, 1979; Cantor & Mischel, 1977; Harris, Teske, & Ginns, 1975; Johnson, Bransford, & Solomon, 1973; Owens *et al.*, 1979; Woll & Yopp, 1978). Thus, covariation judgments may be biased by a tendency for people to overrecall expectation-consistent instances relative to inconsistent instances as well as by a tendency to remember expectation-consistent instances that never occurred.

Several investigators have demonstrated that memory biases distort co-variation judgments (e.g., Arkes & Harkness, 1983; Crocker & Taylor, 1978; Shaklee & Mims, 1982; Trolier & Hamilton, 1986). For example, Alloy *et al.* (1980) found that biased recall of observed evidence contributed to depressed and nondepressed subjects' patterns of covariation judgments. In general, recall biases worked to enhance the biasing effects of information-search strategies. As expected from the discussion above, nondepressives recalled more evidence that confirmed than disconfirmed their initial expectations. That is, when they expected a cause to be correlated with the experimental outcome, they recalled more confirming than disconfirming cases and when they expected the cause to be uncorrelated with the experimental outcome, they recalled more disconfirming than confirming cases. Depressed subjects, on the other hand, recalled more evidence that disconfirmed rather than confirmed their preconceptions.

Step 5. Combining the Evidence to Make a Judgment

The final step in making a covariation judgment involves combining the recalled frequencies of observed cases into a covariation estimate. This is the step that is most clearly specified by the normative or statistical model for covariation assessment. For continuous variables, the statistically appropriate method for assessing covariation involves computing a Pearson r. Given the complicated nature of the formula for the Pearson r, it is highly unlikely that people actually calculate a Pearson r when estimating most covariations. However, the results of covariation-detection studies involving continuous variables suggested that intuitive judgments are highly related to estimates based on the Pearson r, although they are not the optimal estimates predicted by the normative model (see above).

For binary or dichotomous variables, there are several statistical methods for combining evidence into a covariation estimate, including the chi-square statistic, phi coefficient, delta coefficient, or the association coefficient. All of these metrics have in common that they utilize all four cells of the 2×2 contingency table (see Table 10-2). The results of covariation-detection studies employing binary events (see above) indicated that although intuitive covariation judgments were sometimes accurate, much of the time they were biased by strong preconceptions regarding the event relationships in question. We have argued that preconceptions may influence each stage of the covariation judgment process, and Step 5 is no exception. People may rely on the frequency of cases that fit their expectations in computing a covariation estimate. Studies that have reported reliance on confirming cases or positive confirming cases can be interpreted in this manner (Alloy & Abramson, 1979; Arkes & Harkness, 1983; Crocker & Taylor, 1978; Jenkins & Ward, 1965; Smedslund, 1963; Ward & Jenkins, 1965).

Our review of laboratory research suggesting that people's causal attributions and judgments of covariation are jointly influenced by the data of everyday experience and prior beliefs is consistent with contemporary developments in cognitive and social psychology. These developments emphasize the ubiquity with which people "go beyond the information given" and use "schemata" or generalized knowledge about the self and the world in the perception, interpretation, and comprehension of everyday experience (see Taylor & Crocker, 1981, for a review). Importantly, however, whereas work in cognitive and social psychology emphasizes the schema or belief-based nature of information-processing, in the remainder of this chapter we will continue to show that assessments of covariation, both accurate judgments and errors, are influenced jointly by expectations and data.

Motivational/Affective Influences on Covariation Detection

To this point, our perspective on covariation assessment has emphasized the biasing influence of expectations about event relationships on data-based covariation judgments. However, needs and wishes are also likely to play an important role in the covariation judgment process. For example, a growing body of research indicates that people's tendency to attribute success or positive events to internal factors such as ability and failure or negative events to external factors such as luck, usually referred to as the self-serving attributional bias, may stem from a motivation to protect and/or enhance self-esteem (Bradley, 1978; D. Miller, 1978; D. Miller & Ross, 1975; Snyder, Stephan, & Rosenfield, 1978; Weary, 1980; Wortman, Costanzo, & Witt, 1973; Zuckerman, 1979; but see Tetlock & Levi, 1982, for a discussion of the inconclusiveness of the motivation–cognition debate).

D. Miller (1976) provided a convincing demonstration of the role of motivational factors in causal attributions by manipulating both ego involvement in a task (high or low) and task outcome (success or failure). He reasoned that if a motivation to bolster self-esteem mediates self-serving attributional biases, people who are ego involved in a task should be more likely to show this bias than people who are not so involved. As predicted, subjects in the high ego involvement condition made more self-protective attributions when they thought they did poorly on a task than did subjects in the low ego involvement condition. In addition, although less compelling, there was also some evidence that subjects in the high ego involvement condition made more self-enhancing attributions when they thought they did well on a task than did subjects in the low ego involvement condition. Future research and theorizing will need to consider the interaction of beliefs, motives, moods, and situational information in the covariation judgment process (but see the section "Depression: An Example?" in this chapter, for a self-serving motivational account of covariation judgments).

CLINICIAN AS ABERRANT ACTUARY

Given the theoretical framework we have outlined to understand people's covariation judgments in general (Alloy & Tabachnik, 1984), we are now better equipped to examine the impact of covariation judgments in the clinical setting. In this section we will analyze, from a covariation perspective, two of the clinician's tasks. As a psychodiagnostician, the clinician must assess the degree of relation between test signs and symptoms and between symptoms and diagnoses. Consideration of the illusory correlation and labeling biases suggests that clinicians' judgments of covariation evidence expectation-based biases similar to those of people in general laboratory tasks. As a psychotherapist, the clinician must determine the covariation between treatment strategy and patient improvement. In this context we will examine the extent to which expectations about treatment effectiveness influence assessments of therapeutic outcome.

CLINICIANS' ASSESSMENTS OF PATIENTS

Illusory Correlation in the Clinic

Chapman and Chapman (1967) noted a source of much concern for the field of clinical psychology: a persistent and systematic inaccuracy in psychodiagnosticians' assessments of covariation. Despite a massive accumulation of evidence indicating the invalidity of various psychodiagnostic tests—that there is no or minimal correlation between the results of these tests and patient symptomatology—many clinicians share the opinion that identifiable characteristics of test performance are correlated with patient behavior. Chapman and Chapman characterized this systematic error in psychodiagnosis as an example of a broader class of errors, which they term "illusory correlation: the report by observers of a correlation between two classes of events which, in reality, (a) are not correlated, or (b) are correlated to a lesser extent than reported, or (c) are correlated in the opposite direction than that which is reported" (Chapman, 1967, p. 194).

In an attempt to understand the nature and development of illusory correlation among psychodiagnosticians, Chapman and Chapman (1967) conducted an investigation that simulated the conditions a beginning clinician might encounter when obtaining first-hand experience with a diagnostic test (a test of particularly low predictive validity, the Draw-a-Person [DAP] test). In a preliminary survey of practicing psychodiagnosticians, Chapman and Chapman had found empirical evidence of an illusory correlation among them. There was substantial agreement about which DAP test signs were related to which patient characteristics. Despite objective findings to the contrary (Chapman & Chapman, 1967), 80 percent of the clinicians surveyed reported that worry about manliness was associated with manly or muscular DAP drawings and 91 percent reported that suspiciousness was associated with drawings with atypical eyes. Chapman and Chapman then presented naive subjects with a series of DAP drawings. Each drawing was paired arbitrarily with a set of statements about the symptoms of the patient who allegedly drew the picture. After inspecting 45 drawings randomly paired with symptom statements, subjects were asked to determine which DAP responses had been associated with particular patient characteristics. Surprisingly, naive subjects, on the basis of their observations of symptom statements paired *noncontingently* with patient characteristics, "rediscovered" illusory correlates that were virtually identical to those of the clinicians.

Since Chapman (1967) had found that semantic associations were mediating illusory correlations in a verbal learning study, Chapman and Chapman hypothesized that associative strength was underlying clinicians' illusory correlations also. Not surprisingly then, when an independent group of subjects was asked to judge the associative strength between symptom statements and parts of the body contained in DAP drawings, it was discovered that illusory correlates, in fact, frequently had been based on high strength associates. Ironically, this effect was much more pronounced for practicing clinicians than for naive subjects.

Of particular interest for our chapter is the additional finding that illusory correlates corresponded to people's a priori beliefs or expectations about the relationships between test signs and symptom statements. Even when a group of subjects were not shown any stimulus materials, but were asked about the degree of relationship between test signs and symptom statements, their "dataless" judgments closely resembled the judgments of clinicians and subjects who had been given an opportunity to carefully examine relevant data. For example, 91 percent of the subjects in the "data-less" condition expected that a patient who is worried about his manliness would draw a manly or muscular person on the DAP test. Fifty-five percent expected that a suspicious patient would draw a figure with atypical eyes.

The Chapmans' work on illusory correlation in psychodiagnosis is yet another demonstration of the biasing role of expectations on the accurate detection of the objective relationship between events. Indeed, the Chapmans' work seems to point all too clearly to the troubling implications of belief- or expectation-based information-processing. The importance of accurate psychodiagnosis in the clinic cannot be overemphasized. Quite often the treatment of choice for any particular patient will be chosen solely on the basis of his or her clinical diagnosis. Likewise, the reactions of others in the patient's environment will be influenced strongly by their diagnosis.

Moreover, as Chapman and Chapman (1967) themselves have pointed out, the naive subjects in their illusory correlation studies observed the psychodiagnostic materials under conditions far more conducive to accurate detection of the objective contingencies than that usually faced by clinicians. For example, the practicing clinician may be reinforced in his or her detection of illusory correlates by similar observations of fellow clinicians. Yet, as the Chapmans' studies show, such "consensual validation" can often reflect shared systematic error rather than shared accuracy. In addition, in making judgments about the relationships between diagnostic test signs and patients' symptoms, clinicians typically must deal with a much larger number of symptoms over a substantially longer time interval than did the naive observers of the Chapmans' study. Consequently, illusory correlation bias is likely to be even more pervasive in the conventional clinical situation than in the experimental laboratory (See Lueger & Petzel, 1979).

More recently, the illusory correlation paradigm has been applied to an understanding of stereotypes (Hamilton, Dugan, & Trolier, 1985; Hamilton & Gifford, 1976; Hamilton & Rose, 1980; Spears *et al.*, 1986) and phobias (Mineka & Tomarken, in press). However, here we only review additional research that has been conducted on illusory correlations in psychodiagnosis. Although by far the most outstanding finding across these investigations is the robustness of this phenomenon, in fact, under several conditions, illusory correlations were successfully attenuated. In the interest of more fully understanding the role of covariation judgments in the clinic, we evaluate the conditions under which such illusory correlations occur, as well as the conditions under which they may be attenuated.

In a series of experiments following their original demonstration of illusory correlation, Chapman and Chapman (1967) investigated the phenomenon further. In one experiment, subjects' viewing time of stimulus materials was increased from one to three sessions. In another experiment, within one session, subjects were allowed unlimited time to examine the drawing–symptom pairings (although still in sequential order), and were offered monetary incentives for accurate assessment. In a last experiment, subjects were allowed unlimited time to examine test-sign–symptom pairings in whatever order they wished. In addition, subjects were also permitted to rearrange cards, group them, shuffle them, take notes, and so forth; again, monetary incentive was offered for accurate assessment. Under all of the above conditions, illusory correlations persisted. In fact, even when negative correlations between pattern characteristics and illusory correlates were built into the stimulus materials, this phenomenon showed remarkable resistance. It is important to note, however, that the extent to which illusory correlates were reported in each of these experiments was not identical. When subjects were allowed freedom to group cards, there was a statistically significant drop in the percentage of subjects reporting four out of the six illusory correlates. When a negative correlation was built into the stimulus materials, the percentage of subjects reporting each of the five illusory correlates investigated was halved.

Starr and Katkin (1969) extended the work on illusory correlation to a test of considerably more predictive validity than the DAP test—the Incomplete Sentences Blank. They reported that even when demands on information-processing were considerably less than in the Chapmans' studies (see also Lueger & Petzel, 1979), subjects rediscovered in noncontingent data the same illusory correlates that clinicians reported for this test. It is also interesting to note that although Starr and Katkin introduced the possibility of randomness into their instructions to subjects, only 8 of the 60 subjects recognized a random relationship between any of the completed sentences and patient descriptors.

In an even more elegant series of studies than their first, Chapman and Chapman (1969) found illusory correlations for a test which consists of both clinically valid and invalid signs—the Rorschach test. Naive subjects given the opportunity to observe a random relationship between patient characteristics and test signs consistently underestimated the relationship between symptom statements and clinically valid signs having a low degree of associative strength (i.e., between monster signs and the symptom of homosexuality), and/or consistently overestimated the relationship between symptom statements and clinically invalid but "popular" test signs having a high degree of associative strength (i.e., between anal responses and homosexuality). Again, the illusory correlates reported by naive subjects corresponded to the invalid test signs that previously had been reported by clinicians. Even when Chapman and Chapman constructed stimulus materials containing contrived validities (67 percent, 83 percent, 100 percent) between "valid" test signs and symptom statements, the clinically popular but invalid signs were still the most frequently reported correlates. Similarly, Werner, Rose, and Yesavage (1983) found that clinicians' predictions of patients' likelihood of becoming violent were based on invalid patient characteristics that were cognitively associated with violence (e.g., hostility, paranoia). In contrast, patient symptoms that actually do correlate with future violence were not utilized by clinicians in their forecasts of violence.

Although the evidence reviewed thus far seems to point overwhelmingly to expectation-based assessments of covariation in psychodiagnosis, subjects' judgments about the cooccurrence of test signs and symptom statements in these studies were not, in fact, based solely on their beliefs or expectations about sign–symptom relationships (see also Nisbett & Ross, 1980). Rather, consistent with the Alloy and Tabachnik (1984) model, subjects' judgments may be more appropriately described as an interaction between their beliefs and the data of experience.

In a comparison among subjects' judgments under differing conditions of contrived validity between the valid but unpopular test signs and symptom statements (50 percent, 67 percent, 83 percent, 100 percent), it is evident that subjects were not totally unresponsive to situational information. When the popular invalid sign was anality, as the level of contrived validity increased, the percentage of subjects reporting the unpopular valid sign as a correlate increased substantially, and the percentage of subjects reporting the popular but invalid sign decreased. In addition, for all three levels of contrived validity subjects were more likely to report valid than filler signs. It is also important to note that when Chapman and Chapman constructed stimulus materials so that illusory correlates were absent and there was an 83 percent contrived validity between the relevant symptom statements and clinically valid test signs, the two clinically valid signs were the most frequently reported correlates.

It is possible to examine the work on illusory correlation in psychodiagnosis with respect to Table 10-1. Subjects in the typical illusory correlation experiment (and by implication, clinicians) are faced with a Cell 4 (i.e., Case 2 of Cell 4) cognitive dilemma. For example, whereas the situational information presented to subjects in test-sign–symptom pairings indicates that there is no relationship between any particular test sign and homosexuality, subjects have strong expectations that anality and homosexuality are, in fact, associated. In many of the illusory correlation experiments, subjects seem to resolve this cognitive dilemma by weighting heavily their prior beliefs. However, under conditions in which belief-inconsistent information is more compelling (e.g., when a negative correlation between illusory correlates or contrived validities between valid test signs and symptom statements are built into the stimulus materials, or when subjects are allowed to organize stimulus materials in the way they want), although subjects still resolve their cognitive dilemmas in favor of their prior beliefs, their tendency to do so is greatly attenuated.

Given the troubling implications of the illusory correlation phenomenon for the diagnostic enterprise, numerous attempts have been made to develop training strategies by which this phenomenon might be mitigated. If the illusory correlation phenomenon represents another example of expectation-biased covariation judgments, either of two types of remedial strategies might be effective: a strategy that would increase the salience of situational information or one that would decrease the salience of expectations or beliefs.

Golding and Rorer's (1972) investigation attempted to implement the former type of strategy. Subjects in their study examined the relationship between Rorschach test signs and symptom statements under one of two treatment modes. In a simultaneous feedback condition, subjects were presented with symptom statements and test signs at the same time, as in the Chapman and Chapman studies. In a prediction feedback condition, similar to programmed learning, subjects observed the test signs and were required to predict the associated patient symptom, prior to observing the true value of the symptom. It was predicted that focusing subjects' attention on the data in this way would result in more accurate perception of situational information. Surprisingly, Golding and Rorer did not find differential learning as a function of modes of feedback. Under both conditions, subjects showed an illusory bias, although there was significant reduction in the size of this bias from pre- to posttesting sessions.

The prediction feedback treatment implemented by Golding and Rorer represents an attempt to increase the salience of situational information. Apparently, though, regardless of the emphasis placed on accurate assessment of situational information, it was still overcome by people's prior expectations. Waller and Keeley (1978) contrasted a remedial strategy designed to undermine people's expectations about the relationship between illusory correlates (explanation condition) with a strategy designed to increase the salience of situational information (information feedback condition). All subjects in Waller and Keeley's experiment were trained about the illusory correlation effect on a set of Rorschach stimulus materials. Training involved gaining experience with three separate arrays of cue–symptom pairs: one that contained no relationship between illusory correlate pairs, one that contained a strong positive relationship, and one that contained a strong negative relationship. Subjects were then divided into three sensitization or training conditions. In the explanation condition, prior to viewing any cue–symptom pairs, subjects were given an explanation of the illusory correlation phenomenon and its possible relevance to the experimental task. In the information feedback condition, after viewing each set of stimulus materials, subjects were given feedback about the actual cue–symptom relationship in these materials. In a third condition, subjects were given both types of training. To evaluate the effects of training, in the generalization phase of this study, subjects were asked to make judgments about the relationship between cues and symptoms in a set of DAP test materials.

Waller and Keeley found that regardless of the type of sensitization training subjects experienced, they reported illusory correlates when a zero correlation between these cues and symptoms was built into the stimulus materials. However, when there was a strong negative relationship built into the stimulus materials, subjects attended to the evidence, reporting zero or negative rather than positive relationships between illusory correlate pairs. Interestingly, regardless of whether their final judgments on the generalization materials were accurate or inaccurate, subjects became more confident in their judgments from pre- to posttraining (Einhorn & Hogarth, 1978). Kurtz and Garfield (1978) also found that explaining the illusory correlation phenomenon to subjects and warning them to guard against this bias in their judgments was ineffective in actually reducing the bias.

It appears that illusory correlation in psychodiagnosis is a highly robust phenomenon. Both remedial strategies designed to increase the salience of belief-disconfirming situational information and strategies designed to undermine these beliefs have been rather ineffective (but see Anderson, 1982; Arkes, 1981; Kahneman, Slovic, & Tversky, 1982; and Nisbett & Ross, 1980 for ideas of more effective strategies). Only when stimulus materials were constructed to represent negative relationships between illusory correlates, or positive relationships between valid test signs and symptoms, or when subjects were allowed to group or organize stimulus materials in the manner they wanted (all methods that should increase the strength of situational information), were illusory correlations attenuated significantly.

Waller and Keeley (1978) suggested that the consistent finding of an attenuation of illusory correlation bias under conditions of an objective negative relationship between test-sign–symptom pairs indicates that the maintenance of a biased expectation may be determined by the number of confirmations of the expectation relative to the number of disconfirmations perceived in the data. In the typical illusory correlation paradign, only affirmations are explicitly presented. Negations or disconfirmations must be inferred. For example, subjects might be presented with explicit information that a paranoid person had given an atypical eye response on the DAP test, but would have to infer those instances in which a paranoid person did not give an eye response from information that a paranoid person had given a monster response or animal response, and from instances in which a nonparanoid person had given an eye response. Recall from our discussion of the behaviorist bias (the section "The Use of Covariation Information in Causal Attribution" in this chapter) that people are not particularly adept at drawing such inferences.

Mowrey, Doherty, and Keeley (1979) specifically investigated the influence of negation on the illusory correlation phenomenon. In their experiment, subjects were presented not only with affirmations (e.g., that a paranoid person had given an eye response), but also were given explicit negations (e.g., that a paranoid person did not give an eye response, a person who was not paranoid gave an eye response, and a person who was not paranoid did not give an eye response). Unfortunately, Mowrey *et al.* also found that despite negation operations, the illusory correlation phenomenon still persisted.

It is worth pointing out that the illusory correlation phenomenon does not reflect any particular folly on the part of clinical psychologists and psychiatrists. In fact, the "ancestor" of the illusory correlation studies was conducted by Smedslund (1963) and involved erroneous medical diagnoses given by student nurses. In a first experiment, Smedslund's subjects were asked to examine a deck of 100 cards containing a series of letters representing symptoms along with a series of letters representing diagnoses. Subjects were instructed to look through the pack of cards, focusing entirely on symptom A and diagnosis F, to determine whether A was a useful symptom in the diagnosis of F. A unique aspect of Smedlund's experiment is that subjects were additionally asked to give a verbal description of the relationship which they observed between stimuli, as well as a description of the way in which they arrived at their judgment.

Smedslund concluded that not a single subject had an appropriate concept of correlation, because no one indicated that the relationship between A and F depended on information from all four cells of the 2×2 contingency table (see the section "Detection of Covariation," this chapter). More than half of the subjects indicated that the relationship between A and F depended on the frequency of AFs (a result that is not surprising given Smedslund's instructions to focus on A and F—see Crocker, 1982). In addition, Smedslund found that even when subjects were presented with summary tables of the various combinations of A and F, their judgments of covariation were inaccurate and based primarily on the frequency of AFs (positive confirming cases).

In Smedslund's second experiment, the demands made on subjects' information-processing were reduced considerably. The information conveyed on cards was limited to only $+A$ or $-A$ for symptoms and $+F$ or $-F$ for diagnoses (note that subjects were provided with both affirmations and negations) and subjects were given unlimited time to view cards, sort them in the way they wanted, and take notes. However, even when the task was thus simplified, most of the subjects sorted cards very unsystematically and, therefore, arrived at erroneous estimates of covariation. The only subjects who seemed to be relying on any systematic rule for estimating contingencies, were those who based their judgments on the frequency of AF instances (see also Crocker, 1982; Schustack & Sternberg, 1981).

As with all of the research we have discussed thus far on judgments of covariation in the clinic, the results obtained by Smedslund can be viewed as evidence of the biasing role of prior beliefs on people's processing of situational information. As Smedslund noted, nurses are trained to expect an association between symptoms and diagnoses. These prior beliefs hinder their detection of random or chance relationships between the two. Yet Smedslund's research is not entirely consistent with some of the other research on illusory correlation in psychodiagnoses. For example, whereas Chapman and Chapman (1967) found that allowing subjects the opportunity to organize stimulus materials in the way they wished attenuated the illusory correlation effect, Smedslund found no amelioration in subjects' judgments of covariation under similar conditions. Of course, we might speculate that nurses' expectations about symptom–diagnosis relatedness are much more ingrained than naive subjects' expectations about psychological-test-sign–symptom relatedness, and, therefore, nurses' tendencies to misinterpret, misremember, or overlook contradictory situational information may be much stronger. However, until the appropriate experiment is conducted, the plausibility of this argument remains an empirical question.

At this point, let us caution the behaviorist who may be feeling overly smug about the immunity of his or her "diagnostic systems"—behavior rating scales—to expectation-based biases. Berman and Kenny (1976) conducted a study to investigate how observers' beliefs about the cooccurrence of traits or behaviors systematically bias their ideally objective behavioral ratings. In an initial phase of the experiment, subjects in one group were given a questionnaire to assess their expectations about the co-occurrence of events. From this first phase, three types of trait pairs were selected: those which subjects assumed (i.e., expected) were positively related, unrelated, or negatively related. In a second phase of the experiment, subjects in another group were presented with nine series of slides. Each series of slides provided subjects with information about how eight fictitious individuals fared on the same two traits (high or low), and was designed to represent an objectively positive or negative relationship or no relationship between traits. After viewing each series, subjects were asked to recall how each fictitious individual had been rated on both traits. After viewing all nine series, subjects were asked to rate each fictitious individual on the eighteen traits that had been presented over the course of the experiment. Berman and Kenny found that on both immediate and delayed measures, subjects' ratings were generally a function of the actual correlation between traits, but were biased in the direction of the assumed relationship. In other words, people's assumptions about the cooccurrence of traits resulted in a bias in their ratings that was constant over different levels of correlation.

In summary, it would be unfair to suggest that either clinical psychologists or psychiatrists are more susceptible to an illusory correlation bias in psychodiagnosis than other people. Nurses, "objective raters" on behavior rating scales and naive subjects have shown illusory correlation biases as well. We have argued that subjects in illusory correlation experiments (and by implication, psychodiagnosticians) are faced with a Cell 4 cognitive dilemma (i.e., one in which they expect a certain degree of relatedness between events, but the situational information indicates otherwise). Upon careful examination of subjects' judgments of the co-occurrence of events under such conditions, it is evident that although subjects attend to situational information, their judgments are influenced more by prior beliefs than by current data. The psychodiagnostic process appears to be consistent with the theme we have emphasized throughout this chapter: People's judgments of covariation represent an interaction between the data of experience and their prior beliefs or expectations.

Schwartz (1981) has commented that people do not always behave like rational information processors, or "well-oiled machines," in judgment-of-contingency tasks (see also Kahneman & Tversky, 1973; Nisbett & Ross, 1980; Tversky & Kahneman, 1974; Wason & Johnson-Laird, 1972). Instead, he suggests that people impose hypotheses on such tasks, in the form of "If p, then q." Wason and Johnson-Laird (1972), as well as Reber (1967, 1969, 1976), have demonstrated that when people impose hypotheses on a task, they are likely to seek out and weight more heavily those events that confirm their hypotheses than those that do not. From this view, subjects faced with an illusory correlation task in which they are asked to determine the cooccurrence between test signs and symptoms might form several hypotheses on the basis of their prior beliefs, such as "If the test sign of atypical eyes is present, then most likely the person will be paranoid," but "If the test sign of a manly figure is present, then most likely the person will be concerned about his manliness." Given the paradigm of the typical illusory correlation experiment, in which subjects are presented with all the information about which they are to make their judgments, it is clear that in these instances the illusory correlation phenomenon cannot be attributed to biased information search or sampling processes (Steps 1 and 2 of the normative model). It is not yet clear, however, whether subjects in illusory correlation experiments weight too heavily evidence that is consistent with their hypotheses (Step 5 of the normative model), overrecall expectation-congruent instances and underrecall expectation-incongruent instances (Step 4), or whether they actually fail to encode inconsistent evidence (Step 3). The question remains open for empirical investigation.

Labeling Bias

A second area of research that examines cognitive distortions in psychodiagnosis is research on the "labeling bias" phenomenon. Researchers in this area have been concerned with how the general label "patient" (or the more specific labels of depressive, schizophrenic, and so forth) alter the diagnostic process.

Temerlin (1968) conducted an experiment in which psychiatrists, clinical psychologists and graduate students in clinical psychology, as part of a regular staff meeting at their hospital or clinic, listened to and diagnosed a tape-recorded interview of an actor playing the part of a mentally healthy man. Shortly before listening to the interview, however, subjects in the experimental groups were told that a very prestigious person in their field had found this interview particularly interesting because "the patient looked neurotic but actually was quite psychotic" (p. 350). Control groups, matched for professional identity, did not receive this particular prestige suggestion.

Temerlin's results were quite compelling. Whereas not a single control subject reported that the interviewee was psychotic, 60 percent of the psychiatrists, 28 percent of the clinical psychologists, and 11 percent of the graduate students given the prestige suggestion diagnosed psychosis. In addition to indicating the diagnostic category that best fit the interviewee, the clinicians were also asked to write brief clinical reports, delineating the behavioral basis of their diagnosis. It is interesting that only those subjects whose diagnoses were correct, that is, only those who reported that the interviewee was mentally healthy, gave accurate behavioral descriptions. Despite instructions to the contrary, most subjects reported inferences in place of observations (see also Temerlin & Trousdale, 1969).

Temerlin's results may provide another example of expectation-based covariation judgments in the clinic. That the prestige suggestion in this experiment caused subjects to expect psychosis (see Temerlin, 1968, for an explanation of the greater influence of prestige suggestion on psychiatrists than clinical psychologists and graduate students) and therefore biased their objective processing of the information available in the interview seems to be a relatively straightforward conclusion. However, Temerlin's experiment allows us to go a step further than the experiments on illusory correlation, in examining the mechanisms underlying expectation-based biases. Temerlin presents evidence that those subjects who fell prey to the prestige suggestion did so at the level of encoding (i.e., Step 3 of the normative model) by confusing expectation-based inferences with data-based observations. Thus, the belief that the interviewee was psychotic carried with it an expectation that particular "psychotic" behaviors would be observed. Subjects' encoding of the interviewee's behavior, then, was biased in the direction of their expectations, such that they interpreted ambiguous behaviors as indicative of psychosis.

Sushinsky and Wener (1975) have extended the generality of Temerlin's findings to mental health service workers in general and undergraduate introductory psychology students. In Sushinsky and Wener's study, there are two points of interest for our discussion. First, undergraduates asked to rate the pathology evident in a "normal tape" (modeled after the one used by Temerlin) versus a tape of an actual clinical interview of a hospitalized, nonpsychotic psychiatric patient rated the psychiatric patient as more pathological than the normal individual, regardless of the prestige suggestion that they had received. The fact that subjects were sensitive to the objective level of pathology portrayed in the tapes indicates that the labeling bias phenomenon, similar to the illusory correlation effect, is best conceptualized as an interaction between data-based and expectation-based processing, rather than a function of expectation-based processing alone.

Second, Sushinsky and Wener (1975) attempted to determine whether the labeling bias phenomenon is due to complex cognitive processes of "filtering, distorting and categorizing information" (p. 83) or to biased responding processes (i.e., demand characteristics). Subjects were given the prestige suggestion either before hearing the interview or after hearing the interview but immediately prior to making their ratings. These authors concluded that because subjects' rating did not differ significantly between the two conditions, labeling biases are probably due to response biases rather than data filtering or distorting. We would argue, however, that Sushinsky and Wener's conclusion is unwarranted. The similarity of ratings between the label-before and label-after conditions eliminates the possibility that in this situation labeling biases can be attributed to errors in data selection, data sampling, or encoding. It is possible, however, that biases were a function of distortions in data retrieval (Step 4 of the normative model) or in the weighting of the evidence (Step 5) as well as response processes.

Whereas Sushinsky and Wener demonstrated the generality of the labeling bias phenomenon, Langer and Abelson (1974) established its specificity with respect to the theoretical orientations of clinicians. Langer and Abelson reasoned that behavior therapists, who are trained to be skeptical about the usefulness of diagnostic categories and labels, should be less susceptible to labeling biases than their more traditional colleagues schooled in the medical model of abnormal behavior. Two groups of therapists (behavior therapists and traditional therapists) were shown a videotaped interview of a man who recently had applied for a new job. The interviewee presented himself in such a way that he could be seen either as "sincere and struggling or as confused and troubled" (Langer & Abelson, 1974, p. 6). Before viewing the tape, half of the subjects were told that the interviewee was a job applicant and the other half were told that he was a patient. The results were exactly as predicted. When the interviewee was labeled as a job applicant, there was no difference between mean adjustment ratings given by behavioral and traditional therapists. When the interviewee was labeled as a patient, however, the traditional therapists saw the interviewee as more disturbed than did the behavior therapists.

Sushinsky and Wener's results seemed to indicate that labeling biases should be traced to later cognitive processes such as selective recall or weighting of information. On the other hand, Langer and Abelson's results are more consistent with those of Temerlin, that labeling biases begin at the level of encoding. Although all subjects in both patient and employment interview conditions were shown the identical tape, on open-ended questions traditional therapists given the patient label reported having observed different behaviors than traditional therapists given the job interview label. For example, one traditional therapist in the patient condition claimed that the interviewee was unrealistic because he denied, rationalized, and intellectualized. Traditional therapists in the job applicant condition stated that this same person was reality oriented.

Similar to Langer and Abelson's (1974) emphasis on therapist orientation, Berman and Berman (1983) demonstrated that length of experience or training also influences the degree to which mental health professionals exhibit labeling biases (see also Dubnicki, 1977). Berman and Berman found that the more years of training social workers had undergone, the more likely they were to rate a normal client labeled beforehand as "psychotic" as maladjusted. Berman and Berman suggested that increased professional training and experience may increase the extent to which one "buys into" the medical model and the usefulness of diagnostic labels. In other words, increased professional training may strengthen individuals' expectations associated with diagnostic labels, and therefore, their susceptibility to labeling biases.

A consideration of all of the labeling bias experiments taken together suggests that label-produced expectations may exert their influence at several stages of the covariation judgment process (see the section on "Detection of Covariation" in this chapter). When a label is presented before an individual observes relevant data, expectation-based biases may occur in data selection, sampling, encoding, or recall, whereas when the label is presented after observation of relevant data, biases may be limited to memorial or response processes.

The work of Snyder (1977) suggests a possible explanation for the differential susceptibility of traditional and behavior therapists to labeling biases in psychodiagnoses. Upon reanalysis of Langer and Abelson's data, Snyder found that in the patient label condition, psychodynamically oriented clinicians viewed the locus of the interviewee's problem as more person-based than did behaviorally oriented clinicians. In the job applicant condition, however, the two types of clinicians did not differ in their attributions for the locus of the interviewee's problem. Snyder also found that across all subject and label conditions, the more person-based a judge's attribution for the locus of the interviewee's problem, the greater the perceived maladjustment.

Snyder's results imply that the greater susceptibility of traditional therapists than behavior therapists to labeling biases may be due to the differential expectations elicited for each group by the label "patient." Traditional therapists are more likely to expect that psychopathology (indicated by the label "patient") is at least partially caused by dispositional factors. Behavior therapists, on the other hand, tend to expect that psychopathology is relatively more environmentally controlled. Given the high correlation between perceived maladjustment and perceived locus of pathology, it is no wonder that traditional therapists rated the patient interviewee as considerbly more maladjusted than the job applicant interviewee.

In concluding this section on labeling biases in the clinic, let us note the very famous but controversial study conducted by Rosenhan (1973), which so powerfully calls attention to the real world implications of this phenomenon. Rosenhan asked the basic research question, "Do the salient characteristics that lead to diagnosis reside in the patients themselves or in the environments and contexts in which observers find them?" (p. 251). In other words, within the context of psychodiagnosis, Rosenhan was asking a question similar to the one we have been asking throughout this chapter: Does man make sense of or impose sense upon his world?

Rosenhan investigated this question by conducting an experiment in which eight "sane" people (whom we henceforth will refer to as pseudopatients) gained admission to 12 different psychiatric institutions. All pseudopatients were admitted to their respective hospitals with the presenting complaint that they were hearing unfamiliar voices that seemed to say "empty," "hollow," and "thud." During the initial diagnostic interview, aside from this alleged symptom and falsification of name, vocation, and employment, all other information that pseudopatients provided about themselves was reported to have been factually accurate information about their lives. Pseudopatients had been instructed to discontinue feigning any symptoms of abnormality upon admission to the hospital. In fact, because the pseudopatients were told that they would have to utilize their own devices to get out of the hospital, it was assumed that they were motivated to convince the staff of their normality and to be as cooperative as possible. Rosenhan reasoned that if sanity and insanity (or normality and abnormality) were carried within the person, that is, were inherent in the data rather than dependent upon the context in which it occurs, the sanity of the pseudopatients should be discovered.

The results obtained by Rosenhan present a disappointing picture of the clinical acumen that we might hope to find in psychiatric institutions. Of the eight pseudopatients, all were admitted to psychiatric wards, seven with a diagnosis of schizophrenia and one with a diagnosis of manic depression. Despite their normality, the mean length of hospitalization for these patients was 19 days, with a range of 7 to 52 days. Not one patient was discharged as "sane": All were given discharge diagnoses of schizophrenia in remission.

Rosenhan concluded that once patients were diagnosed as schizophrenic, there was little they could do to dispel this label. He presents evidence that when a person is identified as abnormal, other people's perceptions of his or her behavior are biased by that tag. For example, all pseudopatients were instructed to take extensive notes on their experience. Rosenhan points out that rather than questioning patients about their note-taking, staff members automatically interpreted this behavior as pathological; for example, one nurse reported that "patient engages in writing behavior." As another example, one pseudopatient indicated that his relationship with his wife was close and warm, although occasionally they did argue. In the case summary that was prepared about the patient, he was described as a man who attempts to control his environment, although occasionally this is punctuated by bursts of anger. Rosenhan also called attention to the tendency of staff members to attribute any behavior that they considered deviant on the part of patients to dispositional rather than situational factors. Thus, when a pseudopatient paced the corridor, a nurse asked him, "Nervous?" To which he answered, "No, bored."

Similar to other studies on labeling bias, we would interpret Rosenhan's results in the following way: The pseudopatients' diagnoses of schizophrenia elicited certain expectations on the part of the hospital staff who were to work with them—expectations about the covariation between the condition of schizophrenia and particular patient behaviors. Staff members' perceptions of actual patient behavior were then biased, such that they erroneously encoded behaviors as consistent with their expectations rather than giving consideration to alternative explanations for these behaviors (Step 3 of the normative model). However, Rosenhan presented additional data that suggests that labeling biases in the clinic may occur even earlier than the encoding stage of information processing. Rosenhan documented that attendents spent only 11.3 percent of their time outside of the staff cage, interacting with patients. Nurses emerged from the cage on an average of only 11.5 times per shift and physicians emerged on the ward an average of only 6.7 times per day. It is reasonable to assume that staff members would be more likely to intervene in patient activity when there was evidence of aberrant behavior than when everything ran smoothly. Thus, it could be biased sampling of data (Step 2 of the normative model) that led staff members to see patients' behavior as more pathological than it was.

Perhaps Rosenhan's most distressing finding, though, is of patient abuse by staff. If, as in an example provided by Rosenhan, patients were beaten for initiating verbal contact, we might conclude that staff members elicited patient behavior that confirmed their expectations. In this particular case, staff members might have elicited "pathology" in the form of hostility, withdrawal, or abnormal fear.

Although Rosenhan's study has had considerable impact upon the fields of psychiatry and psychology, as well as the general public, it also has been the focus of numerous critiques. In 1975, an entire issue of the *Journal of Abnormal Psychology* was devoted to the controversy surrounding the Rosenhan study. Perhaps, though, the most comprehensive critique was written by Spitzer (1976), who called attention to several weaknesses in the Rosenhan study, only a few of which are relevant to this chapter.

First, Spitzer challenged Rosenhan's assumption that discharge diagnoses of "in remission" for pseudopatients implies inaccurate assessment of pseudopatients' behavior on the part of hospital staff. Spitzer explained that the diagnosis of "in remission" means that the patient is asymptomatic and is, in fact, very rare (for example, 11 out of 12 hospitals that he sampled never used this discharge diagnosis at all). The fact that all eight pseudopatients were discharged as such indicates that the hospital staff was very responsive to the normality of the pseudopatients' behavior.

Spitzer also suggested that the existence in almost every culture of some word or label describing a pattern of covarying symptoms similar to our concept of schizophrenia (Murphy, 1976) indicates that there is some basis in reality for the labels we use. In fact, even behaviorists who presumably are skeptical about the use of diagnostic categories have begun classifying those patients who hallucinate into subgroups corresponding to traditional psychiatric nomenclature. Although it would be difficult to argue that the use of labels in no way biases processing of objective information, clearly Rosenhan has not yet demonstrated that the labels that comprise the psychiatric diagnostic system are entirely in the minds of those who use them.

Finally, Spitzer questioned several of the conclusions drawn by Rosenhan from instances of staff members' behavior towards pseudopatients. He maintained that the nurse who documented one pseudopatient's note-taking as "patient engages in writing behavior" was not necessarily commenting on the pathology of the patient's activities. Typically, nurses take notes on both pathological and nonpathological activities of patients so that other staff members are aware of how patients spend their time. Could it be that Rosenhan is guilty of some of the same biases as the staff members of the hospitals about whom he is writing? It seems that Rosenhan expects staff members of the hospitals to exhibit labeling biases, and, thus, his own interpretation of their behavior has been distorted to confirm those expectations. However, this is not to suggest that in any way Rosenhan has purposely prejudiced his report of the data. Throughout this chapter we have been demonstrating the ubiquity of expectation-based errors in judgments of covariation, and Rosenhan may be no exception.

Spitzer undermined Rosenhan's arguments by showing how Rosenhan himself may be biasing interpretation of his results in the direction of his own prior expectations. Weiner (1975), on the other hand, undermined Rosenhan's argument by illustrating that the decisions made and the inferences drawn by the psychiatric staff in Rosenhan's study were those that logically should have been drawn. First, Weiner explained that pseudopatients who presented with the complaint of hallucinations that were "often unclear" (Rosenhan, 1973, p. 251) were reporting behavior of high consistency and low consensus. Under these circumstances, it would be appropriate for psychiatrists to make dispositional as opposed to situational attributions (see the section on "The Use of Covariation Information in Causal Attribution" in this chapter). In reply to

Rosenhan's claim that it is the inferential leap from a person attribution to a diagnosis of schizophrenia that is unfounded, Weiner pointed out that pseudopatients did not present only with the symptom of hallucinations. They also evidenced a high level of anxiety and expressed a desire to gain admittance to a psychiatric hospital, a desire that should be interpreted as a signal of distress. In addition, the type of hallucinations that the pseudopatients reported typically do covary with other symptoms of mental illness and the presence of schizophrenia. Thus, although the sole diagnosis of schizophrenia may have been unwarranted, it was a very logical inference for the psychiatrists to have drawn.

As for the discharge diagnoses of schizophrenia in remission, Weiner claimed that these too were not unreasonable. An individual who has experienced hallucinations should not be considered identical to one who has not. There is evidence that the former type of person has a much higher likelihood of entering a psychiatric hospital in the future than the latter type of person.

Just as Weiner argued that the errors made by staff members in Rosenhan's study are logical inferences, which according to attribution theory would have been made by anyone, so we would argue that both illusory correlations and labeling biases are not specific to clinicians, but are essentially "the human condition (cognition?)." In the section "Detection of Covariation" in this chapter, we have shown that people's judgments of covariation are dominated by their expectations about the covariation between events more than by the actual degree of covariation present in the data.

Although we have clearly emphasized the negative implications of the illusory correlation and labeling bias phenomena in our discussion thus far, it is important to point out that expectation-based covariation assessments may provide benefits also. Expectations or category labels provide a means by which the multiplicity of stimuli surrounding us in our environment may be organized (Rosch, 1975; Rosch & Mervis, 1975). In addition to guiding the interpretation of previously presented and currently available information, they direct attention to information that is likely to be relevant in the future as well. Along these lines, it may be both necessary and advantageous for clinicians to utilize general theories about psychopathology and specific expectations about individual patients in order to make sense of the bewildering array of patient behaviors with which they are confronted. Moreover, the bias to overweight prior expectations in the covariation judgment process can increase the likelihood of accurate diagnoses if the initial expectations are themselves veridical. Reliance on such expectations may allow the clinician to perceive and comprehend relevant behaviors that he or she would otherwise have not seen or understood. For example, if a professional colleague is, in fact, an expert on psychosis, knowledge that he or she has said that a particular individual "looks neurotic but actually is quite psychotic" can enhance accurate detection of the patient's psychosis by increasing attention to and memory for behaviors indicative of psychosis. In this regard, we might speculate that under certain conditions, behavior therapists' failure to fall prey to the labeling gambit (Langer & Abelson, 1974) could produce erroneous or distorted psychodiagnoses as well. Would behavior therapists fail to notice the pathology in a true schizophrenic's behavior when alerted to do so because they ignored a label?

CLINICIANS' ASSESSMENTS OF THERAPEUTIC EFFECTIVENESS

As we pointed out earlier, the covariation judgment process plays an important role not only in the clinician's task as psychodiagnostician, but also in his or her other role as psychotherapist. Whether a clinician engages in the manipulation of ostensibly intangible, unconscious conflicts, or whether he or she utilizes experimentally derived procedures to modify observable behaviors, periodically during the course of therapy (either explicitly or implicitly), he or she will have to make assessments of the effectiveness of therapeutic techniques. Such assessment can be reduced to the following covariation question: To what extent does a particular treatment or do particular therapeutic strategies covary with desirable therapeutic outcomes?

Throughout this chapter we have pointed out expectation-based biases in judgments of covariation. This section will be no exception. The source of the psychotherapist's biases should be obvious. The practicing clinician has had years of formal education and clinical experience. Typically, by virtue of this experience, he or she has come to expect one or another form of treatment to be more successful than other forms. In fact, even an eclectic therapist is likely to expect that eclectic therapy is most effective or that different types of therapies are most effective in different situations. Thus, we predict that the therapist will be prone to many of the cognitive biases associated with prior expectations as outlined in the previous section on the assessment of covariation. Biased assessment of therapeutic outcome may stem from motivational sources as well. No matter how committed a scientist, the psychotherapist, like the rest of us, will have an emotional investment in viewing himself or herself as competent.

To date, we know of no one study that specifically addresses the issue of clinicians' expectation-based biases in assessment of therapeutic effectiveness (although see Cohen & Oyster-Nelson, 1981, for a study that comes close). We therefore decided to conduct a study of our own. As a starting point we utilized Luborsky, Singer, and Luborsky's (1975) comprehensive review of comparative studies of psychotherapy. In their attempt to determine whether particular forms of psychotherapy were more or less effective, they examined the outcomes of "all reasonably controlled" (Luborsky *et al.*, 1975, p. 995) comparative studies of group versus individual psychotherapy, time-limited versus unlimited psychotherapy, client-centered versus other traditional psychotherapies, and behavior therapy versus psychotherapy.

To make our own task more manageable, we decided to examine only those studies that compared individual psychotherapy to control groups and those that compared different kinds of individual psychotherapy (i.e., behavior therapy versus traditional psychotherapy and client-centered versus traditional). We chose not to look at those studies comparing various forms of drug treatment or studies comparing group to individual psychotherapy. Our task involved tracking down the studies in these categories (of 37 studies we were able to locate 31) and carefully evaluating each to determine whether bias existed in the manner in which therapeutic outcome was assessed. For example, if the individuals who rated patient improvement were the same as those who conducted therapy (and sometimes even the same as the authors of the study), we concluded that there was high probability of biased assessment of therapeutic outcome. Conversely, if the individuals who rated patient improvement were blind to treatment, or if objective criteria such as discharge from the hospital or transfer to a different ward (assuming staff were blind to treatment) were used, we concluded that assessment of therapeutic effectiveness was likely to be unbiased. In Table 10-3 is a box score of our findings.

Studies were grouped into those showing evidence of biased assessment of outcome versus those showing no evidence of bias, and the number of each type in which the favored psychotherapy did better versus the number in which there was no difference between therapies being compared or in which the favored psychotherapy did worse was determined. There were two basic strate-

TABLE 10-3. Box Score of Clinicians' Expectation-based Biases in Assessment of Psychotherapy Outcome

		Therapy Outcome	
		Favored therapy shows greater improvement than alternative therapies or controls	Favored therapy shows less or the same improvement as alternative therapies or controls
Assessment of Therapeutic Outcome	Evidence of biased assessment	CELL 1 10	CELL 2 3
	Evidence of unbiased assessment	CELL 3 6	CELL 4 12

Note. Numbers in the table were derived from an examination of 31 psychotherapy outcome studies selected from those reviewed by Luborsky, Singer, & Luborsky (1975). (See text for selection criteria.)

gies we employed to determine which brand of psychotherapy was favored (and therefore, in which direction expectation-based errors should occur). In many cases, explicit statements in the text of the articles revealed which therapy was favored. In other cases, we determined the favored therapy on the basis of the authors' reputation. For example, in one study comparing behavior therapy to traditional therapy, the person who authored the study and conducted both types of psychotherapy was a noted behaviorist.

Notice that the data in Table 10-3 are markedly skewed, chi-square = 4.5, $p < .05$. Those studies with biased assessment of therapeutic outcome tend to find that the favored therapy does better, whereas those studies with no evidence of bias are more likely to show no difference between the therapies compared. Our study suggests then, that clinicians' expectation-based biases in assessment of therapy outcome are as pervasive as their expectation-based biases in patient diagnosis (and perhaps as problematic to remediate).

As vivid examples of the biasing influence of clinicians' expectations in assessment of therapy outcome, we have selected two studies representative of Cells 1 and 4 of Table 10-3. Albert Ellis (1957), noted for his development of rational-emotive therapy, conducted a retrospective study comparing orthodox psychoanalysis to psychoanalytically oriented therapy to rational-emotive therapy. All data were gathered from Ellis's own notes of cases he had seen over the years and analyzed by him personally. Not surprisingly, given his theoretical bent, Ellis found that significantly more clients treated with rational analysis showed "considerable improvement" than those treated with other techniques (44 percent vs. 18 percent and 13 percent, respectively). We believe that Ellis's study is an example of one in which there was biased assessment of therapeutic effectiveness, where the favored therapy fared better (Cell 1). Note, however, that our conclusion about all of the studies summarized in Table 10-3, should be interpreted with some degree of caution. Because Ellis is considered the founder of rational-emotive therapy, we determined that he was biased in favor of that particular treatment. In fact, though, Ellis claims that he was "favorably disposed" toward each of the three types of therapy he examined.

In contrast to Ellis's study is an investigation conducted by Sloane, Staples, Cristol, Yorkston, and Whipple (1975). In their study comparing behavior therapy to analytically oriented therapy to minimal contact treatment (control group), various measures were taken to ensure unbiased assessment of therapeutic effectiveness. Behavior therapy and psychoanalytic therapy were conducted by experienced practitioners in their respective fields, there was random assignment of patients to groups, and multiple outcome measures of target symptoms and overall functioning were obtained from therapists, patients, relatives, standardized tests, and most importantly, from independent assessors blind to treatment. The data collected in the study were also analyzed by independent and blind assessors. With the results of Table 10-3 in mind, it should come as no surprise that the overall finding of this study was that there was no difference between treatment groups. At a 4-month assessment period, behavior therapy and psychotherapy groups showed equal improvement of target symptoms. Both groups showed significantly more improvement than controls. As for work and social adjustment, behavior therapy, psychotherapy, and wait lists groups improved equally.

Of particular interest are the comparisons Sloane *et al.* made of ratings obtained from therapists, patients, relatives, and independent assessors. In a comparison among group means, although there was considerable concordance among raters, therapists' ratings were somewhat aberrant. Behavior therapists' ratings of patient improvement in work adjustment were significantly higher than ratings made by either the independent assessors or relatives, and also showed a tendency to be higher in ratings of social adjustment. Both groups of therapists gave idiosyncratic ratings of patient improvement in sexual adjustment. The correlations between therapists' ratings and ratings made by independent assessors, patients and relatives were .13, .21, and −.04 respectively. Sloane *et al.* quite vividly demonstrate that biased assessment of therapeutic effectiveness—ratings made by therapists—may be only minimally related to assessment of therapeutic effectiveness made by unbiased sources (i.e., independent and blind raters).

PATIENT AS ABERRANT ACTUARY

Patients' Distortions in Assessment of Covariation

In recent years, a growing number of theorists (e.g., Abramson & Alloy, 1980; Alloy, 1988a; Beck, 1967, 1976; Beck & Emery, 1985; Dodge & Coie, 1987; Ellis, 1962, 1971; Fincham & Bradbury, 1987; Forgus & Shulman, 1979; Ingram, 1986; Kihlstrom & Nasby, 1981; Langer, 1975; Seligman, 1975) have conceptualized psychopathology, including the emotional disorders, in terms of aberrant cognitions. In this section we examine psychopathology, i.e., patient behavior, in terms of the covariation judgment process in particular.

Beck (1976) has argued that psychopathology is rooted in erroneous or irrational thinking about personal experience. Differences in psychopathologies can be attributed to differences in the specific content of this thinking, that is, in the meaning or significance that different groups attach to their experiences. For example, Beck suggests that depressed, hypomanic, and paranoid individuals all exhibit irrational thinking. However, depressed patients' thoughts are concerned with loss. They perceive that they have lost something crucial to their happiness and therefore anticipate that in the future only negative outcomes will occur. On the other hand, hypomanic patients' thoughts are characterized by the expectation of significant gain. They anticipate that in the future only positive outcomes will occur. Paranoid patients are concerned with abuse by others and outside interference with the attainment of personal goals.

The hypothesized thought content associated with each of these psycho-pathologies can be examined from a covariation perspective. Each of these types of patient exhibits deficiencies in the ability to accurately perceive the contingency between events, deficiencies that can be traced to the biasing role of prior beliefs or expectations. The depressed person expects negative out-comes, and therefore either fails to see or severely underestimates the covaria-tion between his or her responses and positive outcomes (e.g., Alloy & Selig-man, 1979; Beck, 1967; Seligman, 1975). The hypomanic individual has an expectation of significant gain and shows an exaggerated "illusion of control." That is, the hypomanic overestimates the covariation between personal re-sponses and positive outcomes (e.g., Langer, 1975). The paranoid person has an expectation that others are "out to get" him or her, and therefore perceives a covariation between his or her responses and the abusive responses of others. Similarly, other psychopathological disorders might also be a reflection of unrealistic assessments of the objecive degree of covariation between events. For example, phobias could be conceptualized as an overestimation of the degree of contingency between certain phobic objects and aversive outcomes (Mineka & Tomarken, in press). Obsessive–compulsive behavior might be based on an overestimation of the contingency between failure to perform certain ritualistic behaviors and aversive outcomes. Anorexia nervosa, de-scribed as a disorder involving lack of awareness of bodily states (e.g., Bruch, 1973), might better be conceptualzed as an inability to detect the contingency between feelings and bodily states.

DEPRESSION: AN EXAMPLE?

Perhaps the most well-articulated theories concerning the role cognitive distor-tions play in psychopathology are theories that describe depression. The cogni-tive theories of depression emphasize that depressed and depression-prone people differ from nondepressed people in their causal attributions and assess-ments of covariation (e.g., Abramson, Seligman, & Teasdale, 1978; Beck, 1967; Seligman, 1975). Therefore, in the development of our covariation perspective for the "patient as aberrant actuary," we have chosen to focus primarily on the depressed patient as an example.

Cognitive Theories of Depression

According to Beck, the affective, motivational, and cognitive symptoms of depression are all consequences of depressed individuals' idiosyncratic cog-nitive patterns. In this view, depressed individuals are characterized by a "cognitive triad" consisting of negative evaluations of the self, negative interpretations of experience, and negative expectations for the future. Beck conceptualizes the depressive triad as a cognitive structure or schema, through which the data of everyday experience are filtered and negatively distorted. For example, depressed people might believe that they are alone and unlovable despite ample evidence of the concern and affection that others feel toward them.

While it is common knowledge that depressed people view themselves and their experiences negatively, the unique aspect of Beck's theory is that it hypothesizes that these negative evaluations stem from specific logical errors in interpreting reality. That is, depressives' inferences are not only negative in content, but are also hypothesized to be the end products of unrealistic, extreme, and illogical cognitive processes. For example, depressives engage in arbitrary inference in which conclusions are drawn with little or no regard for the available facts (e.g., a depressed person might feel incompetent in the face of repeated success experiences). In selective abstraction, the depressive fails to attend to a situation in its entirety and instead concentrates on only a single aspect of the situation (e.g., the depressed person given both praise and criticism might attend only to the criticism). In overgeneralization, the depressive generalizes on the basis of a single episode (e.g., failure to achieve one goal might represent an inability to achieve any goals at all). In magnification and minimization, depressives engage in inaccurate appraisal of life events (e.g., they exaggerate the importance of problems or negative events and underestimate the importance of positive events). In inexact labeling, a neutral interchange might be described in emotionally charged terms (Beck, 1967). Finally, Beck has described the formal characteristics of depressive cognitions. They are automatic, involuntary, seem plausible to the person, and have a quality of perseveration.

We believe that Beck's conceptualization of the cognitive patterns in depression provides an example "par excellence" of expectation-based judgments of covariation in psychopathology. Beck (1967) has argued that "the distinguishing characteristic of the cognitions of the depressed patient is that they show a systematic error, viz., a bias against themselves" (pp. 233–234). In the language of this chapter, depressed people manifest an illusory correlation. In particular, they systematically overestimate the degree of covariation between their own responses and negative outcomes, and systematically underestimate the covariation between their responses and positive outcomes. This systematic error can be attributed to the biasing role of depressive schemata or expectations about the self, the future, and the world.

To examine the nature of this illusory correlation, we refer again to Table 10-1. Beck has specifically noted two types of circumstances in which depressive schemata are likely to be activated and, thus, influence judgments. One is the circumstance in which thinking occurs without any immediate external stimulus, that is, a period of undirected thinking or free association. Another is the circumstance in which the stimuli provoking thought are either vague or ambiguous. Both of these circumstances fall into Cell 2 of Table 10-1: The degree to which generalized beliefs point to a particular covariation is high and the degree to which situational information points to a particular covariation is low. Perhaps it is even more interesting, however, to speculate about depressed people's attributions or covariation judgments under conditions in which both generalized beliefs and situational information are compelling, but indicate opposing inferences (Case 2 of Cell 4). Given Beck's observations of the robustness of depressogenic schemata, we might hypothesize that depressed people would be particularly prone to resolve this "cognitive dilemma" in favor of their generalized beliefs.

It is possible also, to reconceptualize the distorted cognitive processes in depression featured by Beck's theory in terms of the five steps of the normative model of covariation assessment (see the section "Detection of Covariation" in this chapter). Selective abstraction and/or generalization may both be viewed as biases in data selection and sampling (Steps 1 and 2 of the normative model). In both instances, conclusions are drawn on the basis of only a portion of the data that is necessary and available. Magnification/minimization and inexact labeling may both be viewed as errors in encoding or classification (Step 3 of the normative model). In these instances, there is a misrepresentation of the data from which conclusions will be drawn. Likewise, magnification/minimization could also reflect errors in recall of evidence (Step 4 of the normative model). In this regard, depressed people might overestimate the frequency of occurrence of negative events and underestimate the frequency of occurrence of positive events (DeMonbreun & Craighead, 1977; Nelson & Craighead, 1977).

Finally, we can draw parallels between the formal characteristics of depressive cognitions and the formal characteristics of other types of schema or expectation-based judgments. Beck has argued that depressive cognitions are both involuntary and automatic. Harris *et al.* (1975) have shown that schematic processing can be involuntary, while Markus (1977) has demonstrated the rapidity of schematic processing.

To this point it may appear that we are merely redefining Beck's theory into the concepts and vocabulary common to more recent work in cognitive and social psychology. We would argue, however, that it is important to reconceptualize Beck's terms. Although Beck's theory has garnered support from both correlational studies and controlled experiments (see Blaney, 1977, and Coyne & Gotlib, 1983, for reviews), recent developments in cognitive and social psychology have led to conceptual and methodological advances in assessing the content of schemata and their effect on information-processing. If, in fact, depression is rooted in schema-based information-processing, investigators of depression will stand to gain a great deal from consideration of these advances.

Another cognitive theory of depression that has become influential in the past decade is Seligman's learned helplessness theory (e.g., Seligman, 1975). Seligman assigns central importance to perceptions or expectations of no control over important life events (i.e., helplessness) in the etiology and maintenance of depression. He suggests that people (and animals) who experience response–outcome independence come to expect future response–outcome independence. This expectation results in the cognitive as well as motivational and emotional deficits characteristic of depression. Note that whereas Beck has argued that depressed people overestimate the degree of contingency between their actions and negative outcomes (i.e., in terms of self-blame, self-degradation, and so forth), Seligman argues that depressed people underestimate the covariation between their responses and outcomes (See Abramson & Sackheim, 1977, for a discussion of this paradox).

The translation of helplessness theory into the terminology of this chapter should be clear. Individuals who experience no covariation between their responses and outcomes come to expect that in the future there will continue to be no covariation between their responses and outcomes. Subsequent processing of information about objective action–outcome contingencies is then biased by these prior beliefs or expectations.

The original helplessness theory has been revised several times to resolve its major inadequacies as a theory of depression. In the most recent statement of the theory, now referred to as the hopelessness theory of depression, Abramson and colleagues (Abramson, Alloy, & Metalsky, 1988a; Abramson, Metalsky, & Alloy, Chapter 2, this volume, and 1988b; Alloy, Abramson, Metalsky, & Hartlage, 1988a; Alloy, Hartlage, & Abramson, 1988c) hypothesized that the expectation of hopelessness—the expectation that highly desired outcomes are very unlikely to occur or that highly aversive outcomes are very likely to occur and that no response in one's repertoire will change the probability of occurrence of these outcomes—is a proximal sufficient cause of depression. That is, Abramson et al. (1988a, 1988b; Alloy et al., 1988a, 1988c) view only a subset of the cases of helplessness, those involving negative expectations about the occurrence of highly valued outcomes, as a sufficient cause of depression.

The hopelessness theory also specifies a causal chain of events hypothesized to culminate in hopelessness and, thus, depression. The causal sequence begins with the occurrence of negative life events and ends with the onset of depressive symptoms. According to the theory, the kinds of causal attributions people make for particular negative life events they experience and the degree of importance they attach to these events are contributory causes of depression. Hopelessness and, thus, depressive symptoms are more likely to occur when negative life events are attributed to internal (i.e., due to something about me), stable (i.e., enduring or recurrent), and global (i.e., general across many outcomes) factors and viewed as important than when they are attributed to external, unstable, specific factors and perceived as unimportant. The kinds of attributions individuals make for negative life events are, in turn, influenced both by the situational consensus, consistency and distinctiveness information surrounding the occurrence of these events and by their generalized causal schemata or attributional styles (Alloy & Tabachnik, 1984;

Metalsky & Abramson, 1981; see also the section on the "Use of Covariation Information in Causal Attribution" in this chapter). Abramson *et al.* (1978) speculated that some individuals possess a depressogenic attributional style, consisting of a generalized tendency to attribute negative events to internal, stable and global causes and to view negative events as very important. Thus, in the hopelessness theory, a depressogenic attributional style is viewed as a distal contributory cause of depression onset that operates in the presence, but not the absence, of negative life events. In this context, then, it serves as a cognitive diathesis in a diathesis-stress combination (Metalsky, Abramson, Seligman, Semmel, & Peterson, 1982).

A growing body of empirical work supports the hopelessness theory (see Abramson *et al.*, 1988b, and Peterson & Seligman, 1984 for reviews). Of particular relevance for our present purposes is the finding that depressed people make more internal, stable, and global attributions for negative outcomes and more external, unstable, and specific attributions for positive outcomes than nondepressed people (see Sweeney, Anderson, & Bailey, 1986, for a meta-analytic review). In addition, recent evidence suggests that as predicted by the hopelessness theory, attributional styles may actually modulate vulnerability to depressive reactions (Follette & Jacobson, 1987; Kayne, Alloy, Romer, & Crocker, 1988; Metalsky *et al.*, 1982; Metalsky, Halberstadt, & Abramson, 1987).

Recall Kelley's argument (in the section "The Use of Covariation Information in Causal Attribution" in this chapter) that an internal attribution is made when a person perceives low consensus, low distinctiveness, and high consistency for an event. An external attribution is made when a person perceives either high consensus, high distinctiveness, and high consistency for an event, or low consensus, high distinctiveness, and low consistency for an event. It is possible, then that differential use of such covariation information contributes to depressed–nondepressed differences in attributional styles (Metalsky & Abramson, 1981). In addition, we might speculate further that the differential use of explicit covariation information is mediated by differences in implicit covariation information (i.e., prior beliefs or expectations about consensus, consistency, and distinctiveness). Along these lines, Tabachnik, Crocker, and Alloy (1983) have found that people in a depressed state perceive less social consensus for their own traits and behaviors than do people in a nondepressed state (see also Crocker, Kayne, & Alloy, 1985). Moreover, such depressed–nondepressed differences in implicit consensus beliefs do appear to contribute to differences in their attributional styles (Crocker, Alloy, & Kayne, 1988).

To this point, we have presented three of the most influential cognitive theories of depression: Beck's cognitive theory of depression, the original helplessness theory, and the hopelessness theory. Although certainly there are points that distinguish them, they share a common theme. All three theories suggest that depressed people are aberrant actuaries who bias their interpretation of everyday experiences as a function of generalized beliefs. Recently, however, a striking paradox has come to the attention of depression researchers. Whereas the cognitive theories of depression emphasize cognitive bias and distortion in depression, recent empirical work designed to test these theories suggests that depressed people are often more realistic or accurate in their processing of situational information than are nondepressed people. In keeping with this chapter's focus on covariation assessment, below we examine the findings of depressive realism in judgment of contingency tasks, in particular (but see Alloy & Abramson, 1988, for a review of depressive realism findings in other situations as well).

Evidence for Depressive Realism

Alloy and Abramson (1979) conducted a series of studies in which depressed and nondepressed subjects were presented with a series of contingency problems in an instrumental learning situation and asked to quantify the degree of contingency between their responses (pressing or not pressing a button) and an environmental outcome (green light onset). Based on the learned helplessness theory, depressed people were expected to underestimate the contingency between their responses and environmental outcomes relative to the objective degree of contingency or to nondepressed people (Alloy & Abramson, 1979). According to Beck's theory of depression, depressed people should underestimate their control over positive outcomes and overestimate their control over negative outcomes, whereas nondepressed people should make relatively accurate judgments of control. Contrary to the predictions derived from either of these theories, depressed subjects in the Alloy and Abramson experiments accurately perceived the contingency between their responses and outcomes under all conditions. Nondepressed subjects were accurate when presented with some degree of contingency in a hedonically neutral situation, but were surprisingly inaccurate when the outcome of interest was hedonically charged: When noncontingent outcomes were frequent and/or positive, nondepressed subjects overestimated the degree of contingency between their responses and outcomes; when contingent outcomes were negative, nondepressed subjects underestimated the degree of contingency between their responses and outcomes. In summary, Alloy and Abramson's results provided no support for Beck's cognitive theory of depression or for the cognitive component of the original helplessness theory.

Moreover, the findings of depressive realism in judgments of covariation is not limited to the circumstances of this particular series of experiments. A number of studies have replicated the findings of each of the Alloy and Abramson (1979) experiments (e.g., Alloy & Abramson, 1982; Alloy, Abramson, & Kossman, 1985, Experiment 3; Alloy, Abramson & Viscusi, 1981, neutral and no mood induction conditions; Benassi & Mahler, 1985, Experiments 1 & 2; Dresel, 1984, many trials condition; Martin, Abramson, & Alloy, 1984, self condition; Musson & Alloy, 1988, neutral conditions; Vazquez, 1987,

Experiments 1–3). In addition, other investigators have independently discovered similar examples of depressive realism on other illusion of control tasks. Depressed subjects were less likely to succumb to an illusion of control than nondepressed or psychiatric control subjects when elements characteristic of a skill situation, such as personal involvement, were introduced into a chance situation (Golin, Terrell, & Johnson, 1977; Golin, Terrell, Weitz, & Drost, 1979).

Recently, a number of judgment-of-contingency studies have begun to investigate more specifically the conditions under which depressive realism and nondepressive illusions of control occur. For example, Alloy *et al.* (1981) investigated the impact of transient, induced mood states on depressed and nondepressed subjects' judgments of control over a positive, but objectively uncontrollable, outcome. Alloy *et al.* found that nondepressed subjects made temporarily depressed judged accurately that they exerted little control, whereas nondepressed subjects who received neutral or no mood induction or who simulated depression exhibited the typical nondepressive illusion of control. Similarly, depressed subjects made transiently elated succumbed to an illusion of control, whereas depressed subjects who received neutral or no mood induction or who simulated elation gave accurate judgments of control. Although the results of Alloy *et al.* (1981) suggest that current mood state is an important determinant of the accuracy of control judgments, they do not rule out the alternative possibility that individual differences may exist in susceptibility to illusions of control and that those persons who are less susceptible to such illusions may be more vulnerable to developing depressive episodes (Alloy *et al.*, in press; Clements & Alloy, 1988).

Martin *et al.* (1984) asked depressed and nondepressed students to judge either their own or another person's (male or female confederate) control over an uncontrollable, but positive, outcome. Replicating Alloy and Abramson (1979, Experiment 3), depressed students judged their personal control accurately, whereas nondepressed students succumbed to their typical illusion of control. However, with only one exception (depressed males judging a male other's control), depressives overestimated another person's control, whereas nondepressives (particularly nondepressed males) were more likely to judge accurately that the other person did not exert much control. Thus, Martin *et al.* (1984) suggested that depressive realism and nondepressive illusions in judging control may be specific to the self (see Alloy & Abramson, 1988, and Alloy, Albright, & Clements, 1987, for further discussion of self–other differences). Consistent with this line of reasoning, Alloy *et al.* (1985, Experiments 1–3) found that nondepressed students were as accurate as depressed students in judging both positive and zero contingencies between two stimulus events, neither of which involved students' own responses, regardless of the events' frequencies or valence. However, when subjects' own responses were one of the two events in the contingency learning problem (Experiment 3), nondepressives displayed their usual illusions of control while depressives' judgments were accurate.

Other recent studies have suggested that even depressives' judgments of personal control may show illusions under certain circumstances. Vazquez (1987, Experiments 3 & 4) used either depressive or nondepressive content sentences as the outcomes in the Alloy and Abramson (1979) contingency judgment task. He found that when the sentences were contingent on subjects' responses (Experiment 3), nondepressives overestimated their control over positive content sentences but not negative content sentences, whereas depressives gave equivalent and relatively accurate control judgments for both types of sentences. When the occurrence of the sentences was noncontingently related to subjects' responses (Experiment 4), however, nondepressives exhibited an illusion of control for positive but not negative sentences, whereas depressives exhibited an illusion of control for negative but not positive sentences. These effects only occurred when the sentences were self-referent. Benassi and Mahler (1985) found that when depressed and nondepressed students performed a judgment of contingency task alone, depressives accurately judged that they exerted little control over a noncontingent, high frequency outcome whereas nondepressives exhibited an illusion of control (Experiment 1), replicating Alloy and Abramson (1979, Experiment 2). However, when subjects performed the task with an observer watching them, depressed students gave higher judgments of control than did nondepressed students (Experiments 1 & 3).

Alloy, Abramson, and Musson (1988b) examined personal and situational predictors of the illusion of control among students for a noncontingent, positive outcome. They found that larger illusions of control were predicted by younger age, being female, higher grade point average, positive mood, higher trait anxiety, a positive self-schema, low self-consciousness, higher perceived frequency of positive outcomes, and greater experience with and liking for logic and math problems. This set of nine predictors discriminated "realists" (judgment of control ≤ 16) from "illusionists" (judgment of control ≥ 60) with 84 percent accuracy in a discriminant function analysis, and discriminated these two groups with 80 percent accuracy in a cross-validation sample.

In summary, the judgment of contingency studies suggest that depressed individuals generally may be less susceptible to illusions of personal control than nondepressed individuals. However, two important boundary conditions on depressive realism and nondepressive illusions of control may be specificity to the self and private judgment.

How can we explain this intriguing paradox between the depressive distortions predicted by the cognitive theories of depression and the empirical data? Is it really the case that only clinicians, and not patients (or at least not depressed patients), are aberrant actuaries in judging covariation? Below we examine several explanations that have been advanced to explain the "sadder but wiser" (Alloy & Abramson, 1979) phenomenon.

Explanations for Depressive Realism

Four major explanations are proposed here for understanding depressive realism (see Alloy & Abramson, 1988, for additional explanations). First, it is possible that depressed people engage in cognitive distortions, but that investigators have not yet adequately captured these distortions in the laboratory. Second, depressed people may have weaker or less differentiated schemata than nondepressed people and therefore may be less likely to exhibit expectation-based distortions. Third, depressed people may suffer from a generalized motivational deficit that makes them less likely than nondepressed people to selectively filter situational information. Finally, depressed people may suffer from a more specific motivational deficit, that is, a deficit in the motivation to maintain self-esteem. Therefore, they would be less likely than nondepressed people to bias their information-processing in a self-protective manner.

The first account, that depressive distortions exist but have not yet been well isolated is an empirical issue. One might argue that this explanation is improbable, since many, if not all of the experiments demonstrating depressive realism in judgments of control have examined precisely those situations in which cognitive theories of depression predict distortions should occur. However, it is important to note that these studies adopted a nomothetic rather than an idiographic approach. It is quite possible that expectation-based information-processing may not be identical for personally significant versus insignificant content (see also Gong-Guy & Hammen, 1980; Hammen & Cochran, 1981; Klinger, 1975; Klinger, Barta, & Maxeiner, 1981). Differences in information-processing along the continuum of personal relevance may help to resolve the paradox between the predicted cognitive distortions in depressives' judgments and the frequent empirical failures to find such distortions. Beck's theory is based on clinical observations of people in therapy for depression who report cognitions and behaviors in areas of high personal relevance, whereas the empirical studies of cognitive biases and distortions in depression are based on problem-solving situations that may or may not have high personal relevance to each of the subjects involved. An understanding of the situations in which depressed individuals show realistic versus distorted information-processing may require an explicit comparison of information-processing by depressed and nondepressed people in content areas with high versus low personal meaning.

A second view of the depressive distortion/realism paradox is that depressed people are more "aschematic" than nondepressed people and therefore behave more like data-based information processors. The logic of this aschematic hypothesis is relatively straightforward. Recall that research and theorizing in cognitive and social psychology indicates that while schemata facilitate the perception and comprehension of situational information, an important by-product of their operation is bias and distortion (see the section "Detection of Covariation" in this chapter). If depressed people have weaker and/or less consistent schemata about the self, then one would expect their processing of self-relevant situational information to be less biased by schema-based expectations.

Consistent with this hypothesis, a number of studies comparing the self-schemata of depressed and nondepressed individuals have shown that nondepressives possess strong, consistent, positive self-schemata, whereas mildly and moderately depressed subjects' self-schemata appear to contain mixed and rather balanced positive and negative content (e.g., Davis, 1979a, b; Greenberg & Alloy, 1988; Ingram, Smith, & Brehm, 1983; Kuiper & Derry, 1982; Kuiper & MacDonald, 1982; Vazquez & Alloy, 1988; see Greenberg, Vazquez, & Alloy, 1988, and Blaney, 1986 for reviews). One study (Derry & Kuiper, 1981) has suggested that more severely depressed persons may possess self-schemata with more consistent negative content, although this finding is not yet well-established (see Alloy & Abramson, 1988; Blaney, 1986). If severely depressed people do possess strong and consistent negative self-schemata, one would expect their processing of self-referent information to be pessimistically biased. Alloy and Abramson's (1988) review of studies including more severely depressed subjects indicated that their inferences may be as unbiased as those of mildly depressed subjects, although clearly, more evidence is needed on this point.

A clear prediction of the self-schema hypothesis is that even though depressives' weaker, mixed content self-schemata may lead them to be less biased than nondepressives overall, *both* depressives and nondepressives should exhibit both biased and unbiased processing, depending on the relative match of the information to be processed to each group's self-schema. Two recent studies in our laboratory provided evidence consistent with this prediction. Dykman, Abramson, Alloy, and Hartlage (1988) found that both depressed and nondepressed subjects sometimes showed positive biases, negative biases, and accurate encoding of ambiguous personality feedback, dependent upon the relative match between the content of each group's self-schema and the valence of the feedback cue being processed. Similarly, Albright, Alloy, and Barch (1988) found that whether depressed and nondepressed subjects' social comparisons (self versus other ratings) were unbiased or biased in an optimistic or pessimistic direction depended upon the degree of similarity between the content of the subjects' self-schemata and the affective characteristics of the "target other" to be compared to the self. Whether the schema hypothesis can specifically account for differences in depressed and nondepressed subjects' susceptibility to illusions of control remains to be determined (but see Clements & Alloy, 1988).

A third explanation for depressive accuracy is that depressed people suffer from a generalized motivational deficit that makes them less likely than nondepressives to initiate voluntary responses, including voluntary cognitive responses such as hypothesis generation (see Alloy & Abramson, 1980, and

Schwartz, 1981). Recall from earlier discussions (the sections "The Use of Covariation Information in Causal Attribution" and "Clinicians' Assessments of Patients" in this chapter) that when people impose hypotheses on a task, they tend to process available information in such a way as to confirm those hypotheses. If depressives are less likely to generate hypotheses as a function of their general motivational deficit, they should be less subject to this "confirmatory bias" (Schwartz, 1981) than nondepressives. "With the hypothesis generator-evaluator shut down, or severely retarded, data-filtering (be it selective evaluation or selective perception) will also be shut down, and subjects will be accurate. In the Alloy and Abramson situation, they will be perfect Humeans, passively registering all combinations of response and outcome" (Schwartz, 1981, p. 10).

Abramson, Alloy, and Rosoff (1981) provided support for this motivational hypothesis in the judgment-of-control situation. In their experiment, all subjects received a contingency learning problem in which the potential degree of control between responses and outcomes was 75 percent. Abramson *et al.* found that when subjects were required to generate complex hypotheses for controlling the outcome themselves, depressed subjects generated fewer controlling responses and underestimated the potential degree of control relative to nondepressed subjects. However, in a condition in which the experimenter generated a set of potential hypotheses for controlling the outcome for the subjects (including the correct one), depressed subjects did not differ from nondepressed subjects in their judgments of control. If depressives are less likely to initiate hypotheses for exerting control than are nondepressives, in the "real world" they might be less likely to experience control and therefore may never learn the potential degree of control they could exert over outcomes.

Finally, a specific version of this motivational hypothesis is that depression involves a specific deficit in the motivation to maintain or enhance self-esteem (see Abramson & Alloy, 1981; Abramson & Martin, 1982; Alloy & Abramson, 1979). In this view, nondepressed subjects, motivated to protect their self-esteem, overweight successes and underweight failures. Depressed subjects, lacking such a motivation, are more evenhanded in their treatment of successes and failures.

The self-serving motivational hypothesis emerges from several lines of thought. Beck (1976) contends that at the core of depression is a negative view of self. We might speculate that perhaps depressed people are less motivated to protect their self-esteem than nondepressed people because there is less self-esteem to protect (Abramson & Alloy, 1981; Beck, 1976; Laxer, 1964; Nadich, Gargan, & Michael, 1975). Psychoanalysts (e.g., Bibring, 1953; Freud, 1917/ 1957) maintain that depressives actually suffer from a breakdown in the capacity to defend self-esteem. Likewise, the nondepressive "self-serving" attributional style—taking responsibility for good but not bad outcomes—has been conceptualized as a bias stemming from a motivation to defend self-esteem (see Miller, 1976; Miller & Ross, 1975; Snyder *et al.*, 1978; Weary, 1980).

Alloy and Abramson (1982) obtained results consistent with the hypothesis that nondepressed but not depressed people are motivated to preserve self-esteem. Depressed and nondepressed students were assigned to one of three conditions comprising the typical helplessness paradigm. One group of subjects was exposed to controllable noises, a second group of subjects was exposed to uncontrollable noises, and a third group of subjects was not exposed to any noise at all. Subsequent to these experiences, subjects were presented with a judgment of control problem in which the outcome was objectively uncontrollable but associated with success or failure (winning or losing money). Contrary to predictions of the helplessness theory, nondepressed subjects exposed to either uncontrollable noise or no noise exhibited an illusion of control in the noncontingent-win problem. Depressed subjects were accurate under all conditions, and nondepressed subjects exposed to controllable noise were also relatively accurate in both the win and lose problems.

The performance of nondepressed subjects in this experiment was consistent with an egotism hypothesis (Frankel & Snyder, 1978). Exposure to uncontrollable noise posed a threat to self-esteem, which could be regained by attributing subsequent positive outcomes (winning money noncontingently) to internal factors. Nondepressed subjects exposed to controllable noise were accurate because they experienced no such threat to self-esteem. On the other hand, depressed subjects' behavior was inconsistent with self-esteem maintenance. Depressed subjects were less affected by manipulations that seemed to pose a threat to the nondepressed person's self-esteem.

More problematic for the self-esteem maintenance hypothesis is the results of the Benassi and Mahler (1985) study, suggesting that depressed and nondepressed subjects' relative susceptibility to the illusion of control may reverse in public versus private situations. Presumably, nondepressives' motivation to protect self-esteem and the breakdown of this motivation in depressives would be independent of the presence or absence of others' knowledge of their responses. However, Tetlock and Manstead (1985) suggested that public–private manipulations may have self-esteem implications. Thus, the self-esteem maintenance hypothesis remains a viable explanation of depressed–nondepressed differences in covariation assessment.

We began this section on the patient as aberrant actuary by conceptualizing patient behavior in terms of distortions in judgments of covariation. We chose to use the depressed patient as an example precisely because so much theorizing and empirical research on depression has focused on depressed people's biased causal inferences and judgments of covariation. Surprisingly, however, many of the recent findings on depression contradict this view. The more common finding is depressive realism and nondepressive distortion. Although four hypotheses have been advanced to explain these puzzling findings, at this point the current data do not distinguish among the hypotheses very well (see also Alloy & Abramson, 1988). We can only conclude that our working assumption about the cognitive distortions that occur in depression may be wrong. Needless to say, however, until research on judgments of covariation in other psychopathologies is conducted, the possibility still exists that other psychopathologies do involve expectation-based distortions in assessments of covariation.

Finally, we wish to make an important distinction between the concepts of *error*, *irrationality*, and *maladaptiveness* (see Abramson & Alloy, 1981, and Alloy & Abramson, 1988, for detailed discussions of this issue). In many of the experiments we have discussed in this section, depressed subjects were accurate, whereas nondepressed subjects made errors. In the judgment-of-contingency situation, there was a discrepancy between nondepressives' subjective judgments of control and the objective degree of control they exerted over events. However, while nondepressed subjects' judgments were erroneous, the possibility exists that they were based on rational inferential strategies. Perhaps in the nondepressed person's everyday environment, positive outcomes and personal control over these outcomes are in fact highly correlated (see Abramson & Alloy, 1980). Only in peculiar circumstances like that of the Alloy and Abramson experiments are positive outcomes unrelated to personal control. Thus, nondepressives' reliance on the valence of an outcome as an indicator of personal control may provide rational, and even realistic, judgments of control in the real world. In contrast, depressives' failure to utilize outcome valence as a cue indicating degree of control may often lead to inaccurate covariation judgments in their everyday lives.

An alternative possibility is that both depressed and nondepressed individuals' judgments of control are realistic assessments of their everyday environments, because each type of individual makes the world conform to his or her expectations through his or her own behavior. Several investigators have demonstrated that a perceiver's initially erroneous preconceptions about the environment may initiate a chain of behaviors that channel subsequent environmental interaction in ways that cause life events to confirm the perceiver's beliefs (Abramson *et al.*, 1981; Snyder & Swann, 1978b; Swann, 1987; see also Wachtel, 1977). For example, depressives' expectation that they cannot control life events may lead them to try fewer potential controlling behaviors and, thus, they might actually experience the lack of control they originally expected (Abramson *et al.*, 1981). Similarly, nondepressives' belief that they can control life events may lead to extended efforts to exert such control, and these efforts may eventuate in the expected control.

Finally, regardless of whether or not covariation judgments are erroneous and/or irrational, a person who succumbs to illusions may be better able to maintain positive affect and high self-esteem (Abramson & Alloy, 1981; Alloy & Abramson, 1988), may be more likely to persist at behavioral tasks (Greenwald, 1980), and may be less vulnerable to depressive reactions (Alloy & Abramson, 1988). That is, distortions in assessment of covariation may be functional. A comprehensive covariation perspective for patients and clinicians requires a consideration of the error, irrationality, and maladaptiveness of covariation assessments.

INTERACTION OF CLINICIANS' AND PATIENTS' COVARIATION JUDGMENTS

In our formulation of a covariation perspective for the clinic we examined both clinicians' and patients' assessments of covariation. Surprisingly, we found that although clinicians' important assessments of covariations (between test signs and symptoms, symptoms and diagnoses, diagnoses and behaviors, and therapeutic techniques and therapeutic effectiveness) are biased in the direction of preconceived expectations, patients' (at least depressed patients') assessments of covariation may not be biased in this manner.

PERSPECTIVES ON THE THERAPEUTIC INTERACTION

We are now in a position to examine how clinicians' and patients' covariation judgments might interact in the context of a therapeutic relationship. As noted in the first section of this chapter, much of the therapeutic process itself involves changing patients' supposedly erroneous and dysfunctional perceptions of cause–effect relationships. While an attempt to modify patients' maladaptive covariation assessments appears to be a common element in all currently available psychotherapies, it is particularly characteristic of cognitively oriented therapies (Beck *et al.*, 1979; Ellis, 1971; Mahoney, 1974; Meichenbaum, 1977). In support of this statement, we conducted a small, exploratory study to determine the degree to which Beck's cognitive therapy for depression involves the assessment of and attempt to modify depressed patients' covariation judgments. Two independent judges, blind to the hypotheses of this chapter, rated the content of 56 therapist–patient interactions based on actual clinical case material presented for illustration purposes in Beck and colleagues' (1979) book *Cognitive Therapy of Depression*. The judges decided whether or not each reported conversation between therapist and patient involved an attempt on the part of the clinician to either discover the patient's perceptions of contingencies or to modify the patient's existing perceptions of contingencies. Of the 56 therapeutic interactions examined, 35, or 62.5 percent, involved a focus on such covariation perceptions. The interjudge agreement in making these content ratings was 96 percent.

As an example, consider the following vignette, part of an actual therapy session conducted between a cognitive therapist and a depressed patient (Beck *et al.*, 1979, p. 267). The patient in this session has recently been rejected by someone he loved. Note that the patient perceives that there was a covariation between his actions and rejection. The cognitive therapist, who endorses the view that psychopathology (and depression, in particular) is produced by distorted cognitions, encourages the patient to reappraise his "inaccurate" assessments of covariation.

PATIENT: Anyone would be depressed if they were put down by someone they love.

THERAPIST: No one can be put down unless *he is asking someone to hold him up*. Dependence on another person for approval is a form of trying to accept yourself through someone else. "If that person loves me I'm great and if he doesn't, I'm worthless." As long as one is self-sufficient and accepts himself, he will not be depressed if someone chooses not to be with him.

PATIENT: But she rejected me.

THERAPIST: No one can totally reject you. That person can only choose to see you or not to see you.

PATIENT: If there wasn't something wrong with me, she'd be with me.

THERAPIST: It's a value choice. One person might like Cadillacs, another Volkswagens. It is a matter of taste. Some people like classical music, others don't. It doesn't necessarily have anything to do with your personality.

PATIENT: I still think it's something I did.

THERAPIST: That is a possibility. . . . There are a number of other ways of looking at the experience. For example, (a) "I feel sorry for her, she is missing out on me." (b) "Well, someone else will come along." (c) "This is all for the better." or (d) Not to think about it at all.

There are several ways to view this clinical interaction. First, with the research on depressive realism and nondepressive distortion in mind, we might speculate that the depressed patient is accurate in his perception of a relationship between his own behavior and rejection. That is, the patient may be accurately inferring an internal cause for this undesirable life event. Suppose, for example, that the patient really did engage in some objectionable action that resulted in rejection by his lover. In this view, then, the therapist might actually be encouraging the patient to ignore the "real" cause of his rejection and to reinterpret his predicament in a more biased fashion, by constructing for himself the sort of protective illusions that a nondepressed person (and presumably the nondepressed therapist himself or herself) might construct. For example, through reattribution techniques (Beck *et al.*, 1979), the therapist encourages the patient to make external rather than internal attributions (e.g., to feel sorry for his rejector), to make unstable and specific rather than stable and global attributions for his rejection (e.g., to expect that someone else will come along), and to reencode this negative life event in more positive terms (e.g., to think about the possibility that the rejection was all for the better). It is ironic that cognitive therapists strive to assist depressed patients to acquire more realistic perspectives on life, when in fact they may be replacing depressives' realistic perceptions with the more distorted but optimistic perceptions characteristic of the nondepressed person. However, by teaching the depressed patient to distort contingencies in the nondepressive fashion, the cognitive therapist may be successful in reducing depressive symptomatology (see the section "Depression: An Example?" in this chapter, for a discussion of the possible relationship between nondepressive error and adaptiveness).

A second view of this clinical vignette is that the depressed patient is, in fact, engaging in negative schema-based cognitive distortions and overestimating the covariation between personal traits or behaviors and rejection, whereas the therapist is proposing more realistic interpretations of the rejection (see the section cited above, for an explanation of the possibility that depressed people may be unrealistic in their everyday environments, although in certain circumstances, they appear more realistic). Clearly, this view, that the therapist corrects the cognitive distortions of the psychopathological individual, is the cognitive therapist's conceptualization of the therapy process.

Finally, a third view is that both the patient's and the therapist's assessments of covariation are realistic with respect to their own experiences. As previously discussed, individuals' expectations often lead them to engage in behaviors that eventually confirm their original beliefs (Abramson *et al.*, 1981; Snyder & Swann, 1978b; Swann, 1987, Wachtel, 1977). Thus, the depressed person who believes that negative outcomes covary with personal traits or behaviors may actually engage in the sort of self-defeating behaviors that typically do have negative consequences. Likewise, the nondepressed person who believes that personal traits or behaviors covary with positive events might be more likely to engage in behaviors that confirm this belief. It is interesting that in this view, the therapist in the vignette urges the patient to consider alternative explanations for his predicament that would be accurate for the therapist himself or herself, but erroneous for the patient. However, even though the therapist's view may initially be an erroneous perception of behavior–outcome relationships in the patient's world, adoption of this view by the patient may set off a new chain of behaviors that eventually confirms the new view. Thus, what was originally an erroneous perception of the patient's world may become the patient's new reality.

Regardless of which of the three interpretations of the above clinical vignette that one adopts, conceptualizing the therapeutic interaction in terms of clinicians' and patients' covariation judgment processes has enhanced our understanding of the dynamics of therapy. Whether in fact patients are realistic and clinicians have distorted perceptions of covariations, or clinicians are realistic and patients have distorted perceptions of covariations, or both clinicians and patients have accurate perceptions of covariations with respect to their own experiences, an important component of successful therapy entails a change in patients' beliefs about the covariations between important events in their lives.

THERAPY: RECEPTIVITY TO SITUATIONAL INFORMATION

Interestingly enough, although adopting a covariation perspective of the clinical interaction has enhanced our understanding of therapy, this perspective has posed an important problem for our understanding of the covariation judgment process itself. Throughout this chapter we have attempted to show that covariation judgments are jointly influenced by prior beliefs and situational information. However, we have also emphasized that when prior expectations and objective situational information are both compelling but in conflict (Case 2 of Cell 4 of Table 10-1), people's judgments are more heavily influenced by their expectations. That is, people tend to persist in their beliefs despite objective evidence to the contrary. Ross, Lepper, and Hubbard (1975) have labeled this tendency of people to retain beliefs despite disconfirming evidence "belief perseverance" (for a discussion of this phenomenon, see Nisbett & Ross, 1980).

The questions we then pose are the following: Given the fact that situational information provided by the therapist is often effective in changing patients' beliefs about covariations, how does this occur? What are the mechanisms by which a patient's resistance to belief-contradictory evidence eventually breaks down? In other words, why is the clinical interaction special?

Although we are unable to provide definitive answers to these questions, we can speculate about why patients in therapy may be particularly responsive to belief-disconfirming information by referring to other instances reviewed previously in this chapter of sensitivity to situational information despite strong expectations to the contrary. Ward and Jenkins's (1965) subjects, who were provided with information in a summary table about cloud-seeding and rainfall, were able to judge contingencies accurately, whereas subjects provided with the same information serially relied on confirming cases for their judgments, and thus were inaccurate (see the section "Detection of Covariation" in this chapter). Recall also that Chapman and Chapman's (1967) subjects, who were given an opportunity to organize stimulus materials, reported less illusory correlations than those not given this opportunity (see the section "Clinicians' Assessments of Patients" in this chapter). In our analyses of these studies we suggested that the organization of belief-disconfirming evidence may determine the extent to which it is utilized. We now speculate that patients in therapy, like subjects in these experiments, are responsive to information that contradicts their beliefs, because they also receive belief-contradictory evidence in an organized fashion. For example, the patient who believes that he or she is a failure may be responsive to disconfirming evidence provided by the therapist that he or she is not a total failure, because the therapist summarizes relevant information for the patient: for example, "You do poorly on some exams at school, but you are very successful at your job." It is interesting that in this view, patients may resist belief-disconfirming evidence in their everyday experience because typically such evidence is encountered in a serial fashion and cannot be organized into a prior conceptual scheme.

Nisbett and Ross (1980) have suggested two additional factors that may partially account for patients' greater responsivity to belief-contradictory situational information in therapy. First, Nisbett and Ross suggest that in certain situations people's beliefs are modified by "extra-evidential features of information" (Nisbett & Ross, 1980, p. 190), that is, by features of the belief-contradictory evidence aside from its informational value. For example, they note that vivid, concrete, sensory, or personally relevant information may have more impact on a person's belief system than information that is pallid or abstract. Because by definition therapy is focused on patients' behaviors and problems, we might speculate that an important factor contributing to the uniqueness of therapy for changing patients' beliefs about covariations would be the personal relevance of belief-disconfirming evidence provided by the therapist. Patients in therapy may also change their beliefs about covariations because the belief-contradictory evidence supplied by the therapist is particularly vivid, concrete, or sensory.

Second, Nisbett and Ross suggest that people's beliefs may change when they are able to replace their existing theories with new theories that incorporate both initial and contradictory data. Thus, the patient in therapy who believes that he or she is unlikable, may, with the help of the therapist, replace this theory with a more differentiated theory that incorporates both his or her initial beliefs and contradictory evidence (e.g., "I am unlikable when I engage in behaviors A, B, and C, but very likable when I engage in behaviors D, E, and F"). Once the patient in therapy exchanges one set of beliefs about covariations for a more encompassing set, this new set may itself be strengthened by the mechanisms underlying belief perseverance (Nisbett & Ross, 1980). The patient may search his or her memory for additional supporting evidence for the new beliefs (e.g., the patient may recall from his or her past many "long-forgotten" instances in which he or she was a likable person), or the patient may actually generate additional data to confirm new beliefs (e.g., the patient may actually change the way he or she behaves in certain situations so that he or she is liked more).

To this point we have proposed only cognitive accounts of the mechanisms underlying patients' unusual receptivity to belief-disconfirming evidence. These mechanisms are plausible and may in fact operate effectively in the therapy situation. However, emotional and motivational factors as well may contribute importantly to the success of therapy in changing patients' beliefs. An important aspect (to some, the most important aspect) of therapy is the special relationship established between the therapist and patient. It may be that in therapy the patient is able to develop enough trust in the therapist to "try on" a new set of beliefs, even though these beliefs directly contradict his or her own. As discussed above, the person who "tries on" a new set of beliefs may fall prey to the "self-fulfilling prophecy" and engage in precisely those behaviors that eventually lead these new beliefs to persevere as his or her own.

SUMMARY AND CONCLUSION

Our goal in this chapter was to formulate a covariation perspective for the clinic, that is, to develop an overarching framework within which to examine clinicians, patients, and their interaction. To do so, we first examined theoretical and empirical work on people's assessments of covariations in general. The theme that emerged in this section was that people's perceptions of the relationships between events do not merely reflect objective covariations. Covariation-detection processes can be best conceptualized as an interaction between prior beliefs or expectations and currently available situational information. We saw that prior expectations can exert their influence at any of several cognitive steps that may lead to subjective estimates of covariation.

Next, we examined clinicians' assessments of covariation, in their role both as psychodiagnostician and as psychotherapist. Here too, we found that clinicians' assessments of relationships (between test signs and symptoms, symptoms and diagnoses, diagnoses and behaviors, therapeutic techniques and therapeutic effectiveness), although influenced by objective covariations, also seem to be biased strongly in the direction of preconceived beliefs about event relationships. This suggests that many of clinicians' important decisions about patients and therapy will reflect clinicians' expectations to a greater degree than objective situational information.

We then examined patients' abilities to assess covariations. Surprisingly, although cognitive theories of psychopathology suggest that psychopathological individuals (particularly, depressed individuals) may be especially deficient in their abilities to accurately detect covariations, current research has revealed a puzzling phenomenon. A growing body of data suggests that certain psychopathological individuals (i.e., depressed people) are more accurate in their assessments of covariation than are "normal" individuals.

Finally, we speculated about the ways in which clinicians' and patients' covariation judgments might interact in the clinical setting. In therapy, patients are encouraged to adopt their therapist's view of reality. Although initially this view may be erroneous (although more adaptive) for the patient, through the patient's belief-confirming behaviors it may eventually become an accurate reflecton of the patient's new reality. Regardless of which interpretation of the clinical interaction is most fitting, however, we argued that in all cases, therapy can be conceptualized as a process whereby patients change their beliefs about covariations in the world.

In concluding our chapter, an important question became apparent. Why do patients in therapy often come to modify their beliefs about covariations in response to belief-contradictory situational information provided by the therapist (i.e., they resolve their cognitive dilemmas in favor of situational information), when throughout this chapter we have shown that people are typically extremely resistant to information that contradicts their beliefs? We suggested that the answer to this question lies in the fact that therapy is a special situation in which a multitude of cognitive and emotional factors combine to induce belief change.

In conclusion, we believe that our covariation perspective for the clinic provides a useful framework for examining clinicians, patients, and their interaction. Equally as important, we suggest that the interaction between clinician and patient in therapy may represent a microcosm of the interplay between people's beliefs and situational information in covariation judgments in general. Patients in therapy, as well as people in everyday life, appear to both assimilate incoming situational information to their preexisting expectations or beliefs and to accommodate their expectations to the objective data of experience. That is, people both make sense of and impose sense upon the world, simultaneously.

ACKNOWLEDGMENTS

Preparation of this chapter was supported by a MacArthur Foundation Research Grant to Lauren Alloy. Naomi Tabachnik was supported while writing this chapter by a Personality/ Abnormal Psychology Training Grant, NIH 5 T32 MH14636-05, to Northwestern University.

REFERENCES

Abramson, L. Y., & Alloy, L. B. (1980). Judgment of contingency: Errors and their implications. In A. Baum & J. Singer (Eds.), *Advances in environmental psychology* (Vol. 2). Hillsdale, NJ: Erlbaum.

Abramson, L. Y., & Alloy, L. B. (1981). Depression, nondepression, and cognitive illusions: A reply to Schwartz. *Journal of Experimental Psychology: General, 110,* 436–447.

Abramson, L. Y., Alloy, L. B., & Metalsky, G. I. (1988a). The cognitive diathesis-stress theories of depression: Toward an adequate evaluation of the theories' validities. In L. B. Alloy (Ed.), *Cognitive processes in depression.* New York: Guilford.

Abramson, L. Y., Alloy, L. B., & Rosoff, R. (1981). Depression and the generation of complex hypotheses in the judgment of contingency. *Behaviour Research and Therapy, 19,* 35–45.

Abramson, L. Y., & Martin, D. (1982). Depression and the causal inference process. In J. Harvey, W. Ickes, & R. Kidd (Eds.), *New directions in attribution research* (Vol. 3). Hillsdale, NJ: Erlbaum.

Abramson, L. Y., Metalsky, G. I., & Alloy, L. B. (1988b). *Hopelessnesss depression: A theory-based, process-oriented subtype of depression.* Manuscript under editorial review.

Abramson, L. Y., & Sackheim, H. A. (1977). A paradox in depression: Uncontrollability and self-blame. *Psychological Bulletin, 84,* 838–851.

Abramson, L. Y., Seligman, M. E. P., & Teasdale, J. (1978). Learned helplessness in humans: Critique and reformulation. *Journal of Abnormal Psychology, 87,* 49–74.

Adler, A. (1927). *The practice and theory of individual psychology.* Orlando, FL: Harcourt.

Ajzen, I. (1977). Intuitive theories of events and the effects of base-rate information on prediction. *Journal of Personality and Social Psychology, 35,* 303–314.

Albright, J. S., Alloy, L. B., & Barch, D. (1988). *Depression and biases in social comparison: The role of comparison set and target other.* Manuscript under editorial review.

Alloy, L. B. (Ed.). (1988a). *Cognitive processes in depression.* New York: Guilford.

Alloy, L. B. (1988b). Expectations and situational information as co-contributors to covariation assessment: A reply to Goddard and Allan. *Psychological Review, 95*, 299–301.

Alloy, L. B., & Abramson, L. Y. (1979). Judgment of contingency in depressed and nondepressed students: Sadder but wiser? *Journal of Experimental Psychology: General, 108*, 441–485.

Alloy, L. B., & Abramson, L. Y. (1980). The cognitive component of human helplessness and depression: A critical analysis. In J. Garber & M. E. P. Seligman (Eds.), *Human helplessness: Theory and application*. New York: Academic.

Alloy, L. B., & Abramson, L. Y. (1988). Depressive realism: Four theoretical perspectives. In L. B. Alloy (Ed.), *Cognitive processes in depression*. New York: Guilford.

Alloy, L. B., & Abramson, L. Y. (1982). Learned helplessness, depression, and the illusion of control. *Journal of Personality and Social Psychology, 42*, 1114–1126.

Alloy, L. B., Abramson, L. Y., & Kossman, D. (1985). The judgment of predictability in depressed and nondepressed college students. In F. R. Brush & J. B. Overmier (Eds.), *Affect, conditioning, and cognition: Essays on the determinants of behavior*. Hillsdale, NJ: Erlbaum.

Alloy, L. B., Abramson, L. Y., Metalsky, G. I., & Hartlage, S. (1988a). The hopelessness theory of depression: Attributional aspects. *British Journal of Clinical Psychology, 27*, 5–21.

Alloy, L. B., Abramson, L. Y., & Musson, R. F. (1988b). *Who distorts?: Predictors of the illusion of control*. Manuscript in preparation, Northwestern University.

Alloy, L. B., Abramson, L. Y., & Viscusi, D. (1981). Induced mood and the illusion of control. *Journal of Personality and Social Psychology, 41*, 1129–1140.

Alloy, L. B., Crocker, J., & Tabachnik, N. (1980). *Depression and covariation judgments: Expectation-based distortions in information search and recall*. Paper presented at the annual meeting of the American Psychological Association, Montreal.

Alloy, L. B., Hartlage, S., & Abramson, L. Y. (1988c). Testing the cognitive diathesis-stress theories of depression: Issues of research design, conceptualization, and assessment. In L. B. Alloy (Ed.), *Cognitive processes in depression*. New York: Guilford.

Alloy, L. B., Kelly, K. A., Mineka, S., & Clements, C. M. (in press). Comorbidity in anxiety and depressive disorders: A helplessness/hopelessness perspective. In J. D. Maser & C. R. Cloninger (Eds.), *Comorbidity in anxiety and mood disorders*. Washington, DC: American Psychiatric Press.

Alloy, L. B., & Seligman, M. E. P. (1979). On the cognitive component of learned helplessness and depression. In G. H. Bower (Ed.), *The psychology of learning and motivation* (Vol. 13). New York: Academic.

Alloy, L. B., & Tabachnik, N. (1984). Assessment of covariation by humans and animals: The joint influence of prior expectations and current situational information. *Psychological Review, 91*, 112–149.

Allport, G. W. (1954). *The nature of prejudice*. Cambridge, MA: Addison-Wesley.

Anderson, C. A. (1982). Innoculation and counterexplanation: Debiasing techniques in the perseverance of social theories. *Social Cognition, 1*, 126–139.

Arieti, S. Cognition and feeling. (1970). In M. B. Arnold (Ed.), *Feelings and emotions*. New York: Academic.

Arkes, H. R. (1981). Impediments to accurate clinical judgment and possible ways to minimize their impact. *Journal of Consulting and Clinical Psychology, 49*, 323–330.

Arkes, H. R., & Harkness, A. R. (1983). Estimates of contingency between two dichotomous variables. *Journal of Experimental Psychology: General, 112*, 117–135.

Averill, J. R. (1973). Personal control over aversive stimuli and its relationship to stress. *Psychological Bulletin, 80*, 286–303.

Bartlett, F. C. (1932). *Remembering*. Cambridge: Cambridge University Press.

Baum, A., & Singer, J. (Eds.). (1980). *Advances in environmental psychology*. (Vol. 2). Hillsdale, NJ: Erlbaum.

Beach, L. R., & Scopp, T. S. (1966). Inferences about correlations. *Psychonomic Science, 6*, 253–254.

Beck, A. T. (1967). *Depression: Clinical, experimental, and theoretical aspects.* New York: Harper & Row.

Beck, A. T. (1976). *Cognitive therapy and the emotional disorders.* New York: International Universities Press.

Beck, A. T., & Emery, G. (1985). *Anxiety disorders and phobias: A cognitive perspective.* New York: Basic Books.

Beck, A. T., Rush, A. J., Shaw, B. F., & Emery, G. (1979). *Cognitive therapy of depression: A treatment manual.* New York: Guilford.

Bell, L. G., Wicklund, R. A., Manko, G., & Larkin, C. (1976). When unexpected behavior is attributed to the environment. *Journal of Research in Personality, 10,* 316–327.

Benassi, V. A., Knoth, R. L., & Mahler, H. I. M. (1985). Detection of noncontingency in a free-operant situation. *Personality and Social Psychology Bulletin, 11,* 231–245.

Benassi, V. A., & Mahler, H. I. M. (1985). Contingency judgments by depressed college students: Sadder but not always wiser. *Journal of Personality and Social Psychology, 49,* 1323–1329.

Berman, D. S., & Berman, G. J. (1983, August). *Effects of psychiatric labels and training on clinical judgments.* Paper presented at the annual meeting of the American Psychological Association, Anaheim, CA.

Berman, J. S., & Kenny, D. A. (1976). Correlational bias in observer ratings. *Journal of Personality and Social Psychology, 34,* 263–273.

Bibring, E. (1953). The mechanism of depression. In P. Greenacre (Ed.), *Affective disorders.* New York: International Universities Press.

Blaney, P. H. (1986). Affect and memory: A review. *Psychological Bulletin, 99,* 229–246.

Blaney, P. H. (1977). Contemporary theories of depression: Critique and comparison. *Journal of Abnormal Psychology, 86,* 203–223.

Bower, G. H., Black, J. B., & Turner, T. J. (1979). Scripts in memory for text. *Cognitive Psychology, 11,* 177–220.

Bradley, G. W. (1978). Self-serving biases in the attribution process: A re-examination of the fact or fiction question. *Journal of Personality and Social Psychology, 36,* 56–71.

Bransford, J. D., Barclay, J. R., & Franks, J. J. (1972). Sentence memory: A constructive versus interpretive approach. *Cognitive Psychology, 3,* 193–209.

Bransford, J. D., & Johnson, M. K. (1973). Considerations of some problems of comprehension. In W. G. Chase (Ed.), *Visual information processing.* New York: Academic.

Bruch, H. (1973). *Eating disorders: Obesity, anorexia nervosa, and the person within.* New York: Basic Books.

Bruner, A., & Revusky, S. H. (1961). Collateral behavior in humans. *Journal of the Experimental Analysis of Behavior, 4,* 349–350.

Bruner, J. S., Goodnow, J. J., & Austin, G. A. (1956). *A study of thinking.* New York: Wiley.

Bruner, J. S., & Postman, L. (1949). On the perception of incongruity: A paradigm. *Journal of Personality, 18,* 206–223.

Bugelski, B. R., & Alampay, D. A. (1961). The role of frequency in developing perceptual sets. *Canadian Journal of Psychology, 15,* 205–211.

Cantor, N., & Mischel, W. (1977). Traits as prototypes: Effects on recognition memory. *Journal of Personality and Social Psychology, 35,* 38–48.

Cantor, N., & Mischel, W. (1979). Prototypes in person perception. In L. Berkowitz (Ed.), *Advances in experimental social psychology* (Vol 12). New York: Academic.

Catania, A. C., & Cutts, D. (1963). Experimental control of superstitious responding in humans. *Journal of the Experimental Analysis of Behavior, 6,* 203–208.

Chapman, L. J. (1967). Illusory correlation in observational report. *Journal of Verbal Learning and Verbal Behavior, 6,* 151–155.

Chapman, L. J., & Chapman, J. P. (1967). Genesis of popular but erroneous psychodiagnostic observations. *Journal of Abnormal Psychology, 72,* 193–204.

Chapman, L. J., & Chapman, J. P. (1969). Illusory correlation as an obstacle to the use of valid psychodiagnostic signs. *Journal of Abnormal Psychology*, 74, 271–280.

Chatlosh, D. L., Neunaber, D. J., & Wasserman, E. A. (1985). Response-outcome contingency: Behavioral and judgmental effects of appetitive and aversive outcomes with college students. *Learning and Motivation*, 16, 1–34.

Clements, C. M., & Alloy, L. B. (1988). *Affective and behavioral consequences of perception of control styles: Predicting vulnerability and invulnerability to helplessness and depressive reactions*. Manuscript in preparation, Northwestern University.

Cohen, C. E. (1977, September). *Cognitive basis of stereotyping*. Paper presented at the annual meeting of the American Psychological Association, San Francisco.

Cohen, L. H., & Oyster-Nelson, C. K. (1981). Clinicians' evaluations of psychodynamic psychotherapy: Experimental data on psychological peer review. *Journal of Consulting and Clinical Psychology*, 49, 583–589.

Coppel, D. B., & Smith, R. E. (1980). Acquisition of stimulus-outcome and response-outcome expectancies as a function of locus of control. *Cognitive Therapy and Research*, 4, 179–188.

Coyne, J. C., & Gotlib, I. H. (1983). The role of cognition in depression: A critical appraisal. *Psychological Bulletin*, 94, 472–505.

Crocker, J. (1981). Judgment of covariation by social perceivers. *Psychological Bulletin*, 90, 272–292.

Crocker, J. (1982). Biased questions in judgment of covariation studies. *Personality and Social Psychology Bulletin*, 8, 214–220.

Crocker, J., Alloy, L. B., & Kayne, N. T. (1988). Attributional style, depression, and perceptions of consensus for events. *Journal of Personality and Social Psychology*, 54, 840–866.

Crocker, J., Kayne, N. T., & Alloy, L. B. (1985). Comparing the self to others in depressed and nondepressed college students: A reply to McCauley. *Journal of Personality and Social Psychology*, 48, 1579–1583.

Crocker, J., & Taylor, S. E. (1978). *Theory-driven processing and the use of complex evidence*. Paper presented at the annual meeting of the American Psychological Association, Toronto.

Davis, H. (1979a). Self reference and the encoding of personal information in depression. *Cognitive Therapy and Research*, 3, 97–110.

Davis, H. (1979b). The self schema and subjective organization of personal information in depression. *Cognitive Therapy and Research*, 3, 415–426.

Deaux, K. (1976). Sex: A perspective on the attribution process. In J. H. Harvey, W. J. Ickes, & R. F. Kidd (Eds.), *New directions in attribution research* (Vol. 1). Hillsdale, NJ: Erlbaum.

Deaux, K., & Emswiller, T. (1974). Explanations for successful performance of sex-linked tasks: What is skill for the male is luck for the female. *Journal of Personality and Social Psychology*, 29, 80–85.

DeMonbreun, B. G., & Craighead, W. E. (1977). Distortion of perception and recall of positive and neutral feedback in depression. *Cognitive Therapy and Research*, 1, 311–329.

Dickinson, A., Shanks, D., & Evenden, J. (1983). Judgment of act-outcome contingency: The role of selective attribution. *Quarterly Journal of Experimental Psychology*, 36, 29–50.

Dodge, K. A., & Coie, J. D. (1987). Social-information-processing factors in reactive and proactive aggression in children's peer groups. *Journal of Personality and Social Psychology*, 53, 1146–1158.

Dresel, K. M. (1984). *Effects of the Type A behavior pattern, depression, and the duration of noncontrol on the illusion of control*. Unpublished master's thesis. University of Manitoba, Winnipeg.

Dubnicki, C. (1977). Relationships among therapist empathy and authoritarianism and a therapist's prognosis. *Journal of Consulting and Clinical Psychology*, 45, 958–959.

Dykman, B. M., Abramson, L. Y., Alloy, L. B., & Hartlage, S. (1988). *Processing of ambiguous and unambiguous feedback by depressed and nondepressed college students: Schematic biases and their implications for depressive realism*. Manuscript under editorial review.

Einhorn, H. J., & Hogarth, R. M. (1978). Confidence in judgment: Persistence of the illusion of validity. *Psychological Review, 85*, 395–416.

Ellis, A. (1957). Outcome of employing three techniques of psychotherapy. *Journal of Clinical Psychology, 13*, 344–350.

Ellis, A. (1962). *Reason and emotion in psychotherapy*. Secaucus, NJ: Lyle Stuart.

Ellis, A. (1971). *Growth through reason: Verbatim cases in rational-emotive psychotherapy*. Palo Alto, CA: Science & Behavior Books.

Erlick, D. E. (1966). Human estimates of statistical relatedness. *Psychonomic Science, 5*, 365–366.

Erlick, D. E., & Mills, R. G. (1967). Perceptual quantification of conditional dependency. *Journal of Experimental Psychology, 73*, 9–14.

Feldman-Summers, S., & Kiesler, S. B. (1974). Those who are number two try harder: The effect of sex on attributions of causality. *Journal of Personality and Social Psychology, 30*, 846–855.

Fincham, F. D., & Bradbury, T. N. (1987). Cognitive processes and conflict in close relationships: An attribution-efficacy model. *Journal of Personality and Social Psychology, 53*, 1106–1118.

Folkman, S. (1984). Personal control and stress and coping processes: A theoretical analysis. *Journal of Personality and Social Psychology, 46*, 839–852.

Follette, V. M., & Jacobson, N. S. (1987). Importance of attributions as a predictor of how people cope with failure. *Journal of Personality and Social Psychology, 52*, 1205–1211.

Forgus, R., & Shulman, B. H. (1979). *Personality: A cognitive view*. Englewood Cliffs, NJ: Prentice-Hall.

Frankel, A., & Snyder, M. L. (1978). Poor performance following unsolvable problems: Learned helplessness or egotism? *Journal of Personality and Social Psychology, 36*, 1415–1423.

Frederiksen, C. H. (1975). Representing logical and semantic structure of knowledge acquired from discourse. *Cognitive Psychology, 17*, 371–458.

Freud, A. (1946). *The ego and the mechanisms of defense*. London: Hogarth. (Originally published, 1936)

Freud, S. (1950). *Collected papers* (Vol. 3). London: Hogarth. (Originally published, 1909)

Freud, S. (1957). Mourning and melancholia. In J. Strachey (Ed. and Trans.), *The complete psychological works of Sigmund Freud* (Vol. 14). London: Hogarth. (Originally published, 1917)

Freud, S. (1966). *Introductory lectures on psychoanalysis*. (J. Strachey, Ed. and Trans.) New York: Norton. (Originally published, 1920)

Garber, J., & Seligman, M. E. P. (Eds.). (1980). *Human helplessness: Theory and application*. New York: Academic.

Goddard, M., & Allan, L. (1988). A critique of Alloy and Tabachnik's theoretical framework for understanding covariation assessment. *Psychological Review, 95*, 296–298.

Golding, S. L., & Rorer, L. G. (1972). Illusory correlation and subjective judgment. *Journal of Abnormal Psychology, 80*, 249–260.

Golin, S., Terrell, F., & Johnson, B. (1977). Depression and the illusion of control. *Journal of Abnormal Psychology, 86*, 440–442.

Golin, S., Terrell, F., Weitz, J., & Drost, P. L. (1979). The illusion of control among depressed patients. *Journal of Abnormal Psychology, 88*, 454–457.

Gong-Guy, E., & Hammen, C. L. (1980). Causal perceptions of stressful events in depressed and nondepressed outpatients. *Journal of Abnormal Psychology, 89*, 662–669.

Greenberg, M. S., & Alloy, L. B. (1988). *Depression versus anxiety: Schematic processing of self- and other-referent information*. Manuscript under editorial review.

Greenberg, M. S., Vazquez, C. V., & Alloy, L. B. (1988). Depression versus anxiety: Differences in self- and other-schemata. In L. B. Alloy (Ed.), *Cognitive processes in depression*. New York: Guilford.

Greenwald, A. G. (1980). The totalitarian ego: Fabrication and revision of personal history. *American Psychologist, 35*, 603–618.

Hamilton, D. L. (1977). *Illusory correlation as a basis for social stereotypes.* Paper presented at the annual meeting of the American Psychological Association, San Francisco.

Hamilton D. L., Dugan, P. M., & Trolier, T. K. (1985). The formation of stereotypic beliefs: Further evidence for distinctiveness-based illusory correlations. *Journal of Personality and Social Psychology, 48,* 5–17.

Hamilton, D. L., & Gifford, R. K. (1976). Illusory correlation in interpersonal perception: A cognitive basis of stereotype judgments. *Journal of Experimental Social Psychology, 12,* 392–407.

Hamilton, D. L., & Rose, T. L. (1980). Illusory correlation and the maintenance of stereotypic beliefs. *Journal of Personality and Social Psychology, 39,* 832–845.

Hammen, C. L., & Cochran, S. D. (1981). Cognitive correlates of life stress and depression in college students. *Journal of Abnormal Psychology, 90,* 23–27.

Hansen, R. D., & Donoghue, J. M. (1977). The power of consensus: Information derived from one's own and others' behavior. *Journal of Personality and Social Psychology, 35,* 294–302.

Hansen, R. D., & Lowe, C. A. (1976). Distinctiveness and consensus: The influence of behavioral information on actors' and observers' attributions. *Journal of Personality and Social Psychology, 34,* 425–433.

Harris, R. J., Teske, R. R., & Ginns, M. J. (1975). Memory for pragmatic implications for courtroom testimony. *Bulletin of the Psychonomic Society, 6,* 494–496.

Hastie, R. (1981). Schematic principles in human memory. In E. T. Higgins, P. Herman, & M. P. Zanna (Eds.), *Social cognition.* Hillsdale, NJ: Erlbaum.

Hastie, R., & Kumar, P. A. (1979). Person memory: Personality traits as organizing principles in memory for behaviors. *Journal of Personality and Social Psychology, 37,* 25–38.

Hayden, T., & Mischel, W. (1976). Maintaining trait consistency in the resolution of behavioral inconsistency: The wolf in sheep's clothing? *Journal of Personality, 44,* 109–132.

Heider, F. (1958). *The psychology of interpersonal relations.* New York: Wiley.

Hoch, S. J. (1985). Counterfactual reasoning and accuracy in predicting personal events. *Journal of Experimental Psychology: Learning, Memory, and Cognition, 11,* 719–731.

Hovland, C. I., & Weiss, W. (1953). Transmission of information concerning concepts through positive and negative instances. *Journal of Experimental Psychology, 45,* 175–182.

Ingram, R. E. (Ed.). (1986). *Information processing approaches to clinical psychology.* New York: Academic.

Ingram, R. E., Smith, T. W., & Brehm, S. S. (1983). Depression and information processing: Self-schemata and the encoding of self-referent information. *Journal of Personality and Social Psychology, 45,* 412–420.

Jenkins, H. M., & Ward, W. C. (1965). Judgment of contingency between responses and outcomes. *Psychological Monographs, 79*(1, Whole No. 594).

Jennings, D. L., Amabile, T., & Ross, L. (1982). The intuitive scientist's assessment of covariation: Data-based vs. theory-based judgments. In D. Kahneman, P. Slovic, & A. Tversky (Eds.), *Judgment under uncertainty: Heuristics and biases.* Cambridge: Cambridge University Press.

John, D. R., Scott, C. A., & Bettman, J. R. (1986). Sampling data for covariation assessment: The effect of prior beliefs on search patterns. *Journal of Consumer Research, 13,* 38–47.

Johnson, M. K., Bransford, J. D., & Solomon, S. K. (1973). Memory for tacit implications of sentences. *Journal of Experimental Psychology, 98,* 203–225.

Jones, E. E., & Davis, K. E. (1965). From acts to dispositions: The attribution process in person perceptions. In L. Berkowitz (Ed.), *Advances in experimental social psychology* (Vol. 2). New York: Academic.

Jones, E. E., & Nisbett, R. E. (1971). The actor and the observer: Divergent perceptions of the causes of behavior. In E. E. Jones, D. E. Kanouse, H. H. Kelley, R. E. Nisbett, S. Valins, & B. Weiner (Eds.), *Attribution: Perceiving the causes of behavior.* Morristown, NJ: General Learning Press.

Jones, M. C. (1924). The elimination of children's fears. *Journal of Experimental Psychology, 7*, 382–390.

Jung, C. G. (1953). The psychology of the unconscious. In H. Read, M. Fordham, & G. Adler (Eds.), *Collected works* (Vol. 7). Princeton, NJ: Princeton University Press.

Kahneman, D., Slovic, P., & Tversky, A. (Eds.). (1982). *Judgment under uncertainty: Heuristics and biases*. Cambridge: Cambridge University Press.

Kahneman, D., & Tversky, A. (1972). Subjective probability: A judgment of representativeness. *Cognitive Psychology, 3*, 430–454.

Kahneman, D., & Tversky, A. (1973). On the psychology of prediction. *Psychological Review, 80*, 237–251.

Kameda, T. (1985). Stereotype-based expectancy and academic evaluation: The joint influence of prior expectancy and the diagnosticity of current information. *Japanese Psychological Research, 27*, 163–172.

Kassin, S. M. (1979a). Base rates and prediction: The role of sample size. *Personality and Social Psychology Bulletin, 5*, 210–213.

Kassin, S. M. (1979b). Consensus information, prediction, and causal attribution: A review of the literature and issues. *Journal of Personality and Social Psyuchology, 37*, 1966–1981.

Kayne, N. T., Alloy, L. B., Romer, D., & Crocker, J. (1988). *Predicting depression and elation reactions in the classroom: A test of an attributional diathesis-stress theory of depression.* Manuscript under editorial review.

Kelley, H. H. (1967). Attribution theory in social psychology. In D. Levine (Ed.), *Nebraska symposium on motivation* (Vol. 15). Lincoln, NE: University of Nebraska Press.

Kelley, H. H. (1971). Causal schemata and the attribution process. In E. E. Jones, D. E. Kanouse, H. H. Kelley, R. E. Nisbett, S. Valins, & B. Weiner (Eds.), *Attribution: Perceiving the causes of behavior.* Morristown, NJ: General Learning Press.

Kelley, H. H. (1973). The process of causal attribution. *American Psychologist, 28*, 107–128.

Kihlstrom, J. F., & Nasby, W. (1981). Cognitive tasks in clinical assessment: An exercise in applied psychology. In P. C. Kendall & S. D. Hollon (Eds.), *Assessment strategies for cognitive-behavioral interventions.* New York: Academic.

Klinger, E. (1975). Consequences of commitment to and disengagement from incentives. *Psychological Review, 82*, 1–25.

Klinger, E., Barta, S. G., & Maxeiner, M. E. (1981). Current concerns: Assessing therapeutically relevant motivation. In P. C. Kendall & S. D. Hollon (Eds.), *Assessment strategies for cognitive-behavioral interventions.* New York: Academic.

Kuiper, N. A., & Derry, P. (1982). Depressed and nondepressed content self-reference in mild depressives. *Journal of Personality, 50*, 67–79.

Kuiper, N. A., & MacDonald, M. R. (1982). Self and other perception in mild depressives. *Social Cognition, 1*, 223–229.

Kurtz, R. M., & Garfield, S. L. (1978). Illusory correlation: A further exploration of Chapman's paradigm. *Journal of Consulting and Clinical Psychology, 46*, 1009–1015.

Langer, E. J. (1975). The illusion of control. *Journal of Personality and Social Psychology, 32*, 311–328.

Langer, E. J., & Abelson, R. P. (1974). A patient by any other name . . . : Clinician group differences and labeling bias. *Journal of Consulting and Clinical Psychology, 42*, 4–9.

Langer, E. J., & Roth, J. (1975). Heads I win, tails it's chance: The illusion of control as a function of the sequence of outcomes in a purely chance task. *Journal of Personality and Social Psychology, 32*, 951–955.

Laxer, R. (1964). Self-concept changes of depressive patients in general hospital treatment. *Journal of Consulting Psychology, 28*, 214–219.

Leeper, R. (1935). A study of a neglected portion of the field of learning—the development of sensory organization. *Journal of Genetic Psychology, 46*, 41–75.

Levine, M. (1969). Neo-continuity theory. In G. H. Bower & J. T. Spence (Eds.), *The psychology of learning and motivation* (Vol. 3). New York: Academic.

Luborsky, P., Singer, B., & Luborsky, L. (1975). Comparative studies of psychotherapies: Is it true that "everyone has won and all must have prizes"? *Archives of General Psychiatry, 32,* 995–1008.

Lueger, R. J., & Petzel, T. P. (1979). Illusory correlation in clinical judgment: Effects of amount of information to be processed. *Journal of Consulting and Clinical Psychology, 47,* 1120–1121.

Mahoney, M. J. (1974). *Cognition and behavior modification.* Cambridge, MA: Ballinger.

Markus, H. (1977). Self-schemata and processing information about the self. *Journal of Personality and Social Psychology, 35,* 63–78.

Martin, D. J., Abramson, L. Y., & Alloy, L. B. (1984). The illusion of control for self and others in depressed and nondepressed college students. *Journal of Personality and Social Psychology, 46,* 125–136.

McArthur, L. A. (1972). The how and what of why: Some determinants and consequences of causal attribution. *Journal of Personality and Social Psychology, 22,* 171–193.

McArthur, L. A. (1976). The lesser influence of consensus than distinctiveness information on causal attributions: A test of the person–thing hypothesis. *Journal of Personality and Social Psychology, 33,* 733–742.

Meichenbaum, D. B. (1977). *Cognitive-behavior modification: An integrative approach.* New York: Plenum.

Metalsky, G. I., & Abramson, L. Y. (1981). Attributional styles: Toward a framework for conceptualization and assessment. In P. C. Kendall & S. D. Hollon (Eds.), *Assessment strategies for cognitive-behavioral interventions.* New York: Academic.

Metalsky, G. I., Abramson, L. Y., Seligman, M. E. P., Semmel, A., & Peterson, C. (1982). Attributional styles and life events in the classroom: Vulnerability and invulnerability to depressive mood reactions. *Journal of Personality and Social Psychology, 43,* 612–617.

Metalsky, G. I., Halberstadt, L. J., & Abramson, L. Y. (1987). Vulnerability to depressive mood reactions: Toward a more powerful test of the diathesis-stress and causal mediation components of the reformulated theory of depression. *Journal of Personality and Social Psychology, 52,* 386–393.

Miller, D. T. (1976). Ego-involvement and attributions for success and failure. *Journal of Personality and Social Psychology, 34,* 901–906.

Miller, D. T. (1978). What constitutes a self-serving attributional bias? A reply to Bradley. *Journal of Personality and Social Psychology, 36,* 1221–1223.

Miller, D. T., & Ross, M. (1975). Self-serving biases in the attribution of causality: Fact or fiction? *Psychological Bulletin, 82,* 213–225.

Mineka, S., & Tomarken, A. J. (in press). The role of cognitive biases in the origins and maintenance of fear and anxiety disorders. In T. Archer & L. G. Nilsson (Eds.), *Perspectives on aversively motivated behavior.*

Mowrey, J. D., Doherty, M. E., & Keeley, S. M. (1979). The influence of negation and task complexity on illusory correlation. *Journal of Abnormal Psychology, 88,* 334–337.

Murphy, J. M. (1976). Psychiatric labeling in cross-cultural perspective. *Science,* 1019–1028.

Musson, R. F., & Alloy, L. B. (1988). *Depression, self-consciousness and illusions of control: The role of self-focused attention.* Manuscript in preparation, Northwestern University.

Mynatt, C. R., Doherty, M. E., & Tweeney, R. D. (1977). Confirmation bias in a simulated research environment: An experimental study of scientific inference. *Quarterly Journal of Experimental Psychology, 29,* 85–95.

Mynatt, C. R., Doherty, M. E., & Tweeney, R. D. (1978). Consequences of confirmation and disconfirmation in a simulated research environment. *Quarterly Journal of Experimental Psychology, 30,* 395–406.

Nadich, M., Gargan, M., & Michael, L. (1975). Denial, anxiety, locus of control and the discrepancy between aspirations and achievements as components of depression. *Journal of Abnormal Psychology, 84,* 1–9.

Nelson, R. E., & Craighead, W. E. (1977). Selective recall of positive and negative feedback, self-control behaviors, and depression. *Journal of Abnormal Psychology, 86,* 379–388.

Ncunaber, D. J., & Wasserman, E. A. (1986). The effects of unidirectional versus bidirectional rating procedures on college students' judgments of response-outcome contingency. *Learning and Motivation, 17,* 162–179.

Nisbett, R. E., & Borgida, E. (1975). Attribution and the psychology of prediction. *Journal of Personality and Social Psychology, 32,* 932–943.

Nisbett, R. E., Borgida, E., Crandall, R., & Reed, H. (1976). Popular induction: Information is not always informative. In J. S. Carrol & J. W. Payne (Eds.), *Cognition and social behavior, 2,* 227–236.

Nisbett, R. E., & Ross, L. (1980). *Human inference: Strategies and shortcomings of social judgment.* Englewood Cliffs, NJ: Prentice-Hall.

Orvis, B. R., Cunningham, J. D., & Kelley, H. H. (1975). A closer examination of causal inference: The roles of consensus, distinctiveness, and consistency information. *Journal of Personality and Social Psychology, 32,* 605–616.

Owens, J., Bower, G. H., & Black, J. B. (1979). The "soap opera" effect in story recall. *Memory & Cognition, 7,* 185–191.

Peterson, C. R. (1980). Recognition of noncontingency. *Journal of Personality and Social Psychology, 38,* 727–734.

Peterson, C., & Seligman, M. E. P. (1984). Causal explanations as a risk factor for depression: Theory and evidence. *Psychological Review, 91,* 347–374.

Posner, M. I., & Keele, S. W. (1968). On the genesis of abstract ideas. *Journal of Experimental Psychology, 77,* 353–363.

Reber, A. S. (1967). Implicit learning of artificial grammars. *Journal of Verbal Learning and Verbal Behavior, 6,* 855–863.

Reber, A. S. (1969). Transfer of syntactic structure in synthetic languages. *Journal of Experimental Psychology, 81,* 115–119.

Reber, A. S. (1976). Implicit learning of synthetic languages: The role of instructional set. *Journal of Experimental Psychology: Human Memory and Learning, 2,* 88–94.

Reid, E. C. (1910). Autopsychology of the manic-depressive. *journal of Nervous and Mental Disease, 37,* 606–620.

Rogers, C. R. (1961). *On becoming a person: A therapist's view of psychology.* Boston: Houghton Mifflin.

Rosch. E. (1975). Cognitive representations of semantic categories. *Journal of Experimental Psychology: General, 104,* 192–233.

Rosch, E., & Mervis, C. B. (1975). Family resemblances: Studies in the internal structure of categories. *Cognitive Psychology, 7,* 573–605.

Rosenhan, D. L. (1973). On being sane in insane places. *Science, 179,* 250–258.

Ross, L. (1977). The intuitive psychologist and his shortcomings. In L. Berkowitz (Ed.), *Advances in experimental social psychology* (Vol. 10). New York: Academic.

Ross, L., Lepper, M. R., & Hubbard, M. (1975). Perseverance in self perception and social perception: Biased attributional processes in the debriefing paradigm. *Journal of Personality and Social Psychology, 32,* 880–892.

Rothbart, M., Evans, M., & Fulero, S. (1979). Recall for confirming events: Memory processes and the maintenance of social stereotypes. *Journal of Experimental Social Psychology, 15,* 343–355.

Scheier, M. F., & Carver, C. S. (in press). Dispositional optimism and physical well-being: The influence of generalized outcome expectancies on health. *Journal of Personality.*

Schustack, M. W., & Sternberg, R. J. (1981). Evaluation of evidence in causal inference. *Journal of Experimental Psychology: General, 110,* 101–120.

Schwartz, B. (1981). Does helplessness cause depression or do only depressed people become helpless? A comment on Alloy and Abramson, 1979. *Journal of Experimental Psychology: General, 110*, 429–435.

Seligman, M. E. P. (1975). *Helplessness: On depression, development and death*. San Francisco: Freeman.

Shanks, D. R. (1985a). Continuous monitoring of human contingency judgment across trials. *Memory & Cognition, 13*, 158–167.

Shanks, D. R. (1985b). Forward and backward blocking in human contingency judgment. *Quarterly Journal of Experimental Psychology, 37*, 1–21.

Sklar, L. S., & Anisman, H. (1981). Stress and cancer. *Psychological Bulletin, 89*, 369–406.

Sloane, R. B., Staples, F. R., Cristol, A. H., Yorkston, N. J., & Whipple, K. (1975). *Psychotherapy versus behavior therapy*. Cambridge, MA: Harvard University Press.

Smedslund, J. (1963). The concept of correlation in adults. *Scandinavian Journal of Psychology, 4*, 165–173.

Smoke, K. L. (1933). Negative instances in concept learning. *Journal of Experimental Psychology, 16*, 583–588.

Snyder, C. R. (1977). "A patient by any other name" revisited: Maladjustment or attributional locus of problem? *Journal of Consulting and Clinical Psychology, 45*, 101–103.

Snyder, M., & Cantor, N. (1979). Testing hypotheses about other people: The use of historical knowledge. *Journal of Experimental Social Psychology, 15*, 330–342.

Snyder, M. L., Stephan, W. G., & Rosenfield, D. (1978). Attributional egotism. In J. H. Harvey, W. J. Ickes, & R. F. Kidd (Eds.), *New directions in attribution research* (Vol. 2). Hillsdale, NJ: Erlbaum.

Snyder, M., & Swann, W. B., Jr. (1978a). Hypothesis-testing processes in social interaction. *Journal of Personality and Social Psychology, 36*, 1202–1212.

Snyder, M., & Swann, W. B., Jr. (1978b). Behavioral confirmation in social interaction: From social perception to social reality. *Journal of Experimental Social Psychology, 14*, 148–162.

Spears, R., van der Pligt, J., & Eiser, J. R. (1986). Generalizing the illusory correlation effect. *Journal of Personality and Social Psychology, 51*, 1127–1134.

Spitzer, R. L. (1976). More on pseudoscience in science and the case for psychiatric diagnosis. *Archives of General Psychiatry, 33*, 459–470.

Starr, B. J., & Katkin, E. S. (1969). The clinician as an aberrant actuary: Illusory correlation and the incomplete sentences blank. *Journal of Abnormal Psychology, 74*, 670–675.

Strube, M. J., Lott, C. L., Heilizer, R., & Gregg, B. (1986). Type A behavior pattern and the judgment of control. *Journal of Personality and Social Psychology, 50*, 403–412.

Sulin, R. A, & Dooling, D. J. (1974). Intrusion of thematic ideas in retention of prose. *Journal of Experimental Psychology, 103*, 255–262.

Sushinsky, L. W., & Wener, R. (1975). Distorting judgments of mental health: Generality of the labeling bias effect. *The Journal of Nervous and Mental Disease, 161*, 82–89.

Swann, W. B., Jr. (1987). Identity negotiation: Where two roads meet. *Journal of Personality and Social Psychology, 53*, 1038–1051.

Sweeney, P. D., Anderson, K., & Bailey, S. (1986). Attributional style in depression: A meta-analytic review. *Journal of Personality and Social Psychology, 50*, 974–991.

Tabachnik, N., Crocker, J., & Alloy, L. B. (1983). Depression, social comparison and the false consensus effect. *Journal of Personality and Social Psychology, 45*, 688–699.

Taylor, D. M., & Jaggi, V. (1974). Ethnocentrism and causal attribution in a South Indian context. *Journal of Cross-Cultural Psychology, 5*, 162–171.

Taylor, S. E., & Brown, J. D. (in press). Illusion and well-being: A social psychological perspective on mental health. *Psychological Bulletin*.

Taylor, S. E., & Crocker, J. (1981). Schematic bases of social information processing. In E. T. Higgins, P. Herman, & M. Zanna (Eds.), *Social cognition*. Hillsdale, NJ: Erlbaum.

Temerlin, M. K. (1968). Suggestion effects in psychiatric diagnosis. *The Journal of Nervous and Mental Disease, 117*, 349–353.

Temerlin, M. K., & Trousdale, W. W. (1969). The social psychology of clinical diagnosis. *Psychotherapy: Theory, research, and practice, 6*, 24–29.

Tetlock, P. E., & Levi, A. (1982). Attribution bias: On the inconclusiveness of the cognition-motivation debate. *Journal of Experimental Social Psychology, 18*, 68–88.

Tetlock, P. E., & Manstead, A. S. R. (1985). Impression management versus intrapsychic explanations in social psychology: A useful dichotomy? *Psychological Review, 92*, 59–77.

Thompson, S. C. (1981). Will it hurt less if I can control it? A complex answer to a simple question. *Psychological Bulletin, 90*, 89–101.

Thorndyke, P. W. (1977). Cognitive structures in comprehension and memory of narrative discourse. *Cognitive Psychology, 9*, 77–110.

Trolier, T. K., & Hamilton, D. L. (1986). Variables influencing judgments of correlational relations. *Journal of Personality and Social Psychology, 50*, 879–888.

Tversky, A., & Kahneman, D. (1971). Belief in the law of small numbers. *Psychological Bulletin, 76*, 105–110.

Tversky, A., & Kahneman, D. (1974). Judgment under uncertainty: Heuristics and biases. *Science, 185*, 1124–1131.

Tversky, A., & Kahneman, D. (1978). Causal schemata in judgments under uncertainty. In M. Fishbein (Ed.), *Progress in social psychology*. Hillsdale, NJ: Erlbaum.

Vazquez, C. V. (1987). Judgment of contingency: Cognitive biases in depressed and nondepressed subjects. *Journal of Personality and Social Psychology, 52*, 419–431.

Vazquez, C. V., & Alloy, L. B. (1988). *Schematic memory processes for self- and other-referent information in depression versus anxiety: A signal detection analysis*. Manuscript in preparation, Northwestern University.

Wachtel, P. L. (1977). *Psychoanalysis and behavior therapy: Toward an integration*. New York: Basic Books.

Waller, R. W., & Keeley, S. M. (1978). Effects of explanation and information on the illusory correlation phenomenon. *Journal of Consulting and Clinical Psychology, 46*, 342–343.

Ward, W. D., & Jenkins, H. M. (1965). The display of information and the judgment of contingency. *Canadian Journal of Psychology, 19*, 231–241.

Wason, P. C., & Johnson-Laird, P. N. (1972). *Psychology of reasoning: Structure and content*. London: D. T. Batsford.

Weary, G. (1980). Examination of affect and egotism as mediators of bias in causal attributions. *Journal of Personality and Social Psychology, 38*, 348–357.

Weiner, B. (1972). *Theories of motivation: From mechanism to cognition*. Chicago: Rand-McNally.

Weiner, B. (Ed.). (1974). *Achievement motivation and attribution theory*. Morristown, NJ: General Learning Press.

Weiner, B. (1975). "On being sane in insane places": A process (attributional) analysis and critique. *Journal of Abnormal Psychology, 84*, 433–441.

Weiner, B. (1979). A theory of motivation for some classroom experiences. *Journal of Educational Psychology, 71*, 3–25.

Wells, G. L., & Harvey, J. H. (1977). Do people use consensus information in making causal attributions? *Journal of Personality and Social Psychology, 35*, 279–293.

Werner, P. D., Rose, T. L., & Yesavage, J. A. (1983). Reliability, accuracy, and decision-making strategy in clinical predictions of imminent dangerousness. *Journal of Consulting and Clinical Psychology, 51*, 815–825.

Woll, S., & Yopp, H. (1978). The role of context and inference in the comprehension of social action. *Journal of Experimental Social Psychology, 14*, 351–362.

Wortman, C. B. (1975). Some determinants of perceived control. *Journal of Personality and Social Psychology, 31*, 282–294.

Wortman, C. B., Costanzo, P. R., & Witt, T. R. (1973). Effects of anticipated performance on the attributions of causality to self and others. *Journal of Personality and Social Psychology, 27,* 372–381.

Wright, J. C. (1962). Consistency and complexity of response sequences as a function of schedules of noncontingent reward. *Journal of Experimental Psychology, 63,* 601–609.

Yates, J. F., & Curley, S. F. (in press). Contingency judgment: Primacy effects and attention decrement. *Acta Psychologica.*

Zadny, J., & Gerard. H. B. (1974). Attributed intentions and information selectivity. *Journal of Experimental Social Psychology, 10,* 34–52.

Zuckerman, M. (1979). Attribution of success and failure revisited, or: The motivational bias is alive and well in attribution theory. *Journal of Personality, 47,* 245–287.

Index